S0-AAH-840

FLORIDA STATE
UNIVERSITY LIBRARIES

AUG 2 1994

TALLAHASSEE, FLORIDA

THE FACES OF POWER
SECOND EDITION

Constancy and Change
in United States Foreign Policy
from Truman to Clinton

THE FACES OF POWER

SECOND EDITION

CONSTANCY AND CHANGE
IN UNITED STATES FOREIGN POLICY
FROM TRUMAN TO CLINTON

SEYOM BROWN

COLUMBIA UNIVERSITY PRESS

NEW YORK

E
840
B768
1994

Material in chapters 2-21 originally appeared, in somewhat different form, in *The Faces of Power: Constancy and Change in United States Foreign Policy from Truman to Johnson* (Copyright © 1969 Columbia University Press); *The Crises of Power: An Interpretation of United States Foreign Policy During the Kissinger Years* (Copyright © 1979 Columbia University Press); and *The Faces of Power: Constancy and Change in United States Foreign Policy from Truman to Reagan* (copyright © 1983 Columbia University Press)

Columbia University Press
New York   Chichester, West Sussex
Copyright © 1994 Columbia University Press
All rights reserved

Library of Congress Cataloging-in-Publication Data

Brown, Seyom.
The faces of power : United States foreign policy from Truman to
Clinton / Seyom Brown.
p.   cm.
Includes bibliographical references and index.
ISBN 0-231-09668-2 (cloth). — ISBN 0-231-09669-0 (paper)
1. United States—Foreign relations—1945-1989.   2. United States—
Foreign relations—1989–1993.   3. United States—Foreign
relations—1993–   I. Title.
E840.B768   1994
327.73—dc20   93–41945

Casebound editions of Columbia University Press books
are Smyth-sewn and printed on permanent and durable acid-
free paper.

Printed in the United States of America

c 10 9 8 7 6 5 4 3 2 1
p 10 9 8 7 6 5 4 3 2 1

For Two Benjamins

CONTENTS

Contents

PREFACE

This book is for public officials and laypersons as much as for students and scholars of United States foreign policy. It is the product of my continuing effort to discern the basic assumptions held by U.S. policymakers about the country's international interests and purposes and about the power of the United States to protect and further these interests and purposes.

The reason for this undertaking is in part autobiographical.

My principal professional work before joining the faculty of Brandeis University was in the "think tank" world (as a social scientist with the RAND Corporation, a senior fellow at the Brookings Institution, a director of the U.S.-Soviet Relations Project at the Carnegie Endowment for International Peace, and as a consultant to the departments of Defense and State), where most of my efforts were devoted to helping devise foreign policy options for consideration by government officials. In order to get the responsible decision makers to give serious consideration to my suggestions I had to first "get into their heads," so to speak, and try to see the world through their eyes. What did *they* consider to be the country's essential national interests? As *they* saw it, what international developments were most in need of being attended to by the United States? And by what criteria would *they* assess the advantages and disadvantages of pursuing any particular set of policies? Not that I conceived of my role as one of simply catering to the preconceptions of these official "clients," for like any conscientious citizen, and as a scholar of international politics, I had my own views on what was good for the country and what should be done. But I knew that I could best get these views a hearing at the highest levels of the U.S. government if I were able to *connect* my analyses to their ways of looking at the world.

I found that to capture the essence of U.S. foreign policy at any point, and to effectively relate particular foreign policy proposals to the basic policy, requires an understanding of the worldviews not only of the country's current top foreign policy officials but also of their predecessors extending back a number of administrations. I discovered that even among reform-minded foreign policy officials, current policy choices are influenced by inherited policy premises for reasons that have as much to do with the policy-making process as with the substance of the alternatives under consideration. The working out of policies to secure the national interest through a myriad of competing programs is a terribly complex task that requires the mobilization of support from rival agencies within the executive and from a fractious Congress; once this difficult task has been accomplished in a particular field, there is a tendency to deal with issues marginally so as to avoid having once again to open up the whole "can of worms." As a result, standing policy assumptions often carry the day by default—unless a severe crisis or sea change in world conditions forces their reconsideration.

Freshly appreciating the constraining weight of inherited policies, in 1965 (three years into my job as a young policy analyst at the RAND Corporation) I accepted a grant from the Johns Hopkins University Center for Foreign Policy Research in Washington, D.C., to restudy the post–World War II evolution of basic United States foreign policy. The fruits of my self-designed "refresher course" in recent history were published in 1968 in *The Faces of Power: Constancy and Change in United States Foreign Policy from Truman to Johnson.*

The 1983 edition of this book, incorporating insights gained during seven years at the Brookings Institution and two years at the Carnegie Endowment for International Peace, extended the scope of analysis beyond the Johnson administration to the Kissinger era under presidents Nixon and Ford, the Carter years, and the first two years of the Reagan administration. The present edition completes the analysis of the Reagan years, presents an analysis of the Bush foreign policy, and takes an early look at directions being charted by the Clinton administration.

The origins and aims of this investigation have determined the foreign policy episodes selected for examination and the emphasis (reflected in the detail and length of sections) given each of them.

My overriding purpose has been to gain insight into the worldviews prevailing at the highest levels of the United States government, so as to be able to more effectively comment on policy directions and options under consideration in the contemporary period. Thus in delving back into recent history I have functioned less as a historian, interested in illuminating the past for its own sake, than as an active participant in the policy-formulation process, seeking to understand the continuing impact of past policies and precedents on today's responsible decision makers. Accordingly, in each edition of this book, as we move farther away from the origins of the Cold War and its early dramatic episodes, the chapters on the Truman and Eisenhower administrations have become shorter, while retaining much of the material on the early policy demarches (such as the Truman Doctrine, the Marshall Plan, and the New Look military strategy) whose legacies are still very much with us. The searing experience of the Cuban Missile Crisis and the Kennedy administration's effort to develop a more flexible set of instruments for dealing with the turmoil in the Third World are kept essentially as they were in the previous editions, but I have scaled down the attention I previously gave to Kennedy's attempt to manage intra-NATO affairs (today's policy dilemmas with respect to NATO are of an entirely different order). The thinking that got the country involved in the Vietnam War and determined how the war was fought and ended continues to receive extended treatment in the current edition. So does the Nixon-Kissinger effort to move beyond the Cold War by instituting a détente with the Soviet Union and rapprochement with China. Jimmy Carter's efforts to make human rights a centerpiece of U.S. foreign policy, his excruciating struggle to get the Iranians to release the U.S. embassy hostages, and his success in negotiating the Camp David accords between Egypt and Israel are episodes that continue to shape the worldviews of President Clinton's top foreign policy advisers, some of whom played key roles in these events. And, of course, the policies of Reagan and Bush that helped bring the Cold War to an end and began to lay the groundwork for a very different kind of U.S. foreign policy are accorded substantial and detailed attention.

Using this selective prism I seek throughout to illuminate the "defining moments" of U.S. foreign policy since the end of World War II—moments of truth (and occasionally self-deception) for the highest officials, when they were compelled by events to become more conscious than usual about the country's sometimes contradictory values and the kinds of power required to sustain these values in a turbulent world.

The attempt to discover what responsible foreign policy officials think (or thought) they are (or were) doing at the time of making crucial decisions involves a wide variety of sources: official documents that evaluate and argue for or against policy alternatives under consideration, public statements by officials attempting to garner public support, press conferences and testimony before congressional committees, and memoirs and oral history reconstructions by those involved purporting to describe their motives and calculations.

The disclosures by officials of the motives for their decisions are necessarily incomplete. Between the official explanations and the observed behavior there often remains a hazy area: articulated premises do not lead inevitably to the actions taken; nor can one infer the premises backward from the particular actions. Many of the crucial considerations remain unarticulated, not necessarily out of any official design to hide them, but because space and time do not seem to permit a statement of their sometimes complicated interconnections, and also because actions by governments, like actions by individuals, are often the result of conditioned responses, of preprogramming, in which the actor "knows" what to do but is unable to summon into consciousness the reasons.

Thus the search for the determinative policy assumptions cannot stop with public documents, archival materials, or directly elicited interview material. It must go behind the words and between the lines to seek out the *operational* premises—those which do in fact make the difference at forks in the road. The effort is not so much a science as it is an art, a collective art involving the sharing of information and insights among analysts and practitioners alike about the considerations prevailing at crucial junctures.

My informational and intellectual debts are therefore quite large. As indicated in the endnotes, in addition to the standard primary sources in the public record and the published memoirs of policy officials, I have unabashedly drawn on archival-based histories of the administrations under scrutiny and on various excellent "insider" accounts by Washington journalists. Much of my interpretation of these materials, however, is the product of informal and "off the record" exchanges over the years with a great number of individuals who have themselves been involved in the policy process as policymakers or consultants to the responsible policymakers.

Having stated my indebtedness to others in these general terms, I would like to be excused from specifically mentioning here all those from whom I have obtained useful ideas and information. I have two main reasons for this (in addition to preserving the confidentiality of some of the exchanges): First, the acknowledgment ritual can too easily become an attempt to legitimate one's claim to the truth by name-dropping; by the stroke of one's own pen, one becomes the peer of those with more impressive scholarly credentials or more direct access to the pinnacles of political power. Second, acknowledgment lists are hazardous to friendships and cordial associations. Somebody is going to be left out, and no subsequent apologies will remove the suspicion that this was an invidious exclusion. The only way around this risk, for a book like this that is based on hundreds of interchanges, would be to include all the names in my Rolodex. (Perhaps I flatter myself that those excluded would care, but I do not wish to carry the burden of that anxiety.)

Yet I do want to express special appreciation to colleagues who took time to read and comment on drafts of some of the new chapters dealing with the Reagan, Bush, and Clinton administrations— namely, Robert Art, Ethan Kapstein, Christopher Kirkey, and Sidney Milkis. Zoe Fidelman, a doctoral candidate in politics at Brandeis University, provided essential assistance in tracking and analyzing the zigs and zags of Clinton's foreign policy during his first eight months in office. I also want to thank Kate Wittenberg, Leslie Bialler, Julia Kocich and Anne McCoy of Columbia University Press for helping me to shape this project and sharpen the exposition.

Finally, a word of gratitude to my youngest sons, Jeremiah and Matthew, for their skeptical but nonetheless good-humored indulgence of my claim to be doing something important in writing about the goings-on in Washington, D.C.

Seyom Brown
Waltham, Massachusetts
January 1994

THE FACES OF POWER
SECOND EDITION

Constancy and Change
in United States Foreign Policy
from Truman to Clinton

PART I

PURPOSE AND POWER: AN OVERVIEW

Our policy is designed to serve mankind.
—JIMMY CARTER

Our national interest is all that we are really capable of knowing and understanding. . . . If our purposes and undertakings here at home are decent ones, unsullied by arrogance or hostility toward other people or delusions of superiority, then the pursuit of our national interest can never fail to be conducive to a better world.
—GEORGE F. KENNAN

1

CONSTANCY AND CHANGE SINCE WORLD WAR II

Nixon and I wanted to found American foreign policy on a sober perception of permanent national interest.

—HENRY KISSINGER

Between lofty claims that the United States is "doing God's work"[1] and allegations that the government is the handmaiden of capitalist corporations[2] lie the basic objectives of United States foreign policy—objectives so elemental as to constitute an irreducible national interest. The constancy in foreign policy from Truman to Clinton is largely the result of the binding force of these bedrock imperatives. The changes in foreign policy during this period consisted mostly of variations in the means chosen to serve these imperatives, reflecting changes in perceptions by the country's highest decisionmakers about evolving world and domestic conditions.

THE IRREDUCIBLE NATIONAL INTEREST[3]

Every U.S. president is bound by the Constitution and the realities of domestic politics to service first and foremost two essential objectives: the nation's physical survival and the perpetuation of something called the American Way of Life—in the familiar words, "to secure the blessings of liberty to ourselves and our posterity." A third compelling imperative is the injunction to promote the general welfare—the economic well-being of the whole society. From the vantage point of the presidency, there is a good deal of political steam in the passion of the populace to have its liberties and to eat well too.

Yet the understanding by U.S. presidents that they are obligated to serve this irreducible national interest leaves a great deal open. Its implementation varies from administration to administration, depending not only on changing world conditions but also on prevailing definitions of the essential liberties of U.S. citizens, theories about what the economy needs to function well, and convictions about what constitutes a fair distribution of burdens and benefits. These fluctuations, nevertheless, are constrained in each administration by the presidential impulse to lead the nation away from situations where severe trade-offs between survival, liberty, and material well-being have to be made. The central thread of continuity in U.S. foreign policy from Truman to Clinton is in large measure traceable to this popularly sustained impulse.

CHANGING CONDITIONS: THEIR IMPACT AND ATTEMPTS TO INFLUENCE THEM

The foreign policy of the United States comprises efforts to influence conditions outside of the country. These efforts reflect judgments by responsible decisionmakers that: (a) a particular set of conditions is having, or is likely to have, a significant impact on U.S. interests; (b) the behavior of the United States can significantly affect these conditions; and (c) the expected benefits from a particular course of action are worth its expected costs.

The responsible decisionmakers do not always make such policy judgments with forethought and deliberation, let alone systematically—that is, with objectifiable criteria and shared methodologies for assessing the conditions and evaluating the costs and benefits of alternative policies. Often policies are formulated and implemented intuitively ("by the seat of the pants") or by default (where non-decisions allow programs already in place to keep running). But even when policies are chosen or allowed to continue in the absence of considered assessments of their advantages and disadvantages, they still contain (or at least imply) certain assumptions or conclusions about their effects on conditions with a significant impact on U.S. interests.

The larger consequences for policy that have stemmed from such judgments about world conditions are summarized below. Subsequent chapters provide a closer look at the variations in policy, the debates surrounding them, and the changing assumptions on which they were based.

During the Cold War: preoccupation with a hostile superpower

Throughout most of the four decades following the defeat of Germany and Japan, U.S. officials considered the irreducible interest in all three of its dimensions (the country's survival, its basic liberties, and its economic well-being) to be in jeopardy from the Soviet Union. The Soviet leaders were seen to be devotees of a way of life antithetical to the fundamental values of the American nation and bent on imposing their system on the world. But it was widely assumed that a major war to stop the Soviets, given the range and destructive power of the military forces available (especially nuclear weapons), would also place the irreducible national interest in jeopardy. Under eight presidents, these fears sustained the twin imperatives of containing Soviet expansion without starting World War III. This meant: (1) influencing the Soviet Union not to attempt to enlarge its territorial sphere of control and not to try to gain military superiority over the United States, and (2) strengthening the ability of other countries to resist Soviet aggression and pressure.

The major debates within the U.S. foreign policy community during the Cold War were less about these overriding objectives than about the means—the power required—to accomplish them. A consensus coalesced around the necessity of maintaining a favorable U.S.–Soviet balance of power. But, as will be elucidated throughout this narrative, there were substantial differences among and within the administrations over the definition of "power" and its ingredients and thus also over the appropriate "balance" of power in any situation. These differences were central to many of the foreign policy issues that preoccupied the Truman, Eisenhower, Kennedy, Johnson, Nixon, Ford, Carter, and Reagan administrations—issues concerning:

- the size and kind of military establishment to keep in being;
- where to draw the line against Soviet expansion—everywhere around

the world, or only selectively where major U.S. geostrategic interests were
in clear and present danger;
   • the extent to which, and by what means, the United States should
attempt to affect internal developments in other countries, particularly
those that might result in Marxist governments.

My exposition of the constancy and change in U.S. foreign policy
from Truman to Reagan is largely the story of the debates over
these issues between the administrations and their critics and among
factions within the administrations, and of how they were resolved
at the presidential level.

A marked discontinuity in the story appears early in the Bush
administration, with the demise of the Cold War. No longer did the
irreducible national interest demand that primary attention be given
to countering Soviet expansion while preventing World War III.
Without this objective providing a lodestar for navigating the international waters, U.S. officials seemed to be suddenly disoriented.
And they found themselves buffeted by strange and turbulent currents not on their navigational charts. So too my attempt to ferret out
the basic assumptions of particular policy choices and to distinguish
carefully charted courses of action from ad hoc opportunism or drift
encounters more difficulties with Bush and Clinton than it does with
their predecessors.

In the post–Cold War world: the problem of establishing priorities

With the end of the Cold War, the connections between particular
international developments and the irreducible national interest—
never that easy to pin down—became more elusive than ever. Without an identifiable primary "threat" to the country's security and
well-being, the question of which developments abroad were important enough for the U.S. government to attempt to influence
became a major issue in itself. Pundits called for a new "vision" or
"grand design" for U.S. foreign policy in the post–Cold War era to
create generally understood criteria for establishing priorities among
international undertakings, particularly those competing for scarce
resources. It again became politically popular—more so than at any
time since the start of World War II—to argue that United States
foreign policy henceforth should be based on a strict definition of

national self-interest that would thrust the burden of proof, case-by-case, onto those who would advocate that the country devote resources to furthering the security or well-being of other nations, let alone of humankind as a whole.

If anything, U.S. international undertakings became became more variegated and un-prioritized in the aftermath of the Cold War. There has been increased attention at top foreign policy levels to an array of "secondary" international concerns advanced by particular economic sectors or special-interest groups. A related consequence of the end of the Cold War has been the reduced overall priority accorded foreign policy issues in the White House—this in deference to demands that domestic problems neglected during the Cold War now be given their due. A third consequence has been a revival of reliance on international institutions, particularly the United Nations and its associated agencies, to perform world order and international economic management functions that during the Cold War had been largely taken over by the superpowers working through their respective alliance organizations.[4]

REALPOLITIK AND MORAL PURPOSE

Some of the variations in United States foreign policy since World War II have been a function of changing views in Washington on the extent to which the country should be committed to securing the human rights or well-being of other peoples. The extremes on this issue are represented by the realpolitik notion that morality and altruism have no place in international relations and the missionary conceit that it is the divinely given role of the United States of America to root out evil in the world. For the most part, however, the dominant views among influential policy makers have fluctuated across a range considerably short of these extremes.

Policies to advance the human rights or well-being of peoples in other countries have generally commanded widespread support when they reinforced other elements in a grand strategy for securing the irreducible national interest of the United States. By contrast, altruistic policies have been rejected in cases where it was evident that their costs or effects would seriously undermine the ability of the United States to secure the safety and well-being of its own people.

The greatest controversy has surrounded policies of moral intent whose likely consequences for the irreducible national interest were highly ambiguous or unpredictable.

The country's foreign policy leadership feels most secure with the electorate when it can satisfy the popular view of the United States as a country doing good in the world while doing good for itself. Thus, officials of the Truman administration championed the United Nations, the Truman Doctrine, the European Recovery Program, and aid to the Third World as being consistent with American idealism as well as self-interest. John Foster Dulles preached anti-communism as a universal moral imperative. President Kennedy, unsentimental realist he is supposed to have been, proposed that the United States provide help for the world's poor and repressed peoples, "not because the Communists may be doing it, not because we seek their votes, but because it is right."[5] Jimmy Carter claimed that his administration's commitment to human rights was "a beacon of light of something that's clean and decent and proper as a rallying point for us all in the democracies of the world."[6] Ronald Reagan proudly embraced the goal of making all countries safe for free enterprise—for their own good. George Bush claimed to be using force in the Persian Gulf on behalf of a "new world order" where weak states would be protected against military attack from more powerful neighbors. And Bill Clinton promised to develop new programs to further the spread of democracy around the world.

Policies to implement such intentions to do good, however, have been scrapped or postponed when the president discerned that their pursuit would require a major sacrifice of the country's blood and treasure in war, or otherwise take away from the capacity of the United States to tend to its own security and material well-being. This realist constraint on idealist impulses has operated at a number of crucial junctures:

• near the end of the Korean War, when President Truman, and then Eisenhower, decided to accept a stalemate based on the pre-war status quo of a divided Korea rather than pressing for "victory" to allow the United Nations to administer nationwide elections and reunify the country;

• in 1956, when President Eisenhower ruled out intervention on behalf of the Hungarians who, believing Secretary Dulles' earlier "liberation" rhetoric, were dying on the streets of Budapest to assert their independence from the Soviet empire;

• during the 1960s, when the Kennedy–Johnson architects of the "development decade," in contrast to their initial promises, frugally prioritized their congressional foreign aid requests on the basis of the Cold War strategic significance of recipient countries;

• during the Carter years, when noble intentions to make human rights a centerpiece of U.S. foreign policy collapsed in the face of the perceived need to shore up the tyrannical Shah of Iran as a regional bulwark against Soviet expansion;

• in 1981, when President Reagan (having alleged for years that the courtship of Communist China by Nixon, Ford, and Carter was immoral) established a close political-military liaison with Beijing, for the same reason that animated his predecessors: to counter Soviet power;

• in 1991, when George Bush called a halt to the Gulf War after driving the Iraqi forces out of Kuwait and avoided an invasion of Iraq, leaving it to the Iraqi people themselves to decide the fate of (actually, to be at the mercy of) Saddam Hussein.

• in 1993, when newly inaugurated President Clinton, unwilling to open U.S. society to a flood of poor immigrants in a period of high unemployment, reneged on his campaign pledge to reverse the Bush policy of interdicting Haitian refugees on the high seas and returning them to the political repression and economic destitution from which they were escaping.

In the post–Cold War era, responsible decisionmakers lack a clear basis for choosing whether and when U.S. policy should attempt to further the interests of others. There are rarely any directly discernible effects from such altruistic action—either positive or negative—on the basic self-interests of the country. And complicating considerations intrude to muddy up a clear calculus of the material costs and benefits or moral worth of policy, let alone the trade-offs between geopolitics and ethics. Should the United States support national self-determination, including political secession, for ethnic groups that feel repressed within larger multi-ethnic states? Should human rights criteria affect the granting of trading privileges in the U.S. market and the extension of credits? Should the United States, on grounds of the well-being of others, tax its own people to fund sustainable development policies around the world? Should the U.S. armed forces be put in harm's way as a part of peacekeeping operations in remote countries with no significance for U.S. security? How much of a sacrifice in U.S. jobs should be incurred in the short run in the service of the longer-term goal of a open global market?

If these issues can no longer be resolved by appeal to bedrock national interests, neither can they be resolved by appeal to high ground of moral obligation. The new complexities of world politics preclude any such neat and obvious answers.

James Schlesinger (who served in cabinet posts under Presidents Nixon, Ford, and Carter) wrote in *Foreign Affairs* magazine at the outset of the Clinton administration about the hodgepodge that foreign policy had become:

We are urged to advance democracy and all its procedures, human rights, civil liberties, equality before the law, protection of minorities, self-determination, an orderly world, international law, economic growth, free markets, privatization, free trade, limits on environmental degradation, curtailments of arms trade, prevention of the spread of advanced weapons, etc., etc. The list is almost endless. What is ignored is that some of these objectives are flatly in conflict and that all require careful examination of trade-offs. Moreover, striking little attention has been paid to the relations between means and ends.[7]

I have a different perspective on where we have arrived, which I summarize in the next chapter.

2

THE CHANGING ESSENCE
OF POWER

*The United States must maintain a military balance of power . . . .[but] our
military strength, while an essential condition for an effective foreign policy, is
not in itself a sufficient condition. We must nurture and draw on our other
strengths as well—our alliances and other international ties, our economic resources, our ability to deal with diversity, and our ideals. By drawing fully on
these strengths, we can help shape world events in ways that reduce the likelihood
of using military force later.*

—CYRUS VANCE, MARCH 1980

Power is in the eye of the beholder. Its different forms appeal to
different people in different measure, but we can agree on a broad
definition: power is the ability to affect the condition or behavior of
something or someone.

Political power implies getting others to help in the attainment or
protection of one's interests. In the international arena, it usually
requires some degree of consent from other governments and peoples. The ingredients of this ability to induce consent, and their
appropriate weights in particular situations, cannot be set forth in a
tidy formula.

The multifaceted and elusive nature of power is not always taken
into account by statespersons. Indeed, the history of United States
foreign policy from Truman to Clinton is a history of debate among
those charged with developing and wielding the power of the country
as to how gross or differentiated the tools of power ought to be and

on the relative influence to be accorded the military, economic, and cultural, and moral ingredients of power. There have been times during this period when the nation's power was regarded almost exclusively in physical terms—with the ultimate measure being the potential to inflict destruction on other nations. This view held sway in the counsels of decision more often during the early days of the Cold War, when the country was obsessed with the need to maintain an advantageous military balance of power against the Soviet Union, than during the periods of détente and the demise of the cold War. The basic movement from the Cold War foreign policy to the post–Cold War foreign policy can be seen as an evolution from an essentially monotonic concept of international power to a highly differentiated view.

This evolving concept of power was an adaptation—by fits and starts and periodic retrogressions—to the large trends taking place in international relationships: the disintegration of the Cold War coalitions, the rise of nonsecurity issues to the top of diplomatic agendas, and a diversification of friendships and adversarial relationships.[1]

As these trends matured, U.S. policymakers began to conceive of world politics as a system of multiple and crosscutting coalitions formed around a variety of issues, a world in which the properties of power would be significantly different than in the prior, predominantly bipolar, system. In the evolving system, countries with the most influence were likely to be those who were major constructive participants in a wide variety of coalitions and partnerships, since they would have the largest supply of usable political currency—in effect promissory notes that said: "We will support you on this issue if you support us on that issue." Conversely, threats to withdraw support would serve as negative sanctions.

Power in the form of promises to apply or withhold military capabilities—the dominant form of power during the Cold War—would still be of ultimate decisive importance in conflicts over vital security interests. But military power would be of declining use compared with other forms of power, and sometimes even have a negative effect, in bargaining over the nonsecurity issues around which coalitions were forming and reforming. For the threat to apply military power can carry a high risk of devaluing the other bargaining chips in that it would be almost certain to alienate the involved societies from one another, causing them to dismantle their cooperative projects and withdraw from mutual coalition partnerships in virtually all fields. Pairs of countries with few interlocking relationships to start with (as was the case with East-West relations during the period of 1947 to 1967) could afford to be indifferent to such a falling out between them. But active participants in the emerging international system, with elaborate overlapping of interests and coalitions, would be highly constrained by the knowledge that their opponents in one field were often their supporters in another.

If coercive bargaining strategies did have to be resorted to in the new system, the prudent statesperson would conserve his or her overall store of influence by offering, withholding, and withdrawing assets well below the level of military force and avoiding the development of total nation-to-nation or coalition-to-coalition hostility. Rarely should a specific dispute warrant the costs, in loss of influence, that would accompany the escalation to war threats, the mobilization of military alliances, or the repolarization of the international system.

As the system continued to evolve in the 1970s and 1980s, increasing numbers of top U.S. policymakers came gradually to understand—and their learning was dramatically accelerated by the emergence in 1985 of a Soviet leader who also saw what was happening—the new requisites for cultivating and effectively using the revised modalities of power.

• The United States would play down the use of force as a sanction behind diplomacy. This would not preclude the maintenance of the minimal military forces necessary to assure the Soviets or any other potential adversary that it would be futile to resolve their disputes with the United States by force. And to dissuade powerful nations from picking on the weak, it might be necessary occasionally to emphasize the fact that the United States reserves the right to help the victims of military attack. As a minimum, the new situation required demilitarizing the vocabulary of power that had been featured in U.S. foreign policy pronouncements since World War II.

• The United States would seek out special opportunities for practical cooperative projects with countries of diverse cultures, ideological predispositions, and political economies, without making their imitation of the U.S. version of democratic capitalism the litmus test of the new partnerships. Washington would exercise self-restraint against inflating particular conflicts of interest into ideological conflicts over ways of life, and would work

instead to build a world of interdependent and mutually respectful and
mutually accountable communities.

• The United States would promote greater reliance on the United
Nations and regional multilateral institutions to enhance mutual accountability, especially on matters of high international interdependence, such as
the use of the oceans, air space, the atmosphere, and global ecologies.
The United States would support principles of representation in these
institutions that would give voice, in so far as possible, to all communities
affected by multilateral activities.

The growing recognition that power in an increasingly interdependent global society has many dimensions suffered a number of set
backs along the way. But the overall trend—the embrace of complex
ity in the official worldview and of flexibility in the formulation and
implementation of policies—while losing something of the high
drama of the early Cold War years, bespeaks a maturing realism
about power in the contemporary world and augurs well for the
ability of U.S. foreign policy officials to effectively promote the
interests of the nation in the years ahead.

PART II

THE TRUMAN ADMINISTRATION

Do not be deceived by the strong face, the look of monolithic power that the Communist dictators wear before the outside world. Remember that their power has no basis in consent.

—HARRY S. TRUMAN

The course we have chosen . . . involves building military strength, but it requires no less the buttressing of all other forms of power—economic, political, social, and moral.

—DEAN ACHESON

3

THE SHATTERING OF
EXPECTATIONS

Force is the only thing the Russians understand.
—HARRY S. TRUMAN

United States officials emerged from the Second World War in awe
of the physical power nations had been able to develop, but with
little confidence in the power of nations unilaterally to exercise the
self-control required to channel their tremendous physical capabilities to constructive as opposed to destructive purposes. Throughout
the government, there was wide consensus that the survival of civilization required the strengthening of international institutions
and also, but with somewhat less conviction, the eventual reduction of the amount of destructive power in the hands of individual
nations.

To translate these hopes into reality would require the kind of
statesmanship which, in the past, had run afoul of strong American
attachments to the value of self-reliance. Remembering the fate
of Woodrow Wilson's sponsorship of the League of Nations, the
administration started to fully prepare the public, and particularly
the opposition party leadership, for the premises on which the new
postwar diplomacy would be based. Delegations to the founding
conferences for the United Nations were carefully selected on a
bipartisan basis. And, in an appeal to the patriotic, the successful
wartime cooperation between members of the Grand Alliance against

the Axis Powers was held up as the embryo from which the new organs of international cooperation would evolve.

The premise of continued cooperation among members of the Grand Alliance had two faces: its internal, government aspect, where it was viewed as the *most desirable condition* for managing the postwar world; and its public aspect, where the premise of big-power cooperation was viewed as a *prediction* that the presumed harmony would last.

The popular myth that Harry S. Truman, upon assuming the presidency on April 12, 1945, at the time of Franklin D. Roosevelt's death, inherited a set of idealistic beliefs from the Roosevelt administration about Soviet–American postwar cooperation is not borne out by historical research. Rather, FDR, in negotiating with Generalissimo Joseph Stalin at the Big Three meetings in Teheran (December 1943) and Yalta (February 1945), operated from premises very similar to the realpolitik notions of Prime Minister Winston Churchill. Despite differences in style and nuance between the Briton and the American, both viewed Stalin as interested primarily in the security of the Soviet Union, and secondarily in exploiting opportunities for an expansion of Soviet control in the direction of the Mediterranean and the Near East. Both Western statesmen sought to relieve Stalin's paranoid fears—of wartime Anglo-American collusion to weaken Russia and of postwar capitalist encirclement—by granting the Soviet Union a sphere of predominant influence in Eastern Europe and special awards in the Far East (including the Kurile Islands and lower Sakhalin from Japan, an "independent" outer Mongolia, and partial control or leases of key railway networks and ports in northeast China). In return, Stalin was supposed to accept British and American spheres of predominant influence outside of these areas. The basic bargain having been struck, the Big Three could then manage other conflicts over secondary issues through consultation, since none of their vital security interests would be threatened. The new United Nations organization would work on the basis of the essential East–West modus vivendi—an assumption carried into the structure and voting arrangements of the UN itself.[1]

At his Big Three meeting with Stalin and top British statesmen at Potsdam in the summer of 1945, Truman did little more than endorse this basic realpolitik deal worked our earlier with Stalin by FDR and Churchill.[2]

There was soon to be a basic shift in assumptions away from the

Churchill/Roosevelt spheres-of-influence approach and toward what became known as "containment." This took place at the top levels of the Truman administration a good year before being revealed to the public in the Truman Doctrine in 1947. Yet during the first two postwar years the general public got its ideas on the administration's assumptions about international relations from the official rhetoric which for the most part conveyed a set of more optimistic expectations:

1. The expectation that important international disputes would be settled by reasoned debate leading to an expression of majority will through the United Nations;

2. The expectation that in important international disputes the Big Five (the United States, the Soviet Union, Britain, France, and China) usually would find themselves on the same side—i.e., the veto would be an exceptional, rather than a frequently used, device; and

3. The expectation that any required sanctions against international lawbreakers would be organized by this international community.

The real nature of the shift in the operating assumptions of early postwar foreign policy was hidden from the public—the shift from the Yalta view that "we can do business with Uncle Joe" to Truman's confidentially held perspective of 1946 that "force is the only thing the Russians understand."

In less than a year as president, Truman came to believe that the Soviets would expand as far as they could, that they were highly motivated to dominate the world, and that they would aggressively exploit all opportunities to enlarge their sphere of control unless effective countervailing power was organized to stop them. But prior to 1947, Truman felt that a candid presentation to the public of the internal government perception of the Soviet drive for power ascendancy might shock the country into total abandonment of the laborious effort to build up international institutions. This would be tragic, since such institutions, if strengthened by support of most of the peoples of the globe, were truly regarded as the *best* long-term hope for peace. Yet without such candor, the public and their representatives in the Congress would probably not approve the stopgap military and economic measures that might be necessary to induce the Soviets to keep their end of the postwar bargain to become constructive participants in the building of a world order acceptable to a majority of nations.

The effect by Truman's subordinates to reconcile the President's fear of shattering public expectations with his belief that standing up to the Russians now might be a precondition for the eventual realization of these expectations is the central story of the Truman administration's early gropings toward a coherent foreign policy.

TOWARD CONTAINMENT

Truman recalls that during the first weeks of his presidency he gave much weight to the analysis of Soviet policies conveyed to him by Averell Harriman, at that time the United States ambassador to the Soviet Union. Harriman was urging a reconsideration of our policy toward the Soviet Union, fearing that to some extent existing policy might be the product of illusions that the Soviets shared our commitment to an international order based on peaceful national self-determination.

As recounted in Truman's *Memoirs,* the gist of the Harriman analysis as of April 1945 was that Stalin was misinterpreting our generosity and our desire to cooperate as a signal that the United States would do nothing to prevent the extension of Soviet control over its neighbors. The Soviets, reported Harriman, had no wish to break with the United States, as they needed our aid for their program of postwar reconstruction; but Stalin would not hesitate to push his political frontiers westward if he felt he could do so without serious political challenge. We had to disabuse Stalin of his illusion of American softness, counseled Harriman. We could be firm with the Soviets without running serious risks, since they could not afford to alienate their own source of help.[3]

Truman claims to have bought this evaluation and was disposed to follow Harriman's advice that the way to exert a positive influence on Soviet policy was to be tough with them on specific postwar issues as they arose. The assumption was, as Truman put it, "anyway the Russians needed us more than we needed them."[4] The Soviets, because of their economic needs, had more to lose than to gain by the collapse of great-power amicability. We wished to preserve an atmosphere of United States–Soviet cooperation because this was the key to an effective universal collective security system, which in turn, it was hoped, would induce more responsible Soviet behavior. It was not yet considered necessary or desirable to be able to force a general showdown with the Soviet Union over any specific issue by pointing explicitly or implicitly to the military power at our disposal.

When Truman had his first high-level "confrontation" with Soviet diplomats Molotov and Gromyko at the White House on April 23, 1945, and used language that, according to Admiral Leahy, was "blunt" and "not at all diplomatic," he was evidently still leading from a perceived position of presumed *economic* leverage.[5]

The very next day Secretary of War Stimson wrote an urgent note to the President, requesting "a talk with you as soon as possible on a highly secret matter. . . . It . . . has such a bearing on our present foreign relations . . . that I think you ought to know about it without much further delay." The Secretary of War met with the President on April 25 and told him of the nuclear development program, and that in four months a completed weapon would be ready. The discussion with Stimson, reports Truman, centered on the effect the atomic bomb might likely have on our future foreign relations.[6]

The bomb was henceforth to be very much a part of Truman's overall calculus of the balance of military power *behind* his diplomacy, both for ending the war with Japan and bargaining with the Soviets over the postwar arrangements. He knew now that if it became necessary to lay all of his cards on the table in a confrontation with Stalin, he could soon do so from a unique position of strength. But the President was evidently unwilling at this stage— although recent scholarship shows he was pressured hard to do so[7]— to make the bomb a visible and immediate part of his bargaining cards in current diplomatic negotiations. At Potsdam in July he could have done so (having received news of the successful Alamagordo test while the conference was in session), but still chose to rely on the Harriman strategy of catering to the expected Soviet hunger for our economic assistance.

After his face-to-face encounter with Stalin at Potsdam, Truman began to lean toward those in his administration who believed that a diplomacy characterized mainly by firm verbal expressions of disapproval would not disabuse the Soviets of their appetite for expansion. "I'm tired of babying the Soviets," Truman told Secretary of State Byrnes in January 1946. The past nine months have been filled with what he saw as a series of Soviet power plays.

The Soviet Union's failure to implement the Yalta provisions for free elections in Eastern Europe was only part of the story which the

President now recounted to his Secretary of State with evident exasperation: the actual disposition of Soviet-military forces, sheer physical control, was the critical fact in subsequent negotiations over the future of Europe. Under the circumstances, confessed the President, we were "almost forced" to agree at Potsdam to Russian occupation of eastern Poland and the compensatory occupation by Poland of German territory east of the Oder river. "It was a high-handed outrage." The situation in Iran was another case in point— Iran of *all* places! The friendship of Iran had been critical for the Soviet Union's survival in the war; the United States had conducted a major supply operation to the USSR through Iran. Without these supplies furnished by the United States, maintained Truman, the Soviets would have been shamefully defeated. Yet now the Kremlin was stirring up rebellion and keeping troops on the soil of Iran.

Evidently, the original Harriman analysis that the Soviets would respond positively to our blunt talk was inadequate. Stalin, according to Truman's personal reading of events, obviously placed a higher value on expanding the Soviet sphere of control than on maintaining good relations with the United States. The threat of decisive action had to be added to the blunt talk: "Unless Russia is faced with an iron fist and strong language another war is in the making," concluded the President. "Only one language do they understand—'how many divisions have you?' I do not think we should play compromise any longer."[8]

These developing perceptions of Soviet aims were very much a part of the 1946 Acheson–Lilienthal report to the President on the international control of atomic energy, which became, in effect, the plan presented to the United Nations Commission by Benard Baruch in June. In contrast to the Soviet plan, which put destruction of existing weapons stockpiles before inspection and controls, the United States plan demanded *prior* establishments of a comprehensive international inspection and control apparatus with access to and authority over all relevant national facilities, including plants where raw materials could be converted into fissionable materials. Moreover, the veto was not to apply to the operations of the international control authority. Truman's instructions to Baruch unambiguously outlined the considerations that were to be kept paramount: It was in our interest to maintain our present advantage; thus we should attempt to gain a system of reliable international control that

Forrestal, Ickes,
& Stimson pushing
for reversal of policy
&
switch to informing public
of USSR expansion

would effectively prevent the Soviets from proceeding with their own atomic weapons development program. And under no circumstances should we "throw away our gun" until we were sure that others could not arm against us.[9]

If President Truman and a few of his official intimates had an early perception of the dominant means by which the emerging political conflict with the Soviet Union would be waged, they were not ready in late 1945 and 1946 to make it the explicit central premise of our foreign policy. To do so would have required a major reversal of the rapid postwar military demobilization already in full gear. It would have shattered the public's expectations, reflected in the congressional agenda, that the priority business before the nation was to convert to a peacetime economy. James Forrestal's notes of a combined State–War–Navy meeting of October 16, 1945, recount that "it was agreed by all present that . . . it was most inadvisable for this country to continue accelerating the demobilization of our Armed Forces at the present rate." The Secretary of War contended the situation was of such gravity that "the President ought to acquaint the people with the details of our dealing with the Russians and with the attitude which the Russians have manifested throughout."[10]

Appeals to the President for governmental candor with the people about the international situation were made during the next few months by Secretaries Forrestal, Ickes, and others.[11] But Truman apparently needed more than individual instances of Soviet belligerence in order to go before the American people and tell them, brutally, that their fondest hopes for returning to the pursuit of happiness were based on false premises. Even as the increasing newspaper reports of Soviet totalitarianism at home and expansion abroad became a part of the public consciousness, Truman's public posture toward Soviet belligerence continued to stress the mobilization of "world opinion" to back up the principles of the United Nations Charter—issue by issue, situation by situation.

Governmental conceptions of the emerging struggle with the Soviet Union are supposed to have been given new cohesion and direction in February 1946 by George Kennan's eight-thousand-word cable from Moscow. The essentials of the Soviet grand design, the motives (rational and irrational) behind their imperialistic policies, and the meaning of their style of diplomacy were analyzed in historical and psychological depth, and with great cogency (see the end of this chapter for a fuller account). Here was the authoritative and coherent analysis of the Soviet threat that many within the administration, particularly Forrestal, were looking for. But there is no evidence that this early report from Kennan contained, either explicitly or by logical implication, the concrete policy prescriptions Forrestal wanted the President to champion. Kennan did urge, like Forrestal and his colleagues, the importance of having the public "educated to the realities of the Russian situation." And he discounted any deterioration in Soviet–American relations that might result from such a campaign. Yet he saw no urgency for paying particular attention to the *military* components of power. "Gauged against the Western world as a whole . . ." observed Kennan, "the Soviets are still [this was early in 1946] by far the weaker force. Thus their success will really depend upon the degree of cohesion, firmness, and vigor which the western world can muster."[12]

If Truman's *Memoirs* are accurate, he personally, as early as the winter of 1945–46, saw the Russian pressures on Iran and Turkey as an immediate threat to the global balance of power. Russia's failure to withdraw its armies from Iran stemmed from its central geopolitical interests in Iranian oil and control of the Black Sea straits. Russian possession of Iranian oil, the President was convinced, would seriously alter the world's raw material balance, and would be a blow to the economy of Western Europe. But the power play in Iran was also directly related to the demands the Soviets had been making on Turkey for special privileges and territorial concessions. Turkey had been resisting these demands, but would be in a much weaker position to resist if outflanked by the east by Russian armies or a Russian puppet state.[13]

Truman saw Soviet ambitions in Turkey revealed starkly in its proposal to put the Black Sea straits under joint Turkish-Soviet control. Recalling his own studies of Middle Eastern history, the President recognized in the present Communist thrust a continuation of Czarist Russian attempts to gain control of the strategic exits to the Mediterranean Sea. If they were to succeed now, he deduced, it would only be a question of time before Greece and the whole Near and Middle East fell to the Soviets.[14]

There is evidence that this is more than a retrospective reconstruction by Truman of his perceptions at the time. His January

1946 letter to Byrnes expressing exasperation at the way the Soviets were throwing their weight around contained a bald geopolitical evaluation of Soviet aims: "There isn't a doubt in my mind," he wrote less than a year after the close of the Second World War, "that Russia intends an invasion of Turkey and seizure of the Black Sea Straits to the Mediterranean."[15]

Moreover, Truman did begin to "show the flag" in 1946 in his dealings with the Russians on Middle Eastern issues. The battleship *Missouri* was sent to Istanbul to demonstrate support for Turkey's refusal to accede to Soviet demands for joint control over the Straits. Truman has divulged, though not until many years later, that he sent Stalin an ultimatum on the issue of Soviet troops in Iran, informing him that the United States would send troops in if the Russians did not get out, and that he had ordered preparations for the movement of American ground, sea, and air forces.[16] But however effective these moves were as gambits in the management of the particular crisis situations, they were not yet presented to the public as parts of a grand strategy toward the Soviet Union, in which the American military potential would be consciously and more or less continuously displayed in back of diplomatic efforts to moderate Soviet behavior.

Nor was the administration ready to openly embrace the balance of power ideas Winston Churchill was then advancing. When the British leader delivered his sensational "Iron Curtain" speech in March 1946, with President Truman sitting on the platform, the premises he advanced about Soviet motives and behavior were already widely shared in U.S. policy-making circles. But the main policy conclusion he drew, that there ought to be a long-term Anglo-American alliance against the Soviets, was still not acceptable to the highest levels in the American government.

THE TRUMAN DOCTRINE

An early moment of truth was shortly to come for United States policymakers. The February 1947 note from the British government, informing the United States that drastic economic conditions made it necessary for the United Kingdom to withdraw all support from Greece by the end of March, provided the need—and the opportunity. The President's top political and military advisers were of the opinion that it was only the presence of British troops in Greece since the war that had prevented that faction-ridden nation from being swept into the Soviet orbit. The prevailing view within the State Department was that unless the tottering Greek government received immediate assurances of large-scale military and financial aid the regime would lose all authority and the increasingly successful Communist guerrillas would grab control of the country as public disorder mounted. Truman translated the local situation into the starkest global terms: if Greece fell to the Communists, Turkey would become highly vulnerable to Soviet power plays and subversion. Inevitably, the entire eastern Mediterranean would be sealed behind the Iron Curtain.[17]

To save the situation this time more than a White House decision—which had been sufficient for deploying the Navy and sending blunt diplomatic notes in the earlier Turkey and Iran crises—was required. Large-scale economic and military assistance, to be directly administered by American officials, would need congressional authorization and special appropriations. But Republican majorities had just taken control of both houses, and, according to Speaker Joe Martin, were determined to fulfill election promises for a 20 percent across-the-board reduction in income taxes with a collateral reduction in government spending. Administration forces, having suffered badly in the congressional elections, were disposed to regard the Republican spokesmen, as, for once, being in tune with popular sentiment. "Now that an immediate peril is not plainly visible," Secretary of State Marshall told an academic audience, "there is a natural tendency to relax and return to business as usual, politics as usual, pleasure as usual. Many of our people have become indifferent to what I might call the long-term dangers to national security."[18]

The stage was set. The national executive considered matters of high national interest to be at stake. But in order to service these interests it would have to ask the nation at large to reorder its priorities. Such a political context (rather than the logic of the international situation) prompts a democratic leadership to call upon the nation to reexamine existing premises and stimulates it by promulgating new doctrine.

For the public this effort at basic revision of the national premises was associated with Truman's address to the Congress on March 12,

1947, requesting assistance for Greece and Turkey—the so-called "Truman Doctrine." But for many in the administration responsible for foreign diplomatic, economic, and military programs Truman's formal request of Congress was only the exposed tip of an iceberg of massive intellectual and bureaucratic activity.

The seminal statement conceptualizing and catalyzing the new orientation was probably neither Truman's address nor Secretary of State Marshall's at Harvard a few months later, but Under Secretary of State Acheson's effort to educate the bipartisan group of congressional leaders Truman summoned to the White House on February 27, 1947.

According to a State Department official who was present, the leadoff presentation by Secretary Marshall went very badly. Marshall, rather than expounding on the central strategic importance of Greece and Turkey (a subject on which he was very well versed), conveyed the impression that the reasons for extending aid to Greece and Turkey flowed essentially from humanitarian impulses toward these countries and loyalty to Britain. Many of the congressional leaders present were not at all impressed, preoccupied as they were with reducing taxes.

Acheson got Marshall's attention and was given the floor. In bold strokes, he displayed for the congressmen the view of Soviet Middle Eastern strategy that for more than a year had prevailed at the White House and top State Department levels. The Under Secretary described the continuing Soviet pressures on Turkey for territorial cessions and for military and naval bases in the Turkish straits, which if granted would mean "the end of Turkish independence." Soviet pressures on Iran were portrayed as "encircling movements" also apparently focused on the straits. It was only because the Turks, with strong diplomatic backing from Britain and the United States, had stood up to the Russians that these moves had failed for the time being. As a result, the Communists were currently concentrating their pressure on Greece, Acheson explained, where all reports indicated that the Communist insurgents would succeed in seizing control "within a matter of weeks" unless the government of Greece received prompt and large-scale aid.

This was obviously more than helping the British salvage their interests, said Acheson, building up to his main message. The substance and tone of this message are best rendered in the account of the State Department official whose account is the basic public source for the White House meeting of February 27:

> Only two great powers remain in the world, Acheson continued, the United States and the Soviet Union. We had arrived at a situation unparalleled since ancient times. Not since Rome and Carthage had there been such a polarization of power on this earth. Moreover, the two great powers were divided by an unbridgeable ideological chasm. . . . And it was clear that the Soviet Union was aggressive and expanding. For the United States to take steps to strengthen countries threatened with Communist subversion was not to pull British chestnuts out of the fire; it was to protect the security of the United States—it was to protect freedom itself. For if the Soviet Union succeeded in extending its control over two-thirds of the world's surface and three-fourths of its population, there could be no security for the United States, and freedom anywhere in the world would have only a poor chance of survival. The proposed aid to Greece and Turkey was not therefore a matter of bailing out the British, or even of responding on humanitarian grounds to the need of a loyal ally. It was a matter of building our own security and safeguarding freedom by strengthening free peoples against Communist aggression and subversion. We had the choice, he concluded, of acting with energy to meet this situation or losing by default.[19]

Here, full-blooded, were the central premises of what came to be called the cold war: the two-way polarization of the international system around two great powers; an unbridgeable ideological hostility between the two groupings, with the group led by the United States committed to individual liberty and a pluralistic international system, and the group led by the Soviet Union committed to totalitarian statism and a monistic international system organized on the Soviet model; and an intention by the Soviet-led grouping to impose its way of life on the rest of the world.

From these premises it was deduced that any allowance of an extension of Soviet control over additional areas, even if they were limited extensions, would not reduce Soviet aggressiveness, but, on the contrary, would stimulate further aggressiveness by adding to the material and political resources with which the Soviets hoped to impose their will. The policy implications for the United States-led grouping were clear: a balance of power had to be maintained against the Soviet-led grouping, and the intention to apply this power, wherever and to whatever extent necessary, to prevent any further extension of Soviet control had to be unambiguous.

President Truman's address before Congress on March 12, 1947, asking for $400,000,000 in military and economic aid to Greece and

Turkey was based on these premises, but he deliberately refrained from making them as explicit as Acheson had done in the private session. A number of statements that emphasized strategic considerations were deleted from one of the last drafts of the speech on the recommendation of Acheson, whose view is reported to have been that too much emphasis on the strategic considerations might be alarming to the American people, who were not accustomed to thinking in these terms in time of peace. The emphasis in public was to be on the global ideological conflict, and on the economic assistance needed by governments friendly to the United States to successfully combat subversion:[20]

> I believe [Truman told the nation] that it must be the policy of the United States to support free people who are resisting attempted subjugation by armed minorities or by outside pressures.
> I believe that we must assist free peoples to work out their destinies in their own way.
> I believe that our help should be primarily through economic and financial aid which is essential to economic stability and orderly political processes.
> The free peoples of the world look to us for support in maintaining their freedoms.
> If we falter in our leadership, we may endanger the peace of the world—and we must surely endanger the welfare of our own nation.[21]

THE MARSHALL PLAN

The Marshall Plan for the economic recovery of Europe, announced just four months after the promulgation of the Truman Doctrine, was also conceived of by Truman and Acheson as a geopolitical counterthrust to Soviet-sponsored subversion of the West, but it was presented to the public largely as a compound of humanitarian largesse and enlightened economic statesmanship, the latter proceeding from the premise that an economically healthy Europe was a precondition for the world trade required by an expanding United States economy. It was a conscious policy decision to underplay the global balance-of-power considerations.

Between Truman's address to Congress in March 1947 and Marshall's speech at Harvard in June, the Moscow conference of foreign ministers adjourned in recognized failure to make any progress in resolving the East–West discord over the future of Germany and Austria. "The Americans came home from Moscow," Walt Rostow recalls, "firm in the conclusion that the United States should never again negotiate from a base of weakness. . . . The picture of Europe was one of mammoth slow-moving crisis. There was a growing awareness that something big had to be done in Europe to avoid a disaster to the American interest; that a substantial program of economic aid addressed constructively to the problems of economic recovery was required to deal with the multiple threats to the Eurasian power balance."[22] Secretary of State Marshall reported to the country over the radio that "disintegrating forces are becoming evident. The patient is sinking while the doctors deliberate. . . . action cannot await compromise through exhaustion."[23]

In a then-secret memorandum, George Kennan and the policy planning staff recognized that "the communists are exploiting the European crisis and . . . further communist successes would create serious danger to American security." But they advised Secretary of State Marshall that

American effort in aid to Europe should be directed not to the combating of communism as such but to the restoration of the health and vigor of European society. It should aim, in other words, not to combat communism, but the economic maladjustment which makes European society vulnerable to exploitation by any and all totalitarian movements and which Russian communism is now exploiting.[24]

And significantly, there was a brief separate section at the end of the memorandum advising that

Steps should be taken to clarify what the press has unfortunately come to identify as the "Truman Doctrine," and to remove in particular two damaging impressions which are current in large sections of American public opinion. These are:

a. That the United States approach to world problems is a defensive reaction to Communist pressure and that the effort to restore sound economic conditions in the other countries is only the by-product of this reaction and not something we would be interested in doing if there were no Communist menace.

b. That the Truman Doctrine is a blank check to give economic and military aid to any area of the world where Communists show signs of being successful. It must be made clear that the extension of American aid is essentially a question of political economy in the literal sense of the term and that such aid will be considered only in cases where the prospective results bear a satisfactory relationship to the expenditure of American resources and effort.[25]

The Secretary of State heeded this advice. Launching the program for European recovery at Cambridge on June 5, 1947, he claimed, "Our policy is directed not against any country or doctrine but against hunger, poverty, desperation and chaos." And the offer to join in the cooperative effort was made to *all* European nations.[26] There was considerable disagreement over this, and many in the United States government and Western Europe were relieved when Stalin prevented the East European states from joining the effort. But the offer to all European nations was genuine. Marshall and those like him in the State Department had a multifaceted view of the balance of power considerations: they felt that the revival of Western European economic vigor, which was based in large measure on manufacturing, would be facilitated by the raw material resources that once again could be tapped in the Eastern European areas. Eastern Europe in turn could provide a market for the West's manufactured goods. To maintain an advantageous balance of power against the Soviet Union the West needed a strong Western Europe; it did not require an unhealthy Eastern Europe. Moreover, there were some in the United States government who felt that an Eastern Europe largely dependent for its own well-being upon economic relations with the West would be less subject to total Soviet control.[27]

But such questions became academic as the Soviet Union moved even more swiftly during the summer of 1947 to transform the lands it had occupied militarily into dependent units of a tightly integrated economic and political system. The last hopes for some preserve of Western liberalism in Eastern Europe died in February 1948 when the Communist leadership in Czechoslovakia, backed by Soviet armed might, demanded, and was granted, full powers of government.

Meanwhile the public dissemination in the summer of 1947, through the medium of *Foreign Affairs* magazine, of George Kennan's analysis of Soviet grand strategy, and his concept of "containment" as a countervailing grand strategy of the West,[28] provided the missing link for policy-oriented intellectuals who were trying to piece together the real basis, as distinct from the surface rationale, for the Truman Doctrine and the Marshall Plan. Kennan's coherent analysis and prescriptions were, of course, only one of a number of alternative formulations of the emerging official premises about United States–Soviet relations. In some accounts of United States cold war policy the "X" article is treated as the official position of the government. This is incorrect. Many of its premises continued to be debated within the highest levels of the administration. But it did take the public wraps off of a core set of beliefs around which there was an operating consensus among the responsible decision makers: the Soviet's "unfriendliness of purpose," as Kennan put it, was "basic." It proceeded from the inner structure of Soviet-Russian society. Soviet policies over the foreseeable future would reflect "no real faith in the possibility of a permanent happy coexistence of the Socialist and Capitalist worlds, but rather a cautious, persistent pressure toward the disruption and weakening of all rival influence and rival power." Consequently, "if the Soviet government occasionally sets its signatures to documents which would indicate the contrary, this is to be regarded as a tactical maneuver permissible in dealing with the enemy." Moreover, the Soviets, believing in the ultimate triumph of their cause, were as patient as they were relentless. "The Russians look forward to a duel of infinite duration." The implications for American policy needed to be faced: "Sporadic acts" of standing up and talking tough to the Russians were not enough, even if they seemed to produce temporary Soviet retreats. "The main element of any United States policy toward the Soviet Union must be that of a long-term, patient but firm and vigilant containment of Russian expansive tendencies." This policy would require "the adroit and vigilant application of counterforce at a series of constantly shifting geographical and political points, corresponding to the shifts and maneuvers of Soviet policy."[29]

4

THE IMPLEMENTATION OF
CONTAINMENT

The question we have had to face is whether the Communist plan of conquest can be stopped without general war. Our Government and other countries associated with us in the United Nations believe that the best chance of stopping it without war is to meet the attack in Korea and defeat it there.

—HARRY S. TRUMAN

George Kennan's *Foreign Affairs* article displayed important premises about Soviet intentions on which there was an emerging consensus among Truman administration officials. The Secretary of State attempted to lay out the policy consequences of these premises in a report to the Cabinet in early 1947. According to the account in James Forrestal's diary, Marshall stated "that the objective of our policy from this point on would be the restoration of the balance of power in both Europe and Asia and that *all actions would be viewed in light of this objective.*"[1]

There was still a significant lack of consensus, however, on the components of both Kennan's "counterforce" and the "balance of power" that Marshall wanted "restored." The administration was broadly divided between those who regarded the industrial strength of the United States, based on a sound economy, as the weightiest ingredient in the global balance, and those who viewed the extension of Soviet control over new areas of the globe as the most important factor. In the pre–Korean War period, the Bureau of the Budget, the Council of Economic Advisers, and the White House staff tended to stress domestic economic considerations whereas State and Defense tended to emphasize stopping the Soviets.

But even among those who were most oriented toward a global, geopolitical view of the power rivalry with the Soviet Union there was an important divergence of premises concerning both the components of the balance of power and of the American strategies required to stop Soviet expansion. The divergent points of view in 1947–48 clustered around Secretary of State Marshall and Secretary of Defense Forrestal.

MARSHALL VS. FORRESTAL

Marshall's most passionate commitment now was to the success of the European Recovery Program. But he did concede that a militarily strong Western Europe was essential to right the global balance of power and provide the means locally to dissuade the Russians from attempting an easy fait accompli, either by political subversion or military aggression. Western Europe itself could not contain the Soviets in a major war, but it could provide the front line of defense. The United States would have to come to the direct aid of Europe in any such war, but, as in the Second World War, the full weight of American power would be felt in the later stages of the war as mobilization went into high gear. Marshall favored universal military training (UMT) in the United States to provide the base for such mobilization should it ever be required, and to signal in advance the refusal of the United States to tolerate Soviet aggression; but he did not view Soviet aggression as sufficiently imminent to require a major increase to ready forces-in-being. Even in response to the Soviet provocations around Berlin in the spring of 1948, and the blockade of 1948–49, Marshall pressed for priority to be given to *European* rearmament. Marshall, of course, was sensitive to the strong political motivations in the White House and Congress for keeping the lid on expenditures, and very likely saw universal military training plus European rearmament—neither of which would require any sudden major increases in the U.S. budget—as compatible with continued congressional financing of the multibillion dollar project for rebuilding Europe's economy just getting under way.[2]

Secretary of Defense Forrestal gave priority to the rearmanent of the United States as the most effective means of preserving the balance of power against the Soviet Union. To procrastinate on the buildup of an effective United States military posture would be to "deny Marshall the cards to play" in current crisis situations.[3] Strengthening European military capabilities was important, but Forrestal was skeptical of the Europeans' ability to sustain their level of effort on economic reconstruction and simultaneously build the kind of military establishments needed to balance Soviet military power in Europe. In the meantime—he wrote in late 1947—under current budget allocations, reflecting the existing policy of assisting European recovery before American rearmament, we were taking a "calculated risk." That risk involved reliance on the American *strategic* advantage, consisting of American productive capacity, the predominance of American sea power, and the exclusive possession of the atomic bomb. But the last factor, he warned, would be of "indeterminate" duration. "The years before any possible power can achieve the capabilities to attack us with weapons of mass destruction are our years of opportunity."[4] It is clear that had Forrestal been given his way he would have attached greater urgency to the buildup of a balanced United States military posture that did not bank too heavily on either the perpetuation of the atomic monopoly or the rapid recovery of Europe which would allow Europeans to assume the major burden of sustaining the balance of the continent.*

This difference between Marshall and Forrestal over the components of effective international power was in fact resolved in favor of Marshall by the White House and the Bureau of the Budget. Considerations of domestic political economy rather than a systematic analysis of the capabilities needed to carry out the nation's foreign policy commitments seemed to determine the executive choice to stick with military budgets well below $15 billion a year, until the Korean emergency revised the prevailing priorities.

---

*There was yet another consideration that may have weighed heavily with Forrestal. In contrast to the services over which he presided (as the first Secretary of Defense), Forrestal appeared to be more interested in a general increase in the military budget and capabilities than in the implementation of any particular strategic doctrine. He seemed to regard some of the esoteric strategic debates of the military as responses to low budget ceilings, and the consequent need to convince their political benefactors that security could be had only through their particular functions and capabilities. These specious debates were a severe source of embarrassment to Forrestal. In his attempts to achieve harmony within the defense establishment, higher budgets would put him in a position to mitigate the intensity of interservice rivalry.

NSC-68

Actually, a systematic appraisal *was* called for by the President and undertaken by a special State–Defense task force months before the North Korean invasion of South Korea. The Soviet blockade of Berlin during 1948–49 and the collateral negotiations of the North Atlantic Treaty had focused attention in the State Department and the White House on the limitations of the usable military power at the disposal of the West in case of major conflict in Europe. The Soviet atomic bomb detonation in August 1949, three years ahead of United States intelligence estimates, gave immediacy to the alarms Forrestal had been sounding on the temporary nature of our strategic advantage. And the fall of China to Mao Zedong the next month, placing the bulk of the Eurasian heartland under Communist control and raising the spectre of a division of the world's population into two halves, was suddenly seen by many in the administration, as it had not been when only hypothetical, as an immense strategic fact of life. The convergence of these events with the need for Truman to say yes or no to an H-bomb program produced a requirement for some kind of coherent doctrine on our military capabilities, just as the withdrawal of the British from Greece in 1947 produced the need for a doctrine on our intentions. Truman's decision in January 1950 to give the green light, tentatively, to the H-bomb program was accompanied by a directive to the Secretaries of State and Defense to make a comprehensive review of United States foreign and defense policies in light of the developments just mentioned.[5]

In the process of preparing the general strategic appraisal called for by Truman, a dialogue on the components of the global balance of power, analogous to that conducted between Marshall and Forrestal in the 1947–48 period, was now reenacted within the State Department between George Kennan and Paul Nitze.

Kennan laid greater stress on the nonmilitary components of the bipolar struggle, and felt that the Soviets were so reluctant to become involved in a major war against the United States that the most important fact in the strategic equation was a clear *resolve* by the United States not to tolerate piecemeal opportunistic extension of Soviet control. Translating this into military terms was difficult, and apparently uncongenial to Kennan. However, he is reported to have urged the organization of mobile, quickly deployable United States task forces which could be rushed to the scene of "brushfire" conflicts and thus confront the Soviets with the choice of desisting from their provocation or engaging the United States in a military clash which might expand into a major war. Kennan's analysis of the Soviets convinced him that when confronted with such a stark choice the Soviets would back down. Kennan thus did not feel that a general rearmament program was necessary. Moreover, rearmament would further focus national energies on the cruder means of waging the cold war, as opposed to flexible and subtler forms of diplomacy and a stress on improving the quality of life of the Western nations.

Paul Nitze, who became a liaison between State and Defense when Acheson became Secretary of State in January 1949, gave greater weight than did Kennan to the overall balance of military force between the Soviets and the United States. As Director of the Policy Planning Staff in 1950, and chairman of the ad hoc study group which produced the strategic paper requested by the President, Nitze's views were critical in shaping the advanced planning concepts being developed at the time. Kennan retained his influence as State Department Counselor, and his knowledge of the Soviet Union was influential in the deliberations of the study group, but Nitze was known to have the full support of Secretary Acheson, who took the study very seriously. Forrestal's economy-minded successor at Defense, Louis Johnson, was a weak Secretary who provided little support or guidance to Defense Department participants in the study. Any initiative or major departures in overall strategic planning, then, would be responses to the momentum generated by Nitze in fulfilling Truman's desire for a new strategic appraisal.

Nitze felt that the nation's military planning was seriously constrained by the strict budgetary limits imposed by the White House and the Bureau of the Budget. In light of the emergence of a Soviet nuclear weapons capability, the United States would need not only to improve its massive destructive capabilities (as was contemplated in the H-bomb program) but also to balance the Soviet capabilities for conventional war. These ideas emerged as major premises in NSC-68 (the paper's file number upon referral to the National Security Council). For the first time since the war, military planning concepts were tied to an explicit body of assumptions about the political and technological state of the world. On the basis of an analysis of Soviet economic strengths and weaknesses, the study projected that in four years the Soviets would have a nuclear capability sufficient to neutralize the United States nuclear capability for deterring local wars. Moreover, the Soviets would build this capability without any diminution in their local war capability. Thus, by 1954, if the West did not take significant compensating measures, the balance of military power would have shifted in favor of the Soviets. When this happened economic and technical assistance would be insufficient to contain Soviet expansion.

The Nitze group also challenged prevailing premises about the U.S. economy. They argued that the nation could well afford to devote 20 percent of the gross national product to national security purposes as compared with the 5 percent then being spent. In budget terms, defense expenditures could, and ought to, rise as high as $60 billion a year, from the $15 billion then programmed. Nitze and his staff economist, Robert Tufts, had an important ally in Leon Keyserling of the President's Council of Economic Advisers. (Keyserling had consistently urged "expansionist" policies against the views of the Council's Chairman, Edwin Nourse. Nourse resigned in October 1949, and from then on, first as acting Chairman, and as Chairman from May 1950, Keryserling dominated the Council and was an increasingly persuasive force throughout the administration.)[6] In retrospect it is not possible to say whether this alliance of Nitze and Acheson at State and Keyserling in the White House would have moved Truman away from his natural economic conservatism and his political responsiveness to "welfare" demands, and provided a convincing presidential rationale for *implementing* NSC-68, had the Korean invasion not taken place in June 1950.

Acheson had begun to lay the groundwork with his talks in February 1950 on the need to create "situations of strength" vis-à-vis the Soviet Union prior to attempting any kind of global settlement (as was then being suggested by Churchill). But as yet these declarations did not go much beyond making the aspiration explicit to wider public audiences.[7] Any diversion of a larger portion of the nation's resources to affect the global balance of military power was still not administration policy. Truman understood that such a shift in the allocation of resources would have to rest on popular consent; and the people, he believed, did not yet appreciate the current function of the military balance of power in global diplomacy.

The Communist North Koreans, by suddenly taking advantage of a local disparity in military power on June 24, 1950, finally gave Truman a sufficient basis for asking the people to approve militarily "rational" national security policies worked out by his professional foreign policy advisers.

NSC-68 became the conceptual framework on which the rapid expansion of United States armed forces was hung during the first months of the Korean War. Before the war was over military spending had reached a peak of $50 billion a year. The 1,461,000 men in the United States armed forces in June 1950 were more than doubled in two years, with the Army accounting for the largest increase. As compared with 48 Air Force wings in 1950, the Korean Armistice in 1953 left the United States with nearly 100 wings, with another 50 expected to come into the inventory over the coming four-year period. The Navy was floating 671 ships on the eve of hostilities in 1950 and over 1,100 by the summer of 1952.[8] Although administration spokesmen before Congress defended their early Korean War budgets by reference to NSC-68, and although there was an across-the-board doubling of military capabilities, it cannot be inferred that the original premises advanced by the Nitze group about the emerging balance of power now constituted the doctrinal basis of the Truman administration's new national security policy. The Korean War rapidly generated its own priority requirements, and the critical question put by members of Congress to any budget proposal was: How does this help us in Korea?

On the more conceptual military planning level, the Korean War heightened differences rather than produced a consensus. For some the Korean War confirmed the thesis that the Western alliance needed permanent and large-scale conventional armies to deter the Communists from further aggression. This view was reflected most clearly in the NATO force goals formulated during the Korean War, the high point being the February 1952 Lisbon ministerial meeting which called for 96 divisions to be ready or deployable for a European conflict. But the Korean experience also stimulated advocates of an opposing doctrine: namely, that Korea was a model of how *not* to fight a war; that to allow the Communists to engage the United States in conventional land warfare was to allow them to choose the grounds and weapons most favorable to them; that the superior mode of warfare for the technologically advanced West was strategic, relying mostly upon air power to strike deep at the sources of enemy power with weapons of mass destruction; that the way to preserve the balance of power (as the Soviets built up their strategic capabilities) was not to dissipate our resources in an effort to redress the imbalance in armed manpower, but to enhance our capabilities for strategic warfare. The resolution of these antithetical military doctrinal reactions to the Korean War had to await a change in administrations.

Yet the Korean War—the way it was fought by the United States, and the force-posture planning decisions made at the same time— left a material and institutional legacy of progams-in-being not significantly different from those implied in NSC-68. And programs-in-being tend to shape fundamental policy premises just as much as, if not more than, premises tend to shape programs. The perpetuation of existing programs often become a psychological, no less than bread-and-butter, commitment for those with the responsibility for their administration. The fact is that the Korean War *institutionalized* a set of operational (though not necessarily intellectually held) premises:

1. The Soviet Union would resort to military expansion if not checked by visible countervailing military power.

2. Local imbalances of military power which favored the Soviets or a Soviet satellite would lead to further "Koreas."

3. The most appetizing local imbalance to the Soviets was in Central Europe.

4. The global balance of power would shift in favor of the Soviets if they were able to swallow the rest of Central Europe, namely, West Germany and Austria. No other area on the periphery of the Communist world, except for the Greco-Turkish flanks (which were already being buttressed) had such a critical function for the balance of power. The next most critical area on the Soviet periphery was Japan.

5. While attending to the power rations in these primary regions, the United States must not neglect local imbalances in secondary and tertiary areas. The capability and clearly communicated will to defend whatever area the Communist powers might choose to attack, regardless of its intrinsic geopolitical weight in the overall balance, was necessary to prevent the Communists from picking and choosing easy targets for blackmail and aggression. And a number of small territorial grabs *could* add up to a critical

alteration of the global balance. Moreover, our failure to defend one country would demoralize nationals in other localities in their will to resist the Communists. Even in Western Europe people would wonder under what circumstances we might consider them dispensable.

Similar premises, to be sure, antedated the Korean War. But their existence, even in the person, say, of Secretary of State Acheson, did not make them the basis of government policy. It took the Korean conflict to give "validity" to these premises—not by proving them correct, but by making them the assumptions on which important wartime and planning decisions would be reached.

The overriding fear in the White House was not simply that the loss of the Korean peninsula would encourage the Soviets to embark on further aggressions. Rather, it was that the Soviets were now embarked on a pattern of military aggression to pin down the resources of the United States in peripheral battles until the right moment arrived and they could move, virtually unopposed, into Western Europe.

In his *Memoirs* Truman divulges how the strategic (United States–Soviet) situation limited his flexibility in the tactical (Korean) campaign. It was his intention, Truman recalls, to take all necessary measures to push the North Koreans back behind the 38th parallel. But he was unwilling to commit the United States so deeply in Korea that we would not have the resources to handle other situations.[9] The strategic prize was Western Europe, with its skilled manpower and industrial infrastructure. Truman was convinced that Europe was still at the center of the Soviet design for world domination, and he, for one, was not going to allow our attention to be diverted from this dominant feature of the global power contest.[10]

When the Communist Chinese armies intervened, the prospect of becoming bogged down in a huge war in Asia became more immediate, particularly in light of pressure from General MacArthur to attack the Communist staging bases in Manchuria, even at the risk of a general war with China. The administration's view was articulated by Dean Acheson at a November 28, 1950, meeting of the National Security Council. The Soviet Union was behind every one of the Chinese Communist and North Korean moves, said the Secretary of State. We were in competition with the Soviets all around the globe. Thus Korea was a world matter, not merely a regional matter. If we were to lose sight of this fact, he warned, and allowed Russia to trap us on the Asian mainland, we would risk sinking into a bottomless pit.[11]

The Secretary of State presented a similar case to the British a few weeks later during the President's Washington conferences with Prime Minister Attlee. The central enemy was not China, stressed Acheson, but the Soviet Union. The aggression by the North Koreans was not a local, spontaneous maneuver. It was a part of the larger Communist design to get us preoccupied in Asia so the Russians could have a free hand in Europe. We must not and would not distort our global priorities.[12]

This Europe-first emphasis was of course congenial to the British, who were, if anything, afraid that the United States might have already become overcommitted to an increasingly costly Asian conflict and might engage in rash action—such as nuclear bombardment of China. Attlee kept raising reservations about the value of attempting to defend Formosa. Acheson refined the Europe-first emphasis, by pointing to strategic interdependencies among the various forward positions then being sustained. He explained to the British leader that, apart from how we might feel about Chiang Kai-shek, we could not, for geopolitical reasons, allow Formosa to fall into Communist hands. The fall of Formosa would raise severe problems for us in Japan and in the Philippines, contended Acheson; and these countries, being the sites of our bases for conducting operations in the theater, had become essential to our survival as a Pacific power.[13]

General Marshall, present during one of these exchanges, added his weight to the strategic evaluation of Formosa: it was of no particular strategic importance in our hands, but it would be of disastrous importance if it were held by an enemy.[14]

But if hard choices did have to be made in Asia, there was little doubt that priority would have to be accorded the defense of Japan. Such an eventuality was in the minds of the Joint Chiefs during the bleakest days following the Chinese intervention. In the third week of December 1950 they suggested to Truman that consideration ought to be given to ways of withdrawing from Korea "with honor" in order to protect Japan.[15]

The administration's view of the global geopolitical interests and risks involved in the Korean struggle ran head on with General MacArthur's view that decisive military victory in the theater of operations was of overriding importance. But the very intensity of the disagreement between Truman and MacArthur produced a greater self-awareness within the administration of its own objectives and the policies it deemed necessary to implement them.

The much-quoted testimony of General Bradley (to extend the fighting in the mainland of Asia would "involve us in the wrong war, at the wrong place, at the wrong time, and with the wrong enemy"[16]) emphasises the operational effects on the prosecution of the war itself of the premise that the Soviets had their military sights focused on Western Europe. The effects on long-range military planning and alliance diplomacy were no less significant. As Truman telegraphed MacArthur near the final stages of their controversy: "In reaching a final decision about Korea, I shall have to give constant thought to the main threat from the Soviet Union and the need for a rapid expansion of our armed forces to meet this great danger."[17]

The Europe-oriented consequences of those premises led to the rapid transformation of NATO from a security-guarantee pact into an international regional theater army, most heavily deployed at the spot of critical vulnerability in the global balance: the Central European front. This in turn meant that our European diplomacy was to be oriented toward gaining acceptance from the North Atlantic alliance partners of the rearmament of West Germany. And the rearmament of West Germany, in its turn, would require—largely to reassure the French—a United States commitment to the principle of supranational (or "integrated") commands, in which the German units would be unable to take independent action.[18]

Although the stimulus of the Korean crisis was short-lived and, by late 1951, the Europeans had returned to their pre-1950 emphasis on economic recovery, an institutional framework was created for redressing the Central European balance in a future conflict. A supreme commander over allied forces was named, and provided with a large international staff and planning organization, for the purpose of implementing NATO directives on force posture and strategy. Germany was given the major responsibility for providing troops for a "forward defense" under a multinational command directly subordinate to the Supreme allied Commander (Eisenhower). An American military presence—not just bases for the strategic arm, but an overseas army in the forward defense apparatus—was accepted by United States planners as necessary for the indefinite future. (There was some ambiguity with respect to the function and eventual size of these overseas United States deployments, however.

Both General Eisenhower and Secretary of Defense Marshall, in urging congressional authorization of an additional four divisions for Europe in 1951, attempted to delimit their function as largely that of a catalyst for European contributions to a forward ground defense force, in which the Europeans were expected to assume the major burden.)

Moreover, the United States view of the altered scale of priorities, now giving first place to the military components of the power balance, was made explicit to recipients of Marshall Plan assistance. Further economic assistance was made contingent upon the alliance partner's conscientious attempt to fulfill its NATO rearmament obligations.[19] By 1951, the European Recovery Program was formally subordinated to "security" considerations under the omnibus Mutual Security Act.

The way the United States fought the Korean War—particularly our willingness to allow sanctuary status to Communist China even after it became an active belligerent—confirmed and sharpened the premise that mainland Asia was of secondary weight in the balance of global power as compared with Western Europe. But as the United States was willing to fight a high-cost war to keep South Korea out of Communist hands this also gave impetus to the emerging realization that the power contest could be won or lost in the secondary theaters when there was a stalemate in the primary theater.

The Korean War thus marked a globalization of containment in terms of operational commitments as well as rhetoric. The United States finally "intervened" physically in the Chinese civil war by interposing the Seventh Fleet between Mao Zedong's forces and Chiang's last island fortresses. Despite U.S. anticolonial protestations, Washington now financially supported French efforts to suppress the Ho Chi Minh Communist-nationalist insurgency in Indochina. And although the United States *formally* intervened in Korea under a United Nations mandate (by virtue of the absence of the Soviet delegate from the Security Council at the time the votes were taken), henceforth U.S. plans, public commitments, and material undertakings would no longer convey to global adversaries the impression that Washington would hesitate to act unilaterally. Article 51 (the self-defense provision) of the UN Charter now became the operative legal instrumentality of "collective security" arrangements in the secondary as well as the primary theaters.

The globalization of containment—the notion that practically all pieces of territory now had significant, if not decisive, weight in the power balance, that the reputation for being willing to defend each piece was a critical ingredient of our maintenance of allies and deterrence of enemies—rested on solid bipartisan support. The Republican challenge was not to these fundamental assumptions. Rather, they charged that the Truman administration was first too late and then too restrained in countering the threat of Communism in Asia.

The forum for partisan rallying was the 1951 Senate investigation of Truman's recall of General MacArthur from his command.[20] Here, for the first time, the bipartisan Europe-first policy was made the subject of a great debate between the two parties. Secretary of State Acheson's January 1950 statement omitting South Korea from the U.S. "defense perimeter" in the western Pacific was held up to scorn by the opposition (who neglected to note that General MacArthur had traced a similar line in March 1949), who charged that Acheson's statement constituted an "invitation" to Stalin to attack.[21] It became a Republican article of party faith that the Truman administration, out of nearsightedness as to the ultimate power stakes involved, "lost" China to the Communists.

But this breakdown in the domestic consensus over where the stakes in the global power balance lay was a *retrospective* cleavage.

In 1948 no prominent United States politician or China expert rose to challenge Secretary of State Marshall's assessment that:

China does not itself possess the raw material and industrial resources which would enable it to become a first-class military power within the foreseeable future. The country is at present in the midst of a social and political revolution. Until this revolution is completed—and it will take a long time—there is no prospect that sufficient stability and order can be established to permit China's early development into a strong state.[22]

Nor had the critics of the Truman administration's China policies been willing to support United States *combat* operations against Mao in 1948 and 1949 when it became clear that military assistance alone would not suffice. Only marginal increments in aid were offered by members of Congress in the China Aid Act of 1948. The statement of Representative Walter Judd (one of Chiang's staunchest supporters) was typical: "Not for one moment has anyone contemplated sending a single combat soldier in. . . . So it is important to make clear when we speak of military aid . . . it is supplies, training, and advice, nothing further."[23] This had been the period when the rapid postwar military demobilization was in high gear. It was the same atmosphere that led Truman to defer approval of the NSC-68 recommendations, even though he appreciated their strategic soundness.

While the Korean War allowed Republicans and Democrats alike to loosen the purse strings a bit for rearmament, many in the opposition party, now urging a decisive victory in Korea and willing to follow MacArthur into a general war with China, were ready to claim superior wisdom from having been Mao haters since the middle 1940s. This was virtue through hindsight only. Their new charges that the Truman administration had been overly feeble in its approach to the China problem a few years back were regarded by administration policy makers as gratuitous since the critics themselves had cooperated in the enfeeblement process. General Marshall later recalled how he was pressed ad nauseam in the early postwar period to give the Communists hell. "I am a soldier and know something about the ability to give hell," he told a Pentagon audience. "At that time, my facilities for giving them hell . . . was [sic] $1\frac{1}{3}$ divisions over the entire United States. That's quite a proposition when you deal with somebody with over 260 and you have $1\frac{1}{3}$."[24]

Significantly, Marshall did not count among his hell-giving facilities the atomic bomb. If there was to be a military contest with the Chinese Communists, the bomb apparently was of little military utility, nor would it be used as a threat to forestall counterintervention by the Soviets. This was also a part of the atmosphere of the time—especially with respect to any official contemplation in public of its use against Asians so soon after Hiroshima and Nagasaki.

However, the Korean War eroded this constraint on United States calculations of usable power in conflict situations. Truman did not unequivocally rule out the use of the bomb.[25] And the Eisenhower administration went further by hinting that it would have to resort to nuclear weapons if a breakdown in peace negotiations led to a resumption of the war.

In the view of the NSC-68 planners, Korea should have marked the transition to a new era of higher peacetime military budgets, aimed centrally at rectifying local imbalances of power between the Communist and non-Communist nations. The Eisenhower administration also felt it was beholden to a popular mandate against further Koreas and alterations in the existing local military imbalances would be essential for the maintenance of U.S. global commitments and preventing Soviet miscalculations such as Korea. But the plans of the Truman administration for rearmament were seen to be incompatible with the conventional Republican philosophy of reduced government expenditures.

The most appropriate kind of military power for implementing the now globalized "containment" policy was to remain the primary subject of policy-level debate. But for at least another ten years, the policy itself (however much the Republicans disliked associating themselves with it), and the premise that an advantageous military balance of power was its essential prerequisite, was taken as fact in official Washington.

The weight of the non-Communist nations in the global balance of power was to be defined, predominantly, as the product of three variables: United States military forces-in-being, United States industrial and economic strength, and the indigenous military-forces-in-being of allies of the United States. Significantly, the *economic* strength of other non-Communist nations was not to be directly taken into account, in terms of requiring significant outlays by the United States. To the extent that balance-of-power considerations would suppress other considerations in United States foreign policy, policies whose rationale was the socioeconomic development of other nations would receive only marginal attention to top United States decision makers.

PART III

THE EISENHOWER ERA

Occasional pages of history do record the faces of the "Great Destroyers" but the whole book of history reveals mankind's never-ending quest for peace, and mankind's God-given capacity to build.

It is with the book of history, and not with isolated pages, that the United States will ever wish to be identified.

—DWIGHT D. EISENHOWER

I don't expect other nations to love us. . . . But I do expect them to respect us. . . . This means that we abide by our commitments, that we speak only of what we can do, and do what we speak of.

—JOHN FOSTER DULLES

5

A NEW LOOK FOR LESS
EXPENSIVE POWER

*We keep locks on our doors, but we do not have an armed guard in every home.
We rely principally on a common security system so well equipped to punish those
who break in and steal that, in fact, would-be aggressors are generally deterred.
That is the modern way of getting maximum protection at bearable cost.*

—JOHN FOSTER DULLES

The Korean War simplified U.S. foreign policy by giving the maintenance of a balance of power against the Soviet Union and China top spot among previously competing foreign policy objectives and according primacy to the military components of power. Yet the Truman administration left office without resolving the competing doctrines of effective military power put forward by the military strategists.

The Eisenhower administration retained the predominantly military definition of the power balance instituted during the later Truman years; but it carried the process of simplification even further by selecting one of the competing doctrines—and the most narrowly specialized one, at that—as the concept that would guide the allocation of resources to meet the perceived threats to the nation. The military definition of the power balance was leavened somewhat, however, by the prominence given in the Eisenhower administration to the nation's economic health as a critical factor in sustaining the global balance. But here too, the political and economic theories that prevailed in the White House tended toward a simplification and narrowing of the premises governing the choice of national security programs.

The new grand strategy reflected Dwight Eisenhower's determination to implement the philosophy of fiscal conservatism he shared with the Taft wing of the Republican Party (led by Senator Robert Taft of Ohio, whom he had defeated for the party's nomination). Many of Eisenhower's top appointments were fiscal conservatives: George Humphrey at the Treasury Department, Charles Wilson at the Defense Department, Sinclair Weeks at the Commerce Department, Arthur Burns at the Council of Economic Advisers, and Gabriel Hague, the President's administrative assistant responsible for economic affairs. The programmatic expression of their economic philosophy included balanced budgets, fiscal and monetary checks to avoid inflation, tax reduction, and, underlying these, a restoration of the "free market" economy with a minimum of government interference.[1]

THE GREAT EQUATION

Eisenhower's search for a strategic concept that would satisfy the terms of what he liked to think of as the "great equation" (reduced government expenditures *and* military security in the face of expanding Soviet capabilities) had begun shortly after the 1952 election, and continued with intensity, at various levels in the administration, for fifteen months until it emerged full-blown in the spring of 1954.[2]

The notion that defense budget economies could be effected by concentrating on strategic airpower was being urged by the Churchill government during 1951 and 1952. The concept propounded was very similar to that being urged by the United States Air Force since 1948: namely, that strategic air power was now the decisive element in warfare and deterrence, its function being to break the back of enemy power and will at their source. All other capabilities were subsidiary, and, to the extent the other capabilities took away from the resources necessary to maintain strategic superiority over the Soviets, these other capabilities were wasteful. Such strategic monism went against the grain of the balanced defense concepts developed in NSC-68 and implemented on an emergency basis during the Korean War; but they fit in handily with the Republican attempt to exploit popular discontent and confusion with the frustrating military stalemate in Korea. In a *Life* magazine article of May 19, 1952, John Foster Dulles presaged the doctrine which was worked out more fully later by writing of an "instant massive retaliation" capacity as one that provided the United States with the means of taking "action of our own choosing" in contrast to Korea-type engagements where terrain and means were chosen by the enemy.

Eisenhower, at this early stage, still fresh from his NATO role, where it was his job to convince the allies of the necessity for building a significant "forward defense" capability in Europe, did not take too readily to such strategic *avant-gardism*. The presidential candidate is reported to have insisted that the phrase "retaliatory striking power" be stricken from the Republican platform, where it appeared at Dulles' suggestion. However, the general was somewhat enamored of the idea of a mobile strategic reserve based in the United States as the United States contribution to alliance defense, with the forward positions being sustained initially by the forward countries themselves. This hope for allied assumption of the major forward defense burdens had been somewhat dampened by his exposure, as Supreme Allied Commander under NATO, to the economic difficulties the Europeans were encountering in raising and provisioning their armies. As yet, though, Eisenhower himself had propounded no discernibly coherent strategic concept which could serve as an alternative to the programs of the Truman administration.

The initial approach to a new concept is supposed to have begun in earnest in December, before inauguration, as Eisenhower assembled his new Cabinet aboard the U.S.S. *Helena,* on his way back from a trip to Korea. Eisenhower posed the problem: a prolongation of the defense programs then under way would have serious consequences for the American way of life. A free economy with minimal government interference in the life of its citizens would be supplanted by a "garrison state." And the draw upon the resources and finances of the nation would likely lead to serious inflation which would do major harm to the economy. Admiral Radford (soon to be selected by Eisenhower as Chairman of the Joint Chiefs of Staff) and Dulles offered suggestions for effecting savings by more efficient deployment and use of the technologies of atomic-age warfare. Radford is said to have argued that United States military power was overextended—especially in Asia, where it could be pinned down. Instead, he favored a "mobile strategic reserve" based in or near the continental United States. Major reliance for initial local defense would be on indigenous forces. Dulles used the opportunity to argue the virtues of a United States posture based primarily on massive strategic striking power whose function would be to *deter* the Russians instead of trying to contain them all around their extensive perimeter.

These ideas evidently made an impact on Eisenhower, but they were not yet sufficiently gelled to constitute a base for resolution of budgetary issues in the spring of 1953. With a passion to effect dramatic slashes in the Truman holdover budget for fiscal 1954, budget director Dodge, with the President's blessing, instructed all departments to make cuts in existing programs. The Department of Defense was expected to effect reductions of some $4 billion in the forthcoming fiscal year, with a view toward an additional $6 billion reduction for fiscal 1955. The means by which the reductions were to be effected were apparently of little interest to the Bureau of the Budget—that was the business of the defense people; but reductions there must be. Not surprisingly, the Joint Chiefs of Staff reported back to the National Security Council that reductions down to the contemplated ceilings would dangerously affect national security. The civilian officials of the Department of Defense thereupon took matters into their own hands, and largely through not letting any new contracts in 1954 were able to effect paper reductions (actually deferred decisions) to a level more in line with White House requests.

Clearly, a continuation of such leveling off and reduction in expenditures would require a major revision in the concepts upon which the military were then basing their requirements.

One of the earliest of the concepts developed at the White House–NSC level was announced by the President at the end of April 1953. This was the so-called long-haul basis for military planning, which, presumably, was to substitute for the previous administration's method of planning toward some selected "crisis year" or "year of maximum peril." Under this "new" concept a broad base for effecting mobilization when and if needed was to be substituted for high military manpower levels; and an industrial-technological base capable of supporting expanded production schedules was to be maintained along with research and development in new systems, instead of attempting to fulfill specific production goals tagged to some specific year, only to be faced with inventories of technologically obsolete weapons. Actually, the "old" system was not the caricature it was made out to be by the new administration. The target years were meant primarily as a stimulus—as a way of dramatizing the adverse consequences to the global balance of power if corrective action was not well under way by then; and this in no way implied that the provision of mobilization, industrial and research bases for expansion and innovation was to be given short shrift.

The effect of the announcement of the long-haul concept seems to have been primarily to deflate somewhat the sense of urgency underlying existing defense budget levels. This was, of course, part of the effect intended. "It has been coldly calculated by the Soviet leaders," explained Eisenhower, ". . . by their military threat to force upon America and the free world an unbearable security burden leading to economic disaster."[3]

Needless to say, the announcement was very well received in NATO circles, where the NATO Council in its April 1953 session agreed to Dulles' suggestions for a slowdown in the NATO buildup. This was merely a formal recognition of the slackening that had already been taking place in Europe during the previous year; but now their economy-mindedness was dignified as giving emphasis to long-term quality ahead of short-term quantity.[4]

A more drastic revision of strategic concepts was still needed, however, to legitimize the reduced national security expenditures made necessary by the goal of a balanced budget. The vehicle was to be a broad examination of the grand strategy of the United States conducted for the President during the spring and summer of 1953 by three task forces under the overall direction of Under Secretary of State Walter Bedell Smith and Robert Cutler, the President's special assistant for national security affairs. Each task force was to explore the implications of one of three alternative grand strategies: (1) continuation of "containment"; (2) global deterrence by the threat of nuclear punishment; and (3) "liberation" of Communist-held areas through economic, paramilitary, and psychological warfare methods. The National Planning Board of the National Security Council was to integrate the best ideas of the three groups into a single policy paper.

The resulting document, labeled NSC-162, was a reasonably coherent policy paper, but a failure insofar as it did not provide the administration with a new concept that would allow for major reductions in defense expenditures. The policy of containing the Soviet Union—with essentially the kind of balanced forces recommended by the previous administration—was to be retained, with somewhat greater reliance placed on strategic air power for deterrence. The Soviet threat was painted as harshly as ever and as likely to continue over the long term. The Soviet hydrogen bomb explosion in August underlined earlier fears that the Soviets would soon have the capacity to hit the United States with a massive nuclear strike. As a consequence, NSC-162 was unable to recommend a reduction in military forces, ground forces included. National security, in the years ahead, would have to take priority over all policy objectives. [5]

Meanwhile, the newly selected Joint Chiefs of Staff, with Admiral Radford as Chairman, had also been conducting a study under orders of the President, who had made firm his expectation that they would give due weight to domestic economic considerations. Their paper, presented in the late summer 1953, purported to be a statement of general premises which should guide further detailed planning. The critical premises here, in contrast to those of NSC-162, were a combination of those advanced by Dulles and Radford aboard the *Helena* the previous December. The Joint Chiefs of Staff were unanimous in their opinion that United States military forces were overextended, and that the local defense of potentially threatened areas such as Korea and Germany should be the primary responsibility of indigenous forces backed by United States sea and air power. United States force-posture planning should concern itself primarily with two primary functions: defense of the continental United States against strategic bombardment, and the maintenance of a massive retaliatory capability. Mobility, efficiency, and readiness should be stressed for the nonstrategic forces and reserves. [6]

Yet in attempting to translate these premises into substantial budgetary reductions for fiscal 1955, the Joint Chiefs of Staff found little in their respective service programs that they could cut. In National Security Council meetings in the fall of 1953, Treasury

Secretary Humphrey (very much a Taft Republican) and budget director Dodge indicated profound disappointment with the estimates presented by the Defense Department. Admiral Radford reacted by insisting that the only way substantial reductions could be effected would be as a result of a basic decision by the administration on the *kind* of war to be planned for. If the military planners knew that permission would be forthcoming to use nuclear weapons whenever it was militarily advantageous to do so, then there could be substantial dollar savings, since current planning was done on the basis of preparing simultaneously for brushfire and limited conventional wars, conventional wars on the Second World War model, limited nuclear wars, general nuclear wars, and various combinations of these.

By the end of October 1953 there was a consensus on the Radford line, and the President approved a formal paper, NSC-162/2, which specified the critical assumptions that would guide planners throughout the military establishment: it decreed that military commanders could count on using nuclear weapons, tactical and strategic, when militarily required; and it implied that the President would issue the appropriate weapons release orders upon request from the commanders in the field. Force-posture planning was to proceed on this basis, and on the basis that the fundamental objective of national security was to *deter* Soviet aggression—primarily through the massive strategic retaliatory capability of the United States. Greater reliance would be placed on indigenous allied forces to counter local aggression; concurrent with these local buildups some United States overseas forces could return to the United States.[7]

Here, finally, was the set of premises that allowed the Joint Chiefs of Staff to take their "New Look" at the overall level of military spending and the allocation of resources within the total military budget. The document they submitted in December 1953 refined somewhat the general politicostrategic ideas of NSC-162/2. The massive retaliatory power of the United States was seen as a deterrent to *major* aggression, and as a means of fighting general war. Local limited aggression was still a distinct possibility, for which the bulk of ground forces ought to be provided by our allies; but an "educational" effort was needed to convince the allies that such a specialization of functions would benefit everyone. United States ground forces in forward areas in Europe and Asia would eventually be reduced; and U.S. participation in local defense operations would be mainly through tactical air and sea power, and quickly deployable mobile ground units—their functions, presumably, to be built around the new concept of tactical atomic warfare. The recommended force-posture implementations of these concepts were to begin, on an interim basis, with the fiscal 1955 budget and mature by fiscal 1957, resulting in a 25 percent drop in military manpower, and a reduction in the nearly $50 billion annual defense bill to a level under $35 billion.

It was only after the internal administrative tug-of-war had been resolved that the New Look was dressed up in a neat package for public display by the Secretary of State and the President. However, public statements—particularly Dulles'—do distill from the formulation its rather simplified new orientation toward the global balance of power.

As Dulles explained on January 12, 1954, to the Council on Foreign Relations:

> It is not sound military strategy permanently to commit U.S. land forces to a degree that leaves us no strategic reserves.
>
> It is not sound economics, or good foreign policy, to support permanently other countries; for in the long run, that creates as much ill will as good will.
>
> Also, it is not sound to become permanently committed to military expenditures so vast they lead to "practical bankruptcy."

> . . .

> We need allies and collective security. Our purpose is to make those relations more effective, less costly. This can be done by placing more reliance on deterrent power, and less dependence on local defensive power.

> . . .

> Local defense will always be important. But there is no local defense which alone will contain the mighty land power of the Communist world. Local defense must be reinforced by the further deterrent of massive retaliatory power. A potential aggressor must know that he cannot always prescribe the battle conditions that suit him. Otherwise, for example, a potential aggressor, who is glutted with manpower, might be tempted to attack in confidence that resistance would be confined to manpower.

Under the previous policy, maintained the Secretary of State, U.S. military leaders could not be selective in building military power: they needed to be ready to fight in the tropics, Asia, the Near East, and Europe, by sea, land, and air. Such a strategy, he insisted, "could not be continued for long without grave budgetary, economic and social consequences."

In order for the nation's military planning to be put on a more rational basis, said Dulles, it was necessary for the President to make this basic policy decision which he, Dulles, was now announcing to the world: namely, that henceforth this nation would "depend primarily upon a great capacity to retaliate, instantly, by means and at places of our own choosing." Now our military establishment could be shaped to fit *our* policy, instead of having to try to be ready to meet the enemy's many choices: "That permits us a selection of means instead of a multiplication of means. As a result, it is now possible to get, and share, more basic security at less cost."[8]

In one important respect, Dulles had seriously overstated the planning premises agreed upon within the administration. He had talked of the massive retaliatory capacity as if it were to be the primary military means of defense for the entire free community, neglecting to stress adequately the role of indigenous local forces in blocking aggressions during their initial stages. This led to the widespread impression that United States policy had narrowed the choices of the non-Communist world into either accepting local Communist aggressions or turning every local aggression into general nuclear war. Dulles and other administration officials were hard pressed to explain that they had no such extreme policy in mind,[9] and that local defense capabilities would still be important to deny the enemy easy territorial grabs. Moreover, these local forces could be buttressed quickly by rapid deployments from the central mobile reserve here in the United States. The Communist powers would now know, however, that they could not count on drawing the United States into a purely local encounter with a limitation on the weapons employed. The choice would be ours as to when and where to respond with weapons of mass destruction. Backing away from the denigration of a strategy of readiness to fight in all theatres that appeared in the Dulles speech, administration spokesmen explained that programmed reductions in United States military manpower levels were the result of improved local defense capabilities in NATO and the Far East, and the development of tactical nuclear weapons which, it was assumed, would reduce ground manpower requirements.

COMMITMENTS AND COERCION

In his "massive retaliation" speech before the Council on Foreign Relations Dulles had undoubtedly resorted to hyperbole. In failing to give sufficient stress to the role of indigenous military forces he underplayed that which he was later to be accused of overplaying. Indeed, Dulles personally was much more interested in this means of enhancing the non-Communist side of the balance than in the diplomatic exploitation of advanced weaponry.

Dulles believed in the virtues of alliance building for reasons that went beyond the purely military calculus of power. Unity of purpose and coordination of policy were in his view important attributes of strength. The cement for effecting such cohesion was generally thought to be a shared ideology and economic and military interdependence. But in the areas of the Eisenhower administration's most feverish alliance-building—the wide arc through the Middle East and Southeast Asia that connects Europe to Japan, and surrounded the Communist Eurasian heartland—there was thought to be little basis for cultivating strong economic ties.[10]

In the first place, the administration, in its determined effort to reduce all but the most essential expenditures, was in no mood to begin new programs of foreign assistance unless these could be shown to be directly related to crucial United States national security requirements. Second, the Eisenhower Cabinet was skeptical of the ability of the new nations to make productive use of purely economic assistance. Consequently, the dominant basis of Eisenhower—Dulles appeals for military aid between 1953 and 1956 was the supposed comparative economic advantage of the United States of relying on indigenous local forces rather than United States military personnel to contain Communist military expansion.

This narrow basis for alliance building underlay Dulles' offer of U.S. military assistance to Pakistan and Iraq in 1953–54, in the face of outraged opposition from the Arab states and India, and his fashioning of the Southeast Asia Treaty Organization (SEATO) during a period of increasingly assertive neutralism in Asia.

The efforts to sign up military allies in the Middle East, particularly, illustrate that the policy of containment had become submerged in the effort to add overseas weights to the military balance— a departure from the pre–Korean War days when instances of military assistance to countries on the Communist periphery were defined as stopgap emergency efforts, while the most important contributions expected from these peripheral countries were serious strides in their own socioeconomic development.

The military balance-of-power emphasis to containment in the Middle East was, as in Western Europe, stimulated by the Korean War. The Truman administration had always regarded the Middle East as of strategic significance; and in the early 1950s its special attributes—the source of two-thirds of the West's oil reserves, the Suez Canal, and the location of important British military bases—were seen as immediately vital to any global test of strength. The United States, joined by Britain, France, and Turkey, tried to induce the Arabs to participate in a Middle East Defense Command. But Egypt and the other Arab states saw the effort as a plot by the imperialist powers to reestablish control of the area. Their fingers burned in this attempt, Truman and Acheson had to fall back to a less ideological approach, offering technical assistance without "strings" in the hope of maintaining a basis for friendly association.

Dulles, however, was not to be dissuaded by these past failures to fill the Middle Eastern military vacuum. The premises of the New Look gave a new imperative to the organization of indigenous military capabilities. The Middle East may be complicated, but certainly not unmanageable to the skilled diplomatist. In 1953 Dulles made a trip to the area, sounding out, with offers of economic and military assistance, current receptivity to a Middle East Defense Command. Colonel Nasser's unequivocal rejection of the scheme, on the grounds that the new nationalist leaders in the area would be committing political suicide if they entered into external defense alliances, only prompted Dulles to try an end run:

Many of the Arab League countries are so engrossed with their quarrels with Israel or with Great Britain or France [observed Dulles] that they pay little heed to the menace of Soviet Communism. However, there is more concern where the Soviet Union is near. In general, the northern tier of nations shows awareness of the danger.[11]

The most receptive countries were Turkey (a loyal member of NATO concerned with being outflanked on the East by its historic rival) and Pakistan (hardly concerned over Soviet aggression, but willing to exploit the cold war to redress its local imbalance with India). The United States could make direct deals with these two

widely separated nations; but the nations between—Iran and Iraq—
would be less likely to risk antagonizing their Arab neighbors. The
trick was to blur the American role in the Turko-Pakistani association, and then have these two nations establish a mutual security
arrangement with their neighbors, Iran and Iraq.

In February 1954 the United States military assistance agreement
with Pakistan was announced; it was defined only as an arrangement
for handling arms aid, without any formal alliance obligations. Paralleling these negotiations with the United States, Pakistan and Turkey entered into a treaty of friendship and cooperation for security,
pledging to study means of cooperating to defend against external
aggression, and inviting other states in the area to become associated
with this effort. Overt initiatives to bring Iraq into the "northern
tier" arrangements were Turkey's responsibility. The United States
had already effected a bilateral military aid agreement with Premier
Jamali; again, this involved no formal commitments to participate in
collective regional defense. The Turkish–Iraqi agreement signed at
Baghdad in February 1955 was very similar in terms to the previous
year's agreement between Turkey and Pakistan; now, however, a
more concerted attempt was made to draw in other states. The Iraqi
leadership, openly competing with Egypt for influence among the
Arab states, was anxious to increase its regional bargaining power by
extracting the maximum assistance from the West. Britain accepted
the invitation to transform its previously bilateral base agreements
with Iraq into a part of this expanding regional security system—
now called the Baghdad Pact. Pakistan's adherence was a foregone
conclusion. This only left Iran, in 1954 still politically unstable after
the deposition of the anti-Western Mossadegh regime. Although
obvious pro-Western alignment might reignite the extremist fires,
by the fall of 1955 the Shah felt more secure politically, and was
particularly anxious to qualify for the assistance benefits of pact
membership in order to modernize his army.[12]

The result was a polarized Middle East, with the north organized
into the Baghdad Pact, and the south dominated (through subversion
and threat, as well as common ideology and friendship) by Egypt.
Dulles was unwilling to become completely associated with his own
handiwork. Financial and military support, and participation in the
work of pact subcommittees, yes; but full membership, no. Perceiving Soviet attempts to exploit the local bipolarization, Dulles felt the

necessity of preserving some residue of United States influence with Nasser. Thus the simplification of United States diplomacy—attempting to maintain the balance of power by a somewhat indiscriminate adding of military allies—was beginning to produce its own complications.

The American-sponsored proliferation of alliances in the Middle East overlapped the similar effort in Asia to redress the Communist advantage in military manpower by getting signatures to a multilateral Southeast Asian treaty.

The deteriorating French position in Indochina was the immediate stimulus to give an indigenous cast to the existing pattern of special relationships between some of the local states and the United States, Britain, and France. Dulles and Eisenhower had been urging a Southeast Asian "NATO" since 1953. The full-fledged push now was in part the result of the military lessons of the Indochina conflict: the tactical irrelevance of United States strategic power, the unavailability of United States ground forces, and the lack of trained indigenous forces. And in part the new momentum for a local treaty association was an expression of the growing perception that resistance to Communism required support of the indigenous peoples affected, and that this would not be forthcoming if the anti-Communist resistance bore the stigma of colonialism.

The administration had been claiming that a Communist victory in Indochina would have serious consequences for the global balance of power. To the American people, Eisenhower dramatized the strategic considerations underlying his desire to help the French by comparing Indochina to the first of a row of dominoes, which if knocked over would topple the whole row.[13] To Prime Minister Churchill, in an urgent note requesting the British join in the *ad hoc* construction of a Southeast Asian collective defense force, the President wrote:

If . . . Indochina passes into the hands of the Communists the ultimate effect on our and your global strategic position with the consequent shift in the power ratios throughout Asia and the Pacific could be disastrous.[14]

However disastrous the consequences of a Communist victory in Indochina, Eisenhower felt that if the United States took up the major military burden of saving the area the consequences to the U.S. global power position would be even *more* disastrous.

Various schemes for bringing United States military power into play were being advanced by Admiral Radford and Secretary Dulles. The leading option was an air strike from carriers of the U.S. Seventh Fleet. Eisenhower tended to agree with the majority of the Joint Chiefs of Staff that, in purely military terms, this would not significantly help the French situation on the ground. Yet he admitted to feeling "there was some merit in the argument that the psychological effect of an air strike would raise French and Vietnamese morale and improve, at least temporarily, the entire situation."[15] The real barrier, as far as the President was concerned, was the unwillingness of other countries to associate themselves in this or any other military intervention on the side of the French. Dulles, having failed to arrive at a common basis for action with Foreign Secretary Eden, appears at one point to have been willing to go it alone.[16] But Eisenhower claims to have maintained a consistent position throughout that "there would be no intervention without allies." As Eisenhower explained to General Alfred Gruenther, then NATO Supreme Commander:

> No Western power can go to Asia militarily, except as one of a concert of powers, which concert must include local Asiatic peoples.
> To contemplate anything else is to lay ourselves open to the charge of imperialism and colonialism—or at the very least—of objectionable paternalism.[17]

At the climax of the 1954 crisis, with the French under siege at Dienbienphu, a presidential choice between unpalatable alternatives—negotiation from a position of weakness or unilateral United States intervention—could no longer be postponed. On April 29, in a strategy huddle with his top advisers, Eisenhower interposed his military judgment to dispose of all further discussions of forcible United States intervention:

> I remarked [recounts Eisenhower] that if the United States were, unilaterally, to permit its forces to be drawn into conflict in Indochina and in a succession of Asian wars, the end result would be to drain off our resources and weaken our over-all defensive position.[18]

It remained for diplomacy to salvage as much of the situation as possible. Although Dulles would not put his signature to the Geneva accords (which could be read as giving legitimacy to the de facto extension of Communist control), the administration had expected a worse outcome than the one the Communists accepted: a non-

Communist government (albeit temporary) for the southern half of the country. The dire consequences to the power balance, it could be claimed, had been predicated on the fall of the whole of Indochina. Thus, the local balance of power could still be consolidated if the non-Communist countries in the region responded quickly to the challenge.

Dulles immediately committed the prestige of the United States to the construction of a Southeast Asian mutual defense pact to be based primarily on indigenous capabilities. The result was an agreement somewhat short on the provision of capabilities and somewhat unconvincing in its purpose of giving an indigenous, noncolonial cast to anti-Communism.

The Southeast Asia Collective Defense Treaty, dated September 8, 1954, required only *consultation* among its signatories in case one of them were the victim of armed attack or subversion. Each member "recognizes that aggression . . . in the treaty area against any of the Parties . . . would endanger its own peace and safety," but each member pledged no more than to "act in that event to meet the danger in accordance with its constitutional processes" (Article IV). The list of signatories to the treaty was revealing in itself: the United States, France, Britain, Australia, New Zealand, Thailand, the Philippines, and Pakistan. At the most the treaty provided, as Eisenhower claimed, "a moral, legal, and practical basis for helping our friends of the region." At the least, SEATO merely formalized existing power relationships in Asia without significantly altering the three-way balance between the Communists, the anti-Communists, and the nonaligned.

Dulles and Eisenhower were beginning to lose any illusions they might have had that formally committed military allies were one of the most relevant factors in the global balance of power. If anything, SEATO was a face-saving monument to the obsolescence of that simpler conception. Yet, along with the Baghdad Pact, it reinforced the "pactomania" stereotype of Dulles diplomacy. More significantly, these early solemn agreements would later constrain attempts to implement more flexible premises about the functions of nationalism and nonalignment in Asia.

The Eisenhower administration's premises about the ingredients of effective international power in Asia were reflected by the Formosa Straits crisis of 1954–55. Not long after the signing of the

SEATO treaty the Chinese Communists opened their bombardment of the offshore islands remaining in the hands of the Chinese Nationalists. The Communists did not launch their threatened invasions of Quemoy and Matsu (they did take Ta-chen) and Dulles proudly credited those very factors of power with which he was most identified, and for which he was most criticized: formal military alliances, threats of strategic reprisal in response to limited enemy probes, and a willingness to convert a seemingly marginal objective into a life and death matter if this appeared necessary to maintain the objective.

And characteristically for Dulles, the form, more than the material substance, of power received his closest attention.

SEATO was inapplicable to the defense of Taiwan (Formosa) and the offshore islands defined by the administration as contingently necessary to Taiwan's defense. Taiwan was neither a member of the treaty organization nor covered by the treaty provisions, as there was considerable disagreement among the signatories toward the whole China question. All United States moves in the crisis had to be undertaken under the authority of bilateral agreements between the United States and the Republic of China on Taiwan. More important, the definition of the conflict by the United States as vital, involving essential strategic interests of the entire free world, was unacceptable to most U.S. allies. Yet Dulles attempted to give credit to the spirit, if not the letter, of the multination regional security arrangement:

Its [Communist China's] almost unlimited manpower would easily dominate, and could quickly engulf, the entire area, were it not restrained by the mutual security structure which has been erected. But that structure will not hold if it be words alone. Essential ingredients are the deterrent power of the United States and our willingness to use that power in response to a military challenge.[19]

In a news conference on March 15, 1955, the Secretary was asked to indicate how he expected to apply United States military power to the defense of the offshore islands or other points in the Far East and Southeast Asia. "U.S. policy," he replied, "is not to split that power up into fragments." It was rather to preserve the ability to "use our full power." The most effective contribution the United States could make to the defense of the area was by our "strategic force with a high degree of striking power by sea and air."[20]

Eisenhower disclosed in his memoirs that such public hints of strategic retaliation, however vague, were regarded within the administration as more than merely threats. A few days before making the above remarks to the press, Dulles had returned from a two-week Asian trip and reported to the President that the Chinese were determined to capture Taiwan—gaining Quemoy and Matsu would not end their determination.

"If we defend Quemoy and Matsu," advised Dulles, "we'll have to use atomic weapons. They alone will be effective against mainland airfields."

"To this I agreed," recounts Eisenhower. And in response to Dulles' estimate of "at least an even chance" of war growing out of the situation, Eisenhower recalls that "I merely observed that if this proved to be true it would certainly be recognized that the [war] would not be of our seeking."[21]

To take an even risk of general war with Communist China with such equanimity, Eisenhower had to be convinced of two propositions: that the issue was of major importance to the global position of the United States, and that Soviet Russia would refrain from direct involvement. These were the essential propositions of John Foster Dulles. Eisenhower showed his concurrence in two messages to Winston Churchill during the height of the crisis. Never was the Dulles style and substance more evident.

On the vitalness of the interests at stake:

We believe that if international Communism should penetrate the island barrier in the Western Pacific and thus be in a position to threaten the Philippine and Indonesia immediately and directly, all of us, including the free countries of Europe, would soon be in far worse trouble than we are now. Certainly the whole region would soon go.

. . .

Only a few months back we had both Chiang and a strong, well-equipped French Army to support the free world's position in Southeast Asia. The French are gone—making it clearer than ever that we cannot afford the loss of Chiang unless all of us are to get completely out of that corner of the globe. This is unthinkable to us—I feel it must be to you.

On the consequences of a failure to stand firm:

There comes a point where constantly giving in only encourages further belligerency. I think we must be careful not to pass that point in our dealings with Communist China.

. . .

We must show no lack of firmness in a world where our political enemies exploit every sign of weakness, and are constantly attempting to disrupt the solidarity of the free world's intentions to oppose their aggressive practices.

And finally, in discounting the likelihood of Soviet intervention:

I do not believe that Russia wants war at this time—in fact, I do not believe that even if we became engaged in a serious fight along the coast of China, Russia would want to intervene with her own forces. She would, of course, pour supplies into China in an effort to exhaust us and certainly would exploit the opportunity to separate us from your country. But I am convinced that Russia does not want, at this moment, to experiment with means of defense against the bombing that we could conduct against her mainland.[22]

The Chinese Communist decision not to attack after all was for Dulles proof of his premises of power and vindication of his strategic concepts. Emmet Hughes quotes the Secretary of State as claiming, "Of all the things I have done, the most brilliant of all has been to save Quemoy and Matsu."[23] This pride was reflected in the controversial "brink of war" interview he gave late in 1955 to James Shepley of *Life* magazine:

The ability to get to the verge without getting into the war is the necessary art. If you cannot master it you inevitably get into war. If you try to run away from it, if you are scared to go to the brink you are lost. We've had to look it square in the face—on the question of getting into the Indo-China war, and on the question of Formosa. We walked to the brink and we looked it in the face. We took strong action.[24]

Dulles claimed that in all of these situations the ultimate decisions were the President's, which is undoubtedly true. He also claimed that "the President never flinched for a minute on any of these situations. He came up taut."[25] Again, this may very well have been the case, once the alternatives had been narrowed. But Dulles' intended implication that he and Eisenhower had identical premises about the most effective means of dealing with the nation's opponents bears further examination.

6

WAGING PEACE:
THE EISENHOWER FACE

Quite naturally . . . [John Foster Dulles and I] agreed that a determined pursuit of peace with justice should be . . . the foremost objective of the American government. Such an objective . . . could reasonably be pursued, we knew, only if the United States spoke from a position of power.

But the needed power would have to comprehend not only military strength, the age-old single criterion of civilizations long since reduced to rubble, but moral and economic strength as well.

—DWIGHT D. EISENHOWER

The greatest source of Eisenhower's power—in a personal sense—was that he was so well liked. His inclination as a world statesman was to transfer his likeableness to the nation which made him its leader, to make the personal style the national image.

The observation by Eisenhower's speech writer, Emmet Hughes, that there was a "deep conflict of premises" between the President and his Secretary of State refers primarily to the different ways they went about trying to influence men and nations. [1]

Both men were apparently aware of the difference from the beginning of their relationship. Dulles put the matter delicately in a private conference before their official association began: "With my understanding of the intricate relationships between the peoples of the world and your sensitivities to the political considerations involved, we will make the most successful team in history." [2] And in one sense they did; their teamwork was impeccable. Eisenhower, in awe of Dulles' diplomatic credentials, gave his Secretary of State an unusual amount of authority in policy formulation and implementation, while Dulles, in awe of Eisenhower's tremendous domestic popularity and international prestige, was scrupulously deferential and loyal to the President's convictions, to the extent they were expressed in any particular policy.

However, as both the record and the memoirs of the period suggest, Dulles was much more industrious in translating his own predilections into policy than those of the President. And since the translation of a general approach into specific diplomatic moves was, in the Eisenhower administrative fashion, the Secretary's job, the President's general approach often remained unarticulated (in policy as well as speech) while the Secretary's policy premises were well attended. Readers of Eisenhower's own memoirs must fill in a great deal between the lines to glean the essentials of this relationship. With one or two exceptions, such as Eisenhower's questioning the abruptness of Dulles' withdrawal of Aswan Dam assistance (see chapter 7), we are exposed to no differences of opinion. Eisenhower records the version of their relationship which he would like to stand:

It was said . . . that he [Dulles] sought not only to be influential in the conduct of foreign affairs, but to be responsible only to his own convictions and inclinations. What his critics did not know was that he was more emphatic than they in his insistence that ultimate and personal responsibility for all major decisions in the field of foreign relations belonged exclusively to the President, an attitude he meticulously maintained throughout our service together. He would not deliver an important speech or statement until after I had read, edited, and approved it; he guarded constantly against the possibility that any misunderstanding could arise between us. It was the mutual trust and understanding, thus engendered, that enabled me, with complete confidence, to delegate to him an unusual degree of flexibility as my representative in international conferences, well knowing that he would not in the slightest degree operate outside the limits previously agreed between us. The association was particularly gratifying to me because of the easy partnership we developed in searching for the answer to any complex problem. But although behind closed doors we worked as partners, he in all our conversations lived his conviction that he was the adviser, recognizing that the final decision had to be mine.[3]

Sherman Adams also claims that "the Secretary of State never made a major move without the President's knowledge and approval"; but he goes on to make the revealing observation that "the hard and uncompromising line the United States government took toward Soviet Russia and Red China between 1953 and the early months of 1959 [was] more a Dulles line than an Eisenhower one."[4]

Each of the prominent "peace" initiatives of the period was generated and formulated by special assistants or staff aides to the President, not by Dulles, in contrast to the usual pattern.

According to the principal drafter (Hughes), Eisenhower's April 1953 "Chance for Peace" address to the American Society of Newspaper Editors went against Dulles' grain. But because the Secretary of State knew how impatient the President was to follow through on a hunch with a dramatic peace probe in the wake of Stalin's death, Dulles only objected obliquely to the address. To those working on the speech, Dulles spoke plainly:

there's some real danger of our just seeming to fall in with these Soviet overtures. It's obvious that what they are doing is because of outside [Western] pressures, and I don't know anything better we can do than keep up these pressures right now.[5]

Dulles viewed the power struggle between the Communist and non-Communist worlds as a "zero-sum" game: that is, any plus for one's opponents, such as an increase in their military power, general power potential, or even economic well-being, was a minus for oneself—and vice versa. Eisenhower, on the other hand—and this is what worried Dulles—was anxious to reduce the costs and risks of the contest to the United States by finding opportunities for *mutual* gain: a "non-zero-sum" or "win-win" game.

Eisenhower's biggest frustrations at this time came from trying to reduce government expenditures. If only the huge burden of arms spending could be reduced significantly, then budgets could be balanced, taxes could be reduced, and private enterprise could flourish with less government interference! Eisenhower believed these effects would in turn lead to a revival of the American spirit of individual initiative, the basic source of the country's national strength.

Possibly the new Soviet leaders had analogous problems. Eisenhower recalls that his "hope" was that "perhaps the time had arrived when the Soviet leaders had decided, because of the discontent of their subjects, to turn their factories to producing more goods for civilian use and thus to raise the living standards of the Soviet population."[6]

Dulles hoped for the opposite—that the gap between the desires of the Soviet people and the policies of the Soviet regime would become so wide that the Soviet Union would eventually collapse. Dulles did finally go along with the peace probe in April 1953, and hoped for an intensification of the gap between popular aspiration in the Communist countries and Politburo policy. His most optimistic view of the speech seems to have been that it might be a good weapon of political warfare.

But Eisenhower appears to have meant it when he pleaded publicly with the Soviet leaders for "a few . . . clear and specific acts . . . of sincere intent" (such as a finalization of the Korean armistice and the conclusion of an Austrian peace treaty) so as to strengthen "world trust." Out of this could grow "political settlements for the other serious issues between the free world and the Soviet Union," and, concurrently, "the reduction of the burden of armaments now weighing upon the world." This last, Eisenhower truly wanted the Soviet leaders to realize, was his deepest aspiration. The core of the speech, and the part to which Eisenhower gave greatest emphasis, tried to convey his appreciation of the mutual benefits to be derived from substantial disarmament:

> Every gun that is made, every warship launched, every rocket fired signifies, in the final sense, a theft from those who hunger and are not fed, those who are cold and are not clothed.
> The world in arms is not spending money alone.
> It is spending the sweat of its labors, the genius of its scientists, the hopes of its children.
> The cost of one modern heavy bomber is this: a modern brick school for more than 30 cities.
> It is two electric power plants, each serving a town of 60,000 population.
> It is two fine, fully equipped hospitals.
> It is some 50 miles of concrete highway.
> We pay for a single fighter plane with a half million bushels of wheat.
> We pay for a single destroyer with new homes that could have housed more than 8,000 people.[7]

Similar premises underlay the Atoms for Peace proposal, presented before the United Nations on December 8, 1953. This venture, too, which Eisenhower referred to as "my second major speech in the field of foreign relations,"[8] found Dulles on the sidelines. The idea appears to have been very much Eisenhower's own. The early drafts by his special assistant C. D. Jackson for an "Operation Candor" speech on the destructive power of thermonuclear weapons had been disappointing. The Soviet hydrogen bomb explosion in August 1953 reinforced Eisenhower's conviction that some way had to be found to dampen the tensions and suspicion that had now evolved into an ever-more lethal, expensive phase of the arms race. He was disappointed that nothing concrete had come of his speech to the newspaper editors. "I began to search around," Eisenhower wrote to a friend, "for any kind of an idea that could bring the world to look at the atomic problem in a broad and intelligent way and still escape the impasse to action created by Russian intransigence in the matter of . . . inspection."[9]

While vacationing in Denver the idea occurred to the President that the United States and the Soviet Union could each donate fisionable material to the United Nations from their respective stockpiles, with the donations being diverted to peaceful projects under international supervision. This would not be disarmament, but "my purpose was to promote development of mutual trust, a trust that was essential before we could hope for success in the . . [major] disarmament proposals." To generate such trust it was important

to get the Soviet Union working with us in a noncontroversial phase of the atomic field. . . . If we were successful in making even a start, it was possible that gradually negotiation and cooperation might expand into something broader; there was hope that Russia's own self-interest might lead her to participate in joint humanitarian efforts.[10]

Eisenhower delegated the major responsibility for translating this idea into action to General Robert Cutler, his special assistant for national security affairs; Admiral Lewis Strauss, Chairman of the Atomic Energy Commission; and C. D. Jackson. Dulles, busy with a round of diplomatic conferences, was brought in only during the last-minute drafting efforts on the UN speech. But this was not really his cup of tea. "An idealistic venture like the Atoms-for-Peace plan was hardly the sort of thing that would fire the imagination of a man like Dulles anyway," divulges Sherman Adams. "He gave it his tacit approval, but he had some doubts about it."[11]

Eisenhower was to be disappointed again at the lack of a positive Soviet response to his proposals, and nine months later turned Atoms for Peace into a project for joint Western cooperation in research on the peaceful uses of atomic energy. Eventually, Eisenhower could take credit for the creation of the International Atomic Energy

Agency, which the Soviets did join, for the exchange of nuclear information and limited inspection of the nuclear energy facilities of member nations without weapons programs. But the tension-reducing and trust-building premises of the original proposal were eclipsed by more dramatic events of 1954—the Indochina conflict, the formation of the Asian and Middle Eastern military alliances, the acceptance of a rearmed West Germany in the Atlantic defense system—all of which were conducted in the Dulles style and reflected his premises.

Dulles inherited the Acheson attitude that there were in fact no significant negotiable issues between the Soviets and the United States. Each side, for the foreseeable future, was likely to adhere to the position "what's mine is mine; what's yours is negotiable." From the standpoint of the United States the potentially negotiable issue was the Soviet illegal absorption of Eastern Europe, or at least a critical segment of that problem: the division of Germany. But both Secretaries of Sate were convinced that a condition for Soviet willingness to sacrifice some of its control would be global balance of power clearly favoring the West. Acheson does not seem to have had confidence in the emergence of obvious Western superiority. Dulles, at least in his rhetoric, looked forward to an advantageous balance of power developing as a result of the collapse of the Soviet economy and social system. Meantime, however, it was essential to maintain the military strength of the West to deter the Soviets from attempting to alter the balance of power.

To these premises Dulles added the corollary that some amount of East–West tension was an important condition for the maintenance of Western power. As he confided to a State Department colleague:

> If there's no evident menace from the Soviet bloc our will to maintain unity and strength may weaken. It's a fact, unfortunate though it be, that in promoting our programs in Congress we have to make evident the international communist menace. Otherwise such program as the mutual security one would be decimated.
>
> The same situation would probably prevail among our allies [as a result of a détente]. They might feel that the danger was over and therefore they did not need to continue to spend large sums for defense.[12]

The Soviets, Dulles believed, were aware of this susceptibility of the Western democracies and were trying to exploit it. Their calls for negotiations, for relaxation of tensions, for disarmament agreements, were a "Trojan horse" technique to defeat efforts at European rearmament—particularly the integration of a rearmed Germany into the Western bloc, as in the European Defense Community.

Dulles found that other political leaders in the Western alliance (with the possible exception of Adenauer) felt compelled—partly for domestic political considerations—to make a convincing display of peace initiatives before asking their peoples to support major rearmament. From 1953 to 1955, Churchill, and then Eden, advocated a big-power summit meeting. The administration maintained its position that the Soviets would first have to show by deeds, not by promises, that they were interested in serious attempts to reduce tension. As an example of a sincere deed, Dulles and Eisenhower on a number of occasions mentioned Soviet agreement to an Austrian peace treaty. Suddenly, in the spring of 1955, the Soviets reversed their earlier intransigence on Austria and agreed to a mutual withdrawal of troops, demilitarization, neutralization, and a political system contemplating a non-Communist regime. Dulles was apparently surprised and temporarily thrown off balance as the demands for a summit were increasingly heard from most capitals.

The Secretary of State quickly regained his footing by suggesting that the Soviets' willingness to pay the entry price (the Austrian treaty) for a summit meeting was due to the success of his diplomacy. "It is clear we are seeing the results of a policy of building unity and strength within the free world," he said in his May 24, 1955, press conference. "This policy has produced a radical change in Soviet policy, illustrated by new Soviet attitudes toward Austria and Yugoslavia." [14]

Now, in order to continue to play the role of man out front in alliance diplomacy vis-à-vis the Soviets, Dulles took an active part during the next few months in clearing the path to the summit. It is doubtful, however, that he believed the Soviets had made a shift in grand strategy. If anything, the Austrian treaty was a tactical retreat, and Dulles was determined that it should be seen as such. He was skeptical of any important agreements occurring at the summit, particularly to the key question of Germany; but for that very reason Dulles felt it important to have the matter of Germany a prominent part of the agenda. Soviet unwillingness to barter control of East Germany would be exposed, and Adenauer could then convincingly reply to critics of his rigid policy that the Soviets were not really interested in a reunified Germany even if it were neutral. [15]

Although Eisenhower appreciated Dulles' reluctance to have the President drawn into a high-level charade of mutual accommodation and cordiality with the Soviets, once it was decided to go to the summit Eisenhower's inclinations again found an opportunity for expression. "Unlike Dulles, who entertained no such high hopes," writes Sherman Adams, "Eisenhower went to Geneva seeking to make the meeting a solid beginning of a move toward world disarmament." [16]

Adams' characterization of Eisenhower's purposes and expectations may be a slight exaggeration. The President had been somewhat disillusioned by the Soviets' lack of positive response to his Atoms for Peace plan; and, in light of this, particularly angered at the Russian pose as the champion of peace and disarmament. A month before the conference, Eisenhower wrote in confidence to his friend Swede Hazlett: "Personally, I do not expect any spectacular results from the forthcoming 'Big Four' conference." [17] But, in contrast to Dulles, he was unworried about the possibility that the Soviets were engaged in a "Trojan horse" tactic to compel the West to let down its guard. If Soviet tactical considerations required a temporary reduction of tensions, Eisenhower seemed concerned only that the Soviets not take all the credit for the improved atmosphere, especially in the field of disarmament negotiations, as they had been doing recently. Although not particularly hopeful of immediate results, the President was at least determined that this time the propaganda battle would not be won by the Soviets.

Eisenhower did agree with Dulles that in his attempt to convince world opinion that the United States was making a major effort toward peace, he should not create overly high expectations in the American people which would then be followed by extreme disillusionment. Even so, in his address to the nation on the eve of his departure for the conference the former general transformed his peace "probe" into a crusade; and this one, like the others he had led, he must *win:*

If we look at . . . [the] record we would say, "Why another conference? What hope is there for success?" Well now the first question I ask you. "Do we want to do nothing? Do we want to sit and drift along to the inevitable end in such a contest of war or increased tensions?"

Pessimism never won any battle, he reminded his listeners.

But also missing from the previous conferences, said Eisenhower, was "an honest intent to conciliate, to understand, to be tolerant, to see the other fellow's viewpoint as well as we see our own." We must change the spirit in which these conference are conducted, he urged.

Finally, there was emerging "a terrific force"—the common desire for peace on the part of the people of all the world—"to which I believe all the political leaders of the world are beginning to respond." Throughout the world prayers for peace were ascending. These prayers, said the President, could achieve "a very definite and practical result at this very moment":

> Suppose, on the next Sabbath day . . . America, 165 million people of us, went to our accustomed places of worship and, crowding those places, asked for help, and by so doing demonstrated to all the world the sincerity and depth of our aspirations for peace.
> This would be a mighty force. [18]

This demonstrative, symbolic aspect of Eisenhower's speeches for peace also appears to have been the aspect which most appealed to him in the "open skies" plan he dramatically unveiled at Geneva.

Again, this plan was conceived by a group more directly responsive to Eisenhower and his slant on the ways of influencing men and nations than to the Dulles line. A panel of governmental and outside experts headed by Nelson Rockefeller, then special assistant to the President on foreign policy, had been meeting at Quantico Marine base to study various positions which the United States might take at the forthcoming summit conference. The Rockefeller group's terms of reference were very much Eisenhower's: the Soviets were almost sure to offer a disarmament plan at Geneva, and the United States could not afford to appear any less interested in arms control, especially in light of the rising pacifist and neutralist sentiments in Europe. According to the journalist who was given the privilege of writing the "inside" story on the open skies plan, the problem facing the Quantico group was "how the United States could retain its nuclear power but still make it clear for all to see that its purpose was peace." [19] Both of these demands might be met, the panel decided, if the President were to revive and present in a fresh expanded version some of the ideas for mutual aerial inspection and exchange of military information that had appeared in the "control" provisions of United States arms reduction proposals, starting with the Baruch Plan. This time mutual aerial inspection would be presented as a desirable way to reduce the likelihood of surprise attack. The President received the Quantico recommendations on June 10, 1955, and read them with enthusiasm. Dulles was less enthusiastic, but not opposed. After careful discussion, the plan was held in suspension, pending developments at the conference.[20]

When Bulganin tried to attract attention to Soviet disarmament proposals on the first days of the conference Rockefeller pressed Eisenhower to seize the initiative. Eisenhower sought the counsel of Anthony Eden, who immediately saw the virtues of the proposal. It was decided that the President himself would present the idea to the conference, but exactly when was held in abeyance.[21] The search was for the best moment of maximum impact. Everybody in the United States delegation knew the President was going to make some particularly important statement, wrote James Reston from Geneva. "Photographers were alerted ahead of time for the briefing. Plans were made to publicize his remarks."[22] The situation was made for the grand gesture, and particularly for the Eisenhower personality.

As if seized by an inspiration, in the middle of reading from his prepared remarks to the July 21 meeting of the conference, the President took off his glasses, placed them on the table, faced Bulganin and Khrushchev, and said extemporaneously:

> Gentlemen, since I have been working on this memorandum to present to this conference, I have been searching my heart and mind for something that I could say here that could convince everyone of the great sincerity of the United States in approaching this problem of disarmament. I should address myself for a moment principally to the delegates from the Soviet Union, because our two great countries admittedly possess new and terrible weapons in quantities which do give rise in other parts of the world, or reciprocally, to the fears and dangers of surprise attack.
>
> I propose, therefore, that we take a practical step, that we begin an arrangement, very quickly, as between ourselves—immediately. These steps would include:
>
> To give to each other a complete blueprint of our military establishments, from beginning to end, from one end of our countries to the other; lay out the establishments and provide the blueprints to each other.
>
> Next, to provide within our countries facilities for aerial photography to the other country—we to provide you the facilities within our country, ample facilities for aerial reconnaissance, where you can make all the pictures you choose and take them to your own country to study; you to provide exactly the same facilities for us and we to make these examinations—and by this step to convince the world that we are providing as between ourselves against the possibility of great surprise attack, thus lessening danger and relaxing tension. Likewise we will make more easily attainable a comprehensive and effective system of inspection and disarmament, because what I propose, I assure you, would be but a beginning.[23]

The Soviets, possibly sensing the gesture's emotion impact, possibly caught off guard, and quite evidently anxious to allow as much "relaxation of tension" as possible to emerge from the conference, held back their negative response. Contrary to their usual practice, the Moscow papers reprinted the text of the President's speech. Even on the sensitive question of Germany, the Soviets accepted a rather ambiguously worded joint statement that could be interpreted, loosely, as willingness to accept the Western proposals as terms of reference for forthcoming detailed discussions to be held by the foreign ministers in October.

In Eisenhower's final statement at Geneva before the conference adjourned on July 23 he told the assembly, "It has been on the whole a good week." In his judgment, he said, "the prospects of a lasting peace . . . are brighter. The dangers of the overwhelming tragedy of modern war are less."[24] Sherman Adams recalls when the White House staff welcomed the President back to Washington, "he spoke to us with feeling that he had accomplished some real good." and the next day the President told congressional leaders that the Russians seemed to be changing their tactics toward the U.S.[25]

The October foreign ministers' meeting confirmed for Dulles his view that there was really nothing to negotiate about, once having descended from the pleasant atmospherics of the summit to the bedrock of incompatible cold war objectives. On the matters of Germany and European security, there was no desire on the part of the Soviets in 1955 to trade their de facto control for paper guarantees that a reunited Germany would be rearmed and "neutral" (Germany was no Austria). Nor was there enthusiasm on the part of Dulles or Adenauer to trade the presumed stability of the present German situation (resulting from a tight integration of the Federal Republic into the NATO apparatus) for the highly volatile political crosscurrents that would be loosed if reunification, under an Austria-type formula, were an immediate prospect. Schemes for local military "disengagement" were no less suspiciously viewed by the two superpowers. The Soviets were afraid of loosening their main means of keeping the satellites in check. But even if the Soviets should seriously want a mutual thinning out of forces along the Iron Curtain, from the Dulles perspective, this would seriously weaken the overall Western diplomatic position in Europe which now, more than ever, depended upon a large German military contribution to

NATO. The reduction of Western military strength could only follow a general political settlement in Europe; it should never be countenanced as a means for "reducing tensions." "Open skies" was flatly rejected by the Soviets as another Western scheme for espionage; thus it never had to undergo the hard scrutiny (its effect upon the credibility of United States strategic doctrines, for example) Dulles would have felt compelled to give it were it truly negotiable.

This return to the more rigid level of East–West interaction was to Eisenhower a "disillusionment," a "grievous disappointment," which he attributed to "Soviet duplicity." But one of his purposes, he felt, had been fulfilled. "The record was established: All could now see the nature of Soviet diplomatic tactics as contrasted with those of the Free World." In addition,

peoples had been given a glowing picture of hope and, though badly blurred by the Soviets, at least the outlines of the picture remained. Moreover . . . the cordial atmosphere of the talks . . . never faded entirely. Indeed, the way was opened for some increase in intercourse between East and West—there began, between the United States and Russia, exchanges of trade exhibitions, scientists, musicians and other performers; visits were made by Mikoyan and Kozlov to the United States, and returned, by Vice President Nixon and my brother Milton, to the Soviet Union and Poland. These were small beginnings, but they could not have transpired in the atmosphere prevailing before Geneva.[26]

The Geneva episode, more than any other event during the Eisenhower presidency, illustrated Eisenhower's sourness with the coercive tools of the thermonuclear age and a diplomacy premised upon a readiness to use them. The kind of influence he wanted to wield, personally, and as the symbol of the nation, was influence over others derived from their confidence in our goodwill and mutual affection. If the people of the world could only know our sincere purposes they would come to trust and like us—and ultimately their rulers (even in Communist countries) would follow suit. This was the underlying secret of power.

7

CRISES AND COMPLICATIONS

The cement of fear is not so strong to hold us together as it was to bring us together.

—JOHN FOSTER DULLES

While Dulles was pointing with pride to his success in deterring the Communists through the organization and skillful manipulation of the *military* ingredients of the balance of power, the Soviets and Chinese were pushing the competition into new channels. The administration, however reluctantly, would need to develop a more complex conception of the requirements for maintaining the balance.

Since 1953 the Soviets had been quite openly expanding trade and lending with other nations. (China was of course not as active in the economic field; but this was still the period when, in American policy-making circles, the "Sino-Soviet Bloc" was thought to be practicing a largely coordinated strategy.) By 1956 the network of Communist bloc trade and credit agreements extended to practically every nonaligned country in the Middle East and Asia, and even to a few countries supposedly a part of the Dulles alliance system—namely, Pakistan, Iran, and Greece.

The problem was not so much one of *recognizing* the shift in Communist tactics as of *what to do* about it. There was pressure within the administration as early as 1953–54, notably from mutual security administrator Harold Stassen and from Elsworth Bunker, ambassador to India, to expand United States economic assistance to additional nations, without making membership in an anti-Communist military pact a qualification for assistance.

However, in mid-1954, Stassen was replaced at the Mutual Security Administration by John Hollister, whose aim was to reduce foreign aid expenditures. And Dulles gave his newly appointed Under Secretary of State, Herbert Hoover, Jr., overall guidance of foreign economic policy. Innovation was effectively blocked. And orthodox premises were adamantly reasserted: namely, that economic aid to nations not militarily allied with the United States was an unaffordable extravagance; that such nations were essentially hostile, seeking to play off East against West for their own material gain; that many of these new nationalist regimes were more interested in following "Socialist" models of development, and thus had ideological leanings toward the "other side" in the cold war despite their protestations of nonalignment; and, finally, that even discounting these ideological incompatibilities, most of the would-be beneficiaries lacked the administrative and technical talent, economic structure, and will to make significant gains with the additional capital.[1]

In late 1955 and early 1956, with Soviet salesmen in the underdeveloped areas becoming a familiar part of the international scene, Nixon and Nelson Rockefeller added their voices to Stassen's in urging a dramatic response by the United States. The same orthodox wall was encountered again.[2] But now the evidence of Soviet economic penetration, particularly in the Middle East, was more alarming. Dulles was specially worried, as he expressed to a Cabinet meeting on September 30, 1955, over the extent to which the "commercial" transactions involved the provision of obsolete Soviet weapons to the Arab nations.[3] This time Eisenhower and Dulles asked Congress to increase the foreign aid program—then running at about $2.7 billion annually—to $4.9 billion. They also asked for limited authority, in the nature of contingency funds, to support large projects such as Nasser's Aswan Dam.

U.S. economic assistance was viewed primarily as an enticement to the reluctant to join "our side" in the bipolar struggle. However, the premise that the balance of power was essentially bipolar, or ought to be organized on a bipolar basis, was undermined drastically by the Suez and Hungarian crises in the fall of 1956.

THE SUEZ CRISIS

By the time the Baghdad Pact efforts had reached their culmination in 1955, the United States had already begun to act on assumptions antithetical to those underlying its original sponsorship of this "northern tier" alliance system. The network of alliances in the region was based on the premise that the goal of preventing Soviet absorption of the Middle East was best served by building up the indigenous armies of those regimes willing to enter into formal alliance with the West. Nasser's response—the organization of a Pan-Arab alliance system and the bartering of Middle Eastern products for arms manufactured by Soviet Union satellites—shook the foundations of the existing United States approach to the Middle East.

The Soviets were seen to be leapfrogging the northern tier with such success that the administration feared Soviet absorption of the area to the south (including the oil pipelines and the Suez Canal) without a single Communist soldier crossing an international boundary. Ironically, this was happening through the very device that the U.S. had fashioned: the establishment of military-dependency relationships between local regimes and external big powers. The administration was still not ready to throw its established orientation overboard. But its policies increasingly evidenced ambivalence in attempting to demonstrate respect for the nationalisms of the area in order to avoid the local political alienation from the West which was easing the way for Soviet penetration.

This ambivalence was expressed in a series of United States moves in 1955–56 which alienated Britain and France, and contributed ultimately to the split over Suez. The administration avoided formal identification with its own offspring, the Baghdad Pact. The British, who had joined the pact, felt betrayed by this turnabout, which Prime Minister Eden branded an American "failure to put its weight behind its friends in the hope of being popular with its foes."[4] (The British had recently agreed to liquidate their military base at Suez under the assumption that they could still focus military pressure on the area through the instrumentalities of the Baghdad Pact.) France had been disappointed throughout this period in United States unwillingness to demonstrate any sympathy for the French position in North Africa. And now, by offering financial assistance to Nasser's billion-dollar construction of the Aswan Dam, the U.S. was aiding an Egyptian regime that openly supported the Algerian rebel movement.

From Dulles' perspective, the British and French were prisoners of their traditional colonial viewpoint as well as their current economic interests in the area. But the United States was responsible for keeping its eye on the ball: the East–West balance of power. The struggle with the Communists for influence in the Middle East was assuming a new form because of the growth of nationalism and the Soviet attempt to exploit it, and the United States would have to adjust its policies.

To its European allies, the American "adjustment" was crude, unsophisticated, and ultimately disastrous. First, the United States demonstrated a magnanimity to Nasser which the wily politician could only define as New World gullibility. Then, Eisenhower and Dulles, having finally come to the conclusion that Nasser was playing off the United States against the Soviets on the Aswan Dam project, canceled their commitment to the project in such an abrupt, back-of-the-hand manner that Nasser was driven to nationalize the Suez Canal to finance the construction of the dam. In French and British eyes, this act—which led to their subsequent military intervention—was an overreaction; it could have been avoided had Dulles not been so anxious to humiliate Nasser for having taken the United States for a sucker.

Eisenhower subsequently acknowledged that "we might have been undiplomatic in the way the cancellation [of Aswan financing] was handled"; and admitted that if the United States had "avoided a showdown on the issue, we would probably have deprived Nasser of a dramatic and plausible excuse for this subsequent actions affecting the Canal." But Dulles maintained that Nasser got the treatment he was asking for.[5]

But when, in response to Nasser's canal grab, others inflicted their own punishment on Egypt, Eisenhower and Dulles slapped them down. The motives of the administration in demanding that Israel, Britain, and France call off their military action were manifold and complex (indeed, the Europeans appear to have genuinely miscalculated that the United States would support them).

The old policy of buying military allies through military assistance agreements had reached a point of diminishing returns: and to contest with the Soviets for the remaining nonaligned areas required a willingness to back the national development efforts of strident, sensitive, and unpredictable charismatic leaders.

In addition, if such regimes were to qualify for assistance, this would degrade the relative value to our alliance partners of joining us in anti-Communist pacts.

The policies of the United States during the Suez crisis reflected the fact that such considerations had come into play at the highest levels of government, but also that they had not been resolved. First, there was the wooing away of the proud Egyptian nationalists from the Soviet embrace; then came the public altercation in response to being two-timed; then finally, the fear of taking action that would drive Egypt and its allies irreversibly into the arms of Russia.

The British and the French, of course, cast their case *for* military intervention in global balance of power terms and equated any exercise of allied restraint with the appeasement of Hitler prior to 1939.

The Europeans were thinking of their own economic well-being, and equating this with the global balance of power. But Eisenhower and Dulles felt that times had changed. Not only was the most intense United States–Soviet competition shifting to non-European areas, but the strength of the European economies in the face of a squeeze on their oil and commerce was not as enfeebled as the British and French were picturing it. "Foster felt that Anthony's fears of being wholly deprived of Middle East oil were exaggerated," explains Eisenhower.[6] To assuage the fears of the Europeans, the administration worked out an emergency oil pool plan by which the French and British would be supplied by the United States and other nations whose resources were not cut off by the Middle Eastern crisis. A permanent blocking of the Suez to French and British commerce, and an indefinite denial to them of Middle Eastern supplies of fuel, could well have serious consequences for the global balance. The President and Dulles assured the Europeans that this was a central consideration in all our efforts. The question was *how* to avoid such a consequence and, of equal importance in United States calculations, how to do it without turning the entire Arab world against the West. "Obviously we were anxious to sustain our continuing relations with our old and traditional friends, Britain and France," writes Eisenhower. "But to us the situation was not quite so simple as those two governments portrayed it."[7]

The debate between the United States and its principal allies over the consequences of resorting to force against Nasser intensified during the weeks leading up to the British and French military intervention. on October 5, Foreign Ministers Pinay and Lloyd met with Dulles and frankly urged the use of force, maintaining that only by bringing Naser to his knees could Western prestige in Africa and the Middle East be restored. According to Eisenhower's account, "Foster disagreed vehemently . . . setting forth our conviction that Africa, the Middle East, and Asia would be inflamed against the West if we resorted *unnecessarily* to force." [8]

Exchanges of this nature continued between the three governments up to the last minute, when the British and French intervened with troops and planes, ostensibly to separate the Israelis and Egyptians, three days after the Israelis attacked Egyptian positions in the Sinai. Eisenhower's last pleading cable to Eden remained unsent as on October 31 British planes based on Cyprus struck at Egyptian ports and communications centers. The cable, which Eisenhower quotes in part in his memoirs as an example of his thoughts at the time, stressed again the weight the United States was giving to the new anticolonial nationalisms:

I must say that it is hard for me to see any good final result emerging from a scheme that seems to antagonize the entire Moslem world. Indeed I have difficulty seeing any end whatsoever if all the Arabs should begin reacting somewhat as the North Africans have been operating against the French. [9]

The United States reaction, once military action had begun, was consonant with the position developed up to that time. The flat unwillingness to support the British, French, or Israeli action and the sponsorship of United Nations cease-fire and peacekeeping efforts were defended in Eisenhower's election campaign speeches, and in Dulles' addresses to the United Nations, as being required by our morally based adherence to the principles of nonaggression. However, in a letter to Winston Churchill on November 27, following the acceptance of a United Nations-controlled cease-fire, the President was more candid as to our overriding considerations:

Many months ago it became clear that the Soviets were convinced that the mere building of mighty military machines would not necessarily accomplish their purposes, while at the same time their military effort was severely limiting their capacity for conquering the world by other means, especially economic. . . . My point [in communications to Eden counseling against the use of force] was that since the struggle with Russia had obviously taken on a new tactical form, we had to be especially careful that any course of action we adopted should by its logic and justice command world respect, if not sympathy. [10]

The compelling concern had been for the political repercussions of Western military intervention. But there also had been a certain degree of concern that the Soviets might make a direct military response. During the height of the crisis, Eisenhower and Allen Dulles, Director of the Central Intelligence Agency, were worried that the Soviets might try to stage fighter planes from Egypt. The President asked for high-altitude reconnaissance flights over Israel and Syria to see if Soviet planes and pilots had landed at Syrian bases. "Our people should be alert in trying to determine Soviet intentions," he told Dulles. "If the Soviets should attack Britain and France directly we would of course be in a major war."[11]

The President ordered the military to "progressively achieve an advanced state of readiness." These measure were regarded as precautionary signals to the Soviets that the United States would not be taken by surprise. Admiral Radford, in discussing the strategic military context wit the President, observed that the Soviets would find it extremely difficult to undertake any military operations in the Middle East. "The only reasonable form of intervention would be long-range air strikes with nuclear weapons—which seems unlikely."[12]

Eisenhower was suspicious, however, that the Soviets might attempt some ruse to gain a military foothold in the area without running the high risks of direct provocation of the United States. He therefore rejected the Soviet proposal for joint police action by the Soviets and the United States as "unthinkable." The Soviets, Eisenhower told the White House staff on November 5, "seeing their failure in the satellites, might be ready to undertake any wild adventure . . . [they] are as scared and furious as Hitler was in his last days. There's nothing more dangerous than a dictatorship in that frame of mind."[13]

The existing military balance of power, based on United States superiority in strategic nuclear strike capability, gave the administration relative confidence that it could control the military dimensions of the conflict—largely by deterring Soviet military moves. But the military balance was seen to be largely irrelevant to the political dimensions of the conflict, and it was these political dimensions that could very seriously affect the global distribution of power.

The Suez crisis thus drove home, and made operational, the premise that in the power struggle with the Soviets the sentiments of the new nationalist regimes were of critical importance. But as yet the policy implications were drawn primarily in the form of guidelines concerning what *not* to do for fear of alienating the nonaligned nationalists. Policies for positive action—for programs to strengthen the ability of these regimes to counter the socioeconomic sources of Communist subversion within their countries—required the acceptance of additional premises which were still unpalatable to the Eisenhower administration.

EAST EUROPEAN CRISES

The diversity of the opposing bloc was another prominent realization of this period. But again, the problem was what to do about it. The need to solve this problem in concrete policy terms, rather than with the sloganeering rhetoric used to cover lack of action during the Berlin uprisings of 1953, was finally forced upon the administration by the Hungarian uprising. Events in Eastern Europe also served to undermine the reliance by Dulles and Eisenhower on a rather limited set of coercive tools as the primary weights on the Western side of the global power balance.

It is technically correct that in the rhetoric of the 1952 election Dulles and Eisenhower had explicitly disassociated their "liberation" policy from any incitements to armed revolt. "The people [in Eastern Europe] have no arms," said Dulles in a Chicago campaign speech, "and violent revolt would be futile; indeed it would be worse than futile, for it would precipitate massacre."[14] Yet implicit in Dulles' call to "activate the strains and stresses within the Communist empire so as to disintegrate it" was the premise that the Soviets might be dissuaded from violent repression out of a fear that the United States *might* take coercive countermeasures. And this in turn was based on the premise that the balance of coercive power, on a global basis, was such that the U.S. implicit threat was credible.

The standard Republican attack against the Roosevelt and Truman administrations was that the Democrats had been overly respectful of Soviet power. They contended that the Soviets could have been prevented from consolidating their control over the occupied countries of Eastern Europe if the United States had been willing to bring its superior power to bear. This, of course, was the Republican line in hindsight only; from 1945 to 1948 no prominent Republican had advocated that the United States be willing to fight the Soviets on the East European question. Republican campaigners around the country took a tough line in 1952 and pointed to their platform promise to

end the negative, futile, and immoral policy of "containment" which abandons countless human beings to a despotism and Godless terrorism which in turn enables the rulers to forge the captives into a weapon for our destruction. . . . The policies we espouse will revive the contagious, liberating influences which are inherent in freedom. They will inevitably set up strains and stresses within the captive world which will make the rulers impotent to continue in their monstrous ways and mark the beginning of the end. Our nation will again become the dynamic, moral, and spiritual force which was the despair of despots and the hope of the oppressed.[15]

Campaign hyperbole or not, the promises were carried over into the statements Dulles made early in his career as Secretary of State. From his new position of responsibility, in his first public address (January 27, 1953), he again sounded the clarion: "To all those suffering under Communist slavery . . . let us say: you can count on us."[16]

However, no pressure was brought to bear against the East Germans or the Soviets after their violent suppression of the workers' uprisings in East Berlin and East Germany in June 1953. The allied commandants in Berlin protested "the irresponsible recourse to military force" by the Communist authorities, and demanded that "the harsh restrictions imposed upon the population be lifted immediately," but there was no significant coercive sanction implied in these demands.[17]

The Secretary of State used the occasion of the Berlin uprising to reiterate his earlier opinion that "the Communist structure is over-extended, over-riding, and ill-founded. It could be shaken if the difficulties that were latent were activated." But he also insisted he had been saying all along that "this does not mean an armed revolt which would precipitate a massacre."[18]

Congress followed up with its concurrent resolution of August 3, 1953. The hollowness of its operative clause juxtaposed with its statement of conditions in the Soviet sphere came close to being a caricature of administration paralysis on this issue:

WHEREAS the Soviet regime being unable to win the allegiance of the people under its rule, knows no other method of achieving the compliance of the people to their dictatorship than by force of arms, terror, murder, imprisonment, reprisals and mass deportation; and

WHEREAS the cause of freedom cannot be contained and will eventually triumph; Now therefore, be it

Resolved, That the Congress commends and encourages the valiant struggle of these captive peoples for freedom.[19]

The only material assistance offered by the United States during the crisis was the distribution of extra food to the East Berliners who flooded into West Berlin. The pressing problem was whether the United States should prepare to act to greater effect in future contingencies of this sort, which, according to Dulles, were only just beginning.

The abandonment of "liberation" as an operational policy seems to have begun at this time. The grand-strategy task forces appointed by the White House in the spring of 1953 to explore the implications of alternative strategies and to come up with recommendations included one group specifically assigned to the "liberation" alternative. In the initial terms of reference for this group the concept conveyed a "rollback" of existing Communist frontiers through political, psychological, and economic warfare programs, along with paramilitary measures. But when the reports of the groups were integrated into one document and presented to the President for approval in October 1953, no part of the "liberation" alternative was incorporated.[20] And it does not seem to have appeared again as a premise for grand-strategy planning during the Eisenhower years.

Yet the official, and officially blessed, propaganda agencies do not seem to have received the message clearly. Their role was critical in keeping alive and inflating expectations between 1953 and 1956 that the United States would somehow interpose against Soviet repressive measures during a period of major uprisings.

In the fall of 1956 the administration had neither the intention nor the capability of intervening in Poland or Hungary. It is possible that Khrushchev was willing to strike a bargain with Wladislaw Gomulka over the degree of permissible Polish independence from the Soviet Communist Party in part for fear of United States action if the Soviet Army should actually engage Gomulka's troops in battle. (Gomulka made it clear that if Soviet troops were brought in, as threatened, the whole nation would stand and fight. Khrushchev would have been rash to regard this merely as a bluff, since Gomulka had rallied the nation, including the police and the Army, around him.)

But if fear that the administration might feel morally obligated to implement its "liberation" rhetoric was a factor in the Polish situation, it may have been removed prematurely from the Soviet calculus of risks to be incurred by violent repression of the Hungarian revolt. A series of administration statements from October 27 to October 31 seemed very anxious to indicate the United States had no intention of intervening. On November 4 the Soviets returned with 200,000 troops and 4,000 tanks to crush the revolt, reversing their October 30 decision to compromise.

Eisenhower recalls the administration's stark appraisal of the balance of usable force at the time:

> The launching of the Soviet offensive against Hungary almost automatically had posed to us the question of force to oppose this barbaric invasion.
>
> . . . I still wonder what would have been my recommendation to the Congress and the American people had Hungary been accessible by sea or through the territory of allies who might have agreed to react positively to the tragic fate of the Hungarian people. As it was, however, Britain and France could not possibly have moved with us into Hungary. An expedition combining West German or Italian forces with our own, and moving across neutral Austria, Titoist Yugoslavia, or Communist Czechoslovakia was out of the question. The fact was that Hungary could not be reached by any United Nations or United States units without traversing such territory. Unless the major nations of Europe would, without delay, ally themselves spontaneously with us (an unimaginable prospect), we could do nothing.[21]

The weight given by the administration to this essential appraisal of the military situation is corroborated by other writers. Drummond and Coblentz in their book on Dulles tell of a private State Department session at the height of the crisis at which the Secretary of State listed the following reasons against United States military intervention (theirs is a paraphrase, not a verbatim record):

> First, any attempt at limited intervention by the nearest available American troops in Southern Germany would result in their defeat and massacre by the massive Russian forces.
>
> Second, only a full-scale intervention would be feasible from a military viewpoint. It would risk a nuclear war with the Russians, and the American government was not prepared to take this risk on the Hungarian issue.
>
> Third, one of the many ghastly results of a full-scale intervention war would be the total annihilation, rather than the salvation, of Hungary, the country for whose sake the war would be undertaken.[22]

Dulles, according to Drummond and Coblentz, made clear that these considerations would equally have prevailed if the Suez crisis had not been in progress and if the Soviet Union had been the only aggressor on the world stage.[23]

In the aftermath of the Hungarian crisis the tone of administration public statements on Eastern Europe changed, as did the tenor of United States diplomacy.

There were a few lame recitals of the history of the "liberation" doctrine, recalling the exclusion of "armed revolts" as an American policy objective. But the talk of activating stresses and strains in the Soviet empire so as to bring about its disintegration disappeared from high administration statements.

The agitational content of both the official Voice of America and the unofficial Radio Free Europe (which was thought to be the main culprit in arousing expectations of American intervention) was cut down.

The most telling change was in the selective opening of economic relations with the European satellites. Using American experience with Tito since 1948 as the model, the new view was that trade and aid relationships advantageous to a particular Communist regime— Gomulka's Poland was the leading beneficiary of the new policy— could have the short-term result of lessening its need to be subservient to Moscow. In the longer term, greater economic independence in Eastern Europe might affect the global balance of power in our favor. Moreover, the side effects of demonstrating to the people of these areas that the United States had a concern for their well-being and the chance for increased exposure to Western values might indirectly act to moderate the totalitarian characteristics of these regimes.

Loud talk and the stick gave way, at least on an experimental basis, to soft talk and the carrot as tools of power. The Soviets, as well as their satellites and Soviet-leaning neutrals, were to be approached in this vein.

This orientation gain gave prominence to the Eisenhower face, as opposed to the Dulles face, of administration policy—the face associated with the President's welfare-not-warfare speech to the newspaper editors in 1953; with his Atoms for Peace proposal of the same year; and with the smiles, handshakes, and open skies of Geneva 1955.

REACTING TO SPUTNIK

The dramatic Russian space achievements in the fall of 1957, and attempts by the Soviets to exploit diplomatically their potential military significance,[24] riveted American public and official attention, more than ever before, on the military–technological factors of power. From 1957 to 1960 the administration was increasingly pressed to answer opposition-party charges that it was letting the nation fall behind the Soviets in strategic military power *and* in the domestic economic and technological foundations for such power. The prospect of losing the socioeconomic competition to influence the developing nations had also become a part of the policy dialogue, and was reflected in the Mutual Security Administration's renewed emphasis on economic assistance. However, the major controversies surrounding administration decisions for the allocation of resources had to do with the best means of preventing the Soviets from surpassing the United States in strategic military power.

The administration's first public reaction to the Soviet orbiting of their 184-pound Sputnik I on October 4, 1957, was a model of studied nonchalance. The Soviets were congratulated for their scientific achievement, but its military implications were publicly deprecated. When only a month later the Soviets launched Sputnik II, carrying a dog and many instruments, and more than five times heavier than Sputnik I, the tremendous strides the Soviets had been making in technology required something more than sanguine recognition.

The White House announced the appointment of James R. Killian, president of the Massachusetts Institute of Technology, as special assistant for science and technology—a new post described by the President as carrying "active responsibility for helping me to follow through in the scientific improvement of our defense." In addition, Eisenhower gave personal attention to the administrative bottlenecks in the missile program. He directed his Secretary of Defense (Neil McElroy) "to make certain that the Guided Missile Director is clothed with all the authority that the Secretary himself possesses," and announced other changes designed to eliminate overlapping and conflicting service jurisdictions in the rocket and missile programs. These actions were revealed in a major television address on science and defense.

The President's main message was one of reassurance. It was right that the nation should feel concern in light of the Soviet accomplishments; otherwise, we might become complacent and fall behind. But there was every reason for confidence that *existing* programs, with only marginal modifications, would continue to provide the nation with "both a sound defense and a sound economy." The President was certain that "although the Soviets are quite likely ahead in some missile and special areas, and are obviously ahead of us in satellite development, as of today the over-all military strength of the Free World is distinctly greater than that of the Communist countries." He based this conclusion, said the President, on a number of important facts: the U.S. was ahead of the Soviet Union in the nuclear field, both in quantity and quality. Our stock of nuclear weapons was sufficiently dispersed, so that if we were attacked first, "ample quantities would be available for instant retaliation." The United States missile program was well under way, with test shots ranging 3,500 miles already accomplished; and because of our forward system of bases ringing the Soviet Union, an intermediate-range missile would be "for some purposes, as good as an intercontinental missile." In addition to these offensive components, the nation was protected from direct attack by "a complex system of early warning radars, communication lines, electronic computers, supersonic aircraft, and ground-to-air missiles, some with atomic warheads." He also expressed confidence in the combined strength of the ground and naval forces of the United States and its allies. The essential approach of the so-called New Look for serving the nation's security was reaffirmed. It was important to maintain "selectivity" in defense spending, cautioned the President, so as not to neglect priorities and "ride off in all directions at once." [25]

The President's expressed confidence in the adequacy of existing premises and programs in the military sphere, which he said was "supported by trusted scientific and military advisers," was not shared at all by one group of prestigious advisers, whose secret report he had just received. The Gaither Committee report had been briefed to the President and the National Security Council on the morning of November 7. Although recommendations in the report were a direct challenge to the New Look, the committee hoped that the shock of the Sputniks would be utilized by the President, somewhat as Truman had used the shock of the Communist attack in

Korea, to mobilize public support for a larger and more diversified military program.

Though ostensibly secret, the major recommendations of the Gaither Committee, and the premises on which they were based, were known. Newspaper accounts and congressional speeches described the report in detail and leaders of the Democratic Party demanded its declassification.[26] The administration refused to release even a "sanitized" version; but among policy-oriented elites there was general agreement concerning its contents.[27]

The Gaither Committee painted the United States as increasingly vulnerable to Soviet strategic power unless significant corrective action was taken, estimated as leading within a few years to additional annual defense expenditures of at least $8 billion above the current $38 billion. The most critical problem facing the United States, in the eyes of the Gaither Committee, was how to maintain an effective strategic retaliatory capability when, in the early 1960s, the Soviets would have an operational ICBM force. If no corrective action was taken, the Soviet, if they struck first, would be able to destroy the Strategic Air Command. The vulnerability of SAC, rather than its initial destructive capability, was the matter that should be receiving priority attention.

Missiles with intercontinental ranges would have to become the foundation of the strategic force. This would have to be primarily designed as a "second-strike" force capable of surviving a first strike. But the implications of such strategic planning had to be faced: namely, with survivable strategic capabilities on both sides, the non-Communist world would also need to be prepared to fight limited wars. However, for the limited-war capability to be significant, as opposed to that maintained by the Communists, the United States would have to maintain much larger ground forces and airlift capacity than planned for under the New Look.[28]

These proposals, leaked to the press, and given the dramatic context of Sputniks I and II and Soviet claims of an operational ICBM, could not have come at a worse time for the administration. Eisenhower had failed during his first term to keep military expenditures under the New Look ceiling of $34 billion annually. Reluctantly, for the second term, a more realistic ceiling of $38 billion had been agreed upon. But the second term began amid a general price inflation, with the costs of goods and services purchased by the

Defense Department rising faster than those of the economy as a whole. Defense Department officials were now telling Eisenhower that even *without* new programs, military expenditures during fiscal 1958 would rise to about $42 billion.[29] Rather than being able to balance the budget, the President would have to ask Congress to raise the statutory limit on the national debt!

In these circumstances Eisenhower was not at all pleased with the recommendations of the Gaither report, and looked more kindly on arguments showing that with only marginal improvements in existing programs, and with a more selective approach, the U.S. could preserve the existing balance of strategic power against the Soviet Union. He also renewed his interest in the Mutual Security program as a means of saving United States defense expenditures by providing for local defense capabilities with the cheaper-to-provision armies of allies.

Unlike 1950, when Secretary of State Acheson helped provide the President with a grand-strategy rationale for devoting a larger portion of the nation's resources to military programs, the post-Sputnik period found the Secretary of State most effective in buttressing the President's effort to quiet the chorus of demands for greater military outlays. Dulles now joined Eisenhower in deprecating those who would overemphasize military factors in the balance of power. In a top-level meeting that considered the Gaither report, Dulles noted that the committee had confined itself to military problems. "But the international struggle," he observed, "is not just military." By overdevoting its resources to defense the United States could lose the world economic competition. And, in a comment with significance for a whole set of New Look premises, Dulles pointed out that the Soviet Union had made its greatest seizures of territory and people "when only the United States had the atomic bomb."[30]

The implied denigration of the utility of United States military–strategic *superiority* in these remarks was more than polemical. Administration defense planners, fending off pressure to spend more to keep ahead of the Russians in strategic striking power, had as early as 1956 accepted the essentials of mutual strategic deterrence as an operational guideline. As explained by Secretary of the Air Force Quarles in August 1956, looking a few years ahead:

[The] build-up of atomic power [on both sides of the Iron Curtain] . . . makes total war an unthinkable catastrophe for both sides.

. . .

Neither side can hope by a mere margin of superiority in airplanes or other means of delivery of atomic weapons to escape the catastrophe of such a war. Beyond a certain point, this prospect is not the result of *relative* strength of the two opposed forces. It is the *absolute* power in the hands of each, and the substantial invulnerability of this power to interdiction.[31]

Eisenhower was responsive to suggestions, from the Gaither Committee and other experts, that the U.S. maintain at least this minimum deterrent against a massive Soviet strategic strike, and that hardening, mobility, and dispersal were important components of a survivable deterrent. However, he accepted the counsel that this could be done within existing expenditure levels.

The President bristled at suggestions that he was sacrificing national security to economy considerations. But he adamantly refused to be stampeded by those whom he saw as translating every international crisis into a larger appropriation for their pet projects:

The problem was not unfamiliar [Eisenhower recalls]. Our security depended on a set of associated and difficult objectives: to maintain a defense posture of unparalleled magnitude and yet to do so without a breakdown of the American economy.

"We must get people to understand that we confront a tough problem," I said, "but one that we can lick." We could not turn the nation into a garrison state.[32]

Although the President's first reaction to the Soviet space shots was to maintain that we were not in a space race with the Soviets, the United States space effort, centered on the Vanguard project, was accelerated on an emergency basis. By the summer the race was in full swing, with successful United States launches of Vanguard I, Explorer III, and Explorer IV. The Soviets launched heavier satellites (Sputnik III, May 15, 1958, weighed 2,900 pounds) but the United States could claim greater sophistication. In the more immediately critical field of long-range ballistic missiles, the competition also began to be equalized by the end of 1958. The solid-propellant Minuteman ICBM entered its development phase, and the Polaris program for submarine-launched missiles was begun in earnest.

Yet the administration had a difficult time during its last year and a half in office as a growing number of intellectuals, journalists, and politicians were circulating and repeating the phrases "delicate balance of terror" and "missile gap." The thrust of the criticism directed at the administration was that it was overly complacent about the ability of the United States to maintain a retaliatory capability that was not vulnerable to destruction by a Soviet first strike. Journalists, claiming their reports were based on the estimates of high Defense Department officials, predicted a Soviet missile lead of three-to-one by the early 1960s. Administration spokesmen refused to talk "numbers" in public. They insisted that numerical estimates were not as important as the fact that there would be no "deterrent gap"—a vague concept meant to convey the notion that the United States, while constructing its advanced ICBM force, would maintain a diversified capacity (based in part on manned bombers) to inflict unacceptable damage on the Soviet Union in a strategic exchange.

Science, technology, the rate of economic growth, and the esoteric calculus of strategic nuclear deterrence were the dominant terms in which national power was evaluated by administration defenders and critics during the later Eisenhower years. But underneath this dialogue, forces stubbornly resistant to such material factors of power continued to brew and erupt and undermine the peace on which the American pursuit of happiness depended.

RESPONDING TO TURBULENCE IN THE MIDDLE EAST

Dulles and Eisenhower, in opposing the military moves of Britain and France against Nasser in 1956, had taken a very large step in the direction of a United States foreign policy that attempted to work with, rather than against, neutralist nationalism. They expected applause from the middle Eastern Nasserites, but instead encountered jeers. Rather than interpreting United States restraint as respect for the Arab desire to be fully independent, United States opposition to its allies' use of force was seen by the Nasserites and the Soviets as the product of our fear of a Middle Eastern confrontation with the Soviets.

Now with Britain and France thoroughly humiliated in the eyes of the Arabs, and the Baghdad Pact allies more confused than ever as to United States objectives in the area, Dulles felt it essential to reassert the United States interest and intention of keeping the Middle East out of Communist hands. So instead of translating the events of 1956 into an invitation to the Soviets to cooperate in a mutual cold war "disengagement" from the Middle East, the administration redefined the area as critical to the bipolar balance and reaffirmed the nation's resolve to do battle there if necessary.

In his special message to Congress on January 5, Eisenhower went even farther than had Truman in March 1947 in defining the United States interest in the Middle East as one of preventing this critical geopolitical region from falling under the control of the Soviets. Stressing its importance as a transportation and commercial link between continents, and as a source of two-thirds of the world's oil reserves, the President painted the consequences of Soviet domination of the area in global terms:

Western Europe would be endangered just as though there had been no Marshall Plan, no North Atlantic Treaty Organization. The free nations of Asia and Africa, too, would be placed in serious jeopardy. . . . All this would have the most adverse, if not disastrous, effect upon our own nation's economic life and political prospects.[33]

With the stakes this high, said the President, "Nothing is more necessary . . . than that our policy with respect to the defense of the area be promptly and clearly determined and declared. . . . If power-hungry Communists should either falsely or correctly estimate that the Middle East is inadequately defended, they might be tempted to use open measures of armed attack."[34] The greatest insurance against the possibility of major war for control of the Middle East, contended the President, was a clear declaration by the Congress of its willingness to authorize the use of the armed forces of the United States to help Middle Eastern nations "requesting such aid, against overt armed aggression from any nation controlled by International Communism."[35] The President's address also contained requests for congressional authorization of economic and military assistance for regimes in the area. But these were subordinate in emphasis to the request for the declaration of intent to employ United States armed forces directly against Communist encroachments.

The urgency of the need for a clear commitment by the United States to defend the Middle East against Communist aggression was presented in starkest outline by the Secretary of State before the congressional committees handling the proposed resolution:

Soviet ground, naval and air forces are stationed in the areas adjacent to the Middle East—Bulgaria, the Black Sea, the Ukraine, the Caucasus, and Central Asia. These Soviet forces are of a size and are so located that they could be employed at any time with a minimum of warning. This fact is nothing new. But today it takes on new implications.

· · ·

There is ample evidence of Communist infiltration into certain areas, particularly organized labor; and there are plottings of assassinations and sabotage to gain Communist ends. Local Communists have recently obtained small arms. . . . Arab refugees . . . are a special target for Communist propaganda.

Thus the Middle East area is at once endangered by potential military threats against which there is now no adequate deterrent, by a rapidly mounting financial and economic crisis, and by subversive efforts which seek advantage from exceptional opportunities arising out of recent events. This adds up to a new and grave danger.[36]

Dulles rejected charges that in focusing on the Communist threat he was misdirecting American efforts, which should rather be directed at the underlying causes of instability and hatred of the West. He contended that the administration approach to the Middle East was multifaceted and included an intensified program of economic assistance. The United States believed that no efforts should be spared to tackle the root causes of trouble in the area, said Dulles. "But we do not take the pessimistic view that, unless and until these problems can be solved, nothing can usefully be done to prevent the area from being taken over by international communism."[37]

Congress passed the joint resolution, henceforth referred to as the "Eisenhower Doctrine," essentially in the form requested by the administration, in which

The President is authorized to. . . . employ the armed forces of the United States as he deems necessary to secure and protect the territorial integrity and political independence of any such nation or group of nations requesting such aid against overt armed aggression from any nation controlled by international communism.[38]

Under this grant of authority, the Sixth Fleet was ordered to the eastern Mediterranean in April 1957 as a display of United States support for King Hussein of Jordan, faced with political unrest following the dismissal of his pro-Nasser Prime Minister, Suleiman Nabulsi. Egypt and Syria abetted the antiroyalist rebels, and to this extent the conflict was more than a purely domestic affair. King Hussein claimed that the independence and integrity of Jordan were threatened by "International Communism"; and the administration in Washington, conditioned to the sound of its own bell, poised itself to respond. In addition to the naval show of force, $10 million of emergency aid was promptly granted to Jordan.[39] Egypt and Syria failed to intervene on the side of the rebels, nor did Israel move to preempt such intervention. In administration circles, the rapid quieting down of the Jordanian crisis was attributed to the swiftness with which King Hussein was brought under the protective cover of the Eisenhower Doctrine.

A more plausible case of the Communist exploitation of Middle Eastern instabilities occurred in Syria. The Soviets were equipping the Syrian army and, in conjunction with the visit of the Syrian Minister of Defense to Moscow in August 1957, announced large-scale credits for increased trade. The Syrians, meanwhile, charged the United States with complicity in a plot to overthrow the Damascus government. Three United States Embassy and attaché officials were expelled under allegations that they were involved in the subversive conspiracy. The Syrian Army chief of staff, whom Washington regarded as a political moderate, resigned, and his place was taken by a general thought to be a Communist. "The entire action was shrouded in mystery," recalled Eisenhower, "but the suspicion was strong that the Communists had taken control of the government."[40]

In the Jordanian crisis, the Eisenhower Doctrine was implemented simply; it involved only military demonstrations and emergency aid to a regime begging to be saved from Communist subversives. Now, however, although the Communist threat was less of a fiction, implementation of the Eisenhower Doctrine might back the administration into a corner since a failure to reverse the drift of political loyalties in Syria, by whatever means necessary, could undermine the credibility of United States commitments all over the world. The problem was that purging Syria of its Soviet-leaning leadership was likely to be very costly and involve risking war. Direct United States intervention was avoided on the legal grounds that the Eisenhower Doctrine stipulated that United States intervention would come in response to a *request* from a threatened government, and also on the lack of sufficient information concerning the real loyalties of the Syrian regime.

To demonstrate the availability of United States military power in case of need, the Sixth Fleet was again ordered to the eastern Mediterranean; United States aircraft were redeployed from Western Europe to Adana, Turkey; and the Strategic Air Command was placed on alert.[41]

The Soviets were quick in attempting to turn the situation to their advantage. They accused the United States of planning, in collusion with Turkey, Israel, and others, to intervene militarily in Syria, citing the mission of Deputy Under Secretary of State Henderson to the Middle East and the White House press release on his return as evidence. "As for the alleged existence of a danger that Syria will take aggressive action against neighboring states," said the Soviet Foreign Minister on September 10, "why doesn't the U.S. government raise this question in the U.N. Security Council if it has such fears?"[42] The United States was clearly being outmaneuvered, and had little recourse but to deflate the war scare that, it must be admitted, was partly of its own making.

Dulles, as dexterous in backing away from the brink as approaching it, used his September 10 press conference to signal the administration's realization that Syria would not be the arena for a superpower confrontation in the Middle East: "There has been as yet no determination that Syria is dominated by international communism within the meaning of the Middle East resolution." Explained the Secretary of State:

There have to be three findings before there is direct armed intervention by the United States. There has to be a finding by the President that one of the countries was dominated by international communism; secondly, there has to be an act of aggression by that country; third, there has to be a request by the country attacked for that aid. . . . And I might say at the present time I don't think it likely that those three things will occur.[43]

The inappropriateness of the kind of power the United States was trying to apply in the Middle East was driven home once again during the Iraq–Lebanon crisis of 1958. The presidential decision of July 14, 1958 to intervene in Lebanon was precipitated by the bloody coup in neighboring Iraq that transformed the West's only major Arab ally into a Soviet-leaning Nasserite regime, and, it was feared in those early days, possibly a Communist satellite of the Soviet Union. Yet the response—a Marine landing in Lebanon—was undertaken without any real hope of thereby undoing the coup in Iraq.

In the President's public announcement on July 15, 1958, his decision to dispatch United States Marines to Lebanon was presented as a means for preserving the "independence and integrity" of Lebanon against "indirect aggression." The source of this indirect aggression was not identified, but there were strong suggestions that it was the United Arab Republic. There was no reference to "international communism" as the source of aggression, nor was the UAR painted as being "controlled by international communism."[44]

The success of the rebel movement in Lebanon would not in itself have altered the balance of power, materially or geopolitically. But if the United States were again seen as standing by helpless, as it had in Syria, and as it had in Iraq, a profound psychological ingredient of the power of the non-Communist coalition—the reputation of its leader as willing to take potentially costly action—would be disastrously undermined. Without a clear concept of what the consequences of action might be, it was nevertheless essential to *act.*

As it happened, the United States military intervention in Lebanon and the coordinated British intervention to help King Hussein of Jordan incurred less cost and risk than had been contemplated by Eisenhower and Dulles. The Soviets made their usual protests, sent their usual warnings to the Western allies, and made their usual appeals for a summit conference. Nasser, not at all anxious to have a Soviet presence substituted for a western one, apparently assured the Soviets there would be no requirement for Soviet military intervention unless the Western powers invaded Iraq or the UAR. Moreover, the Egyptian leader kept his assistance to the Lebanese rebels to a minimum, and quickly threw his weight on the side of those who sought gains from a political compromise inside Lebanon. The United States and the Soviet Union had little choice but to fall in behind an all-Arab resolution the General Assembly affirming the obligation of the Arab states to respect each other's form of government, and asking the Secretary General to help arrange the withdrawal of foreign troops from Lebanon and Jordan.[45]

The administration was able to claim a major success by retrospectively defining its aims in the Lebanon affair as directed primarily toward keeping Nasser from swallowing up yet another Middle Eastern country, and by attributing Nasser's reluctance to intervene in force to the United States preemptive intervention. Eisenhower maintained that one result of the American action was a "definite change in Nasser's attitude toward the United States." American behavior at the time of the Suez affair had presumably convinced the Egyptian that the U.S. would rarely, if ever, resort to force in support of friends or principles. Now "he certainly had his complacency as to America's helplessness completely shattered."[46]

Eisenhower also claimed that the Lebanon operation was a demonstration—particularly to the Communists—of "the ability of the United States to react swiftly with conventional armed forces to meet small-scale, or 'brush-fire' situations." But he makes the point—curious in light of the difficulty he had in identifying the *source* of the "indirect aggression" in Lebanon—that he was now more than ever convinced that "if 'small wars' were to break out in several places in the world simultaneously, then we would not fight on the enemy terms and be limited to his choice of weapons. We would hold the Kremlin—or Peking—responsible for their actions and would act accordingly." [47]

However, beneath the surface self-congratulation- and reassertion of old strategic doctrine, the Middle East crises of 1957–58 exhibited to those at the helm of United States policy the inadequacy of the predominantly military approach to problems of subversion and "indirect aggression." President Eisenhower's address to the UN General Assembly on August 13, 1958, indicated that "We are living in a time when the whole world has become alive to the possibilities for modernizing their societies." The United States looked with favor upon this trend since "only on the basis of progressing economies can truly independent governments sustain themselves." The President proposed an Arab regional development plan, analogous to the Marshall Plan, to be formulated and managed by the Arab nations themselves, but to be financially and technically supported by the advanced nations. He was ready to pledge United States support now, contingent upon the Arab nations' ability to come up with a plan and willingness to devote their own resources to its implementation. But such an effort would not succeed, warned the President, unless there was simultaneously an elimination from within the area of the chronic fear of violence and of outside interference in the Arabs' internal affairs. To this end, the United States would support the creation of a United Nations peacekeeping force, so that nations of the area "will no longer feel the need to seek national security through spiralling military buildups. These lead not only to economic impotence but to war." [48]

Rather than focusing on a possible Soviet ground invasion of the Middle East, the new orientation was aimed toward productively exploiting the nationalist ambitions of the Arab world. Economic assistance would no longer be conditioned on membership in the anti-Communist alliance system. Neutrality, and even overt anti-

Western postures, would be viewed realistically in their own political contexts—as the necessary credentials for Third World political elites who would lead, rather than be swept away by, the mass demands, frustrations, and explosive anger that accompany the removal of colonial overlordship and the enfranchisement of the newly independent population.

Logically, the recognition of the failure of past policies to harness the emotional steam of Third World nationalism, and the search for new tools, particularly economic ones, for channeling this energy toward tasks of internal development rather than external adventures, should have produced a revolution in United States policies toward Asia, Africa, and Latin America. However, U.S. policies in each of these areas had yet to undergo a crisis of impotence before the Eisenhower rhetoric of August 1958 would become the operational premise of action programs on a global basis.

THE LATIN AMERICAN "PROBLEM"

When the administration faced the prospect of a Communist takeover of Guatemala in 1954 by *political* means, Dulles' diplomatic strategy had been to get the Latin Americans to make an exception to mutual pledges of nonintervention in the case of Communist regimes. The result of his efforts was the "Declaration of Solidarity for the Preservation of the Political Integrity of the American States Against International Communist Intervention," adopted at the Tenth Inter-American Conference in Caracas, Venezuela, in March 1954. (Guatemala voted against; Mexico and Argentina abstained.) The Caracas declaration condemned "the activities of the international communist movement as constituting intervention in American affairs," and declared

that the domination or control of the political institutions of any American State by the international communist movement, extending to this Hemisphere the political system of extra-continental power, would constitute a threat to the sovereignty and political independence of the American States, endangering the peace of America.[49]

Dulles wanted an expansion of the concept of "intervention" to cover political subversion, and this much he got. But he also wanted specific commitments for collective action against the Guzman Jacobo Arbenz regime in Guatemala. In this the Latin treaty partners would not go along. They were not ready to define the situation in Guatemala as one in which the "international communist movement" had taken over a country. Nor were they willing to commit themselves to direct counterintervention when and if such a contingency materialized.

Unable to make use of the hemispheric collective security system to topple the Arbenz regime, the Eisenhower administration took unilateral action—rather unconvincingly cloaked as aid to Honduras and Nicaragua under the bilateral mutual defense assistance pacts just negotiated.[50] The June 1594 invasion of Guatemala from Honduras by Castillo Armas with an army of one thousand men obviously encouraged and assisted by the United States government[51] was so successful, from a tactical point of view, that no fundamental reassessments in the White House of its approach to the growing militancy of the democratic left in Latin America seemed necessary. The United States apparently had adequate power at its disposal to handle Communist insurgency or subversion in the hemisphere, as long as the Dulles example in the Guatemalan affair was followed, unsqueamishly.

This being the perception at the highest levels in the administration of the dimensions of the Latin American "problem," only pro forma attention was given to the appeals of others with ties to the President (such as Milton Eisenhower, Douglas Dillon, and Nelson Rockefeller) that we pay greater attention to the socioeconomic conditions creating a fertile field for Communist cultivation.

The shocked recognition that there was need of a deep reappraisal of U.S. foreign policy toward Latin America came with Castro's overthrow of the Batista regime on January 1, 1959, and the rapid transformation of revolutionary Fidelismo into a harsh totalitarianism as known Communists were given increased responsibility in the Cuban government. Before the year was out, the United States had subscribed $450 million to the new Inter-American Development Bank, and Washington had begun a sweeping policy review.[52]

By early 1960, recalled Eisenhower, the outcome of this policy review was still questionable, but there was "one thing we did know: Fidel Castro was a hero to the masses in many Latin American nations. They saw him as a champion of the downtrodden and the enemy of the privileged who, in most of their countries, controlled both wealth and governments." To counter the Castro *carisma* and the appeal of his expropriation of foreign interests, land reform, and redistribution of wealth, the United States would have to demonstrate its concern for hemispheric development and reform in a more dramatic and convincing manner than heretofore. The personality and prestige of the President would have to be closely identified with these efforts. "I decided by early 1960," writes Eisenhower with cryptic understatement, "that the time had arrived for a presidential journey to South America." [53]

His consultations during his trip made him an ally of those within his administration, led by Douglas Dillon and Milton Eisenhower, who saw the dangers in a failure by the United States to identify itself with the forces of social reform. The premises of this group now came to the fore, and provided United States policy with the first manifestation of the orientation that was to receive fuller elaboration and commitment in Kennedy's Alliance for Progress. At Newport, on July 11, 1960, Eisenhower revealed this new orientation: *change* is the law of life, he said. "Latin America is passing through a social and political transformation. Dictatorships are falling by the wayside. Moderate groups, seeking orderly reform, are contesting with dictators of both right and left who favor violence and authoritarianism." The choice had narrowed. It was now "social evolution or revolution." The President listed those matters requiring the urgent attention of "every American nation": land reform, housing, and a wider share of the national product for the poor majority of the population; the strengthening of institutions for mobilizing resources and promoting economic growth; and greater respect for human rights and the will of the people as expressed in democratic elections. "The United States will not, cannot stand aloof." [54]

These ideas were given expression in a new program drafted by Under Secretary of State Dillon and presented to the special meeting of the economic ministers of the Organization of American States at Bogotá, September 5–13, 1960. Dillon conveyed the offer of the President, backed by congressional authorization, of an immediate loan of $500 million for the purpose of inaugurating "a broad new social development program for Latin America." The Inter-American Development Bank would administer the allocation of subscribed funds and evaluate projects in conformity with agreed criteria. As progress was made through joint and cooperative efforts, the United States would maintain its support with additional funds. [55]

The Act of Bogotá, adopted by the conference on September 13, 1960, incorporated the essential ideas of the Dillon proposal as they appeared in the detailed United States draft. As characterized by President Eisenhower:

"Non-intervention" had given way to a new idea—the idea that *all* American nations had an interest in ending feudalism, the vast hereditary gulf between rich and poor, the system that assured to a handful of families opulence without labor and condemned millions to near starvation without opportunity.[56]

In six short months the White House had moved a long way from its charge that such insidious ideas were "fomented by Communists," and from its insistence that social reform was "purely an internal matter."

Meanwhile the administration's policy toward Cuba, in reaction to Fidel Castro's increasing intransigence, was becoming steadily more rigid. Repeated attempts by the United States to engage his regime in diplomatic discussions concerning such matters as compensation for expropriated United States companies, met with repeated rebuffs and harangues. It was not until about fifteen months after his takeover in January 1959, however, that the United States changed its approach from one of trying to reestablish normal relations to one whose goal was the destruction of the Castro regime. On March 17, 1960, President Eisenhower agreed to a CIA program for the training of Cuban exiles in Guatemala for a possible insurgency operation.[57] In July, the new policy was exhibited in the reduction and subsequent suspension by the United States of the importation of Cuban sugar. And just two weeks before relinquishing the presidency to John F. Kennedy, President Eisenhower broke off diplomatic relations with Cuba in retaliation for Castro's demands that the United States Embassy in Havana drastically reduce its staff. Even serious critics of the Eisenhower administration concede that the deterioration of relations after the Castro takeover was not by United States design, but in reaction to Castro's increasing pugnaciousness, concomitant with the solidification of his ties to the Soviet Union. Most would agree with Arthur Schlesinger that "the policy of the Eisenhower administration lacked both imagination and consistency, but it was certainly not one of purposeful hostility."[58]

The White House apparently believed its own words about the necessity of opposing dictators of the right as well as the left in Latin

America. On August 20, 1960, the United States took a leading role at the San José, Costa Rica, meeting of OAS foreign ministers in passing a resolution condemning the Trujillo government's actions against Venezuela, and calling for a total blockade on the shipment of arms to Trujillo and a partial economic blockade. The United States promptly cut most of the Dominican Republic's sugar quota and broke diplomatic relations with Trujillo.

When the Eisenhower administration left office, Latin America, the area in which the appreciation of revolutionary nationalism as a significant factor in the global power balance was most delayed, had become the field for the greatest experimentation with new tools and a new ideological stance for influencing global alignments.

THE BERLIN CRISIS OF 1958–1959

Throughout the spring and summer of 1958, while the United States was embroiled in the Lebanon crisis in the Middle East and a brief renewal of the offshore island confrontation with Communist China, the Soviets were gradually beginning to tighten the screws in Europe—combining administrative harassments of Western traffic to the city of Berlin with calls for a new summit conference to reduce tension.[59] The Warsaw Pact countries also renewed their campaign for a military disengagement from Central Europe.

American reactions were initially no more than a stale rehearsal of old positions: the U.S. would maintain its rights of access to Berlin; it would not be forced into a summit conference. If the Soviets were serious about reducing tension in Europe, they should be willing to undertake serious negotiations to reduce the sources of such tension—the most outstanding being the unnatural division of Germany. A summit conference would be useless unless substantial progress were made toward a resolution of the German problem at the working diplomatic level. A basis for serious negotiations over the German question had been provided by the Geneva heads of government communiqué of July 1955—namely, reunification on the basis of free elections. But the Soviets had thus far not shown any willingness to negotiate on those terms.

It seems that the Soviets were anxious to test the degree of new diplomatic leverage they had gained as a result of their space success and missile claims. Khrushchev announced on November 10, 1958, that the Soviet Union was committed to put an end to the Western occupation of Berlin and was ready to renounce its Potsdam Agreement obligation unilaterally if the West was unwilling to negotiate an end to the occupation status of Germany and Berlin. Then on November 27, the Soviet Union, in formal notes to the United States, Great Britain, and France, put a time limit of six months for the West to accept its proposals for a termination of the military occupation of Berlin and the "conversion of West Berlin into an independent political unit—a free city . . . demilitarized . . . that . . . could have its own government and run its own economic, administrative, and other affairs." The status of the "free city" of West Berlin, according to the Soviet note, should be guaranteed by the four powers, and possibly by the United Nations. But this free city would lie within the German Democratic Republic. Thus, in order to guarantee unhindered communications between the free city and the outside world, negotiations would have to be undertaken by the four powers with the GDR. The six-month deadline to effect such negotiations read like an ultimatum:

The Soviet Government proposes to make no change in the present procedure for the military traffic of the USA, Great Britain, and France from West Berlin to the FRG for half a year. It regards such a period as fully sufficient to provide a sound basis for the solution of . . . Berlin's situation. . . .

If the above-mentioned period is not utilized to reach an agreement, the Soviet Union will then carry out the planned measures through an agreement with the GDR. It is envisaged that the German Democratic Republic, like any other independent state, must fully . . . exercise its sovereignty on land, water, and in the air. At the same time there will terminate all contracts still maintained between . . . the Soviet Union in Germany and . . . the USA, Great Britain, and France in questions pertaining to Berlin.[60]

The State Department's response to the Soviet proposals was, of course, negative. But this meant the United States had to face the likelihood that the Soviets, in six months, would carry out their threat to abrogate, unilaterally, their Berlin obligations; and this would mean, in turn, that the West would have to deal directly with the East German authorities on all questions of access to Berlin. By such a maneuver, the Soviets apparently hoped to force the West to "recognize" the authority of the GDR, thereby legitimizing the division of Germany and presumably demoralizing the Federal Republic. Dulles attempted to provide some basis for sidestepping a confrontation by hinting in his November 26 press conference that the U.S. might have to deal with the GDR official as "agents" of the Soviet Union.[61]

If a confrontation *were* to arise on this issue, if after the expiration of the six-month deadline the East German authorities were to attempt to control the access routes to Berlin and not let Western traffic through until their authority was recognized, what would be the response? Would the U.S. use force?

Until now, whenever the West had threatened a physical challenge to Soviet administrative harassments on the access routes, the Soviets were able to cease the application of the particular procedure at issue without losing face. The Soviets would usually cover their retreat in advance by claiming that the procedures were made necessary by road repairs or some other temporary technicality.

But in the context of the Soviet ultimatum, a confrontation might be forced on both sides by political considerations. The very real possibility that this time the East German officials, backed by the Soviets, would not retreat under U.S. threats to resort to physical means compelled the administration to reassess the balance of locally applicable force.

Assessing the local military situation, Eisenhower observed that it was "so lopsided as to be ridiculous." He was convinced that if the conflict entered a phase of actual military engagement, "our troops in Berlin would be quickly overrun, and the conflict would almost inevitably be global war." In a White House meeting, critics, particularly leaders of the Democratic Party in Congress, tried to paint this situation as a deficiency of New Look defense policies. But the President was no less adamant in insisting that an attempt to balance Soviet ground troops in Europe was a senseless policy:

"The Soviets are engaged in confronting the United States with a series of crises," I said. "The United States has a need for an efficient military system. But it has to be realized that if we program for the sum total of all recommendations for increasing military strength, the mounting burden would call for full mobilization," putting the nation on a wartime footing. I said that we could not have ground forces to match those that the Soviets could mobilize in Middle Europe.

. . .

I went on to say that we had no intention of opposing, with ground troops only, a full-out attack by a couple of hundred Soviet divisions, but that we would take care of the situation.

He was talking of a third world war, and "for this type of war our nuclear forces were more than adequate." To Speaker Rayburn and Lyndon Johnson (then Senate majority leader) the President reiterated his confidence in United States strategic superiority: "In fact, I said, 'if we were to release our nuclear stockpile on the Soviet Union, the main danger would arise not from retaliation but from fallout in the earth's atmosphere.' "[62]

It was obviously necessary to put a confident face on this assessment of the balance of usable force; for, if the United States had no capabilities or intention of fighting a limited engagement for control of Berlin, the Soviets would win the diplomatic confrontation unless Washington could appear less fearful than they of a general nuclear war. "Possibly, we were risking the very fate of civilization on the premise that the Soviets would back down from the deadline when confronted by force," reflects Eisenhower. "Yet this to my mind was not really gambling, for if we were not willing to take this risk we would be certain to lose."[63]

Eisenhower was very careful to provide himself with alternative courses of action—in the case of a Soviet refusal to back down. The basic contingency plan which the President approved in late January 1959, included these steps:

(a) A refusal to acquiesce in any substitution of East Germans for Soviet officials in checking the Western occupying powers movement to and from Berlin. . . ; (b) A decision to begin quiet military preparations in West Germany and Berlin prior to May 27, sufficient to be detected by Soviet intelligence but not sufficient to create public alarm; (c) Should there be any substitution of East German officials for Soviets, a small convoy with armed protection would attempt to go through, and if this convoy were stopped, the effort would be discontinued and the probe would fire only if fired upon; (d) transit would then be suspended and pressure would be brought to bear on the Soviets by publicizing the blockade and taking the matter to the United Nations Security Council and, if necessary, to the General Assembly. In these circumstances our further military preparations would be intensified by observable means such as the evacuation of dependents from West Berlin and possibly from all Germany; (e) In the event that this moral and other pressure was not sufficient, use of additional force would be subject to governmental decision.[64]

Meanwhile the West would agree, assuming the Soviets would drop their ultimatum, to engage in high-level discussions, but at the foreign ministers' level, not the summit. These discussions, according to the administration, were to provide the Soviets with the opportunity to back away from their November 1958 demands without losing face. The White House and State Department denied any intention to compromise Western rights in Berlin or to review their refusal to accord the Ulbricht regime any formal or symbolic recognition. Yet they did agree to the attendance of the GDR and the FRG at the forthcoming conference, though not as full participants.

Between January and May 11, 1959, the date of the convening in Geneva of the foreign ministers' meeting, the Soviets gave many indications of backing away from their rigid six-month deadline. This made it easier for the West to agree to participate in the foreign ministers' meeting, as it diluted the image of the United States being dragged to the conference table under the grip of an ultimatum.

At the May meeting most of the significant compromises were made by the Western nations. The draft agreement handed by the Western foreign ministers to Gromyko on June 16 provided that (1) the United States, Britain, and France would limit the combined total of their forces in Berlin to 11,000 "and to continue to arm these forces only with conventional weapons;" (2) the "procedures" for controlling access to West Berlin, "without prejudice to existing basic responsibilities . . . may . . . be carried out by [East] German personnel" (it was stated that the access should be "free and unrestricted" and that "basic" responsibilities should remain in the hands of the four powers; but the legitimizing of operational control by the GDR was a major concession by the West); (3) measures should be taken "to avoid in both parts of Berlin activities which might either disturb public order or seriously affect the rights and interests, or amount to interference in the internal affairs, of others." (This curb on propaganda and intelligence activities cut hardest against Western operations and gave in to one of the persistent Soviet complaints against the West Berliners.)[65]

Paradoxically, the administration was saved the embarrassment of a Soviet acceptance of the Western proposals by Khrushchev's assumption that he could press his advantage to get even more. The Soviet leader had let the six-month "deadline" pass without turning over major Soviet responsibilities to the East Germans, explaining to Ulbricht that "conditions are not ripe as yet for a new scheme of things." Finding the West surprisingly malleable, at the June sessions in Geneva the Soviets extended their deadline for a year, but meanwhile intensified their intransigence at the conference to see if there was even more give in the Western position. This reduced the immediate risks to the Soviets of pressing the West too far too soon, while allowing for the possibility of greater rewards later.

Khrushchev must have been encouraged in the assumption that the West believed it was negotiating from a position of weakness when, before the close of the foreign ministers conference, he received a formal invitation from President Eisenhower to visit the United States.

Eisenhower had been consistently trying to deflect the growing popular clamor for a summit (considerably amplified by Prime Minister Macmillan's entreaties) with which the Soviets had identified themselves. As the prospect increased of a collapse of negotiations at the foreign ministers' meeting, Eisenhower reminded Macmillan of their agreement that substantive accomplishments at the foreign ministers' level would have to precede a summit conference. The President confided to his British colleague his fear that "if I surrendered on this point I would no longer have any influence with Khrushchev, who would, thereafter, consider me a 'pushover.' Indeed . . . I would myself interpret such an agreement as an exhibition of weakness."[66]

As Khrushchev pushed his campaign for a summit, Eisenhower thought he found "a device to break the stalemate" in an invitation for the Soviet leader to visit the United States on an "informal basis." This would be no "summit," there would be no "negotiations"; but an opportunity might arise for an informal conversation on matters of mutual concern.[67]

This "informal conversation," held at Camp David, Maryland, on September 25 and 26, 1959, produced an agreement by Chairman Khrushchev to withdraw his time limit for a Berlin settlement in return for Eisenhower's agreement to a Big Four summit conference in 1960 during which the Berlin issue could be discussed. To purists in the delicate area of German-issue diplomacy, this was an American blunder. Clumsier yet was Eisenhower's press conference remark on September 28 that the Berlin "situation is abnormal."[68] The standard Western formulation was supposed to be that the *division of Germany* was abnormal.

The total breakdown of the 1960 summit, ostensibly over the U-2 reconnaissance issue (Khrushchev walked out in anger over Eisenhower's refusal to apologize for the violation of Soviet airspace in which a U.S. plane was shot down.), and the diplomatic hiatus produced by the impending change in United States leadership, saved the Eisenhower administration from further negotiations on the Berlin issue. Significantly, the Democrats, watching from the wings, resolved they would not let themselves be caught in a similar diplomatic confrontation without some redressing of the balance of local military capabilities in Europe.

PART IV

THE KENNEDY–JOHNSON YEARS

Too long we have fixed our eyes on traditional military needs, on armies prepared to cross borders, on missiles poised for flight. Now it should be clear that this is no longer enough—that our security may be lost piece by piece, country by country, without the firing of a single missile or the crossing of a single border.

—JOHN F. KENNEDY

We still tend to conceive of national security almost entirely as a state of armed readiness: a vast, awesome arsenal of weaponry.

We still tend to assume that it is primarily this purely military ingredient that creates security.

We are still haunted by this concept of military hardware.

—ROBERT S. MCNAMARA

8

ENHANCING THE ARSENAL
OF POWER

Power is not a matter of arms alone. Strength comes from education, fertile acres, humming workshops and the satisfaction and pride of peoples.

—DEAN RUSK

The state of the union leaves a lot to be desired, the new President informed the nation on January 30, 1961. "Our problems are critical. The tide is unfavorable. The news will be worse before it is better." With the help of more than twenty-five specialized task forces, assembled during and after the election campaign, he had been taking a close inventory of "our whole arsenal of tools," and had discovered serious gaps—gaps which if not corrected would leave the nation with a deficiency of power for meeting the coming challenges to its very survival. And certainly without attention to the neglected components of our national power, we could not hope to advance beyond these immediate security needs and apply our resources to reducing the misery of others.

The Kennedy foreign policy was centered on the premise that the competition between the Soviet Union and the United States was shifting to a new arena—the competition for influence over the direction of development in the poorer half of the globe; and it was with respect to this competition that we were in greatest danger of falling behind.

Kennedy's view that the Third World had now become the decisive field of engagement was shared by most of the Stevensonians, by Senate foreign policy leaders such as J. William Fulbright and Mike Mansfield, and by ever-renewable Averell Harriman. But the Europe-first emphasis remained strong among Truman State Department alumni, led by Acheson—still the idol of many seasoned top-level career diplomats in the State Department who had survived the Eisenhower–Dulles doldrums. The burden of proof would fall on those arguing for programs allocating a larger proportion of our human and material resource to "containment" in the underdeveloped world. Two weeks before the inauguration, the supporters of the new orientation received their most effective ammunition from an unexpected source.

Premier Khrushchev, in his historic foreign policy speech of January 6, 1961, displayed the Soviet grand-strategy rationale for focusing Soviet efforts on the underdeveloped areas: due to developments in the technology of warfare, "world wars" and "local wars" had become obsolete and, since they would lead to a nuclear holocaust destroying the workers as well as the capitalists, "unjust." The "just wars" of the contemporary period, the inevitable and necessary wars according to the Marxist-Leninist appraisal of the relation between social and material forces, were "wars of national liberation." The phrase was a catchall for anticolonial agitation, popular uprisings against established indigenous regimes, and actual guerrilla wars. Examples were the campaign of the FLN in Algeria for independence from France, the Castro takeover in Cuba, general efforts to mobilize the leftist forces in Latin America, and the insurgency in South Vietnam. "The Communists support just wars of this kind wholeheartedly and without reservations," said the Soviet leader.[1]

Here, in Kennedy's view, was an eminently realistic appraisal by the Soviets themselves of where their best opportunities for expansion lay. It conformed to the strategy shift attributed to the Soviets particularly by Walt Rostow—one of the first in Kennedy's circle of foreign policy advisers to make a serious pitch for a major United States counterinsurgency program. Arthur Schlesinger reports that Khrushchev's January 6 speech "made a conspicuous impression on the new President, who took it as an authoritative exposition of Soviet intentions, discussed it with his staff and read excerpts from it aloud to the National Security Council."[2]

The President was familiar with Mao Zedong's aphorism that power grows out of the barrel of a gun. But he knew there was more to guerrilla warfare than forming new commando-type units. He appreciated and liked to quote Mao's equally important aphorism: "Guerrillas are like fish, and the people are the water in which the fish swim. If the temperature of the water is right, the fish will thrive and multiply."[3] It was critically important to tend the temperature of the water—and as far in advance as possible.

The preventative aspects of counterinsurgency provided the link between those in Kennedy's advisory entourage who saw the balance of power primarily in terms of the distribution of coercive capabilities and those who emphasized the more benign components of international influence. When it was put in this frame of reference, Paul Nitze, Generals Maxwell Taylor and James Gavin, Walt Rostow, Roger Hilsman, Chester Bowles, Averell Harriman, John Kenneth Galbraith, and Adlai Stevenson could all agree on the necessity for a much larger program of long-term development aid to the many potential targets for Communist insurgency in Asia, the Middle East, Africa, and Latin America.

Having agreed that the purpose of foreign assistance was to affect the "temperature of the water" in the recipient countries—to assure economic, social, and political conditions inhospitable to the growth of Communist movements—the next step was to assure application of foreign aid criteria designed by those with credentials in this type of oceanography. The dominant standard that had prevailed during the Eisenhower period, the degree of overt acquiescence on the part of regimes in power to the anti-Communist orientation of United States diplomacy, was now seen to be hopelessly inadequate. Kennedy accepted the need for a much more "technical"—and complicated—analysis for determining the utility of the kinds and amounts of assistance to go to any particular country. As senator and President-elect he sought the counsel of professionals, and they were not to be found within the government. He found them, mainly New Deal–Fair Deal exiles (and professional economist all), encamped along the banks of the Charles River: Galbraith, Carl Kaysen, Edward S. Mason, David Bell, and Lincoln Gordon at Harvard; Rostow, Max Millikan, and P. N. Rosenstein-Rodan at the M.I.T. Center for International Studies.[4] Here, during the 1950s, were developed the propositions on economic assistance that would become official government policy in the 1960s: namely, that operational criteria for evaluating the worth of any particular foreign aid program must be stated in terms of socioeconomic modernization and that the explicit objective of measures sponsored by the United States should be self-sustaining economic growth for each recipient nation. It should be noted that the new President considered the lack of such a concept and objective for determining the flow of foreign assistance to the poorer nations as probably the most critical deficiency in the arsenal of tools by which he hoped to influence the international environment.

Kennedy's economist friends were contending that modernization and the development of greater constitutional democracy and social justice could go hand in hand; that, indeed, economic development required national planning and reliable administration, and these required the kind of political stability that was best sustained in a constitutional system providing for responsible government with the consent of the governed. But Kennedy was also sensitive to the potential gap between the rational political-economics of his advisers and their Western-trained counterparts in the developing countries and the combustible character of the "revolution of rising expectations," particularly when exploited by demagogues. He understood that part of the weakness of the United States in trying to influence the poorer nations from succumbing to totalitarian models for modernization was the lack of passion in the U.S. commitment to egalitarian aspects of social justice. The U.S. had only halfheartedly supported the kind of land reforms and tax reforms that would bring about the structural economic changes necessary for modernization. The excuse, under previous administrations, had been that an open advocacy of such reform measures would constitute an interference in the domestic affairs of those smaller nations—that it was up to those nations, in their own way, however gradually, to take such social reform upon themselves without outside pressure. The effect of this self-denying ordinance, however, had been to identify the United States with the status quo in these countries, and to confirm the suspicions of social revolutionary elements that the State Department was in cahoots with U.S. private interests which profited from privileges extended by entrenched local oligarchies. It was from this concern that the Alliance for Progress evolved. As the President put it on the first anniversary of its launching:

For too long my country, the wealthiest nation on a poor continent, failed to carry out its full responsibilities to its sister Republics. We have now accepted that responsibility. In the same way those who possess wealth and power in poor nations must accept their own responsibilities. They must lead the fight for basic reforms which alone can preserve the fabric of their own societies. Those who make peaceful revolution impossible will make violent revolution inevitable.

These social reforms are at the heart of the Alliance for Progress. They are the precondition to economic modernization. And they are the instrument by which we assure to the poor and hungry, to the worker and the *campesino,* his full participation in the benefits of our development and in the human dignity which is the purpose of free societies.[5]

These are strong words. And strong words might arouse expectations of United States action in support of social reform that outran the *ability* of the U.S. to influence "those who possess wealth and power in poor nations." But, in Kennedy's view of where the stakes in the global struggle for power then lay, he had little choice but to reidentify the United States with the rising demands of the poor and the disenfranchised.

In order to respond to this challenge, the people of the United States would have to feel confident enough of their own productivity to allow a diversion of effort to the needs of others. However, reported Kennedy in his first presidential address to Congress:

We take office in the wake of . . . three and one-half years of slack, seven years of diminished economic growth, and nine years of falling farm income.

. . .

Our recovery from the 1958 recession . . . was anemic and incomplete. Our Gross National Product never again regained its full potential. Unemployment never returned to normal levels. Maximum use of our national industrial capacity was never restored.

In short, the American economy is in trouble. The most resourceful industrialized country on earth ranks among the last in the rate of economic growth.[6]

This lagging state of the U.S. economy reduced both the capacity and will to provide direct help to the poorer nations. Economic stagnation also damaged another very important aspect of U.S. influence: the reputation for successful management of a largely free economy for the well-being of all its people. "We must show the world what a free economy can do,"[7] admonished Kennedy, in recommending a set of economic measures to take up the slack.

Moreover, the United States found itself in a vulnerable diplomatic position with respect to other industrialized nations because of its adverse balance of international payments, which Kennedy felt was partly the result of the sluggishness of the U.S. economy in comparison to the dynamically expanding economies of Western Europe. "Our success in world affairs has long depended in part upon foreign confidence in our ability to pay," he said.[8] And to intimates he confided his anxiety that the payments deficit was "a club that de Gaulle and all the others hang over my head. Any time there's a crisis or a quarrel, they can cash in all their dollars and where are we?"[9]

For Kennedy, programs to "get the country moving again"—his antirecession measures of 1961, the Trade Expansion Act of 1962, and the tax cut of 1963—were as much required by global balance of power considerations as they were by considerations of domestic economic well-being. The continued productive growth of the United States was a value in itself, to be pursued in the basic national interest. But it was also regarded as a means toward the more vigorous exercise of power internationally. The preceding administration seemed to view the requirements of domestic economic productivity as competitive with, and therefore a constraint upon, overseas commitments (we could not raise additional conventional forces because that might bankrupt us). The New Frontier view was that any gap between overseas commitments and the existing domestic economic base needed to sustain them was only an argument for expansion of the domestic economy, not an argument for reduced defense spending. A contraction in commitments or an unwillingness to provide the widest array of diplomatic and military tools to sustain these commitments would further reduce America's ebbing global leadership and, in the long run, would endanger U.S. security.

Similarly, continued reliance on protectionist policy in order to defend the home market from growing foreign competition would have adverse consequences on America's overall power on the international scene. "Economic isolation and political leadership are wholly incompatible," asserted Kennedy in urging Congress to grant him the broad tariff-reducing authority requested in the administration's trade expansion bill of 1962:

If we are to retain our leadership, the initiative is up to us. The revolutionary changes which are occurring will not wait for us to make up our minds. The United

States has encouraged sweeping changes in free world economic patterns in order to strengthen the forces of freedom. But we cannot ourselves stand still. If we are to lead, we must act. We must adapt our own economy to the imperatives of a changing world, and once more assert our leadership.[10]

Pervading most of President Kennedy's major recommendations to Congress, for domestic as well as specifically foreign programs, was this notion of the power of *movement* itself. The key to leadership on the international scene was a creative exploitation of the currents of change. The surge by the new nations, the social and economic egalitarianism of the newly enfranchised masses across the globe, and the unconquerable assertion that the object of government is to protect and extend the exercise of free choice—this was the very stuff of the new international politics. Leadership in this arena called for a renewal of the American experiment in freedom. United States prestige abroad, its influence upon others—i.e., its power— were seriously weakened by the squalor of its cities, the crime on its streets, the overcrowding and low standards in many schools, the shortages of adequate health facilities and medical professionals, and most of all, by the "denial of constitutional rights to some of our fellow Americans on account of race."[11] Kennedy sought to recapture that pride and nerve to explore uncharted frontiers, without which the nation "would trend in the direction of a slide downhill into dust, dullness, languor, and decay."[12]

As much as to help in the spread of literacy and technical know-how abroad—and to improve the American image abroad—the Peace Corps was directed at improving the quality of life in the United States. The Peace Corps typified Kennedy's integrated and long-term approach to the problem of the nation's power, an approach that demanded from the coming generation of leaders, no less than his own, a willingness to pay a price to secure the blessing of liberty: "A price measured not merely in money and military preparedness, but in social inventiveness, in moral stamina, and physical courage."[13]

President Kennedy's decision, after some hesitation, to stress the competitive nature of the space race with the Soviets, not just the potentials for cooperative scientific exploration, was very much a part of his concern for the national fiber. The potential scientific or military payoffs from being "first" in space seem to have impressed him less than the intangible effects on the national spirit. Many of the welfare liberals who supported him down the line on other planks in his program cried "Moondoggle." His reply, best articulated in his September 1962 address at Rice University, reflected the New Frontier's search for that vein of adventuresomeness which had once been, and could again be, a special source of national strength:

> But why, some say, the moon? . . . And they may well ask, why climb the highest mountain? Why, thirty-five years ago, fly the Atlantic? Why does Rice play Texas? . . .
>
> We choose to go to the moon in this decade, and do the other things, not because they are easy but because they are hard; because that goal will serve to organize and measure the best of our energies and skills. . . .
>
> Many years ago the great British explorer George Mallory, who was to die on Mount Everest, was asked why did he want to climb it, and he said, "Because it is there."
>
> Well, space is there, and . . . the moon and planets are there, and new hopes for knowledge and peace are there.[14]

ATTENDING TO THE MILITARY BALANCE

President Kennedy's emphasis on a variegated arsenal of power did not in any way lead him to the conclusion that, short of a major political settlement with the Communists, the United States could reduce substantially the amount of destructive power at its disposal. In fact, the thrust of his remarks on the nation's military posture, during his years in the Senate and during his presidential campaign, was that U.S. forces were insufficient; if anything, a greater proportion of the national effort and product needed to be devoted to strengthening and maintaining our military tools than had been the case under Eisenhower.

Kennedy's general premises about the nation's military requirements were well developed before he assumed the presidency and reflected the "conventional wisdom" among Democrats involved in foreign policy matters. A number of strains of strategic thought had now converged: the ideas generated by Paul Nitze and the Policy Planning Council in NSC-68, the Truman administration document reflecting on the military planning implications of the soon-to-come Soviet intercontinental nuclear capability (see Chapter 4); Air Force–RAND Corporation arguments for a survivable ("invulnerable") strategic retaliatory force (also favored by the Navy as the major rationale for the Polaris submarine-fired missile); the doctrine of "flexible response" put forward within the Eisenhower administration by Army Chiefs of Staff Matthew Ridgway and Maxwell Taylor in opposition to the strategic monism of Secretary of State Dulles and Admiral Radford;[15] the analysis of the possibilities for limited war in the thermonuclear age by scholars such as William Kaufmann, Robert Osgood, Henry Kissinger, and Bernard Brodie;[16] and the recommendations for a balanced defense posture in the reports of the Gaither Committee and Panel II of the Special Studies Project of the Rockefeller Brothers Fund.*

Most reputable American analysts of military policy at the time of Kennedy's election were in agreement on at least the following premises:

1. The temptation of the Soviets and the Chinese Communists to expand into new areas, and otherwise to impose their wills on the non-Communist nations, correlates inversely with their belief in the likelihood of effective counteraction by the leading non-Communist nations.

2. Effective counteraction would impose costs on the Soviets and Chinese disproportionate to their anticipated gain.

3. The Soviets and Chinese determine the probability of such counteraction on the part of the leading non-Communist nations by attributing to them essentially the same calculus: counteraction will be taken by the non-Communists to the extent that the cost of such action would be less than the cost of acquiescence in the Communist moves.

4. Deterrence being the product of these mutual assessments of one another's anticipated costs and gains, an effective strategy and military posture for the United States comprises an ability to respond to each provocation with a degree of violence bearing some reasonable relationship to the value thought to be immediately at stake.

5. The willingness to incur the amount of destruction to the nation that would accompany total war is not a very believable deterrent threat unless it is posed as a counter to the threat of major direct aggression against U.S. home territory.

6. To deter provocations short of direct aggression, the United States must therefore be prepared to respond effectively at levels of violence well below total war; and/or to judge the costs of submitting to such provocations as being as intolerable as the costs of total war. The latter might work for some extraterritorial interests—for example, keeping Western Europe from

---

* See Chapter 7 for recommendations of the Gaither Report. The Rockefeller Panel report, "International Security: The Military Aspect," was first published in January 1958, and then republished as a part of *Prospect for America: The Rockefeller Panel Reports* (New York: Doubleday, 1961).

falling to the Communists; but the Communists were unlikely to believe that every inch of territory in the non-Communist world had a comparable value. Conflicts over territorial objectives which during the cold war had developed a high emotional content for each side might be seen as involving essential psychological components of the overall balance of power. Berlin was one of these conflicts, and with less clarity so were the Chinese offshore islands. But even with respect to these values, the degree of the nation's psychological commitment could fluctuate and they might have to be surrendered to the Communists if the U.S. lacked effective capabilities for at least initial counteraction at lower levels of violence.

7. Lacking capabilities across the entire spectrum of warfare available for measured application relating to the value at stake and the initial intensity of a provocation, firm diplomatic commitments might ultimately have to be restricted to that class of extraterritorial objectives clearly required by the global balance of power. The opportunities for enemy probes beneath the threshold of clearly defined U.S. vital interests would grow accordingly. The non-Communist world would feel increasingly insecure as a result of the uncertainty of U.S. commitment to their defense. The non-Communist world, including the United States, would become increasingly demoralized because of the recognition of the fickleness of these guarantees. The balance of power itself—composed in large measure of the *reputation* for power among the leading nations—would be seen to be shifting drastically against the United States. Such a situation would be ready-made for the kinds of miscalculation and irrationality that would bring on the dreaded thermonuclear holocaust.

A few concrete policy implications were drawn from these general strategic premises. U.S. capabilities for limited war were to be expanded considerably. U.S. strategic nuclear capability was to be seen primarily, if not exclusively, as a last resort, as an instrument of retaliation for a direct attack upon the United States.

But any number of questions remained unanswered: Would the downgrading of the function of the strategic nuclear forces for deterrence of limited conflicts mean that there would be no contingencies in which the United States might be the first to use these weapons? If the strategic forces were to be primarily retaliatory weapons, what should be their targets? Under such concepts, what should be done in advance to deal with the possibility of strategic attack despite American capabilities for retaliation? Did the U.S. want to limit "limited war" to nonnuclear weapons? If so, how would such limitations be enforced? Did the concept of limiting war mean also localizing it? How would the European allies respond to strategies that seemed to reduce the possible costs to the superpowers of a future war over Europe *in* Europe? The President's early statements on his defense policies skirted many of these complicated issues.

President Kennedy's March 26, 1961, special message to Congress on the defense budget contained several explicit, and definitely stressed, pledges "not to strike first in any conflict." These statements were coupled with recommendations for improving the ability of our strategic nuclear forces to survive any attack and strike back with devastating retaliation. The President came closer in this message than did any official spokesman before or afterward to enunciating a doctrine of no first use of strategic nuclear weapons, but he stopped just short of an absolute unilateral inhibition. In light of subsequent statements by him and other members of his administration, the presumption is that this was deliberate. Kennedy undoubtedly understood the disadvantage to the West of pledging not to use its strategic nuclear forces unless the opponent did so first. If the opponent was the Soviet Union, and the battlefield was Central Europe, or, say, Iran, the Soviets would then be accorded military superiority, since the applicable forces would only be the local theater forces in which the United States, by its own admission, was inferior. The view that Kennedy was deliberately ambiguous on the matter of whether the United States would ever launch a preemptive strategic nuclear strike on the Soviets is sustained by his insistence in the same early message that

our strategic arms and defense must be adequate to deter any deliberate nuclear attack on the United States *or our allies*—by making it clear to any potential aggressor that sufficient retaliatory forces will be able to survive a first strike and penetrate his defenses in order to inflict unacceptable losses upon him.[17] (Emphasis added.)

How the United States might respond to a *non*-nuclear attack on friends or allies was left similarly vague. Clearly, the President was recommending a major increase in airlift and sealift capacities, and in Army and Marine Corps personnel, in order to "increase our ability to confine our response to non-nuclear weapons." The ability to fight "limited wars" should be the "primary mission" of U.S. overseas forces, he told the Congress. But a potential opponent must know that "in the event of a major aggression that could not be repulsed by conventional forces," the United States would continue to be prepared "to take whatever action with whatever weapons are appropriate" and that action would be "suitable, selective, swift, and effective."

Not unexpectedly, the emphasis on limited war was not received with enthusiasm by some other members of the North Atlantic Treaty Organization. Since the mid-1950s NATO military doctrine, planning, and programs had been based on the premise that any war in response to Soviet aggression upon Western Europe would be general nuclear war; there would be no serious attempt to repulse a major aggression by conventional means. To be sure, under the leadership of the NATO Supreme Commander, General Lauris Norstad, the automatic nuclear "trip wire" concept had been abandoned as too dangerous, and in its place was put the concept of the "pause"—an initial response to an enemy probe with nonnuclear weapons to demonstrate a determination to resist, and to provide the enemy with time to decide that it had miscalculated; but this new doctrine of a flexible and measured response, coupled with budgetary recommendations for increasing nonnuclear capabilities, immediately aroused suspicions in Europe that in the face of the Soviet intercontinental strategic reach the Americans would regard even a war over Europe as a local war to be fought and won (or lost) in Europe without the United States being subject to devastation.[18] To the Europeans, quite naturally, a war for Europe was total war and they wanted the Soviets to know, in advance, that an attack upon Europe would be just as certainly an act of suicide as an attack upon the United States.

The Kennedy administration sought for ways of reassuring its NATO allies that nuclear weapons would continue to be available for the defense of the entire treaty area. The administration's main fear was that Germany would attempt to follow the lead of Britain and France and develop its own nuclear capability—one too weak to serve as a convincing deterrent to the Soviets while nonetheless making virtually certain that no war over German soil would remain a limited war. Kennedy appreciated the concerns of his alliance partners, and regarded their leaders as patriotic men conscientiously pursuing their national interests. But his responsibility was to pursue United States national interests, and that seemed to require that the United States maintain control over the dimensions of conflict in the NATO area.

The campaign to reassure the European members of NATO was waged on two fronts: doctrinal elaborations of "flexible response" by

McNamara and his subordinates to show that with its adoption by NATO, deterrence of Soviet provocations in Europe would be increased; and offers by the White House to "share" ownership and control of a part of the U.S. strategic arsenal.

The Berlin crisis of the spring and summer of 1961 (see Chapter 11) provided the opportunity for the administration to demonstrate that a buildup of nonnuclear capabilities did not lessen Soviet fears of a general war, but, on the contrary, reinforced expectations on all sides that the United States would resist a Soviet attack with whatever force was necessary to do the job.

To deflect the growing suspicion that the United States was moving toward a "denuclearization" of Europe, the President, in his May 17, 1961, address before the Canadian Parliament, announced that the United States was now committing five Polaris nuclear missile submarines to the NATO Command "subject to any agreed NATO guidelines on their control and use." But anticipating that this would be insufficient—the submarines would still be under the operational command of the United States Navy and direct political control of the President—Kennedy took advantage of his Ottawa address to explicitly hold out "the possibility of eventually establishing a NATO sea-borne force, which would be truly multi-lateral in ownership and control, if this should be desired and found feasible by our Allies, *once NATO's non-nuclear goals have been achieved.*" (Emphasis added.) [19]

The purpose may have been reassurance, but imbedded as it was in the precondition of European increases in conventional fighting capabilities, the proposal for a multilateral force (MLF), from its first mention, merely served to reinforce European anxieties. This early statement probably was one of the most forthright on the issue of nuclear sharing by the administration, representing its real position that flexible intra-alliance arrangements for the management of strategic nuclear weapons were possible as long as there was close agreement on strategy and tactics—presupposing that such close agreement would be in terms of the Kennedy–McNamara doctrine, which would shift the burden of coercion in the most likely contingencies to locally applicable nonnuclear capabilities. The European members of NATO found such an ordering of priorities uncongenial: in their view, if there was to be a reorientation of NATO plans, deployments, and administrative arrangements, priority should be given to the issue of who manages the "deterrent."

First, the political control and military command arrangements of alliance strategic nuclear forces must be such as to give prior assurance that when these forces were needed for the defense of *European* soil the required decisions would be made. Then, and only then, could the Europeans agree that current arrangements for nearly automatic strategic retaliation should be supplanted by a flexible tactical fighting capability.

The MLF was a political control device and an arms control device. It was to be designed as a nonuse military system, with "fifteen finger on the safety catch." From a military point of view, it could be considered an irrelevancy, costing only a small fraction of the United States contribution in vessels and weapons and in no way compromising the essential vast arsenal of strategic nuclear power that would still remain under United States command and control. Because of its presumed political virtues for holding Europe together the project generated much enthusiasm with State Department officials responsible for NATO affairs.

Following de Gaulle's veto of British entry into the European Economic Community, the State Department began more and more to use the promise of United States nuclear sharing with Europe under the MLF scheme to encourage European efforts to form themselves into a true political union. Statements by Secretary Rusk and Undersecretary Ball hinted at an eventual relinquishing of the U.S. absolute veto on any decision to use the weapons in the MLF *after* the Europeans had made "impressive strides" toward political unity, but this condition was never elaborated in detail.[20]

The President, while never very enthusiastic about the MLF as a military instrument or as a prod to European integration, evidently did see value in the offer of the NATO nuclear fleet, or anything similar anyone could come up with, as a way of deflecting, or at least deferring, West German desires to follow France into the nuclear club.[21] As it turned out, only the Germans were seriously interested; but the White House was sensitive to the domestic and international political sentiment against anything hinting of an exclusive military partnership between the United States and Germany, especially involving weapons of mass destruction.

Yet in the absence of an alternative for diverting the Germans and symbolizing the ideal of an "indivisible" strategic nuclear deterrent for all of NATO, the President stayed with it. The greatest pressure was directed toward the British. If they would join the scheme, it would stimulate other members of NATO to join, and, if coupled with a renunciation by Britain of its independent nuclear force, might reverse the trend toward the spread of nuclear weapons. Simultaneously, the independent nuclear weapons programs of France and Britain were deprecated by Washington, and the "credibility" of U.S. pledges to use nuclear weapons on behalf of NATO's vital interests, was affirmed.

As put by Secretary of Defense McNamara, "relatively weak national nuclear forces" operating independently, are "dangerous, expensive, prone to obsolescence, and lacking in credibility as a deterrent." Such a force was likely to be vulnerable to destruction before being launched, and thus, "if a major antagonist came to believe there was a substantial likelihood of its being used independently, this force would be inviting a pre-emptive first strike against it." In the event of war, the Secretary contended, "the use of such a force against the cites of a major nuclear power would be tantamount to suicide, whereas its employment against significant military targets would have a negligible effect on the outcome of the conflict."[22]

By contrast, affirmed McNamara, "the United States nuclear contribution to the alliance is neither obsolete nor dispensable." And the U.S. would continue to make this power available to the defense of NATO interests on a global basis. Moreover, U.S. strategic forces were sufficiently protected, powerful, and accurate to allow them to be used in a controlled and deliberate fashion against military targets at the outset of a general war, thus providing decision time for both sides before engaging in the ultimate folly of mutual population destruction. By spelling out this strategic concept, McNamara was able to drive home his basic argument on behalf of centralized control of the nuclear capabilities of the alliance. To a June commencement audience, the Secretary of Defense explained:

The U.S. has come to the conclusion that to the extent feasible, basic military strategy in a possible general nuclear war should be approached in much the same way that more conventional military operations have been regarded in the past. That is to say, principal military objectives, in the event of a nuclear war stemming from a major attack on the Alliance, should be the destruction of the enemy's military forces, not of his civilian population.

The very strength and nature of the Alliance forces makes it possible for us to retain, even in the fact of a massive surprise attack, sufficient reserve striking power to destroy an enemy society if driven to it. In other words, we are giving a possible opponent the strongest imaginable incentive to refrain from striking our own cities.

In such a strategy, explained McNamara, there cannot be conflicting strategies on the part of the NATO allies, nor can there be more than one list of targets. The nuclear campaign would have to be based strictly on centralized direction and control.[23]

The U.S. was ready, and would continue to be ready, to fulfill its commitments to the alliance, reiterated the Secretary of Defense, and a controlled strategic response "gives us some hope of minimizing damage" in the event of general nuclear war. But there should be no avoiding the fact—"the almost certain prospect"—that severe damage would be suffered in such a war. Thus everything possible should be done to insure that lesser conflicts were controlled and stopped short of the commitment to battle of major force by either side. Because of the strength of the alliance, and the enunciated strategy, it was unlikely that any power would attempt to launch a massive attack, nuclear or conventional, on NATO. But for the kinds of conflicts, political or military, most likely to arise in the NATO area, it was inappropriate, indeed unbelievable, that the U.S. should respond at the outset with nuclear weapons. The Soviet superiority in nonnuclear forces "is by no means overwhelming." Moreover, the NATO countries possessed a potential for successful defense even against the full Soviet nonnuclear potential. "We do not believe that if the formula, $E = mc^2$, had not been discovered, we should all be Communist slaves."[24]

After these public remarks by the Secretary of Defense any remaining European doubts were now resolved. General de Gaulle's most apocalyptic visions were seen to be not entirely fantastic ("who can say that if the occasion arises the two [the Soviet Union and the United States], while each deciding not to launch its missiles at the main enemy so that it should itself be spared, will not crush the others? It is possible to imagine that on some awful day Western Europe should be wiped out from Moscow and Central Europe from Washington").[25]

McNamara's Ann Arbor address may well stand in the history of official strategic thought as a document of seminal theoretical importance, but as an effort at *political* persuasion it was crude, to say the least. It was as if a husband and wife were to try to solve some difference over household management by discussing what they would do in the event the two were lost at sea in a lifeboat with enough food for only one to survive.[26]

Kennedy avoided detailed discussion in public of remote future contingencies, but he was compelled to do so by the ensuing intra-alliance debate over nuclear control. In his news conference of February 14, 1963, he was asked by a reporter whether the government was yet at the stage of making the actual decision to share command and control of nuclear forces with its European allies:

> It is a very difficult area because the weapons have to be fired in 5 minutes, and who is going to be delegated on behalf of Europe to make this judgment? If the word comes to Europe or comes any place that we're about to experience an attack, you might have to make an instantaneous judgment. Somebody has to be delegated with that authority. If its isn't the President of the United States, in the case of the strategic force, it will have to be the President of France or the Prime Minister of Great Britain, or someone else. And that is an enormous responsibility. The United States has carried that responsibility for a good many years. . . .
>
> Now, it is quite natural that Western Europe would want a greater voice. We are trying to provide that greater voice through a multilateral force. But it is a very complicated negotiation because, as I say, in the final analysis, someone has to be delegated who will carry the responsibility for the alliance.[27]

Both Kennedy and McNamara had come too close for their own equanimity to making decisions in a real and terribly immediate context, rather than in the hypothetical world of strategic theory. The Cuban missile crisis had confirmed and refined their premises on the necessity for very tight and unified command arrangements under absolute political control, on the multiplication of risk of miscalculations accompanying a spread of nuclear weapons to additional powers, and on the importance of denuclearizing the United States–Soviet competition.

The President hoped that, having come so close to the fire over the issue of Soviet missiles in Cuba, the United States and the Soviet Union could cooperate in establishing a fresh tone to the language of diplomacy, pushing the strategic nuclear balance into the background where it would still be a restraint-inducing factor, but not a visible element of everyday international discourse. He looked forward to the December 1962 meeting with Prime Minister Macmillan at Nassau as an opportunity to engage in a wide-ranging dialogue in this mood of the Cuban aftermath. Undoubtedly, he would have liked the discussion of United States relations with Europe to get back to economics—the British role in the Common Market, and a more open trading relationship—rather than defense. But out of the blue came Skybolt, a seemingly technical matter in McNamara's defense budget.

Skybolt, a 1,000-mile missile to be carried and launched from a manned aircraft, had been under close scrutiny by McNamara's economists and engineers who found it wanting on "cost-effectiveness" grounds. Its $2.5 billion development costs would be better invested in other weapons system improvements. The U.S. Air Force would be aggrieved at being denied its best hope of extending the role of manned strategic bombers into the missile age; but McNamara was confident of his ability to manage the generals. However, the Royal Air Force was also banking heavily on extending the life of its V-bombers through purchase of the American-produced missile, as agreed to by Macmillan and Eisenhower in 1960. McNamara's confidence that he could placate the British as well as the U.S. Air Force was a gross political miscalculation. The President, evidently unaware of the extent to which the prestige of the British Ministry of Defense and the Prime Minister himself was staked on maintaining their "independent deterrent" with Skybolt, gave McNamara the go-ahead to work out some adjustment with British Defense Minister Thorneycroft.[28]

The "agreement" produced by the Nassau conference was a logical monstrosity and almost worthless as a military planning instrument for either government. But as a diplomatic communiqué meant to give the appearance of unity on fundamental issues where there was none, it was a masterpiece.

The only concrete agreement was that as a substitute for the Skybolt missile program, the United States would make available Polaris missiles for British submarines (the British would construct the submarines and nuclear warheads of the missiles). Lest it appear that the United States was now supporting an independent nuclear deterrent for Britain, British forces developed under this plan would be "assigned a part of a NATO nuclear force and targeted in accordance with NATO plans" (Articles 6 and 8). These forces and at least equal United States forces "would be made available for inclusion in a NATO multilateral nuclear force" (Article 8). But in Article 7 the "multilateral force" was described as more of an end product of these endeavors, and presumably not identical with "NATO nuclear force" described in Article 6, which was specifically designated as the command organization of the new force of Polaris-carrying British submarines. Moreover, the British contribution to the so-called multilateral force was apparently to be taken back under British command in those very situations when it was most likely to be used:

The British Prime Minister made it clear that except where H.M.G. may decide that supreme national interests are at stake, these forces will be used for the purpose of international defense of the Western Alliance in all circumstances. (Article 8.)

If the British were wily in slipping that one in, the Americans could bring something home in the words of Article 10, where

the President and the Prime Minister agreed that in addition to having a nuclear shield it is important to have a non-nuclear sword. For this purpose they agreed on the importance of increasing the effectiveness of their conventional forces on a worldwide basis.[29]

Macmillan could return to London claiming a victory for the concept of an independent British deterrent, which, of course, the Labour Party was not going to let him get away with. Kennedy and McNamara could forget about Skybolt and leave the State Department to plod through the maze that might eventually lead toward some kind of NATO multilateral force.

But what would de Gaulle say? Almost as an afterthought, the conferees at Nassau extended an offer to de Gaulle to contract for Polaris missiles on terms "similar" to those offered the British. The French promptly and curtly, through their Minister of Information, rejected the offer, pointing out that France had neither the submarines nor the nuclear warheads for the Polaris missiles. Deliberately ignoring the rebuff, Kennedy instructed Ambassador Charles Bohlen to inform President de Gaulle that all possibilities were still open for discussion.[30]

By the time Secretary McNamara appeared before the cognizant congressional committees in the early months of 1963 to defend his department's budget request for the coming fiscal year, de Gaulle had blasted the Anglo-American relationship and had vetoed British entry into the Common Market. Macmillan was on the defensive for his handling of the Skybolt affair, and for perpetuating the fiction of nuclear independence while in fact agreeing to become even more dependent upon United States components for England's still-to-be-developed submarine force. Kennedy and Macmillan were both subjected to the charge that their ineptitude at Nassau provoked de Gaulle into excluding Britain from the Common Market. Journalists portrayed the alliance as being in "disarray."

Many in Congress were ready to attribute all of these difficulties to the attempt by McNamara and Kennedy to shift NATO policy against the will of the Europeans, away from deterrence through the threat of all-out war to a posture that would allow substantial fighting to take place on European soil while the homelands of the Soviet Union and the United States were spared. The standard European argument that this would reduce the risks to the Soviets of an attack upon Western Europe and thereby increase their temptation to attack, was reflected in questions thrown at the Secretary—particularly by senators and representatives who were staunch defenders of budgetary requests of the U.S. Air Force.

In defending administration policy and doctrine McNamara went further than any previous spokesman in elucidating official premises about the state of the existing military balance of power and about intentions for applying U.S. power in future military conflicts. Under questioning, the Secretary of Defense maintained that "[our] current strategic superiority . . . does give us a war-winning nuclear capability, in the sense that we are confident that we can completely crush the Soviet Union if forced to do so." But he also warned of the "increasing capability of the Soviet Union to make the United States pay a heavy price for such victories in terms of tens of millions of casualties."[31] Thus when he used the word "win" he meant it only in a technical sense, which should be clearly understood:

We would win in the sense that their [the Soviet Union's] way of life would change more than ours [if the strategic forces of both sides were unleashed against each other] because we would destroy a greater percentage of their industrial potential and probably destroy a greater percentage of their population than they destroyed of ours.

Yet if the calculation also included the destruction inflicted on Western Europe, the total amount in the West "would exceed that of the Soviet Union." His personal opinion, whichever calculation was made, was that "we cannot win a nuclear war, a strategic nuclear war, in the normal meaning of the word 'win.' "[32]

Members of Congress wanted to know if the Secretary's opinion that there could be no real winners in a strategic nuclear war meant he was operating under a doctrine of "nuclear stalemate" or "mutual deterrence." If so, they pressed him to show how the United States could still deter the Soviets from attacking, especially in Central Europe, where the prize was big and the West was presumably still inferior on the ground.

McNamara rejected the terms "nuclear stalemate" and "mutual deterrence" as inaccurate descriptions of U.S. operating strategy, which he kept insisting was to use whatever force was necessary to defend its vital interests. But he was not willing to depend upon strategic forces to deter all Soviet provocations, nor was he sufficiently certain that the Soviets would always get the message in advance which U.S. interests were so vital as to make it risk millions of fatalities in their defense. As to what enemy actions U.S. strategic forces would deter, and what enemy actions might require other kinds of ready responses to make deterrence work:

Now I feel quite certain that if the Soviets are rational, our strategic forces program will deter the Soviets from launching a first strike against this country.

I say that for the very simple reason that, if they did, we would utterly destroy them, and I mean completely destroy . . . the Soviet Union as a civilized nation.

U.S. strategic nuclear capability, however,

is not a deterrent force in the sense that it will deter all political and military aggression by the Soviets. It did not deter them from putting pressure on Berlin when we had a nuclear monopoly in the early part of the 1950's. It did not deter the Communists from invading Korea. It did not deter them from building a wall in Berlin. It did not deter the Communist . . . attempt to subvert Southeast Asia. . . . It did not deter their attempt to move offensive weapons systems into Cuba.[33]

By the time the Kennedy administration took office, "it was clear that, unless we were willing to live under a constant threat of having to choose between nuclear holocaust and retreat, we required major improvements in our less-than-all-out war capabilities."[34]

The "general purpose forces," consequently, were being rapidly improved at an annual cost of over $19 billion. This included an expansion in manpower (the Army went from 11 divisions in the Eisenhower years to 16 divisions); improved equipment and munitions; mobility of the "tactical" forces of all three services; and new, more flexible and functionally integrated command structures, like the multiservice strike command.[35] These programs, McNamara explained, would provide the country with forces that "could, by non-nuclear means alone, counter a wide spectrum of Sino-Soviet bloc aggressions in regions other than Europe."

However, in Europe, "the programmed U.S. forces, together with present forces of other NATO countries, would not be able to contain an all-out conventional Soviet attack without invoking the use of nuclear weapons."[36] This reliance on nuclear weapons for balancing Soviet military power in Europe continued to give the administration trouble diplomatically and doctrinally.

Even if the Europeans were to accept the validity of flexible response and the "conventional option," even if they were to conscientiously fulfill their existing pledges to increase their manpower and equipment levels, NATO would still not be able to contain and repulse a determined Soviet attempt to forcibly absorb Western Europe unless the United States was prepared to redress the local imbalance by turning the war into a global strategic war.

If this was indeed the situation in Europe, asked various senators, then why all the emphasis on strengthening nonnuclear capabilities in Europe? If the Soviets could win an all-out contest of nonnuclear forces, weren't the Europeans right to regard the American stress on the conventional option as a futile use of the West's resources? Reiterating the arguments Paul Nitze had used in connection with the Berlin buildup, McNamara explained that "the purpose of the increase in conventional forces is to deter certain *low-scale* forms of Soviet political and military aggression which they might be tempted to carry out were they not opposed by the type that are being strengthened."[37] (Emphasis added.)

The Secretary's congressional interrogators were not entirely convinced. Suppose the Soviets did try to overwhelm admittedly inferior local forces:

SENATOR THURMOND. If we were fighting a conventional war and we were about to lose it, we would use tactical nuclear weapons, wouldn't we?

SECRETARY McNAMARA. I think a large-scale assault by the Soviet Union and its satellites forces against Western Europe would rather quickly require the use of tactical nuclear weapons in order to preserve the control of Western Europe in the hands of the West. Whether that could be limited to the use of tactical nuclear weapons is an open question in my mind.

McNamara's point was that NATO needed to be prepared to fight in this middle range of conflict between conventional war and strategic nuclear war, particularly to deter the Soviets from escalating to strategic nuclear war: to that end the United States already had "thousands" of nuclear weapons in Europe. But it was important to discourage inflated expectations for the potential role of these tactical weapons in deterring, or repelling, a Soviet nonnuclear attack. As he explained to the House Armed Services Committee in his prepared remarks on the fiscal 1964 budget:

Nuclear weapons, even in the lower kiloton ranges, are extremely destructive devices and hardly the preferred weapons to defend such heavily populated areas as Europe. Furthermore, while it does not necessarily follow that the use of tactical nuclear weapons must inevitably escalate into global nuclear war, it does present a very definite threshold, beyond which we enter a vast unknown.[38]

Some senators pointed to what seemed to be an underlying premise of the whole strategy of flexible response, from its stress on a delayed resort to nuclear weapons through its notion of a city-avoiding nuclear exchange: namely, the premise of a similarly restrained Soviet Union, the notion that the opponent would accept the rules of warfare the U.S. wanted to impose.

McNamara was careful not to answer categorically these questions of likely Soviet behavior in a military conflict. Indeed, the very reason the United States was maintaining such a strong nuclear arsenal in Europe was to *deter* the Soviets from taking it upon themselves to cross the threshold into nuclear war.

With respect to the city-avoidance "option" in strategic nuclear war, again, the hope for Soviet restraint was not based on faith in their willingness to "play fair." It was based entirely on the premise that at the moment of truth, despite previous Soviet protestations to the contrary, they would still want to save the Soviet Union from complete devastation. By holding in reserve the vast American potential to wipe out their cities, the U.S. would be saying: you have not yet lost everything, but whether you do depends on your next move. McNamara was not willing to predict Soviet behavior, only to provide Soviet leaders with an incentive to act more rationally. But this would take advance planning, and he had to admit that, under present circumstances, neither the Soviets nor the United States had the kind of forces-in-being that would allow them to fight a controlled strategic nuclear campaign. McNamara's most careful discourse on this complicated strategic problem was in response to a question by Congressman Leslie Arends before the House Committee on Armed Services:

> I do think we should separate the discussion into two parts: one related to circumstances today and the other related to possible circumstances in the future.
>
> Today we know that the great majority of the Soviet strategic forces, both their bombers and their missiles, are in soft [i.e., highly vulnerable] configurations. Under these circumstances it seems almost inconceivable to me that were the Soviets to attack the United States they would attack other than our cities, because they have no possibility of holding in reserve forces for later use against our cities with any expectation that those forces would survive a U.S. attack. . . .
>
> Now, turning to the future, it is possible, although I think not probable, that . . . Soviet attack might be directed primarily against our military installations. And were that to be the case, it might be advantageous to direct our retaliatory attack primarily against their military installations, thereby giving them an incentive to avoid an attack on our major urban areas.[39]

The point was not lost on the congressmen that McNamara's preferred strategic context seemed to be one in which both the Soviet Union and the United States possessed highly invulnerable "reserve" strategic weapons. He had abandoned as desirable, let alone feasible, a United States first-strike capability powerful enough to destroy the Soviet capability to inflect unacceptable damage upon the United States.

This was precisely the premise of McNamara's statement to Stewart Alsop in an interview published shortly after the Cuban missile crisis. A nuclear exchange confined to military targets seemed more possible, not less, he emphasized, "when *both* sides have a secure second-strike capability. Then you might have a more stable 'balance of terror.' This may seem a rather subtle point, but from where I'm sitting it seems a point worth thinking about."[40]

Senator Stuart Symington, Secretary of the Air Force during the Truman administration, was somewhat disturbed by McNamara's interview with Alsop: "I presume that means the sooner they [the Soviets] have a second strike capability the better. That was the impression I got from the article." McNamara denied that this was a correct interpretation of his remarks. But it was necessary to adjust to the new emerging strategic situation in which the Soviets were moving toward a relatively invulnerable missile force. The point of his comment to Alsop, he explained, was that "we should not assume that our position is worsening as they do that. As a matter of fact, it will put less pressure on them to carry out a pre-emptive strike in a period of crisis, and this is to our advantage."[41]

Senator Margaret Chase Smith was worried that the suggestion that the U.S. resign itself to eventual essential strategic parity with the Soviets was likely to have "serious long-term effects on our national will, our courage and our determination to resist attacks on our way of life."

McNamara granted that the questions raised by his predictions and by the administration's response to this new strategic reality, did go "straight to the fabric of national will and determination." But what was it that sustained this national will and determination and, most important, the perception by the Soviets of the willingness of the U.S. to stand by its commitments? It was the *total* power of the U.S. as a nation, and not simply the measurement of strategic nuclear effectiveness in all-out war (the ultimate unlikely contingency which, regardless of relative "margins of superiority," would be disastrous to both sides). The overall balance of power was what really mattered, and

I don't believe that any time in our lifetime they will reach parity with us in the total power of their system versus ours; particularly, I believe that if you include as an element of that power, the attraction and influence and effectiveness of our political system, but even for the moment excluding that and dealing only with their economic and military power, I don't foresee any situation in which they will reach parity with us.[42]

The Secretary of Defense spoke in precise terms about the military balance and elaborated the sometimes esoteric strategic doctrine that guided his budgetary decisions on the military posture. But his discussions of those matters were often revealingly matter-of-fact and dryly abstract, far removed from the everyday crisis preoccupations of the administration.

Yet those discussions were an essential background to diplomacy, and on occasion the President himself brought them forward as a reminder to friends and foes that Americans were prepared, if driven to it, to pay the highest price in defending their values. The address the President proposed to deliver before the Dallas Citizens' Council on November 22, 1963, was to be one of these occasions. He was going to talk in detail about the various components of the nation's power, "ranging from the most massive deterrents to the most subtle influences."

The need to remain militarily powerful was only a part of the role, thrust upon the U.S. "by destiny rather than by choice," to be "the watchman on the walls of world freedom." But, the President was going to tell his audience at Dallas, to be truly worthy of this power and responsibility, Americans must "exercise our strength with wisdom and restraint," never in the pursuit of aggressive ambitions, and always in the pursuit of peace and goodwill toward men. "For as was written long ago: 'Except the Lord keep the city/the watchman waketh but in vain.' "[43]

9

THE THIRD WORLD AS A PRIMARY
ARENA OF COMPETITION

We live in a very special moment in history. The whole southern half of the world—Latin America, Africa, the Middle East, Asia—are caught up in the adventure of asserting their independence and modernizing their old ways of life. . . . Without exception they are under Communist pressure. . . . But the fundamental task of our foreign aid program in the 1960s is not negatively to fight Communism. Its fundamental task is to help make a historical demonstration that . . . economic growth and political democracy can develop hand in hand.

—JOHN F. KENNEDY

Analysts with an orientation toward military affairs are prone to pay most attention to the so-called Kennedy–McNamara "revolution" in military policy, as if it were the centerpiece of the Kennedy administration's foreign policy. But this is to confuse immediacy with high value. At the center of the Kennedy foreign policy was the premise that the competition between the Soviet Union and the United States was shifting to a new arena competition for influence over the direction of development in the poorer half of the globe; and it was in respect to this competition that the United States was in greatest danger of falling behind.

In his pre–White House years, Kennedy turned much of his fire on the Eisenhower–Dulles approach to the Third World. The Middle East, particularly, had been the scene or "grave errors":

We overestimated our own strength and underestimated the force of nationalism. . . . We gave our support to regimes instead of to people—and too often we tied our future to the fortunes of unpopular and ultimately overthrown governments and rulers.

We believed that those governments which were friendly to us and hostile to the Communists were therefore good governments—and we believed that we could make unpopular policies acceptable through our own propaganda programs.

.   .   .

We must talk in terms that go beyond the vocabulary of the Cold War—terms that translate themselves into tangible values and self-interest for the Arabs as well as ourselves.

It is not enough to talk only in terms of guns and money—for guns and money are not the basic need in the Middle East. It is not enough to approach their problems on a piecemeal basis. It is not enough to merely ride with a very shaky *status quo*. It is not enough to recall the Baghdad Pact or the Eisenhower Doctrine— it is not enough to rely on The Voice of America or the Sixth Fleet. These approaches have failed.[1]

For "terms that go beyond the vocabulary of the Cold War" Kennedy went to his Charles River economist friends. They were putting together a doctrine on the relationship between the structure of societies, the availability of external capital, and the modernization process. Most of these economists had either been government officials, were now consultants to the government, or were participants in overseas technical assistance programs of private foundations. There were the expected intellectual disagreements among learned men of an inexact science; but there was a notable convergence on a set of propositions with important implications for concrete policy.[2]

• The objective of assistance to the underdeveloped nations should be to help them achieve a condition in which economic growth is a normal and self-sustaining process within a democratic political system.

• The attainment of a condition of self-sustaining growth for most of the underdeveloped nations will require fundamental modifications of the economic *and* noneconomic structures of their societies.

• Putting off the fundamental societal modifications until popular demands for change have risen to a high pitch would likely lead to violent upheavals followed by totalitarian rule.

• The required structural modifications can be accomplished peacefully if they are begun early, and are translated into carefully coordinated attacks on the particular roadblocks to modernization found in each nation.

• Frequently· occurring roadblocks are: (1) a lack of sufficient agricultural productivity beyond the subsistence level (sufficient productivity is an important source of investment capital formation); (2) a lack of sufficient investment in social overhead projects (transportation and communication networks especially); (3) the lack of indigenous specialists able to administer these development tasks and to train the rural population in modes of greater productivity; (4) the lack of literacy, which does not allow for the absorption of new values and techniques (including population control) by the population; and (5) the lack of sufficient commitment on the part of elites to greater economic egalitarianism and political democracy.

• Since the need for various expensive projects will arise in advance of the market for them, the governments in these countries, not the free market, will have to be the major determiners of investment during the early stages of economic growth.

• But in many of these countries these people who run the government, who would be responsible for formulating and carrying out national development plans and negotiating for foreign assistance, are themselves very much attached to the existing social structure. Even in those nations where the top political leadership is personally committed to basic structural alterations of their societies (particularly in the new postcolonial societies where mass nationalist parties were the instruments of the independence movements), their continued authority may rest on the support of those groups in the society who still command the bulk of resources in the countryside, and who continue to staff the civil and military bureaucracies. These latter groups, for material and psychological reasons, may be reluctant to bring on the restructuring that would have to accompany true modernization.

• As a source of desired investment capital and foreign exchange, the United States, other developed nations, and international development authorities can exercise some leverage over the otherwise sluggish pace of structural change by making performance in attacking the critical roadblocks to modernization the foremost criterion for continued economic assistance.*

• Military or ideological alignment with the United States should not be a prominent criterion for the flow of assistance.

Many of the scholars involved in generating these propositions were now brought into the government—on the White House staff, the State Department, and as ambassadors to important underdeveloped countries (Galbraith as ambassador to India, Lincoln Gordon as ambassador to Brazil). From their point of view, and from Kennedy's,

---

*The Foreign Assistance Act of 1961 gave legislative sanction to the injection by the President of this criterion when negotiating development loans. The President, in the language of the act, was to take into account "the extent to which the recipient country is showing a responsiveness to the vital economic, political, and social concerns of its people, and demonstrating a clear determination to take self-help measures." (Title I, Sec. 201, *Foreign Assistance Act of 1961*, 87th Congress, 1st session, August 30, 1961.)

they had practically a carte blanche opportunity to reorganize the entire foreign assistance program, its personnel as well as its operational guidelines. A large new foreign aid program for Latin America was to be funded where the new premises would have a proving ground, unencumbered by existing programmatic commitments.

President Kennedy's appreciation of the highly insecure political base of the leaders of the developing nations led him to expunge cold war rhetoric, as much as possible, from the public rationale for foreign assistance. He responded positively to the suggestions from Walt Rostow, David Bell, and others to tone down the anti-Communist appeals appearing in the first draft of his March 1961 foreign aid message.[3] From the outset, however, he was the focal point of the tension between two "constituencies" of the foreign assistance program: the overseas recipients of assistance (whose Washington champions were the development economists in Kennedy's advisory entourage); and, opposing them, the neo-isolationist elements in the American electorate, in portions of the business community, and in segments of organized labor whose congressional brokers have traditionally coalesced to prune administration foreign assistance requests not carrying a simple "essential for national security" rationale. The President did have a basic national security rationale; but it was far from simple. He did see the need to ride with, rather than against, a good deal of the political turbulence in the recipient nations, even when it assumed anti-American, quasi-Marxist overtones; but he was too shrewd a domestic politician to assume that his tactical international apoliticism would get the needed appropriations out of Congress.

The contrary ideological requirements of the overseas recipients as opposed to the domestic provisioners bedeviled Kennedy throughout his presidency, and explains the observed ambivalence in the public rationale of his foreign assistance program—with one tendency represented by the Alliance for Progress, and the other by the Clay report.

To be sure, the Alliance for Progress was very much a part of the grand strategy of the Kennedy administration for frustrating Communist penetration of the Third World. But this aspect of the Alliance's rationale was consciously underplayed in the public rhetoric.

As revealed by Arthur Schlesinger, Jr. (who was heavily involved as a consultant to Kennedy on Latin American affairs), the cold war was a pervasive part of the discussions in the White House on the Latin American aid program. Kennedy's interregnum task force on Latin America (chaired by Adolph Berle*) emphasized the Communist threat, describing it as "more dangerous than the Nazi-Fascist threat [to Latin America] of the Franklin Roosevelt period. . . ." The objective of the Communists, said the task force report, was "to convert the Latin American social revolution into a Marxist attack on the United States itself." As this revolution was "inevitable and necessary," the way to counter the Communist threat was to "divorce" the Latin American social transformation "from connection with and prevent its capture by Communist power politics." The United States needed to put itself clearly on the side of the indigenous "democratic-progressive movements . . . pledged to representative government and economic reform (including agrarian reform) and resistance to entrance of undemocratic forces from outside the hemisphere." The truly democratic social reform groups "should be known to have the good will and support of the United States, just as every Communist group in Latin America is known to have the support of Moscow or of Peiping." It was also necessary for the United States to develop its capabilities for paramilitary and military counterinsurgency operations and to be prepared to offer effective military support to progressive regimes such as Betancourt's in Venezuela. But the U.S. should not try to "stabilize the dying reactionary situations."[4]

The aspect of the Berle report that surfaced in the full-blown Alliance for Progress was the insistence that the United States offer a hemisphere-wide long-range economic development plan, based on the kind of coordinated national planning urged by the Harvard and M.I.T. economists. This was the type of action required to avoid the spread of violent insurrectionary movements in Latin America and also to give credibility to United States professions of being on the side of those working for social justice and democracy.

THE ALLIANCE FOR PROGRESS

After the Kennedy inauguration the momentum for a new departure to Latin American policy accelerated. Berle was appointed to head a

---

*The interregnum task force on Latin America, in addition to Berle, included Richard Goodwin, Lincoln Gordon, Teodoro Moscosco, Arturo Morales-Carrion, Robert Alexander, and Arthur Whitaker.

reconstituted task force on Latin America in the Department of State, where he and Thomas Mann, the new Assistant Secretary for Inter-American Affairs, labored to give the earlier ideas operational content. One of their recommendations was that the President make a major address on United States policy toward Latin America, proposing a ten-year program of continental development.

Richard Goodwin, Kennedy's staff man on Latin America during the campaign, and now a member of the White House staff, was given primary responsibility for drafting the address. The problem was how to sell the economic propositions at home and in Latin America without injecting the cold war rationale, which would alienate the reformist elements in Latin America with whom the administration was trying to align itself.

The "solution," as exhibited in the President's proposal of March 13, 1961 for "a vast new ten-year plan for the Americas," was a coupling of the structural approach to economic development that had been advanced by the Charles River economists with the revolutionary idealism of Thomas Jefferson and Simón Bolívar. Kennedy christened the *Alianza* the contemporary expression of the American revolution (North and South) for the rights of man:

Our nations are the product of a common struggle—the revolt from colonial rule.

. . .

The revolutions which gave us birth ignited, in the words of Thomas Paine, "a spark never to be extinguished." . . . we must remember that . . . the revolution which began in 1776 and in Caracas in 1811 . . . is not yet finished. Our hemisphere's mission is not yet completed. *For our unfulfilled task is to demonstrate to the entire world that man's unsatisfied aspiration for economic progress and social justice can best be achieved by free men working within a framework of democratic institutions.*[5]

The concrete steps "to complete the revolution of the Americas" were to be presented in detail at a ministerial meeting of the Inter-American Economic and Social Council. But the President's speech gave a preview of the criteria which his administration would insist be applied in evaluating a potential recipient's commitments to the ideals of the unfinished hemispheric revolution. Political freedom, said the President, had to accompany material progress, but political freedom must be accomplished by social change:

For unless necessary social reforms, including land and tax reform, are freely made, unless we broaden the opportunity of all our people, unless the great mass of

Americans share in increasing prosperity, then our alliance, our revolution, our dream, and our freedom will fail.[6]

This approach was a product of the analysis of the New Frontiersmen that the weakest chink in the armor of the non-Communist world was the phenomenon of the entrenched oligarchy holding on to privilege in the face of rising demands for social justice. Identifying the United States with the current of social revolution would give it a legitimacy in these countries that would draw responsible professional and middle-class elements into the reform movements, and thereby channel pressures into practical demands and nonviolent modes of agitation. Furthermore, by providing an agenda of practical reforms and insisting that governments in these countries make discernible progress in this direction in order to qualify for development loans, the United States would be providing significant pressure from above to complement and reinforce the popular pressures it was encouraging from below. Progressive regimes would be strengthened against conservative elements in their societies; and oligarchical regimes would be squeezed in an ever-tightening vise. Opportunist leaders would at least know where their bread was to be buttered.

If the Latin American nations took the necessary internal measures, Secretary of the Treasury Douglas Dillon told his fellow delegates at Punta del Este in August, they could reasonably expect their own efforts to be matched by an inflow of capital during the next decade amounting to at least $20 billion. The problem, he said, did not lie in a shortage of external capital, but "in organizing effective development programs so that both domestic and foreign capital can be put to work rapidly, wisely, and well." There were underlying principles to be adhered to: the loan recipients would have to dedicate larger proportions of their domestic resources to national development projects; integrated national programs for economic and social development would have to be formulated, setting forth goals and priorities to insure that available resources were used in the most effective manner, and such national development programs would have to be in accord with the right of all segments of the population to share fully in the fruits of progress.

To implement these principles, said Dillon, difficult and far-reaching changes would have to be instituted by many of the Latin American nations:

It will require a strengthening of tax systems so that would-be evaders will know they face strict penalties and so that taxes are assessed in accordance with ability to pay. It will require land reform so that under-utilized soil is put to full use and so that farmers can own their own land. It will require lower interest rates on loans to small farmers and small business. It will require greatly increased programs of education, housing, and health.[7]

The assembled delegates of the Latin American republics, except for Cuba's Che Guevara, responded with enthusiasm to the United States initiative.

But it turned out to be an *Alianza* mainly at the level of verbalized aspiration. According to Ted Sorensen, the President, after a year or so of little progress, was disappointed:

what disturbed him most was the attitude of that 2 percent of the citizenry of Latin America who owned more than 50 percent of the wealth and controlled most of the political-economic apparatus. Their voices were influential, if not dominant, among the local governments, the armies, the newspapers and other opinionmakers. They had friendly ties with U.S. press and business interests who reflected their views in Washington. They saw no reason to alter the ancient feudal patterns of land tenure and tax structure, the top heavy military budgets, the substandard wages and the concentrations of capital. They classified many of their opponents as "communists," considered the social and political reforms of the *Alianza* a threat to stability and clung tenaciously to the status quo.[8]

Moreover, even when there was the will to reform, there appeared to be a conspiracy of history, natural phenomena, and elemental human forces against essential change. The desire to effect at least a 2.5 percent per capita rate of economic growth just did not conform to the facts. A 3 percent per annum increase in the gross national product was very impressive for a Latin American country, yet with population growth running at 2.5 to 3 percent, the per capita increase was usually all but wiped out even in the best of cases. The lack of Latin American economists with experience in integrated national economic planning was another factor making for sluggishness. By the end of 1962 only five countries were able to submit national development plans for review, and of these only those submitted by Mexico and Venezuela were competently done and within the spirit of the *Alianza*. The lack of sufficiently studied and engineered projects meant that the United States government was able to disburse only two thirds of the $1.5 billion it had already pledged for the first year and a half of the program.[9] Nor was the picture brightened by the worldwide drop in basic commodity prices—the major source of national income for most of the Latin American countries.

Was it all worth the effort anyway? Kennedy continued to think so, but without the earlier euphoria. He admitted that the Alliance for Progress "has failed to some degree because the problems are almost insuperable." In some ways, he said, "the road seems longer than it was when the journey started. But I think we ought to keep at it." [10]

"Perhaps our most impressive accomplishment," said the President on the first anniversary of the Alliance for Progress, "has been the dramatic shift in thinking and attitudes which has occurred in our hemisphere":

> Already elections are being fought in terms of the Alliance for Progress. . . . Already people throughout the hemisphere—in schools and in trade unions, in chambers of commerce and in military establishments, in government and on the farms—have accepted the goals of the charter as their own personal and political commitments. For the first time in the history of inter-American relations our energies are concentrated on the central task of democratic development.
> This dramatic change in thought is essential to the realization of our goals. [11]

The problem was that the dramatic change in thought, if unaccompanied by meaningful changes in government programs in these countries, could create an even larger gap between popular demands and government responsiveness, with governments in turn attempting to stifle demand, and the discontented turning in their frustration to insurgency. The strategy for effecting a "divorce" between Communist and non-Communist social reform movements, and making the latter more powerful by tangible evidence of the success of their programs, was based on the assumption that governments, under prodding by the United States, would respond to the mounting political pressure more quickly than they had in the past.

The prod around which the Alliance for Progress was built was the long-term low-interest loan program for development projects administered in accord with the guidelines set forth in the Charter of Punta del Este. But the diffusion of responsibility to internationally appointed technical experts for implementing the conditions in the charter made it difficult to use this tool as an instrument of reform. Governments could too easily blame their failure to gain the new external capital promised in the Alliance on the bureaucracy and red tape of the inter-American machinery, rather than on their own procrastination. And the United States could be accused of insisting upon complicated technical standards precisely for the reason that it would reduce the projects requiring U.S. financial support. Before the end of 1962 the governments of the Americas, through their delegates to the Inter-American Economic and Social Council, were recommending that "in order to prevent disappointment both on the part of the countries seeking assistance and of the financing institutions, both national and international, it will be advisable to make the conditions and operations of these institutions more flexible." [12]

Latin American diplomats also began to press with greater fervor for international commodity price stabilization agreements, arguing that the instability of their countries' foreign earnings, more than anything else, prevented the amount of domestic capital available for investment in development from being increased. This case was not entirely convincing to the administration, since there was a good deal of "surplus" domestic Latin American private money drawing interest in American and European banks. The people receiving money from the export of basic commodities were very often the same elements least interested in the social reform that would have to accompany true economic development in their countries.

The more conservative Latins, and United States interests, unsympathetic to the national planning approach and the emphasis upon public investment in the original conception of the Alliance, pointed to the decline in the flow of private capital to Latin America since Punta del Este. The obvious implication was that all the talk of dramatic social change, including drastic land and tax reforms, had raised the specter of confiscation of private holdings without sufficient compensation, harassment of foreign-subscribed private enterprise, and political instability leading to unpredictable radical economic experiments. "Taking into account the limitations to the availability of public funds," said the first-year evaluation report of the IA-ECOSOC, "it is clear that the objectives of the Alliance cannot be achieved without the full participation of the private sector and adequate measures must be taken to assure maximum contribution to growth by the private sector." [13] The forces for stability, recovering from the first shock of seeing the White House seriously identifying itself with the forces for change, had begun to regroup.

The President's response to the conservative counterattack was to show as much favor as possible to leaders like Betancourt and Mateos, and to point his finger at those Latin American forces which, in his view, constituted an alliance against progress:

No amount of external resources, no stabilization of commodity prices, no new inter-American institutions, can bring progress to nations which do not have political stability and determined leadership. No series of hemispheric agreements or elaborate machinery can help those who lack internal discipline, who are unwilling to make sacrifices and renounce privileges. No one who sends his money abroad, who is unwilling to invest in the future of his country, can blame others for the deluge which threatens to overcome and overwhelm him.[14]

But the elements of lethargy, obstruction, and despair were not going to prevail this time, affirmed the President four days before his death. These forces should know that he was fully committed, and prepared for a long struggle. "Nothing is true except a man or men adhere to it—to live for it, to spend themselves on it, to die for it," he declaimed, quoting from a poem by Robert Frost.

THE CLAY REPORT: REVIVAL OF THE NATIONAL SECURITY RATIONALE

The Kennedy administration, partly because of its analysis of the sensitivities of the new nations, partly because of its belief that the U.S. was at its best when it gave vent to its altruistic traditions, was initially inclined not to make the national security rationale the be-all and end-all of foreign aid. But gradually, and tragically to some New Frontiersmen, the White House began to trim its approach back to this irreducible national interest as Congress fell back into its habit of trimming the "fat" from foreign aid requests.

Congress went along with the essentials of the administration's program in 1961, creating the Agency for International Development (AID), authorizing the Alliance for Progress and the funds requested for this new venture, and increasing the proportion of foreign assistance appropriations devoted to economic as opposed to military projects. But the next year, the counterattack was in full swing, led by Congressman Otto Passman, chairman of the House appropriations subcommittee on foreign aid.

In 1962, the President asked Congress for a total of $4.9 billion for the various foreign assistance programs. As Congress began to axe the recommended economic development programs, Kennedy appealed to the legislators in the terms of his preferred public rationale: if we were truly for a world of independent self-reliant nations, if we really believed that weakness and dependence for national societies was not a proper environment for the development of political liberty and individual well-being, then in good conscience we could not reduce these foreign assistance programs any further.[15]

Insufficiently impressed, Congress trimmed a full billion dollars off the President's request. There was great disappointment in the White House; AID's first chief, Foweler Hamilton, resigned. Schlesinger portrays Kennedy as "convinced that extreme measures were necessary to get the aid bill through Congress in 1963," and deciding upon "the familiar device of a blue-ribbon panel of bonded conservatives set up to cast a presumably cold eye on the aid effort and then to recommend its continuance as essential to the national interest."[16]

Designated "the Committee to Strengthen the Security of the Free World," the panel was chaired by General Lucius D. Clay, highly respected in banking and financial circles and famed for his cold war toughness toward the Soviets over Germany and Berlin. Fiscal responsibility was represented by Robert B. Anderson, Eisenhower's last Secretary of the Treasury, and before that Secretary of the Navy. Robert A. Lovett, a Secretary of Defense under Truman, and the man most identified in the public mind with the New York "establishment," could never be accused of fuzzy liberalism. Organized labor was represented by the militantly anti-Communist George Meany. Edward S. Mason, of the Harvard–M.I.T. economists circle, was added as an afterthought, but largely as a concession to some of the development economists who may not have appreciated the political gamesmanship of the President. The main economic development aura was provided by Eugene Black of the World Bank. Other members were Clifford Hardin, L. F. McCollum, Herman Phleger, and Howard Rusk.

The Clay committee was more than willing to provide the truest blue ribbon, in the form of a return to the strict national-security-only criterion that had kept economic development assistance to a trickle since the Korean War, and in its insistence that the "private sector" rather than government-owned enterprises should be the favored recipients of assistance. But rather than squaring the circle by arguing that the nation's security interest and interest in expanding overseas private investment would be best served by a long-term continuation of the level of effort the President was recommending, the committee did just the opposite:

> We believe that we are indeed attempting too much for too many and that a higher quality and reduced quantity of our difficult aid effort in certain countries could accomplish much more. We cannot believe that our national interest is served by indefinitely continuing commitments at the present rate to the 95 countries and territories which are now receiving our economic and/or military assistance. Substantial tightening up and sharpened objectives in terms of our national interests are necessary.

> . . .

> For the present . . . we are convinced that reductions are in order in present military and economic assistance programs. Mindful of the risks inherent in using the axe to achieve quickly the changes recommended, the Committee recommends these reductions be phased over the next three years.[17]

The administration released the report reluctantly, in the knowledge that Clay's support was politically indispensable, even if only to salvage the 1963 bill after it was torn apart by Representative Passman and his friends. The Louisiana Democrat could not have been more pleased by the Clay report. And now cautious Republicans like Everett Dirkson and Charles Halleck could vote for cuts in the administration's aid program while wrapped in the mantle of establishment patriotism.

The "national security" standard as wielded by Congress, applying narrower concepts of security and the global balance of power, was in 1963 a keener instrument for whittling down than building up. The actual appropriations bill of $3.2 billion, a slash of $1.7 billion from Kennedy's original request, was the lowest since 1958, and the smallest percentage of U.S. gross national product allocated to foreign assistance since the start of the Marshall Plan.

In an administration that defined the Third World as the major arena of competition, this congressional action was interpreted as a severe curb on the diplomatic power of the United States.

The President, however, was not one to take such defeats without fighting back. If the case for foreign aid had to be made in terms of national security, then that was the way he would make the case. But the connection would have to be more clearly set forth than previously.

In a westward swing through the United States with Secretary of the Interior Udall in the fall of 1963, the President frequently departed from his major theme—the conservation of natural resources—to talk about the preservation of the nation as a whole.

Except for his address during the Cuban missile crisis, probably the hardest-hitting basic national security speech of the President's career was made at the Mormon Tabernacle in Salt Lake City. It was the last week of September 1963. The Senate had ratified the nuclear test ban treaty. There was talk of détente with the Soviet Union. The President, aware that the audience to which he spoke would translate their mood of increasing isolationism into a disapproval of foreign economic assistance, drove home the connections between the security concerns of his audience, the global balance of power, and the array of U.S. foreign commitments. This largely extemporaneous address merits liberal quotation:

I know that many of you in this State and other States sometimes wonder where we are going and why the United States should be involved in so many affairs, in so many countries all around the globe.

. . .

I realize that the burdens are heavy and I realize that there is a great temptation to urge that we relinquish them, that we have enough to do here in the United States, and we should not be so busy around the globe. From the beginning of this country . . . we had believed that we could live behind our two oceans in safety and prosperity in a comfortable distance from the rest of the world.

. . .

I can well understand the attraction of those earlier days . . . but two world wars have shown us that if we . . . turn our back on the world outside . . . we jeopardize our economic well-being, we jeopardize our political stability, we jeopardize our physical safety.

. . .

Americans have come a long way in accepting in a short time the necessity of world involvement, but the strain of this involvement remains and we find it all over the country. . . . We find ourselves entangled with apparently unanswerable problems in unpronounceable places. We discover that our enemy in one decade is our ally the next. We find ourselves committed to governments whose actions we cannot often approve, assisting societies with principles very different from our own.

. . .

The world is full of contradiction and confusion, and our policy seems to have lost the black and white clarity of simpler times when we remembered the Maine and went to war.

. . .

The United States has rightly determined, in the years since 1945 under three different administrations . . . that our national security, the interest of the United States of America, is best served by preserving and protecting a world of diversity in which *no one power or no one combination of powers can threaten the security of the United States.* The reason that we moved so far into the world was our fear that at the end of the war, and particularly when China became Communist, that Japan and Germany would collapse, and these two countries which had so long served as a barrier to Soviet advance, and the Russian advance before that, would open up a wave of conquest of all Europe and all of Asia, and then *the balance of power turning against us we would finally be isolated and ultimately destroyed.* That is what we have been engaged in for 18 years, to prevent that happening, to prevent any one monolithic power having sufficient force to destroy the United States.

For that reason we support the alliance in Latin America; for that reason we support NATO . . . for that reason we joined SEATO. . . . And however dangerous or hazardous it may be, and however close it may take us to the brink on occasion, which it has, and however tired we may get of our involvements with these governments so far away, we have *one simple central theme of American foreign policy* which all of us must recognize, because it is a policy which we must continue to follow, and that is *to support the independence of nations so that one block cannot gain sufficient power to finally overcome us.* There is no mistaking the vital interest of the United States in what goes on around the world. . . .

If we were to withdraw our assistance from all governments who are run differently from our own, we would relinquish the world immediately to our adversaries.[18]

The New Frontier tired to transcend the vocabulary of cold war diplomacy, but found it had often to return to this vocabulary when addressing the American public in order to be granted the resources to develop more flexible programs for the Third World.

10

KENNEDY'S CUBAN CRISES

If at any time the Communist buildup in Cuba were to endanger or interfere with our security in any way, including our base at Guantanamo, our passage to the Panama Canal, our missile and space activities at Cape Canaveral, or the lives of American citizens in this country, or if Cuba should ever attempt to export its aggressive purposes by force or the threat of force against any nation in this hemisphere, or become an offensive military base of significant capacity for the Soviet Union, then this country will do whatever must be done to protect its own security and that of its allies.

—JOHN F. KENNEDY

At this outset of his presidency, Kennedy was unconcerned about a Communist Cuba from a strictly geopolitical point of view. During his campaign he spoke in support of the Miami Cuban exiles' determination to liberate their homeland from Castro's rule; but this was in large measure a bid for support from the politically active Cuban–American community in Florida. It was also partly ideological, as Castro had abandoned his earlier pretenses that he was a latter-day combination of Thomas Jefferson and Simon Bolivar. By opposing Castro, Kennedy could demonstrate his opposition to tyrannies of the left and the right. His opposition to Castro, however, was not yet at the point where he would countenance the use of U.S. military power to depose him. He pulled back from authorizing U.S. combat operations during the Bay of Pigs fiasco due to pragmatism, not to either cynicism or a squeamishness about using military force. Above all, he was unwilling to make Castro a martyr to the Cuban people and the rest of Latin America. More effective, he then thought, to allow Castro to fashion his own noose (albeit with some marginal covert help from the CIA), which would eventually be tightened by the Latins themselves.

The deployment of Soviet missiles to Cuba in 1962 was an entirely different matter. The global balance of power was at stake, and therefore the missiles would have to be removed by diplomacy or by military action. But, as the resolution of the crisis demonstrated, Castro and Communism in Cuba still were not of paramount concern for him, as long as the overall U.S.–Soviet balance of power was satisfactorily restabilized.

THE BAY OF PIGS

President Kennedy hesitated, reversed himself, and was embarrassingly unsure of his footing during the effort to topple Castro in the spring of 1961. But from the outset he was constant in his basic premise that fundamental United States interests would be ill-served if that effort were to directly involve U.S. military power. This premise was a part of the ground rules for Central Intelligence Agency contingency planning as originally approved by the Eisenhower administration. No United States military intervention was explicitly a part of the understanding between the White House and the CIA, and was reiterated and stressed during the secret meetings in March and April between the new President and his chief military, diplomatic, and intelligence advisers.[1] This determination not to apply United States military power was reinforced in a pledge by Kennedy, just five days before the exile landing at the Bay of Pigs:

there will not be, under any conditions, an intervention in Cuba by the United States Armed Forces. This government will do everything it possibly can, and I think it can meet its responsibilities, to make sure that there are no Americans involved in any actions inside Cuba.

The basic issue in Cuba is not one between the United States and Cuba. It is between the Cubans themselves. I intend to see that we adhere to that principle and as I understand it this administration's attitude is so understood and shared by the anti-Castro exiles from Cuba in this country.[2]

This prohibition, in the "moment of truth" where he saw what would be required to make the exile operation succeed, led Kennedy to accept the terrible embarrassment and pain of allowing the 1,400 Cuban exiles to be decimated by Castro's forces.

In everything that has thus far been divulged about the Bay of Pigs crisis, the evidence is that the President thought he had approved an operation whose success would *not* require the use of United States military forces. He accepted the intelligence of the CIA that Castro's hold over the people of Cuba was very unstable, and that the majority of the people, including presumably Castro's own army, would rise against him once a small force of exiles had established a beachhead. The President and his military advisers also accepted the CIA's intelligence on Castro's military forces, and the derived evaluation by the Joint Chiefs of Staff that an insurrectionary beachhead could be established by the Cuban exiles without direct United States military support. In the unlikely chance that the operation did not succeed militarily, it would have been conducted in such a low-key manner that the exiles could disappear into the hills and reorganize themselves for a longer-term guerrilla operation without having to call on the United States to rescue them.[3]

After the assault was underway, the President discovered that all of these critical intelligence and military operational premises were wrong. A good deal of what has been written about the Bay of Pigs explores the bases of these mistaken premises—poor advice, deliberate deception by operatives afraid to tell the President the truth for fear the operation would be called off (but hoping that once it was underway the President would be too heavily committed to reverse himself), the failure of the President to draw out advisers who had important doubts, and Kennedy's inexperience in managing the vast military and intelligence bureaucracies.

Some argue that better generalship on the administration's part would have saved the day: a less-vulnerable landing site; the timing of the exiles' air strikes; supplies of ammunition dispersed rather than concentrated in a single ship which was sunk early in the campaign, and so on. Other critics dwell on the failure of the United States to become militarily involved even in a marginal way—but at the critical margin: if the United States had provided air cover, it is argued, the exiles could have at least established a beachhead from which to mount a major insurgency.

But as the facts came in, the President apparently was convinced that he and his subordinates had made more than a series of technical and marginal errors: the principal agencies and individuals involved in the planning and direction of the venture had jointly constructed a grossly uninformed view of the situation in Cuba. Different pictures of Castro's political and military strength were available from British intelligence, the State Department, and American newspaper reporters. Yet from those within his inner circle, the President received no thoughtful dissent to the premises sustaining the consensus to go ahead, except that offered by Arthur Schlesinger.[4] By Schlesinger's own account, he was ineffectual in advancing counterarguments at meetings when they might have done the most good. Moreover, Schlesinger seems to have overlooked what later, in the midst of the operation, faced the President: namely, that there was no way of avoiding a direct and obvious and substantial United States military involvement if the objective was to take Cuba away from Castro's forces.[5]

When the President belatedly realized that this indeed was the situation, he quickly regained his perspective and evaluated the remaining options—take on Castro directly, or liquidate the Bay of pigs operation—in terms of their implications for the global balance of power. When viewed in this context, liberated from preoccupation with the tactical factors, he knew what he had to do. He was well aware that he, personally, would be subjected to charges of cowardice, of callous disregard for the lives of the exiles on the beach, and of downright political ineptitude; and that overseas these charges would be directed at the nation as a whole. During those critical hours, Kennedy confided to James Reston and Arthur Schlesinger his conception of where the basic national interest lay. In Schlesinger's account:

Kennedy seemed deeply concerned about the members of the Brigade. They were brave men and patriots; he had put them on the beachhead; and he wanted to save as many as he could. But he did not propose to send in the Marines. Some people, he noted, were arguing that failure would cause irreparable harm, that we had no choice now but to commit United States forces. Kennedy disagreed. Defeat, he said, would be an incident, not a disaster. The test had always been whether the Cuban people would back a revolt against Castro. If they wouldn't, the United States could not by invasion impose a new regime on them. But would not United States prestige suffer if we let the rebellion flicker out? "What is prestige?" Kennedy asked. "Is it the shadow of power or the substance of power? We are going to work on the substance of power. No doubt we will be kicked in the can for the next couple of weeks, but that won't affect the main business."[6]

The main business—the substance of power—what was it? The main business was still, as it had been since the days of the Truman

Doctrine, preventing extensions of Communist control that would constitute a significant change in the global balance of power, while containing Communism, if at all possible, without a major war. The U.S. would risk war, even the survival of the United States itself, were that necessary to prevent an imbalance of power. But Kennedy, on this score, found himself in complete agreement with Senator Fulbright, who during the planning stages of the operation had protested, "The Castro regime is a thorn in the flesh; but it is not a dagger in the heart."[7] If the thorn could not be extracted with a tweezer it was surely not worth hacking to pieces the tissue of hemispheric relations being nurtured in the Alliance for Progress, nor worth a major diversion of military resources when trouble was brewing in Laos, the Congo, and Berlin. Sorensen recounts the President's calculations:

> "Obviously," he [Kennedy] said later, "if you are going to have United States air cover, you might as well have a complete United States commitment, which would have meant a full-fledged invasion by the United States."
>
> American conventional forces . . . were still below strength, and while an estimated half of our available Army divisions were tied down resisting guerrillas in the Cuban mountains, the Communists could have been on the move in Berlin or elsewhere in the world.

When the failure of the exile brigade demanded presidential action,

> he would not agree to the military-CIA request for the kind of open commitment of American military power that would necessitate, in his view, a full-scale attack by U.S. forces—that, he said, would only weaken our hand in the global fight against Communism over the long run.[8]

The global fight against Communism had been shifting to the new arena of competition for influence over the development process in the Third World. To allow the U.S. to be panicked into a military intervention in the Americas would be playing the stereotyped role of the hated colossus to the north. The real issue, Castro's betrayal of the ideals of the Cuban revolution, would be submerged in the escalation of battle and emotions. And the fragmentation between left and right, giving the Communists their biggest opportunities for exploiting indigenous revolutions, would block the new lines of communication Kennedy was trying to open with progressive reformists in Latin America, Africa, and Asia.

In his address before the American Society of Newspaper Editors on April 20, the President, while taking full responsibility for the disastrous outcome at the Bay of Pigs, tried to direct the nation's attention to the lessons of the episode. It was clearer than ever, he said, that the U.S. faced a relentless struggle in every corner of the globe "in situations which do not permit our own armed intervention":

We dare not fail to see the insidious nature of this new and deeper struggle. We dare not fail to grasp the new concepts, the new tools, the new sense of urgency we will need to combat it—whether in Cuba or South Viet-Nam. And we dare not fail to realize that this struggle is taking place every day without fanfare, in thousands of villages and markets—day and night—and in classrooms all over the globe.

Too long, he said, the U.S. had fixed on traditional military tools for maintaining the balance of power—on armies prepared to cross borders, on missiles poised for flight. "Now it should be clear that this is no longer enough."[9]

THE CUBAN MISSILE CRISIS

The biggest test during Kennedy's presidency was to occur in 1962, again in the Caribbean, still within the sphere of effective control of the United States, but now, according to the Soviets, part of the environment of dynamic change. From the Soviet point of view, there was no reason, in principle, why a Communist regime, aligned with the Soviet Union, should be regarded as an illegitimate penetration into the U.S. sphere of control.

Khrushchev surely must have feared that the President would deliver on his threat to take countermeasures if the global balance of power was being threatened. This is probably why Khrushchev tried to confuse the issue, and to keep his missile deployments to Cuba clandestine.[10] As it turned out, Kennedy had a clearer notion of the intangible *political* components of the balance of power than Khrushchev anticipated. In retrospect, Kennedy characterized the Soviet missile deployment as

an effort to materially change the balance of power . . . not that they were intending to fire them, because if they were going to get into a nuclear struggle, they have their own missiles in the Soviet Union. But it would have politically changed the balance of power. It would have appeared to, and appearances contribute to reality.[11]

Khrushchev must have thought the President would be constrained from taking action once the missiles became operational, and this continued to bother Kennedy:

> What is of concern is the fact that both governments were so far out of contact, really. I don't think that we expected that he would put the missiles in Cuba, because it would have seemed an imprudent action for him to take, as it was later proved. Now, he obviously must have thought that he could do it in secret and that the United States would accept it. So that he did not judge our intentions accurately.[12]

Khrushchev had broken the ground rules. He had not merely penetrated the American sphere of control, but he had done so in a manner that, if it had been allowed to stand, would tip the global balance of power. Kennedy had insisted publicly that the United States could not allow Cuba to become a base for Soviet "offensive" weapons. This drawing of the line in public, as much as the actual military situation created by the Soviet deployments, underlay Kennedy's definition of the deployment as intolerable. To allow Khrushchev to defiantly step over the line would have been to appear impotent against the Soviets' attempts to do as they pleased. This "appearance" would have "politically changed the balance of power."

The administration seemed to fear that the consequences of such a change in the balance of power would be felt first in a new Soviet squeeze on Berlin. Khrushchev had lessened the pressure on Berlin the previous year at a time when it became generally known that Soviet missile claims had been greatly inflated and that the United States still possessed overwhelming superiority in intercontinental strategic striking power. The deployment of missiles to Cuba might well appear to redress the balance by extending the Soviet strategic reach, reviving that margin of insurance against a United States strategic response to a Soviet probe in Berlin. Throughout the crisis, Kennedy and his advisers were very much on edge in expectation of Soviet retaliation in Berlin (there was some thought that the symmetry of a blockade for a blockade would appeal to the Russians). Their anxiety was eased somewhat when Khrushchev clearly indicated he would not reopen the Berlin issue until after the November congressional elections, which suggested that he did not feel safe enough to move on Berlin until his missiles became operational. Still Kennedy felt it necessary to warn the Soviets in his October 22 speech that "any hostile move anywhere in the world against the safety and freedom of peoples to whom we are committed, including in particular the people of West Berlin, will be met by whatever action is needed."[13]

Once the missiles were detected there was no question in the President's mind but that they would have to be removed. The question was how to attain their removal at the lowest cost in U.S. and Cuban lives without bringing on a major war with the Soviet Union. To avoid a war, Kennedy believed that the U.S. should not attempt to humiliate Khrushchev.

The notion that Cuban lives and Soviet face ought to constrain any plan of action guided the President in his narrowing of options. However, some of his advisers did not appreciate or share the President's convictions. The course of action that was finally selected, and how the issue of the missiles (and bombers) was resolved, was by no means an inevitable derivation from an analysis of the irreducible national interest, the immediate threat posed by the Soviet deployments, or the balance of military capabilities on both sides.

Experienced presidential advisers came to different conclusions about the actions necessary and most desirable to protect the basic national interest and preserve the balance of power. Consequently, the intensive dialogue conducted by the President and his advisers during the period October 16–28, 1962 heightened the administration's self-awareness of the sometimes conflicting premises of power underlying its foreign policy, and contributed to the presidential selection and sharpening of those premises that would govern administration policy henceforth.

One consideration the President found he could not ignore, but which was easier for some of his advisers to bypass, was the moral character of U.S. actions.

The arguments for restraint because of moral considerations were presented most strongly by George Ball and Robert Kennedy in opposing an air strike against the missiles—the option favored at first by most of Kennedy's special executive committee, including the Joint Chiefs of Staff. Ball argued that, regardless of the military outcome, a surprise attack would be against U.S. national traditions. The Attorney General supported Ball, offering, "My brother is not going to be the Tojo of the 1960's."[14] Sorensen quotes Robert Kennedy as contending passionately that the sudden air strike would be "a Pearl Harbor in reverse, and it would blacken the name of the

United States in the pages of history."[15] To knock out the Cuban missiles and aircraft capable of reaching the United States might mean killing 25,000 Cubans.

This argument stressed the political value of action consistent with the presumed moral expectations of others, as well as the U.S. public. It rested on the premise that the reputation for moral restraint by a great power is an important element of political influence. This line of reasoning apparently swayed a number of influential members of the executive committee. "I had wanted an air strike," recalls Douglas Dillon. "What changed my mind was Bob Kennedy's argument that we ought to be true to ourselves as Americans, that surprise attack was not in our tradition. Frankly, these considerations had not occurred to me until Bobby raised them so eloquently."[16] Robert Kennedy later claimed that the ideas which he voiced were really the President's and attributed them to his brother's "belief in what is right and what is wrong."[17]

But the detailed accounts of the deliberations during the thirteen days of the crisis show the President to have been less absolutely constrained by such an absolutist ethic than his younger brother later claimed.[18] The President was not willing to rule out an air strike, or even an invasion of Cuba, if that were what it would take to effect a removal of the "offensive weapons." His position seems to have been that these more costly actions (calculated in part in moral terms) should not be taken until less costly alternatives had been exhausted. He ultimately settled on the naval "quarantine" on weapons-carrying vessels as the least costly alternative, one that would not, as the first move, prevent him from resorting to the higher cost and higher risk alternatives later. He patiently pursued the objective with means least destructive of human life, even though the objective might be more certainly and swiftly attained by more destructive means.

Such moral and ethical questions were taken very seriously by the President. But it would be a distortion to separate them explicitly from the other considerations that weighed heavily upon him. These considerations can be grouped under his general concern for "controlling the risks."[19]

The biggest risk was to do nothing, to accept the presence of Soviet strategic weapons in Cuba as the new status quo. The Soviets would achieve a tremendous victory on which they would then surely capitalize in Berlin or anywhere else that their objectives came into conflict. They would be prone to miscalculate the strength of U.S. commitments and be tempted to take reckless actions that might compel a response in force, possibly at a level where the ability to keep things under control on either side would be severely destabilized.

If there were high risks in doing nothing, there were also high risks in reacting too massively. The White House was not afraid of a "rational" Khrushchev, but a Khrushchev forced to eat humble pie in public was a dangerous unknown. It was important to show the Soviets that the U.S. had the capability and the will to forcibly remove their local threat to U.S. security if necessary, as well as to provide a less-humiliating option than retreat under a public ultimatum. Nor was it desirable to put Khrushchev's pledge to protect Castro to the test by actually invading Cuba. The choices narrowed rather quickly, therefore, to either the naval blockade or to air strikes. Air strikes were finally abandoned by the President as an initial response, though not ruled out as the next step if the blockade failed. The President's reasons, according to Abel, Sorensen, and Schlesinger—which he expressed to his assembled group of advisers[20]—were primarily based on the immediate risks of air strikes as opposed to the naval blockade. Thus, in Abel's account of the final review of the alternatives, on October 21:

The President asked General Walter C. Sweeney, Commander of the Tactical Air Force, whether he could be certain that an air strike would take out all the Soviet missiles at one stroke. Sweeney replied that it should be possible to destroy some 90 per cent of them, though he could not guarantee 100 per cent effectiveness. A clean surgical operation, in short, was a military impossibility. The plan called for bombing Castro's military airports, as well as the missile bases, and several of these were in populated areas. Haunted by the thought that thousands of Cuban civilians might be killed, in addition to the Russians manning the missile sites, Kennedy once again vetoed the air strike. Even if only 10 per cent of the missile sites were to survive, he reasoned, they might be fired against the United States.[21]

The blockade, by contrast, offered Khrushchev the choice of avoiding an immediate military clash by merely keeping his ships away. This would not settle the matter of the missiles already there, but it would, without a direct engagement, establish firmly the U.S. intention to maintain control in the Caribbean. Khrushchev could stall, but once he failed to challenging the blockade, the reality of

U.S. power would have been recognized. If Khrushchev under these circumstances were to make concessions, they would be a temporary acceptance of present realities, a tolerable posture for a Bolshevik; not a humiliating and irreversible defeat.

The strongest public remarks to Khrushchev were made in the President's dramatic October 22 radio-television address, divulging the fact that he knew the Soviet missiles were in Cuba, and outlining his initial low-level response. The only specific reference to a higher level military response was in connection with the hypothetical contingency of an actual launching of nuclear missiles from Cuban soil: "It shall be the policy of this Nation to regard any nuclear missile launched from Cuba against any nation in the Western Hemisphere as an attack by the Soviet Union on the United States, requiring a full retaliatory response upon the Soviet Union."[22] Kennedy made a deliberately vague reference to further action in addition to the blockade, if the missile preparations in Cuba continued, but nothing even approaching an ultimatum. Only through private channels was an ultimatum offered; and, only in conjunction with public acceptance of the formula: you remove the weapons under UN supervision and we will give assurances against invasion. When Robert Kennedy, at the request of the President, handed a copy of this formula to the Soviet ambassador, he accompanied it with a very tough oral message: the point of escalation was at hand. Unless the President received immediate notice that the missiles would be withdrawn, the U.S. was in a position to take strong and overwhelming retaliatory action.[23] That was on Saturday, October 27, six days after the President's address demanding the removal of the missiles, one day after the receipt of the emotional and surprisingly contrite secret letter from Khrushchev, and only hours after a second, stronger Khrushchev letter was broadcast to the entire world.

There had still been no real confrontation. The installation of the missile sites in Cuba, from components already there, continued at a rapid pace. The naval quarantine was in force, but both sides had avoided a clear test: the President had taken his time in actually implementing the blockade. Thursday morning, October 25, the Navy hailed a Soviet tanker and Kennedy ordered it to be passed through without inspection, allowing for the possibility that the ship had not yet received its instructions from Moscow.[24] The Soviet cargo ships with their submarine escorts were to arrive Friday. The

Navy was urging the President to intercept the Soviets far out into the ocean before they reached the Caribbean. But, backed by McNamara, he insisted that Khrushchev be given all possible time to communicate with his ships. The President did, however, stop a ship to symbolically show his resolve: a dry-cargo freighter owned by a Panamanian company, Lebanese registered with a Greek crew, but sailing under a Soviet charter, was halted and boarded at dawn Friday, found to be carrying only trucks and spare parts, and allowed to pass.[25] The Soviets stopped the progress of their cargo ships, and had actually turned them back toward home port by Friday. But would they stop work on the missiles already in Cuba? And, once these were operational, would the Soviet Navy sail toward Cuba more confidently? Or would the Communists invoke a counterblockade around Berlin, where they had tactical superiority? As the President dispatched his brother with his final private ultimatum to Khrushchev, these doubts remained intense. Still, Kennedy stood his ground, and refused to be stampeded into the tempting chest-thumping postures urged by some advisers.

Even after the Soviets agreed to dismantle the missiles in return for a U.S. pledge not to invade Cuba and a secret agreement to dismantle the obsolete U.S. missiles in Turkey,* Kennedy insisted, as Sorensen describes it, that there was to be

no blasting, no gloating, not even a claim of victory. We had won by enabling Khrushchev to avoid complete humiliation—we should not humiliate him now. If Khrushchev wanted to boast he had won a major concession [no U.S. invasion of Cuba] and proved his peaceful manner, that was the loser's prerogative.[26]

It is tempting to overdefine the resolution of the Cuban missile crisis as having reestablished clarity concerning the spheres in which each superpower exercised effective control. The Soviets were kept from establishing an offensive military base in the Western hemisphere. But Castro was not about to accept anything like "normaliza-

---

*President Kennedy overruled most of his advisers in conceding to Khrushchev's demand that the missiles in Turkey be removed. Moreover, he was even prepared to publicly accept the Turkey-for-Cuba trade—despite the doubts this might raise in NATO concerning U.S. commitments—if Khrushchev objected to keeping the deal secret. See transcript of Executive Committee meeting, October 27, 1962. Laurence Chang and Peter Kornbluh, eds., *The Cuban Missile Crisis, 1962* (New York: New Press, 1992), pp. 200–220; and Michael R. Beschloss, *The Crisis Years: Kennedy and Khrushchev 1960–1963* (New York: Harper Collins, 1991), p. 538.

tion" of relations with the neighboring superpower. Castro would not even allow the UN to verify the dismantling of the Soviet missile sites, a condition of the U.S. no-invasion pledge. For three weeks Castro balked at returning to the Soviets their Ilyushin-28 bombers which were within range of the United States. This, not the inspection issue, became the outstanding problem between the United States and the Soviets. When finally the Soviets persuaded Castro to give up the bombers also, Kennedy lifted the naval quarantine, and talked in public with the Soviets as if the crisis was completely resolved. Thus the Soviets could portray the outcome as establishing the legitimacy of the Castro regime, thanks to the Soviet missile ploy.

The United States never explicitly affirmed the no-invasion pledge, but neither did it deny feeling bound by it as a tacit agreement. Indeed, many U.S. actions and statements henceforth suggested that if only Castro would pledge not to export his revolution to other Latin American countries, the U.S. would be prepared to establish normal relations with Cuba again, despite the fact that it was a Communist regime and an ally of the Soviet Union.

Ambiguity remained, but the lines held, and had weathered their most serious threat. Future attempts at interpenetration of one another's sphere would be more subtle and far below the threshold of direct challenge to the other's military dominance in areas of traditional hegemony.

Also—as would materialize in the context of the nuclear test ban negotiations—there could be mutual agreement to refrain from actions, symbolic or material, designed to significantly alter the existing balance of coercive power.

11

BERLIN AGAIN

West Berlin . . . has now become—as never before—the great testing place of Western courage and will, a focal point where our solemn commitments, stretching back over the years to 1945, and Soviet ambitions now meet in basic confrontation.

—JOHN F. KENNEDY

On the issues of Berlin and the missiles in Cuba President Kennedy displayed most clearly his appreciation of the central function played by military power as an arbiter of conflicting goals and wills in international relations. These two crises also indicated the gap between the reality of a bipolar organization of effective power in the international system and the hope for a pluralistic world based on self-determination. Berlin and Cuba compelled Kennedy, at least temporarily, to renew the bipolar basis for coping with the fierce conflicts in a world armed with nuclear power and without a central system of law and order. He could still hope that such a two-sided balance of power, sustained by each superpower's fear of the other's military prowess, could become the basis for a more peaceful phase of competition between the Communists and non-Communists. A period of peaceful competition based on well-defined and mutually respected spheres of control, might eventually lead to depreciation of military power as the currency behind most international transactions, and to a less rigid international order.

The few United States official statements on Berlin in early 1961 conveyed a stiffer posture on Berlin and Germany than had been displayed by the Eisenhower administration during the previous round of negotiations in 1959 (see Chapter 7). In the city, on March 8, 1961, Averell Harriman, the President's roving ambassador, explicitly disassociated the new administration from the Eisenhower administration's concessionary proposals. "All discussions on Berlin," he said, "must begin from the start."[1] At the same time Kennedy, through Ambassador Llewellyn Thompson, sent a personal note to Premier Khrushchev suggesting a meeting between the two leaders to clear the air—not for purposes of negotiation, but rather for each side to better understand the other's basic commitments so as to remove any chance of miscalculations that might lead to war.

At the Vienna Summit (June 3–5, 1961), the Soviet Premier was very tough on Berlin, using language close to the tone of an ultimatum: a peace treaty recognizing East German jurisdiction over access to Berlin would be signed in December and wartime occupation rights would be ended. If the West tried to violate the sovereign rights of the Ulbricht regime, force would be met with force. It was up to the United States to choose whether there would be war or peace.[2] At the close of their talks, Kennedy was handed an official Soviet *aide-mémoire,* somewhat less belligerent in tone, but clearly heralding a resumption of the Berlin conflict.

The *aide-mémoire* called for the immediate convening of a peace conference to "formally recognize the situation which has developed in Europe after the war, to legalize and consolidate the inviolability of existing German borders, [and] to normalize the situation in West Berlin." In the interests of achieving rapid agreement, it would not be necessary to tie the conclusion of a peace treaty to the formal recognition of the German Democratic Republic or the Federal Republic of Germany by all parties to the treaty. If the United States was not prepared to sign a joint peace treaty with the two Germanys, a settlement could be achieved on the basis of two separate treaties. But the peace treaty, or treaties, would have to contain the same kind of provisions on the most important points of a peaceful settlement.

The most important points, the Soviets made clear, involved the status of West Berlin. At present, "the Soviet Government does not see a better way to solve the West Berlin problem than by transforming it into a demilitarized free city." This "free city" of West

Berlin (East Berlin by implication would remain under the complete
control of the GDR) would have

unobstructed contacts with the outside world and . . . its internal regulations
should be determined by the freely expressed will of its population. . . . Token
troop contingents of the United States, the Untied Kingdom, France, and the
U.S.S.R. could be stationed in West Berlin as guarantees of the free city.

This would mean "putting an end to the occupation regime in West
Berlin, with all its implications": namely, the peace treaty or treaties
which provided for the new status of West Berlin would establish
clearly that any questions relating to "communication by land, water
or air within the territory of the G.D.R. would have to be settled
solely by appropriate agreements with the G.D.R."[3]

The Soviets were proposing, in short, an agreement to legitimize
the division of Germany, with East Berlin under the complete authority of the Ulbricht regime and West Berlin an international city.
The Soviets and their allies would be given as much control over the
administration of West Berlin as the United States and its allies.
Access to this international city—located within East Germany—
would be controlled by the East German government. Agreement
would have been to capitulate to the essence of the demands Khrushchev had been making with respect to Germany since 1958.

Why was Khrushchev renewing these demands with such vigor
and confidence now? This question bothered President Kennedy and
his associates in their post mortems on the Vienna conference. Were
the Soviets emboldened by perceptions that the strategic nuclear
balance was such as to make Communist local military superiority in
Central Europe the only relevant factor of power? Had the Bay of
Pigs adventure and Kennedy's backing away from a superpower
showdown over Laos given Khrushchev the impression that the
United States would be the first to swerve off a collision course?

The President, in his discussions with the Soviet Premier at
Vienna, may have sensed that Khrushchev might underestimate the
Kennedy resolve and nerve under pressure. Kennedy was careful to
choose the words and demeanor to disabuse him of such notions.
Sorensen and Schlesinger both recount Kennedy's response to
Khrushchev's insistence that the decision to change the occupation
status of West Berlin by December was irrevocable, whether the
United States agreed or not. If that was the case, retorted the
President, "it will be a cold winter."

The President's instincts were to open up the Berlin issue to a wide set of alternatives, and for the United States to set the terms of reference, rather than always reacting to Soviet proposals. But he was unwilling to enter into negotiations with only the increasingly unbelievable "trip wire" military posture in Western Europe to back him up. Accordingly, he put his foreign policy advisers, including elder statesman Acheson, to work on developing an expanded list of political options while he put the Defense Department to work on increasing his military options.

His advisers found it easier to be creative when proposing military measures than when proposing political approaches. The State Department, designed more to implement and reiterate established policy premises than to generate new ones, responded characteristically: it took exasperatingly long, but it came up eventually with a statement of the U.S. position on Berlin which turned out to be little more than a marginally updated amalgam of positions developed in the 1950s. Acheson's proposals had more substance but were also designed primarily for strengthening the U.S. hand in the status quo, rather than changing the status quo. Backed by Vice President Johnson, Acheson urged a presidential proclamation of national emergency accompanied by an immediate expansion of military manpower, including the calling up of reserves, a $5 billion increase in the defense budget, plus new taxation and standby controls on wages and prices. Openly preparing the nation for the worst and visibly making the economy ready for war would demonstrate to Khrushchev, more starkly than any manipulation of U.S. military capabilities in the vicinity of Berlin, that current Soviet threats were merely stimulating the U.S. to enhance its commitments and to more thoroughly involve the national honor in those commitments.

Acheson's national emergency package was opposed by powerful voices within the administration. Walter Heller and the Council of Economic Advisers were strongly against a tax increase and argued that there was a real danger of serious inflation resulting from the scare buying that would accompany the proclamation of emergency. Heads of the domestic departments were wary of the effects on civilian welfare programs. McNamara, Rusk and even reputedly "tough" White House advisers like Henry Kissinger warned against unnecessarily bellicose reactions which, rather than indicating unflinching resolve, might convey hysteria. Others were concerned that an overemphasis on the Berlin confrontation by measures such as the proclamation might induce Khrushchev, for considerations of his own prestige, to respond in kind with arms increases and menacing postures in preparation for a showdown.

Kennedy rejected the suggestion for an immediate declaration of national emergency, but incorporated some of the major premises underlying the Acheson proposals into his own planning. He knew that words were not enough to dissuade the Soviets. The military increase that the President had already ordered as part of his program for remedying the nation's military deficiencies would be accelerated under the impetus of the Berlin crisis to convince Khrushchev that his bluster could lead only to the firming up of U.S. resolve. The President did not unequivocally reject the more extreme suggestions of a large-scale mobilization and a declaration of national emergency. These might yet have to be used; but not so early in the crisis. The grand strategy should be the classical one of arming to parley; the U.S. *wanted* the parley, in an atmosphere conducive to calm deliberation on terribly complicated conflicts of interest. Showdowns could only revive the simplifications of the cold war, and possibly lead to hot war.

The President's television address on July 25 was designed to be both very tough and more reasonable than previous United States statements on the Berlin issue. The non-Communist presence in West Berlin, and access thereto, could not be ended by any act of the Soviet government, the President told the world. It would be a mistake to consider Berlin, because of its location, as a tempting target: "I hear it said that West Berlin is militarily untenable. And so was Bastogne. And so, in fact, was Stalingrad. Any dangerous spot is tenable if men—brave men—will make it so." The city had become "the greatest testing place of Western courage and will, a focal point where our solemn commitments . . . and Soviet ambitions now meet in basic confrontation." Berlin was no less protected than the rest of the West, "for we cannot separate its safety from our own."

He warned the Soviets not to make the dangerous but common mistake of assuming that the West was too soft, too divided in the pursuit of narrow national interests, to fight to preserve its objectives in Berlin. Too much was at stake for the alliance as a whole: "For the fulfillment of our pledge to that city is essential to the morale and security of Western Germany, to the unity of Western Europe, and the faith of the entire Free World . . . in . . . our willingness to meet our commitments."

Accordingly, in addition to the supplementary defense buildup the President had asked the Congress to approve in March, he was now asking for $3.25 billion more—most of it to be spent on the capability-in-being to deploy rapidly to the Central European front without weakening the U.S. ability to meet commitments elsewhere. The measures included a tripling of the draft calls for the coming months, the ordering up of certain reserve and National Guard units, the reactivation of many deactivated planes and ships, and a major acceleration in the procurement of nonnuclear weapons.

The President wanted to make it clear that "while we will not let panic shape our policy," he was contemplating still more dramatic steps if the situation required them:

in the days and months ahead, I shall not hesitate to ask the Congress for additional measures, or exercise any of the executive powers that I possess to meet this threat to peace. . . . and if that should require more men, or more taxes, or more controls, or other new powers, I shall not hesitate to ask them.

He did however request one additional item, separated from the others in his text, and related more to the overall preparedness of the nation than to the Berlin crisis. This item—his request for a special appropriation of $207 million for a Civil Defense shelter program—came close to creating that national atmosphere of "panic" and overreaction likely to interfere with his efforts to direct attention toward political alternatives and away from military posturing.

Most of what followed this section in the July 25 address was anticlimactic—reversing the emphasis he had intended. The press played up the military measures, including the Civil Defense program, but gave scant attention to his offer "to consider any arrangement or treaty in Germany consistent with the maintenance of peace and freedom, and the legitimate security interests of all nations." The very carefully worded elaboration of this offer was all but ignored in news summaries:

We recognize the Soviet Union's historical concern about their security in Central and Eastern Europe, after a series of ravaging invasions, and we believe arrangements can be worked out which will help to meet these concerns, and make it possible for both security and freedom to exist in this troubled area.

He had said that he was "ready to search for peace in quiet exploratory talks—in formal or informal meetings," but the noisier measures got the headlines in the United States.[4] And these measures dominated Khrushchev's reaction to the President's speech.

Khrushchev, discussing disarmament issues with John J. McCloy, told McCloy in emotional tones that he was angered by the President's speech and professed to find in it only an ultimatum akin to a preliminary declaration of war.

By this time, however, the flow of refugees from East Berlin to West Berlin was seriously damaging Soviet prestige and the manpower resources of East Germany. Khrushchev may have welcomed an atmosphere of imminent explosion as the context for his sealing of the boundary between East and West Berlin just three weeks after the Kennedy address.

On August 7, the Soviet Premier delivered one of the most belligerent speeches of his career, linking "military hysteria" in the United States with an "orgy of revanchist passions" in West Germany, and warning the West against any intervention under the illusion that there could be a limited war over Berlin. Khrushchev, bestowing honors on Cosmonaut Titov, used the occasion to make pointed allusions to the strategic power of the Soviet Union. "Any state used as a springboard for an attack upon the Socialist camp will experience the full devastating power of our blow." The territory of the United States would be crushed. Intervention, an act of war by the West, would be a suicidal act, spelling "death to millions upon millions of people."[5]

When East Berlin was sealed six days later, the specter of thermonuclear holocaust had already been projected. The next move was up to the United States. The U.S. could accept the Soviet claim of acting to stabilize and bottle up the combustible passions on both sides of the boundary to within controllable confines. Or the U.S. could define it as a unilateral abrogation of established four-power responsibility for the city as a whole and a shameless denial of free choice to the Berliners, thus placing it into that category of action the President insisted had to be resisted. Khrushchev was gambling on the vividness of the nuclear backdrop as the main barrier to Western action. The "wall" at first consisted of double strands of barbed wire and other light barricades, backed up by elements of a motorized division of the East German Army at critical crossing points. Western counteraction could have taken the form of a symbolic cutting of the wire, or pushing over of some obstacles. It need not have involved anything as dramatic as a bull-dozing operation with tanks and cannon; and the next move would have been up to the Soviets. Khrushchev still had many options. His gamble, of course, was that the West would not "overreact."

The Soviets launched a well-planned diplomatic campaign, calculated to provide the Western nations with a convincing political excuse for doing nothing. On August 13, the Warsaw Pact countries issued a declaration against "subversive activities directed from West Berlin" against the "socialist countries." The pact members accordingly requested the East Germans

to establish an order on the borders of West Berlin which will securely block the way to the subversive activity . . . so that reliable safeguards and effective control can be established around the whole territory of West Berlin, including its border with democratic Berlin.

And then, in a deft attempt at limiting the issue: "It goes without saying that these measures must not affect existing provisions for traffic control on communications routes between West Berlin and West Germany."[6]

The Ulbricht regime, in its implementing decree issued on the same day, emphasized the point again: "As regards the traveling of West Berlin citizens abroad along the communications lines in the German Democratic Republic, former decisions remain valid." The decree stated explicitly that no former decisions on transit along these routes were being revised.

On the afternoon of August 13, the United States Secretary of State, after checking with the President at Hyannisport, issued a statement which, however causticly, signaled that the United States had gotten the message:

Having denied the collective right of self-determination to the peoples of East Germany, Communist authorities are now denying the right of individuals to elect a world of free choice rather than a world of coercion. The pretense that communism desires only peaceful competition is exposed: the refugees . . . have "voted with their feet" on whether communism is the wave of the future.

Available information indicates that *measures taken thus far are aimed at residents of East Berlin and East Germany and not at the Allied position in West Berlin or access thereto.*. (Emphasis added.)[7]

Rusk did claim that restrictions on travel between East Germany and Berlin directly contravened the 1949 four-power agreements (signed at the conclusion of the Berlin blockade) and indicated that diplomatic protests would be forthcoming. But there was no hint that the unilateral imposition of barriers across the city might constitute a fighting issue. Although many in the West were shocked and outraged at the Communist action, the West Berlin leaders who had foreseen the wall in the writing, as it were, felt themselves helpless and suddenly demoralized. Even Chancellor Adenauer was silent at first.

Kennedy sought advice from advisers at home and abroad, and found a solid consensus that there was not much he could do apart from issuing verbal protests. Sorensen recounts that "not one responsible official in the country, in West Berlin, West Germany, or Western Europe—suggested that allied forces should march into East German territory and tear the Wall down."[8] The mayor of Berlin, Willy Brandt, in a personal letter to President Kennedy, demanded retaliatory actions such as a selective ban on imports from East Germany, a refusal to issue travel permits to East German officials, and the takeover of the portion of the elevated railroad system in West Berlin that was still administered by the East. He also called for special actions to demonstrate renewed support by the United States for the West Berliners, many of whom felt that the West's failure to prevent the erection of the wall meant that the balance had been tipped in the Soviets' favor and it was only a matter of time before the noose was tightened around the entire city. From the symbolic actions suggested by Brandt, four were adopted by the White House during the next few days.

• the reinforcement of the allied garrison in West Berlin;
• the appointment of General Lucius Clay as the American commandant;
• the movement of allied troops along the Autobahn into West Berlin to demonstrate the continuing rights of Western access;
• the dispatch of Vice President Johnson to the city.

The wall remained and was reinforced with bricks and mortar. In a number of incidents refugees trying to escape were brutally mistreated. A confrontation between Soviet and American tanks across the barriers, was among the rather daring demonstrations of resolve by General Clay.[9] West Berlin remained Western and the allies continued to exercise their rights of access to the city while refusing to grant recognition to the East German regime. December 1961 came and went and the Soviets refrained from carrying out the unilateral actions threatened in their July *aide-mémoire.*

The situation seemed to be settling down to an uneasy, but basically stable, equilibrium, based on what now could be tacitly recognized as more clearly defined spheres of effective control. Meanwhile, the "search for peace—in quiet exploratory talks" that Kennedy had called for in his July address got underway in the form of periodic meetings between Secretary Rusk and Soviet Foreign Minister Gromyko, and the Soviet and American ambassadors.

Kennedy was coming to the realization that a major global settlement was probably the necessary correlate of significant "movement" on the German question. As he put it to President Kekkonen of Finland, "Let the Soviet Union keep Germany divided on its present basis and not try to persuade us to associate ourselves legally with that division and thus weaken our ties to West Germany and their ties to Western Europe."[10]

Berlin and the other diplomatic crises of Kennedy's first year could be viewed as tests of the ground rules for coexistence that the President propounded to Khrushchev during their conversations in Vienna: no action by either superpower to alter the existing balance of power and no attempt by either to interfere within the other's sphere of control. At Vienna there seemed to be mutual agreement to these ground rules in principle, but considerable differences over how they might apply in practice: there was no objective definition of the balance of power, nor could the President and the Chairman assent unequivocally to the other's definition of legitimate spheres of control. The Berlin conflict was the product of these differences, not the cause. Neither side could agree simply to a maintenance of the "status quo." Moreover, with so many new nations experimenting with various types of regimes and still determining their international interests and inclinations, there was not even a de facto status quo in the Third World. Consequently a series of tests in a volatile environment would determine who had effective power over what, and where, at any one time, the spheres of control lay.

12

THE VIETNAM QUAGMIRE

The picture of the world's greatest superpower killing or seriously injuring 1,000 non-combatants a week, while trying to pound a tiny backward nation into submission on an issue whose merits are hotly disputed, is not a pretty one.

—ROBERT MCNAMARA

Arthur Schlesinger, Jr., adviser to and sympathetic biographer of the Kennedys, and a critic of President Johnson's policies in Vietnam, claims that "Kennedy had no intention of dispatching American ground forces to save South Vietnam." Schlesinger argues that President Kennedy's 1962 instruction to Secretary of Defense McNamara to start planning for a phased withdrawal of U.S. military personnel from Vietnam, originally only a precautionary contingency plan, "was turning in 1963 into a preference."[1]

Kennedy's serious contemplation of a U.S. withdrawal was the product of his growing disillusion with the policies of the Diem regime in Saigon—especially Diem's ruthless suppression of the civil liberties of opponents, including the jailing of prominent Buddhist leaders. "In the final analysis it's their war," said Kennedy in September 1963, reserving his option to scale U.S. assistance up or down depending upon the extent to which the Diem government demonstrated the political as well as the military capability of sustaining its counterinsurgency effort. "We can help them, we can give them equipment, we can send our men there as advisers, but they have to win it—the people of Viet Nam—against the Communists."[2]

But the option of withdrawal was effectively removed three weeks before Kennedy's death when the U.S. ambassador, Henry Cabot Lodge, and other U.S. officials in Saigon cooperated with anti-Diem elements in the South Vietnamese military who engineered the November 1, 1963, coup in which Diem and his brother Ngo Dinh Nhu were deposed and murdered.[3] Top officials of the U.S. government, although not directly responsible for the coup or the murder of the Diems, felt, like traditional imperialists, implicated in the fate of their wards. After the coup there could be no question of a U.S. pullout, at least not until the regime, with augmented U.S. help, was given a chance to put the counterinsurgency effort back on track.

This was the situation Lyndon Johnson inherited on November 22, 1963, as he assumed the presidency after the assassination of John Kennedy. Until the Gulf of Tonkin crisis of August 1964, Johnson left the direction of Vietnam policy largely in the hands of Secretary of Defense McNamara; but he did approve National Security Action Memorandum 288, authorizing preparations by the U.S. military "to be in a position on 72 hours' notice to initiate . . . Retaliatory Actions against North Vietnam, and to be in a position on 30 days' notice to initiate the program of 'Graduated Overt Military Pressure' against North Vietnam."[4] The President also approved, on McNamara's recommendation, stepped-up covert operations under Operations Plan 34-A, including intelligence collection and graduated "destructive undertakings" against North Vietnam. The 34-A operations, conducted with increasing intensity during the spring and summer of 1964, included commando raids by mercenaries hired by the South Vietnamese to blow up rail and highway bridges and coastal installations north of the 17th parallel, raids by Laotian-marked T-28 fighter-bombers on North Vietnamese and Pathet Lao troop concentrations in Laos, and U.S. naval intelligence-gathering patrols off the coast of North Vietnam.[5]

The clash in the Gulf of Tonkin in the first week of August 1964, which resulted in the first overt U.S. military action in the Vietnam War and the famous Gulf of Tonkin Resolution that set the stage for the subsequent heavy U.S. intervention, was precipitated by the 34-A covert operations. At the time of an amphibious commando raid against a group of coastal North Vietnam islands, the U.S. destroyer *Maddox* was in the area on an electronic intelligence-gathering mission and the North Vietnamese evidently believed it to have been part of the coastal harassment operation. On August 2, when according to Pentagon testimony the *Maddox* was 23 miles from the coast and heading further into international waters, three North Vietnamese torpedo boats began a run at her. The *Maddox* sunk one of the PT boats with a direct hit from its five-inch guns, and the other two were damaged by aircraft from the carrier *Ticonderoga*, crusing to the south of the encounter.

President Johnson ordered another destroyer, the C. *Turner Joy*, to accompany the *Maddox* back into the Gulf of Tonkin up to 11 nautical miles from the North Vietnamese coast and ordered a second aircraft carrier, the *Constellation*, to join the *Ticonderoga* to provide additional air cover. Plans were readied to bomb North Vietnam in the event of another attack on U.S. ships, and the administration dusted off a draft congressional resolution that it had prepared in May to gain legislative support for a commitment of U.S. armed forces to the Indochina conflict.

On August 4, North Vietnamese torpedo boats again made a run at the U.S. naval deployments. In response, in missions approved by the President, U.S. fighter-bombers from the *Ticonderoga* and *Constellation* struck four torpedo boat bases and an oil storage depot in North Vietnam. Johnson met with leaders of the Congress to inform them of his decision to retaliate against North Vietnam for what he claimed was an unprovoked attack against U.S. ships and to enlist their support in passing the Gulf of Tonkin Resolution.[6]

On August 7, by a vote of 88 to 2 in the Senate and 416 to 0 in the House, Congress resolved to "approve and support the determination of the President, as Commander in Chief, to take all necessary measures to repel any armed attack against the forces of the United States and to prevent further aggression"; and declared that "the United States is . . . prepared, as the President determines, to take all necessary steps, including the use of armed force, to assist any member or protocol state of the Southeast Asia Collective Defense Treaty requesting assistance in defense of its freedom."[7]

The ingredients were now in place for major, direct U.S. military intervention into the war in Southeast Asia. Detailed scenarios for systematic bombing of North Vietnam had been developed in the Pentagon. All that was needed was another attack on U.S. forces, either at sea or upon U.S. military bases in South Vietnam, or a formal request for military intervention from the government of South Vietnam, for the President to feel that he was acting legitimately—with the advice and consent of the Congress—in making the United States an active fighting ally of South Vietnam.

Although many of Johnson's political-military advisers were unhappy with the presidential restraint, he was not about to be stampeded into a war that now looked almost inevitable, until he had first validated his own mandate in the presidential elections of 1964—particularly as his election victory would be best assured by making his Republican opponent, Barry Goldwater, appear to be the "warmonger." It was the Republicans, he charged, who were "eager to enlarge the conflict." "They call upon us to supply American boys to do the job that Asian boys should do."[8] As far as he was concerned, said the President,

I want to be very cautious and careful, and use it only as a last resort, when I start dripping bombs around that are likely to involve American boys in a war in Asia with 700,000,000 Chinese. So just for the moment I have not thought that we were ready for American boys to do the fighting for Asian boys.[9]

During the windup of the election campaign, he reiterated unequivocally, "We are not going to send American boys nine or ten thousand miles away to do what Asian boys ought to be doing for themselves."[10]

Even when the Vietcong, on November 1, 1964, in a surprise attack on the Bien Hao air base, killed five Americans, wounded seventy-six, and destroyed six B-57 bombers, Johnson continued to adhere to the escalation restraints, despite the view of principal administration foreign policy experts that the Bien Hao attack was at least as serious as the Gulf of Tonkin incident and therefore deserved a military reply.

Only after the 1964 election Johnson established as policy the premise that the Vietnam conflict was the current flash point of the global conflict between the Communist and non-Communist worlds—the major corollary being that as leader of the non-Communist side the United States had to assume full responsibility for assuring that the Communists did not win. The American commitment, the price the nation would be willing to pay, was unqualified and open-ended. The implications began to be revealed in a series of events and decisions during the first half of 1965.

On February 7 United States fighter-bombers made a reprisal raid on North Vietnamese military barracks north of the 17th parallel in response to Vietcong mortar attacks on United States installations earlier in the day, including the Pleiku airstrip, where 7 Americans were killed, 109 wounded, and at least 20 aircraft were destroyed or damaged. The U.S. had every reason to believe, McNamara explained to reporters, "that the attack on Pleiku, Tuyhoa, and Nhatrang was ordered and directed and masterminded directly from Hanoi." Under Secretary of State George Ball backed him up in the joint press conference on the day of the raids. There is no question, said the diplomat (reputed to be the leading administration "dove" on Vietnam), that "this was a deliberate, overt attempt by the regime in Hanoi to test the will of the South Vietnamese Government . . . and the Government of the United States." This was a situation in which "we could not fail to respond without giving a misleading signal to the . . . regime in Hanoi" as to the strength of American purpose.[11]

The basis for the administration's conviction that Hanoi was masterminding the campaign in the South was further elaborated on February 28, when the State Department issued its White Paper entitled "Aggression form the North: The Record of North Vietnam's Campaign To Conquer South Vietnam."[12] The sixty-four-page text, released to all news media, claimed to contain "massive evidence of North Vietnamese aggression." It did document an increase, especially during 1964, of military aid from the North in the form of weapons and key advisory personnel; but it was certainly no more massive than the increase in U.S. "supporting assistance" to Saigon during the same period.

Hanoi used the increasing American involvement as its justification for increasing its infiltration into the South. And the U.S. government pointed to the evidence of this increasing infiltration as the reason for bringing coercive pressure upon Hanoi and dispatching more men and materials to South Vietnam to redress the deteriorating military balance.

At Kennedy's death Johnson had inherited an American "advisory" force in Vietnam numbering somewhat short of 16,500. By August 1965, before the impact of the major increments ordered that year had been felt, there are already about 125,000 U.S. troops in the field. And decisions made in 1965 and 1966 meant that, barring a political settlement, the number of United States military personnel in South Vietnam could exceed half a million sometime in 1967.

The shift in the mission of these U.S. troops from "advisers" to the main offensive force also occurred between 1963 and 1966. U.S. advice to the South Vietnamese to make extensive use of helicopters for reconnaissance, troop support, and troop transport required, at the outset, training and maintenance bases staffed by Americans. But these bases also required protection (they were obvious targets for the Vietcong). When the South Vietnamese proved incapable of providing the kind of security needed, contingents of U.S. Marines were called to help, and eventually to take over, the base security role. The United States became, willy-nilly, an active co-belligerent, albeit only in "defensive" situations. The next step, as Communist military units and firepower increased, was to expand the perimeters of security of U.S. bases. The actual operations involved in expanding the perimeters were the same as they would be in offensive combat missions. What was indistinguishable in operations easily became indistinguishable in purpose, and the U.S. drifted into full participation in the "clear and hold" missions designed to reduce the proportion of South Vietnamese territory controlled by the Vietcong. Finally, as political instability in Saigon diverted the South Vietnamese military to political tasks including the suppression of Buddhist civil disobedience, the United States found itself the dominant combat force in the Vietnam War.

When Johnson took the situation under intense scrutiny in late 1964, he found the commitments already entered into and the deployments already underway. To fail to approve the increased deployments now being asked for by the Secretary of Defense would be to fail to rectify the deteriorating military situation—it would mean accepting a humiliating military defeat. On the other hand, the increases in infiltration from North Vietnam, which paralleled the increased U.S. involvement during the previous year, gave little hope that the increases in American troops would accomplish anything more than drive the ground war to higher levels of intensity.

From what is known of Johnson-the-political-animal, it would be surprising to find that he would allow himself to be trapped into presiding over a slow war of human attrition on the Asian mainland and the long test of endurance it required. For one thing, the U.S. was likely to be hurt more than its adversaries, who (assuming China was drawn in) had a practically unlimited supply of expendable manpower. For another, the 1964 election results convinced Johnson that he embodied the great American consensus for getting on with the job of tending to the national welfare. The people were tired of the foreign entanglements the country had been sustaining since 1947, particularly those like Vietnam, where the connection with U.S. security was complicated and tenuous. Some means would have to be found for bringing a rapid conclusion to this war. Yet Johnson also sensed that the majority of voters were overwhelmingly against Goldwater because he embodied the pugnacious aspect of American nationalism that risked further expenditure of blood and treasure in "confrontations" with adversaries around the globe. Goldwaterism, as the election showed, was just not the dominant temper in 1964.

But here was LBJ, after having successfully made political capital out of Goldwater's pugnacity, ordering the very escalation strategies that Goldwater had been advocating. The contradiction is at least partially resolved by attributing to Johnson-the-electioneer the very real belief that bombing North Vietnam *would* lead to the larger war (possibly through the entry of the Chinese) that he knew the American public did not want. Whereas Johnson-the-Commander-in-Chief, looking in detail at the developing military situation in late 1964, saw that the United States was already heavily implicated in a rapidly expanding ground war which could easily lead to the intolerable and larger Asian land war. Marginal increments to U.S. forces in the South, then being recommended by the military command in Saigon and endorsed by McNamara in Washington, might not be sufficient to convince North Vietnam and China, and possibly even the Soviet Union, that an expansion of their commitments to Vietnam would involve them in a "deeply dangerous game."

But the way the decision to bring the North under aerial attack was announced and implemented obscured the underlying rationale and possibly interfered with its utility as a signal to the Communist powers. The bombing raid across the 17th parallel following the Vietcong attack on Pleiku—like the air strike in response to the Tonkin incident—was defined as a reprisal. The implication was: don't do what you just did or we'll bomb again. But three days later, on February 10, the Vietcong again found their mark. This time a United States billet at Quinhon was blown up, killing 23 Americans. Now three times as many aircraft were used in retaliation, and the targets were further north, but still in the southern part of North Vietnam. It might appear as if the U.S. were trying to establish a let-the-punishment-fit-the-crime pattern, with the crime being attacks on American installations. However, the White House attempted to blur this impression in its comnuniqué of February 11, which cited, in addition to the Quinhon incident, Vietcong ambushes, raids, assassinations, etc., against South Vietnamese personnel and installations as well as against Americans. These "continued acts of aggression by Communist Vietcong under the direction and with the support of the Hanoi regime," said the statements issued from Washington and Saigon, were the reason for the current air strike. This came a bit closer to displaying the central strategic rationale for commencing the bombing—namely, at least an "equalization" of the pain suffered by the North as compared to the suffering caused by their agents in the South, as a way of convincing Ho Chi Minh that if he continued the insurgency the price would henceforth be much higher than it had been. The selection of targets further north and the increase in intensity were also supposed to communicate that the first blows were only a harbinger of much more damaging blows to come. Yet the full explicit announcement of this rationale was evidently thought to sound too much like an "ultimatum," with all the risks that would involve of provoking counterthreats, even by parties not yet involved. Consequently, in the coming months, as bombing of the North became a regular feature of the war, it was increasingly justified on the narrower grounds of its usefulness in "interdicting" the transport of men and material from the North to the South.

As the insurgency and terror in the South continued and the infiltration from the North increased, the administration was criticized heavily by domestic and foreign opponents of the bombing. The United States had expanded the war, putting pressure on the Soviet Union to aid Hanoi with at least air defense equipment, and incurring the risk of an even greater direct clash with the giant Communist powers, and what did it have to show for it? An even higher level of warfare in the South. The flimsy argument that the U.S. had to bomb the North to buttress the shaky authority of each successive military junta in Saigon was even less convincing.

Meanwhile, with no discernible moves by the Communists to scale down their insurgency, the frequency, scale, and type of target the

U.S. were bringing under aerial bombardment were increasing. In this phase of the conflict the U.S. was also using up its fresh options and settling into a pattern of mutual injury, at a higher level of destruction than that of a few weeks before. Hundreds of thousands of American boys were being sent overseas to fight Asian boys, the casualty lists were growing, the costs were in the billions, and still the end was no closer in sight.

Johnson's instinct to break out of the pattern now resulted in a series of flamboyant peace moves. Up to the spring of 1965 it had been his stance (in reply to promptings from de Gaulle, the UN Secretary General, Asian neutrals, and academic polemicists in this country) that there was nothing to negotiate except the cessation of the violent insurgency by the Communists, and—in any case—negotiations would have to follow a bona fide cease-fire. In April 1965 the White House appeared to change its tune, or at least to be willing to play the counterpoint of negotiations and planning for peace against the continuing din of bombs and mortar and the calls for hawks to expand targets in the North. Some pundits suspected this was another Johnsonian ploy of playing off the hawks against the doves to preserve his options for tactical maneuver in the long and messy conflict that now seemed to stretch endlessly ahead. But the ring of sincerity in his Johns Hopkins address lends greater plausibility to the "break-out" hypothesis.

The case for "why we are there" was reiterated, with considerable eloquence, by the President at Hopkins on April 7. There were references to the "deepening shadow of Communist China," presumably the real stage manager of the insurgency in Vietnam. "It is a nation which is helping the forces of violence in almost every continent. The contest in Viet-Nam is part of a wider pattern of aggressive purposes." He invoked the promises made by "every American President" since 1954 "to help South Viet-Nam defend its independence." If the U.S. failed to honor these promises now, around the world, "from Berlin to Thailand," the confidence of people "in the value of an American commitment and in the value of America's word" would be shaken. "The result would be increased unrest and instability, and even wider war." "To withdraw from one battlefield means only to prepare for the next. We must stay in Southeast Asia—as we did in Europe—in the words of the Bible: 'Hitherto shalt thou come, but no further.' " And there was the posture of unflinching resolve: "We will not be defeated. We will not grow tired. We will not withdraw, either openly or under the cloak of meaningless agreement."

But once this is clear, said the President, "it should also be clear that the only path for reasonable men is the path of peaceful settlement." In a surprise formulation he suggested an acceptable outcome and a range of flexibility in negotiating formats—both a thawing from what seemed to be his preexisting frigid stance. The "essentials of any final settlement," he said, were "an independent South Viet-Nam—securely guaranteed and able to shape its own relationships to all others—free from outside interference—tied to no alliance—a military base for no other country."

This was a considerable departure by the White House from its scornful response to de Gaulle's suggestions for a "neutralization" solution. Moreover:

> There may be many ways to this kind of peace: in discussion or negotiation with the governments concerned; in large groups or in small ones; in the reaffirmation of old agreements or their strengthening with new ones.
> And we remain ready with this purpose for unconditional negotiations.

The peace he wanted, insisted the President, ought not to be incompatible with the desires of the North Vietnamese. "They want what their neighbors also desire . . . progress for their country, and an end to the bondage of material misery." Their Communist ideology and alignment with China were evidently not a bar to their peaceful association in regional economic development schemes: "We would hope that North Viet-Nam would take its place in the common effort just as soon as peaceful cooperation is possible."

Meanwhile, work could begin on projects for regional economic development with those nations among whom peaceful cooperation was now possible. The President would ask Congress to contribute a billion-dollar investment to a program of Southeast Asian economic development to be organized initially by UN Secretary General Thant. U.S. participation would be inaugurated by a team headed by Eugene Black. "And I would hope," said Johnson, "that all other industrialized countries, including the Soviet Union, will join in this effort."

These hopes for development and his dreams for an end to war, claimed the President, were deeply rooted in his childhood experiences. Rural electrification had brought cheer to the ordinary people along the Pedernales—was there any reason why it should not bring cheer to the sufferers along the Mekong? That vast river could provide food and water and electricity "on a scale to dwarf even our own TVA."

> We often say how impressive power is. But I do not find it impressive at all. The guns and the bombs, the rockets and the warships, are all symbols of human failure. They protect and cherish. But they are witness to human folly.

> . . .

> Electrification of the countryside—yes, that . . . is impressive.
> A rich harvest in a hungry land is impressive.
> The sight of healthy children in a classroom is impressive.
> These—not mighty arms—are the achievements which the American nation believes to be impressive. And if we are steadfast, the time may come when all other nations will find it so.[13]

Meanwhile, the arms, symbols of human failure and witnesses to human folly, had to be fully committed "to protect what we cherish." During the month of April the pounding of the North intensified, with 1,500 air sorties against military targets recorded.[14] And in the month following the peace overture at Johns Hopkins, 15,000 additional United States combat troops disembarked in South Vietnam, the largest increase yet for any month. The buildup was proceeding apace.

This was precisely the wrong way to get Hanoi to the negotiating table, charged critics at home and abroad. To bargain while under increasing bombardment would look like surrender. Lester Pearson of Canada, Senator Fulbright, and numerous newspaper editors argued for a bombing pause to convince the Communists of America's sincerity. The administration took counsel and decided to give this gambit a try.

From May 12 to May 18 the bombing raids ceased. Hanoi was informed in advance via diplomatic channels that the U.S. would be watching to see if there were "significant reductions" in actions by the Communist military units in South Vietnam. The message suggested that such reciprocal action would allow the U.S. to half its bombing and thus meet what was assumed to be the essential North Vietnamese precondition for beginning peace talks. When the air attacks on the North were resumed on May 18, the administration claimed disappointment that there had been no reaction from the other side.

But the critics were not silenced. Surely six days was not long enough to give Hanoi an opportunity to make a considered assessment of U.S. intentions and arrange for an appropriate response. In June, Secretary Rusk told the Foreign Service Institute that all that the U.S. government received from Hanoi and Peking were denunciations of the pause as a "wornout trick" and a "swindle." Recent reports, he said, contained clear proof that "Hanoi is not even prepared for discussions unless it is accepted in advance that there will be a Communist-dominated government in Saigon."[15] Only in November did the State Department admit it had received a negotiating offer from Hanoi via the French government just a few hours after the six-day May pause ended. The French government is reported to have suggested that the bombings should cease again after the message had been received but apparently the United States government did not regard the response as a sufficiently serious negotiating offer. The administration was now subject to the charge of being deficient in its credibility.[16]

The failure of the North Vietnamese to give a satisfactory response to peace overtures in the spring of 1965 was stressed by the President in his July 28 "this is really war" speech, announcing an immediate 75 percent increase to U.S. fighting strength in Vietnam. Fifteen efforts with the help of forty nations, he said, had been made to attempt to get the "unconditional discussions" started. "But there has been no answer." The U.S. would persist in its efforts to bring about negotiations, but meanwhile it would also persist on the battlefield, if need be, "until death and desolation have led to the same conference table where others could now join us at much smaller cost."[17]

The President was speaking at a time of extremely low morale in Saigon. Another civilian government had fallen on June 11, and Air Vice Marshal Ky had assumed the reigns of power in the face of increasing antigovernment and pro-neutralism agitation by the Buddhists. Support for neutralism, the new military junta announced, would be punishable by death. It was the beginning of a new time of political troubles in Saigon that would consume the energies of the South Vietnamese military while the United States began to assume the major combat functions. "We did not choose to be the guardians at the gate," said the American President, "but there is no one else."[18]

Thus, by the summer of 1965, the full character of the United States political–military involvement in Vietnam had matured and its underlying premises had been revealed:

1. Global balance of power considerations demanded that the United States do all that was required to prevent the Communists from taking over South Vietnam. Failure to honor U.S. commitments to South Vietnam would weaken resistance to Communist expansion all around the globe—a resistance critically dependent upon the belief by the non-Communist societies that the United States, when called upon, would help them to prevail in their anti-Communist struggles.

2. If the Communist insurgency in South Vietnam were not defeated now, the Communist expansionary drive in the less developed countries would likely require a bigger war, possibly closer to America's shores. Vietnam was a test case for the Communist strategy of expanding through "wars of national liberation" in place of a strategy of direct military aggression. If this strategy of disguised aggression by paramilitary means were allowed to succeed, those within the Communist camp who favored the coercive modes of expansion would be vindicated. If this "war of national liberation" were convincingly defeated, however, those within the Communist world who believed in peaceful forms of competitive coexistence would be strengthened.

3. Those directing the insurgency in Vietnam could be induced to call it off only if they were convinced it would cost them too dearly to continue it and that, even with the higher-cost efforts, they would not succeed. The U.S. strategy in Vietnam, therefore, despite its turns and twists, had an underlying consistent objective: to increase the enemy's costs and diminish their prospects of success. Previous failures to adequately convince them (with only *support* of South Vietnam) that their costs would be excessive and their prospects of success very low led to direct U.S. involvement, and this at increasingly higher levels of violence. The administration had no desire to have American soldiers again fight Asians or to widen the war to include the North, but as lower levels of conflict failed to convince the Communists that the United States was determined to frustrate their designs, the administration was compelled to make its determination even clearer.

4. The strategy of steadily increasing the costs to its opponents carried with it the need to increase U.S. human and material costs; thus, American staying power demanded a national consensus without which the President could not get the congressional majorities needed to provision the war.

Consequently, domestic dissent on the involvement in Vietnam became an ingredient in the test of strength and endurance with the enemy. Hanoi, it was feared, would exploit America's desires to negotiate an end to the violence with a view toward maximizing dissent in the United States. And the Vietnamese Communists would interpret such dissent as an indication that further persistence by them on the battlefield would soon bring about a condition in the United States where a majority could not be found to approve the continued high costs of the war.

THE EROSION OF DOMESTIC SUPPORT

As the buildup in Vietnam by the United States was met by increased Northern infiltration into the South, domestic criticism intensified. Students and professors held stop-the-war "teach-ins", and artists, intellectuals, and religious leaders joined with standard peace groups in petitioning the government, or marching on Washington to demonstrate against the bombing and for negotiations. Hanoi cooperated with hints through third parties that it might be willing to negotiate; each of these hints were picked up in the press, sometimes some months after they had been made, and thrust at the administration as proof of official dishonesty in saying that it was constantly seeking to induce Hanoi to come to the conference table. American leaders were uninterested in negotiations, charged the critics.

The administration's response to domestic criticism was at first testy and tight-lipped. But in the second half of 1965 the White House changed tactics and began to talk back to the critics, to take them seriously—some observers thought too seriously—and to send administration representatives to the teach-ins to present the administration case. The case included the major premises summarized above, including the one about the danger of too much dissent. This was a tactical blunder on the part of the administration, as it would be for any administration in the American democracy, particularly as the argument was only valid if all of the other premises were valid. And serious critics disputed them all.

The President's worst fears of being driven to higher levels of warfare abroad without a sufficient consensus at home to support the greater resource drain seemed to be materializing. But at the end of 1965, he resorted again to a break-out-of-the-pattern move. This time it was a peace offensive the likes of which the diplomatic community had never seen. Prominent American officials made a whirlwind tour of world capitals while the military campaign was dramatically toned down.

Responding to a Vietcong initiative for a Christmas Eve ceasefire, the United States halted air action over North Vietnam simultaneously with the start of a twelve-hour truce on the ground. A similar "natural" truce would be coming up on the Buddhist Lunar New Year (*Tet*), January 20–24. The administration used the month-long interval of military de-escalation to press its diplomatic offensive, meanwhile not resuming the air attacks. This time the critics could not say the pause was too short for Hanoi to make serious contacts. Secretary Rusk issued publicly Washington's fourteen points for negotiation in response to Hanoi's four points, with the claim that the two positions were really not so far apart. Certainly, there was reason for negotiation on the basis of both positions. But the administration's credibility with its domestic critics, already seriously undermined by its past policy ambivalence and rhetorical excesses, was now injured even further by its frantic efforts, probably wholly sincere, to build international support for unconditional discussions between the belligerents. Doubts were raised as to the "unconditional" nature of the discussions as it became clear that the U.S. was quite sticky on the point of *who* was a legitimate spokesman for the other side. "If the Vietcong come to the conference table as full partners," said Secretary Rusk, "they will . . . in a sense have been victorious in the very aims that South Vietnam and the United States are pledged to prevent."[19]

Claiming again to have received no serious offer from Hanoi to negotiate, the administration resumed air attacks with even greater force on January 28. Domestic critics, if they were patriotic in motive, must now finally realize there was no alternative but to rally behind their country's military efforts. And certainly, if American boys *had* to be over there to hold the ground, who could criticize efforts to negate as much of the danger as possible by destroying enemy power while it was still on the trails in Laos, on the bridges above the 17th parallel, or in the storage depots near the factories?

But the new jingoism in the administration's statements accompanying the resumption of bombing in January 1966, particularly the implication that anything less than enthusiastic support was unpatriotic, provoked patriotic men in the President's own party, like Senators Fulbright, Hartke, and Church, to an even greater attack on administration policies. Senator Fulbright's Foreign Relations Committee became the staging ground for this new phase of the domestic debate.

The Senate Foreign Relations Committee hearings in 1966 provided respectability for the serious criticisms—as distinguished from the emotional harangues of the so-called New Left. Convened for the purpose of requiring the administration to justify its requests for supplemental foreign assistance monies (needed to finance the military and economic assistance to Vietnam over and above the amounts previously authorized in the fiscal 1966 budget), these hearings exposed the nation and the world to the profound doubts about U.S. Vietnam policy held by some of the country's most experienced former diplomats and military leaders and some of its most respected scholars.

General James Gavin testified before the Fulbright committee that he feared "the escalation in southeast Asia . . . [will] begin to hurt our world strategic position." This might have "tremendous significance" in the long run, he said. "When we begin to turn our back on what we are doing in world affairs . . . to support a tactical confrontation that appears to be escalating at the will of an enemy we are in a very dangerous position in my opinion." [20]

This policy, offered George Kennan, "seems to me to represent a grievous misplacement of emphasis in our foreign policies as a whole." Not only were great questions of world affairs not receiving the attention they deserved, said the author of the containment policy, but "assets we already enjoy and . . . possibilities we should be developing are being sacrificed to this unpromising involvement in a remote and secondary theatre." Elaborating, he claimed that

our relations with the Soviet Union have suffered grievously . . . at a time when far more important things were involved in those relations than what is ultimately involved in Vietnam. . . . And more unfortunate still, in my opinion, is the damage being done to the feelings entertained for us by the Japanese people. . . . As the only major industrial complex in the entire Far East, and the only place where the sinews of modern war can be produced on a formidable scale, Japan is of vital importance to us and indeed to the prospects generally of peace and stability in Asia. There is no success we could have in Vietnam that would warrant . . . the sacrifice by us of the confidence and good will of the Japanese people.

And, challenging a central pillar of the administration's case, Kennan contended that even in a situation in which South Vietnam was controlled exclusively by the Vietcong, while regrettable, and no doubt morally unwarranted, [it] would not, in my opinion, present dangers great enough to justify our direct military intervention.

Given the situation that exists today in the relations among the leading Communist powers, and by that I have . . . in mind primarily the Soviet-Chinese conflict, there is every likelihood that a Communist regime would follow a fairly independent course.

Yet we were involved now and this raised "new questions" which had to be taken into account. "A precipitate and disorderly withdrawal could represent in present circumstances a disservice to our own interests, and even to world peace." In a courageous statement for a man of Kennan's close establishment associations to make before a congressional committee in the full glare of the television cameras, Kennan confessed that

I . . . find it difficult . . . to believe that our allies, and particularly our Western European allies, most of whom themselves have given up great territories within recent years, and sometimes in a very statesmanlike way, I find it hard to believe that we would be subject to great reproach or loss of confidence at their hands simply because we followed a defensive rather than an offensive strategy in Vietnam at this time.

In matters such as this, it is not in my experience what you do that is mainly decisive. It is how you do it; and I would submit that there is more respect to be won in the opinion of this world by a resolute and courageous liquidation of unsound positions than by the most stubborn pursuit of extravagant and unpromising objectives.[21]

The President, anticipating what was in store in the February sessions of the Fulbright committee, felt it necessary to reassert once more his peace aims as well as his war aims for Vietnam. It was time to show that he meant business about the greater importance of agricultural productivity, rural electrification, and schools than strike aircraft, flamethrowers, and the tremendous military logistics networks.

The televised testimony of the administrator of the Agency for International Development, David Bell, before the Foreign Relations Committee was interrupted on February 4 for President Johnson's announcement of his trip to Honolulu to meet with Prime Minister Ky and President Thieu of South Vietnam. To emphasize that the main purpose of the meeting was to explore plans for the peaceful reconstruction of Vietnam, the President announced he was taking along John Gardner, Secretary of Health, Education and Welfare, and Orville Freeman, Secretary of Agriculture. There would of course be strategy huddles with General Westmoreland and the vietnamese military, but the theme was to be socioeconomic development. And this was the emphasis in the Declaration of Honolulu issued by both governments from Hawaii on February 8. The government of South Vietnam pledged itself to "a true social revolution," to policies designed to "achieve regular economic growth," and to "build true democracy" through the formulation of a "democratic constitution" to be ratified by popular ballot. The United States pledged itself to full support of these aspirations. And to demonstrate their seriousness of purpose, President Johnson persuaded the Vietnamese leaders to extend an immediate invitation to Secretaries Gardner and Freeman to survey the social and economic situation and suggest practical courses of action. On the evening of February 8, the President announced that Vice President Humphrey was leaving immediately for Saigon to join the other Cabinet members and to meet with South Vietnamese officials to discuss these matters. The White House would be represented directly by McGeorge Bundy and Averell Harriman, both of whom would be going along with the Vice President.[22]

The President did get the headlines and the television coverage with this swoop into Asia with Health, Agriculture, and the idealism of Humphrey. But the image came across somewhat differently from what he had hoped. The tone of the television commentators and journalists who covered the event suggested rather strongly that this was Johnson hucksterism more than substance. Juxtaposed against the good-works backdrop was the indelible picture of LBJ embracing Prime Minister Ky as if he were a Democratic Party loyalist in the Texas statehouse. Ky, who had been installed recently by a military coup, was cracking down with authoritarian methods on the Buddhist agitators, and had been making asides to the effect that any negotiations with the Communists would be useless. Rather than Ky's endorsement of the Great Society, Saigon-style, the picture that critics chose to display was that of Johnson's committing himself to support Ky's irresponsible brand of jet-set militarism.

Lyndon Johnson could legitimately claim that the resort to force to move men and nations was the exception, not the norm, of his foreign policies. His preferred mode of influence was that of the prophet Isaiah: "Come now and let us reason together."

It was reason, Johnson would insist, that brought about the resolution of the Panama Canal crisis of 1964–65, and not simply the reason of the weak in accepting the dictates of the strong. The United States government, under Johnson, went further toward recognizing Panama's sovereignty over the Canal Zone and in according Panamanians equitable treatment in United States zone installations than had any previous administration.

It was reason, the objective consideration of the advantages and disadvantages of alternative courses of action, that Johnson could claim to have brought to bear upon the Greeks and Turks to forestall their impending war over Cyprus, and upon the Indians and Pakistanis to persuade them to cease their war over Kashmir. The fact that the United States was in a position to affect the anticipations of advantage and disadvantage of the involved parties (the perquisites and protections of NATO membership to Greece and Turkey, the flow of military and economic assistance to the South Asian countries) was, of course, at the heart of the President's appeals to substitute reason for passion.

Johnson had also shown an ability to practice restraint in situations of extreme local instability, such as in Indonesia, Rhodesia, and the Middle East, where it might have been tempting for a great power to intervene. Rather than attempting to play the world policeman, he prudently allowed events to take their course in response to lesser influences.

The United States support for the Alliance for Progress had been extended indefinitely. Constructive development schemes had been sponsored from the Amazon to the Mekong. The Peace Corps continued to receive the wholehearted support of the White House. A nonproliferation treaty and other arms control accords had been spurred by the personal solicitude of the President. New economic and cultural bridges were being built to Eastern Europe. West Germany had been encouraged to depart from its rigid legalisms vis-à-vis the East. And not a harsh word had been heard from the President against the Soviet regime, despite the many opportunities to retaliate for anti–U.S. diatribes from the Kremlin.

The arts of conciliation and compromise, in the Johnson administration's self-image, were the facts of power now, more so than at any time since the start of the cold war.

Yet an administration cannot escape the massive impressions created on domestic and foreign observers by its most dramatic actions. Regardless of intention, large doses of force in the international environment create a noise level that distorts the sound of other signals. And the effort to get conciliatory messages through the uproar of violence was virtually drowned out by a revival of the more histrionic aspects of postwar U.S. foreign policy—the resort to ideological hyperbole, to moralizing about the basis of U.S. overseas commitments, to lecturing neutrals about their vital interests, and to threats of more violence to come if the enemy persisted in its course.

SECRETARY MCNAMARA JUMPS OFF THE VIETNAM ESCALATOR

By the middle of 1966, the military strategy for getting North Vietnam to call off the war in the South seemed to be producing just the opposite results. The more U.S. forces were deployed into South Vietnam, the more units the North poured down the Ho Chi Minh trail and across the 17th parallel. Sustained bombing of the North only appeared to stiffen the will of Hanoi to persist. The studies Secretary of Defense McNamara called for deeply shocked him: although the bombing had destroyed major weapons storage sites, the flow of men and matériel into the South was undiminished. There was no feasible level of effort, concluded the studies, that would achieve the air war objectives. The only new proposal McNamara's experts could come up with was to build an electronic barrier across Vietnam below the 17th parallel. McNamara's memoranda to the President began to reflect pessimism and the beginning of despair, especially in view of the continual requests from General William Westmoreland for reinforcements that were pushing the number of U.S. troops in South Vietnam up to the 500,000 mark.

The President in turn became more and more suspicious of McNamara. The parting of the ways came in the spring of 1967 and was reflected in the Secretary of Defense's draft memorandum to the President of May 19 on the latest troop and air war requests from General Westmoreland. The substance of its arguments played a pivotal role in crystalizing opposition to the war within the U.S. government. Rejecting the next steps in the military escalation recommended by the Joint Chiefs of Staff as likely to be "counterproductive," McNamara argued that there may be a limit beyond which many Americans and much of the world will not permit the United States to go. The picture of the world's greatest superpower killing or seriously injuring 1,000 non-combatants a week, while trying to pound a tiny backward nation into submission on an issue whose merits are hotly disputed, is not a pretty one. It could conceivably produce a costly distortion in the American national consciousness and in the world image of the United States—especially if the damage to North Vietnam is complete enough to be "successful."

. . .

Mining the harbors would . . . place Moscow in a particularly galling dilemma as to how to preserve the Soviet position and prestige. . . . Moscow in this case should be expected to send volunteers, including pilots, to North Vietnam; to provide some new and better weapons and equipment; to consider some action in Korea, Turkey, Iran, the Middle East or, most likely, Berlin, where the Soviets can control the degree of crisis better; and to show across-the-board hostility toward the U.S. (interrupting any on-going conversations on ABMs, non-proliferation, etc.).

. . .

To U.S. ground actions in North Vietnam, we would expect China to respond by entering the war with both ground and air forces.

Instead, McNamara recommended that the President "limit force increases to no more than 30,000; avoid entering the ground conflict beyond the borders of South Vietnam; and concentrate the bombing on the infiltration routes south of 20°."

With respect to one of the principal purposes of the bombing of North Vietnam—pressure on Hanoi to end the war—McNamara contended that

it is becoming apparent that Hanoi may have already "written off" all assets and lives that might be destroyed by U.S. military action short of occupation or annihilation. They can and will hold out at least so long as a prospect of winning the "war of attrition" in the South exists. And our best judgment is that a Hanoi prerequisite to negotiations is significant retrenchment (if not complete stoppage) of U.S. military actions against them.

And with respect to interdiction of men and matériel,

it now appears that no combination of actions against the North short of destruction of the regime or occupation of North Vietnamese territory will physically reduce the flow of men and matériel below the relatively small amount needed by enemy forces to continue the war in the South. . . . Our efforts physically to cut the flow meaningfully by actions in North Vietnam therefore largely fail.[23]

The President and his national security adviser, Walt Rostow, henceforth categorized McNamara as a dove, which meant that he had to be effectively cut out of the most sensitive deliberations on the conduct of the war, since his rejection of the fundamental premises of the Vietnam strategy meant that he was no longer loyal to basic administration policy. In mid-October 1967, President Johnson informed McNamara that he was nominating him for the presidency of the World Bank, a post that had fallen vacant upon the retirement of the bank's previous president, Eugene Black.

To succeed McNamara as Secretary of Defense, LBJ appointed his friend Clark Clifford, the distinguished Washington lawyer and adviser to presidents since Truman. Johnson was confident Clifford would work well with him, Rostow, and Secretary of State Rusk to reunify the administration (and hopefully also Congress) behind the Vietnam policy. But Clifford, to Johnson's surprise and eventual despair, soon turned out to be an even more effective mobilizer of dissent within the policy establishment against continuing the escalation policy than McNamara.

1968: LBJ BESIEGED

Early in 1968 three developments converged and reinforced each other, culminating in Lyndon Johnson's withdrawal from the presidential race simultaneous with a change in grand strategy for ending the war in Vietnam, and, less visibly, in a willingness by some administration officials to challenge the heretofore sacrosanct premises about the U.S. world role. The first development was the upsurge of violence in the ghettos, stimulated by and in turn stimulating popular discontent because more resources were being devoted to the war in a small Asian country than to the war on poverty at home. The second development was the transference of student militancy from civil rights to the issues of the war and the draft, and the ability of Eugene McCarthy and Robert Kennedy to convert student protest into the energizing force of a powerful antiadministration movement within the Democratic Party. The third development was the ability of Clark Clifford, succeeding McNamara as Secretary of Defense on March 1, 1968, to reach and move the President with evaluations of the military campaign in Vietnam that called into question critical assumptions under which the United States was fighting the war.

Clifford's eyes were opened during his first task as the President's chairman of an interagency task force to evaluate the latest request from General William Westmoreland, American commander in

South Vietnam, for 200,000 additional troops in the wake of the Communist Tet offensive. As later recounted by Townsend Hoopes, Under Secretary of the Air Force from October 1967 to February 1969, Clifford was stunned by the magnitude of the request and accordingly decided to broaden the task force's frame of reference to include the basic question of whether or not the United States was operating under a sensible strategic concept in Vietnam. Although the formal task force report to the President reaffirmed the existing policy, Clifford's doubts deepened during its deliberations, and in presenting the report to the President at the White House on March 7, he felt impelled to express his own new-found reservations, questioning the efficacy of the ground and bombing strategies and wondering what the additional troop buildup would really accomplish. He said that he thought there should be further study before implementing the task force recommendations. The President granted his new Secretary of Defense this delay; but, as Hoopes recalls, "the longstanding friendship between the two men grew suddenly formal and cool." [24]

The President's insecurities were increased by the results of the March 12, 1968, New Hampshire Democratic primary, which gave antiwar critic Senator Eugene McCarthy 42.2 percent of the vote, just a few percentage points behind Johnson's 49.2. And when on March 16, Robert Kennedy announced that he too would seek the presidency, LBJ's worst fantasies about the Kennedy clan's desire to recapture the White House seemed to be materializing. Recalling these days for his biographer Doris Kearns, Johnson confessed that

I felt . . . that I was being chased on all sides by a giant stampede coming at me from all directions. On one side, the American people were stampeding me to do something about Vietnam. On another side, the inflationary economy was booming out of control. Up ahead were dozens of danger signs pointing to another summer of riots in the cities. I was being forced over the edge by rioting blacks, demonstrating students, marching welfare mothers, squawking professors, and hysterical reporters. And then the final straw. The thing I feared from the first day of my Presidency was actually coming true. Robert Kennedy had openly announced his intention to reclaim the throne in the memory of his brother. And the American people, swayed by the magic of the name, were dancing in the streets. The whole situation was unbearable for me. After thirty-seven years of public service, I deserved something more than being left alone in the middle of the plain, chased by stampedes on every side. [25]

But it was not only dovish intellectuals and the people who had no knowledge of foreign affairs who were now challenging the wisdom of Johnson's Vietnam policies. Even veteran cold warriors with impeccable loyalty were calling for a fundamental reassessment. LBJ was particularly shaken by former Secretary of State Dean Acheson's judgment, which he voiced to the President privately on March 15, that the administration was operating under the grossest of illusions about what was possible in Vietnam, that no one believed Johnson's speeches any more, and that he had lost touch with the country which, as a whole, was no longer supporting the war.[26]

Clifford assembled Johnson's senior advisory group on Vietnam, of which Acheson was a member, along with some of the most distinguished former soldiers, diplomats, and policy makers in whom Johnson had great respect. On March 25 they gathered at the White House to read background papers and receive briefings from various high government officials, and on March 26 they met with the President to discuss the issue. Present were Dean Acheson, George Ball, McGeorge Bundy, Douglas Dillon, Cyrus Vance, Arthur Dean, John J. McCloy, General Omar Bradley, General Matthew Ridgway, General Maxwell Taylor, Robert Murphy, Henry Cabot Lodge, Abe Fortas, and Arthur Goldberg. According to Townsend Hoopes' account of this meeting, the President was "visibly shocked" and "stung" by the magnitude of the defection from the existing policy, and especially by the fact that sophisticated pragmatists like McGeorge Bundy and Cyrus Vance were now among those pressing for deescalation, negotiations, and disengagement ahead of being able to assure against a Communist takeover in South Vietnam.[27]

Clifford apparently felt strengthened to intervene with Johnson's speechwriter Harry McPherson to help shape the speech on Vietnam the President was scheduled to deliver to the country on March 31, and through McPherson persuaded the now-demoralized LBJ to announce a unilateral deescalation of the bombing and to imply that there was more of the same to come if Hanoi would enter into serious negotiations. Clifford was gratified to see on his television screen the President finally coming around to the proposals he had been urging over the past weeks. What neither he nor the rest of the nation expected, however, was Johnson's dramatic closing remarks on March 31 that in order to devote all his time and energies to the quest for peace, "I do not believe I should devote an hour or a day of my time to partisan causes. . . . Accordingly, I shall not seek, and I will not accept, the nomination of my party for another term as your President."[28]

The President's personal renunciation of further electioneering and of another term for himself evidently was interpreted in Hanoi as a more credible bid for peace than past efforts by the United States. Accepting the partial bombing halt as a basis for preliminary talks, the North Vietnamese also reciprocated with a temporary cessation of their shelling of cities in the South and a substantial reduction of large unit operations in the demilitarized zone at the 17th parallel. Clifford and his associates felt vindicated in their belief that a U.S. posture looking very serious about deescalating the conflict was better than muscle-flexing for getting Ho Chi Minh to the bargaining table.

Johnson remained skeptical, however, still wanting to believe that the real reason for Hanoi's willingness to negotiate was that they had been hurt by the bombing more than they were willing to let on, and that therefore a credible threat to resume full-scale bombing was essential to induce them to accept an independent South Vietnam. Once again, in late October 1968, against his own instincts he ordered a total bombing halt, yielding to the insistences of Clifford and the two U.S. negotiators in the Paris talks with the North Vietnamese, Cyrus Vance and Averell Harriman. LBJ left office chafing at the bit and full of self-doubts about whether he had shown weakness or strength at the last.[29]

There still were numerous unreconstructed Vietnam interventionists in top policy-making posts in the fall of 1968, not the least of whom were Secretary of State Dean Rusk and national security adviser Walt Rostow. The change—which Clark Clifford was instrumental in bringing about—was that it was now legitimate within the administration to debate the basic policy premises underlying the Vietnam involvement. And the now debatable premises, it would emerge, were part and parcel of the *Weltanschauung* of forward containment of Communism that dominated official Washington's thinking since the late 1940s.

A fundamental tenet from Truman to Johnson was that the *irreducible national interest* ("securing the blessings of liberty to ourselves and our posterity") required that the Communists not be allowed to extend their sphere of control. This policy was based on a set of interrelated assumptions, namely:

——The Soviets and the Chinese Communists are highly motivated to extend their rule to other areas.

——Soviet expansion alone, or the fruits of possible Chinese expansion if added to the Soviet sphere, could eventually give the Communist nations a preponderance of power globally that would enable them to dictate the conditions under which the people of the United States should live.

——The establishment of additional Communist regimes, or the territorial expansion by Communist countries other than Russia or China, would add to the global power of the Soviets or the Chinese and their capacities for expansion.

——The Soviets and the Chinese Communists would resort to military expansion if they were not checked by countervailing military power.

——Against a determined attack by either of the two Communist giants, indigenous military power would be insufficient and United States military power would have to be brought in to redress the imbalance.

——A capability and the clearly communicated will to defend whatever area the Communist powers might choose to attack, regardless of its intrinsic geopolitical weight in the overall balance, was necessary to prevent the Communists from picking and choosing easy targets for blackmail and aggression. Moreover, America's failure to defend one area would demoralize other such localities in their will to resist the Communists. Even Western Europe and Japan, whose advanced industrialization made them critical weights in the global balance of power, would wonder under what circumstances the U.S. might consider them dispensable.

——Even if the Soviets and the Chinese Communists were effectively deterred from direct military expansion, they would attempt to expand their spheres of control in underdeveloped areas through support of subversive movements, insurgencies, and "wars of national liberation."

——Economic underdevelopment and the political disorder that comes from unsatisfied aspirations for betterment provide easy opportunities for Communist takeover of subversive and insurrectionary movements; thus U.S. economic and political development programs, no less than counterinsurgency capabilities, must be prominent parts of the grand strategy of preventing adverse changes in the global balance of power. (An assumption prominent during the Kennedy-Johnson years).

Any questioning of the nature of U.S. security interests in Vietnam, or even questioning—as Clifford did—whether the protection of U.S. interests there was *worth* the high expenditures of human and material resources, would call into question the assumptions just enumerated.

U.S. policy makers had taken for granted that the Soviets and Chinese Communists had unrequited appetites for expansion. Did the record of the past two decades support this proposition? A serious body of revisionist history of the cold war period had emerged during the middle 1960s supportive of alternative propositions. The more extreme revisionists argued that the United States was more clearly the expansionist power since the Second World War, arrogantly attempting to reshape the world in the image of its ideological preconceptions, and that the Soviets and Chinese were only reacting defensively to his "encirclement." Moderate revisionists stressed the likelihood that both sides have been victims of tragic misperceptions of the other's real intentions, which were to assure themselves substantial, but limited, spheres of influence for legitimate reasons of economic and military security. Others, more agnostic with respect to the intentions of the Communists, nonetheless claimed that Soviet and foreign actions as distinct from their rhetoric tended to be prudent if not conservative, that the Communist nations, like the Western countries, had difficult resource allocation problems and unmet domestic needs which placed weighty constraints on their inclinations for foreign adventure.

No less questionable were the forecasts of adverse consequences to the global balance of power if the Communists were allowed to extend their area of control. Changes in the technologies of transportation, communication, basic materials production, and weaponry pointed to the need for a full-scale review of the strategic worth attributed to various peninsulas, straits, island outposts, and sources of raw materials.

Apart from obsolescent notions of geopolitics, the notion of a seamless web of U.S. commitments connecting and sustaining friendly nations of the non-Communist world was also in for hard scrutiny. The implication that United States security was tied vitally to the security of each nation (or was it to regimes?) to which it had made more or less equivocal pledges of protection from internal and external threats might have some utility as a *deterrent* if believed by Moscow and Beijing; but what was its effect upon the behavior of the beneficiaries of U.S. protection? Where they tempted to provocative action themselves, confident the U.S. would bail them out? Were they stimulated to correct the deficiencies in their socioeconomic systems or, rather, were they only encouraged to perpetuate the very injustices and misallocations of resources that made them vulnerable in the first place?

Also due for skeptical examination was the idea that the Third World, especially its nonaligned elements, was up for grabs between the two superpowers. Both the United States and the Soviet Union had undergone the chastening experience during the first half of the decade of finding social, economic, and political forces in the less developed states to be nowhere nearly as malleable as hypothesized in Khrushchev's doctrine of "wars of national liberation" and Kennedy's "decade of development." Political movements and parties receptive to development models and tutelage offered by each of the superpowers often turned out to be politically discredited within their own countries and, if anything, cold war liabilities for their tutors. If this was indeed the emerging pattern, could not the United States afford to be more sanguine at the appearance of Soviet aid or trade missions in Third World countries? But would not such a relaxed attitude also seriously undercut the most politically salable rationale for the U.S. foreign aid program—namely, that it was essential for U.S. security because the Third World was now the new arena for conducting the global power competition?

The consensus underlying the constancy in foreign policy from Truman to Johnson was at an end. On January 20, 1969, there was no basic foreign policy to be handed over intact to the Nixon administration.

The period when policy changes could be attributed to changes in reliance on various tools of power, as distinct from changes in national interests and objectives, seemed to call for an analysis of contending programs and strategies. It now appeared, however, that the analysis of foreign policy choices would have to cut deeper, to contending concepts of national purpose and international order.

PART V

STATECRAFT UNDER NIXON AND FORD

Power used with good intentions, but ineptly, can be as destructive as power used with bad intentions. The greatest tragedy of all, however, occurs when those who have power fail to use it, and because of that failure lives and even freedom itself are lost.

—RICHARD M. NIXON

The most onimous change that marked our period was the transformation in the nature of power. . . . As power had grown more awesome, it had also turned abstract, intangible, elusive.

—HENRY A. KISSINGER

13

AVOIDING HUMILIATION IN INDOCHINA

Our defeat and humiliation in South Vietnam without question would promote recklessness in the councils of those great powers who have not yet abandoned their goals of world conquest.

—RICHARD NIXON

By the time Richard Nixon assumed the presidency, few Americans still believed that Communist domination of the Indochinese peninsula would pose an intolerable threat to U.S. security. The main question was no longer *whether* the United States should slough off responsibility for preventing the North Vietnamese and the Viet Cong from taking over South Vietnam, but *how* to liquidate this costly commitment.

Like Lyndon Johnson at the end of his presidency, the new President and his principal national security adviser believed the prestige of the United States still was heavily at stake in Vietnam, and they discerned a popular mandate that the United States exit from Vietnam "with honor." There were differences, however, between the administration and its critics, and even within the administration, over the ingredients of national honor.

To Nixon and Kissinger, as to Johnson, the nation's honor was bound up closely with its "credibility"—its reputation for keeping promises—and its refusal to be coerced by other nations. "The commitment of 500,000 Americans has settled the issue of the importance of Vietnam," wrote Kissinger in 1968. "For what is involved now is confidence in American promises. However fashionable it is to ridicule the terms 'credibility' or 'prestige,' they are not empty phrases; other nations can gear their actions to ours only if they can count on our steadiness."[1]

But in the view of many other Americans the U.S. was being *dis*honored in Vietnam by its stubborn attempt to keep its promise to stop a Communist takeover. A growing chorus of religious leaders, academics, students, media commentators, and politicians in both parties tried to convince the administration of its folly. It was dishonorable, they argued, for the United States to compel its young men to kill and be killed in a small, faraway country in the vain hope of helping a repressive and corrupt regime defeat the Communists in a civil war. It was dishonorable for the United States to persist in trying to bomb North Vietnam into a submissive withdrawal of its forces in the face of clear evidence that the North Vietnamese were deeply and unequivocally committed to the "liberation" of the South.

According to various accounts, Nixon and Kissinger both recognized, even before taking office, that the honor of the United States was being sullied by its military involvement in Vietnam. They understood that the war was unwinnable and that the United States was being made to look foolish before the rest of the world as it wasted more and more of its substance in a country of minor strategic importance. The trick was to withdraw from the war without having it appear that the United States was giving up. "The basic challenge to the new Administration," wrote Kissinger in *The White House Years,* "was similar to de Gaulle's in Algeria: to withdraw as an expression of policy and not as a collapse."[2] This policy had two essential features: "Vietnamization" and a negotiated settlement with Hanoi. The fighting itself was to be turned over to the South Vietnamese to continue on their own. Meanwhile, Hanoi would agree to pull its forces back into North Vietnam and to support political arrangements that would give the South Vietnamese Communists (the National Liberation Front) a share in the governance of South Vietnam. The negotiating agenda and process, as outlined in Kissinger's January 1969 article in *Foreign Affairs,* would take place on two tracks: North Vietnam and the United States to effect military disengagement, the National Liberation Front and the Thieu regime in Saigon to decide the political arrangement for South Vietnam.

As this became the Nixon administrations' public posture, Hanoi presumably would see that what was being asked for was a "decent interval" to allow the United States to pull out with its honor intact, after which the North and South Vietnamese could settle the fate of their country without outside interference. Hanoi's maximum demand was for an even larger capitulation by the United States and Saigon involving full withdrawal of U.S. forces, without a reciprocal pullback of the North Vietnamese, and the resignation of the Thieu government—prior to a cease-fire in South Vietnam and the start of processes to reconstitute a new government. But Kissinger apparently believed that Hanoi would understand Washington's need to avoid a humiliating exit and therefore could be persuaded to cooperate in choreographing an elaborate finale of mutual concessions.

Only a few days after Nixon's inauguration, the President and Kissinger moved to present their scheme directly to the North Vietnamese through Henry Cabot Lodge, the newly appointed head of the team negotiating with the North Vietnamese in Paris. The proposal Lodge carried to Paris was in essence the two-track process outlined in Kissinger's *Foreign Affairs* article, with the first step being a simultaneous *mutual* withdrawal of U.S. and North Vietnamese troops from South Vietnam—a change from the Johnson administration's position, which had held out for a withdrawal of North Vietnamese troops and a reduction of the level of violence in the South as the preconditions for U.S. troop withdrawal.

Nixon and Kissinger were determined that the Paris negotiations should stop being a charade, and accordingly they pulled out all the stops so as to maximize the incentives operating on North Vietnam to come to the negotiating table with an equally serious intent to conclude a settlement. They set in motion a series of phased, unilateral reductions in U.S. ground forces in Vietnam, but simultaneously revealed a capability and will to bomb North Vietnam and North Vietnamese staging areas in Cambodia and Laos with less squeamishness than the previous administration had shown. Meanwhile, they intensified pressure on Moscow and Beijing to persuade Hanoi to negotiate an end to the war.

The administration pursued this multipronged strategy relentlessly for four years—continuing to make concessions in the U.S.

negotiation position, gradually accelerating unilateral troop withdrawals, applying larger doses of military coercion against North Vietnam, and attempting to thicken the links between Soviet and Chinese constructive influence on their North Vietnamese ally and U.S. responsiveness to Soviet or Chinese interests in other fields. With the signing of a mutually acceptable settlement in 1973, the strategy appeared to have worked, at least in the sense of providing an "honorable" cover for the U.S. military exit.

However, it took only two years for the cover itself to disintegrate completely. In the spring of 1975, with the Cambodian Communists (the Khmer Rouge) marching on Phnom Penh and the North Vietnamese armies closing in on Saigon, President Ford and Secretary Kissinger struck one last pose of support for their now-abandoned allies in Indochina. Knowing full well that the majority in Congress, reflecting a broad popular consensus, had no intention of diverting further national resources to a lost cause, the administration nevertheless asked for a supplemental military aid package for the anti-Communists in Cambodia and Vietnam. It was a transparent effort, at the last, to once again cast the blame for defeat on Congress in a desperate attempt to salvage the honor of the administration.

As the Viet Cong raised their flag over Saigon and renamed it Ho Chi Minh City, the lack of any substantial popular interest in the outcome was, ironically, at least a partial vindication of the administration's strategy.

But this final denouement was a far cry from the Nixon–Kissinger script, which—more clearly in retrospect than during its unfolding—can be seen to have contained two fatal flaws: (1) the assumption that Hanoi would settle for anything less than a total victory over Saigon and (2) the assumption that the North Vietnamese would perceive that Nixon and Kissinger, while sincerely determined to pull U.S. military forces out of Vietnam, could not be party to the total defeat of the anti-Communist forces in Indochina. As it turned out, Hanoi's objectives were unequivocally total, and it remained unswerving in its conviction that the United States would give up even the ghost of a compromise settlement.

The dogged persistence of the belief that Hanoi's settling price was less than its repeated demands and that the positive and negative pressures on Hanoi would convince the Communists that they had to compromise prolonged the agony and brutality of the U.S. involvement four years longer than Kissinger originally promised it would take him to end it. The cost of the delays would continue to haunt all those associated with the effort: more than 15,000 Americans killed and 53,000 wounded from 1969 to 1973, not to speak of the far greater losses by the Vietnamese on both sides.

Overestimation of Hanoi's susceptibility to coercion and positive inducements distorted the U.S. peace efforts at virtually every benchmark along the way to the Communists' final victory. Distorted judgments were present in the basic approach of phasing in "Vietnamization" of the ground war while phasing out U.S. troops, in the graduated U.S. concessions to Hanoi's demands, in the dramatic escalations that followed in reaction to the Communists' rejection or ignoring of these concessions, and even in the Paris Peace Accords themselves.

The administration's unfounded views about the North Vietnamese were paralleled by its overestimation of the humiliation the U.S. government would suffer in the eyes of the American public and other nations if it "precipitously" gave up fighting in Vietnam. By 1971 opinion polls revealed that a substantial majority of U.S. citizens wanted to end the war, even at the risk of an eventual Communist takeover[3] and most of the friends of the United States in Europe and Japan were embarrassed by their powerful ally's irrational squandering of its human and material resources in a theater of secondary geopolitical significance.

Kissinger's attempt to dignify as a "tragedy" his and Nixon's prolongation of the bloodshed to gain an honorable peace in Indochina was transparent charlatanism. They had, primarily through their own rhetoric, backed themselves into a corner from which there was no escape except to admit that they were wrong. But such a noble course was evidently beyond these stubbornly proud men.

THE INVASION OF CAMBODIA: NIXON'S "SEVENTH CRISIS"

The invasion of Cambodia by U.S. troops on April 28, 1970, marked the end of the administration's ability to convince wide segments of the policy community that the White House really did have a workable game plan for ending the war. Clearly, Nixon and Kissinger, no less than their predecessors, had little control over the significant events and actors in Indochina and had lost whatever intellectual or conceptual control over the situation they might have started out with in 1969, not to speak of the emotional control required to implement a strategy of deliberate, cool military disengagement. Nixon called his own agonizing over the invasion decision his "seventh crisis."[4] Kissinger found himself the object of intense animosity on the part of former academic colleagues and members of his own staff, four of whom resigned.

From the point of view of Nixon and Kissinger, the opposition to the Cambodian invasion was a typical expression of the naïveté and spinelessness of the liberal establishment. Cambodia's neutral status had already been systematically violated for more than a year by the belligerents on both sides: North Vietnamese soldiers had been using Cambodian territory over the South Vietnamese border as a base for troops and supplies for their operations in South Vietnam, and U.S. B-52s had been bombarding these staging areas since March 1969 with the acquiescence of the Cambodian ruler, Prince Sihanouk. The bombing had been concealed from the American public and even from many national security officials in the administration. William Beecher, the Pentagon correspondent of the *New York Times,* broke the story in early May; however, it was not until after the spring 1970 invasion of Cambodia that the bombing was officially acknowledged.[5]

Frustrated by the continuing refusal of Hanoi to discuss a mutual withdrawal of "foreign" forces from South Vietnam even as the United States began a good faith withdrawal of its own forces, and genuinely worried that the North Vietnamese might pounce on the South as soon as U.S. force levels got low enough, Nixon and Kissinger evidently felt by the spring of 1970 that they had no alternative but to break out of the pattern of weak signals they were transmitting to Hanoi.

Their opportunity came in March 1970 with the sudden rightwing coup in Phnom Penh that deposed Prince Sihanouk while he was out of the country. Marshal Lon Nol, the leader of the military coup, not only turned against the Cambodian Communists but also attempted to force the North Vietnamese contingents out of his country. The North Vietnamese, no longer constrained to respect the independence of Cambodia, now openly and vigorously supported the Cambodian Communists, who were building up their forces around Phnom Penh in preparation for a countercoup. Lon Nol's desperate plea for U.S. help could not be refused if the North Vietnamese were to be prevented from taking over Cambodia and completely outflanking South Vietnam. "If, when the chips are down," said, Nixon, announcing the decision to attack the North Vietnamese sanctuaries in Cambodia,

the world's most powerful nation, the United States of America, acts like a pitiful, helpless giant, the forces of totalitarianism and anarchy will threaten free nations and free institutions throughout the world. It is not our power but our will and character that is being tested tonight. If we fail to meet this challenge, all other nations will be on notice that despite its overwhelming power the United States, when a real crisis comes, will be found wanting.[6]

Although the foray into Cambodia, like most of the dramatic escalations ordered by Nixon, was designed in part to shock Hanoi into willingness to compromise, the official public explanations stressed a limited military objective. "This is not an invasion of Cambodia," insisted the President. "The areas in which these attacks will be launched are completely occupied and controlled by North Vietnamese forces. Our purpose is not to occupy the areas. Once enemy forces are driven out of these sanctuaries and once their military supplies are destroyed, we will withdraw."[7]

Two months later, on June 30, 1970, the President proclaimed the Cambodian operation a complete success and announced that all American troops had been withdrawn from Cambodia on schedule. He reeled off the indicators of enemy material and human losses, with a curious exactitude: "22,892 individual weapons . . . 2,509 big crew-served weapons. . . . More than 15 million rounds of ammunition. . . . 14 million pounds of rice. . . . 143,000 rockets. . . . Over 199,552 antiaircraft rounds, 5,482 mines, 62,022 grenades, and 83,000 pounds of explosives, including 1,002 satchel charges. . . . Over 435 vehicles . . . over 11,688 bunkers and other military structures . . . 11,349 men killed and about 2,328 captured and detainees."

The "deeper meaning" of these "impressive statistics," said Nixon, was as follows:

We have eliminated an immediate threat to our forces and to the security of South Vietnam—and produced the prospect of fewer American casualties in the future. We have inflicted extensive casualties and very heavy losses in material on

the enemy—losses which can now be replaced only from the North during a
monsoon season. . . .

We have ended the concept of Cambodian sanctuaries, immune from attack,
upon which the enemy military had relied for five years.

We have dislocated supply lines and disrupted Hanoi's strategy in the Saigon area
and the Mekong Delta. The enemy capacity to mount a major offensive in this vital
populated region of the South has been greatly diminished.

We have effectively cut off the enemy from resupply by the sea. . . .

We have, for the time being, separated the Communist main-force units . . .
from the guerrillas in the southern part of Vietnam. This should provide a boost to
pacification efforts.

We have guaranteed the continuance of our troop withdrawal program. . . .

We have bought time for the South Vietnamese to strengthen themselves against
the enemy.

We have witnessed visible proof of the success of Vietnamization as the South
Vietnamese performed with skill and valor and competence far beyond the expectation of our commanders or American advisers.[8]

President Nixon understandably chose not to refer to the fact that
after the sixty-day U.S. incursion into Cambodia the Communist
forces occupied about half of it. Some critics of the Nixon–Kissinger
policies invoke this fact in attempting to show that the U.S. bombing
and incursion into Cambodia *caused* its ultimate takeover by the
Communists and the bloody decimation of its culture and population
which followed. Kissinger effectively refutes this in *The White House
Years* ("Hanoi's insatiable quest for hegemony—not America's hesi-
tant and ambivalent response—is the root cause of Cambodia's ordeal")[9]; but the "success" of the 1970 foray into Cambodia looks
much less impressive when viewed in the context of these developments; and there can be no doubt that the U.S. military incursion
lent a certain credibility to the North Vietnamese claim (however
spurious in fact) that their own massive invasion of Cambodia was
designed to prevent the "imperialists" from reimposing their domination of that country.

Although one immediate purpose of the operation was to shock
Hanoi into facing up to the costs of continuing the war, it had the
boomerang effect of finally shattering whatever confidence remained
in the White House that the administration could revive popular
faith in its competence to bring the war to an honorable end. As it
turned out, Nixon and Kissinger were themselves shocked by the
domestic reaction to their move, and the North Vietnamese leader-

ship only stiffened its intransigence at the negotiating table while intensifying its military efforts throughout Indochina.

The student protest movement, somewhat dormant since the election of Nixon, had been revived overnight by the news of the invasion of Cambodia. The animosity toward the administration for its sluggish exit from Vietnam ignited into a firestorm of anger when four demonstrating students at Kent State University were killed by a trigger-happy Ohio National Guard unit. Efforts were intensified in Congress to limit the executive's war powers.

The Cambodian operation, conceived as a means of widening U.S. options and limiting those of the North Vietnamese, had the opposite effect. Washington, not Hanoi, once again made the next concessions in the diplomatic arena—this time coming almost all the way toward the maximum demands of Hanoi.

Nixon now gave the go-ahead to propose a cease-fire even though the U.S. military and the U.S. Embassy in Saigon believed this would put the Thieu regime in great physical jeopardy and in an untenable political position. "Cease-fire-in-place" was a euphemism for what was, in effect, an agreement to allow Hanoi to keep its forces in South Vietnam and to legitimize their hold on the territory they had already conquered. Here, finally, was the abandonment of the U.S. insistence on a mutual withdrawal of U.S. and North Vietnamese forces from the South. "The decision to propose a standstill cease-fire in 1970," admits Kissinger, "implied the solution of 1972." [10] The U.S. forces alone would leave, being the only "foreign" forces there—a complete capitulation to Hanoi's insistence that the conflict in the South was a continuation of the civil war to liberate Vietnam from imperialism.

The North Vietnamese, more contemptuous than ever of their opponents, would settle for nothing less than an American renunciation of the legitimacy of the Thieu regime. This demand, from the administration's point of view, was surely irrational, for the cease-fire-in-place and accompanying interim political arrangements proposed to the North Vietnamese were clearly only face-saving mechanisms to allow the United States to get out before the final deposition of Thieu and the participation of the Communists in the government in Saigon. Kissinger's military–diplomatic strategy from here on out was designed to convince Hanoi that (1) no matter how sick the United States was of the war, there was no possibility of persuading

President Nixon to cooperate in the final humiliation of Thieu, and (2) the United States was fully committed to a withdrawal of its own forces from Vietnam, and the cease-fire-in-place and interim political arrangements were not any kind of trick to put the North Vietnamese off balance.

THE MINING OF HAIPHONG HARBOR: ATTEMPTS TO WORK THE MOSCOW CONNECTION

From the summer of 1970 through the spring of 1971, terrible pessimism pervaded Washington over the capacity of Nixon and Kissinger to gain that "peace with honor" that would allow the administration to finally get out of Vietnam. With the failure of both the Cambodia invasion and the post-Cambodia negotiating concessions to Hanoi, Nixon and Kissinger appeared to have used up most of their available carrots and sticks.

The U.S. air support for the South Vietnamese Army's 1971 incursion into Laos to cut the Ho Chi Minh trail network was a comparatively insignificant increment of coercion (Nixon was prevented by the Cooper-Church Amendment from using U.S. ground forces, as he had in Cambodia). The South Vietnamese troops were beaten back without accomplishing their mission.

Kissinger once again reached deep into his bag for two further initiatives in his secret negotiations with Le Duc Tho during the spring and summer of 1971: a promise that President Thieu would resign prior to internationally supervised elections under comprehensive peace arrangements, and assurances to Hanoi that all U.S. troops would be out of Vietnam within six months following the signing of the peace agreement. Le Duc Tho countered with his own nine points as the basis for continuing to negotiate in detail. By the fall of 1971, after six intense negotiating sessions in Paris, Kissinger and Le Duc Tho were still deadlocked over details—in essence, the inability of Kissinger and Nixon to agree to an unconditional surrender of South Vietnam. Le Duc Tho attempted to delegate the responsibility for further talks to his deputy. Kissinger's insistence that Le Duc Tho himself continue was ignored, so the negotiations were suspended.

Meanwhile, events along the great power nexus had been maturing. During the summer and fall of 1971 Kissinger had arranged for

Nixon's 1972 summit visits to Moscow and Beijing; and it might now be possible to induce the Communist giants, both of whom were competing for U.S. favor, to lean hard on their Vietnamese comrades to compromise with the United States. But Hanoi began to lay the groundwork for a massive new invasion of the South. U.S. and South Vietnamese military commanders braced for an enemy offensive in February to coincide with the President's trip to China. Instead, Hanoi launched a major spring offensive across the demilitarized zone at the 17th parallel on March 31, a month after the Beijing summit and seven weeks before the Moscow summit.

Nixon and Kissinger now moved to turn the screws on the Russians, to compel them to face the consequences for U.S.–Soviet relations of their continued support of the North Vietnamese war effort. State and Defense Department spokesmen began complaining publicly about the heavy role of Soviet military supplies in the new North Vietnamese offensive.

Meanwhile, North Vietnam was brought under heavy and sustained air bombardment for the first time since the Johnson administration. The port of Haiphong and storage depots around Hanoi were raided by B-52s. Four Soviet merchant ships in Haiphong harbor were damaged by the bombings. U.S. officials hinted of still more destructive escalations to come, including even the mining of North Vietnamese ports which, by putting Soviet supply convoys in jeopardy, would force the issue with the Kremlin.

While the risks of a direct U.S.–Soviet confrontation over Vietnam rose to dangerous levels during April 1972, Kissinger traveled secretly to Moscow to firm up preparations for the May summit between Brezhnev and Nixon. The evident progress in SALT and commercial talks gave both sides reason to hope for a major breakthrough in U.S.–Soviet relations to be unveiled at the summit as long as Vietnam did not ruin it. Each side sensed that the other was most anxious for the summit to take place. But as Kissinger was to find out in Moscow, since both were aware of the other's real priorities, neither could use the threat of postponing or canceling the summit as leverage on the other's role in Vietnam. Kissinger returned to Washington with plans for the May Nixon–Brezhnev meeting intact but with no meaningful Kremlin assurances to bring pressure on the Vietnamese to sign a compromise peace.

Two days after Kissinger returned from Moscow, Nixon went on nationwide television and radio to vent his frustration at the lack of progress in the peace negotiations and to explain the reasons for the resumption of the systematic bombing of North Vietnam. The Easter weekend military offensive by the North, argued Nixon, had stripped away "Whatever pretext there was of a civil war in South Vietnam." Once again escalating his rhetoric on the enormity of the international crime being committed by Hanoi, the President made it more difficult to admit, finally, that the United States had no business continuing to participate in the war: "What we are witnessing here, what is being brutally inflicted upon the people of South Vietnam, is a clear case of naked and unprovoked aggression across an international border." [11] Curiously, this definition of the situation was revived after the United States had repeatedly offered to establish a cease-fire-in-place, to withdraw all its forces, and to establish interim political arrangements in the South based on the military status quo. Washington's willingness to legitimize the fruits of the war had thus already been established, even though at least ten regular North Vietnamese combat divisions were already in South Vietnam. Now Hanoi's movement of three additional combat divisions across the 17th parallel was pointed to as contradicting Hanoi's claim that the conflict was a civil war!

The reescalation of the U.S. stake in Vietnam was backed up by Nixon's promise to continue U.S. air and naval attacks on North Vietnam "until the North Vietnamese stop their offensive in South Vietnam." [12] Other officials hinted that more and more targets in the North would come under attack. Yet at the same time Nixon pledged to continue withdrawing American troops. He claimed to be able to do this because, according to reports he had received from the American commander in Vietnam, General Creighton Abrams, the South Vietnamese forces had demonstrated their ability to defend themselves on the ground against future enemy attacks. "I have decided," said the President, "that Vietnamization has proved itself sufficiently that we can continue our program of withdrawing American forces without detriment to our overall goal of insuring South Vietnam's survival as an independent country." [13]

However, the military reports from the field during the next few days did not support the President's optimistic assessment of the fighting capabilities of the South Vietnamese army. Abandoning Quangtri City, south of the 17th parallel, the South Vietnamese forces virtually turned and ran southward to avoid the advancing North Vietnamese. Hue would be next, and the resulting demoralization of Saigon would bring on a humiliating collapse of the South's effort before the 1972 presidential elections. Something had to be done to break the downhill slide.

Kissinger, again meeting with Le Duc Tho in Paris, offered to accelerate the U.S. withdrawal (all U.S. troops would be removed before the November elections) if Hanoi would agree to a cease-fire and a return of U.S. prisoners of war. In effect, he was saying: Just give us a decent interval to get out under the cloak of an apparent compromise, and you can have the whole country. But riding high now, the North Vietnamese were evidently more confident than ever that they could have it entirely their way: the Americans would have to cooperate in immediately deposing the Thieu regime or else there would be no deal.

Nixon and Kissinger, still hoping to avoid wholesale capitulation to the Communist demands, now attempted to use their incompletely exploited indirect leverage on Hanoi through the Moscow connection. The Navy was authorized to implement one of the favorite options of the Joint Chiefs of Staff: mining Haiphong harbor and other ports in order to drastically increase the risks and costs to the Soviets of supplying North Vietnam. Presumably, this would compel the Kremlin to lean hard on Hanoi to bring the war to an end through diplomacy instead of attempting to win a total military victory. The order to execute the operation was issued on May 8, 1972, only two weeks before Nixon was scheduled to meet with Brezhnev in Moscow. In so forcing the issue of Vietnam with the Russians, Nixon and Kissinger clearly were risking Kremlin postponement, if not cancellation, of the summit. It was a gamble, but Nixon claimed that his back was against the wall and he was left with no alternatives.

In his May 8, 1972, address explaining this decision, Nixon painted his options starkly: "immediate withdrawal of all American forces, continued attempts at negotiation, or decisive military action to end the war." The first course, he contended, "would mean turning 17 million South Vietnamese over to Communist tyranny and terror. It would mean leaving hundreds of American prisoners in Communist hands with no bargaining leverage to get them released." And it would "encourage . . . smaller nations armed by their major allies . . . to attack neighboring nations at will in the Mideast, in Europe, and other areas."

The alternative of negotiating an honorable settlement was his preferred course, said Nixon. But after four years during which "we have made every reasonable offer and tried every possible path for ending this war at the conference table, . . . the North Vietnamese arrogantly refuse to negotiate anything but an . . . ultimatum that the United States impose a Communist regime on 17 million people in South Viet-Nam."

It was plain, Nixon concluded, "that what appears to be a choice among three courses of action for the United States is really no choice at all. . . . There is only one way to stop the killing. That is to keep the weapons of war out of the hands of the international outlaws of North Vietnam"—in other words, a return to the first alternative, decisive military action:

> All entrances to North Vietnamese ports will be mined to prevent access to these ports and North Vietnamese naval operations from these ports.
>
> United States forces have been directed to take appropriate measures within the internal and claimed territorial waters of North Vietnam to interdict the delivery of any supplies.
>
> Rail and all other communications will be cut off to the maximum extent possible. Air and naval strikes against military targets in North Vietnam will continue. [14]

These acts of force would stop, promised the President, once U.S. prisoners of war were released by Hanoi and once an internationally supervised cease-fire had begun. At such time the United States would proceed to completely withdraw all its forces from Vietnam within four months.

Pointedly, Nixon began his address with special reference to the Soviet role. The present massive invasion of South Vietnam, he maintained, "was made possible by tanks, artillery, and other advanced offensive weapons supplied to Hanoi by the Soviet Union and other Communist nations." And he closed with remarks directed at the Soviet leadership:

> We expect you to keep your allies, and you cannot expect us to do other than help our allies. But let us . . . help our allies only for the purpose of their defense, not for the purpose of launching invasions against their neighbors. . . .
>
> Our two nations have made significant progress in recent months. We are near major agreements on nuclear arms limitation, on trade, on a host of other issues. Let us not slide back toward the dark shadows of a previous age. . . .

We, the United States and the Soviet Union, are on the threshold of a new relationship. . . . We are prepared to build this relationship. The responsibility is yours if we fail to do so.[15]

In this pointed rhetoric as well as in the military action, the May 1972 escalation was the biggest gamble Nixon took in Vietnam, for it could have severely alienated the Russians on the eve of the Moscow summit and thereby in one blow shattered the larger diplomatic mosaic the administration was attempting to construct.

The talk around Washington at the time, possibly inspired by Kissinger himself, was that "Henry opposed the President on this one," and it was the vigorous intervention of Secretary of the Treasury John Connally that stiffened the President's determination to up the ante despite the risks.[16]

It is not at all implausible that Kissinger, in order to keep his diplomatic channels open, felt that it was tactically necessary to separate himself somewhat from the administration's new belligerent posture. Kissinger would be the one who would have to reconstitute the summit plans if they were to fall apart temporarily, and it was Kissinger who still would have to meet face to face with his North Vietnamese counterparts when the negotiations resumed.

The basic escalatory ploy, however, was fully consistent with the Kissinger mode of coercive diplomacy. In any event the gamble worked, at least insofar as the Kremlin chose not to scuttle the larger détente relationship, and—to the surprise of most of the Washington policy community—the Russians indicated that the Nixon–Brezhnev summit was still on. But whether the gamble worked in its main objective of pressuring the Soviets to lean hard on the North Vietnamese to finally negotiate a compromise peace remains a question to be illuminated by further historical research.

Defenders of the Haiphong mining operation claimed not only that it broke the back of North Vietnam's spring offensive but that in driving up the risks to the Soviets themselves of a prolongation of the war in Southeast Asia it was the key to a significant Kremlin decision to reduce arms deliveries to North Vietnam and to President Nikolai Podgorny's visit to Hanoi of June 15, presumably to tell the North Vietnamese that they must now negotiate seriously to end the war instead of banking on a total capitulation by their opponents.[17]

If the Soviets did indeed intercede with Hanoi in the spring and summer of 1972 on behalf of the United States, they probably did so

in order to continue the momentum of détente expressed at the
Nixon–Brezhnev summit. There is no evidence, or logic, in the
argument that they did so *because* of the Haiphong mining. Moreover, at the summit Kissinger and Nixon, it has been reported,
inched even closer to Hanoi's maximum demands, reaffirming their
acceptance of a North Vietnamese military presence in South Vietnam, endorsing a tripartite electoral commission that would include
neutralists and the Viet Cong, and conveying their willingness to
call off the bombing of the North prior to a release of American prisoners.[18]

During the summer and fall, Kissinger exhibited great optimism
that the long-sought agreement with Hanoi to end the war was
imminent. In retrospective interviews he attributed the intensification of constructive negotiations with Le Duc Tho to the success of
his leverage diplomacy in putting pressure on both Moscow and
Beijing (each afraid the other would be favored by the United States)
to persuade Hanoi to allow the Americans to leave Vietnam "with
honor."[19]

The sequence of events supports a contrary explanation—namely,
that Nixon and Kissinger, fearful of being outflanked in the coming
U.S. presidential elections by a Democratic peace candidate, conveyed to the Communist powers—more convincingly than ever before—their willingness to give in to Hanoi's demands on virtually all
points. This interpretation is supported particularly by the evident
reluctance of the White House to let the Thieu regime in Saigon
know how completely the United States was now prepared to abandon South Vietnam. During the months following the Moscow summit, the problem of how to persuade Thieu to accept the inevitable
became Washington's central preoccupation. White House military
aide General Haig was dispatched to Saigon to persuade Thieu while
Kissinger and Le Duc Tho labored through August, September, and
October to dot the *i*'s and cross the *t*'s of what was now a basic
Washington–Hanoi accord on most of the essential provisions of the
peace agreement.

THE FINAL BRAVADO . . . AND DENOUEMENT

The hopes of Nixon and Kissinger to successfully conclude the peace
negotiations on the eve of the November 1972 elections were dashed

by Thieu's refusal to accept the terms agreed upon by Kissinger and Le Duc Tho. The South Vietnamese had numerous objections to the draft agreement, but their deepest grievances were over the establishment of a South Vietnamese coalition regime including the Communists, and over the failure to provide for a withdrawal of North Vietnamese troops from South Vietnam. Kissinger urged the President to authorize a separate peace between the United States and North Vietnam; but Nixon needed Saigon's acquiescence to preserve the fiction of an "honorable peace." Accordingly, he had Kissinger delay the final signing. Hanoi thereupon unilaterally disclosed the terms of the draft agreement, probably in an effort to force the issue between Washington and Saigon. Kissinger maintained a public air of optimism by insisting that "peace is at hand," but he surely feared a last-minute disintegration of all his painstaking labors.

When Kissinger and Le Duc Tho met again a few weeks after the November 1972 election in which Nixon defeated George McGovern by an overwhelming margin, the North Vietnamese negotiator seemed to have toughened his stand. Not only did he reject all the points Kissinger presented on behalf of President Thieu, but according to Kissinger's subsequent press briefings he made additional demands to alter the texts he and Kissinger had agreed to in October. In retrospect the new intransigence on the part of the North Vietnamese is understandable, for they could easily have interpreted Nixon's procrastination prior to the elections as a cover for the massive military reinforcements the United States flew into South Vietnam immediately after the election. Although the White House's purpose in this new military infusion may have been to buy off Thieu rather than to alter the military balance of power in South Vietnam before the cease-fire took effect, the North Vietnamese could well have suspected a ruse and decided to stall while engaging in their own reinforcements.

Nixon and Kissinger were more frustrated than ever. Had they slipped back onto a reverse track just as the opening at the end of the tunnel was immediately in front of them? Determined to break out at last, they tried one more dramatic set of moves. They now informed Hanoi that Nixon was ready to agree to a separate peace with North Vietnam if Thieu failed to agree to the October terms. They also informed Thieu of this decision and threatened to cut off all assistance to South Vietnam if Thieu persisted in being an obstructionist. Simultaneously, they delivered a 72-hour ultimatum to Hanoi that unless serious negotiations were resumed immediately they would bomb North Vietnam again with even less restraint than before. With the expiration of the ultimatum on December 18, U.S. bombers commenced a 12-day round-the-clock devastation attack on North Vietnam, including massive attacks on "military" targets in heavily populated areas of Hanoi and Haiphong.[20]

The 1972 Christmas bombing operation was nothing less than an effort to terrorize the North Vietnamese back to the negotiating table. Not incidentally, it would also impress President Thieu. After suffering a rain of bombs for nearly two weeks, the North Vietnamese said they had had enough; they were ready to resume serious negotiations. On December 30 Nixon ordered a halt to the attacks north of the 20 parallel and dispatched Kissinger to Paris for the diplomatic anticlimax.

On January 23, 1973, the Agreement on Ending the War and Restoring the Peace in Vietnam was initialed in Paris by Kissinger and Le Duc Tho. (On January 27 it was formally signed by Secretary of State William Rogers and the North Vietnamese Foreign Minister, Nguyen Duy Trinh, with the Foreign Minister of the Thieu regime and the Foreign Minister of the Communist "Provisional Revolutionary Government" in South Vietnam separately countersigning special copies so that their two names would not appear together on one document.) "The people of South Vietnam have been guaranteed the right to determine their own future without outside interference," announced President Nixon. "Throughout these negotiations we have been in closest consultation with President Thieu and other representatives of the Republic of South Vietnam. This settlement meets the goals and has the full support of President Thieu and the Government of the Republic of Vietnam, as well as that of our other allies who are affected.[21] Neither the history of the negotiations nor the text of the 1973 agreement and attached protocols nor the subsequent fate of South Vietnam supported these claims by Nixon.

The Paris agreement and protocols were transparently a conditional surrender of the non-Communists to the Communists in Vietnam. Coequal status was henceforth to be given in South Vietnam to the "two parties"—the Government of the Democratic Republic of Vietnam (the Thieu regime) and the Provisional Revolutionary Government of South Vietnam (the Communists). The cease-fire would accordingly legitimize all Communist military gains to date and their continuing military–administrative control of these areas, pending the establishment of a new government of South Vietnam. The new government was to be established through "free and democratic general elections," but the two parties would each have a veto in all transitional processes and institutions leading toward the establishment of the new government. Meanwhile, the armed forces of the United States were to be totally withdrawn, regardless of whether the political–governmental provisions of the agreement were working. There was no requirement, however, for the North Vietnamese to remove their forces. Some weak and ambiguous controls were provided on the military reinforcement by North Vietnam and the United States of their respective South Vietnamese allies, but the interpretation and enforcement of these controls would also be subject to the veto of both parties. Kissinger did succeed in getting the North Vietnamese to concede to most of the U.S. demands for the prompt return of all captured military personnel and foreign civilians; the quid pro quo was a U.S. concession on the return of captured Vietnamese civilians, stipulating that the question "will be resolved by the two South Vietnamese parties."[22]

To the surprise of no one who knew the situation in Indochina, the paper peace began to crumble before its ink was dry. Both Vietnams violated the strictures against new military buildups; each blamed the other for the renewed outbreak of fighting and for the failure to set up institutions to govern the transition to free elections. The military balance of power in South Vietnam, Laos, and Cambodia continued to determine the future of these countries, given the prevailing political anarchy in each.

Kissinger, realpolitik statesman that he was, could not have expected anything else. Yet in the first volume of his memoirs he insists that "I believed then, and I believe now, that the agreement could have worked. It reflected a true equilibrium of forces on the ground. . . . We believed that Saigon was strong enough to deal with guerrilla warfare and low-level violations.[23] This assessment proved false, for the violations during the early months of 1973 involved heavy infiltration of military personnel and equipment down the Ho

Chi Minh Trail and across the demilitarized zone, including tanks and surface-to-air missiles. Witnessing this change in the balance of forces, and being prevented by U.S. domestic pressures from re-dressing the growing imbalance, Kissinger recalls, in his second volume, that "in my bones I knew that collapse was just a question of time."[24]

Kissinger denies any naïveté whatsoever about Hanoi's intentions. "I never believed," he recalls, "that Hanoi would reconcile itself to the military balance as it emerged from the Paris Agreement without testing it at least once more." However, Hanoi would be discouraged from actually attempting to topple the military balance because of its fear of U.S. retaliation. "American air power was thus always seen as an essential deterrent to the resumption of all-out war. Nixon gave assurances on this score to South Vietnamese President Nguyen Van Thieu to persuade Thieu to accept the Paris Agreement."[25]

The miscalculation in the White House, then, if we are to take Kissinger's published recollections at face value, was over the ability of the American political process to deliver on the military commit-ment that Nixon and Kissinger gave to Thieu and which Hanoi was supposed to have heard and believed. But how could Nixon and Kissinger have made such a gross miscalculation? Surely, by the fall of 1972, when the basic deal was being struck with Hanoi, the evidence was clear that the majority of the American people wanted an end to the sacrifice of American blood and treasure in Indochina, and that such sacrifice was not warranted to preserve a U.S. client state in South Vietnam. Kissinger still insists that "the people never chose abdication." He cites Nixon's huge electoral victory over George McGovern in November 1972 and opinion polls as endorse-ments of the basic policy of "peace with honor." It is true, says Kissinger, that a majority of the American people came to believe that it had been a mistake to get involved in Vietnam in the first place and that that involvement should be brought to an end, "but an even larger majority rejected the peace movement's policy of immediate and unconditional withdrawal." This larger majority, claims Kissinger, was looking to the nation's executive for the leader-ship that would be crucial in managing the transition to full peace in Indochina in a way that preserved the reputation of the United States as a country that honored its commitments and that did not tempt adversaries to engage in new aggression.[26] But the required executive leadership was not to emerge. The principal reason, according to Kissinger, was Watergate.

During March and April 1973 Kissinger urged Nixon to order a three- or four-day sustained bombing of the North Vietnamese bases and trails in Laos and on both sides of the demilitarized zone separating North and South Vietnam. It was important "to give Hanoi a jolt" to make it clear to the enemy that "we may do something totally unexpected" if it continued to violate the Paris agreement. Kissinger could not get a clear and consistent set of orders out of his chief, however. He portrays Nixon during this period as "uncharacteristically indecisive," as "a distracted man." It was only later, when examining the records, that Kissinger found out the extent of Nixon's preoccupation with the Watergate investigations at the very time that it was most urgent to get him to act decisively to prevent the complete unraveling of the Indochina peace.[27]

"The normal Nixon would have been enraged beyond containment," offers Kissinger, at the mid-April reports that 35,000 fresh North Vietnamese troops had entered South Vietnam and nearby border sanctuaries; "but Watergate Nixon continued to dither."[28] The President did approve U.S. limited bombing of targets in Laos in a two-day retaliation for the North Vietnamese seizure of the Laotian town of Tha Vieng, and he also ordered the suspension of mine-clearing operations around North Vietnamese ports.

The "turning point" for Kissinger—the recognition that it would be futile to expect the beleaguered President to take the retaliatory actions required to deter Hanoi from further violations—came on April 14, 1973, when he heard from one of Nixon's legal advisers that Watergate was beginning to implicate the President himself. "I was appalled by the knowledge, seeing, for the first time clearly, how the Watergate challenges could reach to the heart of the Presidency and destroy all authority," recalls Kissinger. He could no longer urge Nixon to put his diminishing prestige behind a resumption of systematic bombing; the President no longer had the authority or the will to focus his energy on beating down the congressional opposition that was sure to be crystalized by such a renewal of coercive diplomacy.[29] In the following months, antiwar measures that had previously been blocked in the House of Representatives began to pass both houses, culminating in the "nail-in-the-coffin" legislation of June barring all further U.S. military action in Indochina. At the time, Kissinger railed against Congress for denying him any significant sanctions to apply against Hanoi; but in the *Years of Upheaval,* he is more candid, admitting that "the 'window' we had in those few months of early 1973 was closed by Watergate's enfeeblements." [30]

The Soviets, perceiving the paralysis of American will to respond, enlarged their flow of military supplies to the Vietnamese Communists over the next two years. Kissinger and President Ford made the obligatory pleas to a reluctant Congress to match the Soviet effort; but even as the final panic spread in South Vietnam in the spring of 1975 there were few Americans in political life who would define the raising of the Viet Cong flag over Saigon as sufficiently harmful to vital U.S. interests to justify still another futile pretense of honor.

14

THE INSUFFICIENCY OF MILITARY CONTAINMENT

What in the name of God is strategic superiority? What is the significance of it, politically, militarily, operationally, at these numbers? What do you do with it?
—HENRY A. KISSINGER

Détente with the Soviet Union, rapprochement with China—both of these early démarches of the Nixon administration were to a large extent prompted by the realization that Soviet military power could now neutralize the ability of U.S. military power to deter objectionable Soviet behavior short of direct threats to the United States itself. New means for affecting Soviet behavior were required to supplement military deterrence.

Military power was still considered necessary to induce the Soviet Union to respect the range of U.S. interests abroad, for if the Soviet Union, but not the United States, were able and willing to resort to force when the secondary interests of the two superpowers clashed, the Soviets could face down the United States in situation after situation and ultimately achieve a position of global dominance. But U.S. military power was no longer deemed sufficient for containing the Soviet Union within its current sphere of dominance, for military containment was based on confidence that the United States would prevail in any major U.S.–Soviet war—a belief that was eroding by the later 1960s.[1]

Confidence that the United States would prevail rested in some important cases on the credibility of U.S. threats to escalate a conflict to strategic levels—for example, in Berlin—where the Kremlin enjoyed a preponderance of locally applicable force. But now that the Soviet Union as well as the United States was supposed to have a strategic arsenal capable of assuring virtually total destruction of the attacker, no matter how large and well executed its first strike, it was highly unlikely that either superpower would seriously contemplate attacking the other for any purpose except retaliation for a direct attack on itself. With strategic deterrence thus restricted to the ultimate holocaust, lesser Soviet aggressive moves, even against loyal allies of the United States, could not be reliably prevented unless the United States and its allies developed other weighty levers on Soviet behavior.

The raw materials for fashioning such levers were sought by Nixon and Kissinger in the mutual paranoia between the Russians and the Chinese and in the Kremlin's desire to increase the Soviet Union's participation in the international economy. It was uncertain, however, that the contemplated triangular relationship—assuming that both Communist powers, for their own reasons, would latch on—would indeed operate to dissuade the Russians and the Chinese from attempting to take advantage of the new mood of isolationism growing in the United States. And the expectation that expanded commercial contacts would provide substantial U.S. leverage on the Soviets was also still only a hypothesis.

Meanwhile, congressional efforts to reduce U.S. defense expenditures were intensifying, and this, if successful, could shift the global military balance in favor of the Soviets. Nixon and Kissinger, neither of whom had been enthusiasts of arms control before 1969, now felt compelled to seriously negotiate limitations on the arms race.

Arms control thereupon was added to expansion of commercial relations with the USSR and normalization of relations with Beijing as the cornerstones of the "structure of peace" that President Nixon spoke of in his 1969 inaugural address. For Kissinger they became essential elements of global order that otherwise—owing to the inherent weakness of containment based mainly on military deterrence—would become dangerously unstable.

THE ARMS CONTROL DILEMMA

Putting a cap on the strategic arms race proved to be the most difficult of the international restructuring tasks that Nixon and Kissinger set for themselves. It required that both sides abandon the goal of strategic superiority and that each give up attempting to protect its population against the other's nuclear attack. The concepts of parity and mutual deterrence went against the grain of many of the influential military and foreign policy elites in both countries. Moreover, the esoteric strategic doctrine that mutual deterrence required both sides to protect their missiles but not their people was hardly likely to be popular with the general public.

Nixon himself, having frequently rejected strategic parity as an acceptable context for conducting U.S.–Soviet relations and having promised during the 1968 election campaign to restore "clear-cut military superiority" as a planning objective, was not about to frontally contradict hopes in the Pentagon (now free from the planning constraints of the McNamara years) to once again pull well ahead of the USSR. The new presidential assistant for national security affairs, however, provided just the right conceptual finesse. At his first presidential news conference, Nixon was asked by a questioner to distinguish between the planning goal of superiority over the Soviet Union being propounded by Secretary of Defense Melvin Laird and a notion being advanced by Kissinger called "sufficiency."[2] Nixon's answer, while leaving much to later elaboration, deftly chalked out the middle ground:

I think the semantics may offer an appropriate approach to the problem. I would say, with regard to Dr. Kissinger's suggestion of sufficiency, that that would meet certainly my guideline and, I think Secretary Laird's guideline with regard to superiority.

Let me put it this way: When we talk about parity, I think we should recognize that wars occur usually when each side believes it has a chance to win. Therefore, parity does not necessarily assure that a war may not occur.

By the same token, when we talk about superiority, that may have a detrimental effect on the other side in putting it in an inferior position and therefore giving great impetus to its own arms race.

Our objective in this administration . . is to be sure that the United States has sufficient military power to defend our interests and to maintain the commitments which this administration determines are in the interests of the United States around the world.

I think "sufficiency" is a better term, actually, than either "superiority" or "parity."[3]

The new strategic planning concept, as elaborated in subsequent statements by the administration, was supposed to accomplish a number of purposes—not all of them compatible.

Sufficiency first and foremost required enough well-protected strategic forces to be able to inflict a level of damage on the Soviet Union that would deter the Soviet leaders from attacking. In this respect the Nixon administration incorporated the "assured destruction" criterion of former Secretary of Defense Robert McNamara. Assured destruction, however, was deemed insufficient as a force planning concept, for, as interpreted by Nixon, it was "limited to the indiscriminate mass destruction of enemy civilians as the sole possible response to challenges." This would be an incredible response insofar as it involved "the likelihood of triggering nuclear attacks on our own population." As such, it was an inadequate strategic basis for preventing the soviets from coercing the United States and its allies.[4]

It was also essential, explained the President, to maintain "a flexible range of strategic options." Given the variety of possible politico-military situations that could conceivably confront the U.S., "our strategic policy should not be based solely on a capability of inflicting urban and industrial damage presumed to be beyond the level an adversary would accept. We must be able to respond at levels appropriate to the situation."[5]

The Nixon administration had three essential reasons for continuing such potentially destabilizing programs:

1. Deterrence *could* fail, and in such situations—however low their probability—the United States would want to disable as much of the Soviet war-fighting capability as possible and reduce the Soviet capacity to kill Americans.

2. The Soviets were building an impressive counterforce capability that by the late 1970s or early 1980s might be able to destroy most of the U.S. land-based ICBMs; the clear strategic asymmetry that would be produced by the presence of such a Soviet capability and the absence of a comparable U.S. capability could be politically exploited by the Soviets in crisis confrontations between the superpowers.

3. The United States would be more effective in bargaining with the Soviets to alter and reduce the counterforce features of their strategic force programs if the U.S. also had counterforce elements that would need to be sacrificed; moreover, the existence of such U.S. programs would dramatize

for the Soviets the consequences of a failure to agree to their limitation—namely, a counterforce arms race with the United States, whose technological abilities in this field were still far ahead of the Soviets.

The Department of Defense seized upon Nixon's ambiguous concept of sufficiency to establish elastic definitions of what would constitute an adequate military balance of power vis-à-vis the Soviets. During the Kennedy–Johnson years Secretary of Defense McNamara had held down the U.S. strategic force posture with an increasingly strict application of the "assured-destruction" criterion, which he defined as being able to destroy one-quarter of the Soviet population and one-third of Soviet industry. No matter what the Soviets might deploy, it was sufficient to be able to inflict this level of damage in retaliation for a Soviet first strike in order to deter the Kremlin from launching a strategic attack. Now, under Secretary of Defense Laird, the military planning objectives were broadened to ensure (1) that Soviet forces could not inflict substantially more damage on the United States than U.S. forces could inflict on the USSR; (2) that each leg of the strategic "triad" (bombers, land-based ICBMs, and sea-based strategic missiles) would be independently able to survive a surprise Soviet attack and strike back with a society-destroying level of destruction; and (3) that, in addition to these war outcome criteria, the number of weapons deployed on each side should not *appear* to give the Soviet Union an advantage.

Ambiguous rhetoric might obscure the contradictions between the Nixon–Laird notion of sufficiency as a defense planning concept and the Nixon–Kissinger concept of sufficiency as an armament-limiting concept; but when it came to actually negotiating a strategic arms limitation agreement with the Soviets, one or the other had to be given the presidential nod. During the first Nixon administration, 1969–1972, Kissinger—through persuasion, deft bureaucratic infighting, and by setting the proper international events into motion—was able to gain Nixon's endorsement of his version at critical junctures.[6]

The climax of the first phase of the U.S.–Soviet strategic arms limitation talks (SALT), culminating in the Moscow agreements of 1972—the treaty limiting antiballistic missile (ABM) systems and the interim agreement on offensive strategic systems—came very close to institutionalizing a "mutual assured destruction" relationship, dubbed MAD.

According to Article I of the ABM treaty, "Each party undertakes not to deploy ABM systems for a defense of the territory of its country."[7] The limited deployments allowed by the treaty (Article III) restricted each side to two sites of 100 launchers each, one site to protect an offensive missile field and the other to protect the country's capital.[8] Clearly, the populations of both countries were to remain unprotected, consistent with the doctrine that if one's population were exposed to nuclear attack from one's enemy one would not dare to start a nuclear war.

The five-year interim agreement on offensive weapons allowed the Soviet Union to build up its ICBM force to 1,618 while the United States would keep its existing level of 1,054. The Soviets were allowed 950 submarine-launched ballistic missiles (SLBMs) and 62 submarines, while the United States was confined to 710 SLBMs and 44 submarines. Important weapon systems left out of the agreement—bombers, land-mobile ICBMs, forward-based forces of less than intercontinental range, and multiple warheads—were to be the subject of more comprehensive negotiations that were supposed to produce a completed treaty by October 1977.[9]

The allowance of a Soviet numerical advantage in ICBMs and SLBMs was not yet of serious concern to the U.S. Defense Department, for in the items not covered by the agreement the United States was well ahead of the Soviets. But the military preparedness coalition in Congress and the administration was determined to make the subsequent SALT negotiations more responsive to their interpretations of sufficiency. Senator Henry Jackson formulated a Senate resolution which the administration accepted, insisting that in any future strategic weapons agreements with the USSR the United States not accept provisions, such as those in SALT I, that would leave the United States with numerical inferiority.

Kissinger's achievement in satisfying Nixon's political need for a dramatic démarche in U.S.–Soviet relations was made possible by his ability to cater to Brezhnev's political needs and to make these even more intense by the acceleration of détente diplomacy with the U.S.–China rapprochement.[10]

The temporarily suppressed contradictions in the administration's sufficiency concept and in the Soviets' analogous dilemma of simultaneously agreeing to stabilize the arms race while continuing to deploy strategic forces with impressive war-fighting characteristics, were bound to surface again even before the ink was dry on the SALT I agreements.

In the summer of 1972, the Defense Department asked Congress to provide funds for the development of strategic warheads with "hard-target kill capabilities" and programs were accelerated for installing accurate multiple independently targetable reentry vehicles (MIRVs) on U.S. ICBMs and submarine-launched strategic missiles.

In 1973 and 1974, Secretary of Defense James Schlesinger, in a series of candid news conferences, revealed the administration's intention to acquire "precision instruments that would be used in a limited counterforce role" and disclosed that it was refining its strategic targeting doctrine to give the President a "broader range of options." In addition, the administration was prepared to balance any Soviet attempt to obtain a major counterforce option ("We cannot permit the other side to have a relatively credible counterforce capability if we lack the same").[11] Schlesinger's annual defense posture statement to Congress for fiscal year 1975 provided a carefully worded justification for the renewed emphasis on counterforce options:

> To enhance deterrence, we may want . . . a more efficient hard-target kill capability than we now possess: both to threaten specialized sets of targets (possibly of concern to allies) with a greater economy of force, and to make it clear to a potential enemy that he cannot proceed with impunity to jeopardize our own system of hard targets. . . .
>
> To stress changes in targeting doctrine and new options does not mean radical departures from past practice. Nor does it imply any possibility of acquiring a first strike disarming capability. As I have repeatedly stated, both the United States and the Soviet Union now have and will continue to have large, invulnerable second strike forces. . . .
>
> We would be quite content if both the United States and the Soviet Union avoided the acquisition of major counterforce capabilities. But we are troubled by Soviet weapons momentum, and we simply cannot ignore the prospect of growing disparity between the two major nuclear powers. We do not propose to let an opponent threaten a major component of our forces without being able to pose a comparable threat. We do not propose to let an enemy put us in a position where we are left with no more than a capability to hold his cities hostage after the first phase of a nuclear conflict. And certainly we do not propose to see an enemy threaten one or more of our allies with his nuclear capabilities in the expectation that we would lack the flexibility and resolve to strike back at his assets.[12]

Particular stress was now accorded to "essential equivalence" with the Soviet Union in all the basic force characteristics ("throw-weight, accuracy, yield-to-weight ratios, reliability and other such factors") for reasons of military effectiveness *and* political appearances. The requirement was for "a range and magnitude of capabilities such that everyone—friend, foe, and domestic audiences alike— will perceive that we are the equal of our strongest competitors."[13] This meant that even though the Soviets might be exercising bad strategic logic in building forces that could destroy a large portion of the U.S. land-based ICBMs (bad logic in that the Soviet Union could still be destroyed by U.S. submarine-launched missiles and bombers), the United States—to preserve the appearance of symmetry—should also build such a counterforce capability.

Soviet defense programs were even more blatantly at cross-purposes with mutual strategic arms limitation. Consistent with the letter but not the spirit of the 1972 Moscow accords, the USSR continued to deploy heavy-payload ICBMs with substantial counterforce potential, and their military doctrine stressed the requirements of fighting and prevailing in a strategic war more than deterrence. Evidence of continued Soviet reliance on heavy counterforce capabilities spurred U.S. defense planners to go ahead with new systems as a "hedge" against Soviet attempts to achieve strategic dominance. The major consequences were a full-speed-ahead program of retrofitting U.S. missiles with MIRV warheads, efforts to enhance the accuracy of all U.S. strategic systems (including submarine-launched missiles), and "next generation" bomber programs (the B-1 bomber and long-range cruise missiles for the modernized bomber force).

Kissinger and others who hoped to translate the 1972 interim agreement on offensive systems into a solid treaty by its expiration date of October 1977 were dismayed at the continued "qualitative" technological race proceeding on both sides. Not only was that race making a mockery of the quantitative limits agreed to in SALT I, but it was virtually precluding reliable verification of these or future limits. Kissinger's anxiety to put a cap on the accelerating competition before it was too late was reflected in his complaint at a Moscow press conference in connection with Nixon's 1974 visit that "both sides have to convince their military establishments of the benefits of restraint."[14]

The Secretary of State hastily arranged for Brezhnev and President Ford to commit themselves, at their 1974 Vladivostok meeting to negotiating a treaty that would at least freeze their arsenals at a specified number of strategic missile launchers (2,400 for each side), of which only a subset (1,320) could be MIRVed. Within the overall ceiling of 2,400, each side could deploy its own preferred mix of ICBMs, submarine-launched ballistic missiles, or bombers; and there was no specified limit on missile throw-weight.[15] The Vladivostok accord was a political holding action at the top to keep the objective of a mutual-deterrence treaty from being totally subverted by the combined pressures of technology and military doctrine, which, in the United States as well as in the Soviet Union, were tending more and more toward legitimating strategic counterforce and other warfighting capabilities.

When it came to converting the Vladivostok principles into a stable and verifiable treaty, however, the military experts on both sides—even those dedicated to arms control—continued to be baffled by the increasing difficulty of distinguishing offensive from defensive deployments, strategic from tactical weapons, nuclear from conventional munitions, single from multiple warheads, and by the virtual impossibility of determining (in advance of its actually being used) whether a given weapon had a city or a missile complex as its primary target.

Kissinger's skepticism about the stability over time of technical limitations on military hardware led him to concentrate as much on the symbolic benefits of negotiating constructively with the Soviets in the SALT arena as on the presumed military effects of any agreements that might be concluded. And his doubts that close attention to the military balance itself would be sufficient for the purpose of preventing the Kremlin from using military coercion against U.S. interests reinforced his belief in the necessity of non-military levers on Soviet behavior. The China connection and the economic aspects of détente diplomacy were supposed to compensate for the shortfalls in military containment.

THE CHINA ANGLE

The Nixon–Kissinger construction of a new relationship with China preceded and gave impetus to the rapid elaboration of the U.S.–Soviet détente relationship in the early 1970s. The China connection, conceived of primarily as a means of pressuring the Kremlin to be more accommodating to U.S. demands, was also designed to serve other objectives of the administration: an early end to the Vietnam War; a reduction in overseas deployment of American troops; a dismantling of military commitments to Asian regimes that might be unstable or reckless; and simply the need to do something dramatic to convince the American public and international audiences that the government, under Nixon's leadership, did have the capacity to act impressively on the world stage. The new China policy, not incidentally, also could give concrete substance to Kissinger's vague concept of an emerging multipolar world.

However much administration spokesmen might publicly deny that gaining leverage on the Soviet Union was the central purpose of the China connection, this geopolitical *result* of the new triangular relationship was undeniable, and was never really denied. But Nixon and Kissinger apparently calculated that the leverage would be just as great if it was kept implicit and that the Soviets might not be able to bring themselves to be accommodating toward the United States in various fields if it looked to the world as if they were negotiating under coercive pressure.

As Washington and Beijing drew toward each other across the hypotenuse of the triangle from 1969 to 1972, the theatrics of the démarche began to eclipse the geopolitics, but the former in no way undermined the latter. The show business staging of the Nixon visit seemed only to convince the Soviets of the need to stage a more impressive summit spectacular of their own.

Historians will long debate whether this turn in U.S.–China policy was mainly the brainchild of Nixon or of Kissinger (not to mention Mao Zedong and Zho Enlai.) Resolution of this controversy matters little for the present analysis. More important is the fact that both men came to believe by early 1969 that a movement toward normalizing relations with Beijing might now mesh with Chinese calculations and significantly reinforce the Soviets' incentive to explore their own common interests with the United States.[16]

China experts in and out of government had been picking up signs during the late 1960s that Mao and Zho might be reading the tea leaves similarly. The Chinese condemned the Soviet invasion of Czechoslovakia in August 1968 and especially the doctrine of "limited sovereignty" of countries in the Socialist camp by which the Soviets justified their invasion. Tension was heightening along the

Sino-Soviet border in the aftermath of Czechoslovakia. In November 1968 the Chinese Foreign Ministry proposed reconvening the Sino-American ambassadorial talks in Warsaw, which had been suspended since January.[17]

The Nixon administration, while indicating its willingness to resume the heretofore sterile exchanges in Warsaw, was searching for fresh ways to convince the Chinese that the White House might be open to an exploration of some fundamental improvements in the relationship. Early in 1969 Nixon began to hint strongly through French, Romanian, and Pakistani intermediaries that he would like to visit China. Meanwhile, an informal coalition of liberal members of Congress and China experts—perhaps sensing that the administration was exploring a shift in policy—tried to create public support for normalizing relations with the Communist regime. Senator Edward Kennedy, speaking on March 20, 1969 to a conference sponsored by the National Committee on United States–China Relations, urged the Nixon administration to take new initiatives, such as the elimination of U.S. military bases on Taiwan and an offer to reestablish consular offices in the People's Republic. (The conference, chaired by former U.S. Ambassador to Japan Edwin O. Reischauer, took place two weeks after the outbreak of military conflict between Soviet and Chinese forces over a disputed island on the Ussuri River. China experts at the conference speculated that this development might provide an opportunity for a breakthrough in U.S.–China relations.)[18]

Starting in the summer of 1969, the Department of State began to announce various unilateral gestures of reconciliation. In July many travel and trade restrictions that had been applied to China since 1950 were relaxed. Americans traveling abroad would be permitted to bring back $100 worth of items produced in the People's Republic. Members of Congress, journalists, teachers, scholars, university students, physicians, and Red Cross representatives would automatically be cleared by the Department for travel to China. These moves were an effort to "relax tensions and facilitate the development of peaceful contacts," explained State Department spokesmen. These particular actions were chosen because they did not require Chinese reciprocation.[19]

Over the next year the administration continued to signal its intent to put U.S.–Chinese relations on a new basis: in November

1969, U.S. naval patrols in the Taiwan Strait (deployed by Truman at the start of the Korean War) were terminated, removing the most visible symbol of U.S. support for the Nationalist Chinese exiles. In December, the U.S. government partially lifted the embargo on trade by foreign subsidiaries of U.S. firms between China and third countries, again stating that the move was "strictly unilateral." In January 1970, the U.S. and Chinese ambassadors to Poland resumed their suspended talks in Warsaw and explored in a preliminary way the possibility of exchange visits by journalists, students, and scientists. On February 18, in the first of his four annual "State of the World" messages to Congress, President Nixon reiterated that "the Chinese are a great and vital people who should not remain isolated from the international community," and revealed that it was administration policy to "attempt to define a new relationship" for the future. "We have avoided dramatic gestures which might invite dramatic rebuffs," explained the President. "We have taken specific steps that did not require Chinese agreements but which underlined our willingness to have a more normal and constructive relationship."[20] Two days later, at the ambassadorial talks in Warsaw, both sides discussed the possibility of moving the talks to Beijing, and the Chinese hinted that they would welcome a high-ranking official to head the U.S. delegation.[21] This delicate courtship was set back somewhat during the spring and summer of 1970 as U.S. troops invaded Cambodia, while in China a struggle was played out between the Lin Piao faction, which favored a hard line toward Washington as well as Moscow, and the Zhou Enlai faction, which favored a moderate policy at home and abroad, including better relations with the United States in order to put pressure on the Soviets.

Early in the fall of 1970 the atmosphere was suddenly alive with possibility. Mao evidently had thrown his weight decisively behind Zho and seemed to be sending his own signals to Washington that a new era in Sino-American relations might now be appropriate. Official Washington attached significance to Mao's having asked the prominent American chronicler of the Chinese Communist revolution, Edgar Snow, to join him on the reviewing stand for the National Day celebrations on October 1. Nixon and Kissinger intensified their efforts to communicate with the Chinese leaders via the Romanians and Pakistanis. Secret notes, presumably dealing with the possibility of a high-level U.S. visit to China, were carried back and forth through the winter months, except for a six-week hiatus in February and early March surrounding the invasion of Laos by South Vietnamese troops with U.S. air support.[22]

Nixon and Kissinger used all available diplomatic channels to reassure Mao that the Laos operation was not meant to threaten China in any way. And in the second annual state of the world address to Congress the President reiterated his objective of drawing China into "a serious dialogue." He invited the "People's Republic of China to explore the path of normalization of its relations with its neighbors and the world, including our own country." During the coming year, promised the President, "I will carefully examine what further steps we might take to create broader opportunities for contacts between the Chinese and American peoples, and how we might remove needless obstacles to the realization of these opportunities. We hope for, but will not be deterred by a lack of, reciprocity." This effort, the President explained, was part of the main foreign policy approach of his administration: "to create a balanced international structure in which all nations have a stake. We believe that such a structure should provide full scope for the influence to which China's achievements entitle it."[23]

The breakthrough occurred on April 27, 1971, when the Pakistani ambassador to the United States delivered a handwritten note from Beijing, with no signature, inviting an "American envoy" to come to China for high-level talks. The note suggested either Kissinger or Secretary of State Rogers.[24] The invitation and the decision to send Kissinger were closely held secrets. The public was allowed the fantasy that the U.S. ping-pong team, touring China in April 1971 at the sudden invitation of Zhou Enlai, was the vehicle through which the inscrutable Chinese made known to the White House their willingness to explore an improvement in relations. While the ping-pong team was still in China, Nixon announced further relaxation of the twenty-year embargo on trade with the People's Republic. A Chinese ping-pong team was, of course, invited to tour the United States. And at the end of April Nixon began to hint unsubtly to journalists and foreign diplomats that he himself would like to be invited to visit China.

The Chinese cooperated in keeping under wraps Kissinger's secret July 1971 mission to Beijing to arrange for the Nixon visit so that the President himself could make a surprise announcement of the dramatic development. Nixon and Kissinger apparently felt they needed a fait accompli to overcome opposition to such a move from the Taiwan government and its U.S. supporters. In the playing out of this surprise, they knew they would cause anxiety in the Kremlin. The stratagem also shocked and angered the Japanese and other allied governments, but the affronts to established friends were presumed to be ultimately retrievable costs well worth the benefits of the new shift in global power relationships.

It was more than mere coincidence that Nixon's July 15 announcement that he would visit China was followed by his revelation in an August 4 press conference that he and the Soviet leaders had agreed that there should be a U.S.–Soviet summit meeting when there was something substantive to discuss that could not be handled in other channels. Nixon indicated that ongoing discussions with the Soviets were making progress in a number of fields—Berlin, SALT, the Middle East—and added pointedly that "if the time comes, as it may come, and both sides realize this, then the final breakthrough in any one of these areas can take place only at the highest level, and then there will be a meeting. But as far as the timing of the meeting before the visit to Peking, that would not be an appropriate thing to do." [25]

The Kremlin got the message and picked up on the cue. The early fall of 1971 was a particularly congenial season at various U.S.–Soviet negotiating tables. Agreements were reached on procedures for preventing nuclear accidents and on improving the emergency hot line between Washington and Moscow. And most significant, a preliminary accord was reached on the outlines of a Berlin settlement. President Nixon announced on October 12 that he had accepted Chairman Brezhnev's invitation to visit Moscow in May.

Kissinger again traveled to Beijing at the end of October—this time in the full glare of news media—to firm up plans for Nixon to visit China in February. It was more than coincidental that Kissinger would be in Beijing while the issue of China's representation in the United Nations was brought to a vote in New York. The latest U.S. position—ending twenty years of opposition to China's membership in the world organization but still refusing to countenance the expulsion of Taiwan—was announced by Secretary of State Rogers on August 2 and stoutly defended in UN debates by Ambassador George Bush in the face of clear indications that the majority would take an unequivocal pro-Beijing stand. In the key resolution on October 25, the General Assembly decided (by a vote of 76 to 35, with 17 abstentions) to recognize the representatives of the People's Republic as "the only legitimate representatives of China" and to "expel forthwith the representatives of Chiang Kai-shek from the place which they unlawfully occupy at the United Nations and in all the organizations affiliated with it." The White House immediately issued a statement accepting the will of the majority but regretting the explusion of Taiwan.

The year 1972 was to be, in effect, the Year of the Triangle: the year of maximum exploitation by the Nixon administration of its new China connection to pressure the Kremlin on SALT, European security issues, and the conflict in Southeast Asia; the year of maximum exploitation of the growing U.S.–Soviet détente to induce the Chinese to be patient with the United States for continuing to recognize the government of Taiwan and for its slow-paced disengagement from Southeast Asia; and the year of maximum exploitation of Nixon's popularity in both Moscow and Beijing to induce the North Vietnamese to seriously negotiate an all-Indochina peace agreement with the United States. Not incidentally, the simultaneity of all this with the U.S. presidential election campaign was exploited to the hilt.

Uncertain of the strength of the incentives for either Moscow or Beijing to put good relations with the United States ahead of their other international and domestic objectives, the White House was anxious not to appear too blatant in playing on the Machiavellian triangle. Repeatedly, in statements preceding and following the President's trip to China, Nixon and Kissinger insisted that "our policy is not aimed against Moscow. The United States and the USSR have issues of paramount importance to resolve; it would be costly indeed to impair progress on these through new antagonisms." To attempt to use the opening to Beijing "to exploit Sino-Soviet tensions . . . would be self-defeating and dangerous."[26]

The Chinese were more candid with respect to their own reasons for seeking a rapprochement with the United States. The official Beijing journal *Hungchi* reprinted a 1940 article by Mao propounding the wisdom of "uniting with forces that can be united while isolating and hitting the most obdurate enemies."[27]

The Americans succeeded, however, in keeping direct anti-Soviet

statements out of the communiqué issued by President Nixon and
Premier Zhou Enlai in Shanghai at the conclusion of the Nixon
visit. In the language of the communiqué, "The two sides state that
. . . neither should seek hegemony in the Asia–Pacific region and
each is opposed to efforts by any other country or group of countries
to establish such hegemony." And, in a stroke of studied ambiguity,
"Both sides are of the view that it would be against the interest of
the peoples of the world for any major country to collude with
another against other countries, or for major countries to divide up
the world into spheres of interest."[28]

Even in the parts of the communiqué reserved for unilateral
statements by each side, the Chinese, deferring to U.S. sensitivities,
threw their barbs in clever general formulations that could be applied
to either the Americans or the Soviets. Thus,

> The Chinese side stated: Wherever there is oppression, there is resistance.
> Countries want independence, nations want liberation and the people want revolu-
> tion—this has become the irresistible trend of history. All nations, big or small,
> should be equal; big nations should not bully the weak. China will never be a
> superpower and it opposes hegemony and power politics of any kind. The Chinese
> side stated that it firmly supports the struggles of all the oppressed people and
> nations for freedom and liberation and that the people of all countries have a right
> to choose their social systems according to their own wishes and the right to
> safeguard the independence, sovereignty and territorial integrity of their own coun-
> tries and oppose foreign aggression, interference, control and subversion. All foreign
> troops should be withdrawn to their own countries.[29]

For the most sensitive issue between the United States and China—
the problem of Taiwan—the device of including two separate statements in the comminuqué was indispensable. The Chinese reaffirmed their longstanding position that "Taiwan is a province of
China . . . ; the liberation of Taiwan is China's internal affair in
which no other country has a right to interfere; and all U.S. forces
and military installations must be withdrawn from Taiwan." The
Americans attempted to finesse the issue, declaring, in one of the
most carefully crafted statements in the annals of diplomacy, that

> the United States acknowledges that all Chinese on either side of the Taiwan Strait
> maintain there is but one China and that Taiwan is part of China. The United
> States Government does not challenge that position. It reaffirms its interest in a
> peaceful settlement of the Taiwan question by the Chinese themselves. With this
> prospect in mind, it affirms the ultimate objective of the withdrawal of all U.S.

forces from Taiwan. In the meantime, it will progressively reduce its forces and military installations on Taiwan as the tension in the area diminishes.[30]

By granting the legitimacy of even this thin line of disagreement, Mao and Zhou had made a substantial concession in the service of the higher goal they shared with Nixon and Kissinger of normalizing U.S.–China relations in order to gain new leverage on the Kremlin.

The most candid public exposition by a U.S. official of the connection between U.S. policies toward the Soviet Union and U.S. policies toward China was made by Winston Lord, director of the State Department's policy planning staff (and Kissinger's closest aide on China policy). In a statement to a House subcommittee in March 1976, later published in a Department of State *Bulletin* under the title "The Triangular Relationship of the United States, the USSR, and the People's Republic of China," Lord put "improved prospects for global equilibrium" at the top of the list of benefits accruing to the United States from positive relations with China, and "a hedge against Soviet diplomatic and military pressures" as first among the advantages to be derived by the Chinese.

Lord's testimony reiterated the standard official position that an attempt by the United States to manipulate the Sino-Soviet rivalry, to meddle in it, or to take sides, would be dangerous and self-defeating. "At the same time," he observed, "in a triangular relationship it is undeniably advantageous for us to have better relations with each of the other two actors than they have with one another." The United States has no desire to see the Sino-Soviet rivalry escalate into military conflict, said Lord, but "neither can we genuinely wish to see the two major communist powers locked once again in close alliance." In a meticulously formulated qualification, he granted that "a limited thaw in Sino-Soviet relations, however, would not automatically redound to our disadvantage, provided it was not based on shared opposition to the United States." An almost humorous understatement summed up the essence of the approach: "The record to date suggests that improvement in our ties with one does not harm our ties with the others."[31]

Kissinger himself would insist on this public rationale for the China rapprochement through the last days of his tenure as Secretary of State. In an interview with the *New York Times* on the eve of Jimmy Carter's inauguration, he again stressed that "it is a mistake to define the Sino-Soviet relationship in terms of our exploiting their

differences. . . . We didn't create them, we can't exploit them." But
he went on, in a characteristic circumlocution, to place the triangular relationship at the center of his basic geopolitical strategy:

I believe it is important that the People's Republic of China continue to perceive us
as interested in maintaining a world equilibrium. If they feel we have lost our
interest in it or our comprehension of it, or our willingness to preserve it, then they
will draw the inevitable conclusion, which will be to make whatever accommodation
they can get [with the Soviet Union], or they will try to find some other means of
protection, such as organizing the third world against both of us.[32]

THE COMMERCIAL LEVER

During the Kennedy and Johnson administrations policy makers
flirted with the idea of affecting Soviet behavior through commerce.
The hope was to eventually stimulate consumer demand that would
make it more difficult for the Kremlin to sustain high military budgets. Some champions of greater East–West commerce thought it
might also encourage the Soviets to experiment with economic liberalization measures. Presidents Kennedy and Johnson each asked
Congress to approve the sale of wheat to the Soviet Union as a step
toward opening up limited commercial relations in other sectors. But
such moves were tentative and peripheral to the main thrust of U.S.
policy until the Nixon–Kissinger years.

It was not until well into the third year of the Nixon administration that the attempt to construct a commercial relationship between
the two superpowers became an integral part of U.S. policy. As with
the change in policy toward China, the premises of this policy shift
were only partly revealed to the public. Signs that the grounds of
U.S. policy on East–West trade were being altered were picked up
in the fall of 1971 by American firms, which suddenly began to
obtain previously denied licenses to export their products to the
Soviet Union. The coincidence of the export license liberalization
with the firming up of plans for Nixon to visit China and collateral
progress toward a Nixon–Brezhnev summit was hardly accidental.

In the fall of 1971, the Soviets, woefully short of wheat for the
coming winter as a result of a dismal harvest, were allowed to
purchase $1 billion of American surplus food grains. The State
Department indicated its readiness to reduce various discriminatory
shipping regulations on Soviet vessels visiting U.S. ports. The Secre-

tary of Commerce took a highly publicized trip to the Soviet Union surrounded by background stories from government ministries in both countries on the possibilities of pushing U.S.–Soviet trade to the $5 billion-a-year level by the mid-1970s. Appetites on both sides were whetted by visions of cooperative efforts to develop the oil, gas, and hard-mineral riches of Siberia. By the spring of 1972, progress on numerous bilateral commercial negotiations between subordinate levels of the governments was sufficiently advanced for the subject of a general U.S.–Soviet commercial rapprochement to be included as a major item on the agenda for the May summit meeting. Indeed, the Soviets appeared to be more enthusiastic about normalizing economic relations than about any other aspect of détente and this probably was the reason that they refrained from cancelling the 1972 summit in the face of highly coercive U.S. actions against North Vietnam in the spring of 1972 (including the mining of Haiphong harbor, which, not incidentally, interfered with Soviet shipping).

The "basic principles" signed by President Nixon and General Secretary Brezhnev on May 29, 1972, affirmed that "The U.S.A. and the U.S.S.R. regard commercial and economic ties as an important and necessary element in the strengthening of their bilateral relations and will thus actively promote the growth of such ties. They will facilitate cooperation between the relevant organizations and enterprises of the two countries and the conclusion of appropriate agreements and contracts, including long-term ones."[33] By the end of the year, the accomplishments under this accord included an agreement by the Kremlin to pay back $722 million on its wartime Lend-Lease debt by the year 2001, in return for which President Nixon would authorize the Export-Import Bank to extend credits and guarantees for the sale of goods to the Soviet Union; a commitment by the Nixon administration to seek congressional extension of most-favored-nation tariff rates to the Soviet Union; the delivery of 440 million bushes of wheat to the Soviet Union; a maritime agreement opening 40 ports in each nation to the other's shipping; provision for the United States to set up government-sponsored and commercial offices in Moscow to facilitate the work of U.S. business executives seeking contracts, and similar provisions for the Russians in Washington; and the establishment of a Joint U.S.–Soviet Commercial Commission charged with developing and guiding the elaboration of additional arrangements to encourage U.S.–Soviet commerce.

The new policy rested on a number of publicly stated premises, as well as some premises that remained unarticulated, apparently for fear of embarrassing the Kremlin. The openly articulated premises underlying the expansion of U.S.–Soviet commerce were:

——Recent progress on basic political issues (the framework and terms for SALT, and the status of Berlin) made it possible to initiate discussions on a wide range of projects for bilateral cooperation in nonpolitical fields.

——Widened and deepened cooperation in nonpolitical fields would reinforce the trend toward more constructive political relations.

——Bilateral economic arrangements, at first mainly involving trade, could later be broadened to include longer-term cooperative ventures that would "establish an interdependence between our economies which provides a continuing incentive to maintain a constructive relationship."

——As the nonpolitical relationships continued to expand, side by side with continuing progress on arms control and other political issues, there would be created on each side "a vested interest in restraint and in the preservation of peace."[34]

The most elaborate statement of the key premise that a growing web of economic arrangements could reduce political hostility between the United States and the Soviet Union was contained in a report to the President by Secretary of Commerce Peter Peterson, released to the public in August 1972:

Closer economic ties bear both cause and effect relationships to relaxation of political tension. Improvement in political relationships is a prerequisite for improved economic relationships, but, once in place, economic ties create a community of interest which in turn improves the environment for further progress on the political side.

Once set in motion, the cause-and-effect process can portend a downward spiral in political tension, a mutually beneficial economic foundation of the new relationship and tangible increases in the welfare and safety of the peoples of both countries. . . .

Our purpose is . . . to build in both countries a vested economic interest in the maintenance of an harmonious and enduring relationship. A nation's security is affected not only by its adversary's military capabilities but by the price which attends the use of those capabilities. If we can create a situation in which the use of military force would jeopardize a mutually profitable relationship, I think it can be argued that our security will have been enhanced.[35]

One who read between the lines of the public rationale and had occasion to discuss with U.S. policy makers their considerations at the time could ascertain a set of tougher assumptions underlying the effort to open up commerce with the Soviet Union—namely:

——The Kremlin leadership recognized that a continued modernization of the USSR would require a substantial shift of resources into many of the high technology, largely civilian, areas that until recently had been of low priority in comparison with military needs.

——Brezhnev and his comrades also realized that, in order to close the gap in the civilian economy and simultaneously maintain military parity with the United States, the Soviet Union would require substantial inputs from the West, especially in the fields of information technology and electronics.

——The needed Western economic and technological inputs could not be purchased without large credits from the United States and other advanced industrial countries and an improvement in the Soviet Union's export potential.

——Finally, Soviet leaders had come to believe that, despite the Leninist dictum that capitalists would sell the hangman the rope to be used in their own executions, only a fully credible Soviet policy of peaceful coexistence would stimulate the non-communist countries to extend sufficient credits, to liberalize their strategic lists, and otherwise let down their political barriers to East–West commerce.

——In short, the Soviet Union's *economic* need to open up commerce with the industrial countries was greater than their need for commerce with the USSR; therefore, if the United States and its allies wisely bargained with the Soviet Union from this basic position of economic strength, the Kremlin, if not openly backed into a corner, might be willing to pay a *political* price for an expansion of East–West commerce.

Such, undoubtedly, were the unvarnished assumptions beneath the Kissinger gloss that "we have approached the question of economic relations with deliberation and circumspection and as an act of policy not primarily of commercial opportunity." [36] Apparently, the main political price Nixon and Kissinger wanted the USSR to pay was to stop aiding the North Vietnamese war effort in Indochina and to bring pressure on Hanoi to negotiate seriously with the United States to wind down the war.

The U.S. mining of Haiphong harbor took place just two weeks before President Nixon was due in Moscow for his first summit conference with Secretary Brezhnev. The Soviet Minister of Foreign Trade was in the United States at the time for an intense round of presummit commercial negotiations with Secretary of Commerce Peterson and other officials, the results of which were to be unveiled with much fanfare in Moscow. Nixon and Kissinger doubted that the Moscow summit would be allowed to proceed on schedule, but they continued to remind the Russians of what was at stake. Kissinger's May 9 briefing to reporters on the Haiphong mining included a pointed reference to the negotiations in progress with the Soviet Union: "We are on the verge of a new relationship in which, on both sides, whenever there is a danger of crisis, there will be enough people who have a commitment to constructive programs so that they could exercise restraining influences."[37]

During the next few years, when the President or Kissinger publicly observed that détente itself was in jeopardy as a result of Soviet actions—for example, the threat to land Soviet paratroops in the Middle East in 1973 or the Soviet transport of Cuban forces to Angola—they clearly meant to play upon the Kremlin's presumed high motivation for commercial relations with the West. They did not, however, believe that the Kremlin's motivation for commercial relations was so high that U.S. credits and trading privileges could be used as a lever to directly induce changes *within* the Soviet system. This was their objection to the Jackson-Vanik Amendment to the Trade Reform Act of 1974, which sought to deny most-favored-nation trading status and credits to the Soviet Union if the Kremlin did not substantially remove restrictions on Jewish emigration. The administration claimed to be effectively representing the attitudes of the American people toward the denial of human rights in the USSR, but it regarded the Jackson-Vanik Amendment and the Stevenson Amendment (setting a $300 million limit on Export-Import Bank credits to the Soviet Union) as at best unhelpful and at worst likely to revive the bitterness of the cold war. "We have accomplished much," claimed Kissinger in 1974, "but we cannot demand that the Soviet Union, in effect, suddenly reverse five decades of Soviet, and centuries of Russian, history."[38]

The administration did, however, cooperate with the West Europeans in linking East–West economic cooperation to "basket three" human rights issues at the Helsinki Conference on Security and Cooperation in Europe (CSCE). The Soviets probably found it tolerable to go along with such linkage, since the Helsinki language was ambiguous and not explicitly directed at them, nor did the accords themselves contain any sanctions for noncompliance. From the standpoint of the administration, overuse or premature application of economic sanctions (denial of credits and trade) was in any case undesirable, for it would reduce the leverage the United States might obtain from ongoing arrangements.

On the other hand, the administration also belatedly came to the realization that, in the process of attempting to make the Soviet Union more dependent on the non-Communist world by removing political barriers to East–West trade, it may have been creating some cumbersome interdependencies. This problem surfaced most clearly in the concession by both parties' 1976 presidential candidates to demands by U.S. agricultural interest groups that there be no further imposition of embargoes on grain shipments to the Soviet Union. The Ford administration's growing appreciation of the difficulty of operating a policy of economic leverage was reflected in the complaint by a high State Department official that "there has been a tendency in Western countries to let the legitimate quest for commercial advantage in Eastern markets overshadow the need to develop and pursue a purposeful strategy. This has tended to undercut the influences which the economic strength of the industrialized world could exert."[39]

All in all, Kissinger left office on January 20, 1977, with the nonmilitary levers on the Soviet Union that were central to his grand strategy having become objects of growing skepticism in the U.S. policy community. His own doubts about their efficacy, if not supported by a domestic consensus, were reflected in his renewed heavy emphasis in late 1976 (and in subsequent statements as a private citizen) on local balances of military power as essential for containing the Soviets.

15

THE MIDDLE EAST AND THE REASSERTION OF AMERICAN COMPETENCE ABROAD

We could not sit on the sidelines if the Middle East should rage out of control; the world would view it as a collapse of American authority, whatever alibi we might put forward. We had to protect our country's ability to play an indispensable role as the guarantor of peace and the repository of the hopes of free peoples.
—HENRY KISSINGER

For Nixon and Kissinger the liquidation of the Vietnam war was the precondition for the restoration of American international power. They regarded détente with the Soviet Union and rapprochement with China as conducive to the revival of domestic and foreign beliefs in America's dedication to peace and world order, and in its "vision" (a favorite Kissinger word). It was in the Middle East, however, that Nixon and Kissinger could prove the capacity and will to *use* American power effectively during crises in the service of peace and order and, by so doing, re-create international respect for the United States as a constructive and competent superpower.

Their principal Middle Eastern challenges—countering the Soviet buildup of Egyptian military power, controlling the Jordanian crisis of 1970, and stage-managing the termination of the 1973 Arab–Israeli war—provided both men with opportunities to manipulate the most awesome components of American power. In the 1973–74 crisis period, as Nixon became more preoccupied with Watergate,

Kissinger himself had to direct the major military as well as political moves; and by all accounts he loved it.

The Nixon administration inherited the basic dilemma of U.S. Middle Eastern policy: by guaranteeing Israel's security against Arab aggression, the United States had driven many countries into the arms of the Soviet Union and made it more difficult for pro-U.S. regimes in the area to sustain themselves in the face of radical domestic movements. But if the United States were to reduce its support for Israel, the Arabs, with Soviet backing, might soon come to believe they could overpower the small Jewish state. To prevent the crushing of Israel would require U.S. countermoves that would increase the likelihood of a U.S.–Soviet military clash.

Upon assuming the presidency, Nixon attempted to transcend this dilemma by making the United States the active catalyst of the peace process in the Middle East. New initiatives were taken on two levels simultaneously: (1) intense U.S.–Soviet consultations designed to lock the Russians into a joint approach toward an Arab-Israeli settlement and (2) a new "evenhanded" posture toward the demands of the Israelis and the Arabs. Both were reflected in what came to be known as the Rogers Plan—the U.S. draft outline of an Arab–Israeli settlement presented by Secretary of State William P. Rogers to the Soviets for Kremlin endorsement as agreed-upon terms of reference for more specific peace negotiations between Israel and Egypt.

The starting point for the proposed negotiations was United Nations Resolution 242, an ambiguous set of principles passed by the Security Council on November 22, 1967, that both Israel and Egypt said they accepted. Resolution 242 called for a settlement based on "withdrawal of Israeli armed forces from territories occupied in the recent June 1967 conflict" and "termination of all claims or states of belligerency and respect for and acknowledgement of the sovereignty, territorial integrity, and political independence of every state in the area and their right to live in peace within secure and recognized boundaries free from threats or acts of force."[1]

Implementation of Resolution 242 had stalled during the last fourteen months of the Johnson administration, primarily over differing interpretations of the sequence of Israeli withdrawals and the full recognition of Israel's legitimacy by the Arabs. The Arabs, backed by Soviets, insisted on withdrawal first, then peace. The Israelis, supported at least implicitly by the United States, regarded Arab acceptance of Israel as the necessary precondition for relinquishing territories conquered during the last round of the war. The two sides also disagreed over how much of the conquered territory Israel was obligated to give back.

President Nixon delegated Secretary of State Rogers to try to resolve the impasse through a series of diplomatic initiatives aimed at the Soviet Union, the Arabs, and Israel that would compress and dissipate the question of timing in a package of detailed provisions on the rights and duties of the local parties that would form the context for Israeli withdrawals.

The most fully worked out version of the Rogers Plan,[2] as presented to the Soviets on October 28, 1969, provided for indirect negotiations between Israel and Egypt and outlined the key provisions of the agreement that should ensue: (1) a timetable, to be agreed on during the negotiations, for withdrawal of Israeli forces from Egyptian territory occupied during the 1967 war; (2) a formal end to the state of war; (3) specification of the precise locations of the agreed-upon "secure borders," and the establishment of demilitarized zones; (4) freedom of navigation through the Strait of Tiran and an affirmation of its status as an international waterway; (5) nondiscriminatory navigation for the ships of all nations, including Israel, through the Suez Canal; (6) a final settlement of the Gaza strip issue; (7) participation in a process for resolving the Palestinian refugee problem; (8) mutual recognition of each other's sovereignty, political independence, and right to live in peace within secure boundaries free from threats of force; and (9) submission of the final document to the UN Security Council for ratification, and to the United States, the Soviet Union, Great Britain, and France, which would promise to help both sides adhere to the agreement.[3] In December the United States presented to the Big Four a parallel plan outlining a Jordanian–Israeli agreement, including provisions for Jordan's sharing in the administration of Jerusalem.

Despite the elaborate surrounding diplomacy—a preliminary series of meetings on earlier drafts with the Russians, U.S. soundings with Israel, and Soviet soundings with Egypt—the Rogers initiatives got nowhere. Israel flatly rejected the "attempt to impose a forced solution on her . . . [and] appease them [the Arabs] at the expense of Israel."[4] The Soviets, unable to deliver the Egyptians, also rejected the Rogers Plan.

In retrospect, Nixon claims to have known that the provisions for returning the occupied territories to the Arabs meant that the Rogers Plan had absolutely no chance of being accepted by Israel. "I knew that the Rogers Plan could never be implemented," writes Nixon,

> but I believed that it was important to let the Arab world know that the United States did not automatically dismiss its case regarding the occupied territories or rule out a compromise settlement of the conflicting claims. With the Rogers Plan on record, I thought it would be easier for the Arab leaders to propose reopening relations with the United States without coming under attack from the hawks and pro-Soviet elements in their own countries.[5]

THE SAM CRISIS

In January 1970, the Israeli Air Force began to step up its raids on Egypt in retaliation for persisting Egyptian forays across the canal. Raw balance-of-power calculations once again dominated the Middle Eastern scene and the deliberations in the White House. On January 31 Nixon received what Kissinger termed the "first Soviet threat" of his administration—a letter from Premier Kosygin stating that "we would like to tell you in all frankness that if Israel continues its adventurism, to bomb the territory of the UAR and other Arab states, the Soviet Union will be forced to see to it that the Arab states have the means at their disposal, with the help of which a due rebuff to the arrogant aggressor could be made."[6]

Nixon's reply to the threatening Kosygin letter was firm but, by his own characterization, "carefully low-keyed." He warned that increased Soviet arms shipments would draw the major powers more deeply into the conflict, but also proposed U.S.–Soviet discussions on limiting arms supplies to the Middle East.[7] Meanwhile, he postponed responding to Israel's requests for new jet aircraft deliveries. But in the spring of 1970 the deterioration was advancing too rapidly both on the superpower level and on Israel's border to be arrested by benign pleas for cooperation. In April U.S. and Israeli intelligence sources picked up signs not only that the Soviets were accelerating their deliveries of surface-to-air missiles (SAMs), supersonic jets, and tanks to Egypt but also that Soviet military personnel were beginning to man some of the SAM sites and fly some of the planes. Nixon ordered a full investigation of the expanding Soviet role and quietly stepped up the flow of U.S. military supplies to Israel; but he still held back on approving delivery of the supersonic planes that the Israelis now urgently demanded.[8]

As the situation along the Suez became more threatening to Israel, Nixon played on Israeli entreaties for a more forthcoming U.S. response to its military equipment requirements by asking the Israelis to exhibit more flexibility in their terms for a settlement. At the end of May, Prime Minister Meir reiterated Israel's acceptance of Resolution 242 and agreed that it should be the basis of indirect talks between Israel and the UAR. Washington next pressed for an Arab–Israeli cease-fire while talks between the Israelis and Egyptians were conducted under the auspices of UN Special Ambassador Gunnar Jarring. To overcome Israeli fears that a cease-fire would only be exploited by the Russians and Arabs to further strengthen Arab military capabilities, Nixon assured Meir that the United States would continue its arms deliveries at whatever level was needed to prevent a shift in the local balance of power; to that end, in early July he authorized the shipment of electronic-countermeasure (ECM) equipment for Israeli jets to help Israel overcome the Soviet SAMs in the canal zone.[9]

The Israelis were not at all pleased with these marginal and temporizing responses to their requests for decisive U.S. diplomatic and military backing. They feared that the Arabs would use the cease-fire not, as the Americans hoped, as a transition to a negotiated peace but rather as additional time for completing their military buildup while forestalling delivery of a major new round of U.S. military supplies to Israel.

The strongest statement of American intentions during this period came from Kissinger in a June 26 background briefing at San Clemente. "We are trying to get a settlement in such a way that the moderate regimes are strengthened, and not the radical regimes," he told a group of newspaper editors. "We are trying to *expel* the Soviet military presence, not so much the advisers, but the combat pilots and combat personnel, before they become so firmly established."[10]

Egypt was the first to accept the American cease-fire proposal—on July 22, 1970, more than a month after Rogers proposed it. Jordan accepted on July 26. Israel reluctantly acquiesced on August 6. August 7 marked the first day of the cease-fire, which was supposed to last three months and to include a military standstill in a zone thirty-two miles wide on each side of the Suez Canal.

When the Israelis almost immediately began to report Egyptian violations of the truce, in the form of a continuing movement of SAM batteries into the standstill zone, the State Department was unimpressed. But U.S. reconnaissance flights soon confirmed that the Egyptians were indeed systematically introducing new missile launchers into the prohibited area. On August 22 the administration informed the Soviet Union and Egypt that it had "incontrovertible evidence" of the violations, and it followed this up on September 3 by presenting the Russians and the Egyptians with evidence that at least fourteen missile sites had been modified between August 15 and August 27. [11] Nixon now decided to sell Israel at least eighteen of the F-4 supersonic aircraft it had requested. He also ordered rush deliveries to Israel of the latest ECM equipment and conventional Shrike air-to-ground missiles so that the Israeli Air Force could neutralize the SAMs.

At least as important as the resumption of a major flow of U.S. military supplies to Israel was the impact of the Soviet–Egyptian violations of the canal zone truce on the Nixon administration's general policy. At Kissinger's urging, and over the objections of Secretary of State Rogers, there was now a decided tilt toward the Israelis, and a new sympathy for the Meir government's reluctance to make territorial concessions in advance of public and tangible commitments from Egypt indicating plans to live in peace with the Jewish state. Nixon and Kissinger also were freshly determined to reduce Soviet influence over the Arabs and were on the lookout for opportunities to demonstrate American coercive power in the region. Such an opportunity came somewhat sooner than expected. [12]

THE JORDANIAN CRISIS

September 1970 was the month of maximum trauma for King Hussein of Jordan—a situation that presented Nixon and Kissinger with their first full-blown Middle Eastern crisis.

King Hussein was not only the most pro-Western of Arab leaders but also the most cooperative when it came to working for a compro-

mise Arab–Israeli peace. As a consequence he was on the enemies
list of the militant anti-Israelis in the region, particularly the Palestinian commando organizations that wanted to use Jordan's western
border areas as a staging ground for raids into Israel. Moreover,
many of the radical Palestinians living in Jordan were determined to
destroy the Hussein regime and make Jordan the center of their drive
to regain the Palestinian lands controlled by Israel to push the Jews
into the sea.

On September 6, members of the Popular Front for the Liberation
of Palestine (PFLP) hijacked a TWA plane and a Swissair plane and
forced them to land on a airstrip in Jordan twenty-five miles from
the capital, Amman. A third airliner was captured and flown to
Cairo, where its passengers were unloaded just before the plane was
blown up. Still another plane, a BOAC jet, was hijacked the next
day and also flown to the Jordanian airstrip, giving the PFLP a total
of 475 hostages, many of them Americans, in Jordan. The hijackers
threatened to blow up the three planes with their passengers aboard
unless all Palestinian and pro-Palestinian prisoners in Israel, West
Germany, Britain, and Switzerland were released. Beyond this ostensible purpose, the PFLP motive seemed to be to humiliate the
Jordanian monarchy, paving the way for a Palestinian takeover of the
government in Amman. King Hussein was in a double bind: if he
failed to move decisively, the Jordanian army might take matters
into its own hands, thereby undercutting his authority. Yet he was
reluctant to order the army to storm the airstrip, apparently not so
much out of fear that the hostages would be killed as out of anxiety
that Syria or Iraq might move forces into Jordan on behalf of the
Palestinians.[13]

Hussein's dilemma, however, meshed with Nixon's determination
to show resolve and to inject the United States more directly into the
Middle East as a counter to increasing Soviet participation. U.S.
paratroopers of the 82d Airborne Division were placed on semialert
status; a fleet of C-130 air transports was dispatched to Turkey
under an escort of F-4 jet fighters for possible use in evacuating the
Americans from Jordan; and units of the Mediterranean Sixth Fleet
were ordered to sail toward the coasts of Israel and Lebanon.

On September 12, six days after the hijackings began, the PFLP
transferred the hostages to some of their camps and blew up the
three empty planes. In exchange for an Israeli agreement to release

450 Palestinian prisoners, the hijackers began releasing the hostages but continued to hold 55 Jewish passengers. [14]

Three days later what had started out as an extortionary ploy exploded into a raging international crisis with the risk of a direct U.S.–Soviet clash. While holding the hostages in the desert, the PFLP stepped up terrorist attacks against the royal forces. On September 15 the King replaced his civilian officials with a military government, signaling his decision to move in force against the guerrilla strongholds. Jordan was now in a state of civil war.

The immediate question in Washington was whether Syria and Iraq would intervene. The intelligence community tended to discount the likelihood of such intervention, but Nixon spoke and acted as if he considered it imminent. On September 16, in an off-the-record briefing to a group of Midwestern newspaper editors, he said that the United States might have to intervene if Syria or Iraq threatened Hussein. The *Chicago Sun Times* published some of the President's remarks and, surprisingly, was complimented by Nixon for breaking the ground rules. Clearly, Nixon wanted his implied warning to be picked up not only in Arab capitals but also in Moscow. Similar intense concern and hints of U.S. involvement were expressed by Kissinger and Assistant Secretary of State Sisco in background briefings that the press could attribute to "administration officials." [15] The verbal signaling was underscored by a set of military decisions: the aircraft carrier *John F. Kennedy* was ordered into the Mediterranean and the helicopter carrier *Guam*, loaded with 1500 marines, dispatched from Norfolk, Virginia, in the direction of the Middle East. Nixon also authorized half a billion dollars in military aid for Israel and an acceleration of fighter aircraft deliveries. [16]

Nixon recollects his considerations at the time as follows:

We would not allow Hussein to be overthrown by a Soviet-inspired insurrection. If it succeeded, the entire Middle East might erupt in war; the Israelis would almost certainly take pre-emptive measures against a Syrian-dominated radical government in Jordan; the Egyptians were tied to Syria by military alliances; and Soviet prestige was on the line with both Syria and the Egyptians. Since the United States could not stand idly by and watch Israel driven into the sea, the possibility of a direct U.S.–Soviet confrontation was uncomfortably high. It was like a ghastly game of dominoes, with a nuclear war waiting at the end. [17]

On September 18 Kissinger was informed by both the Israeli Ambassador, Yitzhak Rabin, and the Jordanian Ambassador, Abdul

Hamis Sharaf, that Syrian tanks had crossed into Jordan and were headed toward the city of Irbid. Kissinger had Sisco check with the Russians, who offered their assurances that the Syrians had not invaded Jordan. And the State Department received a communication from Moscow telling of the Kremlin's efforts to prevent any outside intervention by Jordan's neighbors.

The next day the White House received firmer evidence that the Syrians had indeed invaded, and it was not a small probe. Some hundreds of tanks were now rolling toward Irbid. Kissinger is reported to have been furious at the Soviets for attempting to deceive him and the President. The Kremlin must have been aware of what was happening and perhaps had even urged the Syrians on, for Syrian tank units were known to have Soviet military advisers. Kissinger reported on the fast-breaking crisis to the President and recommended an alert of American forces. Nixon agreed and ordered a selective alert of American troops in the United States and Western Europe. The Sixth Fleet was also augmented, and the ships with Marine Corps fighting units aboard steamed ominously toward the coasts of Israel and Lebanon. These military moves were coupled with U.S. warnings to the Russians that if the Syrians did not withdraw from Jordan the Israelis might intervene and the United States itself might not be able to stay out.[18]

On September 20 and 21, the Syrians continued to pour military forces into Jordan. Either the U.S. countermoves had not registered or Damascus, with Moscow's backing, had determined that the Americans were bluffing. But in truth Nixon and Kissinger were deadly serious. King Hussein requested Israeli air support and the Israelis in turn asked for U.S. protection in the event that such Israeli intervention provoked an Egyptian/Soviet counterintervention. Additional U.S. military forces in Germany were placed on alert, and transport planes were readied to airlift them to the Middle East. The augmented Sixth Fleet moved in closer. As an indicator of U.S.–Israeli coordination, a small U.S. intelligence aircraft flew back and forth between the advance naval units and Tel Aviv, with the USSR obviously watching.

Finally, the Israelis and Jordanians got the presidential decisions they were waiting for: if Israel were attacked by Egyptian and Soviet forces in response to its military help to King Hussein, the United States would itself intervene militarily to oppose them. On September 22, emboldened by confidence that Israel would indeed join the battle and would be backed by the United States, Hussein threw his own ground and air forces fully against the Syrians. The crisis suddenly broke. Syrian tanks turned around and moved back toward Syria.[19]

Triumphant, Nixon flew to Rome a few days later and spent a night on the aircraft carrier *Saratoga* in the Mediterranean to symbolize his renewed pride in the potency of American military power as a diplomatic instrument.

THE YOM KIPPUR WAR

"The news of the imminent attack on Israel took us completely by surprise," recalls Nixon.[20] This admission itself would not be surprising if it simply referred to the jarring effect the news had on Nixon personally. For the President was already up to his neck in the Watergate tapes by the morning of October 6, 1973, and was also trying to decide how to handle the legal charges of corruption being brought against Vice President Spiro Agnew. But the surprise went deeper, reflecting a massive intelligence failure in the U.S. government, caused less by lack of hard information on the preparatory moves of Egypt and its allies than by the assumptions through which Kissinger and Nixon had processed all information coming out of the Middle East since 1970.

The administration's bedrock assumption was that war was a wholly unattractive alternative to the Egyptians as long as Israel maintained effective superiority and there was a good prospect that it would return the occupied territories as a result of international political pressure. Egypt and Syria might threaten war from time to time, but this was only a ploy to intensify the international pressure on Israel to make concessions.

The premises may have been correct; but even so, they begged the question of how Egypt might assess the pertinent military balance at any time, which would include its judgments about the willingness of other countries to come to the aid of the belligerents in case of war. They also left as a variable the *degree* of Egyptian optimism concerning Israel's willingness to part with territory. In the final analysis the probability of a new Mideast war was to a large extent determined by highly subjective Egyptian judgments that could shift in response to the dynamic political and military situation.

Another unstable variable was Soviet policy. Kissinger and Nixon, however, assumed that the Soviets were firmly opposed to a new round of war between Arabs and Israelis. The Kremlin might still be attempting to gain influence among the Arabs from a no-war-no-peace situation, but a hot war could draw in the USSR and the United States on opposite sides, and this might spell the end of détente. Brezhnev was thought to have too much at stake in détente to put it at risk on behalf of his Middle Eastern clients. As the military supplier of Egypt and Syria, he was in a position to pull the reins on any reckless action they might contemplate. The possibility that Soviet policy might be catalyzed by indigenous Middle Eastern factors, rather than the other way around, was presumably discounted in the White House.

Thus, the general orientation of those at the highest levels of the U.S. government was responsible for the misreading and underweighting of a series of specific developments that, in retrospect, look like inexorable moves toward the October 1973 war: [21]

——On November 14, 1972, Anwar Sadat promised the Higher Council of his Arab Socialist Union party that Egypt would attack Israel sometime within the coming twelve months.

——During the winter of 1972–73, Egypt and the USSR seemed to be repairing the rift that had led Sadat to expel all Soviet military advisers and experts the previous July and to place all Soviet bases and equipment in Egypt under exclusive Egyptian control. Egypt now invited back several hundred Soviet military advisers and allowed the Russians once again to use military facilities in Egypt. In return, Brezhnev agreed to substantially increase the flow of Soviet military equipment to Egypt, this time including the advanced SAM-6 mobile antiaircraft missile. The deliveries also included bridge-building equipment.

——In the spring, Sadat began a series of intensive consultations with King Faisal of Saudi Arabia, who in recent months had been hinting strongly that he was ready to use his oil assets as a political weapon against the friends of Israel, and with President Hafez Assad of Syria, the most prominent war hawk in the Arab camp.

——In June, reports reached Washington of a massive acceleration of Soviet arms deliveries to Syria, including late-model T-62 tanks, sophisticated antitank missiles, SAMs, and MIG-21 fighters.

——In the second week of September, King Hussein of Jordan flew to

Cairo for a summit meeting with Sadat and Assad. Reports on the meeting indicated that war contingencies were discussed.

——During the last week of September, CIA reports to Kissinger spotlighted a number of unusual Egyptian, Syrian, and Soviet military movements. The annual Egyptian military maneuvers (which Kissinger later mentioned in his October 12 news conference) were being conducted with full divisions of Egyptian troops this time. Not only were the Egyptians stockpiling more ammunition and logistical support than ever before; they were also setting up a field communications network more complicated than mere maneuvers would require. The CIA analysts pointed to simultaneous suspicious deployments of Syrian tanks out of their normal defensive formations. U.S. surveillance also detected three Soviet freighters on their way to Egypt, possibly loaded with surface-to-surface missiles that could hit Israeli cities from Egyptian territory. Similar ominous movements were picked up by Israeli intelligence sources.

Then, suddenly, a Palestinian terrorist ambush of Soviet Jews headed through Austria for Israel made Kissinger jittery. He expressed great concern that the Israeli government—outraged and frustrated at the Austrian Chancellor's capitulation to the terrorists' demand that in return for releasing the hostages Austria close some facilities it had made available to transiting Jewish emigrés—might retaliate by attacking Palestinian camps throughout the Arab Middle East. This, Kissinger feared, could set off a cycle of violence that could expand quickly into all-our war; and he warned the Israeli Ambassador of the consequences.

As reports poured in on the intense military posturing now being undertaken by the potential belligerents, Kissinger feared, above all, a major Israeli preemptive strike, in the mode of its lightning raids at the outset of the 1967 war, to hobble the Syrian and Egyptian war machines; but Israeli officials assured him they were not going to strike first this time. The Secretary of State still refused to believe that Egypt and its allies might be planning to start a war as a deliberate act of policy. Even when Kissinger was informed on the night of October 4 that Soviet dependents were being evacuated from Cairo and Damascus, he interpreted this as perhaps another indication of difficulties between the Soviets and their Arab hosts. His intelligence advisers, while disagreeing with this interpretation, still were not ready to predict war.

During the 48 hours preceding hostilities, with evidence from various sources confirming that the Syrian and Egyptian forward armored units were swinging into offensive formations, Kissinger received further assurances from Foreign Minister Abba Eban on the phone that Israel would not preempt. The American Ambassador to Israel, Kenneth Keating, allegedly underscored Kissinger's views in warning his hosts that only if there was irrefutable proof that the Arabs were the aggressors would the United States consider itself morally obligated to help the Israelis.[22] In his memoirs, Kissinger denies the allegation, by Golda Meir among others, that the United States brought great pressure against the Israelis not to preempt in October 1973. He admits having expressed the view in years past to Israeli officials that U.S. support would be impaired if Israel struck first. But as the Yom Kippur War approached, insists Kissinger, all the statements forswearing preemption were initiated by the Israelis themselves.[23]

Regardless of the exact nature of the intense conversations between American and Israeli officials on the eve of the Yom Kippur War, Prime Minister Meir evidently believed that if Israel struck a preemptive blow, it would have to fight alone; and, therefore, against the advice of the Israeli Chief of Staff, she decided to allow her country to accept the first blows. The Arabs struck massively and simultaneously from Syria in the north and Egypt in the south on Yom Kippur morning, October 6, while many Israelis were attending religious services. It was a well-planned, well-coordinated, and efficiently executed attack.

The immediate physical losses suffered by Israel for letting the Arabs strike first were large; but the ultimate gain was presumably of larger significance: namely, a clear moral claim on the United States for support of Israel as a victim of aggression. As it turned out, however, this moral claim had less currency in the White House than the Israelis had been led to believe.

The U.S. leaders, as should have been expected, would always put their own priorities first, and the resumption of hostilities once again made it plain that these were (1) to avoid a major war between the United States and the Soviet Union; (2) to ensure the survival of Israel (Nixon's and Kissinger's sentiments apart, they knew that it would be political suicide to allow Israel to be destroyed); (3) to prevent the Soviet Union from exploiting the conflict to enlarge its influence in the Middle East; and (4) to conduct U.S. diplomacy in the region in such a way as to enhance the regional and global prestige of the United States and to increase domestic support for the Nixon administration. None of these interests required unequivocal U.S. support for Israel's war aims or the underwriting of its military strategy. Rather, Nixon and Kissinger, in assessing the new situation brought about by the onset of war, seemed—to the shock and dismay of the Israelis—to be moving back to the evenhanded approach they had flirted with prior to the 1970 Jordanian crisis.

The White House made no public condemnation during the 1973 war of either the Arabs or Soviet Union. Kissinger articulated the objectives of U.S. crisis diplomacy as, "First, to end hostilities as quickly as possible—but secondly, to end hostilities in a manner that would enable us to make a major contribution to removing the conditions that have produced four wars between Arabs and Israelis in the last 25 years."[24]

Kissinger operated under the assumption—not publicly articulated—that these objectives could not be attained if either side achieved a clear military victory in the hostilities. It was Kissinger's adoption of this assumption, particularly where it looked as if the Israelis might be attempting to conquer more territory than they obtained in 1967, that made him look anti-Israeli to many Israelis and their friends—not to mention the reputation he had gained with many Americans for perfidy and duplicity. Indeed, much of Kissinger's most controversial behavior—his procrastination in moving military supplies to Israel, the timing of his demands for a cease-fire-in-place, and especially his pressures on the Israelis to free the surrounded Egyptian Third Army—would seem fickle, if not irrational, without this premise.[25]

The most detailed account (other than Kissinger's own) of the considerations Kissenger brought to bear on the crucial decisions of the U.S. government during the 1973 war is provided by William Quandt. A member of the National Security Council staff, Quandt attended most of the Washington Special Action Group (WSAG) meetings that Kissinger used as the basic sounding board for exploring and choosing among his options.

According to Quandt, at the outbreak of hostilities Kissinger expected a short war in which Israel would prevail. He was worried, however, that if the Israelis once again began to humiliate the Arabs the Soviets would find it difficult to stay out. Urgent diplomatic initiatives therefore were required to ensure that a cease-fire was reestablished on the basis of the territorial status quo prevailing before October 6. The cooperation of the Soviets would be essential in getting the Arabs to return to the status quo ante, so it was of vital importance that the Soviets understand that the United States would not countenance any new Israel territorial expansion. Accordingly, Nixon sent Brezhnev a letter urging mutual restraint and the convening of the UN Security Council, while Kissinger pressed the case with his counterparts in the Soviet Union, Egypt, and Israel for a cease-fire based on the status quo ante. Otherwise, the United States kept a low profile during the first few days of the war.

Egypt and Syria, with major military units still in the territory they wished to reconquer, were not ready to accede to the cease-fire proposal. Kissinger was confident that once the tide of battle turned against the Arabs they would change their tune, especially if Israel began to cross the canal into Egypt and move beyond the Golan Heights in Syria.

Between the third and sixth days of the war, the WSAG's assessments of the military prospects changed. Israel was finding it difficult to turn back the Arab assault. Suffering heavy losses of aircraft, the Israelis urgently appealed for more American arms and were informed that additional shipments had been approved, including a number of Phantom jets that would soon be on their way. It became impossible to ascertain who was gaining the upper hand as the Israelis launched a smashing counteroffensive on the Syrian front and began bombing Damascus. Assad and Sadat were putting great pressure on King Hussein of Jordan to open up a third front against Israel.

Kissinger's response to the rapidly developing military situation was to call for a cease-fire-*in-place*. Golda Meir immediately refused this revised proposal, insisting that any cease-fire must be tied to the restoration of the territorial dispositions prevailing before Yom Kippur. Sadat was cool to the Kissinger proposal, demanding concrete Israeli commitments to relinquish all land captured in 1967 as the condition for a cease-fire. The Soviets, while not rejecting the cease-fire, and indicating willingness to cooperate with the United States on the diplomatic front, now began a major airlift of arms to the Syrians.

The Israelis pressed their case for accelerated U.S. arms deliveries with greater persistence. Kissinger blamed the Defense Department for the sluggish implementation of the arms resupply effort. The temporizing on the Israeli arms request was consistent, however, with the Kissinger strategy of not having the United States emerge as Israel's ally in opposition to the Arabs and pressuring the Israelis to accept a cease-fire-in-place.[26]

Meanwhile, the shifting fortunes of the belligerents in the war itself were producing a shift in their attitudes toward a cease-fire-in-place. To the Israelis, who were once again on the military offensive and hopeful of more than regaining their lost ground, the idea began to look more attractive, especially if its actual implementation could be delayed for a few days, while to the Arabs it began to look more and more like a trap. On October 12 the Israeli government, still bargaining hard for maximum assurances of American arms supplies, accepted the principle of a cease-fire-in-place. Now Sadat was unequivocally opposed.

Kissinger and Nixon, frustrated by the Egyptian leader's rejection of a cease-fire-in-place, suspecting that the Soviets were encouraging him to dig in his heels, and feeling the need to counter the Soviet airlift of supplies to Syria, were determined to change the Soviet–Arab calculations of gains from allowing the war to continue. Nixon authorized an acceleration and expansion of the delivery of Phantoms and ordered the U.S. military to fly the aircraft and other equipment directly into Israel. The principal purpose was to demonstrate to Sadat and the Kremlin that any prolongation of the war could not possibly operate to the military advantage of the Arabs—despite the flow of Soviet arms, which the United States could easily match. Nor could it be to their political advantage, for it would make it more difficult for the United States to convince Israeli hawks that the Arabs were sincerely interested in an equitable peace. A collateral purpose undoubtedly was to show the Russians, once again, that they would only be embarrassed if they attempted unilaterally to change the balance of military power in the Middle East.

With the American airlift under way, the Israelis launched into a climactic hard-driving offensive on both fronts. The Syrians were decisively thrown off the Golan Heights and pushed back along the Damascus road. To the south the Israeli troops crossed over to the West Bank of the Suez Canal in a maneuver designed to encircle the Egyptian troops still in the Sinai peninsula and cut off their line of retreat back over the canal into Egypt. In a matter of days, Israel was decisively in control of the military situation around its extended borders. Now the Soviets sent out anxious calls for a cease-fire.

Brezhnev invited Kissinger to come to Moscow for "urgent consultations." The moment for a cease-fire might have arrived. Kissinger's premise that it would be counterproductive for the Israelis to humiliate the Arabs had not altered. He left for Moscow on October 20 with his bargaining position strengthened by a presidential request to Congress for $2.2 billion in emergency military aid for Israel.

En route to Moscow, Kissinger received the news of the momentous Saudi Arabian decision to embargo oil shipments to the United States. Not only were the relative bargaining weights on each side of the Arab–Israeli conflict changed thereby, but, as Kissinger was to discover in the months and years ahead, so was the overall world power equation out of which Kissinger had fashioned his realpolitik concepts.

The Kissinger–Brezhnev meeting in Moscow on October 21 produced an agreed-upon superpower approach to an Arab–Israeli truce: a cease-fire resolution to be presented to the UN Security Council, that would call for a simple cease-fire-in-place and negotiations between the parties; and an eventual peace conference, to be chaired by both the United States and the Soviet Union. In effect, the superpowers were agreeing to act jointly to compel their respective clients to stop the fighting.

Despite the Israeli government's protest that it was not adequately consulted, the United States joined the Soviet Union in presenting their agreed-upon text of a cease-fire resolution to the United Nations the very next morning. And after less than three hours' deliberation by the Security Council, Resolution 338 was adopted by a vote of 14 to 0 (China did not vote). The October 22 resolution was a brief but specific statement:

The Security Council:
   1. *Calls upon* all parties to the present fighting to cease all firing and terminate all military activity immediately, no later than 12 hours after the moment of the adoption of this decision, in the positions they now occupy;
   2. *Calls upon* the parties concerned to start immediately after the cease-fire the implementation of Security Council resolution 242 (1967) in all of its parts;
   3. *Decides* that, immediately and concurrently with the cease-fire, negotiations start between the parties concerned under appropriate auspices aimed at establishing a just and durable peace in the Middle East.[27]

The parties stopped shooting six hours after the Security Council passed its resolution, but not without some arm-twisting by both superpowers. Neither Israel nor Egypt was in a position to object too strongly. Israel was now in military control of more territory than before the war started, and was in a strong bargaining position. Egypt was reeling from the Israeli counteroffensive and would probably lose even more ground if a cease-fire were delayed any longer. Syria, too, recognized the new realities and accepted the cease-fire the next day.

Almost immediately after the formal cessation, however, there were charges and countercharges of violations of the truce. Who was responsible was of less concern to Kissinger, however, than the fact that the Israelis were exploiting the opportunity to extend their lines on the Egyptian side of the canal, putting them in a position to capture the city of Suez and completely encircle the 100,000-man Egyptian Third Army Corps.

The new Israeli military thrusts and their noose-tightening around the Egyptian Third Army precipitated a new crisis for Kissinger as the Soviets indicated an intention to intervene directly with their own forces to enforce the cease-fire. Kissinger's response—one of the most daring of his career—was to threaten counteraction against both the Israelis and the Soviets. He would show the Russians that the United States could yet control the Israelis and that therefore Soviet intervention was unnecessary to prevent total humiliation of the Arabs; and he would show the Israelis (and the rest of the world) that the United States still had the will and the power to deter a direct Soviet intervention, but only if the Israelis themselves acted with reasonable restraint.

Kissinger's reasons for insisting on Israeli restraint went beyond the imperative of preventing Soviet intervention. Now, with the Arab oil embargo in effect, it was more than ever important for the United States to demonstrate the capacity to separate itself from the more extreme Israeli actions and to act as an honest broker in the region on behalf of an equitable peace. Accordingly, Kissinger had resolved to at least prevent the Israelis from strangling the Egyptian Third Army Corps, even before the Soviets threatened to intervene.[28] After the Soviet intervention had been deterred, Kissinger insisted that, at a minimum, the Israelis permit humanitarian convoys of food, water, and medical supplies to the surrounded Egyptian soldiers. He hinted that if the Israelis attempted to prevent this, the United States would itself convoy the supplies and threatened to vote in favor of an anti-Israeli resolution the Arabs had introduced in the

UN Security Council. Still the Israelis were not about to give up their advantage. The impasse was finally overcome by Sadat's acceptance of direct military talks between Israeli and Egyptian generals at kilometer 101 on the Cairo–Suez road to implement U.N. disengagement resolution—this in exchange for Israel's permission for a nonmilitary convoy to bring supplies to the Egyptian Third Army under UN and Red Cross supervision.[29]

The threat of Soviet intervention had emerged obliquely. On October 24 President Sadat appealed to the United States and the Soviet Union to send a joint U.S.–Soviet peacekeeping force to police the cease-fire. Kissinger immediately rejected the idea. Soviet troops in the Middle East could only spell additional trouble, with or without a U.S. counterpresence. That night Ambassador Dobrynin phoned Kissinger with a "very urgent" message from Secretary General Brezhnev to President Nixon—so urgent, said Dobrynin, that he must read it over the phone to Kissinger. "Let us act together," said Brezhnev, and "urgently dispatch Soviet and American contingents to Egypt" in order to "compel the observance of the cease-fire without delay." The Soviet leader also went beyond the Sadat proposal with a threat that Nixon later described as the most serious to U.S.–Soviet relations since the Cuban missile crisis: "I will say it straight," Brezhnev warned, "that if you find it impossible to act together with us in this matter, we should be faced with the necessity urgently to consider the question of taking appropriate steps unilaterally. Israel cannot be allowed to get away with the violations."[30]

U.S. intelligence agencies meanwhile were picking up signs of Soviet military movements—"a plethora of indicators," according to Secretary of Defense Schlesinger, that Soviet airborne divisions in the southern USSR and Hungary had been placed on alert. More Soviet ships had entered the Mediterranean, and some unconfirmed reports suggested that they might be carrying nuclear warheads for the missiles sent to Egypt earlier in the year.[31]

While unsure of what the Soviets were really up to—was it a symbolic show of resolve? a bluff? an actual deployment of major military units?—Kissinger acted swiftly to put the Kremlin on notice that any unilateral introduction of Soviet military force into the area at this time would risk a dangerous confrontation with the United States. A toughly worded presidential rejection of Brezhnev's proposals and demands was conveyed to the Kremlin. U.S. forces around the world were put on an intermediate DEFCON (defense condition) level, bringing the Strategic Air Command and other units to a higher-than-normal state of readiness. The 82d Airborne Division was prepared for possible dispatch. And the aircraft carriers *Franklin Delano Roosevelt* and *John F. Kennedy* were ordered to move to the eastern Mediterranean.

The administration's momentous decisions on the night of October 24–25, involving the possibility of a direct military clash between the two superpowers, were made by Secretary of State Kissinger, Secretary of Defense James Schlesinger, and other nonelected officials of the U.S. government. The President, emotionally consumed by the Watergate investigations, was indisposed or sleeping, and the office of Vice President, in the interregnum between Spiro Agnew's resignation and Gerald Ford's confirmation by the Senate, was vacant. (Kissinger asked General Alexander Haig at 9:50 P.M. whether the President should have been awakened. The answer was negative: "Haig thought the President too distraught. . . . From my own conversation with Nixon earlier in the evening, I was convinced Haig was right.")[32]

Kissinger, functioning also in his capacity as presidential assistant for national security affairs, convened the Washington Special Action Group to deliberate with him and Schlesinger in the White House Situation Room between 10:40 P.M. until 2 A.M. and to provide top-level unanimity for decisions taken in the President's name. The attendees included the Director of Central Intelligence, William Colby; Chairman of the Joint Chiefs of staff, Admiral Moorer; presidential chief of staff Alexander Haig; deputy assistant to the President for national security affairs, Brent Scowcroft; and Kissinger's military assistant at the National Security Council, Commander John T. Howe. But for the absence of the President and Vice President, the group comprised the full statutory membership of the National Security Council. In chairing this crisis management group and making the key force-deployment and diplomatic decisions, Kissinger was, in effect, acting President. "It was a daunting responsibility to assume," he recalls.[33]

President Nixon's message to Brezhnev (which Nixon himself did not see until after it was sent) expressed some openness to the idea of having some American and Soviet noncombat personnel go into the area as part of an augmented UN observation team, but it categorically rejected "your proposal for a particular kind of action, that of sending Soviet and American military contingents to Egypt." It is clear, said the presidential reply, "that the forces necessary to impose the cease-fire terms on the two sides would be massive and would require the closest coordination so as to avoid bloodshed. This is not only clearly infeasible, but it is not appropriate to the situation." Moreover, "you must know . . . that we could in no event accept unilateral action. . . . Such action would produce incalculable consequences which would be in the interest of neither of our countries and which would end all we have striven so hard to achieve."[34]

In his October 25 press conference, Kissinger insisted that "we do not consider ourselves in a confrontation with the Soviet Union. We do not believe it is necessary, at this moment, to have a confrontation. In fact, we are prepared to work cooperatively [with them]. . . . But cooperative action precludes unilateral action, and the President decided that it was essential that we make clear our attitude toward unilateral steps."[35]

CBS correspondent Marvin Kalb asked the Secretary of State whether the American alert might have been prompted as much by American domestic requirements as by the diplomatic requirements of the Middle Eastern situation—implying that the Nixon administration, reeling from the Watergate affair, needed its own "missile crisis" to reestablish its prestige with the American electorate. Kissinger's response was angry and defensive: "We are attempting to conduct the foreign policy of the United States with regard for what we owe not to the electorate but to future generations. And it is a symptom of what is happening in our country that it could even be suggested that the United States would alert its forces for domestic reasons." He was absolutely confident, said Kissinger, that when the record was finally made available it would show that "the President had no other choice as a responsible national leader."[36]

An hour after Kissinger's press conference, the Soviet Union joined the United States and the other members of the Security Council in voting affirmatively for Resolution 340, demanding an immediate and complete cease-fire and a return to the positions occupied by the belligerents prior to the recent round of violations, and setting up a UN emergency force composed of nonpermanent members of the Security Council (thus excluding the USSR and the United States) to oversee the cease-fire.[37] The guns fell silent on the Middle Eastern battlefields, and an intricate set of negotiations commenced to separate the forces, return prisoners of war, establish enforceable truce zones, and begin the long process toward an agreed-upon settlement of the underlying Arab–Israeli conflict.

Historians will long debate whether Kissinger played his cards with consummate skill or whether he (and the world) were miraculously lucky to have avoided World War III. Kissinger did, however, establish convincingly that he was neither pro-Israeli nor pro-Arab but genuinely of the conviction that vital U.S. interests required a durable Middle Eastern peace, and that this had to be based on specific political arrangements acceptable to all parties plus a local military equilibrium. This now-secured reputation served him well in the activist-mediator role that became the essence of his subsequent Middle East diplomacy.

KISSINGERS NEW MIDDLE EAST DIPLOMACY

The brink of war, like the hangman's noose, concentrates the statesman's mind. Out of his practical experience in terminating the 1973 war, more than out of his realpolitik concepts, Kissinger finally put together a sophisticated Middle East policy for the United States that corresponded more closely to the complexity and volatility of the area than the administration's diplomacy following the Jordan crisis.

The code term for Kissinger's new Middle East diplomacy became "step by step"—a reference to Kissinger's method of (1) getting Egypt and Israel to disengage their forces in January 1974 from the dangerous overlapping dispositions in which they were left at the cease-fire the previous October; (2) getting Syria and Israel to reestablish a narrow demilitarized buffer zone between them in May 1974; and (3) getting Egypt and Israel to agree in September 1975 to the so-called Sinai II disengagement, which provided for the first substantial relinquishment by Israel of part of the territory it had conquered in the 1967 war, a thick demilitarized buffer zone comprising most of the relinquished territory, to be policed by the United Nations and a special observer team of U.S. civilians, as well as some limited Egyptian indicators of Israel's legitimacy, such as the allowance of nonmilitary cargoes bound for Israel to pass through the Suez Canal.

The step-by-step method separated tangible specific issues, on which they were incentives to achieve immediate agreement, from the larger issues in the Arab–Israeli conflict, which still generated high emotion on both sides. Rather than being asked to agree on a comprehensive set of principles for the settlement at the end of the road as the basis for the immediate specific negotiations, the parties would be induced to start down the road without an agreed-upon picture of their destination any more specific than the highly ambiguous UN Resolution 242. The process of working out an agreement, even on relatively minor matters, would have a salutary effect on the negotiating climate farther down the road. At every step, vested interests would be built up on each side which would not want to see the disintegration of what had already been achieved and therefore would act as a voice of moderation, possibly a peace lobby, for that side.

The step-by-step approach, however, could not be sustained for long if either side began to regard it as a ruse to prevent the attainment of highly valued objectives. This, indeed, soon emerged as a large problem for Sadat, who had to defend himself against militants in his own country and throughout the Arab world—especially against the Palestinians, who charged that he was selling out the goal of regaining the lost Arab territories in order to buy peace with Israel and the good will of the United States. As time went on, therefore, Kissinger was compelled to increase his pressure on the Israelis to make sufficiently meaningful concessions for Sadat to be able to demonstrate to his militant critics that substantial and rapid progress was being made toward the main Arab goal.

Another feature of the matured Kissinger diplomacy was to treat the Arab world not as "the other side" in the Arab–Israeli conflict but as a highly differentiated set of countries with which it was more productive to deal bilaterally on most issues, including relations with Israel. Even categorizing them into moderates and militants was too neat; and acting as if such a division were valid might mean neglecting opportunities for the United States to build special lines of influence with each of the countries. Thus, Syria and Iraq, the leaders of the so-called militants, had their own historical enmities and divergent attitudes toward the Christian–Muslim conflict in Lebanon; and Egypt, Jordan, and Saudi Arabia, leaders of the so-called moderates, had played vastly different parts in the cold war, with Egypt becoming a Soviet client and maintaining a professedly "progressive" regime while the Jordanian and Saudi monarchies built their armed forces around American-supplied equipment. Then again, Saudi Arabia, which along with Iran was a dominant force in the oil producer cartel, was in a different class from Egypt and Jordan when it came to bargaining with the United States and other industrialized countries. Moreover, each of these countries had its own problems with displaced Palestinians and a different set of preferences and priorities when it came to the demands of the various Palestinian guerrilla organizations against Israel.

Of course, if U.S. bilateral diplomacy were conducted crudely, the various Arab countries might see it as a divide-and-rule policy designed to advance Israeli interests and might join to present a united front even if such unity would contradict important national interests. Even the subtle Kissinger found it impossible to sustain the bilateral approach, which involved frequent "shuttling" between the principal Middle Eastern capitals, without creating suspicion that he was playing off one country against another. To mollify such suspicions, especially near the end of his tenure, he began to weave a tangle of complicated reassurances, often in the form of promises of special economic and military-supply relationships, not all of which were likely to be backed up by Congress and some of which required him to make compensatory promises to Israel.

A corollary to the strategy of building multiple relationships in the Middle East was a somewhat more relaxed attitude toward the Soviet role in the region that Kissinger had shown when he promised to "expel" the Soviets from Egypt. If it was now deemed counterproductive to polarize the Arabs into moderate and militant camps, it was even more disadvantageous, from a global geopolitical perspective, to overlay this with pro-Soviet and pro-U.S. groupings. This simply would give the Russians too many automatic clients. It should not be because of U.S. policy that countries ran to the arms of the Soviet Union or were reluctant to come to the United States to satisfy needs that were not adequately attended to by the Russians. The evolution of Sadat's policy should serve as a model: let events run their natural course and Arab nationalism would assert itself against Soviet imperialism. The process might not take this course, however, if the United States acted as if it were illegitimate for Middle Eastern countries to have "peace and friendship" treaties or client–patron relationships with the USSR, or as if in order to build a relationship with the United States one must renounce relations with Moscow; for such an uncompromising U.S. policy would itself cut against the grain of local nationalism and pride, and might only further alienate some of these countries from the United States.

The more permissive U.S. attitude toward a Soviet Middle Eastern presence, however, might have its own pitfalls, particularly where the easiest way for the Russians to get a local foothold was through supplying military equipment. Increased flows of Soviet arms into the area might produce adverse shifts in the local power balance, which the United States might need to counter by further military buildups of Israel or other primary U.S. clients. Thus, what started out as a relaxed approach might result in a new spiral of competitive arming of military clients and even a rigid repolarization of the area.

In short, the new Kissinger strategy of defusing immediately combustible situations and weaving a web of positive relations with virtually all states in the region (regardless of their attitudes toward Israel) might not be sufficient to (1) prevent the expansion of Soviet imperialism in the Middle East, (2) reduce the prospects of a war between the superpowers starting in the region, and (3) ensure the continued survival of Israel. Moreover, the strategy could boomerang, resulting in another Arab–Israeli war with higher levels of armaments on both sides and with the Soviets more ensconced in the area than ever; and unless in the interim the industrial world substantially reversed its growing dependence on Middle Eastern oil, the United States, Western Europe, and Japan might be severely divided among themselves and troubled by internal political dissention over the costs and risks of coming to Israel's assistance during its period of maximum peril.

Kissinger must have known, on the basis of his past historical studies and his baptism in the fire of Middle Eastern politics, that symptomatic firefighting and step-by-step conflict resolution techniques were only surface ameliorants. If any region in the world required a "structure of peace" to prevent events there from severely undermining U.S. external security and internal stability, it was the Middle East. Kissinger had reestablished American competence in the area, but something more was required. Perhaps he had a grand design, some architecture, a "vision"; but this remained unarticulated and could not be inferred from his behavior.

16

THE ANACHRONISM OF
CONSERVATIVE REALPOLITIK

In each period there exist anachronisms, states which appear backward and even decadent to those who fail to realize they are dealing with the most tenacious remnant of a disintegrating world order.

—HENRY A. KISSINGER

The evolution of U.S. crisis diplomacy in the Middle East from 1969 to 1975 reflected the more general metamorphosis in U.S. foreign policy over which Henry Kissinger presided. What was once viewed as a protracted conflict between the forces of radicalism, revolution, and chaos (exploited by the Soviet Union) and the forces of moderation, stability, and order (led by the United States) showed itself to be a more complicated and many-sided interaction of ideological and material forces in which the natural and most effective role of the United States might often be that of sponsor of progressive reform. Similary, the traditional stabilizing mechanism available to those who wanted to preserve the status quo—an advantageous balance of military power—was often insufficient for containing the forces of chaos and frequently inappropriate as a means through which the United States could exert influence on the side of constructive change.

The metamorphosis in U.S. policy was hardly smooth, however, and often found the Nixon and Ford administrations falling back on conservative realpolitik concepts and stances.

• Nixon and Kissinger discounted the humanitarian and moral implications of Pakistani President Yahya Khan's brutal suppression of the Bangladesh independence movement in 1971. They stressed rather the "illegitimacy" of India's reactive intervention and attempt to "dismember" the sovereign state of Pakistan. Reversing the standing U.S. policy of scrupulously avoiding taking sides in India–Pakistan conflicts, the administration aligned itself diplomatically with Pakistan in the Bangladesh conflict, threatened to call off the Nixon–Brezhnev summit scheduled for the spring of 1972 if the Kremlin did not put restraining pressure on India, and dispatched a Marine intervention task force, ostentatiously escorted by the nuclear aircraft carrier *Enterprise,* into the Bay of Bengal. This was a symbolic show of force, apparently with no real intention to directly participate in the fight. The administration was most worried that a decisive Indian victory over Pakistan (China's diplomatic ally in its own border conflicts with India), with the United States standing idly by, would destabilize the Asian balance of power and might cause China to reconsider its opening to the United States. As it turned out, the Indians prevailed in effecting the separation of Bangladesh from East Pakistan despite the U.S. action. Nevertheless, Nixon and Kissinger claimed success in deterring India from pressing its advantage to the point of military attacking West Pakistan and occupying Pakistani-claimed areas of Kashmir.[1]

• In authorizing covert CIA programs to support Chilean opponents of the Marxist government of Salvador Allende Gossens, and implicating the United States indirectly in the violent military ouster and death of Allende in September 1973 (Kissinger denies allegations of active U.S. government complicity in or encouragement of the coup), Nixon and Kissinger reembraced the ideological anti-Communist definitions of U.S. interests that they claimed to be discarding in the "structure of peace" concepts. Kissinger himself had previously ridiculed claims by the U.S. military that Chile had vital strategic importance, and is reputed to be the originator of the quip that a Communist Chile would be a dagger pointed at the heart of Tierra del Fuego. But now he argued that "if Chile had followed the Cuban pattern, Communist ideology would in time have been supported by Soviet forces and Soviet arms in the southern core of the South American continent."[2]

• Kissinger's policy of politically quarantining Portugal—of acting as if that country had a contagious disease during the seventeen months of political turmoil following the April 1974 reformist coup in Lisbon—had the ostensible geopolitical rationale of insulating NATO military organs, especially the Nuclear Planning Group, from possible subversion by Portuguese leftists. The ruling Cabinet of the provisional government, although led by a popular general and a prominent liberal, included two leaders of the Portuguese Communist party as well as several Socialists. Actually, it was rather easy for the NATO organization to protect its essential functions against Communist subversion by setting up special subcommittees, excluding Portugal, to deal with sensitive matters. Kissinger's fears apparently went deeper: a Communist victory in Portugal would profoundly destabilize the European equilibrium, providing the Soviet Union for the first time with a major presence in Western Europe and on the strategically located Iberian peninsula. (The Portuguese Communists, under Alvaro Cunhal, were openly pro-Soviet and not part of the liberalizing "Eurocommunist" movement.) Accordingly, as the Communists intensified their efforts to take over the central and local governing apparatus of Portugal, Kissinger made it known that he intended to subject that country to virtually complete diplomatic and economic isolation from the West unless the Portuguese Socialists and liberals expelled the Communists from official positions of influence in Lisbon. Non-Communist leaders in Portugal, the U.S. ambassador in Lisbon, and some of America's European allies tried to dissuade Kissinger from such a coercive approach, arguing that it would only gain the Communists greater sympathy among the Portuguese people. (Kissinger's coercive diplomacy was never put to the test. Cunhal overplayed his hand by attempting a military *putsch*. This rash Communist bid for total power was defeated by a coalition of moderate military officers and democratic Socialists, who now had sufficient grounds of their own for denying the Communists important positions in the government.)

• Kissinger's response to the phenomenon of "Eurocommunism" was also a product of a persisting cold war mindset. Kissinger was mistrustful of pledges by Communist Party leaders in Italy, France, and Spain to respect freedom of expression and association and democratic political processes, including the rights of opposition parties to openly oppose a Communist-controlled government and the obligation of governments to turn over power to other parties when the electorate so decides. He regarded such pledges as a deceptive stratagem to undercut the reluctance of the non-Communist parties in Western Europe to form electoral alliances and coalition governments with the Communists. Once the Communists were allowed to share power, argued Kissinger, they would have no scruples about reneging on their promises and, like the Communists in Eastern Europe in the late 1940s, would decisively suppress all opposition parties and deal brutally with anyone who cried foul. Moreover, the Western hope that, once in power, the European Communist parties would remain nationalist and pursue international policies distinct from those of the Soviet Union was regarded by Kissinger as a dangerously näive basis for relaxing the barriers to their attaining power. It would be damaging enough, from Kissinger's viewpoint, if any of the key NATO countries turned neutralist. His strategy, therefore, was to allude openly to the international economic and political costs that would be incurred by any Western European country that turned toward Communism—a drying up of foreign investments of private capital, and second-class status in or expulsion from NATO—as a deterrent to any power-sharing experiments with the Euro-communists.

• Kissinger's vacillation and delay in responding to the July 1974 Greek nationalist coup in Cyprus that deposed Archbishop Makarios was perhaps attributable in part to the Secretary of State's preoccupation with the Middle East crisis and the climatic traumas of Watergate. But the fact that, when preoccupied, Kissinger gave the benefit of the doubt to the Greek military junta that engineered the coup, and then remained aloof as Turkey, using U.S. arms in violation of congressional restrictions, invaded Cyprus to protect the island's Turkish minority, was revealing of his natural, almost instinctual, biases: suspicion, even contempt, of democratic reformers and populist politicans (into which category he placed Archbishop Makarios) and faith in the reliability of decisive, militaristic, disciplined leaders such as might be found in a Greek military junta or in NATO-loyal Turkish governments.

• In May 1975, two weeks after the final Communist takeover of Saigon, U.S. marines stormed a Cambodian Communist stronghold on Tang Island in the Gulf of Thailand to rescue the American crewman from the freighter *Mayagüez*, which had been seized for penetrating what Cambodia claimed to be its territorial waters. Fighter planes from the U.S. aircraft carrier *Coral Sea* bombed the Cambodian mainland. By this swift use of force, Kissinger and President Ford impatiently preempted their own diplomatic initiatives through the UN and neutral channels. They found out afterward that the Cambodian government had decided to release the crew before the marine and air assault had started. If that information had been in Ford's hands, the lives of the thirty-eight Americans who died in the operation, not to mention the larger number of Cambodians, could have been saved. But Kissinger and Ford, having just shown themselves unable to prevent the Communists from attaining total military victory in Vietnam in violation of the Paris agreements of 1973, were particularly anxious to demonstrate that the United States, under their leadership, was still not to be trifled with. By seizing the *Mayagüez*, Cambodia provided them with the opportunity for a show of the old machismo without the risk of major war.

THE CRISIS IN THE WORLD ECONOMIC ORDER

The destabilization of international economic relations that resulted from the embargo and oil price increases imposed by oil-exporting countries in 1973 and 1974 was initially perceived and responded to by Kissinger mainly as an element in the East–West balance of power and as a critical variable in the Arab–Israeli conflict. To the extent that he regarded the economic and political actions of the Organization of Petroleum Exporting Countries (OPEC) as serious threats worthy of his attention, it was insofar as (1) the denial of oil to the Western industrialized nations or Japan might bring about the economic and political collapse of key members of the anti-Communist alliance, and (2) the Arab members of OPEC, using such a denial threat, could coerce the industrialized nations into supporting the Arab side in the Arab–Israeli conflict. The emergence of these threats in connection with the Arab–Israeli war of 1973 riveted Kissinger's attention on the economics as well as the politics of the global energy situation and, because the energy situation was now so closely linked with the overall workings of the international economy, compelled him to educate himself quickly on the structure and condition of the world economic order. ("From the start I had not expected to play a major role in international economics, which—to put it mildly—had not been a central field of study for me. Only later did I learn that the key economic policy decisions are not technical, but political.")[3] What he found significantly complicated his views on geopolitics and effected a transformation in his statesmanship. Global equilibrium, the structure of peace, the security of the United States itself—all of these depended as much on the distribution of economic power as on the distribution of military power and the pattern of political loyalties. It was therefore part of the art of high statesmanship to be able to manipulate the international economic variables, not simply as adjuncts to U.S.–Soviet détente but as elements in the very essence of international power. In this field too, responding to crisis situations Kissinger was able to seize the reins and perform most effectively while others were confused and demoralized.

During the first Nixon administration (1969–1972) the driver's seat for U.S. foreign economic policy was usually occupied by Secretary of the Treasury John Connally or the President himself. The U.S. domestic economy was in deep trouble in 1971—"stagflation," it was called—in ways that could have damaging effects on Nixon's chances for reelection: unemployment was dangerously high, simultaneously with abnormally high increases in the prices of goods and services. U.S. labor unions had turned protectionist, arguing that a large part of the unemployment problem was due to the influx of foreign goods produced by cheap foreign labor, sometimes in foreign subsidiaries of U.S. multinational corporations. Trade and monetary experts were alarmed at the rapidly deteriorating U.S. balance of international payments, reflecting the lag of U.S. exports behind imports and the increasing outflow of U.S. dollars in the form of overseas investments. Monetarists claimed that the dollar was highly overvalued in relation to other currencies and that this was dangerous for the health of the U.S. economy; it artificially made U.S. goods more expensive than they should be on the world market, and made foreign goods cheaper in the United States. There was growing pressure in international financial circles for the United States to devalue the dollar, but this would mean that the domestic economy would have to absorb the first shocks of the international readjustment; moreover, such talk could cause a dangerous collapse of the whole monetary system as holders of U.S. dollars—the most widely held of all currencies—rushed to cash them in for other currencies or, worse yet, demanded that the United States exchange their dollars for gold at the established price of $35 per ounce. (There was nowhere near that amount of gold in the U.S. Treasury.)

Under the circumstances, argued Secretary of the Treasury Connally, the United States should insist that others in the system assume some of the burdens of making the international economy work. The West Europeans and the Japanese, having recovered from World War II to become major competitors of the United States, should no longer be babied. Speaking in Munich in Maya 1971, Connally bluntly told the Europeans that the United States was losing patience with the other industrialized nations, which it was still protecting in the NATO alliance, for not pulling their weight in the economic system. Questions were beginning to arise in the United States, he warned, over how the costs of NATO and other mutual security arrangements should be allocated. "I find it an impressive fact, and a depressing fact, that the persisting underlying balance of payments deficit which causes so much concern, is more than covered, year in and year out, by our net military expenditures abroad." Financing the free world's military shield was part of the burden of leadership that the United States should not cast off, said the Treasury Secretary, but

the comfortable assumption that the United States should—in the broader political interests of the free world—be willing to bear disproportionate economic costs does not fit the facts of today.

. . .

No longer does the U.S. economy dominate the free world. No longer can considerations of friendship, or need, or capacity justify the United States' carrying so heavy a share of the common burdens.

And, to be perfectly frank, no longer will the American people permit their government to engage in international actions in which the true long-run interests of the U.S. are not just as clearly recognized as those of the nations with which we deal.[4]

Ten weeks after Connally delivered this stern lecture, President Nixon announced a "new economic policy" to "blaze the trail to a new prosperity." In addition to domestic measures to create new jobs (mainly tax breaks for industry to stimulate investment in new plants), to stimulate more consumer demand (a repeal of the 7 percent excise tax on automobiles and an increase in personal income tax deductions for dependents), and to control inflation (a temporary freeze on all wages and prices throughout the United States), Nixon ordered a set of measures designed to coerce the other industrialized nations into reconsidering their reluctance to allow the United States to openly compete with them in the international economy.

On the advice of Secretary Connally, he temporarily suspended the convertibility of the dollar into gold or other international reserve assets. This technical action, dubbed by journalists as "slamming the U.S. gold window," was taken, the President explained, to prevent the international money speculators from "waging an all-out war against the American dollar." Also on the advice of Connally, Nixon imposed a temporary tax of 10 percent on goods imported into the United States. This action was taken, he said, "to make certain that American products will not be at a disadvantage because of unfair currency exchange rates. When the unfair treatment is ended, the import tax will end as well." Now that the other nations had regained their vitality and had become competitors, argued Nixon, "the time has come for them to bear their fair share of defending freedom around the world" and maintaining a stable international economic order.

The time has come for exchange rates to be set straight and for the major nations to compete as equals. There is no longer any need for the United States to compete with one hand tied behind her back.[5]

The European allies and Japan were shocked at Nixon's harsh tone and uncompromising posture. Kissinger and Nixon both had criticized the Kennedy and Johnson administrations for their arrogant unilateralism on matters of concern to the alliance and had pledged a more consultative approach. Now Washington, without prior consultation, was not only changing key structural elements in the international monetary system but was also unilaterally imposing a special tariff (the 10 percent "import surcharge") on goods from its trading partners—in effect, twisting their arms until they gave in to U.S. demands to revalue their currencies.

The damaging effects of such coercive unilateralism to an overall system of mutual accountability among the economically advanced noncommunist countries alarmed the chairman of the Council on International Economic Policy, Peter Peterson, who implored Kissinger to intervene with Nixon against Connally's Texan shoot-it-out style. Kissinger, although almost totally preoccupied with Vietnam and still unfamiliar with the intricacies of international economics, nonetheless weighed in on behalf of a less confrontationist approach.[6]

Nixon softened the U.S. position somewhat in subsequent negotiations with the Europeans and the Japanese by agreeing to devalue the U.S. dollar as the others revalued their currencies upward. The result was the agreement concluded at the December 1971 meeting of the International Monetary Fund (IMF) to realign all major currencies and subsequently allow them too "float"—that is, to have their values set by supply and demand on the world money markets within rather broad margins. Collaterally, the European Economic Community agreed to a new round of extensive trade negotiations with the United States. Japan also exhibited a cooperative attitude in implementing the "voluntary" restraints on its exports to the United States and the import barrier liberalizations it had accepted earlier in the year in exchange for U.S. cooperation in returning Okinawa.

The official tone of mutual accommodation surrounding the December 1971 meeting of the IMF was capped by Nixon's appearance at the meeting to bless what he termed "the most significant monetary agreement in the history of the world." But this could not erase the fact that the United States had used not only economic coercion but also hints of a withdrawal of military protection to compel its allies to accede to its desires.

If the international system was now to feature intense competition and coercive bargaining within the anticommunist alliance as well as East–West rivalry, America's partners would make their own adjustments to this new reality. Perhaps General de Gaulle was right after all, and Europe (and even Japan) would have to seek a unique role in the system that would maximize its bargaining advantages vis-à-vis both superpowers. Kissinger would reap the bitter harvest of 1971 when, at the conclusion of the Vietnam war two years later, he turned his attention to the disintegrating "Atlantic community." The potentially disastrous geopolitical implications of the disintegrative trends would be driven home during the Yom Kippur War, when he tried to obtain allied cooperation against Arab oil blackmail and Soviet military threats.

By 1973 the differences in membership and purposes between the North Atlantic security community on the one hand and the West European economic community on the other hand were prominently exposed and crucially affecting relations between the United States and Europe. With the new era of détente reducing the immediacy of the common-defense purposes of NATO, the principle that everyone should do his part for the good of the whole was difficult to enforce. Those with the greatest military power did not automatically exercise the greatest authority, and conflicts within the community were harder to resolve than previously. Where nonmilitary matters were at issue—trade barriers, currency exchange rates, the terms of technological cooperation, access to energy supplies, environmental controls—there was now more opportunity for special-interest groups to press their demands on their own governments and on the deliberative assemblies and bureaucracies of the European and Atlantic communities. Even when it came to military issues, such as determining the size, composition, and strategy of NATO forces, the debates were less over how best to defend against military attack from the East than over the distribution of the economic burdens of alliance membership. Previously, when the United States had insisted that the economically thriving NATO countries provide more for their own defense and purchase military equipment from the United States to offset the U.S. balance-of-payments costs of American forces in Europe, it had been easier to compel agreement on the basis of the overriding imperatives of mutual security. But as the question of sharing military burdens became linked to monetary and trade issues (as it had been by Nixon and Connally in 1971), the

United States found itself bargaining against a coalition of European countries in NATO.[7]

Against this background Kissinger proclaimed the "Year of Europe" in an address before Associated Press editors meeting in New York City on April 23, 1973. The formulation was remarkably patronizing, leading French wags to complain that it was as if an inconstant husband had suddenly announced a "year of the wife." Smarting from the insensitive and indifferent treatment they had been getting from top officials of the Nixon administration, European governments were predisposed to read the worst implications into the appeal for transatlantic cooperation, which Kissinger had meant as a sincere offer to make amends. His ringing call for a "new Atlantic charter" that would "strike a new balance between self-interest and common interest, . . . identify interests and positive values beyond security in order to engage once again the commitment of people and parliaments, . . . [and set forth] a shared view of the world we seek to build" was received skeptically by the Europeans. They read his indelicately phrased observation—"The United States had global interests and responsibilities. Our European allies have regional interests"—as a reassertion of the hegomonic conceit that the United States had an obligation to consult with the Europeans only on specifically European matters but that the Europeans should consult with their superpower protector on all matters of significance. And they squirmed uncomfortably at the unintended irony of a Nixon administration official preaching to them that "we cannot hold together if each country or region asserts its autonomy whenever it is to its benefit and invokes unity to curtail the independence of others."[8]

As a realist, Kissinger understood the inevitability of such tensions, given the centrifugal forces pulling the international system away from the bipolar abnormalities of the early cold war period and back toward a more normal pattern of multiple and shifting coalitions. He was disappointed at the cool European response to his call for a new Atlantic charter, but not terribly surprised. Yet he still hoped that in times of profound challenge to their common values from the Soviet Union or some other source, the NATO nations would bond together to protect Western civilization.[9] He was therefore deeply dismayed at the Europeans' failure to rally around the alliance leader in the fall of 1973, when the very fabric of society was threatened by OPEC's quadrupling of the price of oil and the embargo imposed by the Arabs on oil exports to Israel's supporters. Not only did France, Britain, and Japan, conducting their own bilateral negotiations with the Arab producers, undermine Kissinger's efforts to organize a united front of the major consumer nations to break the producer cartel, but some of the NATO countries were so anxious to disassociate themselves from actions in support of Israel that they refused to allow U.S. planes to use their bases or even to overfly their territory to transport military supplies to Israel during the 1973 war. The American Secretary of State regarded such weakness in the face of Arab pressure as spineless and craven, reminiscent of the way European governments caved in to Hitler's demands on the eve of World War II.

Kissinger was able to adapt to this reality too, recognizing that the European and Japanese economies were more vulnerable to price changes and limited oil supplies than the United States, and that the Europeans had developed considerable experience, still lacking in the United States, in diplomatic dealings with the Arabs and Third World raw materials producers on such matters. He also had to recognize how little he knew about the economic side of the world energy situation, and accordingly he quickly recast his staff to give it intense study and began personally to avail himself of governmental and nongovernmental counsel on the subject. This crash self-improvement course was paralleled by a series of urgent consultations with the major oil-consuming countries and with representatives of the producer countries so that, upon the termination of the Arab–Israeli war and the lifting of the oil embargo, the United States would be ready to propose a set of international rules for rational and fair commerce in this vital resource. Failure to resolve the energy problem on the basis of international cooperation, Kissinger warned, would threaten the world with a vicious cycle of competition, autarchy, rivalry, and depression such as had led to the collapse of world order in the 1930s.

The basic approach to the energy problem that Kissinger would follow during the rest of his tenure as Secretary of State was presented to him in broad outline to a conference of major oil-consuming countries summoned by the United States in February 1974: [10]

1. *Conservation.* Kissinger called for a "new energy ethic" designed to promote the conservation and efficient use of energy supplies by all coun-

tries. The United States, being the world's most profligate country, bore a special responsibility in this regard, admitted Kissinger, and he pledged an expansion of crisis-stimulated conservation measures and offered to collaborate in a mutual review by the energy-consuming countries of one another's programs.

2. *Alternate fossil energy sources.* Sources neglected during the era of low-cost oil now needed to be exploited—coal, of course, but also shale and offshore oil. The United States would be ready to coordinate its programs of new exploration and exploitation with the other consumer countries, and this might involve multilateral efforts to encourage the flow of private capital into new industries for producing energy, as well as governmental arrangements to accelerate the search for new energy sources.

3. *Research and development.* The United States was prepared, said Kissinger, "to make a major contribution of its most advanced energy research and development [technologies] to a broad program of international cooperation," including technologies to promote the use of nuclear reactors under controls to prevent the spread of nuclear weapons.

4. *Emergency sharing of petroleum.* The most generous of the Kissinger proposals, but also the most problematic in view of likely opposition in Congress, was his offer "to share available energy in times of emergency or prolonged shortages. The United States would be prepared to allocate an agreed portion of our total petroleum supply provided other consuming countries with indigenous production do likewise."

5. *International financial cooperation.* New international measures, and above all a spirit of international responsibility, were needed to cope with the accumulation of petrodollars and their "recycling" back into the consumer countries. These measures, said Kissinger, should include "steps to facilitate the fuller participation of producing nations in existing international institutions and to contribute to the urgent needs of the developing countries."

As we look toward the end of this century, said America's arch-practitioner and conceptualizer of conservative realpolitik,

we know that the energy crisis indicates the birth pains of global interdependence. Our response could well determine our capacity to deal with the international agenda of the future.

We confront a fundamental decision. Will we consume ourselves in nationalistic rivalry which the realities of interdependence make suicidal? Or will we acknowledge our interdependence and shape cooperative solutions?[11]

This was not simply posturing. Kissinger understood that the essence of statesmanship in the emerging international system was the ability to deal with the politics of economics and technology. He who had once dubbed such matters the province of second-rate minds now seemed to relish demonstrating his mastery of his new specialty. Confidently embodying a synthesis of finance minister and geopolitician, he grabbed the international ball back from the departments of Treasury and Commerce and made it clear once again to foreign governments that the President's principal adviser and spokesman on all matters of foreign policy—including economics—was Henry Kissinger.

This was a more complicated policy arena than Kissinger had written about or operated in during his first four years as a high government official. At home there were more players in the multiple legislative and bureaucratic games in the field of foreign economic policy making than there were in the field of national security policy and U.S.–Soviet relations. Kissinger was to find that the commanding position of the United States in the global economy was not readily cashed in for bargaining chips on the specific issues he wanted to deal with.

The United States was a leading producer of goods for which there was high international demand, such as high technology and food, but the free market principles to which the United States was officially committed, combined with the opposition of domestic sellers to export controls, blocked Kissinger's efforts to convert these assets into flexible instruments of diplomacy. Kissinger flirted with using the position of the United States as the largest exporter of food grains to exert leverage against the oil producer cartel. But the 1974–75 famines in India and the African Sahel removed this option. To hold back food from the international market at a time of vast starvation, and by so doing to further drive up world prices, would be regarded as an act of the grossest cruelty. Kissinger was resourceful, however, in turning U.S. dominance as a food producer into more general world political leadership by proposing a World Food Conference and, at its meeting in Rome in November 1974, offering a comprehensive scheme for nationally held but internationally coordinated stocks of surplus grain to stabilize grain prices and help the countries with the greatest need.[12]

Still, Kissinger's lack of tangible and effective leverage against the energy producers continued to bother him, and he found it hard to resist the temptation to reach for the familiar political–military bargaining chips.

At the end of 1974, Kissinger, unsuccessful in his effort to form a solid consensus among the major consumer countries for bargaining with OPEC, allowed himself to be quoted in *Business Week* on the pitfalls, but also the possibilities, of political and military power plays against the Arab oil producers. The only way to bring oil prices down immediately in the absence of consumer solidarity, Kissinger told his interviewers, would be to "create a political crisis of the first magnitude." When probed to describe what he meant, Kissinger talked of

massive political warfare against countries like Saudia Arabia and Iran to make them risk their political stability and maybe their security if they do not cooperate. That is too high a price to pay even for an immediate reduction in oil prices.

If you bring about an overthrow of the existing system in Saudi Arabia and a Qadaffi takes over or if you break Iran's image of being capable of resisting outside pressures, you're going to open up political trends which could defeat your economic objectives. Economic pressures or incentives, on the other hand, take time to organize and cannot be effective without consumer solidarity. Moreover, if we had created the political crisis that I described, we would almost certainly have had to do it against the opposition of Europe, Japan and the Soviet Union.

His interrogators persisted:

BUSINESS WEEK: One of the things we . . . hear from businessmen is that in the long run the only answer to the oil cartel is some sort of military action. Have you considered military action on oil?

KISSINGER: Military action on oil prices?

BUSINESS WEEK: Yes.

KISSINGER: A very dangerous course. We should have learned from Vietnam that it is easier to get into a war than to get out of it. I am not saying that there's no circumstance where we would use force. But it is one thing to use it in the case of a dispute over price, but it's another where there is some actual strangulation of the industrialized world.

BUSINESS WEEK: Do you worry about what the Soviets would do in the Middle East if there were any military action against the cartel?

KISSINGER: I don't think this is a good thing to speculate about. Any President who would resort to military action in the Middle East without worrying what the Soviets would do would have to be reckless. The question is to what extent he would let himself be deterred by it. But you cannot say you would not consider what the Soviets would do. I want to make clear, however, that the use of force would be considered only in the gravest emergency.[13]

When Kissinger's references to remote possibilities when force might be considered caused a stir in Arab and European capitals, he claimed to be "astonished." He insisted in a television interview that "no nation can announce that it will let itself be strangled without reacting. . . . I find it very difficult to see what it is that people are objecting to." He was simply saying that the United States would not permit itself or its allies to be strangled. "Somebody else would have to make the first move to attempt the strangulation. . . . There would have to be an overt move of an extremely drastic, dramatic and aggressive nature" before the United States would seriously consider using military force against the oil producers.[14]

Only against economic actions that in their effects and intent would be akin to the use of force would the United States respond militarily; but in not totally ruling out such contingencies Kissinger obviously was attempting to warn the Arabs that at some point even their oil pricing policies, let alone another embargo, could seriously provoke the United States.

It was evident to Kissinger and other Western statesmen that an important shift in the global balance of power was taking place, in that key nations in the Third World were able to crucially affect the security and well-being of most of the countries in the non-Communist industrialized world. He was not at all pleased with the tacit bargain between the OPEC countries and other Third World countries to support one another's demands in international forums to maximize their bargaining leverage. Professedly nonaligned African, Latin American, and Asian nations now ganged up in the United Nations and its subsidiary organs to help the Arab countries pass anti-Israel resolutions. In return, the Middle Eastern Arab countries and Iran lent their support to some of the most radical demands emanating from the Third World for a restructuring of the international economic order and a global redistribution of income to the economically disadvantaged nations. "It is an irony," said Kissinger in an angry speech in July 1975,

that at the moment the United States has accepted nonalignment and the value of diversity, those nations which originally chose this stance to preserve their sovereign independence from powerful military alliances are forming a rigid grouping of their own. The most solid block in the world today is, paradoxically, the alignment of the nonaligned. This divides the world into categories of North and South, developing and developed, imperial and colonial, at the very moment in history when such categories have become irrelevant and misleading.

He warned those in the majority in the UN General Assembly and its specialized bodies not to operate under the illusion that they could use their voting power coercively without paying a large price, "for the coerced are under no obligation to submit. To the contrary, they are given all too many incentives simply to depart the scene, to have done with the pretense." Those who abused the procedures of the organization to isolate or deny the full privileges of the United Nations to members they dislike, as the majority, prodded by the Arabs, was now doing to Israel, "may well inherit an empty shell."

The United States had been by far the largest supporter of the United Nations, Kissinger reminded the Third World voting bloc; but

the support of the American people, which has been the lifeblood of the organization, will be profoundly alienated unless fair play predominates and the numerical
majority respects the views of the minority. The American people are understandably tired of the inflammatory rhetoric against us, the all-or-nothing stance accompanied by demands for *our* sacrifice which too frequently dominate the meeting halls
of the United Nations.[15]

As if to drive home his growing anger, Kissinger had President Ford appoint Daniel Patrick Moynihan as the new U.S. ambassador to the United Nations. Moynihan had recently published in *Commentary* a scathing attack on the Third World advocates of a new international economic order, whom he lumped together as the "Fabian socialist" international party of "equality," and their applogists in the United States. The United States should take the offensive, argued Moynihan, as the leader of the "liberty party" and speak out loudly against those who would sacrifice freedom and condone tyranny in the pursuit of professedly egalitarian ends.[16]

Kissinger's hardening rhetoric and the appointment of Moynihan raised apprehension in UN circles about the Seventh Special Session of the General Assembly, scheduled for the fall of 1975. The Special Session was to consider means of implementing the principles of the "new international economic order" formulated by the General Assembly majority in the Charter of Economic Rights and Duties of States voted the previous December. The Third World coalition was demanding

——international commodity agreements to assure the producers of the Third World of remunerative and "equitable" prices, perhaps by indexing commodity prices to prices of manufactured goods;
——debt relief in the form of cancellation or postponement of the repayment obligations of the poor countries to their international creditors;

———preferential treatment for developing-country exports in the markets of the industrialized world;

———increased official development assistance from the rich countries amounting to at least 0.7 percent of the gross national product of each rich country;

———increased allocations of special drawing rights (SDRs), the International Monetary Fund's reserve assets created to alleviate the balance-of-payments deficits of member countries;

———technology transfers from the technologically advanced countries to developing countries at concessionary prices;

———the right to nationalize and expropriate any foreign holdings within their territories without compensation (a demand directed at the current *bête noire* of the Third World militants, the multinational corporation);

———greater representation and voting rights for developing countries in international funding and lending institutions.

To the relief of all countries, save perhaps the Soviet Union, China, and some of the more intransigent Third World militants such as Algeria and Libya, the feared North–South confrontation failed to materialize. The big struggle took place before the convening of the Seventh Special Session, not between the diplomats of the industrial and developing nations but within the U.S. government, between State Department officials sympathetic to the demands of the Third World and Treasury officials anxious to protect the international economic status quo. Kissinger was converted to the reformist position sometime during the summer of 1975; and in the weeks immediately preceding the UN meeting he reportedly was engaged in a major dispute with Secretary of the Treasury Simon over the official U.S. posture toward the Third World's demands for a new international economic order. Kissinger won out and, with the blessing of President Ford, the new American policy was presented to the United Nations in a historic address of September 1, 1975. It fell to Ambassador Moynihan, of all people, to deliver the Secretary of State's address to the General Assembly. (Moynihan, it became clear in subsequent months, never agreed with the philosophy he was now instructed to expound.)

The specific proposals put forward in Kissinger's address to the Seventh Special Session went only part way toward meeting the grievances of the developing-country coalition; but they did imply substantial acceptance of the legitimacy of international compensation to the poorer countries for their comparative disadvantage in the international market.[17]

Granting the obligation of the international community to protect vulnerable economies against dramatic drops in their export earnings, Kissinger proposed the creation of a new "development security facility" within the IMF with the mandate and financial resources to give concessionary loans and grants to developing countries to make up for their export shortfalls. (However, the United States rejected the standing demand of the Third World militants for an indexing system to peg the price of basic commodities to price changes in industrial goods.)

Conceding that many of the poor countries, in all fairness, did deserve special help in raising development capital, Kissinger urged expansion of the lending programs of the World Bank and the regional development banks as well as the creation of an international investment trust to mobilize portfolio investment capital for local enterprises. In addition, the United States would be willing to provide technical assistance and expertise to developing countries ready to enter long-term capital markets, and asked other developed countries to provide similar assistance.

On the touchy issue of the role of multinational corporations, Kissinger recognized the concerns of many host countries regarding the ability of foreign-controlled firms to dominate their economies, evade local laws, and intervene in their politics. He affirmed that "countries are entitled to regulate the operations of transnational enterprises within their borders." But, contended Kissinger, host governments had an obligation to treat transnational enterprises equitably and responsibly.

Finally, with respect to developing-country demands for a greater role in international institutions and negotiations, Kissinger agreed that "participation in international decisions should be widely shared, in the name of both justice and effectiveness. . . . No country or group of countries should have exclusive power in areas basic to the welfare of others. This principle is valid for oil. It also applies to trade and finance."[18]

Kissinger was to be frustrated in his attempts to implement these proposals in the form of specific agreements between the developed and developing countries. In part, this was because of the lack of enthusiasm in the departments of Treasury and Commerce. In part,

it was because of the lingering suspicion among Third World leaders
that Kissinger wanted to split the developing-country coalition from
the OPEC countries and was attempting to co-opt the poor militants
with cosmetic generosity. But as Kissinger's policies toward Africa in
1976 were to show, there was a shift taking place in his grand
strategy that was both fundamental and genuine.

AFRICA AND THE REALPOLITIK OF CHANGE

On April 26, 1976, at a luncheon hosted by President Kenneth Kaunda
of Zambia, Kissinger once again surprised the world with a bold recast-
ing of U.S. policy on southern Africa, identifying the United States
for the first time as unequivocally on the side of black majority rule.

The new U.S. policy that Kissinger outlined comprehensively in
Lusaka was clearly a dramatic turnabout from the assumptions of
the so-called tar baby policy the Nixon administration had decided
on during its first year in office. The policy had been nicknamed "tar
baby" by its State Department opponents to express their judgment
that it was a sticky policy that the United States would be unable to
abandon if it did not work.[19] "Tar baby" had called for "selective
relaxation of our stance toward the white regimes" while maintaining a public posture of "opposition to racial repression." The
policy had been based explicitly on the premise that "the whites are
here to stay and the only way that constructive change can come
about is through them. There is no hope for the blacks to gain the
political rights they seek through violence, which will only lead to
chaos and increased opportunities for the communists." Increased
U.S. economic aid would be provided to the black states "to focus
their attention on their internal development and to give them a
motive to cooperate in reducing tensions." The Republic of South
Africa would also be encouraged to provide economic assistance to
the black states of Africa. Concrete measures to implement the
policy were to include a selective liberalization of the arms embargo
against South Africa and the Portuguese territories, plus the other
relaxations of sanctions that had been imposed against the white
regimes in conformity with U.N. resolutions; and flexible aid programs for the black states, including "nonsophisticated arms" in
response to "reasonable requests," while opposing the use of force by
insurgent movements.[20]

In approving this policy, President Nixon had set a U.S. course in southern Africa over the next five years that was to end ingloriously with the Angola crisis of 1975–76. The United States got stuck on the tar of its policy of improving relations with the white regimes while the Soviets were left to pick and choose among black clients. Kissinger's first response to this larger geopolitical consequence of "tar baby" was to counterintervene "covertly" against the Soviets and the Cubans in Africa; in Angola this only produced the further embarrassment of associating the United States with the losing blacks.

Angola provided the shock of recognition for Kissinger that conservative realpolitik would no longer work in Africa. He resisted learning this lesson, however, until U.S. incompetence in Angola was exposed before the entire world.

The leading claimant to head the new, post-Portugese regime in Angola was Agostino Neto and his Popular Movement for the Liberation of Angola (MPLA)—a movement supported by the Soviets.

In January 1975 the CIA had been authorized by the Forty Committee (the top-level review board that controlled covert operations abroad during the Nixon and Ford administrations) to funnel $300,000 worth of assistance secretly to Neto's principal opponent, Holden Roberto, the leader of the National Front for the Liberation of Angola. In the spring of 1975, the CIA requested more funds as well as authorization to expand its political and economic assistance into covert military aid to counter the growing Soviet shipments of military equipment to Neto and his increasing reliance on Cuban military advisers in the escalating civil war. It also asked for authorization to initiate a new program of support for another of Neto's opponents, Jonas Savimbi.

The CIA plan was strongly opposed by the NSC task force on Angola and by Assistant Secretary of State Nathaniel Davis. The covert military actions the CIA recommended might lead to increased intervention by the Soviet Union and other foreign powers, argued Davis. The level of violence in Angola would probably increase and, especially if there were widespread tribal or racial massacres, U.S. support for one or more of the rival groups would become a major political issue in the United States and an embarrassment internationally. It would be impossible to ensure that the CIA operations could be kept secret, and their exposure would have a negative impact on U.S. relations with many countries as well as with large segments of the U.S. public and Congress. Moreover, the United States would be committing its prestige in a situation over which it had limited influence and one whose outcome was highly uncertain. If the MPLA did come to power, the chances for the United States to establish working relations with it would have been greatly damaged.[21]

Davis' protestations were to no avail. Kissinger endorsed the CIA action plan, and President Ford gave Kissinger and the CIA the go-ahead to implement it in July 1975. Over the next six months, virtually all of Davis' predictions came true. The Soviets transported over 10,000 Cuban troops into Angola by air and sea and flew in massive amounts of combat equipment for use by the Cubans and the MPLA, while South Africa and Zaïre intervened against Neto's forces. In December the Senate voted to prohibit all further covert aid to Angola. The Soviets and the Cubans pressed their advantage. Neto trounced his opponents in the north of Angola, who had been aided by forces from Zaïre. The South Africans withdrew their forces from the South. By the end of January 1976, it was all over except for the recriminations.

On January 29, 1976, Kissinger appeared before the Subcommittee on African Affairs of the Senate Committee on Foreign Relations in one last defense of his Angola policies. The blame for failure, he insisted, lay not with the Ford administration but with Congress for failing to provide the wherewithal for standing up to the Soviets in the crunch. His testimony was a string of castigations of the congressional majority for their naïveté and lack of spine.[22]

Senator Dick Clark, chairman of the Subcommittee on African Affairs, disagreed profoundly. The important lesson of Angola, he maintained, is that the U.S. should not ignore the African black liberation movements until their victories against minority regimes are imminent and then back particular factions simply because their opponents are backed by the Soviet Union. The United States should make a new beginning in its African policy, by establishing connections between U.S. and African commitments to human rights and racial equality and between the U.S. commitment to international pluralism and African concepts of nonalignment. If the United States pursued such a new African policy, contended Clark, "our cold war interests in Africa may very well take care of themselves."[23]

In February the Organization of African Unity—the regional association of black African states—officially recognized the Neto regime as the legitimate government of Angola. Kissinger said little about Africa in public during the next two months. Only when he unveiled his new African policy in Lusaka at the end of April was it evident that he had taken to heart some of the criticism leveled at him by Senator Clark and others.

He had come to Africa, he said, "to usher in a new era in American policy." This new American policy endorsed the black African premise that racial justice and majority rule were the prerequisites for peace in Africa. This endorsement, however, was "not simply a matter of foreign policy but an imperative of our own moral heritage."

Specifically, with respect to Rhodesia, the United States unequivocally supported the British insistence that independence was illegal unless it was based on majority rule. "The Salisbury regime must understand," Kissinger warned, "that it cannot expect U.S. support either diplomatically or in material help at any stage in its conflict with African states or African liberation movements. On the contrary, it will face our unrelenting opposition until a negotiated settlement [to institute majority rule] is achieved." Accordingly, the United States was taking steps to insure its own and other nations' strictest compliance with UN resolutions on economic sanctions against Rhodesia consistent with U.S. nonrecognition of the Ian Smith regime in Salisbury. In addition, the United States was ready to provide special economic assistance to countries bordering on Rhodesia that might themselves suffer economic hardship as a result of closing their borders to normal trade with Rhodesia. The Ford administration was prepared to immediately provide $12.5 million to Mozambique under this policy. Looking toward a successful transition to majority rule in Rhodesia and then full independence, Kissinger promised that the United States would join other nations in a program of economic and technical assistance to the "newly independent Zimbabwe." (Kissinger's use of the African name for the country was symbolic of the basic shift in policy he was attempting to convey.)

On the Namibia question, Kissinger strongly reiterated the standing U.S. position that the Republic of South Africa's continued occupation of its former mandate territory was illegal and that the South African government should withdraw and allow the United Nations to supervise the Namibian people's attainment of full self-determination and independent statehood.

On the matter of South Africa's internal racial policies, Kissinger associated the United States with the position of the black African states more clearly than any previous top U.S. official had. "The world community's concern with South Africa is not merely that racial discrimination exists there," said Kissinger. "What is unique is the extent of which racial discrimination has been institutionalized, enshrined in law, and made all-pervasive.[24] The white South Africans must realize that the world would not tolerate the continued institutionalized separation of the races being enforced under the "apartheid" policy.

The Secretary of State backed up his new political orientation toward African issues by pledging to triple U.S. economic support for development programs in southern and central Africa over the next three years.

The evolution of Kissinger's North–South policy—now focused primarily on Africa—was remarkably analogous to the evolution in U.S. Latin American policy associated with the Kennedy administration. Kissinger had vituperatively criticized Kennedy's Alliance for Progress as naïve in its premise that democratic socialists rather than the conservative military elite of the Third World would provide the best bulwark against instability and Soviet attempts at capture leftist movements. Now he was embracing movements and concepts that he had previously branded as romantic and soft, as insufficiently based on hard balance-of-power realities to be able to effectively counter the unsentimental and often brutal Marxist-Leninists.

"Has Henry lost his nerve?" asked critics on the right. "Is he merely up to his old deceptive tricks?" asks critics on the left. Both suppositions were wrong. The Kissinger policy shift emanated largely from realpolitik considerations: how best to compete with the Soviets for influence in the Third World and how best to prevent the oil-producing nations from organizing the Third World into a block that would play off the superpowers against each other, particularly in the Middle East and Africa, and undermine the economic strength of the West and Japan.

In his "progressive" responses to the international populist demands for a global redistribution of wealth and political power, Kissinger was still acting essentially as a conservative. But in acting to conserve both American power and Western civilization he adopted an international posture analogous to the progressive responses of Theodore Roosevelt and later of Franklin Roosevelt to the domestic populist and Marxist movements in the first half of the twentieth century—or indeed, analogous to the way one of his heroes, Otto von Bismarck, had responded to the liberal and egalitarian agitations in Germany in the 1870s.

PART VI

THE CARTER PERIOD

I was familiar with the arguments that we had to choose between idealism and realism, between morality and the exertion of power; but I rejected those claims. To me the demonstration of American idealism was a practical and realistic approach to foreign affairs, and moral principles were the best foundation for the exertion of American power and influence.

—JIMMY CARTER

It is not a popular thing to remind people that power is important, that it has to be applied, that sometimes decisions which are not fully compatible with our concepts of what the world ideally ought to be like need to be taken.

—ZBIGNIEW BRZEZINSKI

17

THE MANY FACES OF
JIMMY CARTER

I am a farmer, an engineer, a father and husband, a Christian, a politician and former governor, a planner, a businessman, a nuclear physicist, a naval officer, a canoeist, and, among other things, a lover of Bob Dylan's songs and Dylan Thomas' poetry.

—JIMMY CARTER

In his campaign for the presidency, Jimmy Carter latched on to the popular discontent with Kissinger's realpolitik—a discontent prominent on the ideological right as well as on the left, and which nearly lost Gerald Ford the 1976 Republican nomination to Ronald Reagan. Carter was more effective than any of his rivals for the Democratic nomination, and more believable than Ford, in putting himself forward as the embodiment of a revived national consensus that U.S. foreign policy should reflect basic American values.

The divisions and bitterness of the period of Vietnam and Watergate would be overcome by giving fresh expression, at home and abroad, to the country's traditional dedication to the achievement by all of God's children of political self-determination, freedom from oppression, and a decent material life. "World order" politics would supplant "balance-of-power" politics. It was time to move beyond arms control and toward the abolition of nuclear weapons. The bonds of trust between the people of the United States and the officials who conduct U.S. foreign policy would be restored, as would the trust by other countries in the word of the United States, by avoiding secrecy in the formulation of policies and in negotiations with other countries.

Carter carried these themes forward into his early presidential prenouncements on foreign affairs—his inaugural address ("Our commitment to human rights must be absolute"; the ultimate goal of U.S. arms limitation policy is "the elimination of all nuclear weapons from the Earth"[1]); his maiden speech to the United Nations ("I have brought to office a firm commitment to a more open foreign policy. . . . No member of the United Nations can claim that mistreatment of its citizens is solely its own business"[2]); and his address at the 1977 commencement exercises of Notre Dame University:

I believe we can have a foreign policy that is democratic, that is based on fundamental values, and that uses power and influence, which we have, for humane purposes. We can also have a foreign policy that the American people support and, for a change, know and understand.

. . . Because we know that democracy works, we can reject the arguments of those rulers who deny human rights to their people. . . .

We are confident that the democratic methods are most effective, and so we are not tempted to employ improper tactics at home or abroad.

We are confident of our own strength, so we can seek substantial mutual reductions in the nuclear arms race.

And we are confident of the good sense of the American people, and so we let them share in the process of making foreign policy decisions. We can thus speak with the voices of 215 million, and not just an isolated handful.

. . . Being confident of our own future, we are now free of that inordinate fear of communism which once led us to embrace any dictator who joined us in that fear. . . .

For many years, we've been willing to adopt the flawed and erroneous principles and tactics of our adversaries, sometimes abandoning our own values for theirs. We've fought fire with fire, never thinking that fire is better quenched with water. This approach failed, with Vietnam the best example of its intellectual and moral poverty. But through failure we have now found our way back to our own principles and values.[3]

These idealistic aspects of Carter's world view were championed most vocally—inside the administration and in public—by Andrew Young, protégé of Martin Luther King and devotee of his pacifist philosophy, former congressman for Georgia, early supporter of Carter's presidential candidacy, and Carter's ambassador to the United Nations.

But Zbigniew Brzezinski, Carter's principal tutor in world affairs during his campaign for the presidency and his national security adviser in the White House, was always at Carter's elbow to insist that the idealistic impulses conform to thee geopolitical realities of international relations—at least when it came to the actual conduct of policy. Brzezinski was a persistent advocate of the view that the necessary condition for the preservation of American values at home and their propagation abroad was the limitation of the power of the primary adversary, the Soviet Union. And he echoed Henry Kissinger's "linkage" approach to the Soviets in maintaining that the Kremlin could not expect the United States to sustain cooperative relationships with the USSR in some fields—arms control, trade, technology transfer—while the Soviets engaged in aggressive power plays in Africa and the Persian Gulf area. Détente, insisted Brzezinski, "cannot be conducted on a selected and compartmentalized basis."[4] Indeed, Brzezinski was even more inclined than Kissinger to threaten a reduction in U.S.–Soviet cooperative arrangements as a punitive sanction for aggressive Soviet behavior, and to play upon Soviet fears of a Sino–American alliance against the Russians.

In contrast to Kissinger, Brzezinski advocated visible policies on behalf of human rights and Third World development as essential thrusts of an activist global policy that would be more than just a reaction to Soviet initiatives. In these respects he often could present himself as a soul brother to Andrew Young and other social-justice activists in the administration, even though he tended to shape his human rights and Third World policies to serve the geo-political imperatives of the U.S.–Soviet competition rather than as ends in themselves.

A third approach was that of Carter's Secretary of State, Cyrus Vance. A former high government official (Secretary of the Army in the Kennedy administration, Deputy Secretary of Defense and then diplomatic trouble-shooter in the Johnson administration) and prominent New York lawyer, Vance was skeptical of grand designs, reformist or geopolitical, urging rather that each international situation be examined on a case-by-case basis to determine which U.S. interests might be implicated, and which policy options might best serve those interests. His preferred options, even with adversaries, usually stressed problem solving through negotiations aimed at narrowing points of difference and solidifying common interests instead of the pressure tactics of linkage and confrontation. Perceiving that vital U.S. interests would be served by limiting the strategic arms race, he resisted all attempts in Washington to hold back SALT negotiations and ratification unless the Soviets reversed their interventions in east Africa and Afghanistan. Nor did Vance believe that U.S. relations with most other countries should be determined with primary and explicit reference to the global power rivalry between the United States and the USSR. Rather, the United States should deal with countries "on the merits" of the particular needs of each country and the capacity of the United States to relate to these needs.

Jimmy Carter could be swayed by the world views and preferred style of each of these approaches; and at times during his campaign for the presidency and during his tenure in the White House he would appear to have adopted one or the other, and at times some confusing hybrid of all of them. An uncharitable explanation of Carter's apparent vacillation between these various approaches is that he had no deeply held views of his own and was simply a politician attempting to secure the support of diverse factions in the body politic and the policy establishment. A charitable explanation is that Carter, faithful to the country whose values he was attempting to embody, was a complex person, whose own deep impulses and commitments were sometimes at cross-purposes, particularly when it came to concrete policy implications, and that the various approaches he appeared to vacillate between were indeed facets of the real Jimmy Carter.

Carter's presidential campaign had been unabashedly populist, claiming that the common people were his constituency and that it was their common sense that guided him in what was good or bad public policy, rather than the recommendations of experts or the calculations of Washington lawyers or power brokers.* Of course, having been Governor of Georgia, Carter knew as well as anyone that "the people" are hardly unified in their common sense, and more often than not are divided into bitterly opposed self-seeking

---

*Carter himself was proud to apply the term "populist" to his political philosophy, calling his speech accepting the Democratic presidential nomination "a populist speech designed to show that I derived my political support, my advice and my concern directly from the people themselves, not from powerful intermediaries of special interest groups. 'Populist' is a word, as you know, that comes from *populus*—people—and I think that people have been the origin of my own political incentives and my political strength." Interview with Jimmy Carter, *U.S. News & World Report* (September 13, 1976). See also Jimmy Carter, *Keeping Faith: Memoirs of a President* (New York: Bantam Books, 1982), p. 74.

interest groups who themselves employ lawyers, power brokers, and experts to advance their demands.

His more private campaign had been a skillful effort to maintain and establish contacts in the world of the materially and politically powerful elites, and to engender in them confidence in his intelligence, worldliness, nonideological pragmatism, and sophisticated experience in dealing with corporate and governmental power. An important vehicle for this campaign had been his membership in the Trilaterial Commission, a nongovernmental organization of prominent influentials from North America, Western Europe, and Japan, to promote cooperation among the advanced industrialized countries. Founded by David Rockefeller and directed by Zbigniew Brzezinski, the Trilateral Commission included among its members many exiles from past Democratic administrations (Cyrus Vance, George Ball, Paul Warnke, Harold Brown, Paul Nitze), media executives (Arthur Taylor of CBS, Hedley Donovan of *Time*), and prominent multinational corporation directors. It was largely from his Trilateral Commission contacts that candidate Carter formed his Foreign Policy and Defense Task Force, and subsequently his top-level and sub-Cabinet appointments to his administration.

Carter's success as presidential candidate was largely attributable to his ability to present himself variously as populist and establishmentarian, human rights idealist and geopolitical realist, country boy and impeccably mannered dinner-party host, Bible-quoting "born-again Christian" and devotee of existentialism. He was credible in each of these roles, depending upon whom he was talking with, and—most remarkably—credible also in his professions of guileless honesty.* The aura of credibility undoubtedly was a reflection of the fact that all these facets were the real Jimmy Carter, that he indeed was an amalgam of all of them, and a true believer in the mystical ethos that this was the essence of the nation he felt called upon to represent. With Walt Whitman's America, he could proclaim: "Do I contradict myself?/Very well then I contradict myself, (I am large, I contain multitudes.)"

---

*Carter's promise never to lie catered to a people who, following the systematic lying at the highest levels of the U.S. government in connection with Vietnam and Watergate, wanted to trust their leaders again. His effort to demonstrate such credibility was taken to lengths unusual for a political in his admission, near the end of the election campaign, to an interviewer for *Playboy* magazine that he had "looked on a lot of women [other than his wife] with lust." Interview with Jimmy Carter by Robert Scheer in *Playboy* (November 1976).

Some of Carter's main problems as President appear to have stemmed from his continuing to display in his executive role the all-things-to-all-people quality that got him elected. To give vent in the Oval Office to the contradiction-laden instincts of Mr. Everyman was to fail to establish and stick to priorities among values and objectives without which consistent and credible policy is impossible to sustain. Each of Carter's most trusted advisers sensed that the chief was most sympathetic with one's own approach, and would carry back to subordinates and sometimes to the public such presidential guidance as one wanted to (and did) hear. Moreover, the President himself, often giving expression to the formulations of his different advisers, frequently would deliver himself in policies and pronoucements of a sequence of inconsistent moves and postures.

In foreign policy, the part of Jimmy Carter that was a Baptist preacher-politician was in tune with the moral sloganeering and simplications of Andrew Young. But the engineer in Carter, always seeking structural principles and formulas to resolve problems, was particularly susceptible to the geopolitical grand designs and abstract formulations of Brzezinski, which provided a sense of intellectual control over otherwise confusing events. Yet Carter was also a shrewd and pragmatic businessman who understood the pitfalls of being carried away by emotion, ideology, or overly abstract logic. This part of Carter admired the case-by-case, corporate-lawyer approach of Cyrus Vance, who patiently and coolly could work through a complicated negotiating sequence with adversaries without getting trapped in a confrontation over general principles.

When it came to dealing with the Soviet Union, Carter's own pradoxical qualities and his susceptibility to the approaches of his various advisers would produce a confusing series of policy stances—confusing not only to the American public and allies but also to the Soviet leadership.

As a deeply religious man, Carter found strategies of polarization and alienation uncongenial; his preferred mode of dealing with adversaries was to discover bonds of common humanity as a context for attempting to harmonize, or at least reconcile, their conflicting interests. But such pacifist impulses were hardly as absolute for him or for Andrew Young as they had been for their hero, Martin Luther King. Carter increasingly expressed in words as well as action an appreciation for maintaining an adequate arsenal of coercive power in order to defend one's interest against aggressive adversaries.

A self-made millionaire farmer, Carter could switch as required to a stance of toughness and decisiveness in dealing with the Soviets, especially when buoyed by Brzezinski's counsel that these were the qualities that the Russians respected most. Brzezinski advised the President not to shirk from aggressively taking the diplomatic offensive against the Soviets, for they feared an America aroused and, despite their boasting, admired its economic and technological prowess and its military potential.

But Secretary of State Vance's cool professionalism, his insistence on considering the manifold implications of any course of action, would appeal to Carter's self-concept as businessman-turned-chief-executive and sophisticated modernist statesman. He was particularly receptive to Vance's cautionary advice against unnecessarily provoking the Russians or stimulating a full-blown arms race, thus destroying the basis for U.S.–Soviet cooperation—which was still new and fragile—by reviving a cold war psychology on both sides.

Carter's first major address devoted to U.S.–Soviet relations, delivered at the June 1978 Annapolis commencement, revealed his ambivalence so openly that it was an embarrassment to many in the administration.[5] It was widely believed, recalls Hodding Carter III, the State Department's press spokesman under Vance, that the President "took speech drafts offered by the State Department and the National Security Council and simply pasted half of one to half of the other. The result was predictably all over the lot, offering the Soviet Union the mailed fist and the dove's coo simultaneously."[6]

The Third World policies of the administration revealed a similar ambivalence at the top, once again reflecting the differing world views of the President's principal advisers. Brzezinski viewed the Third World much the way it was viewed in the Kennedy White House, as an arena of competition between the United States and the Soviet Union for influence over those demanding self-determination and equalization of wealth and power. To compete effectively, the United States should try to get on the side of the "new forces." However, the United States should not simply accept losses where the Soviets had already established a local power base; in such cases it was imperative to organize local balances of power against those within the Soviet camp, even if this meant backing conservative or reactionary forces. Nor should the United States stand idly by and accept defections from the U.S. camp toward nonalignment, for this, as viewed by Brzezinski, would weaken the global power position of the United States vis-à-vis the USSR. Especially in the case of regional bulwarks against Soviet influence—most notably Iran—it was important to prevent a collapse of regimes friendly to the United States.

Brzezinski and Andrew Young were frequent allies on the importance of putting the United States on the side of movements for national self-determination and economic development in the Third World, even if their basic reasons for this posture differed. Their joint championing of U.S. support for the Marxist Robert Mugabe who took power in Zimbabwe was a notable case in point. Brzezinski saw that the real alternative was not a perpetuation of the more conservative black-white Rhodesian regime backed by former white Rhodesian Prime Minister Ian Smith, but rather the Soviet-supported faction of the black liberation movement. By backing the dominant Mugabe group (also supported by China), the United States retained considerable influence with the new Zimbabwe government, while the Russians were left out in the bush. Andrew Young's reasons converged here with Brzezinski's insofar as he too saw the Mugabe faction as the strongest among the liberationist forces. But Young was opposed to injecting cold war considerations prominently into decisions about whom to support or oppose in the Third World. U.S. support, rather, should go to the "progressive" forces, which in the African context, meant those most capable of establishing and sustaining black majority rule in those areas still dominated by the white minority, and which in the Third World generally meant those attempting to redistribute wealth and political power to broader segments of the population. Young was against treating Third World countries and movements as pawns in the U.S.–Soviet rivalry—a policy he branded a form of racist condescension—and argued for giving the benefit of the doubt to Third World "progressives," whose judgments about their own interests should be respected, even when this meant accepting help from the Soviets and Cubans. Brzezinski, of course, regarded such a Third World policy as geopolitically naïve and dangerous.

Cyrus Vance, as aware of the geopolitical realities as any of Carter's advisers, and hardly indifferent to Soviet expansionism, often differed with Brzezinski over the best means of limiting Soviet influence in the Third World. Vance held that Soviet expansion could be contained best by the development of strong, proud nations, unwilling to sacrifice their independence to the imperial purposes of a superpower. The United States should resist getting pulled into the game of competitive imperial expansion in the Third World. Rather, it should respond primarily to the development needs of Third World countries in a way that conveyed respect for their own ability to define and deal with their indigenous problems. The problems of the Third World should not in the first instance be defined as cold war issues. The United States did not have to preach to the natives to save them from the Communist devil. American practical know-how and its pluralistic ideology would speak for itself. Influence would come from good works. The Soviets would lose out in the larger competition through their crude power plays.

Carter, in part, evidently wanted to be like Cyrus Vance, while sharing Andrew Young's compassion for the oppressed and poor peoples of the world. He wanted to be the kind, wise world leader who puts the human dignity of all God's children uppermost. But another part of him apparently wanted desperately to be admired as tough and unsqueamish in adversity, and perceived that the largest part of his domestic American audience identified with the machismo image more than the saint.

One of Carter's speechwriters during his first two years in office summed up the problems: "Carter has not given us an *idea* to follow. The central idea of the Carter administration is Jimmy Carter himself, his own mixture of traits, since the only thing that gives coherence to the items of his creed is that he happens to believe them all. . . . I came to think Jimmy Carter believes fifty things, but no one thing. . . . Values that others would find contradictory complement one another in his mind."[7]

Carter was perhaps all too faithfully a man of the season—the season of confusion in U.S. foreign policy goals following the country's misadventure in Vietnam; the season of popular backlash against the immorality of Watergate and against the amorality and elitism of Kissinger's brand of geopolitics; the season of realization that the Soviet Union, its arrogance revived by the attainment of full strategic equality with the United States and global military mobility, was not going to play détente according to the rules of mutual restraint; the season of adjustment to dependence on the Middle Eastern oil producers, most of whom were hostile to the U.S. for what they perceived as its past attempts to dominate them economically and politically and for its friendship with Israel.

Neither Carter nor Brzezinski nor any other influential official had the genius to translate the mood of confusion and apprehension which brought Carter to the presidency into a coherent foreign policy. A semblance of coherence developed out of the perceived need to more effectively prosecute the rivalry with the USSR, especially after the Soviet invasion of Afghanistan in late 1979—but haplessly this turn reinforced the larger impression of vacillation, for it appeared to contradict Carter's earlier pledges to reduce America's preoccupation with the Soviet Union.

The departure from the administration of Andrew Young in August 1979 and finally Cyrus Vance in April 1980 was the necessary correlate of this shift by Carter toward the primary orientation of Brzezinski. Vance's resignation marked the ascendancy of the Brzezinski approach—the renewed preoccupation with the Soviet threat and the tendency to resort to confrontationist postures in dealing with adversaries. The Secretary of State said in resigning that he had been overruled in his objection to the attempt to rescue the American Embassy hostages in Iran by helicopter. This explicit reason, of course, was only a symptom of his more basic disagreement with the direction U.S. foreign policy was taking under Brzezinski's increasing influence. As Vance stated in his address at the 1980 Harvard commencement exercises: "Our real problems are long-term in nature. It will not do to reach for the dramatic act, to seek to cut through stubborn dilemmas with a single stroke." But it was also a "fallacy" to seek "a single strategy—a master plan" to yield "answers to each and every foreign policy decision we face. Whatever value that approach may have had in a bipolar world, it now serves us badly. The world has become pluralistic, exposing the inadequacy of the single strategy, the grand design, where facts are forced to fit theory."[8]

Ironically, it was Vance's patient, soft-spoken approach that was primarily responsible for most of the dramatic foreign policy successes of the Carter administration: the successful negotiation and ratification of the Panama Canal treaty; the Camp David accords between Israel and Egypt and their subsequent treaties; the husbanding of the installation of a black majority regime in Zimbabwe; and, finally, the deal with Iran to free the embassy hostages, consummated during the last hours of the Carter administration. The major accomplishment of the administration for which Brzezinski could claim credit were the establishment of full diplomatic relations with China and the revival of serious efforts in NATO to balance the Soviet military buildup; but these two elements were already in the pipeline, so to speak, and it would have been surprising had they not materialized.

The largest disappointment of the Carter administration—its inability to gain congressional ratification of SALT II—can be blamed primarily on the Soviets, who by invading Afghanistan on Christmas 1979 and brutally occupying that country throughout 1980, ruined whatever chance Carter might have had to gain Senate concurrence to the treaties. A President with substantial political clout who believed, as Carter did, that SALT II was still in the national interest, despite Afghanistan, might have been able to successfully prosecute the ratification battle in 1980. Carter's international and domestic reputation as a statesman stayed too low to give him the kind of charisma that could convert wavering senators. Reluctantly, Carter backed away from a ratification fight which he was sure to lose.

Brzezinski would later complain that "SALT lies buried in the sands of Ogaden," a reference to the unwillingness of the United States to support the Somalis in 1978 in their war against the Ethiopians, who were being helped by Cuban troops and Soviet military advisers and equipment. In Brzezinski's view, SALT could have been ratified if the Carter administration had been able to sustain a reputation of not being "soft" toward the Soviets, willing to "compete assertively" with them. "The argument that the phrase [about SALT and the Ogaden] is meant to capsulate," explained Brzezinski, "is that, unless we stand up to the Soviet drive by proxy soon enough, we'll not do well in the competition and will lose chances for effective cooperation."[9]

Vance, from retirement, would rebut Brzezinski's assertions and their implications. "The charge that some are making that there was an unwillingness to consider the use of force if necessary when our vital interests were concerned is hogwash," he declared. The trouble was, rather, that Brzezinski gave too much emphasis to "the use of military power or bluff, ignoring, in my judgment, the political, economic, and the trade aspects of our relationship with the Soviet Union." Brzezinski's epigram about SALT being "buried in the sands of Ogaden" was symptomatic of the grand strategy's neglect of the details of particular circumstances. It was "a catchy phrase without any substance," said Vance. Somalia had violated Ethiopian territory by invading the Ogaden in 1978, and the Soviet Union and Cuba had sent troops into Ethiopia to help an ally defend itself. The United States got what it wanted, Vance recalled, as the Soviet Union and its allies, heeding the U.S. warning, held back from invading Somali territory.[10]

Having lost the election to Ronald Reagan, Carter might at least have been spared further public altercations by those closely associated with his presidency. It was a measure of the weakness of his administration that his associates felt the need to absolve themselves of Carter's supposed failures by blaming each other.

18

IDEALISM AS THE HIGHER REALISM

We seek these goals because they are right—and because we, too, will benefit. Our own well-being, and even our security, are enhanced in a world that shares common freedoms and in which prosperity and economic justice create the conditions for peace. . . . Nations, like individuals, limit their potential when they limit their goals.

—CYRUS VANCE

The impulses to bring justice to the world reflected in Jimmy Carter's campaign rhetoric were not the stuff that could be readily translated into programs and actions. Secretary of State Vance, in particular—the most experienced foreign policy official at the top level of the new administration—was wary of the pitfalls of an ideologically crusading policy. It should not be the business of the United States, in the words of John Quincy Adams, to roam the world "in search of monsters to destroy."

But Vance, and other experienced hands, were also aware of the pitfalls in the realpolitik posture of aloofness from the "domestic" politics of countries the United States was supporting for geopolitical reasons. The manifestations of such support—generous financial credits, technology transfers, military and police training programs, and weapons sales—all constituted, in fact if not by design, a rather significant intervention in the domestic policy of the client country. Thus, in practice, the ideological neutrality that was supposed to underlie the realpolitik policy was vitiated, for the governments that came forward as the most willing clients were usually rightist regimes, dependent for their domestic political survival on commercial and military classes, and resistant to egalitarian reforms.

FASHIONING A WORKABLE HUMAN RIGHTS POLICY

The earliest attempts by Carter to show the world that his human rights posture was more than rhetoric were fashioned for him by eager White House aides. A public letter by the President to the Soviet dissident Andrei Sakharov and the media event of a White House meeting with the recently exiled Vladimir Bukovsky portended a resourceful cooptation of the human rights policy by Brzezinski and his staff of young activists. The Office of Human Rights and of Humanitarian Affairs under Assistant Secretary of State Patricia Derian was slow in getting its act together, and its initiatives, which would be equally directed against oppressive right-wing oligarchies in the Third World, were eclipsed by what appeared to be a cold war revivalism in the White House. State Department officials spent much of the spring trying to reassure the Soviets that this was not the case, especially after Brezhnev and Foreign Minister Gromyko insisted that serious negotiations on arms control and other matters would be distorted, if not precluded, in such an environment.

A concerned President Carter asked Secretary Vance to sort things out and to fashion a coherent and workable human rights policy. The results of this first effort by the administration to think through systematically the policy implications of its human rights posture were presented in a major foreign policy address by Secretary Vance at the University of Georgia Law School on April 30, 1977.

"In pursuing a human rights policy," said Vance, "we must always keep in mind the limits of our power and wisdom. A sure formula for defeat of our goals would be a rigid, hubristic attempt to impose our values on others. A doctrinaire plan of action would be as damaging as indifference." We must be realistic, he said. "Our country can only achieve our objectives if we shape what we do to the case at hand." In each reported case of a country violating basic human rights norms, therefore, the administration would ask a number of specific questions in determining whether and how to act:

First, what is the nature of the particular case?

What kinds of violations or deprivations are there? What is their extent?

Is there a pattern to the violations? If so, is the trend toward concern for human rights or away from it?

What is the degree of control and responsibility of the government involved?

And finally, is the government willing to permit outside investigation?

A second set of questions concerned the prospect for effective action.

Will our action be useful in promoting the overall cause of human rights?

Will it actually improve the specific conditions at hand? Or will it be likely to make things worse instead?

Is the country involved receptive to our interests and efforts?

Will others work with us, including official and private international organizations dedicated to furthering human rights?

Finally, does our sense of values and decency demand that we speak out or take action anyway, even though there is only a remote chance of making our influence felt?

A third set of questions focused on the difficult policy dilemmas and tradeoffs.

Have we been sensitive to genuine security interests, realizing the outbreak of armed conflict or terrorism could itself pose a serious threat to human rights?

Have we considered *all* the rights at stake? If, for instance, we reduce aid to a government which violated the political rights of its citizens, do we not risk penalizing the hungry and the poor, who bear no responsibility for the abuses of their government?

The Secretary of State did not want to prejudge how such trade-offs would be made in any specific case, for this might encourage some countries to repress political dissent for the ostensible reason of more effectively implementing an economic development plan, or to rationalize draconian police tactics in the service of security against terrorism. His listing of the types of human rights the United States would work to advance around the world placed civil and political liberties third, behind

First, . . . the right to be free from governmental violation of the integrity of the human person. . . . [such as] torture; cruel, inhuman, or degrading treatment or punishment; and arbitrary arrest or imprisonment. . . .

Second, . . . the right to the fulfillment of such vital needs as food, shelter, health care, and education.

The civil and political liberties generally associated with liberal democracies, such as freedom of speech and press and freedom to run for elective office, could not, realistically, be accorded equal priority with the physical security and economic subsistence needs of peoples. Elementary respect for the basic integrity of the human person was another matter, and the Carter administration was putting all, including its allies, on notice that this administration would not condone, and certainly not allow itself to be associated with, violations of this fundamental norm of decent society.

Just as a variety of circumstances had to be carefully assessed in determining if a country was guilty of human rights violations, so too a variety of possible responses would have to be assayed on a case-by-case basis. The means available ranged "from quiet diplomacy in its many forms, through public pronouncements, to withholding assistance. Whenever possible, we will use positive steps of encouragement and inducement." There could be no mechanistic formulas, no automatic answers. "In the end, a decision whether and how to act in the cause of human rights is a matter for informed and careful judgment."[1]

Opponents of giving human rights a central emphasis in U.S. foreign policy pointed out that, with all the qualifications, dilemmas, and tradeoffs in the Secretary of State's exposition of the policy, the Carter administration could not really claim to be offering the country and the world anything new. In their opinion, that was all to the good. Some opponents, however, would hold up the Carter administration's highly circumscribed performance in the human rights field to the standards of Carter's own earlier, more absolutist rhetoric, not to Vance's refinements, and, accordingly, took delight in vilifying the administration for hypocrisy.

Many human rights idealists agreed, but with sadness, with the allegations of hypocrisy, as they witnessed Carter showering praise on dictators like the Shah of Iran and President Somoza of Nicaragua; continuing high levels of military support to the oppressive military regime in South Korea; taking a "hear no evil, see no evil, speak no evil" stance toward the People's Republic of China; and backing off quickly from his initial criticism of the Soviet regime for its treatment of dissidents in the USSR.

Despite the unpopularity of the pragmatic and quiet approach, the President remained committed to Vance's logic, with few exceptions, throughout his term of office. The President and the Secretary of State made it clear that they were making human rights a central consideration in U.S. foreign policy, and that they expected the bureaucracy to be resourceful in seeking and adapting policy instruments to give this commitment effect. Much legislation was already on the books, reflecting congressional attempts to get the executive to act during the Kissinger years. Part of the effort would be simply to organize the administration to implement the law, particularly in foreign military and economic assistance programs.

The seriousness of the Carter–Vance commitment was reflected in the designation of Deputy Secretary of State Warren Christopher to head an interagency group on human rights and foreign assistance. The group's mandate, backed by the authority of the NSC directive of April 1, 1977 that set it up, was to approve, delay, limit, or deny any proposed project on the basis of the recipient country's human rights record. Bureaucratic opponents of the new human rights emphasis might be able to undermine the efforts of Assistant Secretary of State Derian and her newly enlarged Office of Human Rights and Humanitarian Affairs; but the Secretary of State's trusted second-in-command presided over a powerful interagency group with members from the departments of Defense, Treasury, Commerce, Labor, Agriculture, and the NSC. Decisions of the Christopher group were tantamount to an executive order, and were backed up by the appropriate White House and Cabinet-level endorsements when required.

As a result of the actions of the interagency group, assistance levels were lowered, on grounds of poor human rights performance, to Afghanistan, Guinea, Central African Empire, Chile, Nicaragua, Paraguay, and El Salvador. And the group's findings of positive human rights developments resulted in increased levels of assistance for India, Sri Lanka, Botswana, Gambia, the Dominican Republic, Peru, and Costa Rica.[2]

Under Carter, the U.S. government also opposed loans by international financial institutions to countries in gross violation of basic (especially "integrity of persons") human rights, but much less consistently or automatically than human rights zealots in the Congress wanted. The Carter administration inherited a congressionally imposed requirement (denying it the case-by-case flexibility it thought essential) that the U.S. governors to both the Inter-American Development Bank and the African Development Fund must vote against loans to any country engaging in "a consistent pattern of gross violation of internationally recognized human rights unless such assistance will directly benefit needy people." This legislation, an amendment sponsored by Congressman Thomas Harkin of Iowa to the May 1976 bill authorizing funding to these regional banks, became the model for congressional attempts during 1977 to extend human rights provisos to development loans from the World Bank and other international lending institutions. The Carter administration lobbied hard against such legislation, arguing that it reflected an overly rigid approach, and that it would actually handicap U.S. efforts to encourage human rights improvements in other countries, since by making the U.S. vote against loans to specific countries automatic, it would weaken U.S. bargaining power. A compromise bill passed the Congress on September 2, 1977, instructing U.S. officials to international financial institutions to "oppose" any loans to rights violators unless the loans directly benefited the needy. The requirement to "oppose" rather than to "vote no" was more consistent with the flexibility the administration wanted.[3]

Despite dissatisfaction in Congress, and a public generally confused by the administration's pragmatic pullback from Carter's earlier rhetoric and some glaring contradictions (such as Carter's support for the Shah of Iran), the Carter administration could properly take some credit for positive human rights developments in several countries: substantial numbers of political prisoners were released in Bangladesh, Sudan, Indonesia, South Korea, the Philippines, Brazil, Nepal, and Cuba. In Ghana, Nigeria, and Thailand significant steps toward the transfer of power from military to civilian governments were taken. More freedom was granted to the press in various countries. As put by one administration official in his congressional testimony, "Both dissidents and governments have acknowledged—the former favorably and the latter at times less so—our inclusion of human rights issues into U.S. foreign policy. The wall posters of China, the statements of Sakharov and others, and the declarations of groups concerned with political prisoners in Asia, Africa, and Latin America, demonstrate that the U.S. human rights policy is a constant reality."[4]

PANAMA, NICARAGUA, AND ZIMBABWE

In four situations during the Carter administration, the United States was faced with challenges to the status quo that would have inevitable consequences for regional balances of power, and which provided the country the opportunity to put its ideals of self-determination and human rights in the service of its geopolitical interests. One of these, the revolution in Iran, because of the depth of the trauma it produced, and the consequences of its outcome for the global balance of power, will be treated in a separate chapter. The other three—the maturing of the negotiations on the Panama Canal treaties, the success of the Sandinista movement in Nicaragua, and the failure of halfway measures toward black majority rule in Rhodesia/Zimbabwe—were not as traumatic for the U.S. nor as consequential in their immediate effects; yet their management by the Carter administration also sparked considerable domestic controversy over the power and purposes of the United States in the world.

The Panama Canal Treaties

The domestic controversy was most intense over the two treaties signed with great fanfare on September 7, 1977, by President Carter and Brigadier General Omar Torrijos Herrera, ceding sovereignty over the Panama Canal and the Canal Zone to Panama and guaranteeing the United States future peacetime and wartime use of the canal.* For the treaties to become law, the Senate had to vote its consent with at least a two-third majority, or 67 votes; at the outset of the Senate deliberations, a United Press International poll reported only 36 senators for or leaning toward approval, 27 against or leaning against, and 37 uncommitted.[5] Moreover, popular passion and organized pressures were running against approval.

The administration won few converts by pointing out that technically the United States never had formal sovereignty over the canal

---

*The Panama Canal Treaty established a staged devolution of control of the canal and the zone to Panama, to be completed by the year 2000. Until then, the United States would retain its military base rights in the zone as well as full responsibility for the defense of the canal. The treaty also established schedules of fees to be paid Panama during this period and stipulated canal administrative procedures in detail. The Neutrality Treaty, which takes effect in the year 2000, was a guarantee by Panama to assure all nations the right to use the canal in peace and war, stipulating that only Panama was to operate the canal and to maintain any required military forces on its territory for the purpose, but implying a residual right of the United States to take matters into its own hands if Panama failed to live up to its treaty obligations. The United States also was given the status of first among equals by the provision that warships of the United States and Panama were entitled to transit the canal "expeditiously."

and Canal Zone, but only a grant from Panama, through the original 1903 treaty, to act "as if it were sovereign," and that even this was extracted from Panama by a coercive power play which, by today's standards, would be universally condemned as imperialistic and illegitimate. The popular ground in the debate was occupied by those like Ronald Reagan, who argued for a revival of the kind of American patriotism that took pride in Theodore Roosevelt's aggressiveness in securing the canal, and by those like Senator S. I. Hayakawa, who, with his quip "We stole it fair and square," gave vent to a cocky American jingoism pressing for release from the post-Vietnam restraints on such impulses.

Accommodating to the all-too-evident popular mood and senatorial reluctance to buck it, President Carter, during the seven-month battle for legislative approval of the treaties, shifted his own ground from invocations of the country's traditions of fairness, nobility, and self-determination for all peoples, to predictions of disastrous geopolitical consequences for the United States if the treaties were rejected. And to assure senators that the United States was relinquishing neither any tangible military and commercial rights to use the canal in war or peace nor any real power to enforce these rights should Panama someday be hostile to the United States, the President accepted some ninety "reservations," "understandings," and "conditions" demanded by senators, as well as two amendments that required General Torrijos' consent, in the process coming perilously close to pushing the Panamanian into a repudiation of the whole effort.

Despite the amendments and reservations—some of (which like the Deconcini reservation providing that if the canal were closed for any reason, *either* the United States or Panama could take military steps to put it back into operation) almost killed both treaties—the President and all the heavies he could muster in the administration and outside, including Kissinger, persuaded the Senate to approve the treaties by only a slim two-vote margin over the required two-thirds.

Ousting Somoza

In Nicaragua, the United States was unavoidably implicated by the challenges to the legitimacy of the oligarchical Somoza dynasty, which, because of its own staunch anti-Communism and tangible cooperation with U.S. anti-Communist interventions in Central America and the Caribbean, was heavily supported throughout the post–World War II period by U.S. economic and military assistance. Now, with the dictator Anastasio Somoza Debayle confronting a rapidly expanding revolution against his rule, the United States government—even with Carter's commitment to human rights— found itself trapped by its past obligations.

By the time of Carter's inauguration, opposition to Somoza had become broadly based with Managua's large and thriving middle class organized in the Unión Democrática de Liberación, led by the respected editor of *La Prensa,* Pedro Joaquin Chamorro. The militant leftists, whose spearhead was the Frente Sandinista de Liberación Nacional, were still not the dominant force, but Somoza's strategy of focusing on the Sandinistas as the main threat and his allegations that their Cuban and Soviet connections (still rather thin) meant that an international Communist conspiracy was behind the effort to undermine his regime, gave the leftists more visibility and influence in Nicaragua and internationally than they might have had other- wise. The Sandinistas thus became a partner with Somoza in polariz- ing Nicaragua, as their acts of terrorism and hostage-taking led to increased brutality by Somoza's National Guard against suspected opponents of the regime. In the two years before Carter's election, the escalation of the brutal civil conflict had led Somoza to declare a state of siege; an elite "counterinsurgency force," supported by an 80 percent increase in U.S. military aid, launched a reign of terror in the countryside, committing torture and mass executions, uprooting and forcibly resettling 80 percent of the rural population in the northern regions of the country.[6]

The gross and systematic brutality of the Somoza regime was brought to the attention of the Christopher interagency group and led to a restriction of military and economic aid to Nicaragua in April 1977, in one of the first acts by which the Carter administration demonstrated its seriousness of purpose on human rights. It was a minor slap on the wrist to the Nicaraguan dictator who had over the years developed influential allies in the U.S. Congress and State and Defense Department bureaucracies. Somoza banked on the effi- ciency with which his reign of terror had reestablished his invulnera- bility and domestic order to allow him to dispense with those acts that offended the sensibilities of the Carter administration. And, indeed, in September 1977 the administration relaxed the restrictions it had imposed only five months before.

The moderates now stepped up their activities to mobilize support for peaceful electoral and constitutional change, and tried to forge links with some of the less fanatic elements of the Sandinista front. But the assassination of the moderate leader, Chamorro, in 1978 led to a new flareup of popular outrage and violence directed against Somoza. The country's business leaders called a general strike to demand Somoza's resignation, and terrorists launched attacks throughout the country. The Sandinistas were revived, and so were the harsh, repressive tactics of the National Guard. The moderates placed their hopes in the Carter administration, anticipating a reimposition of sanctions on Somoza coupled with pressure for the establishment of genuine constitutional representative government.

The severe deterioration of Somoza's ability to control events in 1978 posed a more stark dilemma for the Carter administration— sanctions might further undercut Somoza's legitimacy at a time when the consequence would be the coming to power of the revolutionary elements. Yet to do nothing, given the widespread knowledge that the situation was even worse now than in the previous year, would be an embarrassing retreat for the Carter human rights policy. The result was the Carter administration's 1978 decision to reimpose sanctions and to insist upon a "dialogue" between Somoza and the moderates. Once again, surface calm returned to the cities and countryside of Nicaragua, and by summer the Carter administration decided to reduce the sanctions. In addition Carter sent a letter to Somoza congratulating the dictator on his improved human rights record.[7]

The U.S. reconciliation with Somoza had just the opposite effect of that intended by Carter. Rather than stimulating movement toward the liberalization of the government in Nicaragua, it demoralized most of the moderates and drove them in desperation into an alliance with the radicals under a new umbrella organization, the Broad Opposition Front.

With the country now polarized, the militant Sandinistas were able to set the pace and call the shots for the broad anti-Somoza coalition. In August 1978, they stormed the National Palace while Somoza's rubber-stamp Congress was in session and took 1,500 hostages, in exchange for whom they were able to force Somoza to release 59 jailed Sandinistas. Another general strike was called, and in September the Sandinistas launched attacks on National Guard garrisons in five provincial cities.[8] The National Guard, insecure on the ground, retaliated from the air with bombing and strafing attacks on rebel strongholds in which thousands of innocent civilians were killed. By the end of the month Somoza had again established his power, at the cost of totally losing his authority.

The events of bloody September 1978 finally convinced U.S. officials that Somoza must be persuaded to step down in favor of a constitutional regime. They still hoped to accomplish this by negotiations between Somoza and the moderates to arrange for a plebiscite and in this way to prevent the Sandinistas from dominating the post-Somoza government. Somoza agreed to participate in such negotiations, but his attempts to manipulate and subvert them provoked even the moderate elements to walk out in protest. In the meantime the Sandinistas had been reorganizing and rearming for what was to become the final, successful stage of their insurrection.

The decisive anti-Somoza uprising began on June 4, 1979. Virtually the entire population of Managua cooperated in bringing to a halt all commercial and professional activity. The National Guard again retaliated with bullets and bombs, but this time the insurrection only spread. Well-equipped Sandinista forces that had been arming themselves and training in neighboring Costa Rica reentered the country. American and other foreign observers began to talk of an impending Sandinista victory.[9]

On July 21, 1979, Secretary of State Vance finally announced a change in United States policy during a meeting of the Organization of American States in Washington. "We must seek a political solution which will take into account the interests of *all* significant groups in Nicaragua," he told the assembled Latin American diplomats (emphasis added).

Such a solution must begin with the replacement of the present Government with a transition government of national reconciliation, which would be a clear break with the past. It would consist of individuals who enjoy the support and confidence of the widest possible spectrum of Nicaraguans.

. . .

We propose that this meeting insist on a cease-fire within Nicaragua and on its borders and a halt to all shipments of arms and ammunition into Nicaragua.

· · ·

All of the member nations of this organization must consider on an urgent basis
the need for a peacekeeping force, to help restore order and to permit the will of
Nicaraguan citizens to be implemented in the establishment of a democratic and
representative government.[10]

The Organization of American States almost unanimously rejected
the U.S. proposals for a cease-fire and a regional peacekeeping force.
It was clearly too little and too late, and—besides—the OAS was
itself not well structured to perform this function.

The Sandinists pressed forward, set up a provisional government,
and Somoza, denied further U.S. backing, went into exile. The
United States government, having lost virtually all credit with the
Sandinista-dominated regime in Managua, proved incapable of influencing events in that country during the remainder of the Carter
presidency to prevent it from moving in a pro-Castro and pro-Soviet
direction; if anything, the record of U.S. timidity in dealing with
Somoza made such a radicalization likely.

Zimbabwe

The Carter administratino looked considerably more consistent
and competent in dealing with Rhodesia/Zimbabwe than it did with
respect to the Panama Canal treaties or the Somoza ouster. The
policy dilemmas were no less profound nor was conservative opposition to a reformist policy lacking, but Carter's relatively impressive
success on matters in southern Africa was partly the result of there
being an active constituency for change in Congress and among his
appointees to high foreign policy positions. The U.S. government
was also able to take a back sat to the British, who bore the principal
international responsibility for bringing about a durable regime
change in Harare.

The reformist constituency in the administration, a part of what
UN Ambassador Andrew Young called "the new Africa coalition,"
consisted of Young himself, Assistant Secretary of State for Africa
Richard Moose, and director of the Policy Planning Staff Anthony
Lake. Building on the American black constituency support that
Young was instrumental in bringing into the Carter camp in the
1976 campaign and the emergence of African issues as a post-Viet-
nam foreign policy concern among American liberals, this group was

instrumental in getting Congress to repeal the Byrd Amendment (providing for U.S. imports of Rhodesian chrome), allowing Carter to fulfill one of his campaign promises, and to bring U.S. diplomacy back in concert with Britain's on the Rhodesia/Zimbabwe issue.[11]

The repeal of the Byrd Amendment, said Carter in signing the legislation, "puts us on the side of what is right and proper." By allowing the United States to join in the UN-authorized boycott of Rhodesian exports, to which the American delegation had originally subscribed, "it puts us back on the side of support for the United Nations. It puts us in the strategic position to help with the resolution of the Rhodesian question."[12]

Carter soon came under renewed pressure from conservatives in Congress to lift the boycott of Rhodesian materials to indicate approval by the U.S. government for the racially mixed government Rhodesian Prime Minister Ian Smith put together in 1978 and successfully submitted to electoral referenda in January and April of 1979. The President, following the advice of the African coalition in his administration, continued to concert U.S. policy with that of Britain, which even under the Conservative government of Margaret Thatcher refused to accord legitimacy to the new Muzorewa regime. The British urged a more deeply cutting change in Rhodesia/Zimbabwe that would bring the most popular and vigorous elements of the black liberationist movement, the Patriotic Front for the Liberation of Zimbabwe, into the new black-run government. If not, the British argued, the Marxist leadership of the Patriotic Front would come increasingly under the sway of the Soviet Union, and eventually stage a full-blown insurrection to install a pro-Soviet regime in Salisbury.[13]

It was thus essentially a realpolitik rationale of dealing with those who have the power (in this case potential power) that allowed Carter to sustain the boycott and to cooperate with Britain in inducing the Patriotic Front leader, Robert Mugabe, to lay down his arms and participate constructively in the formation of the new government of independent Zimbabwe. By so doing, the United States salvaged for itself in southern Africa, more than it had been able to do in Nicaragua or Iran, a position of influence with the ascending political forces. A not inconsiderable side benefit was the parallel diminution of Soviet influence.

The new regime in Salisbury/Harare would hardly be a model of liberal democracy, respecting human rights. But at least Carter could point to the outcome as, on balance, a plus for the United States. He was properly pleased to find that the newly installed leader of Zimbabwe, "who was formerly looked upon as a Marxist and a hater of the United States—Mugabe—has now, I think, become one of our strong and potentially very good and loyal friends." [14]

19

THE CAMP DAVID ACCORDS:
CARTER'S FINEST HOUR

We offer our good offices. I think it's accurate to say that of all the nations in the world, we are the one that's most trusted, not completely, but most trusted by the Arab countries and also by Israel. I guess both sides have some doubt about us. But we'll have to act kind of as a catalyst to bring about their ability to negotiate successfully with one another.

—JIMMY CARTER

President Carter's foreign policy advisers, and Carter himself, had anticipated that the Middle East would provide the new administration with its greatest challenges *and* opportunities. The momentum of Kissinger's shuttle diplomacy, after the Sinai II disengagement agreement, had begun to run down. Between Israel and each of its antagonists other than Egypt there were not the ingredients for the kinds of quid pro quo compromises that were needed to keep the peace process alive, nor did any of the other principal antagonists of Israel have the added incentive to play ball with the United States that President Sadat had after his falling out with the Soviets.

It was of the utmost importance to regain the lost momentum of the peace process, for in the Middle East the status quo itself was too dangerously volatile. The bitter resentments and impatience of the Arabs toward Israel and its deepening consolidation of the territories captured in the 1967 war, plus the readiness of the Soviet Union to exploit Arab grievances in order to expand its own influence, would surely present Carter, like Nixon, Johnson, Eisenhower, and Truman before him, with another round of war in the Middle East. Renewed war would confront the United States with more profound dilemmas than ever: Israeli military superiority, if indeed it still existed, would be less than before, and the United States would probably need to come to Israel's assistance more heavily than in the past; but now with the clear prospect of the Arabs cutting off the flow of oil to Israel's supporters. Even short of a resumption of hostilities, continued high tension between the Arabs and the Israelis might at any time stimulate the Arab oil producers to use their resource a a political weapon.

A dramatic breakthrough from the status quo was required. Carter and company thought they had a plan for bringing this about.

THE BROOKINGS REPORT AND THE OCTOBER 1977 INITIATIVE

The new administration's plan for getting the Middle East peace process moving again was brought with them into office, essentially made, in the form of a 1975 Brookings Institution study group report titled *Toward Peace in the Middle East.*[1] Co-directed by former U.S. Ambassador Charles Yost and Professor Morroe Berger of Princeton University, the Brookings study group had included Zbigniew Brzezinski among its sixteen members.* Brzezinski brought the report to candidate Jimmy Carter's attention and got him to endorse it during the 1976 presidential election campaign.

The Brookings study group concluded that the approach followed since the 1973 war, emphasizing interim steps designed to reduce tension and to move the parties gradually toward a comprehensive settlement, was no longer feasible. To avoid a dangerous stalemate it was imperative that "peacemaking efforts should henceforth concentrate on negotiation of a comprehensive settlement, including only such interim steps as constitute essential preparations for such a negotiation." The negotiations should aim at a "package" of agreements on boundaries, the nature of a Palestinian entity, and

---

*The complete membership of the Brookings Middle East study group was Morroe Berger (co-director), Robert R. Bowie, Zbigniew Brzezinski, John C. Campbell, Nijeeb Halaby, Rita Hauser, Roger Heyns (chairman), Alan Horton, Malcolm Kerr, Fred Khouri, Philip Klutznick, William Quandt, Nadav Safran, Stephen Spiegel, A. L. Udovich, and Charles W. Yost (co-director).

the regime for Jerusalem, and should involve all the nations which would be affected, plus the principal external guarantors.

In exchange for Arab assurances to Israel of peaceful relations and the security of its territory and borders, Israel should withdraw to the boundaries prevailing prior to the start of the 1967 war, with only such modifications as might be mutually accepted. Israel also should accept the principle of Palestinian self-determination, and should not rule out the possibility that the Palestinian entity would be an independent state; but in return the Palestinians should recognize the sovereignty and integrity of Israel, and should accept whatever security arrangements, mutual guarantees, demilitarized zones, or UN presence was embodied in the peace settlement. The Brookings group felt it was premature to stipulate the precise nature of the regime for Jerusalem, and granted that it might be wise to leave this question, particularly the issue of Israel's sovereignty over the whole city, to a late stage in the negotiations. But it was not too early to obtain agreement on the minimum criteria for governing the city— namely, that there should be unimpaired access to all the holy places and that each would be under the custodianship of its own faith; that there should be no barriers to the free circulation of populations throughout the city; and that each national group, if it so desired, should have substantial political autonomy within the area of the city where it was predominant.

Some of the elements of the proposed comprehensive Arab–Israeli peace settlement could be implemented in stages. But, advised the Brookings study group, "In order that a settlement be sufficiently attractive to all the parties to induce them to make the necessary compromises, all aspects of the settlement will have to be spelled out explicitly in an agreement or agreements that will be signed more or less simultaneously as part of a 'package deal.' "[2]

Such a comprehensive package would have to be considered and approved, if not actually negotiated, in a "Geneva"-style conference at which all of the parties directly involved were represented along with the big-power guarantors of the settlement. The "Geneva" format refers to the December 1973 conference in Geneva co-chaired by the United States and the Soviet Union and attended by Israel, Egypt, and Jordan, which broke up after only two days. If Geneva were to be reconvened, perhaps with a larger membership, Israel could obtain its objective of negotiating face to face with its Arab neighbors. Such a conference would again commit the USSR to the negotiating process in a way that would make it difficult for the Kremlin to reject the settlement that would emerge.

The idea of a general conference also had inherent difficulties: How would the Palestinians be represented, and would they first have to recognize Israel and its right to exist in peace and security? How could such a general conference be structured and conducted so as not to degenerate rapidly into a polarized polemical debating arena, with the Soviet Union playing to the militant Arab galleries?

Such obstacles to a successful general conference are serious, admitted the authors of the Brookings report, but they should not be insurmountable if the nations involved could be persuaded that there is no viable alternative to a comprehensive settlement.

These were the assumptions underlying the initiative early in the Carter administration to get the Soviets committed to the broad principles in the Brookings report as the terms of reference for a reconvened Geneva Conference. The Soviets were more than willing to be brought back into the picture as a partner in the Middle East peace process, and jumped at the chance of joining the United States in a call to reconvene the Geneva conference.

In their formal joint statement of October 1, 1977, issued simultaneously in Moscow and Washington, the United States and the Soviet Union, as co-chairs of the Geneva conference, maintained that "a just and lasting settlement of the Arab–Israeli conflict . . . should be comprehensive, incorporating all parties concerned and all questions." The settlement should resolve

such key issues as withdrawal of Israeli armed forces from territories occupied in the 1967 conflict; the resolution of the Palestinian question, including insuring the legitimate rights of the Palestinian people; termination of the state of war and establishment of normal peaceful relations of the Palestinian people; termination of the state of war and establishment of normal peaceful relations on the basis of mutual recognition of the principles of sovereignty, territorial integrity and political independence.

The only right and effective way to achieve a fundamental solution to these issues, said the U.S.–Soviet statement, was through

negotiation within the framework of the Geneva Peace Conference, specifically convened for these purposes, with participation in its work of the representatives of all the parties involved in the conflict, including those of the Palestinian people.[3]

Although the statement departed somewhat from the standard Arab formulations (it did not name the Palestine Liberation Organization as the representative of the Palestinians, and it did not insist on Israeli withdrawal from *all* territories occupied in the 1967 war), it outraged the government of Israel and its supporters in the United States by referring to the "legitimate rights" of the Palestinian people, the code words for a claim to statehood, rather than their "legitimate interests"—the more innocuous phrase which Israel over the years had been willing to accept. The joint statement also alarmed Egypt's President Anwar Sadat, who wanted least of all to bring the Soviet Union back heavily into the peace process. Sadat had only recently made his historic shift away from being a principal client of the USSR and did not trust Soviet motives; and now here was the Carter administration unwittingly becoming an accomplice in subordinating Egypt's interest to the Kremlin's geopolitical designs in the Middle East.

The negative reactions by Israel and Egypt to the October 1, 1977, joint statement were no real surprise to the Carter administration's Middle East experts. Prime Minister Begin and President Sadat each had previously voiced objections to reconvening the Geneva forum and suspicions of Soviet designs. Nevertheless, Brzezinski and Carter were determined to shake loose the logjam; they were convinced that Soviet leverage was needed to get the recalcitrant Arabs to negotiate with Israel, and felt that they could keep the Kremlin honest by making it clear that Soviet cooperation in bringing about a Middle East peace was an essential link in the overall détente relationship. Begin and Sadat, as well as the rest of the parties in the region, could be brought along if the two superpowers operated in concert.

What the Carter administration did not know, however, was that simultaneously with the dialogue between the Soviets and the Americans that produced the October 1 statement, the highest levels of the Begin and Sadat governments were in secret dialogue to explore the prospects of a direct and substantial accommodation between Israel and Egypt. (The secret Israeli-Egyptian dialogue during the fall of 1977 had grown out of the decision by Begin to share Israeli intelligence information with Sadat about a Libyan terrorist plot to assassinate the Egyptian leader, which allowed Sadat's secret police to capture the terrorists in Cairo. Sadat was doubly grateful when

Begin announced to the Knesset that Sadat could go ahead with a military attack across the Egyptian–Libyan border without fear that Israel would take advantage of the situation on the Sinai front while Sadat's forces were preoccupied with the situation on Egypt's western front).[4] Sadat's dramatic decision to accept Begin's rhetorical invitation to come to Jerusalem to talk peace could not have been predicted (even Sadat's closest associates were surprised); but it is doubtful that the Carter administration would have so easily discounted the anticipated Israeli and Egyptian objections to the concerted Soviet–American move to reconvene the Geneva conference if they had been aware of the rapport that was developing between Begin and Sadat.

Sadat's historic visit to Israel on November 9, 1977, completely pulled the rug out from under the U.S.–Soviet October 1 démarche. In some measure, however, it may have been provoked by that démarche. The resulting negotiations between Israel and Egypt gave Jimmy Carter the opportunity to play his sought-for role as peacemaker.

CARTER AS MEDIATOR

The United States government, temporarily knocked off balance by the decision by Sadat and Begin to begin a dialogue themselves, once again was able to resume the role of provider of good offices to Egypt and Israel in their efforts to overcome the still-wide divergence in their terms for peace. This mediating role would be played less through the peripatetic shuttling of high U.S. officials between Cairo and Jerusalem, than through the President of the United States encouraging the leaders of each country to visit with him personally in the United States to work out, at the highest level, ways of consummating real peace.

Begin came first, in mid-December 1977, to talk with Carter, and the following week traveled to Ismailia, Egypt, to negotiate directly with Sadat. Still, neither the two Middle Eastern leaders nor their technical working groups were able to resolve the impasse.

Next it was Sadat's turn to visit with Carter. Meeting at Camp David in early February 1978, the two Presidents of humble rural beginnings and deeply religious sentiments apparently established an easy rapport (in contrast to the reportedly poor chemistry between each of them and Begin), with Sadat commenting that the United States was no longer simply a "go-between" but was now a "full partner" in the peace process. There was more than personal rapport involved, however. This first Carter–Sadat meeting marked a return to the geopolitical understanding between Kissinger and Sadat that the United States and Egypt shared a priority interest in reducing the Soviet Union's influence in the Middle East; and that momentum in achieving an Arab–Israeli settlement was crucial for this purpose, but so was the assumption by the United States of the role, previously played by the Soviets, of Egypt's principal arms supplier.

Four days after Sadat left the United States, the Carter administration proposed that Congress authorize sales of $4.8 billion worth of military jet aircraft to Israel, Saudi Arabia, and Egypt. The Egyptian portion of the package (Cairo could purchase fifty F-54E short-range fighter bombers) would be the first transfer of U.S. weapons to Egypt since the 1950s. Speaking for the administration, Secretary of State Vance argued that "Egypt, too, must have reasonable assurance of its abilty to defend itself if it is to continue the peace negotiations with confidence."[5]

Prime Minister Begin came to the White House again at the end of March 1978; this time President Carter gave him a deliberately cool reception. The administration was now growing impatient with what it regarded as Israel's increasing intransigence on the West Bank and Gaza Strip issues. Begin had stated on March 4 that his government did not regard UN Resolution 242 as obligating Israel to withdraw from the West Bank and Gaza. Moreover, the White House was especially irked at the Begin–Sharon* policy of encouraging Israeli settlements on the West Bank to give corporeal substance to Begin's biblical and ancient legal claims of Israeli sovereignty over this area. Carter himself apparently was also miffed at the Israelis for their mid-March invasion of southern Lebanon in retaliation for a PLO terrorist raid near Tel Aviv.

Sadat too was growing more and more impatient by the summer of 1978, calling Begin "an obstacle to peace." On July 30, citing the

---

*Begin's Minister of Agriculture, the flamboyant hawk General Ariel Sharon, was the principal architect of the settlements policy, pushing Begin to more substantial and even irreversible colonization of the occupied areas than apparently was the Prime Minister's preference.

"negative" and "backward" moves of Israel, Sadat opposed resuming their bilateral peace talks.

President Carter now interjected himself even more actively into the process, inviting Begin and Sadat to meet with him in a three-way summit at Camp David to work out the peace agreement they all wanted. The Egyptian President and the Israeli Prime Minister accepted immediately and without conditions.

The negotiations at Camp David between September 5 and 17, 1978, were more like a compressed version of Kissinger's shuttle diplomacy than the famous summits between the leaders of the United States, the USSR, and Britain during World War II, where important bargaining took place in face-to-face sessions among the Big Three. Carter and his aides "shuttled" between the cabins of his two guests at the Maryland mountain retreat to hammer out a mutually acceptable agreement. And representatives of Begin and Sadat held working sessions with Carter in his cabin. Vice President Mondale, Secretary of State Vance, and National Security Adviser Brzezinski were also actively involved in the cabin-to-cabin shuttle. Carter, Begin, and Sadat met together only twice during the thirteen-day marathon before they appeared together on September 17 to announce their success.[6]

It was an extremely difficult and delicate task of mediation for the Americans, for in the ten months since Sadat's visit to Israel, Sadat and Begin had retreated back to positions the other side found offensive, and it was with these positions that they opened the Camp David negotiations. Begin came prepared to return all of the Sinai to Egypt (with the proviso that some Israeli settlements be allowed to remain there), but Israel would not, he said, cede sovereignty over the West Bank and Gaza, nor the right to maintain Israeli forces and settlements in these areas. Moreover, Israel could not agree to an independent Palestinian state. Sadat's opening demands were that Israel withdraw totally from all the territory occupied during the 1967 war (which implied, in addition to the Sinai, the West Bank, Jerusalem, the Gaza Strip, and the Golan Heights) and recognize the right of full self-determination for the Palestinians on the West Bank and in Gaza. In short, Israel was bargaining for a separate peace with Egypt—the only Arab country willing to negotiate with it— but Egypt was insisting on linking any bilateral agreement to a broader Arab–Israeli settlement, without which Sadat knew he would be branded a traitor throughout the Arab world to their common cause.

The central impasse was overcome by separating the Sinai issue, on which explicit and detailed agreements were immediately possible, from the West Bank and Gaza issues, on which agreement still seemed remote. The Sinai agreement would constitute the core of a peace treaty between Egypt and Israel to be concluded before the end of the year, whereas only general principles for settlement of the West Bank and Gaza issues would have to be agreed upon at this time. Both sets of issues, however, would be linked by virtue of their being two parts of an agreed "Framework for Peace in the Middle East" to be issued by the three governments as the fruit of their Camp David meetings, and by having the Egyptian–Israeli peace treaty preamble commit both parties to work diligently toward a comprehensive settlement of the Arab–Israeli conflict in all its aspects.[7]

Given this crucial breakthrough, there were still numerous difficulties to be worked out in each part of the draft Camp David "Framework" as Begin and Sadat each threatened to walk out of the negotiations and return to a confrontational relationship. The thorniest obstacle to agreement on the draft Egyptian–Israeli peace treaty was the issue of Israeli settlements in the Sinai—a pet project of the popular General Sharon. Carter adamantly supported Sadat's demand that the Sinai settlements be removed, and reportedly painted for Begin the stark consequences of a refusal by the Israelis to acquiesce: a renewal of war in the Sinai in which Israel could not count on U.S. help.[8] Begin's backdown in agreeing to dismantle the Sinai settlement if the Knesset approved, broke the final serious logjam and allowed the full-speed-ahead drafting of the final Camp David accords that were announced by the smiling trio of Carter, Sadat, and Begin at the White House on September 17, 1978.

The Camp David accords were published as two documents—the "Framework for Peace in the Middle East," and the "Framework for Conclusion of a Peace Treaty Between Egypt and Israel"—each signed by President Sadat and Prime Minister Begin as the parties and by President Carter as the witness. The first, more general document included the agreed principles for negotiating "autonomy" and a "self-governing authority" for inhabitants of the West Bank and Gaza. The second document stipulated the key points of agreement on the Sinai that would constitute the core of the peace treaty to be concluded within three months.

The framework for settling the West Bank and Gaza issues outlined a negotiating process to establish a "self-governing authority" within five years—"the transitional period." During this transitional period negotiations were to be undertaken among Egypt, Israel, and Jordan and elected representatives of the inhabitants of the West Bank and Gaza "to agree on the final status" of these areas.

The transitional "self-governing authority" for the West Bank and Gaza was to be established by negotiations to begin immediately between Egypt, Israel, Jordan, and "representatives of the Palestinian people," with the Palestinians included in the Egyptian and Jordanian delegations. The "self-governing authority" would be an "administrative council" that would be "freely elected by the inhabitants of these areas to replace the existing military government." A local police force would be established which could include Jordanian citizens. Israeli armed forces would be withdrawn, but there could be a redeployment of some Israeli forces into specified "security locations." During the five-year "transition period," "representatives of Egypt, Israel, Jordan, and the self-governing authority will constitute a 'Continuing Committee' to decide by agreement on the modalities of admission of persons displaced from the West Bank and Gaza in 1967, together with the necessary measures to prevent disruption and disorder."

Thus, while granting the right of eventual self-determination to the Palestinians, the terms of the "Framework" preserved basic Israeli sovereignty over the West Bank and Gaza for at least the five-year transitional period: no devolution of authority to the Palestinian administrative council would take place beyond what it would be granted in the yet-to-be-undertaken "autonomy talks" to institute the period of limited self-government; some Israeli forces would remain in the area, albeit at specially designated locations; and Israel would retain a veto over any developments through its membership in the Continuing Committee along with Egypt and Jordan. Yet these provisions could be interpreted by the Egyptians (as Sadat did when other Arabs accused him of selling out the Palestinians in order to achieve his separate peace with Israel) as a significant erosion of Israeli sovereignty over the West Bank and Gaza. Israel was more answerable than ever before to others—the United States,

Egypt, and Jordan (if King Hussein agreed to participate in the process)—for its dealings with the inhabitants of the West Bank. The burden of proof would be on Israel to demonstrate why it could not move toward granting full self-determination and statehood to the Palestinians. Real, tangible, increases in administrative (including police) powers were to be given to the resident Palestinians during the transitional period; and although the tripartite Continuing Committee would give Israel a veto over major changes in the status of the area, it also would give Egypt and Jordan vetoes over attempts by Israel to reassume local powers it had alraedy relinquished.

The Camp David "Framework" for the peace treaty between Egypt and Israel was a much briefer, more specific, document, committing the parties to a rapid conclusion of the treaty negotiations begun at Camp David, and recording details already agreed, including the withdrawal of Israeli armed forces from the Sinai; limitations on deployments of Egyptian and Israeli military units on their respective sides of their common border; limitations on Egyptian armed forces to be stationed in the Sinai immediately east of the Suez; provision for United Nations forces adjacent to the Egyptian–Israeli border near the Strait of Tiran; and guarantees of rights of free passage to Israeli ships through the Gulf of Suez, the Suez Canal, the Strait of Tiran, and the Gulf of Aqaba. The Israeli troop withdrawals would be phased over a period of two to three years, but the two countries would establish full diplomatic and economic relations three to nine months after the signing of the peace treaty and upon the completion of an "interim withdrawal" of Israeli troops from the Sinai to lines yet to be determined.[9] The decade-long impasse between the two countries in implementing Resolution 242 had been overcome at last—truly an historic achievement. But between the raising of the goblets of peace and being able to drink their wine there was still much to be worked out.

The overarching issue was the degree of linkage between the Egyptian–Israeli peace treaty and the negotiations over the status of the West Bank and Gaza. Sadat, anxious to counter the intensifying drumbeat of charges by other Arab leaders that he was a traitor to their cause, wanted a stronger link to be stated explicitly in the preamble to the treaty than did the Israelis, who worried that the preambular linkage could be interpreted to mean that the provisions in the body of the treaty were inoperative until substantial progress had been achieved in the autonomy talks. In the months following Camp David the Carter administration was even more insistent than Sadat that collateral progress on the Palestinian autonomy arrangements was an essential content for a durable Egyptian–Israeli peace. Assistant Secretary of State Harold Saunders was dispatched in October to convince King Hussein of Jordan to join the negotiations, and to persuade Palestinian leaders in the West Bank that the "autonomy" promised in the Camp David accords was only an interim step toward more complete self-determination. While on his trip Saunders angered Begin by saying that Israel would dismantle its settlements on the West Bank—there had been no such commitment at Camp David—and by calling East Jerusalem "occupied territory."[10] A provoked Israeli government hardened its opposition to what looked like new American pressures for a comprehensive peace and announced plans to "thicken" the Israeli settlements on the West Bank.

It began to appear as if Begin had never really intended to transfer substantial power to the Palestinians in the West Bank and Gaza, and that his limited concessions on the matter at Camp David were only for the purpose of getting the Egyptian–Israeli peace treaty moving, and need not ever to be concretely delivered. Sadat could not allow the rest of the Arab world to gain the impression that he had been diddled by Begin, and began to toughen his stand on various details in the draft bilateral peace treaty. When Carter suggested in February 1979 that Begin and Sadat come to Camp David for a second summit to resolve their differences, both leaders declined. Begin saw Carter in Washington in March, but left complaining that the Americans were now supporting Egyptian proposals that were totally unacceptable to Israel.

Carter decided to inject himself even more forcefully into the bargaining than he had done through the means of the Camp David summit. He personally would fly between Jerusalem and Cairo in the type of meditational diplomacy Kissinger had pioneered, but with an immense difference—the prestige of the President of the United States would now be implicated in the success or failure of the effort. This was Carter's daring gamble, and it gave his insistence on constructive negotiation added weight, for now Carter would be viewed in the media worldwide as a principal participant in the negotiations with high political values of his own immediately at stake, not just as a detached go-between providing "good offices." Carter was gambling on the assumption that the Israelis and Egyptians were fundamentally committed to a consummation of the peace between them essentially on the terms outlined at Camp David, and that the outstanding disagreements were negotiable details which, as part of the end game of the bargaining, had been inflated into matters of "principle" by each side.

In Jerusalem and Cairo, Carter created the impression that his failure to bring home peace was intolerable to him and that noncooperation at this point by either Sadat or Begin would result in a deterioration of relations between the United States and whichever country was most responsible for preventing final agreement. Any deterioration in relations with the United States was a particularly fearsome prospect for the Israelis given the growing strategic interest of the Americans in securing access to Persian Gulf oil and therefore in cultivating friendly relations with many of Israel's hostile neighbors. The West Europeans and the Japanese had already put good relations with their Middle East oil suppliers ahead of friendship with Israel; it would be suicidal for the Begin government to alienate the American President. Sadat too was in a bind: increasingly isolated from other Arab governments, most of whom had severed diplomatic relations with Egypt in relation to his trip to Jerusalem and subsequent negotiation of the Camp David accords, Sadat had to turn to the United States for economic credits to rescue the faltering Egyptian economy and for arms to maintain a military balance not only against Israel but against his Soviet-armed enemy on Egypt's western border, Libya's Muammar Qaddafi. Sadat, of course, did retain the option of another dramatic turnaround, to embrace the Pan-Arab cause and to junk his Nobel Prize–winning peace initiatives with Israel, so Carter could not push him to accept terms that would sacrifice vital Egyptian interest, or that would personally humiliate the proud Egyptian President. But Carter saw that Sadat would be doubly humiliated if he were to crawl back to the militant Arab fold; and that therefore any implied threat to do so in response to reasonable Israeli demands backed by the United States was a bluff.

By purposefully inflating his own, and thus the United States government's, stake in an Isareli–Egyptian settlement, thereby maximizing the pressure on Begin and Sadat to converge on the terms of their treaty, Carter's Middle Eastern shuttle of March 8–13, 1979, should be ranked as one of the most impressive démarches in the annals of diplomacy—less infused with emotional drama than Sadat's 1977 trip to Jerusalem, but, as it turned out, the crucial element in transforming Sadat's initiative from simply an act of political theater into a major branch point in world history.

The terms of the "Treaty of Peace Between the Arab Republic of Egypt and the State of Israel" signed in Washington on March 26, 1979, by President Sadat and Prime Minister Begin and by President Carter as "witness" were remarkable. Usually peace treaties codify the results of war, giving international legitimacy to control over territory established by battle, attempting to give de jure durability to the new de facto situation and to resolving marginal issues not settled by war that could provoke new hostilities. The Egyptian–Israeli treaty, by contrast, substantially changed territorial dispositions established twelve years previously by war, and instituted a fundamentally new status quo, effecting a revolutionary change in the thirty-year-old situation in the Middle East in which the leading Arab country, among others, had refused to grant legitimacy to the State of Israel.

As anticipated in the Camp David framework, Israel agreed to evacuate its military forces and civilians from the Sinai Peninsula in a phased withdrawal over a three-year period; the state of war between Egypt and Israel was terminated; and the parties agreed to establish normal and full diplomatic relations after the initial nine months of Israeli military withdrawal; Israeli ships were accorded the right of free passage through the Suez Canal and its approaches, and all normal international navigational rights through the Strait of Tiran and the Gulf of Aqaba. The parties agrees to negotiate special security arrangements, including the deployment of United Nations forces to monitor the implementation of the peace treaty. They also agreed "not to enter into any obligation in conflict with this treaty."

On the controversial issue of the linkage of the Egyptian–Israeli peace treaty to the negotiations on the regime for the West Bank and Gaza, as provided for in the Camp David framework, the text of the treaty itself was mute, except for a vague clause in the preamble committing the parties to continue "the search for a comprehensive peace in the area and for the attainment of the settlement of the Arab–Israeli conflict in all its aspects." The Israelis won their determined fight to keep all clauses out of the treaty that might make its implementation conditional on the settlement of the Palestinian problem. Sadat's need to demonstrate to the other Arab countries and the Palestinians that his peace with Israel was only the opening move in a larger strategy of getting the Israelis to give back all of the territories conquered in 1967 was catered to, on the insistence of President Carter, in the form of a "Joint Letter" to Carter signed by Begin and Sadat in which they agreed to continue good faith negotiations according to the Camp David framework for "the establishment of the self-governing authority in the West Bank and Gaza in order to provide full autonomy to the inhabitants."

It was more than politeness or the requirements of protocol that was reflected in the accolades paid by Sadat and Begin at the signing ceremony to Carter's role in the negotiations. As put by Sadat, "the man who performed the miracle was President Carter. Without any exaggeration, what he did constitutes one of the greatest achievements of our time. . . . There came certain moments when hope was eroding and retreating in the face of pride. However, President Carter remained unshaken in his confidence and determination. . . . Before anything else, the signing of the peace treaty *and the exchange of letters* is a tribute to the spirit and ability of Jimmy Carter."[11] (Emphasis added.) Begin agreed.

20

HOSTAGES IN IRAN

I don't know what historical assumptions guided Carter's or Vance's approach . . . , but I assumed that their assumptions were different from mine and involved a somewhat different scheme of the world. To me, principled commitment to a more decent world order did not preclude the use of power to protect our most immediate interests.

—ZBIGNIEW BRZEZINSKI

The Carter administration inherited the dominant view in the policy establishment of U.S. interests in the Persian Gulf. "Under the Shah's leadership," recalls Kissinger, "the land bridge between Asia and Europe, so often the hinge of world history, was pro-American and pro-West beyond any challenge. . . . The Shah's view of the realities of world politics paralleled our own. . . . Iran under the Shah, in short, was one of America's best, most important, and most loyal friends in the world."[1]

Nixon and Kissinger had themselves built upon the legacy of U.S.–Iranian relations that went back to World War II and that had been elaborated during the Truman, Eisenhower, and Johnson administrations.

President Roosevelt perceived it to be the American mission to prevent the USSR and Britain from transforming their wartime zones of military occupation in Iran into a permanent postwar partition of the country. It was on U.S. insistence that the two occupying powers signed a treaty with Iran in January 1942 to withdraw their troops from Iranian territory within six months after the end of the war. Roosevelt was concerned, with Britain no longer able to perform her historic geopolitical role of containing Russian expansion into the oil-rich Persian Gulf, to solidify a posture of determined independence within Iran—a substitute, as it were, for the traditional British presence.[2] In any event, by being in favor of an independent Iran, the United States would not have to assume an anti-Soviet posture.

The geopolitical, rather than the idealistic, basis for U.S. attempts to assure Iranian independence took over U.S. diplomacy during the first year of the Truman administration when, in the first major U.S.–Soviet altercation of the postwar period, the United States brought maximum diplomatic pressure on the Soviets to get Stalin to honor his commitment to withdraw Russian occupation troops from northern Iran after the cessation of hostilities. The geopolitical considerations henceforth dominated U.S. policies toward Iran; but the assessments of the best means for keeping Iran out of the Soviet sphere kept fluctuating between efforts to induce the Shah to liberalize his regime and efforts to bolster his internal and external power by aiding him to build up his security forces and his military establishment.

The larger movement of U.S. policy was toward catering to the Shah's preference for a powerful military establishment and other trappings of monarchic, even imperial, grandeur and for glamorous industrialization projects and away from insistence on basic socioeconomic and political reforms.

The Truman–Acheson policy of trying to convince the Shah that he needed to modernize and democratize Iran lest it suffer a fate analogous to Chiang's China and of making loans and arms transfers at least partly contingent upon a sincere effort by the Shah to institute domestic reforms, gave way to the Eisenhower–Dulles policy of relying on the Shah to make Iran the centerpiece of the U.S. anti-Communist alliance system in the Middle East and of intervening to help the Shah combat his domestic enemies.[3] The Eisenhower administration feared that Mohammed Mossadegh, the nationalistic Prime Minister appointed by the Shah in 1951, was by 1953 demogogically catering to extremist and pro-Soviet elements, especially the Marxist Tudeh Party, and that Mossadegh's nationalization of the Anglo-Iranian Oil Company was only the first step toward a complete radicalization of Iran's political economy and a turn toward alignment with the Soviet Union. As Mossadegh moved in 1953 to dissolve the Parliament and to assume dictatorial powers, the Eisenhower administration felt justified in authorizing the CIA to proceed with its plan to topple Mossadegh and reinstate the Shah, who already had fled to Italy. Although, at the time, the overthrow of Mossadegh and the restoration of the Shah was more popular than unpopular in Iran, the recollection by Iranians of the CIA engineered coup, more than any event in the relationship between the two countries, provided the source of the hysterical charges during the 1979–1980 hostage crisis that the United States was a full accomplice in all of the crimes committed by the Shah against his countrymen.

While the restoration of the Shah in 1953 hardly produced the reign of terror that the 1978 revolutionary leaders would allege was the immediate result, and while many participants in the Mossadegh government willingly went to work for the Shah, the 1953 coup decimated the sociopolitical infrastructure that was gradually maturing in Iran, and which, given time and encouragement, might have provided a stable structure for a moderate democracy. In the post-Mossadegh period all political authority was concentrated in the monarchy; the bureaucracy and Parliament became rubber stamps for the Shah's decrees, and in the name of securing the regime against a resurgence of Tudeh radicalism from the left and Muslim fundamentalism from the right, the Shah delegated more and more enforcement powers to the armed forces and police. With the Shah less inclined than ever to accept foreign advice on the basic structure of his regime, the bargaining between Washington and Teheran tended to concentrate during the remaining years of the Eisenhower administration on the material inputs and technical assistance the United States could contribute to Iran's economic, administrative, and military modernization and on the role Iran should play in the regional "mutual security" network being constructed in the Near East by John Foster Dulles. The Shah shrewdly calculated, as did other leading U.S. clients in the Third World, that by catering to Dulles' preoccupation with the U.S.–Soviet rivalry he could get maximum support from the United States for building up his own domestic and regional power, even though this was targeted more against the Shah's local adversaries than against hypothetical Soviet aggression.

The Eisenhower administration was not at all sanguine about

Iran's future stability and pro-Western orientation; in the White House there was particular concern that the Shah's emphasis on expensive military projects was dangerously retarding the evolution of a balanced domestic economy capable of supporting his attempts to rapidly industrialize the country. But Eisenhower and Dulles were loath to threaten a reduction in military or economic assistance as a lever on Iranian domestic reform for fear of undercutting the Shah's authority and stimulating the anti-Shah groups.

Iran's economic and military programs went even more against the grain of the economic development philosophies influential among John F. Kennedy's New Frontiersmen in the White House and in the Agency for International Development, as did the Shah's reputation as a ruthless autocrat. The President's own determination to move away from the previous administration's policy of deference to the Shah was apparently crystalized by Khrushchev's prediction at the 1961 Vienna summit that the Shah would fall victim to a popular uprising. In 1962 the Kennedy administration conditioned its contributions to Iran's economic plan and military modernization upon the Shah's agreement to reduce his army from 240,000 to 150,000 men and to institute various economic and political reforms. Displeased with such meddling, the Shah nevertheless went along with most of the new U.S. insistences, meanwhile attempting to increase his bargaining power vis-à-vis the United States by accepting Soviet economic and military aid, and by attempting to exploit the increasing dependence of the United States, Western Europe, and Japan on Iranian oil.

During the Johnson administration the Shah, perhaps sensing the opportunity arising out of the U.S. preoccupation with Vietnam, became increasingly manipulative of his U.S. patrons. U.S. financial aid was being rapidly phased out due to Iran's soaring oil revenues, and therefore provided virtually no leverage by the late 1960s. The Shah's main requests now were that he be permitted to purchase the most sophisticated military equipment: ground-to-air missile systems and radars, supersonic aircraft, and surface-to-surface missiles. The Shah perceived that many top U.S. officials, alarmed at Soviet arms deliveries to Iraq and Egypt, were ready to support his requests before congressional committees and within the bureaucracy despite growing skepticism about the Shah's purported needs and worries about the distortions the arms transfers would produce in Iran's economic and social system. Whatever opportunities there might have been for U.S. officials to capitalize on the divisions in Washington by way of hard bargaining with the Shah were bypassed in the latter years of the Johnson administration; instead the President and Secretary of State followed the counsel of Under Secretary of State Eugene Rostow that the Shah not be "alienated," lest he turn to the Soviets.[4]

The Shah's star reached its zenith in Washington during the Nixon–Kissinger years. The "Nixon Doctrine"—devolving frontline containment and regional stabilization tasks to selected U.S. allies who would be well supplied with U.S. military equipment—was precisely suited to the role of Iran as conceived of by the Shah. In the wake of the British military withdrawal from the Persian Gulf at the end of 1971, Kissinger recalls that "there was no possibility of assigning any American military forces to the Indian Ocean in the midst of the Vietnam war and its attendant trauma." But with Iran as a willing military client, "the vacuum left by British withdrawal, now menaced by Soviet intrusion and radical momentum, would be filled by a local power friendly to us. . . . And all of this was achieved without any American resources, since the Shah was willing to pay for the equipment out of his oil revenues."[5]

Despite this mutuality of interests between Washington and Teheran, the Shah was not averse to playing hardball diplomacy to extract the maximum possible out of the American arsenal. In 1971 he indicated a willingness to join with the Arab majority in OPEC in its threat to use the oil cartel as an instrument of international leverage against Israel unless the United States was fully responsive to Iran's security needs. The result was Nixon's promise in Teheran in May 1972 to allow the Shah to buy virtually any and all nonnuclear weapons he wanted.[6] Kissinger objects to journalistic characterizations of the 1972 arms transfer agreement as "open ended," branding these accounts "hyperbole."[7] But the fact of a nearly totally open spigot on the American arms pipeline to Iran after 1972 is indisputable.

From 1973 to 1977 more than a third of all U.S. military sales were to Iran, whose military budget rose fourfold during this period, consuming over a quarter of the Iranian government's expenditures. The increase in the value of arms exports from $1 billion annually in the early 1970s to $10 billion annually in the mid-1970s was attributable in large part to the Shah's insatiable appetite for new weapons.

THE "ISLAND OF STABILITY" ERUPTS

The public face of United States policy toward Iran throughout Jimmy Carter's first presidential year was one of unwavering support for the Shah, despite growing concern within the administration and in Congress over the vulnerability of the Shah's regime and his use of his secret police, SAVAK, to brutally suppress political opposition. On November 15, 1977, the President and the Shah stood together on the White House south lawn, exchanging expressions of mutual admiration and respect while blinking and wiping their eyes from the tear gas fired by Washington police breaking up a fierce riot north of the White House between 4,000 anti-Shah and 1,500 pro-Shah demonstrators. And on January 2, 1978, U.S. news media carried reports of Carter's New Year's Eve toast in Teheran to the Shah's regime as "an island of stability" in one of the more troubled areas of the world. "This is a great tribute to you, Your Majesty, and to your leadership and the respect, admiration and love which your people give to you."[8]

Critics of the policy of continuing to support the Shah with mawkish flattery and lavish arms sales wondered how an administration professing dedication to human rights and arms control could justify these actions. However, the reasons for special support of the Shah, especially during his time of troubles, were convincing to the new President, just as they had been convincing to Carter's predecessors. The Shah's Iran had become the most important of the "regional influentials" (Brzezinski's phrase) upon which the United States had to rely, particularly in the post-Vietnam era of opposition to overseas U.S. military deployments, to provide an adequate forward defense against Soviet impulses to expand the USSR's sphere of control. Both the human rights and the conventional arms transfer policies of the Carter administration provided explicitly for geopolitically determined exceptions such as this. The legacy of past commitments and the lack of current alternatives to the Shah continued to tilt sentiment in the administration, including Carter's, in favor of supporting the Shah—until the foundational premises of the policy had already crumbled beyond repair.

The Carter administration inherited more than the arms sales contracts of its predecessors; it also inherited career bureaucrats in the departments of State and Defense who, in approving the sales, had made judgments about the basic viability of the Shah's rule, and about his regime's suppression of political opposition. The prevailing consensus among the careerists was that the Shah was without peer among Middle Eastern leaders in his ability to maintain domestic order while instituting major socioeconomic reform of a traditional society, and that the draconian measures he sometimes used were hardly unusual among regimes in the region or indeed throughout the Third World. The careerists had to contend against Carter appointees who were committed to helping the President implement his campaign promises to reduce arms sales and promote human rights, but the old hands found a powerful ally in Zbigniew Brzezinski, who accepted the Kissingerian argument that a constriction of weapons transfers to Iran, especially if it were an expression of discontent with the monarchy's human rights record, would be against U.S. interests, since it could only alienate the Shah and turn him toward other arms suppliers.

As evidence mounted during the first half of 1978 that opposition to the Shah's regime was spreading in Iran, this bureaucratic coalition in Washington continued to successfully resist a fundamental reassessment of U.S. policy by arguing that any criticism of the Shah at this time would play into the hands of his opponents and exacerbate the turmoil, and this in turn could only increase the Shah's tendency to rely on SAVAK's brutal techniques of repression. Consistent with Secretary of State Vance's cautionary guidelines on implementing the President's human rights policy, pressures exerted on other governments should be constrained by the realization that in some circumstances good intentions may produce pernicious results.

In the fall of 1978, when it began to be evident that the growing instability in Iran was more serious than anything that had been seen since the Mossadegh period, Brzezinski himself began to argue that the overthrow of the Shah was a real possibility. Strikes were endemic in essential public service industries; the economy was near collapse; wealthy Iranians were sending their money out of the country; and Ruhollah Khomeini was calling from exile in Paris for civil war. Carter's national security adviser's response to the impending crisis was predictable: back the Shah all the way and let him and his opponents know that this was U.S. policy.[9]

The view from the American Embassy in Teheran was quite different. Ambassador William Sullivan sent a message to Washington on November 9, 1978, recommending that since the Shah's regime might collapse, the United States should begin to look for alternative means to preserve its interests. The unity of the armed forces and their willingness to support a post-Shah regime would be crucial to preserving the territorial integrity and independence of Iran, and therefore the United States should attempt to use its influence to "broker an arrangement" between the Khomeini group and the leading military officers about the makeup of the new regime and on the role of the armed forces under it. Receiving no reply to his message, and believing his views were no longer welcome at the White House, Ambassador Sullivan, through talks on his own with the revolutionary leaders and the military, began to explore the possibility of acceptable post-Shah arrangements.[10]

By the end of the first week of December 1978, reports reaching the White House on the disastrous crumbling of the Shah's support in Iran moved Carter to publicly urge the Shah to broaden the base of his government in an effort to restore its legitimacy. And the President, in response to questioning by the press, allowed himself to express some doubt about the Shah's ability to hang on to power unless he instituted a major effort to transform his regime into a constitutional monarchy with free elections and a decentralization of power.[11]

Behind the scenes, a fierce debate raged among Carter's inner council of top foreign policy and national security advisers.

Brzezinski and James Schlesinger (Carter's Energy Secretary, and formerly Secretary of Defense under Nixon and Ford) wanted the President to make clear to the Shah that the United States encouraged and would back him in a major mobilization of the Iranian armed forces to put down civil disturbances, take over the provision of essential services, and root out and incarcerate subversive groups—in short, anything that was necessary to decisively smash the revolution.

Secretary Vance, on the other hand, felt the time had come for the President to distance the United States from the Shah. There was no saving him anymore, and he should be urged to leave the country. The United States should back a transition government that would be supported by the armed forces and could rely on them to restore public order and establish procedures for instituting a constitutional, popularly legitimized regime.

By the end of December, events in Iran appeared to validate the Vance approach. The Shah appointed Shahpour Bakhtiar, an opposition leader and former deputy minister in the Mossadegh government, to the post of Prime Minister. Bakhtiar's conditions were that he be allowed to release political prisoners, dissolve SAVAK, and reinstitute freedom of the press—and that the Shah should leave the country.

The announcement on December 29, 1978, of the Shah's appointment of Bakhtiar as Prime Minister was followed by great confusion and near chaos. The militant National Front, heady with the developing revolutionary situation, expelled Bakhtiar for being too willing to compromise. The Shah's spokesman denied that Reza Pahlevi had actually consented to leave Iran. Seemingly credible rumors were rife about coups being hatched by the right, the left, and various factions of the armed forces. And increasing attention—Iranian and international—was focused on the charismatic Khomeini to determine to whom he might throw his support. Ambassador Sullivan urged a meeting between U.S. officials and Khomeini, but Brzezinski vetoed the idea. Khomeini rejected the Bakhtiar government and himself named a shadow government with a religiously oriented leader of the National Front, Mehdi Bazargan, as its Prime Minister. Meanwhile the United States government had declared its support for Bakhtiar. Finally, on January 16, 1979, the Shah left for Egypt, telling Bakhtiar that his departure would result in a worsening of the situation and that the people would soon call him back to rule.

The White House, taking up some of the suggestions made by Ambassador Sullivan, appointed its own emissary to the Iranian military to negotiate their cooperation with the new Bakhtiar regime. Brzezinski's designee for this mission was General Robert Huyser, a deputy to General Alexander Haig, then Supreme Allied Commander in Europe, who knew little about Iran. Ambassador Sullivan, however, continued to urge to no avail that Bakhtiar was despised by the Khomeini group, and that the crucial negotiations should be with them.

Ambassador Sullivan's recollections of this chaotic period reveal the gap between White House and embassy perspectives about what was actually happening in Iran:

I received terse instructions telling me that the policy of the U.S. government was to support the Bakhtiar government without reservation and to assist its survival. I replied . . . that the Bakhtiar government was a chimera that the shah had created to permit a dignified departure, that Bakhtiar himself was quixotic and would be swept aside by the arrival of Khomeini and his supporters in Tehran. Moreover, I argued that it would be feckless to transfer the loyalty of the armed forces to Bakhtiar because this would cause the destructive confrontation between the armed forces and the revolutionaries that we hoped to avoid. It would result in the disintegration of the armed forces and eventually in the disintegration of Iran.[12]

Sullivan's warnings were discounted, and he soon would be relieved of his ambassadorship. The revolutionaries worked assiduously to develop converts in the armed forces and, as Sullivan had predicted, there were mutinies and defections as confrontations between junior officers and loyal Army elements began to occur. SAVAK was also riddled with defections.

In the midst of this crumbling of the Bakhtiar regime, the Ayatollah Khomeini finally landed in Iran on February 1, 1979, and appointed Medhi Bazargan his Prime Minister. On February 11, the Army declared itself neutral. As revolutionary machine gunners began to close in around the prime ministerial office, Bakhtiar made good his escape and soon afterward fled the country. The Khomeinists were exultant, but obsessed with the idea that the United States was yet plotting a counterrevolution to reinstall the Shah.

ATTEMPTING TO CONTROL THE UNCONTROLLABLE

Despite the extreme hostility against the United States being whipped up in Iran by the Marxists and the Khomeinists, U.S. officials in Teheran and Washington remained optimistic during the first ten months of 1979 that the Khomeinists, who seemed to have the upper hand, would realize that the main threat to their goal of turning Iran into a fundamentalist Islamic state came from the Marxists and their external patron, the Soviet Union, and that therefore after they consolidated their power they would soon move to reestablish cordial relations with the United States. An early sign that the Khomeinists knew where their real interests lay was their denunciation of the February 14, 1979, armed attack and capture of the United States Embassy by the radical Fedayeen-i-Khalq group, many of whom had been trained by Palestinian guerrillas. The armed militants were persuaded to give up control of the embassy and the American officials they had taken prisoner by the new regime's Deputy Premier, Ibrahim Yazdi, and its Foreign Minister, Karim Sanjabi.

On February 21, 1979, the United States officially recognized the Bazargan government, and Ambassador Sullivan met with the regime's military and political leaders to facilitate the resumption of American arms transfers to Iran. The United States would also continue its oil purchases and business activities in Iran to the extent desired by the new regime.

But as the revolution, in the classic mold of revolutions, began to take revenge on members and supporters of the old regime, voices were raised in Congress against the retributive brutality; and in May the Senate passed a resolution deploring the executions. Khomeini and his followers were furious and vilified the United States for its double standard of indifference to the brutalities of the Shah's regime.

The Khomeinists now competed with the leftist militants in stirring the Teheran street crowds into mobs of screaming frenzy against the Americans; and moderates who wanted to preserve cordial contact with U.S. diplomatic and commercial representatives in Iran had to defend themselves against allegations of conspiring with American CIA agents who allegedly, as in the time of Mossadegh, were posing as embassy officials, journalists, and corporate representatives while really organizing a countercoup for the Shah.

The question of whether or not to grant the deposed Shah political asylum in the United States occasioned intense controversy at the top levels of the Carter administration. Predictably, Brzezinski was for inviting the Shah, Vance was opposed. "It was my view from the beginning," a *New York Times* interviewer quotes Brzezinski as recalling, "that we should make it unambiguously clear that the Shah was welcome whenever he wanted to come. Our mistake was to ever let it become an issue in the first place."[13]

When the Shah left Iran in January 1979, he apparently felt he had a firm invitation from the United States. Walter Annenberg, the wealthy publisher and former U.S. Ambassador to England during the Nixon administration, was to let the Shah use his estate in Rancho Mirage, California. But while in transit in Egypt, the Shah was informed that there had been a cooling of enthusiasm in the United States for his arrival. The Beverly Hills home of his mother had been stoned, and the U.S. government was getting worried about its ability to provide adequate protection for the Shah and his family. Offended by this as yet unofficial rebuff, the Shah himself cut off further discussion and decided to go instead to Morocco, where he would be more welcome. After two months in Morocco, however, demonstrations against the Shah by university students had reached such a pitch that his embarrassed host, King Hassan, felt compelled to request him to find another place of exile before the forthcoming Islamic summit conference in Marrakesh. Humiliated, the Shah now inquired whether the United States was ready to receive him, and was told by the U.S. Ambassador in Morocco that the United States government was concerned for the safety of Americans in Iran if the Shah came to the United States. The embassy in Teheran was particularly vulnerable. There would be demonstrations in the United States itself, and there would be various legal complications. In short, it would no longer be "convenient" for the Shah to come.[14]

David Rockefeller and Henry Kissinger now found the Shah temporary refuge at a resort in the Bahamas, and then in Cuernavaca, Mexico. Rockefeller and Kissinger also stepped up their efforts to get the Carter administration to reconsider the decision to refuse the Shah's request to come to the United States, and enlisted a senior member of the policy establishment who was highly respected by the Democrats, John J. McCloy, to join them in personal interventions with Vance, Vice President Mondale, and Carter himself (Brzezinski needed no persuading). Rebuffed by the President, Kissinger took to the public podium to voice his outrage at the Carter administration's treatment of the Shah as reducing the monarch to "a Flying Dutchman looking for a port of call."[15]

Another try was made by the Shah's twin sister, Princess Ashraf, in an August 10, 1979, letter to President Carter in which she stressed "the quite noticeable impairment of his [my brother's] health" as a consideration Carter should take into account. The response, conveyed by Deputy Secretary of State Warren Christopher, expressed concern for the welfare of the Shah and his family, but once again denied the request on grounds of there being "a reasonable chance that the United States can in the months ahead improve the relations with the new government [in Iran] on the basis of mutual respect and cooperation." Christopher's letter referred to "the still serious risks to the safety of our people in Iran" with the clear implication that admitting the Shah to the Untied States would exacerbate those risks. When relations with Iran were established again on a better course, "we will be reviewing our position on the best timing of your brother's move to the United States."[16]

The Shah had been suffering from cancer for the past seven years, but had kept it a secret from the world, and extensive tests and diagnoses were required by cancer specialists to determine how far the disease had progressed.

After a report from the State Department medical officer, Secretary Vance advised that, despite the political difficulties it would cause, the Shah should be admitted to the United States, not to take up residence, but only for required emergency medical observation and treatment. Carter agreed, and on October 22 the Shah flew from Mexico to the United States, where he was taken immediately to New York Hospital.[17]

Although angry at Washington's decision, the Iranian officials promised that the embassy would be protected against assaults by militants, such as the armed attack the previous February. After the February assault on the embassy, U.S. personnel had been reduced from over 1,000 to less than 100, a few extra Marine guards had been assigned to the embassy, and steel doors had been installed. These new security measures would be insufficient to defend the embassy from a determined siege by armed militants, but the assumption in Washington was that the Iranian government, as it did in February, would intervene in case of a serious threat to the premises or to U.S. officials.

By the time of the Shah's arrival in the United States for medical treatment, the Bazargan regime, for the very reasons that Secretary Vance and others thought it could be trusted—its moderation and desire to normalize the situation—had lost its revolutionary legitimacy not only with the left but, more importantly, with the Muslim fundamentalists. Khomeini's continuing authority over the revolution required him to separate himself from the Barzagan government that he had originally installed and blessed, thus further undermining its crumbling authority.

The Carter administration, by deciding to work with the Bazargan government, was only contributing to its increasing difficulties. Zbigniew Brzezinski, meeting with Bazargan in Algiers on October 31 on the anniversary of Algerian independence, allowed a photograph to be taken of them and inflicted the proverbial kiss of death on the Bazargan regime. The next day, the Ayatollah Khomeini broadcast an appeal to the Iranian people to take to the streets on November 4 to demonstrate and to "expand with all your might your attacks against the United States and Israel."

The November 4 demonstration had originally been the idea of the Society of Islamic Students (the date being the first anniversary of an invasion by the Shah's troops of Teheran University that resulted in the killing of several students) to demand that the Shah be returned to Iran to stand trial for torturing his political opponents and other crimes. Khomeini was now taking over the demonstrations, but the students would yet force the pace of events, for they had decided, apparently without Khomeini's knowledge, to seize the American Embassy.[18]

THE TEST OF AMERICA'S HUMANITARIANISM: STRENGTH OR WEAKNESS

Demonstrators started circling the embassy early in the morning of November 4. At midmorning some of them began scaling the gate, at which time the guards locked the recently installed steel door to the chancellery. But the mob broke open the steel door. The few Marine guards held off the Iranians by pointing shotguns at them while embassy employees gathered on the second floor, access to which was barred by a second steel door. On the second floor, employees began to shred secret documents and destroy computer circuits. Meanwhile the embassy's security officer attempted to talk with the leaders of the militants, but was taken captive and apparently forced to order a Marine to open the steel access door to the second floor. The militants rushed upstairs and immediately took all the Americans captive, except three officials who had locked themselves in a steel vault to complete the shredding of documents. The officials within the vault were coerced into surrendering before they had finished their shredding job as the militants held a knife to the throat of one of their American captives before a television monitor on view within the vault.

Sixty-three American officials were now at the mercy of a group of young Iranian militants in physical control of the embassy; and three more—including chargé d'affaires Laingen—who had been at the Iranian Foreign Ministry blocks away and were in telephone contact with the embassy during its siege, were also taken captive. The militants, a small group of hitherto virtually unknown young radical Muslim activists, suddenly found themselves in a position to bargain with one of the global superpowers—that is, as long as they kept their American captives alive and as long as Jimmy Carter continued to place a high value on the lives of these American officials.[19]

"I listened to every proposal, no matter how preposterous," recalls Carter, "all the way from delivering the Shah for trial as the revolutionaries demanded to dropping an atomic bomb on Tehran."[20] One proposal was a rescue attempt in emulation of Israeli methods of freeing hostages held by airplane hijackers, such as the famous rescue at Entebbe, Uganda. The Joint Chiefs of Staff pointed out the pitfalls of such an attempt in the present situation: Tehran was not like the Entebbe airport; there was no way to pull off such a commando raid in the middle of the city without getting the hostages killed in the process. Even so, this option might yet have to be used, and thus the military was ordered to prepare for such a rescue effort and to put the people most knowledgeable about this kind of operation to work in devising ways of minimizing injury to the hostages in case a rescue was decided upon. A "show of force" in the form of massing naval units near Iran was discussed, but dismissed: to work as a coercive ploy it would have to be a visible and dramatic deployment which might provoke the militants into either a wholesale slaughter of the hostages or killing them one at a time to pressure the United States to give in to their demands while there was still some chance of saving the rest.

Carter early on decided to shift the responsibility for bloodshed onto the captors: "I am not going to take any military action that would cause bloodshed or arouse the unstable captors of our hostages to attack or punish them," he announced, as long as they were not harmed or put on trial. The clear implication was that he would feel compelled to take military action under such circumstances, but yet this kind of formulation stopped short of an ultimatum which locked the United States into a military response. On the other hand, it left open the definition of "harmed," and "put on trial" so that he would not have to tolerate the hostages' being tortured or otherwise abused, and the captors would be put on notice not to push their luck.[21]

Carter's initial restraint on the use of any force that would endanger the lives of the hostages was consistent with the dominant public sentiment at the time as reflected in public opinion polls and editorial opinion, which in turn was shaped by media attention given to the families of the hostages, their anguish, and their fears. The President himself met periodically with these families and thereby helped create a national empathy with their plight, so that it was not a group of faceless U.S. diplomats and embassy guards whose lives were at risk, but the sons and daughters of one's neighbors.

Having rejected a military move against Iran or a rescue operation as immediate responses to the taking of the hostages, the Carter administration moved quickly to exploit the nonlethal forms of pressure at its disposal that might sway those in control in Iran to induce the militants to release the hostages. Who those in control were, apart from Khomeini himself, was not at all clear; and Khomeini was still an enigma. Would international diplomatic and economic pressures really make any difference to him? It was decided to try anyway, under the assumption that there were large segments of Iranian society that did want Iran to be an accepted member of the larger society of nations, and did realize that their own material well-being was dependent upon the government of Iran and Iranian citizens being able to buy and sell normally in the international market. If most of the internationally connected and internationally sensitive elements in Iran could be made to realize that the hostage-holding would hurt them, then perhaps even the xenophobic Khomeinists could be prevailed upon to intercede to get the hostages released.

On November 7, the President prohibited U.S. companies from buying oil from Iran. A week later the President enlarged the scope of proscribed economic transactions to include various other imports as well as certain U.S. exports to Iran. But to have any real pinch in Iran, these sanctions would require concerted action by other countries so that Iran could not simply shift its commerce elsewhere; and such cooperation with the United States proved hard to induce. The most important economic sanction proved to be a freeze on Iranian assets on deposit in U.S. banks in the U.S. and abroad—some $12 billion in all.

On the diplomatic front, the Carter administration, now defined by the Iranians as the enemy, had to rely on intermediaries to press its case that normalized U.S.–Iranian relations would be of substantial benefit to the post-Shah regime; that the United States had no plans or intentions to reinstall the Shah; that the United States was willing to hear the claims of the Iranians against alleged U.S. crimes in Iran, and even to discuss the Shah's future, but not with a knife at the throats of American officials. Carter himself contacted as many as thirty foreign leaders personally, among them Leonid Brezhnev, to request such intercession.[22]

To the surprise of most Americans, but not to Carter and his advisers, one of the early intermediaries, and probably the most effective, was the PLO leader Yasir Arafat. The Palestinian guerrilla chief was not asked directly by the Carter administration to use his influence with Khomeini, but Carter was apprised of the initiative of Congressman Paul Findley (Republican of Illinois), a known champion of Palestinian causes, to get Arafat to intercede, and that Arafat wanted the U.S. leadership to know that he was engaging in an action that might be politically costly for him. On November 19 and 20, thirteen hostages—the women and blacks—were released upon Khomeini's orders, evidently as a result of Arafat's intercession.

The diplomatic intercessions were also for the purpose of finding out precisely what the Khomeini government would settle for to release all of the hostages. In mid-November, in secret "proximity talks" at the United Nations between Vance and an envoy of the Iranian government (Vance and the Iranian, Ahmad Salmatian, sat in separate rooms and passed papers to each other through Secretary General Kurt Waldheim), it was determined that the Iranian government would no longer insist on the extradition of the Shah. The hostages might be released if three conditions were met: (1) the U.S. government would arrange for the Shah's wealth to be returned to Iran; (2) the U.S. government would pledge never to interfere again in the internal affairs of Iran; and (3) the U.S. government would agree to participate in an international forum in which Iran could present its charges against both the Shah and the United States and have these examined before the world. Vance indicated his desire to pursue negotiations on each of these demands and his hope of reaching a settlement with the Iranian Foreign Minister, Bani-Sadr, at the time of the Security Council meetings on the crisis scheduled for the end of November.[23]

Before the delicate negotiations could resume, however, there was another shakeup in the government in Teheran. Khomeini denounced the forthcoming UN Security Council meetings as staged by and for the United States. Foreign Minister Bani-Sadr was dismissed and replaced by Sadegh Ghotbsadeh—a vocal proponent of forcing the extradition of the Shah. The Carter administration was disheartened by this regression, but surmised it might be a part of the Byzantine political maneuverings among the revolutionaries, and that the real settling price had been revealed by Bani-Sadr's representative in New York. Patience and further diplomatic skill might yet return the Iranians to this more reasonable bargaining posture.

Each passing day of the hostages' captivity was being counted off on the TV evening news. Opposition politicians were demanding a reassertion of American will and power to protect the country's honor. Editorial writers were complaining that the President had drastically weakened the U.S. bargaining power by making the lives of the hostages the highest national interest and thereby giving the world to believe that the U.S. was an easy target for blackmail.

Then, to make matters worse, the Mexican government announced that it could not allow the Shah to return to Mexico upon completion of his medical treatment in New York. Medical reports issued from New York Hospital indicated the Shah was ready to leave at the start of December. If he remained in the United States the credibility of Carter's original rationale for admitting him would be destroyed and efforts to free the hostages might collapse.

The Shah was flown to Lackland Air Force Base in Texas— "temporarily" and "en route" to his next place of residence outside the United States—while the White House and State Department frantically attempted to locate another country for his exile. Panama's General Torrijos, who had developed a close rapport with the White House during the successful negotiations on the canal treaty, bailed out the administration by inviting the Shah to reside in Panama.

In January 1980, UN Secretary General Waldheim intruded himself into the situation. Waldheim's inquiries in Teheran convinced him that what the Iranians wanted most from the United States now as a condition for the release of the hostages was an admission of past complicity in the Shah's crimes, and that this might be accomplished through an international commission of inquiry whose findings the

United States would agree to accept. Exploiting this information, the White House attempted to get things moving again by indicating a receptivity to the commission idea and by trying to institute specific discussions about the modalities: would the hostages be released simultaneously with the formation of the commission? upon the commencement of its hearings in Teheran? or only after it had reported its findings? The outlines emerged of a partial scenario: an independent distinguished-persons commission would go to Iran before the hostages were released, and this commission, in addition to hearing charges against the Shah and the United States, would be able to talk with the hostages. The President of the United States and the President of Iran (now Bani-Sadr) would deposit statements with the United Nations expressing understanding of the particular grievances of the other. The United States by agreeing to this scenario hoped to set in motion a dynamic process in which the Iranian government itself would take over control of the hostages from the young militants, and a quick release would follow before the publication of the commission's report. But would the regime in Teheran so commit itself?

Despite the uncertainties on the precise tasks of the commission when it arrived in Teheran and the timing of the hostages' release in relation to the commission's report, Iran and the United States agreed in early February to the appointment of the five-member commission and to its membership: Andrés Aguilar Mawdsley of Venezuela, Mohammed Bedjaoui of Algeria, Adib Daoudy of Syria, Hector Wilfred Jayewardene of Sri Lanka, and Louis-Edmond Pettiti of France. But the artful drafting of ambiguous terms defining the commission's role thrust its five members into an embarrassing situation when they discovered that the Iranians and the Americans had not resolved their essential differences over what the commission was supposed to do.[24]

The Iranians stage-managed the scenario in Iran, providing hundreds of victims of brutal treatment by the Shah's government and police for the commission to interview. By the end of the first week in March, after the investigation of the past had been performed, the Iranian government, to implement its end of the bargain, was supposed to take control of the hostages from the militants. But the young militants at the embassy refused and the Iranian government claimed to be in no better a position than the United States to use force against them without provoking a slaughter of the hostages. The Iranian officials appealed to Khomeini to attempt to salvage the affair without great international embarrassment to Iran, whereupon the Ayatollah proposed that the commission be allowed to see the hostages at the embassy without the students having to relinquish control; but as a condition for being able to interview the hostages, the commission should *first* make a declaration of its findings about the brutality of the Shah's regime and the past interference by the United States in the internal affairs of Iran.

The commissioners properly refused to be manipulated so crassly and, despite frantic appeals from the United States and the UN Secretariat to stay on, refused to continue their work under such terms, nor would they publish their report. It looked as if the Ayatollah's timetable—no action on the hostages until the new parliament was convened in the spring and decided what to do—would prevail. It would take great diplomatic skill to restore a climate for resuming negotiations on the hostages' release, for now all parties were angry and highly suspicious of one another.

Now Carter's own domestic political troubles (Senator Kennedy won the New York presidential primary on March 26), coupled with his anger at the Iranians' sabotage of the UN commission's work, began to erode his patient and meticulous approach. On March 29, he sent a warning to Bani-Sadr that if the hostages were not transferred to the control of the government in Teheran within 48 hours, the United States would inflict new and harsh sanctions on Iran. With the failure of this ultimatum to produce results, Carter was in a corner. Graduated diplomatic and economic sanctions were no more likely to work than before; and given the ugly mood in Iran at not being able to get at the Shah or have his and the American "crimes" revealed by the UN commission, a major escalation, such as a naval blockade of Iran, might provoke the Iranians into staging a show trial of the hostages and demanding their execution.

THE ABORTIVE RESCUE MISSION

Administration hints that the use of force was now seriously contemplated punctuated a stiffening of diplomatic and economic sanctions during the first half of April 1980. On April 7 the United States formally broke diplomatic relations with the government of Iran; and on April 17 the President announced a ban on all exports to Iran and the U.S. government's seizure of the Iranian assets frozen in U.S. banks.

The members of the European Economic Community reluctantly voted sanctions of their own under the assumption, reinforced by U.S. officials, that such concerted U.S.–European action would make it unnecessary for the United States to resort to force at this time, and that the resulting international isolation of Iran should be the basic pressure on Teheran for a while; the failure of the Europeans to join the United States in applying diplomatic and economic sanctions, U.S. officials had strongly suggested, would compel a resort to military action before the summer.

Behind the scenes, Carter was closely reviewing his military options and, even before the EEC had voted to cooperate in the nonmilitary sanctions, he decided, at an April 11 National Security Council meeting with Brzezinski, Harold Brown, Deputy Secretary of State Warren Christopher (Vance was in Florida on a four-day vacation), General David Jones (Chairman of the Joint Chiefs of Staff), Stansfield Turner (Director of the CIA), Vice President Mondale, and White House aides Hamilton Jordan and Jody Powell, to go ahead with the helicopter rescue of the hostages.

Upon his return from Florida, Secretary Vance, in a private meeting with Carter, objected to the rescue plan, arguing that even if it succeeded with minimal injury to the hostages (which he thought improbable), the raid would place at risk the approximately two hundred other Americans still living in Iran, who might themselves be seized as hostages, and it would jeopardize U.S. relations with other countries in the region as well as with the EEC countries, which had joined in the diplomatic and economic sanctions. A follow-up meeting of the National Security Council was convened to hear out Vance's objections, but Carter had already made up his mind to go ahead with the rescue. On April 17, Vance told Carter that even if the raid succeeded he would resign.[25]

Why did the President feel he had to resort to the rescue raid just then? Couldn't he have waited so as to satisfy Vance and the Europeans that all other options short of force had been exhausted? Evidently, a few key details determined the timing: the hostages were still being held in the embassy compound (once they were dispersed to other places it would be almost impossible to try a rescue); the desert nights were getting shorter and the desert temperatures hotter as summer approached; thus each passing week would degrade the efficiency of the helicopter operation and reduce nighttime concealment—two crucial elements of the plan. Carter was convinced it was now or never.[26]

The President was strengthened in his conviction that this was the time to try a more dramatic option by reports of a shift in public attitudes toward the use of force against Iran. A *Washington Post* nationwide poll conducted from April 9 to 13 showed nearly a two-to-one majority in favor of military action even if it imperiled the lives of the hostages (this in contrast to a similar poll taken in January showing 51 percent rejecting the use of force on grounds that it could result in harm to the hostages).[27]

The rescue scheme authorized by the President on April 11 had been carefully worked out to minimize the chances of its being discovered by the Iranians in time for them to first move or kill the hostages. Early in the evening of April 24, 1980, six transport planes carrying 90 commandos, helicopter fuel, and weapons-jamming equipment took off from Egypt. At the same time eight Navy helicopters took off from the aircraft carrier *Nimitz* in the Arabian Sea and headed for a rendezvous point in the Dasht-i-Kavir salt desert 200 miles southeast of Teheran. The commandos were to be carried in the helicopters to a staging site just outside of Teheran, where they would be met by other commandos who had been infiltrated into Iran over recent months and had obtained local trucks in which they would drive the raiding party, unnoticed, blending with Teheran city traffic, to the embassy compound. In the middle of the night, the force, equipped with nonlethal chemical weapons, was to scale the compound wall, cut telephone and electricity lines, incapacitate the Iranians, and evacuate the hostages in helicopters that meanwhile had landed on the embassy grounds. The helicopters would escape to another desert rendezvous with the transport planes, which would then fly the hostages and the raiding party out of the country, leaving the helicopters behind. Some Americans would be likely to die in the operation.*

The mission was aborted in midcourse, after three malfunctioning

---

* A CIA evaluation of the plan estimated that most probably 60 percent of the hostages would lose their lives in the rescue attempt.

helicopters reduced the fleet available for the final evacuation efforts from the embassy to five instead of the original eight helicopters. Receiving this information and an evaluation from the mission commanders at the desert airstrip that at least six operational helicopters would be required to implement the rescue plan, Carter had no choice but to call off the attempt. No one had yet been killed. But tragically, while the helicopters were refueling for their return flight, one of them collided with a transport plane on the ground, igniting both planes and killing eight men. Knowing that the failed raid could no longer be kept secret, the President sadly informed the nation on television of the abortive rescue operation and freak desert collision that killed the eight men. But he expressed no regrets for attempting the mission, and thereby implied that this was not the last of such efforts, or of other military moves contemplated against Iran, especially if the hostages were now harmed by the angry Iranians.[28]

To the relief of the Carter administration and the American public, the Iranians contented themselves with verbal anger and ridicule at the desert debacle, including a warning to Carter from the Ayatollah "that if he commits another stupid act we won't be able to control the youths now holding the . . . spies and he will be responsible for their lives," and a statement from President Bani-Sadr that to make a second rescue attempt impossible, the hostages were being transferred outside the embassy.

THE DIPLOMATIC DENOUEMENT

Domestic politics in Iran and the United States preoccupied both countries for four and one half months after the abortive rescue attempt. The Shah died in an Egyptian military hospital on July 27, and no high official of the U.S. government attended his funeral (former President Nixon did attend, in a private capacity). The Iranians were electing their first parliament since the revolution. The United States was in the final stages of the nominating process for the fall's presidential elections. The hiatus on the diplomatic front was an opportunity for Carter to follow the strategy, recommended by European diplomats and some professionals within the State Department, of turning the spotlight off the hostages and thus reduce the bargaining leverage the Iranians could gain from their incarceration. The American press, with its tendency for single-minded emphasis on the issue of the day, obliged by indulging in its typical obsession with the presidential election.

The Iranian parliamentary elections, completed in August, were a popular victory for the Khomeinists, legitimizing their revolution and making it less important for them to show their power and curry favor with the masses by exploiting the hostage issue. Moreover, electoral success left the Islamic leaders with a new set of imperatives—namely, restoring civic order and economic stability to the country for which they were now officially responsible, and resurrecting its international respectability. The role of "kidnapper" served none of these purposes, and Khomeini, still titular leader and elder statesman of the revolution, sensing this, now sanctioned the first serious negotiations to free the hostages since the embassy takeover the previous November.

The Carter administration was made aware of this in early September when German diplomatic intermediaries informed Secretary of State Edmund Muskie (Vance's successor) that the Iranians now wanted to meet urgently to work out a deal to release the hostages. A close associate of the Ayatollah, Sadegh Tabatabai, met in Bonn with Deputy Secretary Warren Christopher to get down to specifics; and at these meetings it was immediately apparent that Iran's demands were now within the range of negotiability. There was no mention of ransom, or even of an apology from the United States. The Iranians still wanted a U.S. pledge of noninterference in Iran; but the principal talking points were over the release of Iran's financial assets that had been seized by the United States and the size and repayment modalities of Iran's obligations to its U.S. creditors. The credibility of the negotiating positions Tabatabai presented to Christopher was established in a speech by the Ayatollah stating essentially the same conditions.

The negotiations, which took place mainly in Algeria, with the Algerians acting skillfully as mediators, resembled complicated international commercial negotiations rather than the highly charged political encounters of the earlier stages in the crisis. High politics was an ever-present background factor, but now the political context worked to reinforce Iran's incentives to settle with the United States. Iraq's attack on Iran on September 22, and the ensuing war, made it all the more urgent for Iran to establish international respectability with its Western arms suppliers (especially the United States) to counterbalance the new arms Iraq had been receiving from the Soviet Union. Ronald Reagan's election in November also increased the incentives in Teheran to settle before January 20, for the President-elect had revealed himself during the campaign to be a more confrontationist type than Carter, unwilling to grant that Iran had any legitimate cause whatsoever for its actions over the past year. Reagan, moreover, had pledged to freeze the negotiations when he assumed office and to reassess the whole strategy of dealing with the hostage issue. The Carter administration played on the Iranians' fears of Reagan by convincing them that a finalized official agreement with the Carter government, capped by a return of the hostages before Reagan was inaugurated, would very likely be honored by the new administration, whereas an uncompleted agreement could be easily torn up.

The negotiating end game, typically, involved efforts by both sides to extract maximum face for themselves, as well as some nontrivial differences over the financial settlement. As late as December, the bargaining was almost derailed by Teheran's surprise insistence that its frozen assets plus the wealth removed from Iran by the Shah required $25 billion to be handed over to Iran. Patient negotiation by Christopher, with helpful intercessions by the Algerians, moved the Iranian demands back to the more reasonable level—of approximately $8 billion in exchange for the hostages—which appeared in the final agreement of January 20. After setting aside $5.1 billion that Iran owed in debts to American banks, some $3 billion in cash was to be released to Iran simultaneously with the freeing of the hostages. The $3 billion was to be held in escrow until the hostages were safely airborn in a U.S. Air Force jet. This final exchange of fifty-two lives for cash, as the two Air Force craft carrying the hostages cleared Iranian airspace, was consummated just after 12:30 P.M. on January 20, 1981. Ronald Reagan had become President at noon.

21

AFGHANISTAN AND THE REASSERTION OF GEOPOLITICAL IMPERATIVES

I warned the President that the Soviets would be in a position, if they came to dominate Afghanistan, to promote a separate Baluchistan, which would give them access to the Indian Ocean while dismembering Pakistan and Iran.

—ZBIGNIEW BRZEZINSKI

More than any other event, the Soviet military invasion of Afghanistan at the end of December 1979 appeared to bring Jimmy Carter's view of the USSR into congruence with Zbigniew Brzezinski's and to cause the President finally to discard his 1976 election campaign promise to supplant balance of power politics with world order politics. "It's only now dawning on the world the magnitude of the actions that the Soviets undertook in invading Afghanistan," said Carter in a New Year's Eve television interview. "This action of the Soviets has made a more dramatic change in my own opinion of what the Soviets' ultimate goals are than anything they've done in the previous time I've been in office."[1]

The President's admission of being moved to reassess his views of the Soviet Union was jumped at by critics as evidence of Carter's shallowness and naïveté when it came to the hard facts of geopolitics and Soviet strategy: the inevitability of Soviet–American rivalry all around the Eurasian rimland, or what Brzezinski called the "arc of crisis." In fact, the President had moved considerably toward adopting Brzezinski's geopolitical views well before the Soviet action provided a provocation of sufficient weight and drama to justify a formal resurrection of a U.S. foreign policy directed centrally at containing Soviet expansion.

THE TOUGHENING STANCE IN 1978 AND 1979

Brzezinski had pushed for a tough stance against Soviet expansion during the first year of the Carter administration in response to the open Soviet support of Ethiopia in its border war with Somalia and the Kremlin's exploitation of this conflict to move Soviet naval and air power and a hefty contingent of Cuban troops into the strategically significant Horn of Africa. Secretary of State Vance argued that this was the wrong place to draw the line against the Soviets, since it was the Somalis, not the Ethiopians, who were widely regarded by other Africans as the expansionary aggressors in the border conflict. The strongest statements in opposition to the Soviet–Cuban activities in Africa came from Brzezinski, not the President, as did the administration's warnings to the Kremlin that such Soviet power plays might threaten the negotiating climate for SALT II and that the Senate, in response to public anger at Soviet behavior, might be reluctant to ratify whatever agreement was negotiated.[2]

The fact that Carter could have muzzled Brzezinski and didn't was taken by the administration's critics as evidence of a leadership gap at the top of the administration. A more plausible explanation is that Carter found it useful to have the stern-faced Brzezinski surface the hawkish impulses within the administration without the President yet having to adopt this demeanor himself—thus preserving room to maintain the cordial relations with Brezhnev that might be crucial for progress on SALT and other matters, such as the Arab–Israeli conflict, where the administration was anxious to gain Soviet cooperation.

Carter accepted the need to display credible capabilities and intentions to oppose Soviet moves to take advantage of their military prowess and mobility, and to disabuse the Kremlin of any beliefs that this administration had a "soft" approach to world order and might be squeamish about employing military counters to Soviet aggression. The capacity to act tough if driven to it was conveyed in two major presidential addresses in 1978—the March 17 speech at Wake Forest University calling for increased defense spending, and the June 7 commencement address at the Naval Academy in Annapolis, on U.S.–Soviet relations.

Reiterating the doctrine that a Soviet strategic nuclear attack on the United States "would amount to national suicide for the Soviet Union," the President took cognizance, from the podium at Wake Forest, of impending improvements in Soviet missiles that could make U.S. ICBMs increasingly vulnerable to a Soviet first strike during the coming decade. However remote their attempting to launch such a first strike, cautioned Carter, "it is a threat on which we must constantly be on guard." He pointed out the accelerated development and deployment of cruise missiles for U.S. strategic bombers and decisions to work on the MX intercontinental ballistic missile and Trident II submarine-launched ballistic missile "to give us more options to respond to Soviet strategic deployments. If it becomes necessary to guarantee the clear invulnerability of our strategic deterrent, I shall not hesitate to take actions for full-scale development and deployment of these systems."

The President also pointed to the enlargement and modernization of Soviet theater deployments in Western Europe, charging that these were "beyond a level necessary for defense." In response the United States was developing new force augmentation and modernization plans with its NATO allies, focusing on efforts for speedy reinforcements in wartime and to plug specific gaps in deployed NATO defenses. Additionally, announced the President, "the Secretary of Defense, at my direction, is improving and will maintain quickly deployable forces—air, land, and sea—to defend our interests throughout the world."[3]

Paralleling this concern with Soviet military capabilities, the President's remarks at the June commencement exercises at the Naval Academy were hardly a sanguine characterization of Soviet intentions:

To the Soviet Union, détente seems to mean a continuing aggressive struggle for political advantage and increased influence. . . . The Soviet Union apparently sees military power and military assistance as the best means of expanding their influence abroad. Obviously, areas of instability in the world provide a tempting target for this effort, and all too often they seem ready to exploit any such opportunity.

As became apparent in Korea, in Angola and also, as you know, in Ethiopia more recently, the Soviets prefer to use proxy forces to achieve their purposes. . . . The

Soviet Union can choose either confrontation or cooperation. The United States is adequately prepared to meet either choice.[4]

Carter's acknowledgment that the containment of Soviet expansion still required a visible readiness and impressive capability to use force was reflected in a number of programs and actions during the second and third years of his administration.

• Reversing his campaign promise to reduce defense expenditures by as much as 7 percent from the last Ford administration budget, Carter pledged to increase the real level of defense spending by some 3 percent each year and persuaded most of the NATO allies to make the same pledge.

• The administration initiated and gained alliance cooperation in a new NATO Long Range Defense Program to rectify European theater deficiencies in a number of fields—especially the growing Soviet tank superiority (against which NATO now planned to deploy a new generation of conventional and nuclear antitank weapons) and the Soviet deployment of new intermediate-range missiles such as the multiple-warhead SS-20 targeted on Western Europe (against which the United States would deploy the Pershing II and the ground-launched cruise missile.

• The Defense Department was authorized to improve the U.S. strategic arsenal in two major respects: reducing the vulnerability of the ICBMs to a Soviet strategic first strike (the preferred option was a mobile deployment of the new MX missile); and improving the accuracy and other effectiveness of U.S. strategic weapons so as to give them a capability for rendering *Soviet* ICBMs more vulnerable. Without these improvements, maintained Secretary of Defense Brown, the Soviet Union might appear to have a "warfighting" strategic arsenal while the United States was prepared only for a mutual-suicide type of strategic war, and this might give the Soviets an intimidating edge in a future intense U.S.–Soviet confrontation.*

• The military services were ordered to organize a Rapid Deployment Force (RDF) for quick military intervention in crises outside the NATO area. When finally fleshed out in the 1980s, the RDF was supposed to be ready to inject up to 150,000 troops with fighting equipment into a trouble spot, say, in the Persian Gulf, with the leading contingents arriving in a matter of days from the "go" order. (This idea, popular with military strategists as far back as the Eisenhower administration, was thought to have been buried by the post-Vietnam antipathy to U.S. military interven-

---

*The flexible targeting doctrine for U.S. strategic forces was formulated in the summer of 1979 in Presidential Directive 59, but the go-ahead for the associated improvements in U.S. strategic forces to make them at least equivalent to the Soviets in "war-fighting" capability was obtained by Brown in late 1977 and was featured in his unclassified budget presentations to Congress in January and February of 1978.

tion in the Third World; but it had been revived in a classified study of the country's global military requirements directed by Samuel P. Huntington out of Brzezinski's office in 1977, and Brzezinski himself became one of the strongest backers of an RDF. Brzezinski argued that without such a capability, the Soviets could present the United States with local military faits accomplis in areas of strategic importance like the Horn of Africa or the Persian Gulf.)

• In the aftermath of the fall of the Shah's government in Iran, the Carter administration announced in March 1979, without waiting for congressional review, that it would sell $400 million worth of advanced military equipment to North Yemen, including jet aircraft, tanks, and antitank guided missiles, to help that country—an ally of Saudi Arabia—defend itself in its ongoing war against South Yemen, a Soviet client state. To punctuate U.S. support for the North Yemenis and the Saudis, the aircraft carrier *Constellation* and its escort ships set sail from the Philippines toward the Arabian Sea. Administration spokesmen explained that this was part of a larger strategy to demonstrate that stability in the Middle East and the Arabian peninsula was a vital U.S. interest, and that the decisions involving Yemen were only the first steps toward an enlarged U.S. military presence in the region. (By the end of March 1978, the two Yemens agreed to a cease-fire, after the South had been strongly pressured by the Soviets to call off the war. Although the administration would have liked to be able to claim that its tough stance was decisive in stopping the war, the more weighty consideration with the Soviet Union seems to have been the embarrassment its backing of South Yemen was causing other Soviet clients in the area, especially Syria and Iraq.)

REDRAWING THE CONTAINMENT LINE

The sudden and swiftly executed Soviet military takeover of its Muslim neighbor in the last week of 1979 and first week of 1980 was the kind of fait accompli about which Brzezinski had been warning. Once it had been substantially accomplished (the Soviets had difficulty in completely subduing fierce Afghan tribesmen in the mountainous parts of the country), there was little the United States could do. The immediate question was whether or not the Soviet move (the first combat use of Soviet troops outside of the Warsaw Pact area in Eastern Europe since World War II) was only the first phase of a larger plan of aggressive expansion targeted on the oil-rich Persian Gulf. The answer was a large question mark. The rest of the states in the region, even unstable Iran, were apparently not in immediate jeopardy of military attack; the Soviets were concentrating tens of thousands of troops in their Afghanistan operation; these troops would be pinned down as an army of occupation for months if not years; and it was highly unlikely that the Soviets could afford to make additional major diversions from their primary military deployments in Eastern Europe and along the China border. But the longer-term threat posed to other states in the region by a consolidated Soviet military presence on Iran's eastern border and Pakistan's northwestern border could not be discounted; a failure of the United States to react strongly to the invasion of Afghanistan would undoubtedly shake the confidence of those Persian Gulf countries that depended ultimately on U.S. protection against an imperially expanding Soviet Union and would vindicate those who had signed peace and friendship treaties with the USSR.

An immediate military countermove by the United States was not a seriously considered option. Afghanistan itself was simply not that important a geopolitical prize to deny the Soviet Union, and it therefore would have been grossly imprudent to climb on to an escalation ladder of military threat and counterthreat that would dangerously commit the prestige of the United States to a Soviet military withdrawal. A regime in Afghanistan that would not allow that country to be used by Islamic revolutionaries as a base for building anti-Soviet links into the Muslim populations of the USSR, was, afterall, a more substantial interest to the Soviet Union than a free Afghanistan was to the United States, if that's as far as things went.*

Thus the Soviet military takeover, while illegitimate, shocking, and even outrageous, was in itself not really intolerable to the United States. An obviously ineffectual U.S. response would be intolerable. As put by President Carter, "If the Soviets are encouraged in this invasion by eventual success, and if they maintain their dominance over Afghanistan and then extend their control to adjacent countries, the stable, strategic, and peaceful balance of the world will be changed. This would threaten the security of all nations including, of course, the United States, our allies and friends. Therefore, the

---

*The United States had already indicated its willingness to tolerate the Soviet Union's conversion of Afghanistan from a nonaligned country to a client state by acquiescing, without much visible diplomatic protest, to the Soviet-engineered coup in 1978 that installed a pro-Soviet Marxist regime in Kabul.

world cannot stand by and permit the Soviet Union to commit this act with impunity."[5]

Accordingly, the administration immediately applied a wide range of punitive but nonlethal sanctions: the President asked the Senate to delay further consideration of the SALT II treaty; licensing of high-technology items for sale to the USSR was suspended; fishing privileges for Soviet ships in U.S. waters were severely curtailed; an embargo was placed on 17 million tons of grain already purchased but not yet shipped to the USSR; planned openings of new American and Soviet consular facilities were canceled; and most Soviet–American cultural and economic exchanges then under consideration were deferred. The President also announced that he was considering asking U.S. athletes not to participate in the Olympic Games scheduled for Moscow in the summer.

Critics charged that the sanctions were too little and too late to effect a reversal of the Soviet aggression, but they were unable to propose stronger alternatives that were feasible. Collateral moves to shore up the region against *further* Soviet encroachments were feasible; the administration made a point of its determination to redraw the containment line deeply in the sands of Southwest Asia. Pakistan was offered $400 million in military aid. Discussions with Kenya, Oman, Somalia, and Egypt were intensified to arrange for the establishment of service facilities for U.S. naval units deployed in the region.

The President firmed up his public rationale for these actions in his State of the Union address of January 23, 1980. "The implications of the Soviet invasion of Afghanistan could pose the most serious threat to world peace since the Second World War," said the President.

The Soviet effort to dominate Afghanistan has brought Soviet military forces to within 300 miles of the Indian Ocean and close to the Strait of Hormuz—a waterway through which much of the free world's oil must flow. The Soviet Union is now attempting to consolidate a strategic position that poses a grave threat to the free movement of Middle East oil.

He then voiced the warning that was labeled by journalists, with the approval of the White House, as the Carter Doctrine:

Let our position be absolutely clear: Any attempt by any outside force to gain control of the Persian Gulf region will be regarded as an assault on the vital interests of the United States. It will be repelled by use of any means necessary, including military force.[6]

The administration's two-pronged response—imposing current economic and diplomatic sanctions on the Soviet Union; and building up, over five years, a military capability to confront future Soviet power plays in the Persian Gulf region—was designed to tell the Kremlin, the world, and not incidentally the American electorate, that the Soviet invasion of Afghanistan was based on a miscalculation of the American will to resist Soviet aggressive expansion, especially in the geopolitically crucial "rimland" area between the Mediterranean and China. Despite the grumblings of wheat farmers and some Olympic athletes the domestic response was generally favorable. It was virtually assured that the 1980 elections would be contested in a post-détente atmosphere, with the candidates competing over who could best stand up to the Russians.

Afghanistan also—more than any event in Carter's tenure in the White House—reordered the priorities in the Carter foreign policy from those indicated at the outset of the administration. Human rights, global economic development, reducing arms sales, preventing the spread of nuclear weapons, even the Soviet–American strategic arms agreements, were all subordinated to the imperative of preventing the Soviet Union from gaining global dominance. Allies with dubious human rights records, like Pakistan, would be courted and built up; economic aid would be allocated on the grounds of the consequences for East–West alignment; conventional arms transfers would be increased to countries opposed by arms clients of the Soviet Union; adherence to the nuclear nonproliferation treaty and safeguards would not be rigidly imposed as a precondition for military or economic aid when such insistences might alienate an anti-Soviet ally; and, finally, the Soviets would be put on notice that the U.S. was prepared to resume the arms race in all categories of weapons if driven to it, and that the USSR would be substantially worse off at the end of the next round.

Ironically, a national consensus was being created by the Carter administration's new rhetorical and policy preoccupations with the Soviet threat that appeared to legitimize the complaints of the unreconstructed cold warriors in the Reagan camp. The Reaganites, who had never accepted even Kissinger's détente approach, had charged that the Carter foreign policy was inexcusably naïve in its emphasis on human rights and world order, and had contributed to the decline of the West's ability and will to stand up to the Soviet Union. It was time, argued the Reaganites—with impressive success first in their own party and then in the November 1980 general election—to install in Washington a group of leaders who had never been duped by Soviet professions of peaceful coexistence, who had always understood the crucial relevance of military power to the security of the American way of life, and who had been willing all along to engage in higher defense expenditures and a confrontationist policy toward the Soviet Union and its allies. Thus the Carter administration, adopting many of the foreign policy views of its earlier critics, helped reinforce the backlash that removed it from office.

PART VII

THE REAGAN ERA: REALISM OR ROMANTICISM?

Suppose we were at the point of deploying the SDI system and we alone had it; our research is done but it is going to take months, maybe years, to deploy. We are also sitting with a great arsenal of nuclear weapons and the world knows it; we'd realize it might seem very tempting for them to push the button on their weapons before our defense is installed because of a fear we'd soon be able to blackmail the world.

When the time comes to deploy SDI, the United States would have no rational choice but to avoid this situation by making the system available to all countries, so they know we wouldn't have the power to blackmail them. We're not being altruistic.

—RONALD REAGAN

In truth, Ronald Reagan knew far more about the big picture and the matters of salient importance than most people—perhaps especially some of his immediate staff—gave him credit for or appreciated. He had blind spots and a tendency to avoid detail. . . . But he had a strong and constructive agenda, much of it labelled impossible and unattainable in the early years of his presidency.

. . .

You couldn't figure him out like a fact, because to Reagan the main fact was a vision.

—GEORGE SHULTZ

22

HIGH PURPOSE AND
GRAND STRATEGY

I think that . . . it is important that the Soviets and the world know that the U.S. has changed, and that we . . . will acquire much greater strength as well as greater firmness and resolve during this administration.

—CASPAR WEINBERGER

Ronald Reagan was convinced that his 1980 election victory, in addition to being a mandate to reduce the role of government in the domestic economy, was a mandate on foreign policy: a mandate to regain for the United States the reputation of a country that could not be pushed around; to revive the clear definition of what America was for and against internationally (as had been articulated in the Truman Doctrine and in the rhetoric of John Foster Dulles); to reestablish the United States as the leader of the "free world" coalition; and to organize the required programs under a grand strategy that would bring U.S. power, especially military power, back up to the level needed to effectively assert U.S. interests.

These foreign policy imperatives, like Reagan's domestic policy imperatives, were appropriately seen by both supporters and critics as conservative in that they looked to the country's past for models and inspiration. His inaugural address heralded a "new beginning" in the form of "an era of national renewal." The "heroic dreams" he called for were of an America again standing tall after the decay and self-doubts of the 1960s and 1970s. "Let us renew our determination, our courage, and our strength. And let us renew our faith and our hope."[1] But whereas the more glorious past as a model for Reagan's domestic policy was the laissez-faire era preceding the New Deal (even though ex-Democrat Reagan continued to admire Franklin Roosevelt), the model era for his foreign policy was the early Cold War of the late 1940s and early 1950s when U.S. leaders were willing to define the international struggle against Communism as a conflict between good and evil.

Drawing his inspiration from a simpler past, Reagan's rhetoric (and foreign policy for Reagan was rhetoric more than operational planning) was rich in metaphors of war, the mythical cowboy West, and, most nostalgically, sports. His heroes were those who, in real life or Hollywood fantasies, facing defeat and death, summoned the strength to lead their side on to victory.

Reagan's favorite story was of another great storyteller, Notre Dame football coach Knute Rockne, and the ailing football hero, George Gipp. The most famous version of the tale, a concoction of fact and coach Rockne's fertile imagination, was reflected in the 1940 movie *Knute Rockne—All American*. The last words of the dying Gipp, played by Reagan, were that Coach Rockne should tell the team, then losing, to "win just one more for the Gipper." Rockne rouses the team to victory with this message. The Notre Dame player who makes the winning touchdown is carried off the field severely injured, saying: "That's the last one I can get for you, Gipper." Reagan liked the story so much that he made it his own, embellishing it to suit the occasion, from rallying political campaign workers, to mobilizing his aides to lobby a close vote in the Congress, to encouraging a graduating class to tackle the challenges ahead. "Win one for the Gipper" became synonymous with win one for Reagan; and Reagan himself became "the Gipper" for many in his administration and in his admiring audiences. Even Nancy Reagan began to refer to her husband by the name when she sensed it would make him appear more heroic.

Sports also provided the metaphoric support for the strategic paradigm of the Cold War the incoming Reagan administration was determined to revive: the view of the U.S.–Soviet rivalry as a global struggle for ascendancy in which there was no substitute for victory. The object of the game was to win—to be "number one," as sports fans typically proclaim.

THE GRAND STRATEGY OF PEACE THROUGH STRENGTH

The goal was a peaceful world where Americans, with a minimum of government interference, could once again attend to their domestic pursuits in a free capitalist society. But the restoration of this simpler, better America was threatened by the hostile forces of Marxism, now championed by an ever more aggressive superpower. In a mirror image of the Marxist dictum that peace would come only with the worldwide revolutionary eradication of class conflict, the Reaganites believed that peace and freedom for Americans required the worldwide victory over the proponents of Marxism-Leninism.

Reagan's grand strategy for victory was heralded by the Republican national platform of 1980. Written largely by Reagan ideologists, it committed the next Republican president to "achieve overall military and technological superiority over the Soviet Union" and to "nonmilitary means to roll back the growth of communism." The goals of military superiority and the rollback of Communism had not been so openly promulgated as U.S. policy since 1956, when they were discarded as too expensive and dangerous by their earlier Republican advocates in the Eisenhower administration.

Once again opposition to Soviet power and influence would unambiguously top the list of U.S. international objectives. And military power—U.S. equipment and training for its allies, backed by credible threats to directly employ the awesome U.S. arsenal—would provide the principal means for asserting U.S. influence and limiting Soviet expansion. It was time to leave behind the Vietnam-era squeamishness about the decisive application of U.S. military force. Economic power and the attractiveness of the American way of life would also be exploited with confidence and pride, not with the equivocation and apologetics of the Carter years, in a worldwide assault on the false prophets of socialism.

THE "FULL COURT PRESS" ON THE SOVIET UNION

The various strands of the peace through strength strategy as they developed during the first year of the Reagan administration were brought together and publicly articulated in national security adviser William Clark's May 21, 1982 address at Georgetown University's Center for Strategic and International Studies. Administration officials (speaking anonymously) called attention to the speech in background briefings for reporters. One invoked the analogy of the basketball stratagem of a full court press, wherein the opposing team is aggressively harassed in their own half of the court to prevent them from moving the ball into your half of the court where they can score. The Reagan strategy, explained Clark, included "diplomatic, political, economic, and informational components built on a foundation of strength." Its objective was to "convince the Soviet leadership to turn their attention inward" instead of engaging in expansionary international moves.[2]

The administration's embrace of a projected $1.7 trillion in military expenditures for the period 1982–1987, amounting to a real annual increase (corrected for inflation) of 7 percent a year, was the centerpiece of this "full court press" on the Soviets. Adopted and openly proclaimed by Reagan and Secretary of Defense Weinberger over the objections of Budget Director David Stockman even before the Pentagon had come up with plans for spending the money, the extravagant increase in defense outlays was dictated less by considerations of military effectiveness than by the grand strategy of pricing the Soviets out of the superpower competition. Accordingly, a key Defense Department planning document urged the development of weapons that "are difficult for the Soviets to counter, impose disproportionate costs, open up new areas of military competition, and obsolesce [sic] previous Soviet investments."[3] The intention of this early stance by the administration, Reagan recalls in his memoirs, was

to let them [the Soviets] know there were some new fellows in Washington who had a realistic view of what they were up to and weren't going to let them keep it up. . . . I intended to let them know that we were going to spend whatever it took to stay ahead of them in the arms race. We would never accept second place. The great dynamic success of capitalism had given us a powerful weapon in our battle against Communism—*money*. The Russians could never win the arms race. We could outspend them forever. Moreover, incentives inherent in the capitalist system had given us an industrial base that meant we had the capacity to maintain a technological edge over them forever."[4]

Would the Soviet Union recognize the challenge of a very expensive arms race? "Someone in the Kremlin had to realize that in arming themselves to the teeth, they were aggravating the desperate economic problems in the Soviet Union, which were the greatest evidence of the failure of Communism. Yet, to be candid, I doubted I'd ever meet anybody like that."⁵

In other words, the Soviet Union could not realistically be expected to reform before it experienced a total collapse, perhaps in the aftermath of losing a war with the capitalist West. Not that the U.S. would start such a war. "They had nothing to fear from us if they behaved themselves," insisted Reagan. But in a reverse of the standard Marxist-Leninist prophecy, it was the Communists (not the beleaguered capitalists) who, at the moment of truth about the failure of their system, might initiate another World War—even a nuclear war—in a last gasp of desperation. The Americans would have to arm themselves to the teeth not simply to deter such a war, but to limit damage to themselves and prevail in the event deterrence failed.

Meanwhile, access by the USSR to the markets of the West would be severely constricted, not encouraged under the naive belief, propagated by Kissinger, that trade with the capitalist West would give the Kremlin a stake in international equilibrium. The policy of isolating the Soviet Union from the international economy, however, proved difficult to implement for it required the cooperation of the other advanced industrial countries, many of which opposed this both on grounds of national economic interest and coalition grand strategy.

The intra-alliance differences over commerce with the USSR surfaced most dramatically in public altercations with the governments of Germany, Britain, France, and Italy over their arrangements with the Kremlin to provide technology and financing for construction of a Soviet pipeline for transporting natural gas from Russia to Western Europe. Reagan's unilateral announcement at the end of December 1981 of a suspension of U.S. export licenses for sales of pipeline equipment to the Soviets was not echoed by the allies.⁶ At a time of economic recession in the West, and with the United States having recently cut back on its steel imports from the European Community, the Europeans were in no mood to forego job-generating orders for their pipeline equipment or a source of natural gas not prone to Arab embargoes or price hikes.

The Reagan administration tried to persuade its European counterparts that their assistance to the Soviets in building the gas pipeline had geopolitical implications transcending immediate economic considerations: the U.S. call for an embargo was part of the grand strategy of denying the Soviet Union goods and technology that contributed to its warmaking capabilities.

The Europeans did not take kindly to the charge that in the gas pipeline deal they were letting commercial objectives override the common defense needs of the West, particularly in light of the recently lifted embargo on U.S. grain sales to the Soviets. The White House admitted that lifting the embargo on grain sales was a response to domestic economic considerations (actually, it was a political payoff to the farm lobby for its support of Reagan in the election), but argued that the grain made no contribution to Soviet military capabilities. Moreover, by purchasing the grain the Russians would be depleting their hard currency reserves; by contrast, in the gas pipeline deal the Soviets stood to earn over $10 billion a year once the gas began to flow, and this would increase their capacity to continue their dangerous military buildup and to pursue an aggressive foreign policy. Even more ominous, the Western countries would become dependent on the gas they received through the pipeline, and thus would be vulnerable to Soviet threats to turn off the spigot in East–West crises.

The Europeans rejected these arguments and took special umbrage at the allegation that by becoming consumers of Soviet natural gas they would be making themselves susceptible to Soviet pressures. At most, they pointed out, supplies from Russia would constitute 5 percent of their total energy consumption, a gap that could be filled from other sources in the event of a cutoff from the East.

At the suggestion of Secretary of Defense Weinberger, President Reagan issued instructions in the summer of 1982 prohibiting European-based subsidiaries of U.S. companies from selling or delivering equipment to the USSR for the pipelines and banning the use of American equipment or technology in the pipeline project by foreign companies. The European governments, supported by powerful elements in their business communities with a stake in expanding East-West commerce, charged that the extra-territorial prohibitions by the U.S. were an infringement of national sovereignty. "The question," explained Reagan's usually loyal friend, Prime Minister Thatcher, "is whether one very powerful nation can prevent existing contracts from being fulfilled. I think it is wrong to do that."[7]

It fell to Secretary of State George Shultz, newly appointed to succeed Alexander Haig, to resolve the intra-alliance confrontation. Shultz negotiated a face-saving agreement for Reagan in which the allies agreed to enlarge the list of items in the NATO category of technology and equipment with military applications that could not to be sold to the USSR and its allies in return for the U.S. looking the other way while the Europeans consummated their gas pipeline deal with the Russians.[8]

The President was more successful in sustaining the pressure on the Soviets at the level of ideological rhetoric. He did perhaps over-state the revived Cold War orientation, and embarrass allied govern-ments, in some off-the cuff press conference remarks at the start of his administration. Most notorious was his charge that "the only morality" for the Soviets is what will further "their goal of . . . a world revolution and a one world Communist state . . . , meaning they reserve unto themselves the right to commit any crime, to lie, to cheat, in order to obtain that."[9] But the great communicator clarified his meaning in a number of artfully crafted and flawlessly delivered speeches designed to seize the political high ground from the Soviet propagandists.

Reagan's proudest effort of this kind was his rousing address in London to the British Parliament on June 8, 1982. In an open castigation of the Soviet system more extreme than anything since John Foster Dulles railed against "atheistic communism," the Presi-dent attributed what he called "the decay of the Soviet experiment" to the inherent flaws of Marxist state socialism. He predicted that the repressiveness of the Soviet system would ultimately drive its people to resist it—possibly by violent revolution. "While we must be cautious about forcing the pace of change," he cautioned, "we must not hesitate to declare our ultimate objectives and to take concrete actions to move toward them." It was time to launch a new "crusade for freedom" to "leave Marxism-Leninism on the ash heap of history." The President pledged to cooperate with various on-going international efforts for helping democratic political movements as well as a new action program by the United States that implied an increase of covert activities by U.S. intelligence agencies. "This is not cultural imperialism," insisted the President. "It is providing the means for genuine self-determination and protection for diversity."[10]

The anticommunist convictions at the core of Reagan's foreign policy were evident nine months later in his address to the National

Association of Evangelicals in Orlando, Florida. Calling the Soviet Union "the focus of evil in the modern world," the President castigated arms control advocates who, he implied, were inadvertently assisting the devil by spreading the pernicious doctrine that both sides were equally at fault for the Cold War. This was "to ignore the facts of history and the aggressive impulses of an evil empire." To "simply call the arms race a giant misunderstanding," he said, was to "remove yourself from the struggle between right and wrong and good and evil." [11]

SDI: AN ARMS PROGRAM ON THE SIDE OF THE ANGELS

While thinking about good and evil in connection with the arms race, Ronald Reagan was disturbed by the fact that his military advisers continued to operate within the inherited strategic orthodoxy of mutual assured destruction (MAD). According to the MAD orthodoxy, if neither superpower could hope to escape a devastating retaliatory strike on its centers of population and industry no matter how large and well-executed its first strike against the other side, then each side would be deterred from starting a strategic nuclear war. The MAD relationship, codified and secured in the SALT treaties, was thought to be the realization of Winston Churchill's prophecy of a situation in which "safety will be the sturdy child of terror and survival the twin brother of annihilation."

The President's principal national security advisers were aware of the President's deep dislike of the inherited deterrence doctrine, but they were taken aback on March 23, 1983 when he publicly promulgated a diametrically opposed strategy for defense and arms control. In a speech that reported favorably on the administration's defense program and strategic arms reduction talks with the Soviets, Reagan added a section that was a surprise even to the Secretary of Defense, whose office had drafted the body of the speech. At the end of the mostly "nuts and bolts" disquisition on the intricacies of the superpower military balance, the President reflected that it was

still . . . necessary to rely on the specter of retaliation, on mutual threat. And that's a sad commentary on the human condition. Wouldn't it be better to save lives than to avenge them?

.   .   .

Let me share with you a vision of the future which offers hope. It is that we embark on a program to counter the awesome Soviet missile threat with measures that are defensive.

. . .

What if free people could live secure in the knowledge that their security did not rest on the threat of instant U.S. retaliation to deter a Soviet attack, that we could intercept and destroy strategic ballistic missiles before they reached our own soil or that of our allies?

I know that this is a formidable technical task; one that may not be accomplished before the end of the century. Yet, current technology has attained a level of sophistication where it is reasonable for us to begin this effort.

. . .

My fellow Americans, tonight we're launching an effort which holds the promise of changing the course of human history. [12]

The President's expression of moral anguish about the need to base deterrence on the threat to devastate the enemy's society, as well as his endorsement of efforts to limit damage to American society in case deterrence failed were not novel. Similarly, there was nothing revolutionary in urging expansion of efforts to develop an antiballistic missile (ABM): indeed, while adhering to the prohibitions in the 1972 ABM treaty, the Nixon, Ford, and Carter administrations had all continued research and development programs on ballistic missile defense. Many officials in the Reagan administration wanted the President to repudiate the ABM treaty as being too inhibitory of essential development and testing programs; but even the Pentagon proponents of a more vigorous ABM effort looked toward deployments that protected U.S. retaliatory forces and command and control centers from nuclear destruction. Few, if any, U.S. defense planners assumed that either the United States or the Soviet Union now, or in the foreseeable future, whatever the research and development efforts, would be able to protect the bulk of their populations in a major U.S.–Soviet nuclear war. But this was precisely what the President was now advocating.

In his memoirs, Reagan reconstructs the reasoning that led him to embrace the goal of a comprehensive defense of the American people in the event of a nuclear war between the superpowers.

One of the first statistics I saw as president was one of the most sobering and startling I'd ever heard. I'll never forget it: The Pentagon said at least 150 million

American lives would be lost in a nuclear war with the Soviet Union—even if we "won."

.   .   .

Even if a nuclear war did not mean the extinction of mankind, it would certainly mean the end of civilization as we knew it.

.   .   .

My dream, then, became a world free of nuclear weapons. Some of my advisers, including a number at the Pentagon, did not share this dream. They could not conceive of it. They said a nuclear-free world was unattainable and it would be dangerous for us even if it were possible; some even claimed that nuclear war was "inevitable" and we had to prepare for this reality. . . . But for the eight years I was president I never let my dream of a nuclear-free world fade from my mind.

Since I knew it would be a long and difficult task to rid the world of nuclear weapons, I had this second dream: the creation of a defense against nuclear missiles, so we could change from a policy of assured destruction to one of assured survival.[13]

On the basis of interviews with Reagan friends and aides, Reagan's biographer Lou Canon finds the President's obsession with protecting the American people in a nuclear war as at least partly reflective of Reagan's belief in Armageddon prophecies. Nuclear World War III might well be the manifestation of that prophecy.[14] But where did the President suddenly get the idea that a space-based nationwide defense against ballistic missiles was feasible? In fact, this was a vision Ronald Reagan had nurtured for more than fifteen years.

In 1967, as Governor of California, Reagan visited the University of California's Lawrence Livermore National Laboratory for a briefing on nuclear defense technologies by Edward Teller. One of Dr. Teller's pet projects was utilization of X-ray lasers for destroying ICBMs early in their trajectories. The idea appealed to Reagan, who over the next dozen years on his way to the White House was repeatedly briefed by Teller and other proponents of spaced-based defenses.

Upon becoming President, Reagan continued this special interest in exotic ABM options despite the skepticism of most of the profes- sional military strategists and planners in his administration. He was backed by his young adviser on domestic politics and eco- nomics, Martin Andersen and the presidential science adviser, Dr. George A. Keyworth, an associate of Dr. Teller enthusiastic about the potential of X-ray lasers. Anderson and Keyworth were joined by National Security Adviser Richard Allen in a series of private White House meetings in 1981 with leading advocates of space-based defense, including Teller and former deputy director of the Defense Intelligence Agency, General Daniel Graham (an advocate of an alternative concept called "high frontier"). This intensification of interest coincided with a study issued by the Heritage Foundation, a Washington-based conservative think tank urging that a nationwide system to defend against ballistic missiles be adopted as a high-priority goal for the country. Dr. Teller and General Graham were prominently involved in the study.[15]

The new National Security Adviser, William Clark, and his principal military deputy, Robert McFarlane, became converts to the idea and found sufficient rationale for a presidential endorsement in a number of political developments: the peace movement was proposing a freeze on nuclear weapons deployments; the administration had failed to gain congressional authorization for MX multiple-warhead missile deployments because it could not come up with an acceptable basing plan for the vulnerable missiles; the Soviets were dragging their feet in the strategic arms negotiations while augmenting their own super-missiles; and the Conference of American Catholic Bishops was disseminating a major moral critique of the prevailing nuclear deterrent strategy.

The peace through strength strategy was faltering. McFarlane later revealed in interviews with Lou Canon that he worked through the Joint Chiefs of Staff, particularly Chief of Naval Operations James D. Watkins, who shared Reagan's repugnance of the assured destruction doctrine, to create the appearance of military support for taking a serious look at ballistic missile defense options. Reagan misinterpreted the new openness of the Chiefs as tantamount to a recommendation that the administration get to work on his dream. McFarlane later claimed to have envisioned the large new research and development program as a "bargaining chip" in the strategic arms negotiations with the USSR—a bargaining chip the Americans would be willing to trade in for major Soviets concessions.[16] This turned out to be a gross miscalculation of Reagan's intentions.

The President continued to make clear, in public and in the councils of his administration, that he believed deeply in the moral and strategic necessity of defending the U.S. population—the entire

country—against nuclear attack. A strategic defense initiative organization (SDIO), directly under the authority of the Secretary of
Defense, was given overall management responsibility, while the
media and the Congress were fed fancy descriptions and visuals of
alternative SDI systems. The White House favored a multilayered
defense "umbrella" of orbiting spacecraft that would use lasers to
destroy as many Soviet multiple-warhead ICBMs as possible in their
boost phase (before the warheads had separated) and then knock out
any surviving warheads in mid-trajectory and terminal intercepts.

Reservations of the Administration's Strategic Experts

The President's optimism was not supported, however, by the
results of the administration's newly ordered feasibility studies.
Whether conducted within the Pentagon or contracted out to think
tanks, they showed the President's dream of physically defending the
population of the United States from a major Soviet strategic attack
to be an unrealizable fantasy. Even if 99 percent of the Soviet
strategic nuclear warheads could be destroyed by the defense shield
(a wildly optimistic premise), and even if official Washington were
spared, that would still leave the continental United States vulnerable to well over 100 nuclear explosions, each on the average 50 times
as powerful as the explosion that devastated Hiroshima. Moreover,
SDI did nothing about nuclear bombs that could be delivered by
Soviet strategic aircraft, low-trajectory missiles launched from Soviet
submarines deployed near American coasts, and terrorist "suitcase"
bombs. The costs of SDI would run into the trillions of dollars; and
even after deployment of the most comprehensive system, the country would still lack a leakproof defense: even only 10 warheads (less
that 1/10 of one percent of the available Soviet arsenal) leaking
through the umbrella would cause millions of fatalities. If the contemplated systems—popularly known as Star Wars—had any strategic utility at all, according to most of the new studies, it was in their
potential role in protecting the deterrent forces themselves and in
"complicating" enemy attacks.[17]

The President did not want to hear the gloomy assessments and
Secretary Weinberger was glad to shield him from the devastating
conclusions of the studies, for by now the Joint Chiefs and the
Pentagon generally saw the opportunity of funding other missile and
exotic technology projects through Star Wars. Within the Pentagon,

to think tank strategists, and to congressional experts on military matters, SDI's potential for protecting the deterrent was emphasized; while in their public and media presentations administration spokespersons sustained a facade of confidence in eventually being able to deploy systems that could protect the population.

Reagan himself took to the public rostrum to counteract the spreading impression that SDI had a more modest purpose. Typical was a 1985 speech before the National Space Club in which he insisted that "We're not discussing a concept just to enhance deterrence, but rather a new kind of deterrence." The capability "to intercept ballistic missiles during their early-on boost phase of trajectory," claimed the President, "would enable us to fundamentally change our strategic assumptions." The revolutionary significance of the initiative should not be underestimated:

We seek to render obsolete the balance of terror—or Mutual Assured Destruction, as it's called—and replace it with a system incapable of initiating armed conflict or causing mass destruction, yet effective in preventing war. Now, this is not and should never be misconstrued as just another method of protecting missile silos.[18]

One of the most worrisome aspects of the Star Wars program to arms control specialists was not simply that it contradicted the ABM treaty, but that in posing a potential negation of the Soviet Union's assured destruction deterrent, it would only stimulate the Soviets to augment their offensive strategic arsenal (numerically and with sophisticated countermeasures) to neutralize whatever antimissile defenses the United States might eventually deploy. But some strategic hardliners in the administration, most notably Assistant Secretary of Defense Richard Perle, saw this as all to the good: it would strain Soviet resources to the breaking point and weaken the USSR's ability to sustain its superpower rivalry with the United States.

At least one of Reagan's top advisers, arms control negotiator Paul Nitze, was not all that confident that the objective of pricing the Soviets out of the arms race would be that easily attained. His February 1985 public speech to the Philadelphia World Affairs Council, created quite a stir among the national security policy cognoscenti. Ambassador Nitze laid out the consideration of a criterion for any defense system:

New defensive systems must . . . be cost effective at the margin—that is, they must be cheap enough to add additional defensive capability so that the other side has no incentive to add additional offensive capability to overcome the defense. If this

criterion is not met, the defensive systems could encourage a proliferation of countermeasures and additional offensive weapons to overcome deployed defenses, instead of a redirection of effort from offense to defense.[19]

All these reservations and debates, however, missed the most
important function of SDI for Reagan. The very dream quality that
earned it the ridicule of critics was its primary appeal for this
President whose power lay in his capacity to reach and identify with
the people through fantasy. The fantasy of Armageddon, which
served to revive both the fear of God and the imperative of fighting
the devil in an overly secular world, was complemented by the
fantasy of salvation by America's technological imagination and skills
applied to noble purposes.

THE REAGAN DOCTRINE

The worldview articulated in the London and Orlando speeches was
later dubbed the Reagan Doctrine. This was merely a journalistic
label (willingly accepted by the President) for policy premises and
actions that were essential to the administration's approach to world
affairs from the outset of the Reagan presidency:

• The United States was the global leader of the forces of good against
the forces of evil.

• On every continent and in virtually every country this struggle was
manifest in the post–World War II contest between the supporters of
democratic capitalism and the supporters of Marxist-Leninist state socialism.

• The vital interest of the United States worldwide lay in strengthening
governments and anti-government forces on the side of free democratic
capitalism and weakening governments and anti-government forces on the
side of Marxism-Leninism.

The Reaganites came to office convinced that their predecessors
has lost sight of these fundamentals and therefore could not distinguish friend from foe, particularly in the volatile Third World. Their
principal mission in foreign policy, which Reagan had been openly
preaching during five years of campaigning for the presidency, was
to put the United States back on the basic course from which it
had strayed under both Kissinger's realpolitik and Carter's human
rights policies.

During Reagan's first term, however, the administration attempted to keep secret the most controversial part of the revived Cold War policy toward the Third World: namely, efforts to over-throw existing Marxist-oriented governments, by force if necessary. The Reaganites admired President Eisenhower's successful use of the CIA's covert capabilities in the 1950s to organize renegade elements of the Guatemalan military to overthrow the Marxist Arbenz regime in Guatemala, and to stage a coup in Teheran to restore the Shah's power (interventions which Eisenhower proudly took credit for in his memoirs).

A new globally extensive covert operations policy against Marxist governments (or Soviet client states) was presented by Director of Central Intelligence Casey in March 1981 in a top secret briefing to the National Security Planning Group—the Reagan administration's highest level foreign policy directorate, which at this date comprised, in addition to the CIA Director, only President Reagan, Vice President Bush, Secretary of State Haig, Secretary of Defense Weinberger, and NSC adviser Allen. Casey's plan called for covert U.S. support to anti-government groups in pro-Soviet states, including Afghanistan, Cuba, Nicaragua, Laos, and Libya.[20] However, Casey advised that there would be too much opposition in the Congress to the renewed interventionist policy if it were made public. Casey's initiative led to a series of "findings" signed by the President (as required by Congressional legislation on covert operations) to authorize the CIA to start down the road that Congress did indeed attempt to block when information on the full extent of the covert activities began to leak out.

The administration's reaction to congressional restrictions on the covert action, particularly Casey's program of arming and training the Nicaraguan Contras (see Chapter 25), took two forms: the low road of flouting the law and lying to the Congress and the high road of public rhetoric designed to create popular pressure on Congress to support the policy of overt actions and sanctions to destabilize Marxist regimes. The Reagan Doctrine was the principal expression of the campaign to gain legitimacy in the form of public support and Congressional authorization for what the administration was doing covertly.

In his State of the Union Address on February 6, 1985, the President enunciated what supporters hoped would stand as both a reaffirmation and enlargement of the Truman Doctrine—now expanded to encompass support not only for governments under attack by Communist rebels but also for rebels against Communist rulers:

We must not break faith with those who are risking their lives—on every continent, from Afghanistan to Nicaragua—to defy Soviet supported aggression and secure rights which have been ours from birth. . . . Support for freedom fighters is self defense.[21]

Then, at Bitburg, Germany on May 5, 1985, the President gave the doctrine a special emotional twist:

Twenty years ago President John F. Kennedy went to the Berlin Wall and proclaimed that he, too, was a Berliner. Well, today freedom loving people around the world must say: I am a Berliner. I am a Jew in a world still threatened by anti-Semitism. I am an Afghan, and I am a prisoner of the Gulag. I am a refugee in a crowded boat foundering off the coast of Vietnam. I am a Laotian, a Cambodian, a Cuban, and a Miskito Indian in Nicaragua. I, too, am a potential victim of totalitarianism.[22]

The principal intellectual guru behind the Reagan Doctrine was United Nations Ambassador Jeane Kirkpatrick—William Casey's closest ally in the Cabinet. A political science professor and former Democrat, she owed her appointment as Ambassador to the UN to the president-elect's admiration for her November 1979 article in *Commentary* magazine urging vigorous support for anti-Marxist elements in the Third World. Titled "Dictatorships and Double Standards," the essay provided conceptual muscle and seemingly tight logic—an intellectual wrapper, as it were—for Reagan's intuitions. Professor Kirkpatrick argued that a naive set of deterministic and essentially apolitical misconceptions about "modernization" and "development" prevalent in the Carter administration had led to mistaken reformist pressures by the United States on reliable Cold War allies such as the Shah of Iran and Anastasio Somoza of Nicaragua, undermining the legitimacy of these rulers within their own countries; and then when these friends were most in need of American support against radical revolutionary movements, the U.S. pulled the rug from under them, at the end even aligning itself with their (and ultimately America's own) enemies. In Kirkpatrick's words:

the Carter administration brought to the crises in Iran and Nicaragua [and elsewhere in the Third World] several common assumptions each of which played a major role in hastening the victory of even more repressive dictatorships than had been in place before. These were, first, the belief that there existed at the moment of crisis a democratic alternative to the incumbent government; second, the belief that the continuation of the status quo was not possible; third, the belief that any change, including the establishment of a government headed by self-styled Marxist revolutionaries [or left-leaning clerics], was preferable to the present government.[23]

Moreover, in attempting to force the pace of human rights progress and democratic development on the part of traditional autocrats like the Shah and Somoza, the United States was operating with a double standard. "Assisting 'change'," complained Kirkpatrick, "did not lead the Carter administration to undertake the destabilization of a *Communist* country"—an inhibition the Carterites cloaked in "selectively applied" principles of self-determination and nonintervention. "We accepted the status quo in Communist nations (in the name of 'diversity' and national autonomy), but not in nations ruled by 'right wing' dictators or white oligarchies."[24]

Kirkpatrick located the source of this double standard in what she saw as the Carter administration's failure to comprehend the essential differences between "traditional autocracies" and "revolutionary [or totalitarian] autocracies" and the relation of each to U.S. national interests. Traditional authoritarian governments are not only "less repressive" than totalitarian governments, they are also "more susceptible of liberalization." A realistic policy, consistent with U.S. geopolitical interests as well as the American commitment to freedom and democracy, would operate on the premise that "there is a far greater likelihood of progressive liberalization and democratization in the governments of Brazil, Argentina, and Chile than in the government of Cuba; in Taiwan than in the People's Republic of China; in South Korea than in North Korea; in Zaire than in Angola; and so forth."[25]

The policy implications for the incoming Reagan administration were clear. Foreshadowing what would later emerge full-blown as the Reagan Doctrine, Kirkpatrick advised that "a posture of continuous self-abasement and apology vis-à-vis the Third World is neither morally necessary nor politically appropriate. Nor is it necessary or appropriate . . . for our leaders to forswear unilaterally the use of military force to counter military force."[26]

Later, when the White House decided to go public with what it had been attempting covertly in the Third World, not surprisingly Ambassador Kirkpatrick provided the most intellectually compelling geopolitical and moral justifications for U.S. policy. Typical was her address before the National Press Club on May 30, 1985, in which she contended that Soviet military aid, often including Cuban and other Soviet-block military and paramilitary personnel in Angola, Ethiopia, Mozambique, Nicaragua, and Cambodia, let alone the Soviet military occupation of Afghanistan, internationalized the struggle for power in these countries. Only the narrowest reading of the UN Charter's prohibitions on intervention in violation of national sovereignty would argue against the legitimacy of U.S. support for indigenous opponents of such Soviet-supported regimes. "It seems clear," she said:

> if client rulers have the "right" to ask for external assistance to maintain their rule, citizens deprived of rights have the right to ask for external aid in reclaiming them.

> .   .   .

> In aiding those who resist Communism are we adopting the same concepts of morality in reverse?
> The answer is, assuredly not.
> To suggest otherwise is to deny the relevance of context and consequences to moral and legal judgment: it is like asking us to look only at the knife that cuts into an abdomen without taking account of whether the man wielding it is a surgeon or Jack-the-Ripper, or whether the patient is likely to be cured by the knife or destroyed.

> .   .   .

> Suggestions that force is force is force deny . . . that there is an objective difference between liberation and conquest and treats them if it were merely a matter of whose ox is being gored.

> .   .   .

> A government which takes power by force and retains power by force has no legitimate grounds for complaint against those who would wrest power from it by force.
> A government whose power depends upon external support has no legitimate grounds for complaining that externally supported force is used against it.
> Obviously it is legitimate for the U.S. to support an insurgency against a dictatorial government that depends on external support.[27]

Kirkpatrick was speaking in 1985. During Reagan's first term, such an open embrace of the interventionist logic prevailing in the administration had been deliberately avoided. Many of the actual operations of the United States government in the Third World were kept secret from the public and the Congress until it was evident that they would be exposed by journalists and congressional investigators. White House public relations specialists feared a public and congressional backlash (there was still a considerable hangover of the "Vietnam syndrome") to implications that the United States was girding itself up for new military interventions against Communists in the Third World. But the policy of intervening with money, equipment, and training on behalf of Third World anti-communists, and preparing to do so with U.S. military force if necessary, would go forward regardless of growing congressional efforts to rein in the zeal of the President's and Casey's men.

When Reagan decided to use the occasion of the 1985 State of the Union address to make overt the premises that had been governing the covert operations, the State Department (reflecting the cautious approach of Secretary Shultz) fought to water down the passages pledging worldwide support for "freedom fighters." But the President was enthusiastic about declaring his deeper convictions and the speech was delivered as written. [28]

With or without the rhetoric, with or without congressional approval, a marked alteration in U.S. Third World strategy coinciding with the ascension of Reagan to the presidency was evident in country after country in the thrust of U.S. operations, both overt and covert. Egalitarian reformers, from democratic socialists to Marxist-Leninists, were isolated and opposed—not courted as they had been during the Carter (and Kennedy) years in the hope of driving a wedge between nationalist leftists and those who were agents of the Soviets. The qualification for U.S. favors, funding, equipment, and training was whether the recipients, governmental or anti-governmental, had creditable anti-Communist credentials; such governments, autocratic or not, were defined (consistent with the Kirkpatrick distinctions) as part of the "free world," and all anti-Communist insurgents, even those in league with the most anti-democratic elements in their countries, were seen as "freedom fighters."

Remarkably, given the fact that the cultural, ethnic, and tribal determinants of the most intense indigenous conflicts in the Third World cut across the Manichean worldview of the Reagan Doctrine, U.S. diplomats and operatives in virtually every country were expected to implement the doctrine's imperatives in their areas of responsibility. The actual local configuration might not conform to the policy premises, but more often than not U.S. officials faithfully persisted in trying to bend local realities to the President's known predilections.

In Afghanistan, the stated purposes of the Reagan Doctrine and the behavior of the involved parties corresponded quite closely—if one squinted (as Reagan did) to make the fanatical Muslim mujahadeen look like fighters for democratic freedom while blurring their connections with and affinity to the radical theocratic government in neighboring Iran. Their opponents, the Soviets and their puppet government in Kabul, did measure up to their billing as an evil presence that the United States was fully justified in helping the mujahadeen resistance remove by force. The Soviets had blatantly invaded the country with major military force in 1979 "to restore order" on the invitation of an Afghan government installed in a brutal coup engineered by the KGB. To this extent the mujahadeen were truly "freedom fighters" on behalf of national self-determination against Soviet imperialism. U.S. assistance to the Afghani rebels was initiated by the Carter administration and its expansion to some $600 million worth of military equipment during the Reagan years, including highly effective Stinger anti-aircraft missiles, was popular with both parties in the Congress.

In southern Africa Reagan found worthy "freedom fighters" in the UNITA rebels led by Jonas Savimbi against the Marxist regime in Angola. Dr. Savimbi, a loser to his Soviet-supported rival Agostino Neto in the struggle for power in Luanda after Angola achieved independence from Portugal, had been accepting aid from the white apartheid regime in South Africa (Pretoria was furious at the Neto government for harboring the outlawed anti-apartheid African National Congress and radical factions of the Namibia independence movement). The incoming Reagan administration was anxious to directly aid Savimbi, but was prevented from doing so by the Clark Amendment, passed by Congress in the 1970s in the aftermath of Vietnam. The Soviets had dramatically enlarged their presence in Angola and the other ex-Portuguese colony, Mozambique—going so far as to airlift thousands of Cuban troops into Angola to help Neto redress the balance of power against militarily powerful South Africa.

The Soviet-supported Cuban troops in Angola were a major case in point for the four-year lobbying effort by the Reagan administration to repeal the Clark Amendment. After the repeal of the Clark

Amendment in the spring of 1985, following the President's vigorous defense of an interventionist policy in the State of the Union and other speeches, U.S. diplomats in discussions with their Soviet counterparts reported an apparent willingness by the Soviets to explore a quid pro quo comprising the withdrawal of Cuban troops in exchange for U.S. and South African withdrawal of support for the Savimbi rebels and credible progress toward Namibian self-determination. In the White House the presumed new willingness of the Soviets to pursue diplomatic resolutions of the conflicts in southern Africa was attributed to the enlarged and more vigorous support for Savimbi, and perhaps also for rebel elements in Mozambique, that the repeal of the Clark Amendment made possible.

The motivation for peaceful settlement was not all on the Soviet side, however. There was considerable apprehension in the State Department and among the U.S. military—who did worry about "another Vietnam" in the making—that the increasing U.S. involvement with Savimbi carried the high risk of escalation to a direct U.S. confrontation against Cuban, and possibly even Soviet, forces. Additionally, the deepening U.S. involvement was likely to produce a severe domestic political backlash against the administration's policy of "constructive engagement" toward the government of South Africa; for now, in going beyond the theory of Assistant Secretary of State Crocker that association with the regime in Pretoria, not its economic and diplomatic isolation, would produce reform of the apartheid system, the United States was becoming, willy-nilly, an open and direct ally of that government's racist military and police actions against the African National Congress and militant factions of the Namibian independence movement.

In Cambodia, the Reagan administration could claim it was on the side of human dignity and freedom only by obscuring the fact that the pro-Chinese rebels it was supporting (including the genocidal Khmer Rouge) were at least as brutal in areas they controlled as were the Cambodian puppets who ran the government in Phnom Penh under Vietnamese military occupation. Administration officials attempted to maintain the appearance of consistency with the Reagan Doctrine by emphasizing the right of the Cambodians to national self-determination against imperialistic, Soviet-backed Vietnam. But this was a transparent justification for siding with China in its regional power rivalry vis-à-vis the Soviet Union.

In the Philippines, even as the nonviolent "people power" resistance to the corrupt dictatorship of Ferdinand Marcos gained the admiration of Democrats and Republicans alike, the White House stubbornly clung to the Kirkpatrick version of the Reagan Doctrine: autocratic dictators loyally allied with the United States in the larger struggle against the Marxist-Leninists needed understanding and support when in political trouble; precisely at such times the U.S. should avoid undermining them by providing either tangible or rhetorical assistance to their domestic opponents. Marcos's fraudulent interference with the 1986 elections (which he allowed to take place only after urgings from Washington) and his refusal to accept his electoral defeat by Corazon Aquino, the widow of the assassinated opposition leader Benigno Aquino, was finally too much for Secretary of State Shultz and other officials. The President's special emissary to Manila, Senator Paul Laxalt, and diplomatic troubleshooter Philip Habib both confirmed the allegations of fraud and urged Reagan to sever the embarrassing association with the corrupt dictator; still Reagan resisted abandoning his friend, with the lame excuse that the election involved "fraud on both sides."[29] Reagan's reluctance was perhaps personal as well as ideological. Lou Canon points out that Marcos, a World War II Medal of Honor winner who concocted legends of his own bravery, had long been a hero to Reagan, who now found it "nearly impossible to adjust to the idea that Marcos had become a corrupt and discredited despot."[30] Only the imminent prospect of a bloody civil war between pro- and anti-Marcos factions of the armed forces pushed Reagan at last to ask Marcos to abandon his dictatorship in exchange for protected exile in Hawaii.[31]

The principal Third World arena for attempting to implement the Reagan Doctrine was in Latin America, specifically the conflicts in El Salvador and Nicaragua. The Latin American policies of the administration are given extended treatment in Chapter 25.

23

THE TENSION BETWEEN FOREIGN AND DOMESTIC IMPERATIVES

He has two religions: free enterprise and God.
—FRANCOIS MITTERRAND ON RONALD REAGAN

One of the most beguiling features of Ronald Reagan's worldview was his faith in the free market economy—beguiling not only his constituency but Reagan himself. Ironically, Reagan was no less an economic determinist than the Marxists in whose atheistic materialism he saw the work of the devil: the free market was the engine of economic development and national and world prosperity, the fairest dispenser of social justice, and the essential precondition for political democracy. Overlooking the early history of U.S. governmental protection and subsidies to its infant industries, Reagan never tired of preaching to Third World countries that they should follow the example of the United States, where a commitment to "the magic of the marketplace" produced rapid and spectacular growth and prosperity.[1]

Supported by the ideas of distinguished economists such as Milton Friedman of the University of Chicago, Reagan claimed that a principal source of the world's social maladies was government policy that distorted the natural economic relationships among supply, demand, and price. Whatever interfered with the freedom of sellers to market their goods and services at the highest profit to themselves and of buyers to make purchases at the lowest prices they could find was both inefficient and unjust. Accordingly, it was counterproductive and morally wrong for government policy to inhibit capital from being invested where otherwise the factors of production (land, natural resources, labor, managerial and entrepreneurial skills, and marketing outlets) were most conducive to the highest output per unit of capital invested. The greatest good for the greatest number of people the world over would flow from the unfettered workings of the free market.

These were self-evident economic (and moral) truths to the core of ideologues in the Reagan administration (not all of the President's aides were true believers) who saw themselves as the vanguard of a policy revolution. But their determination to translate this laissez faire economic philosophy into practice ran up against the aggressive nationalism and special-interest politics that—in addition to the popular clamor for reduced taxes—were responsible for the right-wing Republican revival and the ascendancy of Ronald Reagan. Revealingly, one of the most committed of the true believers—David Stockman, Director of the Office of Management and Budget from 1981 to 1985—titled his memoir on "why the Reagan revolution failed" *The Triumph of Politics*.[2]

Even among the true believers, the Reagan revolution, like most revolutions, had its rival factions. The radical "supply-siders" put their faith in a drastic reduction of taxes, particularly those taxes that inhibited entrepreneurial risk-taking, thought to be the engine of the new economic growth that would generate the revenues needed to balance the federal budget; the supply-side ideologues were willing to accept increased budget deficits (the probable immediate effect of major tax reductions), convinced that these would be only temporary. The more cautious "monetarists" in the Reagan vanguard felt that the movement toward the laissez-faire economy needed to be steered via Federal Reserve Board controls on the money supply and interest rates so as to avoid the wide swings in the unfettered business cycle that once again (as during the 1930s) could produce a backlash against the free market system. The "fiscal conservatives"—in the tradition of anti-welfare state Republicanism from Herbert Hoover to Barry Goldwater—were first and foremost anxious to reduce federal spending.[3]

Where did Ronald Reagan stand on the fractious disputes among those purporting to launch a revolution in his name? His rhetoric, happily for the image of a united Republican party and administration, soared above the fray. However, to the chagrin of administration aides who wanted more precise guidance, so did his own thinking. As put by William Niskanen, member of the Council of Economic Advisers, and for a period its acting chairman:

The primary problem of advising Reagan was his incurable optimism. . . . One important consequence of this optimism was the impossibility of preparing realistic economic and budget forecasts. . . . He wanted all good things to come in a package and was reluctant to signal priorities when there was a trade-off among his objectives.[4]

Reagan's basic economic goals were clear enough, and widely shared throughout his administration: to remove the heavy hand of the federal government off the economy, so that the free market could once again reward those who were most competitively efficient (and not subsidize the inefficient), thereby stimulating product innovation and overall economic growth that would benefit everyone; to induce other countries to follow the example of the U.S., thus giving Americans an even larger market in which to compete and spreading the benefits of the free enterprise system to more of the world's peoples; to bring the federal budget into balance, but without raising taxes; and to reduce corporate and individual income taxes as soon as possible, especially those that discouraged entrepreneurship.

It was up to his subordinates to work out among themselves how all this was to be accomplished and present it to him as a comprehensive program that he, with the aura of the presidency and his great communicative skills, would sell to the country.

Reagan's zealous young budget director, David Stockman, was at first astonished at how his hero ran the administration, but then seized the opportunity to fill the vacuum himself. Reagan "seemed so serene and passive," Stockman recalls,

He conveyed the impression that since we all knew what needed to be done, we should simply get on with the job. Since I *did* know what to do, I took his quiet message of confidence to be a mandate. If the others weren't going to get his administration's act together, I would.[5]

By the end of Reagan's first term, however, Stockman was convinced that the White House had become "a dreamland." Those who had the President's ear and were crafting his optimistic rhetoric were "holding the American economy hostage to a reckless unstable fiscal policy based on the politics of high spending and the doctrine of low taxes." Orwellian doublespeak had been given a new lease on life. "In 1984 we were plainly drifting into unprecedented economic peril," but the "brash phrasemakers of the White House . . . had the audacity to proclaim a golden age of prosperity." And worst of all, the President seemed to actually believe what he was saying.[6]

NATIONAL SECURITY VS. REAGANOMICS

Stockman's disillusionment with the President in the spring and summer of 1981 came to a head in the battle over the defense budget. It was no secret in Washington that Secretary of Defense Caspar Weinberger's announced pledge to increase defense spending at an average real (corrected for inflation) rate of 7 percent annually during the coming five years was a quantitative projection picked out of the air for political reasons, not the product of serious Pentagon studies of essential force requirements. From Stockman's perspective, the Defense Department's initial budget submissions were obviously still soft, containing items that could be cut.

However, Weinberger, Reagan, and Secretary of State Haig were determined to best the outgoing Carter administration's fiscal 1982 request for a 5 percent increase in the defense budget. To maintain the patriotic enthusiasm that was a crucial factor in Reagan's election it was important to appear deadly serious about reversing the relative decline in U.S. military power vis-à-vis the Soviet Union. A dramatic increase over the Carter defense budget was also an essential element of the full court press on the Soviet Union, designed in large part to shock the Kremlin into recognizing that it could not hope to keep up with the United States in the next round of the arms race.[7]

Once he realized that the President would reject any reductions in the defense budget that would undercut this grand strategy, Stockman's fall-back position was to develop a more efficient spending plan to achieve a roughly equal military buildup. But his alternative—projecting a modest cut of only $13 billion in Weinberger's proposal to spend $1.46 trillion over five years—was characterized by the Secretary of Defense as subversive of national security. Stockman was livid at what he regarded as Weinberger's disingenuous debating tactics in front of the President:

The none-too-subtle implication was that anyone proposing even to nick his budget wanted to keep us behind the Russians.

As he droned on, my temperature went above 98.6. If he wanted to question my patriotism, fine; but almost all the red versus blue comparisons on his charts involved weapons categories I wasn't even proposing to change.

.   .   .

His briefing was so intellectually disreputable, so demeaning, that I could hardly bring myself to believe that a Harvard-educated cabinet officer could have brought this to the President of the United States. Did he think the White House was on Sesame Street?[8]

By the end of the first budget-planning cycle, Stockman was convinced that "the President didn't have it in him to overrule his Secretary of Defense."[9] Reagan's typical suggestion that "you fellas get together and see if you can work it out" was merely a wink and a nod to his old crony Weinberger. Barely nine months after the inauguration, the new administration's key official for translating ideology into programs had already reached the point "when I ceased to believe that the Reagan Revolution was possible."[10]

Clearly, however, Secretary of Defense Weinberger was serving the President in stubbornly acting on behalf of the Reagan imperative to stand tall again against the Soviets. Those who thought that the President, simply because he seemed to know more about domestic economics than international relations, would give higher priority to balancing the budget than balancing Soviet power, didn't know their man. In giving the highest priority to the U.S.-Soviet rivalry, Reagan, in the early 1980s, embodied the nation's psychic need to rebound from its withdrawal reactions to the Vietnam fiasco. And other politicians knew this to be the case. Thus, in the 435-member House of Representatives, only fifty-four Democrats and seven Republicans voted against Weinberger's defense appropriations bill of November 1981, and in the 100-member Senate only four Democrats and one Republican voted against it.[11]

Yet, as the deficit grew, the President—while adamantly opposed to reversing his tax-relief policies, let alone imposing new taxes—required at least the political gesture of frugality from all departments, in the sense of eliminating wasteful and unnecessary expenditures. After the 1984 elections, an internal review of the second-term agenda and the fiscal year 1986 budget by the so-called "core group" of Ed Meese, James Baker, Donald Regan, Malcolm Baldrige, David Stockman, Richard Darman, William Niskanen, and Jack Svahn, produced a defense budget proposal that would have led to no Pentagon increases in the coming year and a 3 percent real growth in successive years without any basic change in Weinberger's projected force capabilities. (Weinberger was invited to participate in the deliberations of the "core group" but declined.) Once again, when Weinberger was presented with these recommendations in a Cabinet meeting with the President, he insisted that national security required that the defense budget should be determined only with reference to the Soviet threat and should be exempt from domestic economic considerations. In this setting, Weinberger would again carry the day. Niskanen recounts, for example, how Secretary of the Treasury Donald Regan, who had supported a lower defense budget in the core group, was now "a tower of jelly on this issue in front of the president."[12] Regan, in his memoirs, claims to have been more of a true-blue Reaganite than such accounts suggest, being both a devotee of the strategy of pricing the Soviets out of the arms race and a believer in the supply-side philosophy of stimulating the economy through tax reductions instead of drastic budget cuts (especially in the military).[13]

However, in Ronald Reagan's second term (perhaps even late in his first term, though he would not admit it before the 1984 elections), there appears to have taken place in the President's mind a reassessment of the prospects of pulling off the economic miracle of financing the lavish arms buildup through reduced tax rates. The accumulated deficit was careening off the charts as the gap between government expenditures and revenues continued to widen. In Congress former supporters were abandoning the badly listing supply-side ship and swimming for rescue devices like the Gramm-Rudman mandatory budget-cutting bill. It was more than coincidence that just about this time, and over Weinberger's objections, Reagan began to pursue U.S.–Soviet arms control agreements in earnest. During his last two years in office, and despite his oft-repeated admonitions against trusting the Marxist-Leninists, Reagan was ready to credit Mikhail Gorbachev with a sincere interest in negotiating a truce in the increasingly expensive cold war.

The relationship between national security and economics turned out to be more complex than Reagan had anticipated. The imperatives of his peace through strength policy interfered from the very first with his domestic dream of restoring America's mythical laissez-faire economic system. And the real predicaments of the contemporary American economy led him eventually to embrace the very kind of East–West détente policies for which he had so roundly condemned his predecessors.

THE DOMESTIC BACKLASH AGAINST INTERNATIONAL FREE TRADE

At the outset of the Reagan administration there was a rather solid consensus among the top officials in the Departments of State, Defense, and Treasury, and the National Security Council, supportive of the President's free trade posture. The President and Treasury Secretary Regan were committed to global free trade as one of their articles of faith in the market economy. In addition, Secretaries Haig (and his successor, Shultz) and Weinberger buttressed Reagan's conviction that he was right to resist the rising pressures in Congress to retaliate against the Japanese and Western Europeans for subsidizing their own export sectors while discriminating against U.S. imports: the early argument from State and Defense was that since America's principal competitors in the global market were also its principal allies in the cold war, it was not in the security interest of the United States to play rough with them in the trade and monetary arenas—especially at a time when the U.S. was attempting to persuade its allies to assume a greater burden of the collective defense effort.

But others in the administration more directly responsive to aggrieved domestic interests, notably Secretary of Commerce Malcolm Baldrige and U.S. Trade Representative William Brock, as well as the Secretaries of Agriculture and Labor, argued that it was time to stop babying economically prospering allies, particularly Japan and members of the European Community, who were simultaneously failing to assume their fair share of the common defense burden and preventing Americans from competing freely in their markets. Moreover, unless the administration took the lead in demanding that the allies agree to compete on "a level playing field" in the international economy, Congress was sure to take matters in its own hands with counterproductive protectionist legislation.

President Reagan and other advocates of free trade for a time could feel content that they were taking both the moral and geopolitical high ground in resisting the popular rise of protectionist sentiment. But the free market had its own natural laws—which rhetoric might obscure but which could not be violated without severe consequences.

With the government required to borrow heavily simply to keep functioning, the rates of interest the government had to pay to attract lenders were bound to rise. By raising the value of the dollar in relation to other currencies, foreign goods were made cheaper for American consumers and U.S. goods more expensive for foreigners. The competitive advantage handed to foreigners threatened not only those U.S. industries that produced mainly for the home market, but also those dependent on sales abroad. Declining U.S. exports and rising U.S. imports combined to produce the largest trade deficits in the country's history.

The shock of the conversion during the 1980s of the United States from the world's biggest creditor into the world's biggest debtor nation severely weakened the case within the government against protectionism. Early in Reagan's second term Treasury Secretary Donald Regan and White House chief of staff James Baker switched jobs. At the White House, Donald Regan's ideological predilections were overtaken by his obsession to become the President's right hand man, while at Treasury the politically sophisticated Baker was now in a strategic position to compel the previously feuding Commerce Secretary and U.S. Trade Representative to form a common front with him for bargaining with the Congress.

Starting in mid-1985, under the leadership of the new Secretary of the Treasury, the administration's foreign economic policies took a noticeable turn away from rhetorical absolutism on free trade toward managed relationships with various trading partners in the service of "fair trade"—a euphemism for governmental interventions in the market. An early expression of the new pragmatism was the agreement (engineered by Secretary Baker) among the finance ministers of the United States, Japan, France, West Germany, and the United Kingdom to devalue the dollar. Announced at the Plaza Hotel in New York on September 22, the so-called Plaza Accord committed Japan and the European governments to "some further orderly appreciation of the main nondollar currencies."[14] The five leading industrial countries, by authorizing aggressive central bank intervention in currency exchange markets, were openly legitimizing a significant departure from the laissez-faire philosophy heretofore propounded by the Reagan administration. Although the other members of the Group of Five were not all that pleased with having to increase their own risks of recession in order to relieve the balance-of-trade deficits being borne by the United States, the Plaza accord signalled a healthy step back toward the principal of multilateral accountability in monetary matters that had been at the core of the Bretton Woods system established at the end of World War II.

The September 1985 Plaza accord was welcomed by industry leaders who had been appalled at the Reagan–Regan "America is back!" sloganeering about the "strong" American dollar (the reality was that the high exchange rate of the dollar had given foreign competitors a 30 to 40 percent pricing advantage in the U.S. market). Yet many trade-embattled sectors of the economy regarded the international monetary adjustments as too indirect and uncertain in their effects. From an administration purportedly responsive to business interests they expected a vigorous approach to trade-affecting mechanisms already on the books, and were angry and frustrated that the administration was apparently paralyzed—either by an extreme free trade ideology or bureaucratic infighting, or both—from giving American industries even a fraction of the protection that their competitors were provided by their governments. In frustration, disadvantaged industry groups formed a tacit alliance with organizations representing affected labor to pressure Congress to defend their interests.[15]

Reagan therefore felt compelled to compromise, if not virtually abandon, one of the central commitments of his faith, or else see the control of U.S. trade policy fall almost totally into the hands of Congress. Not that the President had been all that steadfast in his defense of free trade during his first term. But the departures from the path of economic righteousness had been finessed and called something else. Thus, under threat of Congressional action to put a quota on the importation of Japanese autos, the administration let the Japanese government know early in 1981 that it would have no objections to a "voluntary" limit by the Japanese on the amount of cars they shipped to the United States. The quota agreed on was 1.67 million cars per year. By this device, recalls a former Reagan

administration trade negotiator, "the United States was able to maintain the fiction of being a free-trader without having to be one." [16]

At the start of his second term, President Reagan finally admitted
that he had no other alternative, in the face of the surge of protectionist legislation pending in Congress, but to assume a more aggressive posture toward Japan and other countries to get them to abandon
their "unfair" trading practices. The new strategy was reflected in
the President's major speech of September 23, 1985, in which he
reiterated his faith in free and open markets and his opposition to
programs that were "purely protectionist," but went on to argue that:

Above all else, free trade is, by definition, fair trade.

When domestic markets are closed to the exports of others, it is no longer free
trade. When governments subsidize their manufacturers and farmers so that they
can dump their goods in other markets, it is no longer free trade. When governments permit counterfeiting or copying of American products, it is stealing our
future, and it is no longer free trade. When governments assist their exporters in
ways that violate international laws, then the playing field is no longer level, and
there is no longer free trade. When governments subsidize industries for commercial advantage and underwrite costs, placing an unfair burden on competitors, that
is no free trade.

And he warned:

I will not stand by and watch American businesses fail because of unfair trading
practices abroad. I will not stand by and let American workers lose their jobs
because other nations do not play by the rules. [17]

The new get-tough attitude was manifested in high tariffs imposed
by the administration (under existing laws) against Japanese electronic products in response to Japanese "dumping" of semiconduc-
tors; special duties on various Canadian lumber products in response
to Canadian government subsidies to its lumber industry; threats by
administration officials of retaliatory barriers against food imports
from Europe in response to European bans against meat from ani-
mals treated with growth hormones; and threats of tariffs on Brazil-
ian goods in response to Brazil's import restrictions on U.S. computer hardware and software.

By the last year of the Reagan administration—whatever the ostensible reasons—U.S. trade policy had taken a decided protectionist
turn: 35 percent of the goods produced in the United States (as
compared to 20 percent at the start of Reagan's presidency) were
helped to compete against foreign goods by U.S. government-imposed

import barriers and duties and by "voluntary" controls by foreign governments on their own exporters following strong pressure from Washington.[18]

Neither America's trading partners nor many economists were persuaded by the administration's excuse that the new protectionism was being forced upon it by the unfair trading practices of others. The major culprits, in fact, were the huge federal deficit and the heavy allocation of the country's innovative energies into defense research and development. The deficit, because of its effects on interest rates and the value of the dollar, was making many U.S. goods more expensive than their foreign counterparts. Meanwhile, the federal government was sucking investments into elaborate military research and development projects through all manner of subsidies favoring U.S. industries, while (being ideologically averse to an "industrial policy") government spending on commercial research and development was in drastic decline, as were public outlays for upgrading the country's deteriorating transportation infrastructure. Also consequential for any prospect of recovery of basic American competitiveness was the constriction in federal funding of higher education.

The Japanese and the West Europeans, less constrained by ideological aversions to public spending in order to enhance the competitiveness of industries involved in international commerce, were thus handed a substantial trading advantage by the Reaganites. All too obviously there was hypocrisy or self delusion (or both) in complaints from Washington that the Japanese and West Europeans were violating the moral norms of the free enterprise system; for the standing U.S. industrial policy—conducted largely under the rubric of national security—was persisted in and enlarged upon by the Reagan administration. Administered by the Pentagon and its sister agencies, America's high technology industrial policy had become such a staple of the country's economic life that Reagan and other laissez faire ideologues were apparently able to delude themselves that it was not the highly intrusive complex of subsidies that it was. But, unlike the industrial policies of the Japanese and West Europeans, the U.S. policy did not produce innovative technologies that were sufficiently convertible into products that could compete effectively in consumer-goods markets.[19]

Although America's economic rivals complained about the new

protectionism, they were hardly disappointed by the opportunity
provided by the U.S. compulsion to allocate its own resources—as
well as award contracts to foreign firms—in illusory high tech military projects (including SDI). Yet thoughtful foreigners were increasingly concerned about the implications for the United States
and international stability; as put by the British strategist and historian Michael Howard,

There is little comfort in a situation where the economy is in ruins but defenses
remain intact. . . . The absence of prudent management that resulted in the United
States becoming a debtor nation on a Third World scale, and the inability of the
American leadership to tackle the problem when the crisis made further prevarica-
tion impossible, did more to destroy European confidence in American leadership
even than the Reykjavik summit or the Iran-contra affair.[20]

Rather than negotiating from strength, the Reagan administration,
in the international economic sphere, found itself—with increasing
embarrassment—negotiating from weakness. In the decades of U.S.
economic hegemony, American administrations could be credibly
committed to free trade as serving the national interest, both in the
long term and the short term. But now, as revealed in the President's
slide into the rhetoric of "fair trade" (which, not incidentally, was
artfully applied to the "free trade" agreement with Canada), and
despite the continued insistence by U.S. economic policy makers
that all they wanted was an international "level playing field," the
White House copies of Adam Smith and Ricardo became, like the
Bible, a source of homilies to be quoted in Sunday sermons to assuage
the guilt of workday actions.

24

MIDDLE EASTERN COMPLEXITIES: THE ARAB–ISRAELI CONFLICT, TERRORISM, AND ARMS FOR HOSTAGES

As every president since World War II has learned, no region of the world presents America with more difficult, more frustrating, or more convoluted problems than the Middle East.

—RONALD REAGAN

The Middle East, a crucial theater of great power rivalry throughout history, was high on the Reagan administration's list of arenas in which to stand tall against the Soviets. In the eyes of the Reaganites, the nations of the region were needlessly dissipating their energies in communal conflicts, diverting their attention from the mammoth imperialist beyond the mountains who posed a potentially fatal threat to all of their various ways of life as well as to the petroleum lifelines of the industrialized West and Japan. Here in particular it was imperative to forge the "consensus of strategic concerns" that Secretary of State Haig was insisting on, to reverse the potentially disastrous shift in the balance of power resulting from the defection of Iran from the anti-Communist coalition and the occupation of Afghanistan by Soviet troops—both of which, according to the Reaganites, had been brought on by the Carter administration's distortion of priorities and indecisiveness.

The traditional Anglo–American geopolitical thinkers whom Alexander Haig studied at West Point had warned against allowing a would-be Eurasian "heartland" hegemon to establish a position of dominance on the Near Eastern "rimland," for this would allow the Eurasian imperialist to interdict the oceanic powers' lines of global navigation for essential commerce and military operations. A heartland power that also controlled the rimland could rule the world. Yet this was exactly what loomed ahead unless the United States urgently took up the challenge of reconstituting a vigilant coalition of states in the region to counter the growing Soviet presence.

Secure access to and transit through the rimland had been a key strategic premise of virtually all U.S. national security officials since the 1940s: George Marshall, Dean Acheson, George Kennan, Paul Nitze, John Foster Dulles, President Eisenhower, Dean Rusk, McGeorge Bundy, Walt Rostow, Henry Kissinger, and Zbigniew Brzezinski. The problem (from the perspective of the Reagan grand strategists) was that in recent years softer notions—most disastrously, Carter's vision of a human rights based world order supplanting the balance of power—had increasingly emasculated U.S. foreign policy. The Carter Doctrine reaction to the Soviet invasion of Afghanistan had been a too-little, too-late response to a too-narrowly defined threat from the Marxist-Leninist enemy.

Reagan, Weinberger, Haig and their principal foreign policy aides were all agreed that the Soviets and their friends were up to no good in the Middle East. The geopolitical understanding of the stakes in the region reflected in the Truman Doctrine had to be restored. The Reagan cold warriors apparently believed that it was both vital and politically feasible for the non-communist countries of the Middle East to subordinate their internecine conflicts—Muslim vs. Jew, Shiite vs. Suni, Arab vs. Persian, Palestinian vs. Hashemite, radical socialist vs. monarchist, current-demand oil producers vs. supply-conservation producers—to the imperative of containing Soviet expansion.

In his memoirs, Haig attempts to refute allegations that the administration's concept was a geostrategic abstraction distant from the vital concerns of the peoples of the region. "There was, in a real rather than a theoretical sense, a strategic consensus in the region," he insists.

This had nothing to do with American phrase making or with an American tendency to turn the Middle East into a theater for East–West confrontation. Three great fears ran through the region: fear of terrorism, which was endemic; fear of Islamic fundamentalism, which had broken out in Iran in fanatical form; and fear of the Soviet Union.

Yet in the next breath he again subordinates all of this to the singular overriding threat:

In reality, this was one consolidated fear: that terrorism and fundamentalism so destabilize the region that the Soviets would either subvert the Islamic movement for their own purposes or seize control of Iran and possibly the whole gulf in a second revolution after the Iranian revolution collapsed under the political and economic weight of its own excesses.[1]

The strategic consensus approach would impel the anti-Communist governments of the area to focus on what united them rather than what divided them; presumably, when they did, each would rediscover that its natural geopolitical inclination was aligned with the United States.

ISRAEL'S RAID ON IRAQ'S NUCLEAR REACTOR

The fact that those who were expected to adhere to the strategic consensus had their own very different priorities, and would be highly resistant to joining in a revived cold war coalition, flashed dramatically on Ronald Reagan's global viewing screen on June 7, 1981 as the Israeli Air Force, using American F-15 and F-16 combat aircraft, destroyed the Osirak nuclear reactor the Iraqis were constructing ten miles from Baghdad. Washington was neither consulted nor informed in advance of the raid, and questions were immediately raised in Congress concerning Israel's apparent violation of the law prohibiting the offensive use of U.S. arms transferred to other countries without the express consent of the United States government.

While many U.S. officials privately appreciated Prime Minister Menachem Begin's rationale for ordering the raid—the reactor could have given Iraq a usable nuclear weapons capability within five years and destroying it before it was "hot" removed the risk of lethal radioactive fallout—the Reagan administration was placed in the awkward position of having to mollify both outraged Arab governments and angry members of Congress. UN Ambassador Jeane Kirkpatrick maneuvered to have the Security Council pass a resolution strongly condemning Israel but without provisions for sanctions. The administration suspended delivery of four F-16s about to be shipped to Israel. President Reagan publicly expressed strong displeasure with Israel's unilateral use of force but also granted that "Israel had reason for concern in light of the past history of Iraq."[2]

The Israeli attack also made it extremely difficult for the administration to insulate its arms transfer policies to the region (meant to be directed almost exclusively against the Soviet threat, not as a means of maintaining a local military balance) from the Arab–Israeli conflict. Saudi Arabia openly justified its arrangement for advanced U.S. military surveillance aircraft as dictated by the need to warn its Arab friends of Israeli attacks. And the Israelis used such Arab statements to buttress their case against the Reagan administration's policy of increasing the flow of arms to Saudi Arabia and other "moderate" Arab countries.

BOMBING THE PLO IN DOWNTOWN BEIRUT: HARBINGER OF THINGS TO COME

On July 17, 1981, the day the Reagan administration was to announce the resumption of the F-16 shipments to Israel, the Israelis again unleashed their air force unilaterally in a brutal attack on Palestinian Liberation Organization (PLO) headquarters in downtown Beirut, reportedly killing more than 300 people and wounding more than 800. Again, although there may have been some appreciation in the Reagan administration of the Israeli motive and strategy (the Begin government was retaliating against increasing PLO rocket and artillery attacks across the border on villages in northern Israel and signaling that Israel would no longer allow the PLO sanctuary in Lebanon), Washington's official reaction was one of shock and condemnation.

Many strong supporters of Israel in Congress openly warned of the erosion of popular support for Israel. Secretary Weinberger was quick to brand the Beirut raid as immoderate; and Deputy Secretary of State William Clark, reflecting Haig's worries, stated that such actions by the Begin government were "making it difficult for us to help Israel."[3]

Not only did the administration not resume delivery of the four F-

16s held back in June, but it now put on hold ten more F-16s previously scheduled to have been delivered to Israel in the summer. Meant to put Israel on notice that the United States would not countenance any additional unilateral moves of this sort, these "punishments" by Washington only convinced Begin that Israel would have to take matters into its own hands and present the world with a fait accompli if it was ever to remove the PLO threat to its northern borders.

AWACS AND ALL THAT

Arms proffered, arms withheld—if you love me, send me arms. The Reagan administration, like its predecessors, became ensnared in the game of international courtship in the contemporary Middle East. Naively, Haig, Weinberger, and Reagan expected the recipients of U.S. arms to be monogamous (love us, keep away from the Soviet Union) while the U.S. remained free to develop "special relationships" with various attractive Middle Eastern partners. It was quite some time before Reagan understood why everyone was so resentful while he was trying to be so nice. Part of the problem was that early in his administration, he had emerged from heavy arms negotiations with the supposedly aloof Saudi Arabians under the impression that he had "scored"—a view not shared in the Middle Eastern bazaars.

That Reagan should become involved in an arms courtship of Saudi Arabia was understandable. The Khomeini revolution, which took Iran out of the U.S.-led Mideast coalition, left only two reliable anti-Soviet Islamic pillars in the region: Saudi Arabia and Egypt. The oil-rich sheikdom was much weaker militarily than Iran (which was now the center of the Shiite fundamentalist threat to the conservative theocracy of Riyadh) or than either of the Soviet Union's principal Middle Eastern clients, Iraq and Syria. The Saudis' military capabilities needed to be significantly strengthened for the country to play its new and larger role in the regional balance of power. Accordingly, the Reagan administration requested congressional approval of sales of Sidewinder air-to-air missiles and refueling equipment to enhance the combat effectiveness of the sixty F-15 fighter aircraft the Saudis had bought in 1978. The Israeli government was opposed, but Secretary of State Haig was convinced that in his forthcoming trip to the Middle East to champion the new strategic consensus he could persuade Jerusalem to acquiesce—particularly if he carried an offer to sell the Israeli Defense Forces forty additional improved F-15s (Israel already owned twenty-five) and a promise to increase U.S. grant aid to Israel to help finance the purchases.

Israel and its supporters in the Congress might have accepted the F-15 bargain were it not for the April 3, 1981 announcement that the Reagan administration also intended to sell five Airborne Warning and Control System (AWACS) aircraft to the Saudis. Preliminary negotiations on the AWACS deal had begun in the latter days of the Carter administration. Saudi expectations of being able to buy these top-of-the-line reconnaissance/combat control systems— ostensibly needed to protect Saudi oil fields from Iranian air attack— could not be denied without engendering Arab suspicions that, beneath the surface of even-handedness, Reagan and Haig were in reality more pro-Israel than their predecessors. For their part, the Israelis were alarmed not only at the military implications of an Arab AWACS capability (which could reduce Israel's prime advantage of being able to control the airspace in another Arab–Israeli war), but also at the ominous implication that the Reagan administration's obsession with countering the Soviets in the Middle East could translate into a decided tilt by official Washington toward the Arab side in the Arab–Israeli conflict generally.

By the summer of 1981, Israel's supporters in the Democratic-controlled House of Representatives had mobilized a majority against the Saudi possession of AWACS, but Reagan was depending on the Senate, where the Republicans had a slim majority, to sustain his policy. (Under the governing Arms Export Control Act, the executive was authorized to make such weapons transfers to friendly countries as long as Congress, by concurrent resolution, did not explicitly block a proposed sale; thus, if one house defeated the negative resolution, the administration could consummate the AWACS deal.)[4]

The President, recovering from his gunshot wound and basking in the enhanced aura of toughness this gave him, was ready to make the AWACS sale a high-stakes issue worthy of engaging the prestige of the presidency. In his autobiography, Reagan recounts his feelings and determination:

Unfortunately, . . . Israel and some of its supporters in Congress . . . chose to take on the administration over the AWACS sale and created a donnybrook in Congress that we could not afford to lose. I believed it was a battle that *had* to be won to advance the cause of peace in the Middle East. I also knew that if we lost on AWACS, it might undermine our ability to persuade Congress to approve our domestic programs and the rearmament of the Pentagon.[5]

The President's ire was raised further by the behavior of Israeli Prime Minister Menahem Begin during his visit to Washington early in September. In their White House meeting Reagan said that the United States was as ever committed to Israel's survival and would do nothing to reduce its military superiority over the Arabs. The Pentagon had given its assurances, he told Begin, that the AWACS would not alter the Arab–Israeli military balance. At the end of the day's meetings and ceremonies Reagan contentedly recorded in his diary that his assertive Israeli guest had "mellowed." But Reagan was subsequently told that Begin, upon leaving the White House, went to Capitol Hill to actively lobby against the AWACS sale. Reagan took it as a personal affront: "after he told me he wouldn't do that. . . . I felt he'd broken his word and I was angry about it."[6]

The assassination of Egyptian President Anwar Sadat on October 6, 1981 was invoked by both sides in the AWACS debate. The administration contended that now, more than ever, with the future of Egypt highly uncertain, it was crucial that the United States solidify its ties with moderate Saudi Arabia. Critics of the Saudi arms deal countered that Sadat's murder demonstrated the instability of all regimes in the Arab Middle East and the danger of relying on any of them to provide durable links in the containment chain around the Soviet Union.

Reagan recalls that in his efforts to beat back congressional opposition to his decision to sell AWACS to the Saudis, he "experienced one of the toughest battles of my eight years in Washington. . . . I spent more time in one-on-one meetings and on the telephone attempting to win on this measure than on any other."[7] The Saudis didn't make the President's job any easier when one of their spokesmen in Riyadh admitted that, as far as they were concerned, their principal opponent was Israel, not the Soviets.

In response to reports from Senate Majority Leader Howard Baker that the vote was too close to call, the administration pressured the Saudi government to agree to a list of stringent restrictions on how the AWACS would be used. Reagan's five-page letter detailing these stipulations stated that the Saudis had agreed that their AWACS would be operated solely within Saudi Arabian air space except with the prior, explicit mutual consent of the two governments and solely for defensive purposes as defined by the U.S. With these assurances in hand, on October 28 the Senate narrowly defeated (by a 52–48 vote) the resolution to block the sale.

THE MEMORANDUM OF UNDERSTANDING

Secretary Haig and President Reagan tried to limit the damage to U.S.–Israeli relations from the AWACS controversy by responding positively to Begin's desire for a comprehensive agreement of strategic cooperation, just short of a formal military alliance, to solidify the special Washington–Jerusalem relationship against the erosive trends now evident. But the Memorandum of Understanding signed without fanfare in Washington at the end of November 1981 by Israel's Minister of Defense, Ariel Sharon, and Secretary of Defense Weinberger (who never liked the idea, and successfully watered it down) turned out to be more of an embarrassment to the Begin government than an asset.

Not only did the memorandum fail to provide many of the tangible arrangements the Israelis wanted—most important, a prepositioning of U.S. military equipment at Israeli bases to assure U.S. dependence on Israeli cooperation in a future crisis—but its core commitments clearly favored U.S. priorities. The document obligated both governments to cooperate in meeting threats in the Middle East "caused by the Soviet Union or Soviet-controlled forces from outside the region," but it did not commit the United States to help Israel defend itself against attack by its Arab enemies.[8]

Israel's Annexation of the Golan Heights

The differences between Washington and Jerusalem were exposed once again as the Begin government moved in December 1981, without consulting the United States, to extend Israeli civil law to the Golan Heights—the strategic high ground between Israel and Syria that the Israelis had captured in 1967. The Reagan administration charged this was inconsistent with the memorandum of strategic understanding and suspended implementation of the terms of the memorandum. In turn, Begin gave the U.S. Ambassador to Israel a vitriolic lecture against efforts by the United States to treat Israel like a "vassal state."[9]

Eight months before the June 1982 Israeli invasion of Lebanon, at the funeral of Egypt's Anwar Sadat, Prime Minister Begin had informed Secretary Haig of the plan under consideration in the Israeli cabinet to take control of a swath of Lebanon up to 40 kilometers (25 miles) beyond the Israeli border. The ostensible purpose of the military operation was to push PLO artillery and rockets out of range of settlements in northern Israel. Haig, known for blunt speaking, did not unequivocally object. Instead, he told Begin, "If you move, you move alone." And in a remark that Begin chose to interpret as a qualified endorsement, Haig added: "Unless there is a major, internationally recognized provocation, the United States will not support such an action"; moreover, the Israeli military response would have to be "strictly proportional" to the provocation.[10]

In the months following, the Begin government kept probing for how the U.S. government would react if operation "Peace for Galilee" were carried out, and each time it received the same studiously ambiguous reply. Even when the director of Israeli military intelligence informed Haig on February 3, 1982 of the larger dimensions of the Lebanon invasion plan, which included a drive to Beirut, Haig reiterated the now standard U.S. formula.

The final failure of communication—inadvertent or deliberate—took place in a conversation between Haig and Defense Minister Sharon in Washington late in May. Sharon had just outlined the more ambitious version of Israel's planned Lebanon operation, shocking a roomful of State Department officials. As Haig recounts in his memoirs:

after the meeting, so that there could be no question that I was playing to an audience, I invited Sharon into my office and told him privately what I had repeated to him and Begin and their colleagues many times before: unless there was an internationally recognized provocation, and unless Israeli retaliation was proportionate to any such provocation, an attack by Israel into Lebanon would have a devastating effect in the United States. "No one," Sharon replied, in his truculent way, "has the right to tell Israel what decision it should take in defense of its people."[11]

In this crucial face-to-face encounter the U.S. Secretary of State apparently let the Israeli Defense Minister have the last word.

Begin and Sharon were handed the "provocation" they required on June 3, 1982, when a Palestinian terrorist group acting on its own, not on behalf of the PLO, shot and gravely wounded the Israeli Ambassador to Britain on a London street. Three days later the Israeli Defense Forces invaded Lebanon as Begin invoked the right of self defense in Article 51 of the UN Charter and compared the operation to the British military action in the Falkland Islands, then underway with the tacit support of the United States. Even as Israeli paratroopers were landing on the coast well above the 40 kilometer line and beginning to advance north toward Beirut, Begin publicly (and in a personal letter to President Reagan) defined the operation as being only for the purpose of clearing out the PLO contingents in southern Lebanon which had been attacking the Israeli settlements in the Galilee.

In fact, the Israeli move into Lebanon was nothing less than the full assault Sharon had described to Haig and his staff. By June 13 the Israelis had surrounded and laid siege to the Lebanese capital, bombarding the western sections of the city and demanding the surrender of the PLO headquarters there. Meanwhile, despite Israeli assurances to Syria via the United States and other diplomatic channels that its forces would not attack Syrian military units in Lebanon unless the Syrians attacked the Israelis, there were intense ground and air battles between Israeli and Syrian forces in the Bekaa valley. In this Bekaa valley war, which raged for several weeks punctuated by temporary cease-fires, the Israelis trounced the Syrians, to the great embarrassment of the Soviet Union, which had supplied Syria with most of its military equipment.

The White House was shaken by its inability to anticipate, let alone control, events in the Middle East. An intense battle for the mind of the President ensued over how to deal with Begin and Sharon. Most of Reagan's foreign policy advisers, including Secretary of Defense Weinberger, national security adviser Clark, CIA Director Casey, and Vice President Bush, wanted to discipline Israel; they favored support for UN resolutions condemning the Israeli invasion and they urged Reagan himself to demand Israel's unconditional withdrawal. On the other side, standing virtually alone, was Secretary of State Haig, who saw the new situation as a "great opportunity to make peace." Haig's "strategic plan," as he called it, was to exploit the Israeli military stranglehold on Beirut to negotiate a removal from Lebanon of the PLO and all other foreign forces—namely, the Syrian and Israeli armies—and to restore the country to the Lebanese under international guarantees and protection. Henry Kissinger's protegé, sensing his chance to emulate the great diplomatic impresario, was convinced that "if we acted quickly and with a sure hand, the United States could achieve all this." Moreover, "such a moment might never come again if it was not seized."[12]

Haig was working through special envoy Philip Habib to effectuate PLO, Israeli, and Syrian agreement to a mutual withdrawal at the same time that Caspar Weinberger, Vice President Bush, and deputy national security adviser Robert McFarlane were assuring the Saudis and other Arabs that Israel would not be allowed to get away with its aggression. Haig was livid at the Weinberger faction for undercutting his diplomatic démarche, but his anger only isolated him from the President, who hated to deal with infighting among his subordinates. Frustrated by his failure to obtain the trust and support necessary, he believed, to his effectiveness as Secretary of State, Haig resigned on June 25, 1982, leaving the seasoned negotiator and Middle East expert Philip Habib in effective control of U.S. Lebanese diplomacy while the new Secretary of State, George Shultz, settled into his job.

The U.S. efforts at mediation during the summer of 1982 eventually bore fruit, but not before Israeli armored units entered West Beirut in force on August 4. Over the next two weeks, with the Israelis intensifying their air and ground military operations in and around Beirut, Habib hammered out an agreement among the various governments and parties providing for the immediate evacuation of PLO forces from Lebanon and their relocation in neighboring Arab countries simultaneously with the withdrawal of Israeli and Syrian forces from Beirut and an agreement in principle to free Lebanon from all foreign military intervention. The PLO evacuation was to be monitored by a multinational peacekeeping force not under UN control (at Israel's insistence), composed of troops from France, Italy, and the United States.

Secretary of Defense Weinberger and Chairman of the Joint Chiefs of Staff John Vesey argued against U.S. participation in the multinational force (MNF), but they were overruled by the President who, increasingly unhappy at the carnage in Beirut, now became a visible player in the unfolding drama. After a particularly devastating series of military assaults by the Israelis into West Beirut culminated in an eleven-hour aerial bombardment on August 12, Reagan was photographed delivering a telephone reprimand to Begin, demanding an end to the attacks. Begin called back in a few minutes to tell the President that he had ordered a stop to the bombings. Michael Deaver reports the President's surprise at the Israeli Prime Minister's acquiescence. "I didn't know I had that kind of power," said Reagan.[13] The President's willingness to publicly criticize the Israeli escalation gave Ambassador Habib the added leverage he needed to gain Syrian, PLO, and Israeli adherence to his plan for a mutual withdrawal from Beirut under MNF supervision.[14]

The President enthusiastically supported U.S. participation in the MNF operation. Eight hundred U.S. Marines came ashore on August 25, 1982 to join the contingents from Italy and France. In a little over a week the PLO, including Yasir Arafat, were out of Beirut and on their way to neighboring Arab countries willing to host them.

Ambassador Habib and Secretary of State George Shultz thought the Marines should stay on to help stabilize the situation and to oversee the full Israeli and Syrian withdrawals from the country. However, Weinberger and Vesey prevailed on Reagan: mission accomplished, quick in, quick out, no mess, plus new prestige for a job well done. Less than three weeks after landing the Marines were back on their ships. France and Italy also decided to pull out their MNF contingents.

Secretary Shultz didn't weigh in as heavily as he might have against such a quick withdrawal of the Marines from Lebanon. New to the job, he was seized with the idea of turning his own intense orientation in Middle Eastern politics and Reagan's new-found willingness to focus on the issues into an all-out presidential effort to bring peace to the region. The result was the President's surprise September 1, 1982 speech on the Middle East. The Reagan plan was fanfared in a well-orchestrated White House and State Department media blitz. In content it did little more than reiterate the moribund Camp David formula for bringing "autonomy" but not statehood to the Palestinian inhabitants of the West Bank and Gaza Strip.[15]

Reagan had hoped that with the departure of the Marines from Lebanon he could leave the tangled politics and diplomacy of that country to underlings while he concentrated on grand strategy. But no sooner had the Marines left than chaos broke out. On September 14 Lebanon's Christian president-elect, Bahir Gamayel, was assassinated. The Israeli military immediately moved back into Beirut with the declared mission of preventing a new cycle of violence in the city, while Gamayel's Christian paramilitary Phalange went on a retributive rampage of Palestinian refugee camps. On the might of September 16 the Phalange massacred more than 700 unarmed Palestinians at the Sabra and Shatila camps. Neither the Israelis nor the Italians, whose forces had not yet been withdrawn, did anything to stop the slaughter.

National security adviser William Clark and his principal deputy Robert McFarlane urged Reagan to send a larger U.S. force back to Lebanon, again as part of a multinational operation, to restore order and to effect the full withdrawal of Israel and Syria. Secretary of Defense Weinberger and General Vesey again opposed what Weinberger criticized as a "passionate desire to use our military." The new MNF would not have a mission that could be defined, he argued, and its "objectives were stated in the fuzziest possible terms." The Joint Chiefs complained that it would be very difficult to determine the proper size and weaponry and rules of engagement for such a force.[16] But once again the President was persuaded that a visible U.S. presence could be a crucial stabilizing element. Exactly what the defined mission of the U.S. forces was to be—nobody told him, nor did he ask.

"After the decision was made to go back in," General Vesey recalls, "then we debated this business of what are we going to do."[17] No matter: by the end of September 1982, only two weeks after their previous departure, an augmented U.S. Marine contingent numbering 1,200 rejoined their French and Italian counterparts in a reconstituted MNF deployed in the outskirts of Beirut. Over the next year, as the number of U.S. Marines grew to 1,800, this presumedly neutral presence was transmuted in the eyes of many of the Muslim factions in the civil conflict into the status of allies of the Christian government and, therefore, appropriate targets of attack.

The Shiites escalated their holy war against the United States on April 18, 1983 with a truck-bomb attack on the U.S. Embassy that killed more than fifty-seven (seventeen of whom were U.S. citizens). To Weinberger and the military brass in the Pentagon it was beginning to look like Vietnam all over again. By the end of June the

Marines were conducting joint patrols with the Lebanese Armed Forces. Vulnerable to snipers and grenade attacks, the Marines began to carry loaded weapons on patrol. These visible changes in behavior by the Marines further confirmed the view that the United States was a party to the civil war. Yet the Marines remained constrained by their formally defined mission as a neutral presence from engaging in active perimeter defense operations which were now becoming essential to their self-defense.

Weinberger intensified his arguments for removing the Marines from Lebanon or at a minimum to remove them from the line of fire by redeploying them on Navy ships 500 yards offshore. His memoirs recount his anguish at not being able to covert the President to his belief that "we were totally unable to accomplish anything with this second Multinational Force" because it had been "sized and structured" to serve "only as an interposition force, as a buffer between withdrawing armies," not to perform the other actions they were being drawn into. "I urged that our Marines were in a position of increasing vulnerability as they sat, in effect, in the middle of a target, unable to do what was required to protect any occupied position." Again, Weinberger found himself on the wrong side of Reagan's sensibilities:

The arguments raged back and forth, with the President always being concerned about how it would look to the rest of the world if the MNF were removed. The State Department and the NSC played to that worry of the President's by telling him that it would always appear that we had "cut and run," that we had been "driven out," and similar phrases designed to encourage the belief that only if we stayed in Lebanon could we demonstrate our manhood.[18]

At the end of the summer of 1983, reacting to increasing incidents of U.S. units coming under fire, including an artillery attack from Druze Muslim forces that killed two Marines, members of Congress attempted to invoke provisions of the 1973 War Powers Resolution. A legacy of the Vietnam War, the War Powers Resolution established a ninety-day limit on any foreign commitment of U.S. combat troops by the President without explicit congressional authorization. The administration resisted such a limitation on its flexibility, arguing that the Marines were not combat troops but part of an international peacekeeping operation; that the War Powers Resolution was an unconstitutional infringement on the separation of powers (an argument made by previous administrations); and that any such establishment of a time limit on the U.S. participation in the MNF would undercut the restoration of the political independence and territorial integrity of Lebanon. The administration and the congressional leadership worked out a compromise resolution endorsing the Marine deployment in Lebanon but mandating their withdrawal after eighteen months. The resolution explicitly invoked the War Powers Resolution, but when President Reagan signed it on October 12, 1983 he stated in writing that he did not recognize the constitutionality of the 1973 act and that as Commander in Chief he retained full constitutional authority to deploy U.S. forces.[19]

Just eleven days later, the worst fears of Weinberger, Vesey, and many congressional opponents of the Marine deployment were realized. Early Sunday morning, October 23, 1983, a terrorist driving a Mercedes Benz stakebed truck accelerated through the public parking lot south of the U.S. Marine compound at the Beirut International Airport. The truck drove over a barbed- and concertina-wire obstacle and passed between two Marine guard posts. Speeding toward the headquarters and sleeping quarters of the Battalion Landing Team, the vehicle flattened the guard booth at the building's entrance and penetrated into the central lobby where it detonated with the force of 12,000 pounds of TNT. The building collapsed, killing 241 U.S. military personnel and wounding over 100.[20]

The high-flying abstractions of the strategic consensus bore no correspondence to the deceptive and treacherous realities of Middle Eastern politics. Drawn in by the romantic illusion that the temporary presence of an honest American sheriff would assure a stable self-determined Lebanese order (thereby enhancing both Israeli security and the containment of communism), the White House was now faced with the avoidable massacre at the Beirut airport.

The bombing of the Marine barracks in Beirut, Reagan recalls, produced "the lowest of the low" points of his presidency, "perhaps the saddest day of my life."[21] But in the manner of a fast-paced Hollywood adventure movie, before the end of the week, while the full story of the Beirut disaster was being absorbed by the American public, Reagan was able to present the nation with a dramatic catharsis in the form of the swift and apparently efficiently executed Marine invasion of Grenada (see Chapter 25)—"one of the highest of the high points of my eight years in the presidency."[22]

Reagan used a speech in which he conflated the pushover intervention in Grenada with the futile sacrifice of American lives in Lebanon to extract from these events a grander meaning than either warranted in any realistic geostrategic calculus. In a televised address from the Oval Office on October 27, 1983, the President told the nation that the "events in Lebanon and Grenada, though oceans apart," were "closely related." Not only had "Moscow assisted and encouraged violence in both countries," but the Kremlin had provided "direct support through a network of surrogates and terrorists." The U.S. interventions in both countries were thus necessary to prevent the ultimate incorporation of the Middle East and Central America into the Soviet bloc.[23]

Having staked out his position with heroic oratory, Reagan became impervious to the logic of extracting the remaining U.S. forces from Lebanon, despite the virtual consensus among his national security advisers (Shultz was still a holdout) behind Weinberger's proposal that the Marines be redeployed to their ships and despite growing bipartisan pressure for their withdrawal in Congress.

The case for withdrawal was strengthened at the end of the year by the release of the findings of a special Department of Defense commission on the Beirut Airport fiasco. The presidentially ordered investigation laid part of the blame on inadequate security at the Marine headquarters in the airport. But the commission's most damning indictments were directed at the highest policy levels of the administration:

The Commission concludes that U.S. decisions as regards Lebanon taken over the past fifteen months have been, to a large degree, characterized by an emphasis on military options and the expansion of the U.S. military role, notwithstanding the fact that the conditions upon which the security of the USMNF were based continued to deteriorate as progress toward a diplomatic solution slowed. The Commission further concludes that these decisions may have been taken without clear recognition that these initial conditions had dramatically changed and that the expansion of our military involvement in Lebanon greatly increased the risk to, and adversely impacted upon the security of, the USMNF.[24]

These findings further raised Congressional and public anxieties about the sacrifice of American lives in the confused Lebanese civil conflict. By appealing to Reagan's growing frustration with the failure of Shultz's diplomatic initiatives, the Secretary of Defense and the Chairman of the Joint Chiefs finally, in early February 1984, were able to obtain presidential authorization to get the Marines out of Lebanon.

The White House did not talk of "withdrawal" but emphasized the "redeployment" of the Marines to their ships offshore, coupled with vague threats of new military steps if the situation warranted. During the week that the decision was publicly announced, Reagan was on a Western speaking and vacation trip. Usually accessible on such trips, the President was kept away from reporters.[25]

But there was no way to avoid the negative outcome. The final withdrawal of U.S. forces from Lebanon, followed by the withdrawal of the French and Italian contingents of the MNF, left Lebanon in greater communal turmoil than ever. Even the Israelis abandoned their strategy of attempting to directly affect the political-military balance of power in the country as a whole and returned to their more limited objective of making sure that southern Lebanon could not be used as a base for attacks against Israel.

There were surely no gains to the people of Lebanon from the failed U.S. foray into their country. The only beneficiary was Soviet client Syria, which augmented its military deployments while persisting in Machiavellian maneuvers to divide and dominate the feuding Lebanese. The Reagan administration was saved from a major cold war loss in Lebanon by the fact that the Soviets were no more successful in forging their own strategic consensus among their fiercely nationalistic Middle Eastern clients and would-be clients— many of whom (Syria, Iraq, Iran, and the PLO) were as determined to dominate one another as they were to counter Israeli power. The Soviets could not identify themselves too closely with Syrian ambitions in still ungovernable Lebanon without alienating the others in Moscow's fragile sphere of influence in the region.

During Reagan's second term, with the development of his symbiotic relationship with Mikhail Gorbachev, the U.S. and Soviet governments began to explore the possibility of a bilateral "strategic consensus" (though never calling it that) to bring order to Lebanon. This was hardly the result of the success of either superpower's assertive policy, but rather the beginning of an accommodation to the reality that they both were being manipulated in embarrassing and potentially dangerous ways by their respective Middle Eastern clients.

TAKING OFF AFTER THE TERRORISTS

The popular discontent with the Carter administration's careful, almost respectful, dealings with the captors of the U.S. embassy personnel in Teheran had been fanned and exploited by Ronald Reagan on his way to the White House. And he did nothing to discourage the journalistic speculation that the coincidence of his inauguration with the release of the 52 U.S. officials the Iranians had held hostage for 444 days was due to the Iranian regime's fear that he would have dealt harshly with Iran if the hostages were still in captivity when he assumed the presidency. Reagan had intoned at a White House lawn celebration of the hostages' return that never again, certainly not during his presidency, would the United States allow itself to be humbled by terrorists: "Let terrorists beware that when the rules of international behavior are violated, our policy will be one of swift and effective retribution."[26]

Reagan's newly installed Secretary of State was also ready to make the war on terrorism one of his central charges. Himself a target of an assassination attempt in 1978 while serving as NATO Supreme Commander, Alexander Haig brought a special animus, bordering on an obsession, to the new administration's determination to go after international terrorists. Whereas the Carter administration had made human rights a centerpiece of its foreign policy, the Reagan–Haig foreign policy would make the war on terrorism one of its highest priorities. As Haig explained in his first press conference as Secretary, "International terrorism will take the place of human rights in our concern because it is the ultimate abuse of human rights."[27]

Haig claimed that the government's intelligence on the terrorist threat demonstrated conclusively that the Soviet Union was the principal sponsor of international terrorist activity. "They [the Soviets] today are involved in conscious policy, in programs, if you will, which foster, support and expand this activity which is hemorrhaging . . . throughout the world."[28] Unlike Carter's human rights policy, which was a diversion from the persisting cold war rivalry with the Soviet Union, Reagan's anti-terrorist policy, according to Haig, would be fully integrated with the geopolitical grand strategy.[29] Accordingly, the United States need not wait until the next hostage crisis to act against the international terrorist conspiracy. By building up its covert counterterrorist capabilities, the United States could preempt the international conspiracy by moving against key operatives in the terrorist network whenever and wherever they might be located—in Teheran, Tripoli, Havana, or PLO strongholds in Lebanon—while making it clear to the leaders of the Kremlin that they would be held ultimately responsible for any intensification of the global campaign of terrorism against the West.

The President's 1981 inaugural-week statements on allowing terrorists no quarter[30] and Secretary of State Haig's public diagnosis of the terrorist threat as a global Marxist-Leninist conspiracy masterminded by the Kremlin[31] created the expectation of dramatic action. The showman's instinct in the White House sought the appropriate scene, the right villain to target. But a dramatic antiterrorist victory proved to be more elusive than anticipated.

There were plenty of international terrorist incidents to grab the headlines, but—frustratingly for the administration—none of these could convincingly be traced directly to governments or groups against whom the United States could take dramatic and effective reprisal. There was the additional problem of fashioning an appropriate military response that would not obviously violate international rules of noncombatant immunity. This latter consideration was present at the time of the suicide truck attack on the U.S. Marine barracks at Beirut airport. Reagan retrospectively complained:

I've pounded a few walls myself when I'm alone. . . . It is frustrating. But . . . you can't just start shooting without having someone in your gun sights. . . . Retaliation in some people's minds might just entail striking a blow in a general direction, and the result would be a terrorist act in itself and the killing and victimizing of innocent people.[32]

The administration's reputed "moderate," Haig's successor as Secretary of State, George Shultz, emerged, in response to the Marine barracks massacre and subsequent terrorist acts, as the champion of swift and dramatic military responses—even preemptive strikes. And Secretary of Defense Weinberger, widely regarded as one of Reagan's most hawkish advisers, became the most insistent defender of the proposition that military force should be used only as a last resort.

The Shultz strategy was given its most elaborate public airing in a speech at the Park Avenue Synagogue in New York City on October 25, 1984. In order to deter terrorist acts, said the Secretary of State, terrorists must face the certainty of punishment. There should be "no question about our ability to use force where and when it is needed." This would require that the American public be prepared for the risks:

The public must understand *before the fact* that there is potential for loss of life of some of our fighting men and the loss of life of some innocent people.

The public must understand *before the fact* that some will seek to cast any preemptive or retaliatory action by us in the worst light and will attempt to make our military and our policymakers—rather than the terrorists—appear to be the culprits.

The public must understand *before the fact* that occasions will come when their government must act before each and every fact is known—and decisions cannot be tied to the opinion polls.[33]

In this and related statements both within the councils of the administration and from the public platform Shultz tried to overcome the general reluctance with regard both to the preemptive use of force and the killing of noncombatants. An effective counterterrorism policy, he argued, "will have to have an element of unpredictability and surprise." There would not always be time for national debate.

We may never have the kind of evidence that can stand up in an American court of law. But we cannot allow ourselves to become the Hamlet of nations, worrying endlessly over whether and how to respond.[34]

The prerequisite for the required swiftness and flexibility was "a broad public consensus on the moral and strategic necessity for action."

Fighting terrorism will not be a clean or pleasant contest, but we have no choice but to play it. . . . If terrorism is truly a threat to Western moral values, our morality must not paralyze us; it must give us the courage to face up to the threat. . . . There is no room for guilt or self-doubt about our right to defend [our] way of life.[35]

Shultz's speech, which he had reason to believe reflected the President's views, was a surprise to Secretary of Defense Weinberger and Vice President Bush—both of whom had argued against some of its premises within the administration. Reporters aware of the cabinet-level controversy asked the President (then in New York for a re-election campaign appearance) for his views on the Shultz statement. The President's immediate reply was that Shultz's remarks represented Reagan's own thinking. But the Vice President, campaigning in the midwest, took issue with Shultz's advocacy of military responses to terrorism that might kill innocent people. "I don't agree with that," Bush said. "I think you have to pinpoint the source of the attack. . . . It has not been our policy to needlessly risk the lives of innocent civilians. This makes it difficult to retaliate." Bush was echoing the President's remarks of the previous Sunday in his debate with the Democratic candidate, Walter Mondale. Reagan had said that "we want to retaliate, but only if we can put our finger on the people responsible and not to endanger the lives of innocent civilians there." Alerted by his staff to these various contradictory remarks coming out of his administration, and reminded of the unresolved debate within it, the President pulled back from his initial flat endorsement of the Shultz speech, saying that he did not think it represented a statement of policy. This infuriated Shultz, since it publicly undercut his role as the administration's principal spokesman on foreign policy. White House press secretary Speakes shortly added to the confusion by saying the speech by the Secretary of State "was Administration policy from top to bottom."[36]

Weinberger was chagrined at Shultz's unilateral policymaking on an issue in which the Defense Department's views were crucial. But he waited until after the presidential election to publicly air his views. Speaking to the National Press Club in Washington on November 28 on the broad subject of the criteria for the use of military force, the Secretary of Defense took oblique swipes (reportedly his remarks in internal debates were more pointed) at the Secretary of State's readiness to commit the country's military power to undertakings before the consequences had been fully explored.

There are six tests to be satisfied before undertaking a major military operation, said Weinberger: (1) the use of force must be deemed vital to U.S. national interest or that of its allies (Shultz regarded this criterion as unnecessarily vague and likely to engender endless debate, producing just the paralysis he was trying to overcome); (2) the use of force, once decided upon, must be premised on the intention of winning and the military must be guaranteed the full material, financial, and political backing of the other agencies of government in using as much force as necessary to win (Shultz only disagreed with the need to get such guarantees in advance); (3) both the military and political objectives of the military operation must be clearly defined (Shultz wanted an option of reprisal even where there was no compelling military objective); (4) a clear plan of precisely how the military action will accomplish the objectives must be in place (Shultz was willing to act in advance of meeting this stringent requirement); (5) there must be reasonable assurances of public support—in advance (this in contrast to the Shultz view that in military responses to terrorism the public should be prepared not to be consulted); and (6) military action must be undertaken only as a last resort after an assessment that alternative means could not accomplish the objective (Shultz felt that the use of force, even when alternative action was available, might nevertheless be justified as a signal that the United States was ready for a major military encounter should the adversary choose to escalate the conflict).[37]

Weinberger's views reflected the deeply held convictions of the military after their searing experience in the Vietnam War. Never again should the leaders of the armed services allow the top political levels of the government to drag the country into a war without full exploration of the implications and the requirements for victory. And never again should the conduct of military operations be hamstrung by untested, intellectually conceived theories of deterrence, graduated escalation, and the like. In articulating these views more consistently and vigorously than any of his predecessors the SecDef enhanced his influence within the Pentagon. The issue also provided Weinberger with a "hard-nosed" military basis for waging his protracted bureaucratic battle with Secretary Shultz for Reagan's favor, in this case on an issue in which the Secretary of State could be shown to be amateurishly venturing into turf where military expertise was crucial. But Shultz had no intention of backing off. He persisted in castigating Weinberger's position as "the Vietnam syndrome in spades, carried to an absurd level, and a complete abdication of the duties of leadership."[38]

Weinberger rejected any suggestion that he was a dove on the question of tough and unsqueamish responses to terrorism. His stance was, before using force, you had better choose the circumstances carefully and make adequate provision to carry through what you start to a successful conclusion. Reluctant to use force until all the planning criteria were satisfied, the Pentagon would show itself the most determined once the threshold had been crossed and would be ready to err on the side of overkill.

The gap between the brave posturing at the outset of the Reagan administration and the more equivocal actions required by the complex realities of the 1980s was starkly revealed in the U.S. government's response to the hijacking of TWA flight 847 in June 1985. The President found that his standing pledge to inflict "swift and effective retribution" upon those who resorted to terrorism against the United States and, above all, his promise never to negotiate with them, were simply not appropriate premises of action in this case. Neither this nor the Byzantine dealings the administration undertook to obtain freedom for some seven American citizens (including a CIA covert operations agent) being held hostage by various militant Shiite groups in Lebanon prevented Reagan from frequent public reiteration of the absolutist no-deals stance.

The TWA Hijacking

After it became clear to the White House that the young Shiite hijackers of TWA flight 847 were prepared, if their demands were not met, to murder the airplane crew and its American passengers (as demonstrated by their beating and shooting of one of the passengers and dumping his body onto the tarmac at Beirut airport) and the Joint Chiefs of Staff advised that a commando rescue operation was unfeasible, Reagan was left with two bitter options: to take his chances and threaten military reprisal against governments in the area thought to be sponsors of the hijacking group; or to explore the possibility of obtaining the hostages' release by meeting at least some of the demands of their captors.[39]

The first option would have compelled Reagan to distance himself emotionally from the media-fanned public sympathy for the hostages and their families. The White House staff, aware of his susceptibility to individual human appeals, tried their best to prevent any face-to-face meetings between relatives of the hostages and the President. But at various speaking engagements Reagan's staff was unable to dissuade him from meeting with hostage family members backstage.[40] (*The Wall Street Journal* pointed out the parallel between Reagan's increasing emotional involvement with the hostages and his predecessor's plight in an editorial under the caption "Jimmy Reagan.")

The hijackers' highest priority demand was the release by Israel of the remaining 700 Shiite civilians captured by the Israeli Defense Forces during their invasion of Lebanon. The Israelis had already released some 300 of the 1,000 they had imprisoned; but the process of releasing the prisoners had been suspended after the kidnapping of some United Nations soldiers in southern Lebanon.

Since this demand could be satisfied by Israeli action and would not require the U.S. government to make any direct concessions, the President was provided with an alternate course of action. If the release of the remaining prisoners could induce the hijackers to free the TWA passengers and crew, the Israelis would oblige a public request by the U.S. government, so that the Israelis would not be seen capitulating to Shiite blackmail.

While the official definitions of who was acceding to whose requests were being worked out between Washington and Jerusalem, the prominent Shiite Lebanese lawyer Nabih Berri negotiated on behalf of the hijackers. The United States also prevailed upon President Assad of Syria to intercede against more radical Muslim groups in Lebanon which were hoping to exploit the TWA incident to embarrass Israel and the United States.

Pressure was brought on Reagan at this point by the families of the "forgotten seven" American hostages in Lebanon (who had been captured one by one by pro-Iranian militants in recent years) to link their release to the arrangements being worked out. Even though such linkage would have required coordinated negotiations with diverse rival groups in Lebanon, Reagan spoke publicly as if the U.S. government were demanding the release of all Americans held hostage in the Middle East.

The more limited deal was salvaged by a special statement by President Reagan—suggested by the Syrians—affirming U.S. respect for the sovereignty of Lebanon. When he announced the release of the TWA crew and passengers, Reagan struck his standard rhetorical posture: "The United States gives terrorists no reward and no guarantees," he insisted. "We make no concessions. We make no deals."[41] He followed this with an even more bellicose statement a week later in his address to the American Bar Association:

Let me make it plain to the assassins in Beirut and their accomplices that America will never make concessions to terrorists. . . . The American people are not going to tolerate . . . intimidation, terror, and outright acts of war against the nation and its people. And we're especially not going to tolerate acts from outlaw states run by the strangest collection of misfits, Looney Tunes, and squalid criminals since the advent of the Third Reich.[42]

Paradoxically, the President's unshakable determination to obtain the release of all the Americans being held hostage in the Middle East led to the two greatest embarrassments of his administration: the sale of arms to Iran and the clandestine diversion of profits from these sales to the Contras in Nicaragua (see Chapter 25).

Arms for Hostages

The office of the national security adviser was the center of the effort, begun in earnest in the summer of 1985, to exploit the Khomeini government's need for U.S. antitank and antiaircraft missiles and parts during the Iran–Iraq war in exchange for Iran's help in getting the Shiite militants in Lebanon to release their American hostages. Initially the weapons came from Israeli stocks; subsequently some of the equipment came directly from the United States. The brainchild of the Israelis who were already supplying arms to Iran, the idea caught the fancy of the President when it was first broached to him in a private meeting by national security adviser Robert McFarlane.[43]

McFarlane had been informed in May 1985 that the Peres government in Israel was worried about Soviet-backed Iraq and wanted American approval to sell artillery shells originally obtained from the United States to Iran. McFarlane was persuaded by Israeli arguments that this might be a way to support the anti-Khomeini factions in Iran with whom the Israelis were dealing and also insure against any temptation in Iran to cultivate relations with the Soviets. In July Iranian agents proposed to the Israelis that in return for U.S. approval of Israeli sales of antitank missiles to Iran the hostages being held by pro-Iranian groups in Lebanon could be released.

The President, intrigued, presided over a discussion at the White House on August 6, 1985 with McFarlane, Secretary Weinberger, Secretary Shultz, Vice President Bush, and White House chief of staff Donald Regan on Israel's request for authorization to sell 100 of its antitank TOW missiles. McFarlane reported that the Iranians were prepared to release four of the seven hostages as part of the deal. Weinberger and Shultz opposed the plan, arguing that it would contradict the basic policy of isolating Iran and undermine U.S. efforts to get other countries to cooperate in the embargo. Shultz was adamant against "falling into the arms-for-hostage business."[44]

Despite the objections raised by the Secretaries of State and Defense, Reagan—obsessed by the need to free the hostages and backed by CIA Director William Casey's opinion that the plan was worth a try—authorized McFarlane and his associates to arrange for a sequence of arms sales to Iran. In the words of one of the authorizing Findings signed by the President,

> I hereby find that the following operation in a foreign country (including all support necessary to such operation) is important to the national security of the United States, and due to its extreme sensitivity and security risks, I determine it is essential to limit prior notice, and direct the Director of Central Intelligence to refrain from reporting this Finding to the Congress . . . until I otherwise direct.

> SCOPE Iran
> DESCRIPTION Assist friendly foreign liaison services, third countries, which have established relationships with Iranian elements, groups, and individuals sympathetic to U.S. Government interests and which do not conduct or support terrorist actions directed against U.S. persons, property or interests, for the purpose of: (1) establishing a more moderate government in Iran, and (2) obtaining from them significant intelligence not otherwise obtainable, to determine the current Iranian Government's intentions with respect to its neighbors and with respect to terrorist acts, and (3) furthering the release of the American hostages held in Beirut and preventing additional terrorist acts by these groups.

The presidential Finding went on to elaborate that the U.S. government would:

> Provide funds, intelligence, counter-intelligence, training, guidance and communications, and other necessary assistance to these elements, groups, individuals, liaison services and third countries in support of these activities. The USG will act to facilitate efforts by third parties and third countries to establish contact with moderate elements within and outside the Government of Iran by providing these elements with arms, equipment and related material in order to enhance the credibility of these elements in their effort to achieve a more pro-U.S. government in Iran by demonstrating their ability to obtain requisite resources to defend their country against Iraq and intervention by the Soviet Union. This support will be discontinued if the U.S. Government learns that these elements have abandoned their goals of moderating their government and appropriated the material for purposes other than that provided by this Finding.[45]

Until the arms sales to Iran were exposed by a Lebanese magazine article in November 1986, the initiative was supported among

Reagan's principal foreign policy advisers by CIA Director Casey, national security adviser McFarlane, and his successor, Admiral John Poindexter; and opposed by Secretary of State Shultz and Secretary of Defense Weinberger. (The President himself was strongly in favor of the initiative; Vice President Bush evidently did not attempt to change Reagan's mind.) Casey worked with McFarlane and Poindexter, both of whom relied increasingly on NSC action officer Oliver North in implementing the policy and conspiring to keep the details of what they were doing from Secretaries Shultz and Weinberger.

Remarkably, the formulators of the arms-for-hostages plan persisted with it secretly even when it should have become evident to them that they were being "snookered" (White House chief of staff Donald Regan's term) by the Iranians. They expected at least four hostages would be released in September 1985 in return for Israel's shipping 504 TOW antitank missiles to Iran but only one was released. They allowed themselves to be persuaded by Iranian agents that the rest of the hostages would be released after Israel shipped Iran Hawk antiaircraft missiles; none were released. They were persuaded that Iran would deliver the hostages once the United States itself delivered Hawk missile parts in 1986; but, again, only one hostage was released. Finally, they believed they had obtained a credible promise from the Iranians to turn over one more hostage and to exert pressure on their friends in Beirut to obtain the release of one other after the United States shipped 500 more TOWs in October 1986: once again they were humiliated as the Iranians demanded additional weapons before making any real effort to fulfill their promise.

The failure to obtain the release of the hostages by arms sales should have been enough to terminate the sales before the disclosures in the fall of 1986 embarrassed the White House. Casey, Poindexter, and North kept the operation going because it had taken on another function of high value to the administration by generating millions of dollars in profits from the arms sales—funds that then were diverted secretly into the coffers of the "enterprise" set up by Casey and North to funnel military assistance to the Nicaraguan Contras. Once the secret Iran–Contra diversion was exposed, the White House suffered a double embarrassment. There were flat denials, sustained for the duration of the Reagan administration, that the President or any Cabinet-level officials (other than Casey) had any knowledge of the diversion, and Poindexter and North were promptly fired for acting beyond their authority. The President's knowledge of the arms sales to Iran could not be denied. But the administration insisted that it had not engaged in any "arms for hostages" deals.

Ten days after the release of one of the hostages, David Jacobson, director of the American Hospital in Beirut, in the first week of November 1986, the Iranians disclosed the secret May 1986 visit by McFarlane, North, and others to Teheran to sell arms. Before the disclosure, Larry Speakes' press briefings on the release of Jacobsen were carefully crafted by national security adviser Poindexter to maintain the fiction that the Iranians and their friends in Lebanon received nothing in exchange for Jacobsen. Speakes was instructed to say, "As long as Iran advocates the use of terrorism the U.S. arms embargo will continue." The effort to sustain these denials proved too much for the President's skillful press secretary, Larry Speakes, and ultimately led to his resignation.

After the Iranian announcement, Speakes and others in the administration tried to persuade the President that, rather than risk the charge of an "Irangate" coverup, he should admit to the public that he was wrong and apologize for his mistake. But it was not clear to the President exactly what the basic mistake was: trying to obtain the release of the hostages through selling arms (after all, Jacobsen had just been released and it was possible that further releases might follow), or the rigid posture against any deals and the duplicity of conducting such negotiations while publicly denying it.

The most the President allowed himself to admit publicly was that "mistakes were made" and that, as President, he was responsible. But, as Speakes complains in his memoir, the President "could never bring himself to say that *he* had made a mistake . . . he did not think he had done anything wrong and was not about to concede that he had, as a matter of principle." Speakes offers the judgment that "It was just the makeup of the man."[46] The President was receiving contrary advice from his trusted advisers as to what was right and wrong about the Iran initiative; moreover, those like Speakes and Shultz who wanted the President to take certain public positions do not appear to have been clear even in their own minds why he should do so—for the good of the hostages? for the geopolitical interests of the country? to avoid another Watergate?

The result was a hodgepodge of confusing remarks from the President, some of them containing not only halftruths but also major inaccuracies. Thus, in his televised address of November 13, 1986, Reagan said:

> The charge has been made that the United States has shipped weapons to Iran in ransom payment for the release of American hostages in Lebanon, that the United States undercut its allies and secretly violated American policy against trafficking with terrorists. Those charges are utterly false. . . . We did not trade weapons or anything else for hostages—nor will we.[47]

In his press conference six days later, fending off a question alleging that the United States had condoned Israeli arms shipments to Iran, Reagan insisted, "Bill, everything you've said here is based on a supposition that is false. We did not condone, and do not condone, the shipment of arms from other countries." Knowing that the U.S.–Israel–Iran connection was being uncovered, Poindexter drafted a hasty correction that was immediately issued in the President's name, admitting: "There was a third country involved in our secret project with Iran." But the statement still claimed that "all of the shipments of the token amounts of defensive arms and parts that I have authorized or condoned taken in total could be placed aboard a single cargo aircraft."[48]

As the Tower Commission and congressional investigations of the Iran–Contra affair began to reveal the true extent and modalities of the administration's Iran arms-for-hostages initiative, the President countered with denials that this was not "ransom" since the U.S. government had not dealt directly with the captors of the hostages but only with intermediaries.

Speakes, in his memoir, still could not bring himself to suspect Reagan: "Frankly, I don't believe the man can tell a lie. The man can make a mistake and the man can hear something so many times that he believes something is true when it really isn't, but he simply isn't a liar."[49] Gary Wills is probably closer to the mark in showing Reagan to be capable of believing things to be true if they are true to him in an emotional sense (in particular, his tendency to confuse roles he played in the movies with what actually happened to him) even though they may not withstand empirical validation. Wills quotes a revealing confession by Reagan: "I told the American people I did not trade arms for hostages. My heart and my best intentions still tell me it is true, but the facts and the evidence tell me it is not." [50]

The Achille Lauro *Saga: A Hostage Crisis Made to Order* [51]

On October 7, 1985, the Italian cruise ship *Achille Lauro* en route from Alexandria to Israel, was hijacked by four members of the Palestine Liberation Front (a faction of the PLO) who demanded the release of 50 of their fellow terrorists from Israeli prisons. The captured ship contained a mostly Italian crew of 344 and 97 passengers (the remaining passengers were to have boarded that night at Port Said), among them a few retired Americans.

The hijackers asked Syria for permission to dock the *Achille Lauro* at the port of Tartus where they planned to negotiate with diplomatic representatives of the hostages' countries to put pressure on Israel to agree to their demands; but Syrian President Hafez Assad, apparently anxious to undermine PLO chief Yasir Arafat, cooperated with the United States and Italy and refused the ship permission to dock.

This left the ship in open waters vulnerable to seizure by antiterrorist commandos. Deputy national security adviser John Poindexter and Oliver North, acting through the interdepartmental terrorist incident working group which Poindexter chaired, quickly established themselves in the White House situation room to coordinate the U.S. response under direct authority of the President. This time it would be a military response—swift and decisive, like an Israeli operation.

The Joint Special Operations Command (JSOC) was mobilized and deployed specially trained SEAL frogmen and DELTA helicopter assault units—500 men in all—in a dozen giant air transports to forward NATO bases on Sicily and Cyprus. To the disappointment of those itching for action, the terrorists were ordered by their more realistic superiors in the Palestinian Liberation Front to release the hostages. The *Achille Lauro* headed back to Egypt, where the PLO struck a deal with the Mubarak government and the Italians to provide the hijackers safe passage out of Egypt. The American government objected that the hijackers should be brought to justice in

U.S. courts for murdering and throwing overboard an elderly American passenger. But the Mubarak government, determined not to provoke the Palestinians (President Anwar Sadat had been assassinated in 1981 by Palestinian fanatics), was anxious to facilitate safe passage for the hijackers out of Egypt in return for releasing the hostages in Port Said. An EgyptAir 737 was made available to fly the hijackers to Tunis.

North and Poindexter saw an irresistible opportunity in a scheme concocted by a Navy captain on the NSC staff. Appropriated by Col. North as his own, the plan called for intercepting the Egyptian airliner with U.S. fighter planes from the carrier *Saratoga* as it flew from Egypt to Tunis through international airspace over the Mediterranean. After forcing it to land at the NATO base at Sigonella, Sicily, U.S. authorities would apprehend the hijackers for transport to the United States to stand trial. In addition to the hijackers, the airliner would be carrying an additional prize: Abu Abbas, head of the faction of Palestinian radicals that had directed the hijacking. Poindexter briefed McFarlane on the scheme and McFarlane obtained the President's approval despite Secretary Weinberger's effort to dissuade Reagan on the grounds that the interception would damage U.S. relations with Egypt.

The technical aspects of the operation over the Mediterranean were carried out brilliantly. But a complication arose during the attempt to escort the airliner to the NATO base in Sicily, which was under the sovereign jurisdiction of Italy. The Italian air control tower at Sigonella had not received authorization from President Craxi, who was reluctant to antagonize Mubarak and to make Italy the target of another round of terrorism. The control tower was withholding permission for EgyptAir flight 2843 to land. An American Navy lieutenant grabbed the microphone from the Italian controller and talked the plane down onto the runway. As American troops surrounded the aircraft, Italian troops surrounded the Americans, outnumbering them five to one.

American diplomats in Italy implored President Craxi to order his troops to withdraw and to allow U.S. authorities to take the hijackers into custody. Craxi stood firm, insisting that Italian courts had jurisdiction over crimes committed aboard an Italian ship. The White House ordered the American troops to allow the Italians to assume custody over the hijackers. President Reagan, speaking to

Craxi, had to content himself with saying that the U.S. government
would submit a formal petition to the Italian government for extradition of the four hijackers. Reagan also asked that the United States
be allowed to arrest the two Palestinian leaders also on board; but
Craxi demurred after checking with the Egyptian government,
which wanted the two returned to Egypt. Craxi ordered his troops
to take the four hijackers into Italian custody while allowing Abbas
and his companion to remain onboard. As the Egyptian aircraft took
off with its remaining passengers for another airport in Italy, it was
buzzed by a small U.S. Navy jet. Later the two Palestinian leaders
were secretly transferred onto a Yugoslav airplane for a flight to
Belgrade where they took refuge in the PLO embassy.

Overlooking the confrontations with the Italians and the Egyptians and ignoring the fact that the United States was not able to get
its hands on the hijackers, Reagan was publicly and privately ecstatic
over the dramatic mid-air intercept. The President, delivering one of
his most memorable lines, crowed that the "these young Americans
[who flew the Navy jets] sent a message to terrorists everywhere.
The message: *You can run but you can't hide.*"[52] In fact, Abu Abbas,
who masterminded the *Achille Lauro* hijacking, both ran and hid.
Within the administration, Reagan had found his Rambos, Poindexter and North, who for a time could do no wrong and were given
broad discretion to implement the administration's counterterrorism
policy. The Secretary of Defense, who had opposed the aerial interception, could only praise the President for authorizing it: "He has
better judgment than all the rest of us put together."[53]

Taking it out on Qaddafi

The demonstration of American derring-do in the aerial intercept
of the *Achille Lauro* hijackers had virtually no impact on the pattern
of terrorism. Again there was a buildup of frustration in Washington.

In the third week of November 1985, members of the Abu Nidal
organization attempted to hijack an EgyptAir jetliner. A courageous
effort by the crew to foil the hijacking resulted in a forced landing in
Malta, where the plane was stormed by Egyptian commandos and
sixty people were killed in the exchange of fire. The CIA was
convinced, on the basis of communications intercepts, that the Lib-

yan government had financed and in other ways abetted the failed hijacking.

Abu Nidal, protected and financed by Qaddafi, was also believed to be behind two attacks at El Al ticket counters at the Rome and Vienna airports on December 27, 1985, in which five Americans were among nineteen travelers killed. In response the United States suspended economic relations with Libya and ordered all Americans to leave that country. Pressure was brought on the NATO allies to follow suit, with the U.S. hinting that plans were being readied to use force against Libya if the efforts to isolate Qaddafi economically did not work. Reagan stated publicly that "if these steps do not end Qaddafi's terrorism, I promise you that further steps will be taken."[54] Actually, the White House did not expect economic sanctions to succeed. In resorting to these measures along with the public threats of tougher sanctions to come, the administration was attempting to lay the groundwork for domestic and allied support for more dramatic actions.

The President wanted irrefutable evidence of Libyan involvement in terrorist acts—a "smoking gun"—in order to justify a direct U.S. blow at Qaddafi. This was provided to his satisfaction by the early morning terrorist bombing of La Belle disco in West Berlin on April 5, 1985. It was a weekend night and the disco was crowded with U.S. servicemen. One American soldier was killed, another was mortally wounded, and over 200 people were injured. Earlier that night British intelligence intercepted the latest in a series of messages between the Libyan Intelligence Service in Tripoli and a known Qaddafi terrorist network in Europe, the People's Bureau. The messages indicated that the network was preparing attacks against U.S. military installations and other targets where Americans congregated. During the previous week Libya had exchanged fire with American naval forces in the Gulf of Sidra. In the April 4 message intercept the People's Bureau predicted an imminent "joyous event." The full texts of these interceptions were never made public and West German investigators did not conclude that the La Belle bombing was in fact ordered by Libya. Nor did the circumstantial evidence unequivocally indict Qaddafi—for instance, the disco was a favorite of black servicemen and the Libyans avoided targeting blacks and other minorities.[55]

Despite the lack of evidence, the President felt that Libyan involvement was clear enough to authorize the Navy and Air Force to undertake an airstrike against Libya. The targets were military facilities and aircraft at the Tripoli airport, a frogman school and Qaddafi's own principal compound in Tripoli, and the military airfield and Qaddafi's compound in Benghazi. The prime target was the Qaddafi compound in Tripoli, comprising communications facilities, the staff headquarters of the Libyan military, barracks for Qaddafi's personal security guards, and the residence in which Qaddafi lived with his wife and seven children. Although officially denied from the President on down, the pattern of bombings and subsequent interviews of personnel involved in the operation left no doubt that one of the purposes of the airstrike was to kill Qaddafi.[56] President Reagan personally approved the targeting of Qaddafi's compound, convincing himself that it did not violate his standing policy against assassinations since the principal objective was to destroy the military communications facility; the risk to Qaddafi's life, if indeed he was there at the time, would be a side effect of an attack with a compelling military rationale.

Before proceeding with the airstrike on Libya it was necessary to obtain Margaret Thatcher's permission to use F-111 fighter planes deployed in Britain. The British Prime Minister wanted to help her friend in the White House, especially in light of Reagan's support during the 1982 Falkland Islands war. Given her public position against retaliation that was simply punitive reprisal, she had to be convinced that each of the targets was an important component of Libya's terrorist capability and therefore could be destroyed under the rationale of legitimate self-defense.

French President François Mitterrand was not convinced of the need and efficacy of the bombing raid. He refused permission for the American warplanes to fly over French territory. The warplanes had to circle the continent from England and come through the Strait of Gibraltar in order to reach Libya—doubling the flying time and fuel requirements. The mission thus included—in addition to short range air attacks from U.S. carriers in the Mediterranean—eighteen fighter-bombers and accompanying refueling tankers on a fourteen-hour, 5,400–mile roundtrip from Lakenheath Air Base in Britain: a big, noisy, malfunction-prone operation.

The strike at Tripoli airfield, which was supposed to catch Qaddafi's entire fleet of Ilyushin-76 transports on the ground, found less than half there (the others had been dispersed). In the attack on the other airfield, two of the Navy's nine fighter-bombers had to turn back because of equipment failure. Only two of the six targeted MIG hangers sustained significant damage. The aircraft that struck at the military barracks complex got only ten percent of their weapons on target. And in the prime target area—Qaddafi's own compound—the operation was particularly sloppy: bombs landed no closer than 30 yards from the leader's residence, but the blasts and flying debris injured two of Qaddafi's little sons and killed his fifteen-month old adopted daughter. Qaddafi himself escaped major injury. Meanwhile, six bombs, totaling five tons of explosives, missed their targets completely and landed in residential streets, killing thirty-seven, according to the Libyans, and injuring ninety-three.[57]

President Reagan proudly addressed the nation from the White House. "Today we have done what we had to do. If necessary we shall do it again. . . . Self-defense is not only our right, it is our duty, and that's the purpose of tonight's mission."[58]

The bombing raid on Libya was popular with the American public but not with America's European allies. Margaret Thatcher had to defend herself for allowing British bases to be used and asked the Reagan administration, which was reportedly preparing a repeat operation, not to ask such a favor of Britain again. It was clear to America's allies that the effort was not really an act of self-defense. An effort to deter future terrorist acts, yes; and perhaps, as suggested by George Shultz, a pointed demonstration to potential anti-Qaddafi elements in Libya that the flamboyant, megalomaniacal ruler was leading their country down a suicidal path and needed to be deposed.

The President, however, stuck to his explanation that the airstrike was an act of self-defense:

We Americans are slow to anger. We always seek peaceful avenues before resorting to the use of force, and we did. We tried quiet diplomacy, public condemnation, economic sanctions and demonstrations of military force—and none succeeded. So we were driven to strike against the headquarters, terrorist facilities, and military assets that constituted the nerve center of Qaddafi's international network for terrorism and subversion against U.S. citizens and facilities around the globe.[59]

In actuality, as American and allied intelligence services were reporting, to the extent that there was a nerve center of globally active terrorism and subversion against the United States, it was located in Teheran, not Tripoli. But Iran was for the time being out of bounds for U.S. military reprisals due to the arms-for-hostages effort. The underlying cathartic rationale for going after Qaddafi was well put by Admiral William Crowe, Chairman of the Joint Chiefs of Staff. "There comes a time in the events and affairs," he said, "when you've got to retaliate just because people are doing things to you they don't have a right to do, and you've got to stand up."[60]

25

CONTRADICTIONS IN LATIN AMERICA

What may be aptly called the "cabal of zealots" was in charge.
—U.S. CONGRESS, *IRAN–CONTRA REPORT*

U.S. leaders of various foreign policy persuasions—expansionary nationalists, human rights reformers, realpolitik strategists—have been strongly disposed to treat Latin America as within their country's (hemi)sphere of influence. When threats to important U.S. interests are located in or targeted on Latin America, particularly if hostile extra-hemispheric powers are seen to be involved, there tends to be a coalescence across party lines of righteous indignation, and even isolationists are inclined to support the commitment of economic and military resources abroad for the purpose of exorcising such threats. The Reagan administration's obsession with Marxism in Latin America was only the latest expression of a foreign policy tradition extending back to its classic statement in the Monroe Doctrine of 1823. This is a tradition running through the Mexican–American War of 1846–1848, the Spanish–American War of 1898, the construction of the Panama Canal, Woodrow Wilson's military interventions in Mexico, the 1954 CIA-engineered uprising against the Marxist government in Guatemala, the Alliance for Progress as well as the Kennedy administration's covert and overt efforts to get rid of Fidel Castro, the Cuban missile crisis, Lyndon Johnson's dispatching of the Marines to the Dominican Republic in 1965, the Nixon administration's complicity in the Chilean coup against Salvador Allende in 1973, and even the Carter administration's support of the Nicaraguan Sandinistas against Somoza in 1979.

But this picture of historical continuity overlooks a metamorphosis in U.S. policy from the anti-communist simplicities of the early 1950s to a rather sophisticated set of assumptions about the connections between socioeconomic underdevelopment and Marxist inroads in the Western hemisphere. Near the end of his presidency, Dwight Eisenhower, in a major speech at Newport in July 1960, defined the choice facing the United States throughout most of Latin America as whether to support "social evolution" or to face "revolution." Among "evolutionary measures" he listed land reform, housing, a wider distribution of national income, the strengthening of institutions for promoting economic growth, and greater respect for human rights and the will of the people as expressed in democratic elections. In the Act of Bogota of September 1960, the Eisenhower administration offered an immediate loan of $500 million to inaugurate "a broad new social development program for Latin America." The Kennedy Administration carried forward the new orientation in its Alliance for Progress. Presented to the public in idealistic terms as a dramatic re-identification of the United States with the global struggle for freedom and equality, the *Alianza* was defended in the counsels of government as a strategy for driving a wedge between Soviet clients and other leftist movements in the hemisphere. Viewed from this perspective, the Reagan administration's kneejerk anti-Marxism represented a great leap backward from the evolving realism in U.S. Latin American policy.

COUNTERINSURGENCY IN EL SALVADOR

The incoming Reagan administration saw the conflict in El Salvador as a flashpoint of the intensifying East–West struggle. The U.S.-backed regime headed by Jose Duarte was trying to put down a leftist insurrection that appeared to be supplied through Marxist Nicaragua with active support from Cuba and other Soviet bloc countries. In early February 1981, the Department of State issued an elaborate white paper, "Communist Interference in El Salvador," which laid the groundwork for a series of requests to Congress for emergency aid for the Duarte regime as well as for possible moves against

governments in the Caribbean and Central America—particularly
Cuba and Nicaragua—alleged to be giving support to the rebel
forces. The white paper purported to show conclusively that "over
the past year, the insurgency in El Salvador has been progressively
transformed into a textbook case of indirect armed aggression by
Communist powers through Cuba." The evidence was "definitive"
that "Cuba, the Soviet Union, and other Communist states . . . are
carrying out . . . a well-coordinated covert effort to bring about the
overthrow of El Salvador's established government and to impose in
its place a Communist regime with no popular support."[1] Complicating the new administration's anti-communist strategy was the undeniable fact that the Duarte government was itself unpopular and
unable to restrain Salvadoran military death squads from brutal,
repressive tactics against the insurgents and their suspected civilian
supporters. The Reagan White House inherited a report prepared for
President Carter in December 1980 by a distinguished nonpartisan
committee of lawyers headed by William D. Rogers and William G.
Bowdler (former Assistant Secretaries of State for Latin America in
the Ford and Carter administrations, respectively) on the killing of
four American churchwomen by members of the Salvadoran National Guard. The Rogers–Bowdler report had concluded that "there
is a high probability that an attempt was made [by the Salvadoran
authorities] to conceal the deaths."[2]

Early comments by Reagan administration officials attempted to
shift the blame for the nuns' murder away from the Duarte regime.
Secretary of State Haig suggested that the nuns may have provoked
fire on themselves by trying to run a roadblock. UN Ambassador
Jeane Kirkpatrick claimed that "the nuns were not just nuns; the
nuns were political activists . . . on behalf of the [revolutionary]
Frente."[3] President Reagan hoped the public would view the episode
"that happened before I took office" in the perspective of reforms
being instituted by the Duarte government: "One of our reasons for
the support of this government is because we believe they do hold
out the best hope for improving the conditions of the people of El
Salvador. . . . We think we are helping the forces that are supporting human rights in El Salvador." Reagan claimed it was wrong to
focus exclusively on alleged excesses by the Salvadoran military
when "the terrorists themselves, the guerrillas, boast of having killed
. . . somewhere above 6,000 people in the last year." The important

thing was to realize that the situation in El Salvador and the U.S. response to it were part a larger struggle:

> What we're doing . . . is [to] try to halt the infiltration into the Americas by terrorists, by outside interferences and those who aren't just arming El Salvador but I think, are aiming at the whole of Central and possibly later South America—and I'm sure eventually North America. . . . What we're doing, is trying to stop the destabilizing force of terrorism and guerrilla warfare and revolution from being exported in here, backed by the Soviet Union and Cuba and those others that we've named.[4]

This line was echoed by administration officials trying to deflect the growing concern in Congress over human rights abuses by the Salvadoran military. Assistant Secretary of State Thomas Enders in his March 6, 1981 testimony before the House Foreign Affairs Committee on behalf of continuing aid to the Duarte government insisted that the legislators keep their eye on the big picture: "Here you have, in fact, Shafik Handel [the leader of the Salvadoran resistance], requesting assistance from the Soviet Union . . . and getting assistance from Vietnam. . . . You have the Cubans shipping arms and organizing the political leadership of the El Salvadoran insurrection."[5] Secretary Haig appeared before the Foreign Affairs Committee on March 18, 1981 to outline what he called a "four-phases" operation by the Soviet Union in Central America. The first phase, "the seizure of Nicaragua," had already been completed. "Next is El Salvador," he said, "to be followed by Honduras and Guatemala." This was not necessarily a domino theory, said Haig: "I would call it a priority target list—a hit list, if you will—for the ultimate takeover of Central America."[6]

The most eloquent, and revealing, explanation of the administration's attitude came from UN Ambassador Kirkpatrick:

> Speaking generally, we must make it perfectly clear that we are revolted by torture and can never feel spiritual kinship with a government that engages in torture. But the central goal of our foreign policy should not be the moral elevation of other nations, but the preservation of a civilized conception of our national self interest.[7]

The congressional majority was not persuaded by such rationalizations. In the International Security and Development Cooperation Act of 1981, Congress included El Salvador among those countries that would qualify for aid only if the President of the United States certified every six months that that country's government was making a genuine effort to comply with internationally recognized standards of human rights. Not surprisingly, the President, starting in January 1982, provided the required periodic certification: "I hereby determine that the Government of El Salvador is making a concerted and significant effort to comply with internationally recognized human rights."[8] When skeptical members of Congress brought up contrary testimony by human rights organizations and individuals with direct knowledge of the situation in El Salvador, such as former Ambassador Robert E. White, the standard rebuttal was that "accurate information is hard to establish" (Assistant Secretary Enders) and "responsibility for the overwhelming number of deaths . . . cannot be found in the majority of cases" (Ambassador Deane Hinton).[9] Fifty-seven members of Congress, outraged at the administration's see-no-evil, hear-no-evil stance, sent a letter to the President charging that his certification of El Salvador's human rights compliance "is contrary to documented fact" and urging him "to withdraw that 'certification' and provide a more accurate assessment of the junta's actions with respect to human rights . . . so that your determination on providing military assistance may be credible."[10]

The congressional objections signalled to the White House that future authorizations of military aid for the Duarte government might be held back unless there was, at a minimum, a more candid admission of the deficient human rights situation in El Salvador. Accordingly, subsequent presidential certifications were imbedded in rather detailed accounts of repressive and even brutal actions by factions of the Salvadoran military, along with claims that the Duarte government, with prodding from the United States, was taking steps to make its military more aware of the need to observe human rights.

Reagan hailed the March 1982 elections in El Salvador as an indication that the country was on the road to genuine democracy. The election results gave four right-wing parties sufficient votes in the Salvadoran Constituent Assembly to allow Roberto D'Aubuisson, the militant rightist leader alleged to be connected with the death squads, to become the new president. Knowing that a D'Aubuisson presidency would galvanize Congress to cut off military aid, the Reagan administration let in be known in influential political circles in San Salvador that, unless they formed a centrist government, they would risk losing further aid from the United States. A deal was

struck among the centrist and rightist parties in which Dr. Alvaro
Magana, a centrist, became interim president of El Salvador until
the elections of 1984 and D'Aubuisson was made president of the
Constituent Assembly.[11]

These efforts to limit D'Aubuisson's ascendancy marked the beginning of the realization in the White House and State Department
that, Jeane Kirkpatrick's theories to the contrary, unqualified support for autocrats who happened to be on the anti-communist side in
the Cold War could be counterproductive. As human rights abuses
by the Salvadoran military continued in 1983, U.S. Ambassador
Hinton and his successor Thomas Pickering publicly as well as
privately stepped up their criticisms of the political establishment in
that country, including the business community, for remaining
silent.

The high point of official U.S. criticism was Vice President Bush's
visit in December 1983 to warn Salvadoran officials that the Reagan
administration held the government in San Salvador responsible for
human rights abuses.[12] At a dinner hosted by President Alvaro Borja
Magana and attended by all the government leaders including the
Minister of Defense and the high military command, the American
Vice President pulled no punches. The cause of defeating the anti-
government guerrillas "is being undermined by the murderous violence of reactionary minorities," said Bush:

These rightwing fanatics are the best friends of the Soviets, the Cubans, and
Sandinista *comandantes,* and the Salvadoran guerrillas here. Every murderous act
they commit poisons the well of friendship between our two countries and advances
the cause of those who would impose an alien dictatorship on the people of El
Salvador. These cowardly death squad terrorists are just as repugnant to me, to
President Reagan, to the U.S. Congress, and to the American people as the terrorists of the left.

                              .   .   .

    I ask you as a friend not to make the mistake of thinking that there is any division
in my country on this question. It is not just the President, it is not just me or the
Congress. If these death squad murders continue, you will lose the support of the
American people, and that would indeed be a tragedy.[13]

Bush's rhetoric had more effect on the political process in Washington than in San Salvador. The administration's public posture of
opposition to the death squads was sufficient to undercut congres-

sional criticism of the President's certifications of human rights progress, and future aid requests for El Salvador moved through Congress with relative ease. Meanwhile, in February 1984, the Salvadoran Constituent Assembly passed Decree 50, justified as a state of siege emergency measure that had the effect of legitimizing the denial of basic rights to persons apprehended by government security forces. A suspect could be detained for fifteen days without being charged with a crime and without access to legal counsel. In its report of 1984–1985, the Inter-American Commission on Human Rights of the Organization of American States stated

The maintenance of the state of siege . . . has virtually deprived the Salvadoran people of [their] . . . rights since March 1980 when the state of siege was declared. *This situation has become worse since the implementation of Decree 50 of February 1984, which regulates the treatment of political prisoners.*[14]

As public and congressional attention in the mid and late 1980s turned from El Salvador to the situation in Nicaragua—as the government in San Salvador was once again headed by the moderate (but increasingly ineffective) Duarte—the administration had virtual carte blanche in its Salvadoran policies for the remainder of the Reagan years.

THE FALKLAND ISLANDS FAUX PAS

Ronald Reagan's good guys vs. bad guys view of the world (and Jeane Kirkpatrick's distinction between authoritarian and totalitarian regimes) also clashed with hard reality in the case of the Falkland Islands—one of Britain's remaining imperial possessions, claimed for Argentina by the rightwing military regime in Buenos Aires. CIA Director Casey was favorably disposed toward General Leopoldo Galtieri's junta for providing military training in Honduras to the anti-Sandinista Contras. Casey's ally, Ambassador Kirkpatrick, had championed the Argentine dictatorship by meeting with General Galtieri and lobbying the State Department and Congress to obtain a favorable human rights rating for Buenos Aires so that Argentina could again qualify for the U.S. arms sales that had been denied on grounds of human rights violations.

Miscalculating the degree of support for him in Washington, General Galtieri in April 1982 sought to take the Falklands from Britain in a swift invasion, under the assumption that the United

States, in the name of anti-communist solidarity in the hemisphere, would dissuade Britain from military counteraction. Indeed, for almost a month after the Argentine invasion of the Falklands, the Reagan administration refrained from taking sides on the competing sovereignty claims. As the British task force sailed toward the Falklands, Secretary of State Haig tried to act as mediator, proposing that Britain commit itself to negotiating with Argentina over the future political status of the islands in return for a pullout of Argentina's military forces and suggesting some kind of international presence to administer the islands during the negotiations and transition period. But neither side was willing to compromise its claim to the islands. Haig could not persuade Prime Minister Thatcher to rescind her demands that the status quo ante be restored as a precondition for negotiations, nor could he persuade General Galtieri to withdraw the Argentine occupation troops before negotiations began over the Falklands.

As the British warships reached the Falklands on April 30, Secretary Haig announced that because his mediation effort had failed and since Argentina had violated the international rules against the use of force to settle international disputes, the United States had no choice but to back the United Kingdom. But the U.S. shift to the ground of higher principle was too late to avert a bloody battle. The British, with their advanced air and naval units, decisively overpowered the defending Argentine occupation force.

President Reagan, addressing the British Parliament in June as British troops tightened the noose around Galtieri's beleaguered garrisons on the islands, warmly embraced the British effort as part of a great "crusade for Freedom." Voices had been raised, said the President, against the sacrifice of British young men "for lumps of rock and earth" so far away in the South Atlantic. "But these young men aren't fighting for mere real estate. They fight for a cause, for the belief that armed aggression must not be allowed to succeed and that people must participate in the decisions of government under the rule of law."[15] The last phrase was an endorsement of the British claim that in a free plebiscite the Falkland Islanders would show an overwhelming preference for retaining British sovereignty.

Reagan's praise of Thatcher's deployment of the royal armed forces as a noble defense of freedom solidified his relationship with his friend at No. 10 Downing Street. But the Falklands episode removed

Argentina from the thin roster of Latin American players on the U.S. team combating Marxists in Latin America and exposed the fact that the Reagan administration's formula for ascertaining its friends and enemies in the Third World had not worked as clearly as intended.

URGENT FURY IN GRENADA

Reagan could see the enemy clearly on the small Caribbean island of Grenada, as clearly as Cervantes' hero Don Quixote could see them on the Spanish plain. No episode of the Reagan presidency approximates tilting at windmills better than operation Urgent Fury, the Marine and Army paratroop invasion of Grenada during the last week of October 1983 in response to the civil chaos in Grenada following the assassination of the island's Marxist Prime Minister, Maurice Bishop, by rival Marxists. With the U.S. Marines already landing in Grenada, the President on October 25 dispatched a letter to the Speaker of the House of Representatives and the President Pro Tempore of the Senate officially informing Congress of his decision to use armed force in response to a call from members of the Organization of Eastern Caribbean States (OECS) to help them counter the "threat to the peace and security of the region created by the vacuum of authority in Grenada." Of overriding importance, he stated, was "protecting the lives of the United States citizens in Grenada." [16]

Speaking on television on October 27, Reagan provided his larger rationale for ordering U.S. combat forces into Grenada:

Grenada was without a government, its only authority exercised by a self-proclaimed band of military men.

There were then about 1,000 of our citizens on Grenada, 800 of them students in St. George's University Medical School.

. . .

Six members of the Organization of Eastern Caribbean States, joined by Jamaica and Barbados . . . sent an urgent request that we join them in a military operation to restore order and democracy to Grenada. . . . These small peaceful nations needed our help. Three of them don't have armies at all, and the others have very limited forces. The legitimacy of their request, plus my own concern for our citizens, dictated my decision. I believe our government has a responsibility to go to the aid of its citizens, if their right to life and liberty is threatened. The nightmare of our hostages in Iran must never be repeated.

Grenada, we were told, was a friendly island paradise for tourism. Well, it wasn't. It was a Soviet–Cuban colony, being readied as a major military bastion to export terror and undermine democracy. We got there just in time.[17]

The invasion resulted in the deaths of eighteen U.S. soldiers, 45 Grenadans (37 of them civilians), and 24 Cubans; 116 Americans, 337 Grenadans, and 59 Cubans were wounded. To Reagan this cost was more than worth the returns. In his memoirs, he recalls that his "eyes got a little misty" watching the television coverage of the rescued medical students landing in the United States, seeing them step off the airplanes and "lean down and kiss American soil." On November 7, the White House staged a ceremony for the students and the soldiers who had rescued them. When some of the students embraced the soldiers, Reagan marked the contrast with his experience as governor of California when he had "seen college students spit on anyone wearing a military uniform." In his diary entry he wrote that it was "the most wonderful South Lawn ceremony we've ever had . . . heartwarming, indeed thrilling to see these young people clasp these men in uniforms to their hearts."[18] Reliable assessments of the invasion, however, disclosed that most of the students and their parents in the United States felt it was unnecessary to remove them from the island. And questioning of the administrators of St. George Medical School showed that neither at the time nor subsequently did they believe the students were actually in danger.[19]

The Reagan administration eventually came to rest its case on the grander strategic considerations: the Soviets and Cubans were transforming the island country into a military base. Grenada's neighbors, their independence and security threatened by the presence of an aggressive Soviet–Cuban outpost, had requested U.S. military action under the aegis of regional collective security arrangements which the United States was obligated to honor.

According to the administration, the major indication of the intention of the Grenadan Marxists to turn the island into a Soviet base was the construction of a new airport in Grenada that could handle Soviet and Cuban military traffic. But the new airport had in fact been designed mainly to promote and handle Grenada's increasing tourist traffic. The project was supported and financed by the governments of Canada and Britain, among others; nor did the project involve construction of facilities that would have signaled military use: protected fuel dumps, antiaircraft defenses, hardened shelters for warplanes, or the like.

What about the request for U.S. military intervention by the OECS, the group consisting of Antigua, Dominica, Grenada, Montserrat, St. Kitts–Nevis, St. Lucia, and St. Vincent? A March 1984 report by the British House of Commons concluded that the way in which this OECS request came about remained "shrouded in some mystery."[20] The request was drafted in Washington and delivered to the members of the OECS by special U.S. emissaries. Although the OECS Treaty stipulates that collective action requires a unanimous decision by all seven parties to the Treaty, the Reagan administration chose to interpret a request from only four of the seven members as an official act of the OECS. There is no doubt that at least these four members were alarmed by the radicalizing trends on Grenada and regarded the murder of Bishop as a portent of greater violence, possibly directed against them. Yet it is equally clear that the U.S. government planted the idea with these governments that they should ask for an immediate U.S. military intervention: U.S. ships had been diverted into the area a day before the OECS met.[21]

Reagan repressed these messy details. He chose rather to recall the heroic imagery of "one of the highest of the high points of my eight years in the presidency":

The people of Grenada greeted our soldiers much as the people of France and Europe welcomed our GIs after they liberated them from Nazism at the end of World War II. The Grenadans had been captives of a totalitarian state just as much as the people of Europe. . . . I think our decision to stand up to Castro and the brownshirts on Grenada not only stopped the Communists in their tracks in that part of the world but perhaps helped all Americans stand a little taller.

When Reagan later visited Grenada to personally experience the gratitude of its people, he was delighted to find

no YANKEE GO HOME signs . . . , just an outpouring of love and appreciation from tens of thousands of people—most of its population—and banners proclaiming GOD BLESS AMERICA

I probably never felt better during my presidency than I did that day.[22]

The President was angered by editorials and congressional comments implying that he ordered the invasion of Grenada to distract attention from the massacre of 241 U.S. Marines in their barracks at the

Beirut airport on October 23. He had reason to resent such innuendoes, for although the final order for the actual invasion of Grenada probably was not transmitted until October 24, the preliminaries of Operation Urgent Fury were already underway with presidential approval days before the terrorist attack at Beirut airport. Yet Reagan was partly to blame for the widespread suspicion that his motives were more cathartic than strategic, since he made a special point of linking the two events. "The events in Lebanon and Grenada, though oceans apart, are closely related," he said in his television address of October 27, the first half of which was devoted to the Beirut airport massacre, the second half to the military action still underway in Grenada. "Not only has Moscow assisted and encouraged the violence in both countries, but it provides direct support through a network of surrogates and terrorists." He closed his address with an emotional invocation of the Marine Corps motto, Semper Fidelis, calling on all Americans proudly to "stand shoulder to shoulder in support of our men and women in the armed forces."[23]

CONTRABAND IN NICARAGUA

The Sandinista takeover in Managua had been a favorite issue for Republicans eager to demonstrate the Carter administration's indecisiveness and ineptitude. Now Nicaragua would become the centerpiece of the Reaganites' determination to make the hemisphere inhospitable to Soviet-supported Marxists.

When in the summer and fall of 1980 the Sandinista-dominated government in Nicaragua signed military and intelligence assistance agreements with Soviet bloc countries, Carter's reelection campaign was put on the defensive by Republican allegations of neglect of U.S. interests in Central America. Candidate Reagan demanded a cessation of further U.S. support for the Sandinistas. Before leaving office Carter felt compelled to suspend aid to the now openly pro-Soviet government.

By the time Reagan assumed the presidency, there was renewed and rapidly growing support in the U.S. foreign policy establishment for new vigilance against Soviet-sponsored Marxism in Central America. The political pragmatists in the new administration saw that it would take time for congressional action to reverse the legislative inhibitions against the policies that would be required to oust the Sandinistas from power; but the zealots were impatient to go against the Marxists immediately, even while the pragmatists were trying to forge a broader consensus and a set of policy instruments behind the yet-to-be-named Reagan Doctrine.

The contest between the political pragmatists and the zealots over Reagan's Nicaragua policy allowed Thomas Enders, the experienced diplomat appointed Assistant Secretary of State for Latin America, to operate as point man for Washington–Managua relations at the start of the new administration. Enders, like Secretary Haig a Kissinger protegé, favored a carrot-and-stick realpolitik bargaining approach to the Sandinista government, alternating hints of renewed economic support and threats of U.S. military action to get the Ortega regime to cease its support of the insurgency in El Salvador and to reverse its increasingly close ties with Cuba and the Soviet Union. The elitist diplomatic style and the substance of the early Enders initiatives went against the grain of both the leftist populism in Managua and the new rightist populism that was the animating spirit of the Reagan administration. The Enders approach, involving a flurry of diplomatic shuttles between capitals and overly clever bureaucratic maneuvering in Washington to keep Congress and rivals in the administration from hampering his flexibility, alienated the anti-Communist zealots and stimulated countermoves by Enders' bureaucratic rivals to block his influence.[24]

Casey into the Breach

The new Director of Central Intelligence, William J. Casey, set the pace and direction of policy for rooting the Marxist-Leninists out of Latin America. Casey's case for stepping up covert operations to pro-U.S. elements all around the globe prompted the President to sign a secret Finding on March 9, 1981 authorizing covert CIA anti-Marxist operations in Central America. (The law required the President to formally "find" that national security required covert actions in a particular situation before Congress, acting through its Select Committees on Intelligence, would authorize the release of funds for such operations.) On November 17, with Thomas Enders presenting the comprehensive brief, Casey persuaded Reagan to issue National Security Decision Directive 17 authorizing covert support to the Nicaraguan anti-Sandinistas (who called themselves Contras). This was followed on December 1 by another presidential Finding that identified the Sandinista government as the target; to ward off possible objections from members of the intelligence oversight committees who would see the Finding and who might not be ready to support covert operations against a government with whom the United States maintained formal relations, the objective of the anti-Sandinista program was defined as the interdiction of the arms flow from Nicaragua to the Marxist rebels in neighboring El Salvador.[25]

Countering Congressional Attempts to Restrain the CIA

As newspaper reports of U.S. activities in Nicaragua increased in 1982, the administration released cover stories admitting to aiding the Contras only to prevent the Sandinistas from exporting revolution to El Salvador and not for the purpose of overthrowing the Nicaraguan government. Some members of Congress and editorial writers were skeptical of the official explanation, quoting Contra leaders who claimed their goal *was* the overthrow of the Sandinistas. Other members of Congress and opinion leaders urged that, in the service of bringing democracy to Nicaragua, the U.S. government should openly oppose the Sandinista government.

The debate in Congress resulted in the passage of a restrictive amendment introduced by Representative Edward Boland to the December 1982 defense appropriations bill. Later referred to as Boland I, this amendment prohibited the CIA from using funds "for the purposes of overthrowing the Government of Nicaragua." This was, of course, precisely the raison d'etre of the Contras, as their supporters in the Reagan administration knew very well.

In the months following the enactment of Boland I, reporters filed stories from Nicaragua detailing the deep involvement of the CIA with the Contras. Members of congressional intelligence committees and their staffs also returned from visits to Nicaragua with reports strongly suggesting that the administration's covert action program was operating beyond the limits set by Congress.

The growing suspicions prompted thirty-seven members of the House of Representatives to write to President Reagan on March 24, 1983 warning that CIA operations in Nicaragua could be in violation of the law. Reagan responded to the letter and to the growing chorus of editorial allegations by asserting publicly and unequivocally that "We are complying with the law, the Boland Amendment, which is the law." Whatever "I might personally wish or what our government might wish," he said, "still would not justify us violating the law of the land." Was the administration doing anything to overthrow the government of Nicaragua, journalists probed? "No," replied Reagan, "because that would be violating the law."[26]

In his address on Central America before a joint session of Congress on April 27, 1983, the President further attempted to quiet such concerns:

Let us be clear as to the American attitude toward the Government of Nicaragua. We do not seek its overthrow. Our interest is to ensure that it does not infect its neighbors through the export of subversion and violence. Our purpose, in conformity with American and international law, is to prevent the flow of arms to El Salvador, Honduras, Guatemala, and Costa Rica.[27]

Suspicious congressmen on the intelligence committees were not at all reassured. They introduced legislation in the summer of 1983 threatening an aid cutoff to the Contras in the absence of more concrete indications, secret as well as public, that CIA activities were in fact confined to the President's publicly stated policy objectives.

Fearing a complete congressional cutoff of aid for the Contras, Director Casey devised a new Finding for the President that expanded the rationale to include the more vague and open-ended purpose of pressuring the Sandinista government into negotiating a treaty with its neighboring countries committing them all to cease subversive action against each another and committing the Sandinistas to hold free elections in Nicaragua. Casey's stratagem worked. Intelligence committee members, flattered into believing they finally were being taken into the confidence of the administration, voted in September to support continued covert operations in Nicaragua. Opposition in the House of Representatives, however, resulted in a congressionally imposed cap of $24 million to support the Contras for the coming fiscal year. The $24 million appropriation fell far short of the amount needed to accomplish the administration's larger agenda for Nicaragua. The President's counselors were divided as to whether to rely on the great communicator's speechmaking talents to create a national consensus on behalf of the administration's real policy of ousting the Sandinistas from power or to do an end-run around the Congress. Casey did not wait for the issue to be resolved and pushed ahead with intensified activities designed to escape congressional monitoring.

The Casey–North Connection

Convinced that Casey's schemes had the President's blessings, the new National Security Adviser, Robert McFarlane, assigned his most vigorous and resourceful action officer, Marine Lt. Colonel Oliver North, to serve as the NSC's liaison with the CIA, to provide a conduit for Casey's increasing reliance on the NSC to accomplish in Nicaragua what Congress would not let the CIA do. It is doubtful that the President, with his aloof executive style, fully comprehended the constitutional significance of what was being done under his authority: the Casey–North connection in effect turned North into Casey's principal deputy for operations in Nicaragua. The Director of the CIA created for himself a satellite office within the NSC that took on the special privileges and immunities from accountability that were supposed to be lodged in the CIA itself.

The arrangement was quickly reflected in stepped-up activities by the Contras and their U.S. advisers in Nicaragua. In January and February 1984, with the approval of the President, mines were laid by the CIA in Corinto and Sandino harbors. Col. North served as the NSC staff liaison for this operation, keeping National Security Adviser McFarlane well briefed. An air raid to destroy a Sandinista communications and arms depot was successfully carried out through essentially the same clandestine grouping and earned North a "well done" from NSC Deputy Director Poindexter. [28]

Avoiding Boland II

When a *Wall Street Journal* story on April 6, 1984 revealed that the CIA had been responsible for the mines in Nicaraguan harbors that damaged a Soviet oil tanker and several other ships, there was outrage in the Congress, especially from members of the intelligence committees. Barry Goldwater, the Republican chairman of the Senate Select Intelligence Committee, normally a loyal supporter of the administration, wrote an angry letter to his friend Bill Casey:

I've been trying to figure out how I can most easily tell you my feelings about the discovery of the President having approved mining some of the harbors in Central America.

It gets down to one, little, simple phrase: I am pissed off!

. . .

Bill, this is no way to run a railroad and I find myself in one hell of a quandary. . . .

The President has asked us to back his foreign policy. Bill, how can we back his foreign policy when we don't know what the hell he is doing? Lebanon, yes, we all knew that he sent troops over there. But mine the harbors of Nicaragua? This is an act violating international law. It is an act of war. For the life of me, I don't see how we are going to explain it.[29]

Casey apologized to the congressional committees for inadequate disclosure, but this was insufficient to head off new efforts to rein in the administration's covert operations. In addition to refusing the President's request for an additional $21 million for the Contras, Congress voted another restrictive amendment by Senator Boland to the fiscal 1985 omnibus appropriations bill, which the President reluctantly approved when he signed the whole bill on October 12, 1984. Boland II included the provision that:

During fiscal year 1985, no funds available to the Central Intelligence Agency, the Department of Defense, or any other agency or entity involved in intelligence activities may be obligated or expended for the purpose or which would have the effect of supporting, directly or indirectly, military or paramilitary operations in Nicaragua by any nation, group, organization, movement or individual.[30]

Casey and North, convinced they were operating under a presidential mandate to keep the Contras' "body and soul together," as Reagan put it, would now run the Contra operation almost entirely through the NSC staff—which under their legalistic interpretation of Boland II was not an "agency or entity involved in intelligence activities." And they would bypass the congressional withholding of funds by raising money from private sources and from other governments anxious to do the President of the United States a favor. More than ever, this put North in charge of U.S. policy toward Nicaragua. Casey and North needed and got the full cooperation of the Assistant Secretary of State for Latin American Affairs, Elliot Abrams, and of North's superiors at the NSC, Robert McFarlane and his deputy John Poindexter. Of this group, only McFarlane claimed to have any reservations about the legality of the maneuvers for evading Boland

II. Asked during the Iran–Contra investigations why he did not so advise the President, McFarlane confessed that "probably the reason I didn't is because if I had done that, Bill Casey, Jeane Kirkpatrick and Cap Weinberger would have said I was some kind of commie."[31]

By the end of October 1984 all the elements of what later became known as the Iran–Contra affair were in place: an unshakable conviction at the pinnacle of the administration that removing the Sandinistas from power in Nicaragua was a current imperative in the global struggle against Soviet-sponsored Communism; a determination to use the Contras in the vanguard of that project; a refusal to accept congressional interference with this presumed vital national interest; a small cadre of totally dedicated and resourceful activists, convinced they were loyally serving the President and willing to bend the law and if necessary evade it; an administration pervaded by careerists and sycophants who, even if they doubted the efficacy and legality of what they were asked to facilitate, were too awed or too intimidated by those who claimed to be working directly for the President to blow the whistle.

"The Enterprise"

The President, convinced that the end was right, characteristically left it to his subordinates to devise the means, which included writing the script for his performance. Between the summer of 1984 and early 1986, the President, the National Security Adviser, and the NSC staff secretly raised $34 million for the Contras from other countries—the leading contributor was Saudi Arabia. In addition, North raised $2.7 million in 1985 and 1986 from private contributors who were delighted to help the President fight the good fight, especially when rewarded by an invitation to come to the White House for a personal thank-you and photo opportunity with the President.[32]

Casey and North assigned the job of converting the "third country" and private funds into practical assistance to the Contras while avoiding congressional scrutiny of "the Enterprise"—a clandestine group involving retired military officers with experience in covert operations, soldiers of fortune, and entrepreneurs active in arms sales. Run by retired General Richard Secord and his associate Albert Hakim, an international arms dealer, the Enterprise reported directly to Col. North. According to the congressional report on the Iran–Contra affair:

By the summer of 1986, the organization that Richard Secord ran at Lt. Col. Oliver North's direction controlled five aircraft, including C-123 and C-7 transports. It had an airfield in one country, warehouse facilities at an airbase in another, a stockpile of guns and military equipment to drop by air to the Contras, and secure communications equipment obtained by North from the National Security Agency (NSA).

Flying the planes were veteran pilots and crew, many experienced in covert operations. At any given time, about 20 airmen were paid consultants to a Panamanian corporation formed by Secord and Albert Hakim at North's direction; their salaries were paid from secret Swiss accounts controlled by Secord and Hakim.[33]

The Enterprise and its activities were concealed from Congress and the public. It functioned without any of the accountability required of government activities—even of covert intelligence operations. By maintaining the fiction that it was "private" or funded from foreign sources, Casey, North, and numerous other high officers of the administration—including President Reagan and Vice President Bush—apparently convinced themselves (or at least thought they could convince others) that they were not acting contrary to the Constitution's most basic check on executive action—the power of Congress to grant or deny funding for official U.S. government programs.

In early October, 1986, a Sandinista SAM-7 missile downed one of the aircraft of the Enterprise flying supplies to the Contras. The surviving crew member, Eugene Hasenfus, admitted to his captors that he was employed by an organization with ties to the CIA, but senior U.S. officials categorically denied any U.S. government connection with the supply effort. Two days later, the Secretary of State told interviewers that "The people involved were not from our military, not from any U.S. government agency, CIA included."[34] The next day the President was equally emphatic in responding to questions from skeptical reporters about the Hasenfus plane. "There is no government connection with that at all," he said. But he did allow: "We've been aware that there are private groups and private citizens that have been trying to help the Contras—to that extent— but we did not know the exact particulars of what they're doing." He used the exchange with reporters as an opportunity to praise the courage of those who were trying to get arms to the Contras, comparing them to the "Abraham Lincoln Brigade in the Spanish Civil War."[35] (A curious analogy, since that 1930s group of mainly leftist volunteers aided a Soviet-supported Spanish government holding out against the rightist insurrection led by General Francisco Franco and supported by Hitler.)

In the congressional Iran–Contra hearings the following year, the activities of the Enterprise were held up to the public spotlight. Secord and Hakim detailed their relations with Oliver North and North confirmed most of what they revealed. But North vigorously defended his role in setting up and giving direction to the Enterprise as being required by the highest national interests and as entirely within the law—basing his legal argument on the grounds that the funds for the operation were all raised from private or third country sources, and thus could not be a misuse of public funds in violation of the congressional proscriptions; and that his NSC office, from which he guided and facilitated the work of the Enterprise and related pro-Contra activity, was a part of the President's NSC staff and was not one of the named agencies in the 1984 Boland Amendment prohibited from assisting the Contras.

North justified the Enterprise on the basis that the President was determined the Contras should be kept alive despite opposition in Congress, and that the President's obduracy was repeatedly confirmed orally and in documents by his immediate superiors in the White House, Robert McFarlane and Admiral John Poindexter. North also invoked the national interest in defense of his having withheld information from Congress about his pro-Contra activities: such scrupulous secrecy was necessary, he argued, for the safety of those involved in the dangerous covert operations.

McFarlane and Poindexter, in their testimony, backed up North's claims about the President's commitment to the Contras and admitted their own complicity with Casey and North in avoiding full disclosure to Congress. At the same time, they were especially protective of the President and other high officials who claimed a lack of detailed knowledge of the covert operations, particularly those actions that might raise questions of legality.

When it came to explaining the whys and wherefores of the diversion to the Contras of the profits from the secret sale of arms to Iran (see Chapter 24), Poindexter and North denied they had done anything fundamentally wrong (while taking responsibility for all

U.S. government actions on behalf of the Contras); they insisted they were acting only to loyally implement the President's policies (indeed, Poindexter testified he believed the President would have approved the diversion if he had been asked), yet denied that the President ever explicitly authorized the messy operational details.

The hubris of noble ends justifying corrupt means was perhaps most revealingly expressed by Oliver North's impeccably efficient and loyal secretary, Fawn Hall. She did feel a bit uneasy, she admitted, in helping her boss alter, destroy, and smuggle documents out of the White House that might incriminate North and his associates. But Hall was convinced that "protecting the initiative" required these unusual measures. Didn't she know, asked Congressman Tom Foley, that such handling of official documents was considered a violation of one's legal responsibilities as a public servant? Hall responded that she did know this, but that she believed in Colonel North and what he was doing. "Sometimes you have to go above the written law," she said.[36]

Fawn Hall's statement was doubly revealing in that it stripped away North's pretense that he always thought he was acting within the law: Hall was obviously reflecting her boss's philosophy. But from how far up in the Reagan administration did this philosophy emanate?

The Growing Circle of Culpability

In the hierarchy above North there was no such willingness to admit publicly to such a disdain for the law—the Watergate affair was too deeply seared into the consciousness of this generation of high officeholders. The official posture at the cabinet level was one of scrupulous legal rectitude. As the story of the Iranian arms for hostages initiative surfaced in the world press in November 1986 and American journalists and congressional staff began to close in on the truth, the President acceded to Attorney General Edward Meese's suggestion that the Justice Department fully investigate any possibility of legal improprieties. Despite tactical warnings to Poindexter, North, and Casey, the Meese investigation inadvertently uncovered Poindexter–North memoranda on the secret diversion to the Contras of profits from the Iran arms initiative. The Attorney General reported this immediately to the President. White House chief of staff Donald Regan, the President's wife, and others in Reagan's inner circle persuaded the President to preempt Congress and the press by going public with what was known and firing Poindexter and North. (Officially, the President accepted Admiral Poindexter's resignation and Col. North was reassigned to the Marine Corps.)

After informing the full National Security Council and the congressional leadership on November 25, 1986, President Reagan and Attorney General Meese faced the press to tell about Meese's discovery of the Iran–Contra diversion and what they intended to do about it. The President's opening statement was as cryptic as it was brief. He told of not being fully informed about an activity undertaken in connection with the Iran initiative that raised "serious questions" about its propriety. The two officials most directly responsible, National Security Adviser Poindexter and Col. North, were being relieved of their duties at the NSC. But the President still defended his administration's "policy goals toward Iran" as "well founded." It was only the implementation that was "seriously flawed" in this case. Measures were being taken to avoid mistakes of this sort in the future by assuring that such initiatives proceeded only under his authorization. He then turned the rest of the press briefing over to Meese.[37]

The Attorney General was not about to grant that any U.S. official had actually violated any law. The Department of Justice, he said, was still looking into whether there was any criminality involved. All those associated with the Iran initiative claimed that the questionable transactions were conducted by Israel, and therefore, "So far as we know at this stage, no American person actually handled any of the funds that went to the forces in Central America."[38]

Reagan's public relations staff and Meese's lawyers quickly went into action to undercut any attempt by the President's opponents to suggest that the administration, and not simply a few misguided functionaries in the NSC, was guilty of impropriety, let alone illegalities. The President appointed a special review board comprising Senator John Tower, Edmund Muskie, and former National Security Adviser Brent Scowcroft, with the mandate to assess the procedures of the National Security Council staff. A distinguished jurist, Lawrence E. Walsh, was appointed independent counsel to investigate the Iran–Contra diversion.

Congress would not allow the administration to stage manage its own self-investigation. North and Poindexter should not be allowed to simply walk off into the obscurity of anonymous jobs somewhere: they owed it to the country to reveal what they were really doing and at whose direction. The public hearings of the House Select Committee to Investigate Covert Arms Transactions with Iran and the Senate Select Committee on Secret Military Assistance to Iran and the Nicaraguan Opposition, although allowing Oliver North a national stage from which to galvanize popular support for his patriotic zealotry, also kept public attention focused on the scandalous aspects of Iran–Contra. Reagan left office on January 20, 1989 with nagging questions still ringing in his ears: How high in his administration did the malfeasance extend? How much did the President know of what was being done in his name?

The White House hope that the rather anodyne findings of the Tower Commission—its strongest criticisms were directed at the President's overly aloof management style—would cool the public's enthusiasm for the intensifying spectacle on Capitol Hill was not to be realized. Its very blandness consigned the Tower Commission report to relative obscurity in contrast to the televised Iran–Contra hearings, with their parade of charismatic witnesses and duel of legal gladiators.

Meanwhile, the tenacious investigations by independent counsel Lawrence Walsh uncovered sufficient evidence of indictable criminal offenses by North, Poindexter, and others associated with the Enterprise to warrant bringing them to trial. Walsh obtained criminal convictions of North, Poindexter, and ex-CIA agent Thomas Clines. North was convicted in May 1989 on three felony counts: aiding and abetting obstruction of Congress, destroying National Security Council documents, and accepting an illegal gift. He was fined $150,000 and sentenced to two years' probation and 1,200 hours of community service. Poindexter was convicted the following April on five counts involving charges that he obstructed and made false statements to Congress and was sentenced to six months in prison. Clines was convicted of various financial crimes, sentenced to 16 months in prison, and fined $40,000. All three men appealed their convictions and in July 1990 a Federal appeals court suspended all three of North's felony convictions—a ruling that independent counsel Walsh unsuccessfully appealed to the Supreme Court. Robert

McFarlane, Richard Secord, Albert Hakim, and two of the Enterprise's private fundraisers, Carl Channell and Richard Miller, all pleaded guilty to various charges in the Iran–Contra affair. Each was sentenced to probation and some were required to pay fines or perform community service.

Walsh's initial prosecution of those most directly involved portended the possibility of more indictments of a much wider network of administration officials. But Walsh's further investigations were severely inhibited by the wall of secrecy surrounding the CIA and by the death of CIA Director Casey of a brain tumor in the midst of the congressional Iran–Contra hearings, and by the immunity from future prosecution offered witnesses by the congressional Iran–Contra committee.

26

THE REAGAN–GORBACHEV
SYMBIOSIS

JOURNALIST: *Sir, yesterday you did say you no longer believed the Soviet Union is an "evil empire." You said that was another time, another era. What's changed? Is is just Mr. Gorbachev's succession to the General Secretaryship, or have you yourself changed or expanded your view of the Soviet Union?*
THE PRESIDENT: *No, I think that a great deal of it is due to the General Secretary, who I have found different than previous Soviet leaders have been.*

—REAGAN NEWS CONFERENCE

The official line from Washington explaining the rapid thaw in the superpower cold war relationship during the last three years of the Reagan administration was that the President's peace through strength policy worked. The basic premises of the full court press against the USSR had been validated: by challenging the Soviets to an expensive arms race with exotic technologies, by refusing the Russians and their allies normal commercial access to capitalist markets, by putting the Kremlin on the defensive both with respect to human rights abuses and the failure of economic modernization in the Soviet sphere, and by countering Marxist-Leninist movements and regimes in the Third World, the United States had forced the Soviets to severely constrict their external expansionary activities. In short, Reagan produced Gorbachev. The record of the administration's policymaking, however, reveals a considerably more complex story.

REAGAN'S PRE-GORBACHEV MELLOWING

More than a year before Gorbachev ascended to power in the Kremlin, the White House was faced with the contradictions between the increasing federal deficit and the full court press strategy against the Soviet Union. Looking toward the 1984 elections, domestic political advisers were telling the President that he needed to find a way to prevent the Democrats from exploiting the peace issue. The President's foreign policy advisers counselled that the Soviets were still in a post-Brezhnev torpor and might be amenable to a relaxation of international tensions while they worked on their domestic problems.

On January 16, 1984, Reagan delivered an uncharacteristically conciliatory speech on U.S.–Soviet relations. It included the usual self-congratulatory claims of American economic recovery and restored military strength and the standard characterization of the adversary as "a government that does not share our notions of individual liberties at home and peaceful change abroad." Deterrence would remain essential to preserve peace and the American way of life, but

deterrence is not the beginning and end of our policy toward the Soviet Union. We must and will engage the Soviets in a dialogue as serious and constructive as possible.

The new U.S.–Soviet dialogue, said the President, should concentrate on three broad areas:

First, we need to find ways to reduce, and eventually eliminate, the threat and use of force in . . . regional conflicts. . . . As a first step, our governments should jointly examine concrete actions that we can both take to reduce the risk of U.S.–Soviet confrontation in these areas. . . .

Our second task should be to find ways to reduce the vast stockpiles of armaments in the world. . . . We must accelerate our efforts to reach agreements that will greatly reduce nuclear arsenals, provide greater stability, and build confidence.

Our third task is to establish a better working relationship with each other, one marked by greater cooperation and understanding. . . . We're prepared to discuss the problems that divide us and to work for practical, fair solutions on the basis of mutual compromise.[1]

The President affirmed that the United States was ready to resume serious arms limitation negotiations on strategic weapons and to continue to work with the Soviets on East–West confidence-building measures, including advance notification of missile tests, military maneuvers, and the like, to avoid dangerous miscalculations and to diminish the risk of surprise attack. "We will negotiate in good faith," he promised. "Whenever the Soviet Union is ready to do likewise, we'll meet them halfway."[2]

He returned to this theme in his 1984 State of the Union address on January 24, saying that he wanted "to speak to the people of the Soviet Union" to tell them that if their government wanted it, "We can come together in faith and friendship to build a safer and better world." In contrast to the standard strategic and NATO concepts that the Secretary of Defense would reiterate to the Congress a few days later,[3] Reagan intoned:

People of the Soviet Union, there is only one sane policy, for your country and mine, to preserve our civilization in this modern age: A nuclear war cannot be won and must never be fought. The only value in our two nations possessing nuclear weapons is to make sure they will never be used. But then would it not be better to do away with them entirely?[4]

Over the next few months, prior to the 1984 elections, the administration's posture toward the Soviet Union mixed continuing toughness and clear indications of a willingness to make another try at détente (though the administration would never use that word). This mix was less the product of a calculated carrot-and-stick policy than the result of different agencies and elements within the administration getting Oval Office endorsement for their particular projects. Washington's seeming ambivalence was also in part simply a reaction to Moscow's erratic and unsettled foreign policy during Brezhnev's last tottering years until the installation of Gorbachev in the spring of 1985.

Throughout the spring of 1984, the Pentagon kept hammering away at Soviet violations of arms control agreements: the construction of a radar facility in Krasnoyarsk, Siberia and the encoding of missile tests to avoid detection. In March, the new Soviet Communist Party General Secretary Konstantin Chernenko, succeeding Andropov, called for a renewed U.S.–Soviet dialogue. U.S. administration spokesmen welcomed the conciliatory tone. In Vienna, NATO and Warsaw Pact negotiators resumed their talks on conventional force reductions; but the strategic force negotiations, derailed by the Soviet walkout in reaction to the new U.S. intermediate nuclear force deployments in Europe, were still not back on track. Instead, the Soviets announced deployment of a new intermediate-range missile of their own.

Public receptivity to better East-West relations suffered a setback with the imbroglio over the Los Angeles Summer Olympic games when the U.S. government denied visas to certain Soviet officials because of their ties to the KGB; in May the Soviets and most of their allies announced they were pulling out of the games, claiming inadequate security for their athletes. Nevertheless, on a broad, and less visible, front, efforts to restore detente went forward. In July, the superpowers agreed to modernize the "hot line" between Moscow and Washington, the Reagan administration rescinded the 1980 ban on Soviet fishing in U.S. waters, and U.S. and Soviet trade officials again began exploring ways of resuming more normal commercial relations.

Reagan's public effort to outflank Walter Mondale on the peace issue almost came undone with his gaffe at the start of his August 11 weekly radio broadcast. Mistakenly believing he was only testing the microphone prior to air time, the President joked, in mock confirmation of the charge he was a warmonger: "We begin bombing in five minutes!" Hardly anyone thought it funny, least of all Reagan's campaign managers, as editorial writers around the world expressed alarm over trusting the fate of the planet to someone with such a cavalier attitude toward his responsibilities.

Opinion polls at the end of the summer indicated that Reagan's most unpopular trait was his harsh anti-Soviet stance. Secretary Shultz accordingly suggested the President should have Soviet Foreign Minister Andrei Gromyko pay a visit to the Oval Office in connection with his trip to New York to attend the United Nations General Assembly meeting in September.[5] Nancy Reagan was apparently instrumental in convincing her husband to extend the invitation.[6]

The President addressed the United Nations General Assembly on September 24. Building on the themes of his January address, he issued a ringing call for the "new beginning" of a more cooperative superpower relationship. He invited the Soviets to join the Americans in multiple negotiating arenas to reduce international tensions—particularly to resolve regional conflicts, to reverse the arms race, and (in a departure from previous "linkage" strategies) not to allow setbacks in one field to hold up progress in others. Toward this end, Reagan proposed to the Soviets (who at the outset of his administration he insisted were too deceitful to negotiate with seriously) that "we institutionalize regular ministerial or cabinet-level meetings between our two countries on the whole agenda of issues before us, including the problem of needless obstacles to understanding." Identifying himself at the end of his speech with humanity's greatest peacemakers, Reagan quoted the "vision" of Mahatma Gandhi: "Think on it . . . always. All through history the way of truth and love has always won."[7]

Gromyko, whose General Assembly address followed Reagan's, used the occasion to strongly denounce U.S. foreign policy. The Soviet foreign minister met with Secretary Shultz in New York, where he also met with the Democratic presidential candidate. The White House meeting between the President and Gromyko the next day, while providing the photo opportunities Reagan's campaign managers wanted, turned out to be a frigid affair, but no matter—foreign policy issues had virtually no effect on the November election results. An overwhelming majority of the voters, evidently agreeing with Reagan that they were "better off now than you were four years ago," gave the Republican ticket a landslide victory.

GENEVA 1985: THE FIRST ENCOUNTER

The domestic economic recovery helped re-elect Reagan; but despite his upbeat rhetoric, the President was by now aware of the deep risks of continuing to finance the recovery by getting the country deeper and deeper into debt. Moreover, he knew that even under the most optimistic supply-side assumptions about increasing revenues without raising taxes, the federal budget could not be brought into balance without drastic cuts in expenditures, including substantial reductions in defense outlays. Meanwhile, the huge national debt was driving up interest rates and making it virtually impossible to erase the country's international trade deficit, while the principal economic competitor of the U.S., Japan, unburdened by huge defense obligations, was outpacing the United States in the production and marketing of attractive high-tech consumer goods.

Michael Deaver and Nancy Reagan in particular were concerned by new public opinion surveys reflecting a widespread belief that the President was too hawkish for the safety of the nation. Mikhail

Gorbachev's accession to power in the spring of 1985, and the evident determination of this relatively young pragmatist to modernize Soviet society, plus his recognition that a less threatening international environment was required for sufficient resources to be allocated to this task, could well provide the opening for Reagan to take center stage as the great peacemaker.

Michael Deaver gives Mrs. Reagan much of the credit for getting the Reagan–Gorbachev show underway. "It was Nancy who pushed everybody on the Geneva summit. She felt strongly that it was not only in the interest of world peace but the correct move politically. She would buttonhole George Shultz, Bud McFarlane, and others, to be sure that they were moving toward that goal."[8] In her memoirs, Nancy Reagan explains that:

With the world so dangerous, I felt it was ridiculous for these two heavily armed superpowers to be sitting there and not talking to each other. I encouraged Ronnie to meet with Gorbachev as soon as possible, especially when I realized that some people in the administration did not favor any real talks. So yes, I did push Ronnie a little. But he would never have met Gorbachev if he hadn't wanted to.[9]

Shultz and McFarlane wanted the President to meet with Gorbachev while Secretary of Defense Weinberger, CIA Director Casey, and Ed Meese did not. The pro-summit faction had a crucial ally in White House Chief of Staff Donald Regan, at this point the person who, apart from Nancy, had the most influence over Reagan's plans. The former Treasury Secretary weighed in with arguments about the relationship between Soviet economic troubles and Gorbachev's grand strategy. The key was SDI: to stay equal, the Soviets would either have to build a defensive shield of their own or develop a new generation of offensive weapons capable of penetrating it. To match SDI, Regan told the President, "Gorbachev would have to mortgage the whole future of communism." That was why Gorbachev wanted to negotiate, and that was why Reagan would be "holding the trump card" in the negotiations.[10]

The Geneva Summit

The first U.S.–USSR summit in six years began in Geneva on November 19, 1985 and lasted four days. Secretary of Defense Weinberger in particular was concerned that the President, even under the tutelage of Secretary Shultz and NSC adviser McFarlane, might be too eager to come away with a dramatic breakthrough in arms control without understanding the full strategic implications. A Weinberger letter to the President advising him not to give in to the Soviets on arms control was leaked to the *New York Times* and the *Washington Post* while the presidential party was en route to Geneva. McFarlane and others around the President believed it to have been a deliberate leak by disgruntled Pentagon hardliners— perhaps even Weinberger himself—designed to sabotage the summit.[11]

Although neither Reagan nor Gorbachev made any compromise of substance on any of the major outstanding issues in U.S.–Soviet relations, the hawks were nonetheless disconcerted, fearing that Reagan, like Franklin Roosevelt, was possessed of the hubristic illusion that he could charm his Soviet counterpart into a mutually trusting relationship and that such personal trust between the two could overcome the hostility between the two nations. In his memoirs, Reagan confirms that this was indeed the way he felt. "I believed that if we were ever going to break down the barriers of mistrust that divided our countries, we had to begin by establishing a personal relationship between the leaders of the two most powerful nations on earth. . . . I wanted to convince Gorbachev that we wanted peace and they had nothing to fear from us."[12] Even before Gorbachev came to power:

I'd dreamed of personally going one-on-one with a Soviet leader because I thought we might be able to accomplish things our countries' diplomats couldn't do because they didn't have the authority. Putting that another way, I felt that if you got the top people negotiating and talking at a summit and then the two of you came out arm in arm saying, "We've agreed to this," the bureaucrats wouldn't be able to louse up the agreement. Until Gorbachev, I never got an opportunity to try out my idea. Now I had my chance.[13]

In their formal concluding statement the two leaders agreed to an exchange of visits in the near future and to accelerate the negotiations on nuclear and space arms. They endorsed the principle of halving their nuclear arsenals; directed their experts to study the idea of jointly staffed nuclear risk-reduction centers and other confidence-building measures; reaffirmed their commitment to the Treaty on the Non-Proliferation of Nuclear Weapons and agreed to continue their bilateral consultations on this problem; agreed to accelerate efforts to ban chemical weapons; and encouraged increased U.S.–Soviet cooperative endeavors in various environmental, scientific, and transportation projects. Picking up a theme from Reagan's address to the United Nations, the joint statement approved the idea of regular meetings between the Soviet Minister of Foreign Affairs and the U.S. Secretary of State as well as between the heads of other agencies. The joint statement also adopted Reagan's statement that "a nuclear war cannot be won and must never be fought." A related departure from the U.S. government's internal planning premises was the phrase that the superpowers "will not seek to achieve military superiority" over one another.[14]

Generalities. No substantive agreements. Still, the chemistry that began to develop between these two vastly different personalities had the potential for more substantial results, and they and their immediate aides were excited by it. The White House press secretary recounts that as the two leaders prepared to sign the final summit statements, Reagan whispered to Gorbachev, "I bet the hardliners in both our countries are squirming," and that Gorbachev nodded in agreement.[15]

Donald Regan's account of the Geneva summit captures some of the chemistry between the two men, as revealed in particular in their informal conversations. The White House Chief of Staff, attuned to the President's preferences, arranged to have the informal one-on-one sessions as often as possible. During these, "The President, speaking in anecdotes as is his way, sprinkled his conversation with memorable phrases from past presidents and other famous Americans. Gorbachev was almost wholly impersonal in his own statements. . . . his interest ran to issues rather than personalities, and he seemed to have a detached rather than a narrative style."[16] Given this characterization, Regan's report, a few sentences later, that "Both Gorbachev and his wife were spellbound by Reagan's stories of his Hollywood days" seems somewhat exaggerated. But clearly the Soviet leader gave the President to feel that he held them spellbound, laughing appreciatively at Reagan's jokes.

Reagan came away from the summit liking Gorbachev and—which was to prove significant for their subsequent encounters—wanting to trust the Soviet leader and wanting desperately for Gorbachev to trust him. Nancy Reagan recalls an "unmistakable warmth" between the two men. And with this achieved, "Ronnie's main objective for the Geneva summit had already been met. Above all, he had wanted to establish a personal working relationship with Gorbachev. Everything else would follow from that."[17] Reagan would refer to "our personal liking for each other" and in his memoirs he gives great weight to the "chemistry between Gorbachev and me that produced something very close to a personal friendship."[18] A few days after returning to Washington, Reagan recalled for his press secretary how in one of his private chats with Gorbachev they had reflected on their immense mutual power, not only to bring about World War III, but to prevent it. "I think I'm some judge of acting, and I don't think Gorbachev was acting. He, I believe, is sincere, as we are, in wanting an agreement."[19]

THE EMBARRASSMENTS OF REYKJAVIK

On October 9, 1986 (the day Nancy Reagan's astrologer thought most auspicious[20]), only ten days after deciding to go, after putting aside his prior insistence that he would not participate in another summit meeting before the 1986 midterm elections—certainly not one without a clear agenda of issues already thoroughly prepared at lower diplomatic levels—the President and a hurriedly assembled entourage departed on Air Force One for Reykjavik, Iceland.

Administration officials refused to call it a summit; but their awkward locutions (pre-summit, preparatory meeting) were unconvincing and were belied over the next few days as the extent to which Reagan and Gorbachev became engaged in strategically momentous negotiations became known. The President had every intention—misguided or not—of conducting serious negotiations. He was looking to build on the exchange of letters he had been conducting with Gorbachev over the past four months, which culminated in a letter hand-delivered by Foreign Minister Shevardnadze to Reagan on September 19. In this letter, Gorbachev not only proposed a meeting between the two at the earliest time possible to resolve the deadlock of the professional arms control negotiators, but also moderated a number of previously rigid Soviet positions on intermediate range missiles (particularly with respect to British and French missiles). Reagan sensed an opportunity for a "historic breakthrough."[21]

Historic it was. Reykjavik now appears in the diplomatic lexicon as a symbol for amateurish, ill-prepared, and romantically naive summitry. As put by John Newhouse, "There can have been no stranger meeting between leaders of big powers . . . in modern history. . . . Two high rollers were matching idealistic visions and raising each other. They reached a higher and more rarefied place than anyone had been, and then fell off the cliff."[22]

Gorbachev brought with him to Reykjavik a proposal with which, he told Reagan, they could "wrench arms control out of the hands of the bureaucrats." He and the President could now agree to the principles of a treaty which the specialists would then prepare for their signatures at a forthcoming Washington summit. Gorbachev's proposal featured a halving of strategic offensive forces, distributed across all categories of weaponry, including—and this was sure bait for Reagan—substantial cuts in heavy missiles. Another Soviet concession (foreshadowed in his letters to Reagan) concerned NATO intermediate-range missiles and bombers, even those capable of striking the Soviet Union: these would no longer be included in the total from which the 50 percent reduction would be calculated. We will accept "your definition" of "strategic," he told the Americans. Along with the strategic arms reductions, all Soviet and U.S. intermediate-range missiles in Europe would be eliminated—"your own zero option," Mr. President. There was even a concession on SDI: in consideration of how strongly Reagan was attached to it, said Gorbachev, the program could go forward as long as it complied with the ABM treaty for ten years (the Soviets up to then had been demanding a fifteen year adherence).[23]

As Reagan's and Gorbachev's advisers discussed the Gorbachev proposals, it emerged that the only issue blocking agreement was the ABM treaty; the Soviets insisted that the ABM treaty be strictly interpreted, and the Americans insisted on a broad interpretation. The disagreement revolved around the technical question of the extent to which tests of SDI components had to be confined to laboratories. The anti-arms control, anti-détente members of the U.S. delegation, led by the Pentagon's Richard Perle, were not anxious for this deadlock to be broken, and counselled that the President should stick to his guns; but they were sensitive to the position into which Gorbachev had skillfully maneuvered the President—one of looking obstructionist before the world in the face of his counterpart's remarkably generous concessions.

Perle accordingly got Secretary Shultz to endorse a dramatic démarche for Reagan to put to Gorbachev: the superpowers would agree to eliminate all ballistic missiles over a ten-year period. During the first five years, the arsenals would be cut in half, and the ABM treaty would remain in force. At the end of the ten-year period, with no ballistic missiles on either side, deployments of antimissile defenses would be permitted as "insurance" against cheating or accidents and against the missiles of other countries. Gorbachev would be bound to reject the American counterproposal—thought Perle—since the Soviets would be divesting themselves of their strategic advantage in ballistic missiles while the United States retained its advantage in strategic bombers and cruise missiles.

No stranger to this political game, Gorbachev was not about to be branded the naysayer. In the final Sunday evening session, he upped the ante, proposing the elimination of all nuclear weapons over a ten year period. The American president's startling acceptance of this proposal, which Reagan and his aides later denied, has since been confirmed by various sources. Chief of Staff Regan's verbatim account is the key source:

Nuclear weapons? Reagan said. Well, Mikhail, that's exactly what I've been talking about all along. That's what we have long wanted to do—get rid of all nuclear weapons. That's always been my goal.
"Then why don't we agree on it?" Gorbachev asked.
We should, Reagan said. That's what I've been trying to tell you.[24]

The President reportedly thought a great historical moment had arrived. But then Gorbachev suddenly ruined it all by adding that the abolition of nuclear weapons had to be in conjunction with a ten-year extension of the ABM treaty and a ban on the development and testing of SDI outside the laboratory. "He threw us a curve," the President later wrote. "I couldn't believe it and blew my top."[25] Abrupt and unequivocal in his angry refusal, the President gathered up his papers. Gorbachev tried to dissuade him from leaving. Reagan said it was too late. The summit was over.

Donald Regan recalls the President's distress:

In the limousine Reagan was somber, and for the first time since I had known him I felt I was in the presence of a truly disappointed man.

. . .

Reagan sat in silence . . . Then he said, Don, we came so close. It's just such a shame. . . .
His frustration was palpable.

Laboratory, laboratory, laboratory, the President said, repeating the word over and over again.[26]

Speakes remembers it as "a crushing blow" for Reagan. "Now he saw time running out. I believe when he told Gorbachev 'It's too late,' he was—for once—confronting his own mortality."[27] Reagan himself, in his otherwise cheerful memoir, confesses that "At Reykjavik, my hopes for a nuclear-free world soared briefly, then fell during one of the most disappointing—and ultimately angriest—days of my presidency."[28]

The administration's massive public relations machine undertook "the biggest effort we ever made to get out the White House side of the story," says Speakes. Administration officials made some ninety press appearances in the first three days after the summit. At the end of the exhausting post-summit week of spin control, Don Regan quipped to the *New York Times*: "Some of us are like a shovel brigade that follows a parade down Main Street, cleaning up."[29]

National security policy analysts of all persuasions, in and out of government, feared that Reagan and his aides were themselves spinning out of control—losing the capacity to distinguish between the hard realities of geopolitics and the illusions of presidential greatness they were weaving. In a scathing article in *Foreign Affairs*, former Secretary of Defense James Schlesinger, one of Washington's most respected and sober hardliners, inveighed against the "casual utopianism" that marked the President's performance at Reykjavik and that turned the summit into a "near disaster from which we were fortunate to escape." Schlesinger pointed to the "astonishing irony" that it was "the President's preoccupation with SDI" that "saved us from the embarrassment of entering into completed agreements from which subsequently we would have had to withdraw." The U.S. was lucky. The President was lucky. But he was reckless:

At Reykjavik he was prepared apparently to sacrifice our entire strategic nuclear-armament, but unprepared to compromise on outside-the-laboratory testing of SDI. One finds it hard to believe that preserving the freedom to test SDI is by itself of sufficient importance to determine whether to jettison or salvage the entire Western system of security based on nuclear deterrence.[30]

Many in the peace movement felt that a wonderful opportunity had been stupidly squandered. But in the eyes of most of Washington's defense and arms control community, the country could thank

Reagan's Star Wars for inadvertently preventing an ignominious diplomatic defeat. John Newhouse reports that Allied leaders, including the usually supportive Margaret Thatcher, were shaken, judging "the what-might-have-been as constituting a near abandonment of the American commitment to defend Europe."[31]

Most of the criticism of Reagan's performance at Reykjavik was based on the premise that the global balance of power restraining Soviet international aggressiveness depended crucially on the credibility of the NATO (primarily U.S.) threat to respond with overwhelming power, including nuclear weapons, to any Soviet military move against a country outside its sphere of control. To eliminate nuclear weapons from the equation, prior to rectifying the conventional force imbalance favoring the Soviets and their Warsaw Pact allies, would be to grant the Soviet side overall superiority in the global balance of power. Moreover, without having to face the likelihood of military conflict escalating to nuclear war, the Soviets would be tempted to engage in aggression, under the assumption of being able to control the risks.

After Reykjavik, and having to fend off the rising chorus of neo-conservative criticism that he was, like the detentists in the Nixon, Ford, and Carter administrations, too easily beguiled by Soviet promises rather than deeds, Reagan for a while shied away from positions that might confirm fears that he was turning soft. He retrieved the heroic high ground in June 1987 in a speech at the Berlin Wall on his return from the G-7 economic summit in Vienna. "We hear much from Moscow about a new policy of reform and openness," he said. "Are these the beginnings of profound changes in the Soviet state? Or are they token gestures, intended to raise false hopes in the West, or to strengthen the Soviet system without changing it?" There was one sign that the Soviets could make of real change:

General Secretary Gorbachev, if you seek peace, if you seek prosperity for the Soviet Union and Eastern Europe, if you seek liberalization: Come here to this gate! Mr. Gorbachev, open this gate! Mr. Gorbachev, tear down this wall![32]

Reagan admits in his memoirs that this was a rhetorical gambit. "I never dreamed that in less than three years the wall would come down and a six-thousand pound section of it would be sent to me for my presidential library."[33]

THE INF BREAKTHROUGH

In Gorbachev's comprehensive opening proposal at Reykjavik on October 11, 1986, the Soviets had indicated a readiness to accept the essentials of Reagan's zero option for intermediate-range nuclear forces (INF). The INF offer was taken seriously by Reagan's advisers, for it was consistent with what Gorbachev had stated to Reagan in their exchange of letters leading up to the summit. Perhaps at least this part of the convergence between the two leaders could be retrieved.

The elimination of INF from their arsenals would be a natural, strategically risk free, yet dramatic, first step by the superpowers toward mutual nuclear disarmament. It would remove weapons that were essentially superfluous for both sides. Any targets now assigned to the INF could be covered by only a small fraction of their intercontinental-range forces. The United States would insist on stringent verification procedures; but even if one side cheated, it would not attain a decisive strategic advantage. But would Gorbachev be willing to "de-link" an INF treaty from the impasse over SDI? The answer came from the Soviet leader on February 27, 1987, in a statement offering to separate the INF negotiations from all other issues, including SDI.

But there was still opportunity for mischief. Two additional ploys remained for Richard Perle and others in the administration opposed to arms control: the United States would insist on a "double-zero" INF ban—not only on all U.S. and Soviet deployments in Europe, but all such intermediate-range nuclear forces worldwide, thus compelling the Soviets to dismantle their anti-China systems deployed in Siberia. The U.S. would also demand verification procedures the Soviets would be bound to reject as too intrusive.

Once again, however, Gorbachev showed himself to be master of the technique of throwing the adversary off balance by suddenly removing all resistance. The Soviet negotiators were given instructions in the spring of 1987 to accept the premise of the U.S. proposal that all Soviet and American intermediate-range land-based missiles should be banned: there should be no deployment anywhere in the world; indeed, the missiles in the inventories of the superpowers would be dismantled or destroyed. In addition, the Soviet negotiators argued for even more intrusive on-site inspection procedures:

whereas the Americans had insisted on stationing inspectors at suspected missile production or storage sites on the basis of spur-of-the-moment challenges, to monitor what was coming in and out, the Soviets now urged inspections of the interiors of such facilities as well, "any time, any place," including on the territory of "third countries."

This was exactly the opposite of what the Pentagon authors of the toughened verification requirements had expected: the Russians were supposed to find the requirements incompatible with national sovereignty. The negotiations would have gotten nowhere. Now, however, it was the turn of the American hardliners to invoke fears of espionage: suppose the Soviet inspectors insisted on entering sensitive intelligence facilities or ICBM bunkers; this was verification run wild.[34]

Clearly neither side wanted anything near this degree of intrusive inspection. But each leader, for his own reasons, really did want the INF negotiations to produce an arms reduction treaty for them to sign in a Washington summit meeting before the end of the year. Gorbachev was determined to reduce the drain on Soviet resources from the persisting global rivalry with the United States; an INF ban would involve the dismantling of already-deployed Soviet forces and could mark a turn toward a substantially reduced arms competition. And Reagan, who also sensed the positive fiscal implications of success in arms control, now had the additional incentive of diverting public attention away from the Iran–Contra scandal.

As it turned out, the verification experts on both sides found they could transcend the negotiating impasse, once it was agreed that all U.S. and Soviet missiles with ranges of between 500 and 3,000 miles would be eliminated; even the discovery of one missile in this comprehensive class of weapons would be proof of violation, so a somewhat less intrusive inspection regime would suffice. Accordingly, the White House and Kremlin approved treaty wording providing for short-notice inspections at sites on mutually agreed lists of installations—which was hailed by Reagan as "the most stringent verification regime in history."[35]

Reagan and Gorbachev finally had the positive international accomplishment each had been seeking. Their signing of the INF treaty was the centerpiece of their summit meeting of December 7–10, 1987 in Washington.

In the signing ceremony, the President shared credit with the Soviet leader for effectuating a "dramatic shift in thinking, to which it took conventional wisdom some time to catch up." The two of them had been more creative than their respective experts. "To some the zero option was impossibly visionary and unrealistic; to others merely a propaganda ploy. Well, with patience, determination, and commitment, we've made this impossible vision a reality." General Secretary Gorbachev stated that this "first-ever agreement eliminating nuclear weapons . . . offers a big chance at last to get on the road leading . . . toward a nuclear-free world. . . . We can be proud of planting this sapling which may one day grow into a mighty tree of peace." And not to be outdone by the President's hyperbole, he offered: "May December 8, 1987, become a date that will be inscribed in the history books, a date that will mark the watershed separating the era of a mounting risk of nuclear war from the era of a demilitarization of human life."

The Reaganesque scene at the signing ceremony included lump-in-the-throat emotion, warm handshakes, and the good fellowship of light-hearted repartee:

THE PRESIDENT: We have listened to the wisdom in an old Russian maxim. And I'm sure you're familiar with it, Mr. General Secretary, though my pronunciation may give you difficulty. The maxim is: *dovorey no provorey*—trust but verify.
THE GENERAL SECRETARY: You repeat that at every meeting. [Laughter]
THE PRESIDENT: I like it. [Laughter] [36]

TOWARD THE END OF THE COLD WAR?

Seven months before the end of his presidency, Ronald Reagan finally made a trip to the capital of what early in his first term he had branded the "evil empire." There on a balmy day in May he strolled Red Square laughing and bantering with the leader of the system he had earlier castigated for producing leaders trained to lie and cheat in the service of their Marxist-Leninist revolutionary goals. Out of the Moscow summit came a spate of new agreements on arms control, cooperative nuclear research, maritime affairs, transportation, and student exchanges.

Had America's most articulate cold warrior changed, as some of his most ardent early supporters angrily charged? On the contrary, Reagan insists in his memoirs, it was precisely his administration's worldwide and relentless opposition to Marxism-Leninism that finally brought home to Gorbachev and his associates the fundamental contradictions in the Soviet system and the futility of their persisting in a global struggle against democratic capitalism. If the Cold War was about to come to an end, it was because the Soviets, subjected to the full court press, were finally ready to say uncle. Reagan does of course give some weight to the inherent internal weaknesses of the Soviet system:

When Gorbachev came into power in March 1985, I believe, he would have continued on the same path as his predecessors if Communism had been working, but it wasn't. . . . Seventy years of Communism had bankrupted the Soviet Union economically and spiritually. Gorbachev must have realized it could no longer support or control Stalin's totalitarian empire; the survival of the Soviet Union was more important to him. He must have looked to the economic disaster his country was facing and concluded that it couldn't continue spending so much of its wealth on weapons and an arms race—as I told him at Geneva—we would never let his country win. [37]

In Reagan's view, the world was blessed by having the right leaders in the right places at the right time: in the West, a leader wise enough and tough enough to make the Soviet Union more aware than it had ever been before of the stark choices it faced; and in the East a leader with "the intelligence to admit Communism was not working, the courage to battle for change, and, ultimately, the wisdom to introduce the beginnings of democracy, individual freedom, and free enterprise." [38]

Reagan left office heady with the conviction that his relationship with Gorbachev had profoundly changed the course of history.

PART VIII

PRUDENCE AND POWER IN THE BUSH YEARS

We're not going to overexcite the American people or the world. And so we will conduct our diplomacy in a prudent fashion, not driven by excess, not driven by extremes.

—GEORGE BUSH

We should always be skeptical when so-called experts suggest that all a particular crisis calls for is a little surgical bombing or a limited attack. . . . This approach has been tragic for the nation. . . . Lincoln perceived war correctly. It is the scourge of God. We should be very careful how we use it. When we do use it, we should not be equivocal: we should win and win decisively.

—GENERAL COLIN POWELL

27

PRESIDING OVER THE END
OF THE COLD WAR

We've got to slow this thing down. We can't let ourselves be driven by Moscow at breakneck speed.

—BRENT SCOWCROFT

Vice President George Bush was one of those in the Reagan administration alarmed at the breathless pace of President Reagan's rush toward full reconciliation with the Soviet Union. Whereas during Reagan's first term Bush had worried that the President's good versus evil approach to U.S.–Soviet relations could provoke unnecessary confrontations between the nuclear superpowers, Bush looked on in troubled amazement at Reagan's fascination after 1985 with the idea that total mutual nuclear disarmament had become feasible and desirable since Gorbachev's Soviet Union was no longer an enemy of the West. Unlike some in the Reagan administration who were convinced that Gorbachev's bid to end the Cold War was only the latest Soviet attempt to dupe the West, Bush was willing to suspend judgment while the United States probed Soviet intentions—experimentally, pragmatically—in the arms control arena and in various regional conflicts, such as Afghanistan, Angola, and Nicaragua.

If elected President, Bush would have an open mind toward the prospect of reviving the détente relationship initiated by Nixon and Kissinger; like them, he could be indifferent to the form of government and human rights situation in the Soviet Union as long as the Kremlin was willing to play by the rules of the game internationally. But first he would have to win the Republican nomination against a field of more hawkish contenders, including Senator Robert Dole and ex-Secretary of State Alexander Haig. Bush privately cautioned Gorbachev in late 1987 to ignore the anti-Soviet rhetoric of his forthcoming election campaign.[1]

TESTING THE WATERS . . . PRUDENTLY

After the election Bush encountered an impatient Gorbachev willing to forgive his campaign statements but anxious to take up the building of the post–Cold War relationship where he and Reagan had left off. On December 7, 1988, in a remarkably forthcoming speech before the United Nations, the Soviet leader threw down a dramatic challenge to the President-elect to move beyond the Cold War. "New realities are changing the entire world situation," said Gorbachev. "The differences and contradictions inherited from the past are . . . being displaced." It had become obvious that "the use or threat of force no longer can or must be an instrument of foreign policy." The superpower disarmament process had commenced in earnest with the intermediate-range nuclear forces (INF) treaty eliminating U.S. and Soviet intermediate-range nuclear forces. The INF treaty was but one expression of "a new historic reality—a turning away from the principle of superarmament to the principle of reasonable defense sufficiency." In accord with this principle, Gorbachev announced, the Soviet leadership had decided to unilaterally reduce its armed forces by 500,000 men and to withdraw and disband six tank divisions from Germany, Czechoslovakia, and Hungary by 1991, along with comparable reductions in artillery and combat aircraft in the European theater.[2]

But rather than reciprocate, Bush instinctively held back. He would consult with his top foreign policy aides and order studies of possible responses. If this was a historic juncture in world politics, he wanted some breathing space to formulate an appropriate set of policies. His cautious reaction was backed by both his designated Secretary of State, James Baker, and his designated National Security Adviser, Brent Scowcroft—each skeptical of Gorbachev's motives; they still viewed the charismatic Soviet leader as a master manipulator of international public opinion and a coldly calculating Marxist-Leninist. Gorbachev's rhetorical embrace of a kind of "global humanism," of détente and arms control, and his domestic *perestroika* (restructuring) were all possibly a rational grand strategy to provide for a temporary reallocation of resources and reordering of priorities to allow the Soviet Union—aided by Western technologies and financial credits—to renew its bid in the near future for global dominance from a stronger base.

A different perspective came from Henry Kissinger. Bush's former boss from the Nixon era proposed that Bush boldly seize the initiative with respect to the implications that Gorbachev's new policies had for the situation in Eastern Europe, and by so doing help bring the Cold War to an end. As with Khrushchev's efforts at liberalization two decades earlier, Gorbachev's policies could unleash a degree of revolutionary chaos among the East Europeans, particularly in East Germany. The results might lead to Soviet military intervention and West German threats to counterintervene. To prevent such situations, Bush should offer Gorbachev the following deal: the Soviets would agree not to use military force to suppress anti-Communist regime uprisings in Eastern Europe in exchange for a NATO promise not to intervene or otherwise attempt to exploit the ferment there at the expense of "legitimate" Soviet security interests. This mutual forbearance accord would help Gorbachev hold off the Soviet hardliners who were opposing his efforts to reduce Soviet foreign obligations and it would allow the East European countries greater leeway to gradually dislodge themselves from Soviet hegemonic control. Bush should understand, however, and so should Gorbachev, that any public knowledge of such a deal at this time would be inadvisable, for it would invite charges from the American right wing that Bush and Gorbachev were engaging in a "Yalta" type arrangement to preserve a sphere of Soviet influence in Eastern Europe. Bush liked the idea and suggested that Kissinger explore it with Gorbachev and his advisers during Kissinger's forthcoming trip to the Soviet Union.[3] Meeting with Gorbachev in Moscow two days before Bush's inauguration, Kissinger encountered a wary response. Still mistrustful of the incoming administration's intentions, the Soviet leader suspected a ruse to get him to reveal too much of his own plans for Eastern Europe.

The new administration did not have an agreed-upon basic policy toward Gorbachev. Over the next ten months, Bush's lieutenants often contradicted one another while the President himself awkwardly straddled various positions—both in public and in deliberations with his advisers.

Two days after the inauguration, Scowcroft publicly cautioned that "the Cold War is not over" and warned that Gorbachev's plan (dubbed the "peace offensive") might be a calculated strategy to get the West to let down its guard while the Soviet Union built up its power for a new global offensive.[4]

At his first presidential press conference on January 27, Bush was asked about these expressions of mistrust by his National Security Adviser. He replied that the administration was engaged in a "reassessment" of U.S.–Soviet relations:

Let's take our time now. Let's take a look at where we stand on . . . our bilateral problems with the Soviet Union; formulate the policy and then get out front. . . . I want to try to avoid words like 'Cold War' if I can because that has an implication. If someone says Cold War to me, that doesn't properly give credit to the advances that have taken place in the relationship. So I wouldn't use that term. But if it's used in the context of—do we still have problems; are there still uncertainties; are we still unsure in our predictions on Soviet intentions—I'd have to say, yes, we should be cautious.[5]

The sub-cabinet and working level officials who played an influential role in the administration's Soviet policy review included unreconstructed cold warriors like Robert Gates (Scowcroft's deputy) and Robert Blackwill (who had the Soviet portfolio on the NSC), skeptics like Lawrence Eagleburger (the impeccably professional Deputy Secretary of State), and pragmatic détentists like Dennis Ross (director of the policy planning staff at State). Of this group, Gates and Blackwill were the only ones who could claim to be experts on the Soviet Union. The analytical balance thus tended to tilt toward the naysayers and skeptics, with the burden of proof borne by those who believed the end of the Cold War was in sight. During the first few months of the Bush administration, the center of gravity of U.S. Soviet policy shifted back from the venturesome latter-day Reagan approach to a cautious conservatism—reflected neatly in Scowcroft's remark that "There may be . . . light at the end of the tunnel. But I think it depends on whether the light is the sun or an oncoming locomotive."[6]

The hardline ex-CIA cold warriors, Gates and Blackwill, tended to discount the depth of the transformation taking place under Gorbachev. Well into the spring of 1989, as Bush began to appreciate the pervasiveness of the turbulence spreading through the Soviet sphere, they continued to voice doubts even of Gorbachev's commitment to fundamental reform, citing his statements that he was still a loyal Communist. By contrast, Dennis Ross, increasingly influential with Secretary Baker, saw the survival of Gorbachev as crucial to the dramatic positive changes that were taking place. But Eagleburger and other State Department professionals, including Ambassador Jack Matlock in Moscow, although persuaded that the revolutionary ferment was transforming the societies in the Soviet sphere from top to bottom, worried that Bush and Baker were becoming overly enthralled by Gorbachev and Foreign Minister Eduard Shevardnadze, overlooking the shallowness of their domestic political base in the vast country they were trying to restructure.

The hawks attributed Gorbachev's pleas for an end to the Cold War (which they saw as only a temporary truce) almost entirely to Reagan's U.S. military buildup and "full court press" on the Soviet Union. This was no time to let up on the pressure. But Ross and his analysts understood Gorbachev's *perestroika* to be the product of a recognition by the new leaders in the Kremlin of fundamental contradictions in the Soviet system. The Gorbachev modernizers wanted to reorient the country's material and human resources away from the arms race and worldwide power rivalry with the United States to the enormous task of restructuring facing them. For the United States to take a hard line would make it very difficult, if not impossible, for Gorbachev and his associates to pursue the historic transformation of Soviet society they were determined to bring about. Rather it was important to try once again, as Nixon and Kissinger had done, but now with a more enlightened group in the Kremlin, to give the Soviets positive stakes in a stable peace.

Bush's ambivalent posture toward the Soviet Union during the early months of his administration reflected these internal policy debates. He received no help from a vague mid-March report on the policy review he had ordered. And the lack of clear guidance from the Oval Office was license for others in the administration to put their own interpretations on what was happening in the Soviet Union and the implications for U.S. foreign policy. Thus Secretary of Defense Cheney offered a "guess" in a television interview on April 29 that Gorbachev would ultimately fail in his reform efforts and would be replaced by a leader more hostile to the West. Secretary of State Baker's anger at this comment prompted an explanation by White House Press Secretary Marlin Fitzwater that Cheney was only expressing "personal observations."

Finally, chafing at the criticism that he was dragging his feet in responding to a historic opportunity to bring the Cold War to an end, the President used a commencement address at Texas A&M University on May 12 to announce that his administration's review of U.S.–Soviet relations had just been completed and had produced a "bold" and "ambitious" new policy:

Our review indicates that 40 years of perseverance have brought us a precious opportunity, and now it is time to move beyond containment to a new policy for the 1990s, one that recognizes the full scope of change taking place around the world and in the Soviet Union itself. . . . The United States now has as its goal much more than simply containing Soviet expansionism. We seek the integration of the Soviet Union into the community of nations.

But the President made it clear he was not yet ready to fully welcome the Soviets into the world order. This would be the ultimate result of a process of which "we are only at the beginning." Rhetoric and promises were not enough:

The Soviet Union says that it seeks to make peace with the world and criticizes its own postwar policies. These are words that we can only applaud. But a new relationship cannot be simply declared by Moscow or bestowed by others; it must be earned. . . . The Soviet Union has promised a more cooperative relationship before, only to reverse course and return to militarism. Soviet foreign policy has been almost seasonal: warmth before cold, thaw before freeze.

Similarly, with respect to Gorbachev's domestic reforms, the President was positive with respect to the potential, while maintaining his posture of wait-and-see before committing the United States to any initiatives to assist in the Soviet system's modernization:

We hope perestroika is pointing the Soviet Union to break with the cycles of the past—a definitive break. . . . And let no one doubt our sincere desire to see perestroika succeed. But the national security of America and our allies is not predicated on hope. It must be based on deeds. And we look for enduring, ingrained economic and political change.

The President then proceeded to outline the deeds the Soviets would have to perform to qualify for full participation in "the world order." These included:

First, reduce Soviet forces . . . to less threatening levels [than those already announced by Gorbachev] in proportion to their legitimate security needs. Second, adhere to the Soviet obligation, promised in the final days of World War II, to support self-determination for all nations of eastern and central Europe. And this requires specific abandonment of the Brezhnev doctrine. . . . And third, work with the West in positive, practical—not merely rhetorical—steps toward diplomatic solution to . . . regional disputes around the world. I welcome the Soviet withdrawal from Afghanistan, and the Angola agreement. But there is much more to be done. . . . And fourth, achieve a lasting political pluralism [in the Soviet Union] and respect for human rights. We are impressed by limited but freely contested elections. We are impressed by a greater toleration of dissent . . . Mr. Gorbachev, don't stop now. And fifth, join with us is addressing pressing global problems, including the international drug menace and dangers to the environment.[7]

The President, with an eye to the headlines, proposed an additional test of Gorbachev's commitment to change and openness—a variation on the Open Skies proposal offered thirty-four years earlier by President Eisenhower to a post-Stalin leadership also professing a readiness to change. "Open skies" would allow unarmed aircraft from the United States and the Soviet Union to fly over each other's territory to open up military activities of each side to mutual scrutiny. In 1955, said Bush, the Kremlin had failed the test by refusing Eisenhower's offer. The willingness of the present Soviet leadership to embrace such a concept would "reveal their commitment to change." In fact, the United States and the Soviet Union were already conducting such "open skies" military surveillance via orbiting reconnaissance satellites. But the President evidently realized he needed a dramatic gesture to counteract the impression that the rest of his speech was a rigidly unimaginative and unreciprocal response to Gorbachev's bid to end the Cold War. As it turned out, the revived Open Skies proposal was a public relations failure: journalists, having interviewed Pentagon experts, revealed that it lacked any serious arms control or strategic rationale.

The Texas A&M speech was reassuring to conservatives in the administration and Congress. But it was disappointing to those who wanted the President to step out boldly with a new, dynamic definition of the post–Cold War era. The aura of global leadership was gravitating toward the magnetic Gorbachev. Clearly, George Bush was no Ronald Reagan.

THE PUBLIC RELATIONS GAME

The President's increasing irritation at Gorbachev's ability to upstage him was reflected in a public complaint by Fitzwater that Gorbachev was "throwing out in a kind of drugstore cowboy fashion one arms control proposal after another."[8] Privately, Bush complained to Scowcroft that he was "sick and tired of getting beat up day after day for having no vision and letting Gorbachev run the show."[9]

Looking toward the NATO summit in Brussels at the end of May, Bush wanted to steal a march on the Soviet leader in the European arms control arena with new proposals that were both militarily prudent and imbedded in a vision of a post–Cold War Europe that would appeal to European and U.S. public opinion. Bush's determination to push for a breakthrough on European arms control was welcomed by French President François Mitterrand and German Chancellor Helmut Kohl who themselves were increasingly frustrated with the Americans for failing to appreciate the extent to which the NATO–Warsaw Pact military balance had become a matter of political symbolism rather than military security, and that the West was losing the contest of public opinion to Gorbachev.

The Soviets had captured the public imagination with their proposal to follow up the INF treaty with an agreement to remove all short-range nuclear weapons from the European theater. The United States had opposed any negotiations on short-range nuclear weapons, arguing that this would countenance the very de-nuclearization of Europe that had been a major part of Soviet grand strategy for decades. But sophisticated strategists understood the anachronism of the old rationale for the deployment of battlefield nuclear weapons on the Central European front. This rationale had become obsolete with the realization that the Soviets no longer had any inclination to start a European war, and that whatever residual deterrence was still needed to prevent a Soviet squeeze on West Berlin or attack on West Germany was best provided by a continued U.S. commitment to become militarily involved and by the maintenance of a capability to inflict unacceptable damage on the Soviet Union itself in a U.S.–Soviet war. Moreover, in a volatile post–Cold

War period in which violent incursions across the East-West border in Germany were quite conceivable, Germans on both sides of the divide had the highest incentive to do away with deployments that guaranteed that local military encounters would trigger explosions of nuclear weapons on their soil.

If the military balance of power in Europe still had relevance to important political issues, then why not respond positively to the Soviet bid to finally do away with Warsaw Pact superiority in conventional forces? There was a limit to what Gorbachev could do unilaterally without provoking a backlash from his own military; if he needed some reciprocal concessions from the West, perhaps this was the time for NATO to be more forthcoming in the conventional forces in Europe (CFE) negotiations. If one-upsmanship in arms control was now the name of the game and if the NATO partners didn't mind—indeed, if they wanted it—then why not be truly bold? These considerations were reflected in the package of arms control proposals the President brought with him to Brussels and championed in speeches in Germany. The key elements of the new package were the invitation to the Soviets to agree to a ceiling of 275,000 troops each for the United States and the Soviet Union to station in the European theater, along with similarly substantial reductions down to common numerical ceilings on tanks, troop carriers, artillery, helicopters, and land-based combat aircraft. Although the Soviets had already agreed in principle to common numerical ceilings in some of these categories, the new levels Bush was proposing would require the Soviets to make vastly disproportionate reductions, particularly in troops and tanks. The President called on the U.S. and Soviet negotiators to reach a comprehensive conventional arms control agreement within six months to a year, with the reductions to be implemented at the latest by 1993. There was no reason, he said, for the five-to-six year timetable suggested by Gorbachev. Bush also let it be known that the United States was dropping its opposition to a ban on the deployment of short-range nuclear weapons on the continent.

Bush told his European audiences that his new proposals for a "less militarized Europe" were based on the premise that the Cold War could finally be brought to an end. But it would end, he said, only when Europe because "whole and free." At Mainz, Germany, on May 31, he gave special emphasis to these themes. One idea was sweeping across Eurasia, he said, the "passion for freedom." This was why the entire Communist world was in ferment. This was why the very concept of a divided Europe was under siege. And in an attempt to take the high ground from Gorbachev's slogan of "a common European home," he intoned: "There cannot be a common European home until all within it are free to move from room to room." [10]

To the surprise of the administration, the Soviets, instead of objecting to the asymmetrical U.S. formulae for arms reductions in Europe, agreed to proceed with the accelerated negotiations Bush was urging. Encouraged, Bush sent Gorbachev a parallel set of asymmetrical proposals in June for the strategic arms reduction talks (START): large cuts in heavy ICBMs, relatively minor reductions in submarine-launched ballistic missiles and cruise missiles, and no concessions on SDI. And once again, although reports had it that Gorbachev was angered, the Soviets conceded to a resumption of negotiations basically under the U.S. terms of reference.

THE SMELL OF VICTORY

Bush drew two lessons from his initial foray into the European disarmament arena with Gorbachev: the first confirmed the assumption of the detentists that Gorbachev was in fact sincere in wanting to call off the Cold War; the second confirmed the assumption of the anti-Soviet hawks that the Soviet economy was in such dire straits that the Gorbachev regime was willing to do virtually anything the West demanded in order to get out of the arms race. In other words, the time was ripe to press on to a full victory in the Cold War and to lock in Soviet concessions so that a post-Gorbachev regime would find it very costly to attempt to regain anything approaching military and geopolitical parity with the United States. Secretary Baker appeared to have some qualms, fed by Shevardnadze's expressed concerns that humiliating Gorbachev would play into the hands of hardliners in the Soviet military and the Communist Party who were alleging that the Soviet reformer was a dupe of the West.

Bush took these concerns seriously enough to deny himself any public gloating over his victories, but when it came to the larger issues still outstanding—the role of Germany in a post–Cold War Europe, a new pan-European security system, and the conditions under which the Soviet Union would be granted membership in the International Monetary Fund—he allowed Gorbachev no quarter. Indeed, the more the Soviet sphere of control began to crumble, the more imperious Bush became about the right of the United States— the only remaining superpower—to define the arrangements of the post–Cold War order.

A dramatic indication of the depth of Gorbachev's intentions to renounce a hegemonic role in Eastern Europe came in Poland in June 1989 with the stunning electoral victory of Lech Walesa's Solidarity movement over the ruling communist party of President Wojciech Jaruzelski. Whereas in 1981 the Reagan administration had assumed that General Jaruzelski had been directed by Leonid Brezhnev to impose martial law to control the challenge to Communist rule posed by the Solidarity Workers' party, now the tables were completely turned. Jaruzelski had been prompted by Gorbachev to allow Solidarity to legally contest for seats in the June 1989 parliamentary elections; upon Solidarity's victory, Gorbachev let Jaruzelski and the world know that, as far as the Soviet Union was concerned, the election results had to be accepted, and the non-communists had to be given power in the government commensurate with the election results.[11] Bush, jumping the gun, suggested that it was time for the Soviets to pull their troops out of Poland; but when it got back to him that Gorbachev regarded this as meddling, he claimed no intention of trying to call the shots in Eastern Europe. Ironically, when Bush visited Poland a few weeks later (on a previously scheduled trip) he got along better with President Jaruzelski, still head of state, than he did with Walesa, and implied in some of his remarks and body language that he was more comfortable with order, even Communist order, than he was with the potential chaos of revolutionary change, even toward liberal democracy.[12]

The historically most significant test of Gorbachev's determination to end the Cold War centered on East Germany—since 1945 the Soviet empire's most strategically significant, heavily fortified, and tightly controlled forward bulwark against the West. The East German Communist leadership was not responding well to Gorbachev's insistence on "new thinking." The Honecker regime went so far as to censor from the country's press passages of Gorbachev's speeches it considered too liberal; but East Germans received the information through television broadcasts from the West. Beginning in May

1989, hundreds of thousands of East Germans eventually took advantage of the decision of the Hungarian government to remove its barbed wire barriers along the Austrian border (a decision countenanced by Gorbachev), and made their way into West Germany through Austria. Thousands of others encamped temporarily in the West German embassies in Hungary, Czechoslovakia, and Poland while awaiting entry visas from the West German government. In the past, when Communist East Germans had fled in any numbers, the Kremlin had provided decisive help in stanching the flow (e.g., the erection of the Berlin Wall in 1961); now the leader in the Kremlin was talking about a "common European home" and the free movement of people.

In June, Gorbachev further energized the incipient reform movement in East Germany by signing a joint declaration with Chancellor Kohl of West Germany expressing "unqualified adherence . . . [to] the right of self determination." On their television screens, East Germans along with viewers in Western Europe and the United States saw the Soviet leader being welcomed by West German crowds as if he were a conquering hero.[13]

The situation in East Germany came to a head in October 1989. Crowds numbering in the hundreds of thousands took to the streets in Berlin, Leipzig, and Dresden. Gorbachev let Honecker know that Soviet troops in East Germany would not participate in any effort by the East German government to suppress the demonstrations, warning his host that "life punishes those who come too late."[14]

Amid continuing demonstrations, the East German Politburo replaced the elderly Honecker with a younger party leader, Egon Krenz, who pursued a surprisingly reformist policy—legalizing freedom of travel to the West, forcing many of Honecker's associates to resign, and promising democratic elections. Bush administration officials saw the hand of Gorbachev in all of this.

Then on November 9, 1989—in an act that more than anything else symbolized the end of the Cold War—the East German military, acting under directives from Krenz, began to dismantle the Berlin Wall. But the sudden opening of the wall only increased the force of the turbulent pressures. It was too late to salvage any legitimacy for the Communist regime. The urgent question now for Germany's neighbors, the United States, and the Soviet Union was how to contain the potentially explosive consequences of a total collapse of civic order. The old nightmare of West Germans and Soviets counterintervening in East Germany had become all too real a prospect.

A logical alternative to anarchy and bloodshed was another "unthinkable"—now suddenly quite plausible—the voluntary reunification of Germany. For the rest of 1989, the West German politicians themselves did a dance around the issue, ever sensitive to the historic fear of the reappearance of a powerful German superstate in the center of Europe (the Germans during these months were careful to talk only of the possibility of "unification," never "*re*unification"). But the popular enthusiasm for the prospect became irresistible, and by the turn of the year Kohl and his Christian Democrats were ready, despite the awesome economic burdens.

It was not enough that the Germans were ready. The next question was whether the Soviets would agree to Germany's unification on terms that were acceptable to the United States. For more than four decades, neither Washington nor Moscow would contemplate a reunification that would add the great material and human resources of Germany to the other side's power. Nor, given the record of German imperialistic aggression, had the World War II victors been ready to countenance a totally independent and "neutral" Germany.

Something had to give, and as far as Bush was concerned that meant Gorbachev's opposition to NATO. The Soviets were now talking about the need to rethink their objections to a neutral Germany—belonging to no alliance but subordinated into a pan-European security system evolving out of the Conference on Security and Cooperation in Europe (CSCE). Neither Kohl nor Mitterrand opposed such a revamping of the entire European security apparatus once the Cold War was over. But Bush, convinced that Gorbachev was leading from weakness, would have none of it. He lobbied Kohl in particular to insist on NATO membership for a reunified Germany, hinting that the United States might rather see a perpetuation of two Germanies than see Germany defect from the alliance. Baker made it clear to Shevardnadze that NATO membership for a reunited Germany was a prime condition for U.S. acquiescence to full Soviet participation in world economic institutions and for direct U.S. economic help. As a World War II victor power over Germany the Soviet Union would have a role in defining the new Germany. The Soviets would be a part of the authorizing group of four in the "two plus four" process for achieving unification—a formula generated in the U.S. State Department by which the details of the

incorporation of the East into an expanded Federal Republic would
be negotiated by the two Germanies and then ratified by the United
States, the Soviet Union, Britain, and France.[15] Some policy planners at the State Department, and perhaps Baker himself, worried
that this tough posture on the NATO issue would severely weaken
Gorbachev's ability to stand up to his hardline reactionary opponents; but Bush sensed a virtually unconditional victory in the Cold
War.

Simultaneously with the efforts to settle the German issue, the
United States and the Soviet Union were engaged at all diplomatic
levels (from Bush-Gorbachev summitry to private meetings between
Baker and Shevardnadze and working-level commissions) in resolving
the still outstanding Cold War issues. The frenetic diplomatic activity was taking place against a backdrop of growing turbulence in the
USSR, as Gorbachev found himself caught up in a chaotic stampede
towards political decentralization and economic privatization which
was swifter and more radical than he could have anticipated or
was capable of modulating effectively.[16] Gorbachev needed some
international success or, at a minimum, continuing international
recognition of his importance in order to buttress his declining popularity at home. The Bush administration, playing on this need, was
willing to give him the recognition but not the success—catering
rather to the President's own need to enhance a reputation for
toughness in presiding over the end of the Cold War.

At the Malta summit of December 2–3, 1989—nicknamed the
"seasick summit" for its shipboard sessions in the storm-tossed harbor—the wide-ranging discussions between the two leaders encom-
passed the CFE and START negotiations, the still volatile German
question, Soviet and Cuban support for the Sandinista regime in
Nicaragua, and the sensitive issue of self-determination for the three
Baltic republics. Bush came away from this exercise in personal
diplomacy confident that Gorbachev, more than ever anxious to
obtain most favored nation trading status (MFN) and qualification
for Export-Import Bank credits, was prepared to cooperate on all of
these issues. More so than in any of the previous discussions between Bush and the intellectually aggressive Soviet leader (on the
phone or in person), Gorbachev was now equally a listener, a respon-
dent, with Bush increasingly setting the agenda and defining the
parameters for future negotiation.

By the time of the summit held in Washington and Camp David

from May 30 to June 3, 1990, the shift in the relationship between the two countries was manifest in the contrast between Bush's relaxed, almost imperious confidence and Gorbachev's tense and often irritated demeanor at being reduced to the role of supplicant. In response to Gorbachev's repeated emphasis on the importance for *perestroika* that the United States finally provide the USSR with MFN status and government backing for commercial credits, Bush continued to invoke his demands: in addition to the longstanding requirement that the Soviets rescind their restrictions on Jewish emigration, he included the new demands that Gorbachev accede to NATO membership for a reunified Germany, stop subsidizing Cuba and the Sandinistas, show more progress in instituting a market economy, and lift the economic sanctions that had been imposed on secessionist Lithuania.

As the results of this Cold War endgame materialized over the next year, Bush was sustained in his view of himself as the impresario of the new world order. After all, during his presidency:

• Eastern Europe had been released from political and economic bondage to the USSR, and Soviet military forces had been largely withdrawn from the region.
• The Warsaw Pact had been disbanded.
• The Berlin Wall had been torn down.
• East Germany had been peacefully reunited with (actually absorbed into) the Federal Republic of Germany, which, Gorbachev finally agreed, could remain in NATO.
• Soviet troops had been totally withdrawn from Afghanistan.
• Cuban troops had been withdrawn from Angola at the behest of the Soviets as part of a U.S.-brokered settlement between Luanda and Pretoria on independence for Namibia.
• The Nicaraguan Sandinistas, responding to Soviet pressures, had consented to an internationally monitored election which they lost.
• The Soviets had ceased subsidizing Cuba's economy.
• In the United Nations, the Soviets had cooperated in obtaining Security Council authorization for the United States to lead a military coalition to force Saddam Hussein out of Kuwait.

REACTING TO THE COLLAPSE AND DISINTEGRATION OF THE SOVIET UNION

By the spring of 1991, the Soviet Union itself was on the brink of economic and political collapse. The gross national product was in a precipitous decline, Gorbachev was under challenge from both the "right" (unreconstructed Communists) and the "left" (believers in radical decentralization of the political economy, rapid privatization, and full embrace of market capitalism), and most of the fifteen member republics of the Soviet Union were threatening secession so as to become fully sovereign independent countries.

Washington's cold warriors were congratulating themselves: not only had the Soviets been forced to release their empire, but the whole Marxist-Leninist experiment was imploding at its very core. At the highest levels of the Bush administration the elation was tempered by the realization that some of the spoils of such a total victory could be bitter, even dangerous—and fraught with great financial burdens for the United States.

Gorbachev and his emissaries were now privately imploring the United States for massive aid—on levels comparable to the Marshall Plan assistance for the reconstruction of war-torn Europe. Without such help, the democratic restructuring that had been going on would be reversed, civic order would collapse, and a new Stalinist or fascist-nationalist dictatorship would be highly likely. Moreover, unless Moscow were provided the wherewithal for exercising major economic leverage over the restive republics, the USSR might well disintegrate into rival ethno-nationalistic states, some of which (particularly Ukraine, Belarus, and Kazakhstan) might try to gain control of the nuclear weapons and facilities on their territories.

Academic experts on the Soviet Union and editorial writers in the U.S. also weighed in. The Bush administration was once again being accused of procrastinating and dragging its feet when the situation cried out for bold vision and decisive action. But the administration saw itself in a bind: if it poured resources into the existing, still largely unreformed Soviet political economy, the very sources of the worsening economic downturn would only be reinforced; on the other hand, if the administration continued to condition any substantial U.S. economic assistance on a more rapid adoption of democratic capitalism in the USSR than the Gorbachev regime was able to deliver, the increasingly unpopular Gorbachev would be further discredited without any real prospects that the necessary reforms would materialize in the near future. Given Bush's understanding that the huge U.S. budget deficit would be a major issue in his bid for reelection, the administration was not prepared to ask Congress to authorize a massive U.S. financial bailout of the USSR—with or without new performance conditions.

With the administration seemingly paralyzed by its inability to choose among unpalatable alternatives, some U.S. academic economists and political scientists, collaborating with a handful of radical free market reformers among Gorbachev's advisers, worked up and energetically promoted a "grand bargain" designed to break the impasse. Graham Allison of the John F. Kennedy School of Government and his colleague, Robert Blackwill, formerly of the NSC staff, published the proposal in *Foreign Affairs* on the eve of the July 1991 economic summit, the Group of Seven (G-7) meeting, in London. The industrial democracies, wrote Allison and Blackwill, should offer the Soviet Union a bargain of Marshall Plan proportions with substantial financial assistance to Soviet reforms conditioned upon continuing political pluralization and a coherent economic program for moving rapidly to a market economy.

• The "political pluralization" provisions of the bargain would require Soviet reaffirmations of commitments to respect human rights, including the right of the republics to decide whether to stay in the Union or to become independent states. The more onerous and difficult provisions were in the economic realm, where the major steps included: (a) sharp reductions in fiscal and monetary deficits by cutting defense spending and subsidies to state enterprises; (b) legalizing private, individual economic initiative; (c) moving in stages to total price decontrol in which prices would reflect scarcity values, first within the Soviet Union and soon thereafter in the world economy; and (d) demonopolization and privatization of state enterprises.

• The G-7 side of the "grand bargain" would entail a commitment of "$15 billion to $20 billion a year for each of the next three years in grants, not loans" to both the central government and the republics "to motivate and facilitate the rapid transition to a market economy." The funds would go for balance of payments support, infrastructure projects (like transportation and communication), and the maintenance of a "safety net as a part of a general 'conditionality program' that followed basic IMF–World Bank principles." The funds would not simply be given over to the Soviets; rather they would be allocated "step-by-step" and be "strictly conditional" on the recipients' adherence to their side of the bargain.[17]

Although much of the U.S.–Soviet dialogue on economic matters during the late spring of 1991 was informed by the "grand bargain" proposal, neither the Bush administration nor the Gorbachev government tried to have it become an official part of their negotiations. Bush and Baker appreciated the logic of the idea, but felt that it was politically unfeasible for either side to make the contemplated commitments. They were told that some of the young radicals in Gorbachev's cabinet favored it, as did Gorbachev's political rival, Boris Yeltsin; but they were also aware that Gorbachev himself, now struggling to avert the breakup of the USSR into separate states, was mending fences with moderate elements in the Communist Party; nor were there any signs from the author of *perestroika* that he was willing to abandon his preference for a state-managed transition to a hybrid form of market socialism. Moreover, Bush knew that to be able to credibly offer the Soviets up to $20 billion a year in grant aid from the G-7 (some economists were estimating the Soviet bailout would take five times as much) the United States would need to promise to contribute at least a quarter of that amount. While it was almost certain that the bargain would have been rejected by the Soviets, it would have been political suicide for Bush to publicly make the offer.

Still, Gorbachev would be a guest at the G-7 London summit in July, hoping to charm and cajole his Western counterparts into helping him make the still-intact Soviet Union safe for capitalist investment. Fighting for his political life at home—Yeltsin just a few weeks previously had been elected president of Russia—Gorbachev's aura was considerably diminished. The leaders heard him out but offered no substantial tangible assistance. Gorbachev reportedly left feeling humiliated and angry; even his petition for Soviet membership in the International Monetary Fund had been denied (the G-7 said they would agree to "associate membership" for the Soviets in the IMF, which Gorbachev found demeaning).

The London encounter was not a complete failure—Bush and Gorbachev gave final approval to the START accord and confirmed plans for the treaty signing a few weeks later in Moscow. The treaty required both sides to reduce their strategic arsenals by roughly a third, leaving the United States with 8,556 and the USSR with 6,163 long-range nuclear warheads. A few years earlier this would have been celebrated with toasts all around; and prior to its approval, the highest officials on both sides would have pored over the details of the sublimits in various weapons categories to make sure the other side had not achieved even the slightest marginal strategic advantage. But it was a measure of the radical change away from their superpower rivalry that START had come to be regarded by the White House and the Kremlin as a sideshow to the central arena, which now featured negotiations on their economic relationship.

The Moscow summit of July 29–31, 1991 was an awkward affair for Bush. Gorbachev was still smarting from his rebuffs by the G-7 and accused Bush of undermining the success of *perestroika*. Most embarrassing was Boris Yeltsin's manipulation of Bush. The Russian president used Bush's presence in Moscow to enhance his own prestige: he refused to attend a reception for the American President where he would be merely a leader of one of the republics and instead obtained a private session with Bush, after which—to Bush's dismay—he briefed the press on the progress of their talks about economic cooperation. The principal reason for the summit, the START signing ceremony, got good press coverage as Bush and Gorbachev both made the appropriate statements about reversing the arms race and exchanged pens made from the metal of missiles dismantled under the Intermediate Nuclear Force Treaty.[18]

The next leg of Bush's trip—a visit to Kiev, the capital of secessionist Ukraine—proved to be a public relations disaster. Gorbachev wanted Bush to cancel the planned Kiev trip, given the explosiveness of the self-determination issues throughout the USSR. But Bush and his aides thought that to cancel would only inflame the Ukrainians more and would make Bush look weak back home. He reworked his speech to help produce a conceptual framework for both sides, the Ukrainians and Gorbachev, to come to a modus vivendi. Instead, the speech angered his Ukrainian hosts and received highly critical coverage back in the United States. The most controversial passages were obviously late additions to an earlier draft: "Some people have urged the United States to choose between supporting President Gorbachev and supporting independence-minded leaders throughout the USSR," Bush intoned from the lectern in the Ukrainian parliament.

I consider this a false choice. In fairness, President Gorbachev has achieved astonishing things, and his policies of glasnost, perestroika, and democratization point toward the goals of freedom, democracy, and economic liberty. . . . We will maintain the strongest possible relationship with the Soviet Government of President Gorbachev. But we also appreciate the new realities of life in the USSR. And

therefore, as a federation ourselves, we want good relations—improved relations—
with the Republics."

The President proceeded to give the Ukrainian legislators a lecture
on the American concept of freedom as the ability of people to live
without fear of government intrusion and without fear of harassment
by their fellow citizens. The U.S. would support those who want to
build democracy, "a system that derives its just power from the
consent of the governed." But first there was the pointed interjec-
tion that:

freedom is not the same as independence. Americans will not support those who
seek independence in order to replace a far-off tyranny with a local despotism. They
will not aid those who promote suicidal nationalism based upon ethnic hatred.[19]

To Bush's dismay, these remarks and the lack of any invocation of
the concept of national self-determination earned for this thoughtful
address disparaging references as the "chicken Kiev" speech.

Bush wanted to deal with those who were in power, in control.
But this did not always serve him well where *who* was in control was
up for grabs. Bush was vacationing at Kennebunkport on August 18
when he received the news that leaders of the Soviet army and
several high government officials had staged a putsch in Moscow and
put Gorbachev under house arrest in his holiday home on the Cri-
mean coast. Bush's initial reaction in a statement early in the morning of August 19 was that it was "a disturbing development" and that
the leaders of the coup seemed to be "a very hardlined group" that
had taken over by "extra-constitutional means." He was concerned
about the possible setback to democracy in the Soviet Union and to
the new era of U.S.–Soviet cooperation. But he wanted "to watch
the situation unfold" before fashioning any particular response.

I think it's . . . important to know that coups can fail. They can take over at first,
and then they run up against the will of the people. . . . All this stuff is unfolding,
it just happened. . . . And let's just remain open on this as to whether it's going to
succeed or not. . . . And it's not a time for flamboyance or show business or
posturing on the part of any countries, certainly [not] the United States. . . . We're
not going to overexcite the American people or the world. And so, we will conduct
our diplomacy in a prudent fashion, not driven by excess, not driven by extremes.[20]

Bush's first response to early reports that Boris Yeltsin was opposing
the coup and calling for a general strike were also somewhat equivo-

cal. "Well, we'll just see what happens on that," he said. "I think what he is doing is simply expressing the will of the people there to have . . . reforms and have democracy. . . . I hope that people heed his call."[21]

Concerned that his reactions during the early hours of the crisis might be misconstrued as fence-sitting, the President had his staff issue a formal statement later on August 19 branding the coup as "illegitimate" and affirming "support [for] President Yeltsin's call for 'restoration of the legally elected organs of power and the reaffirmation of the post of USSR President M.S. Gorbachev.' "[22] In his press conference the following morning Bush was even stronger, contending that the "unconstitutional seizure of power . . . puts the Soviet Union at odds with the world community and undermines the positive steps that have been undertaken to make the Soviet Union an integral and positive force in world affairs."

When pressed by reporters to indicate what kind of support he was going to give Yeltsin or whether he was just going to "stay on the sidelines and offer verbal encouragement," Bush held back: "Well, we're certainly going to offer encouragement in every way we can," he said. "And we're making it clear to the coup plotters and the coup people that there will not be normal relations with the United States as long as this illegal coup remains in effect." He was putting all economic relations "on hold." What did this mean? Was he going to suspend grain credits? Was he going to delay most favored nation status? The President's answer: "Its simply—we've got to just take our time. We've got to be prudent, a word I think is applicable here. And I think we've got to be strong."

The journalists also questioned the failure to give Gorbachev any hope of obtaining the financial help he had requested, particularly at the last G-7 summit, implying in their questions that this might have been part of the reason for the coup. The President bristled:

You get this from the left saying if you'd written out a better check this wouldn't have happened, and I don't believe that for one single minute. And you get hit on the other side by people that are suggesting that if we hadn't been supportive of the duly constituted President of the Soviet Union that things would have gone more swimmingly for democracy. I reject that.[23]

Over the next few days as the coup fell apart—after Yeltsin's courageous public defiance of the coup, massive demonstrations on the streets of Moscow, defections in the Soviet military, Gorbachev's refusal to resign, a chorus of international condemnation, and simple ineptitude on the part of the coup leaders—Bush felt that his prudential posture had been vindicated. But he also realized that he had become too heavily vested in Gorbachev's leadership. Over the next few months, the administration and its emissaries paid just as much attention to the Russian president as they did to the president of the weakening center of the Union and became increasingly supportive, openly, of Yeltsin's policies favoring the dismantling of the USSR into a loose "commonwealth" of fifteen sovereign states and a radical and rapid "shock therapy" conversion to a market economy.

On the weekend of December 20–21, 1991, the former republics of the USSR formed the Commonwealth of Independent States (CIS). On December 25, Mikhail Gorbachev resigned as president of the expired Soviet Union. That night, George Bush addressed the world from the Oval Office for a Christmas reflection of the meaning of these events. "For over 40 years," he said, "the United States led the West in the struggle against communism and the threat it posed to our most precious values. . . . That confrontation is now over."

The President took a few minutes to praise Gorbachev for his contributions to world peace and to the revolutionary transformation of the Soviet Union, and then proceeded to recognize the independence of each of the former Soviet republics, citing each by name. He closed by asking God to "bless the people of the new nations in the Commonwealth of Independent States" as well as the United States of America.[24]

The Cold War, as far as the President of the United States was concerned, had ended.

28

GEORGE BUSH AND THE RESORT
TO MILITARY POWER

All right George, all right, but this is no time to go wobbly.
—MARGARET THATCHER

f you're a genteel New England aristocrat, the way you handle a
bully who has been harassing you is to attempt to befriend him:
invite him for a ride in your boat, buy him a drink, joke with him
about sports and girls, even get him a job in the family business.
Some people might say you're a wimp, but you don't let that bother
you. You've taken boxing and wrestling lessons and regularly use the
weight room at the country club. If despite your efforts he persists
in his provocations and a fight becomes unavoidable, you go all out
and give him the thrashing of his life.

George Herbert Walker Bush was disappointed that even some
members of his own party should still think him a wimp after the
way he knocked off the overly aggressive Bob Dole in the presidential
primaries and then went on to smash Michael Dukakis in a no-holds-
barred campaign. Disappointed, but not deeply bothered, because
George Bush knew himself; and when push came to shove, he would
behave as President as he had before: he would stand tall and give
the bullies the punishment they deserved.

As it turned out, when sufficiently provoked—by Manuel Noriega,
by Saddam Hussein, by the Somali warlords—Bush responded, for
the most part, true to character. These episodes bear close examina-

tion, not only for what they reveal about the Bush approach to the use of military power, but also as harbingers of new concepts emerging in the policy community about the role of the United States as enforcer of law and order in the post–Cold War world.

President Bush had reasons that went beyond the national interest in protecting the Canal or breaking Panama's link with international drug cartels for going after General Manuel Antonio Noriega. Noriega had almost ruined the Bush campaign for the Republican nomination in 1988 by telling reporters of their contacts, dating back to 1976 when Bush was director of the CIA and Noriega was the head of Panamanian intelligence, and including the December 1983 visit to Panama by then Vice President Bush when, according to Noriega, Bush had asked for his help with the Reagan administration's Contra operations in Nicaragua.

In February 1988, as Bush was putting his election campaign into high gear, U. S. grand juries in Miami and Tampa indicted Noriega for drug trafficking and money laundering; and stories surfaced in the press alleging that the Vice President had known about these illegal activities even as he was enlisting Noriega as an agent for U.S. covert activities in Central America. Bush vehemently denied any such early knowledge of Noriega's narcotics dealings; but reporters on the campaign trail kept bringing up the allegations. Bush's main rival for the nomination, Senator Robert Dole, ridiculed Bush's denial of knowledge of Noriega's drug connections: "People have been playing footsie with this guy," said Dole, "people who knew, or by virtue of their jobs and resumés ought to have known, that he was up to his eyeballs in dirty drugs and anti-American politics."[1]

Bush found an opportunity to exploit all the fuss to the benefit of his campaign for the nomination when, in May, it became publicly known that the Reagan administration was offering to drop U.S. court proceedings against the Panamanian dictator if he would resign his office. Uncharacteristically (as Vice President he had till then scrupulously refrained from differing in public with President Reagan), Bush's office let it be known that he had been arguing against this in White House meetings; and in a Los Angeles campaign appearance, Bush took the high ground: "Drug dealers are domestic terrorists, killing kids and cops, and they should be treated as such. I won't bargain with terrorism and I won't bargain with drug dealers either, whether they're on U.S. or foreign soil."[2] Noriega wasn't interested in the deal; but Bush meanwhile had established his determination to punish the Panamanian dictator.

The picture of Bush leading the battle within the Reagan administration for a tough anti-Noriega policy was contrived. By the summer of 1987, Noriega's double dealings (his relations with Castro, with Marxist revolutionaries in Columbia, and with Qaddafi) and reports that he rigged the Panamanian elections had angered Reagan. During the ensuing months political instability and attempted coups dominated the news out of Panama and the Pentagon reviewed its contingency plans for protecting the Canal. In April 1988, following a series of brutally suppressed attempted coups, Reagan ordered economic sanctions against the dictator. Secretary of State Shultz urged military intervention, but Reagan was not ready to authorize an operation of the size the Pentagon claimed would be necessary to protect the lives of U.S. citizens in Panama. Finally, in July Reagan authorized covert operations against Noriega.

During the first weeks of his presidency, Bush found an appropriate opportunity to turn the screws on the corrupt Panamanian leader. Noriega had reluctantly agreed to hold elections in May in response to rising domestic opposition to his dictatorship. In February, President Bush signed a secret finding authorizing the CIA to covertly help the opposition candidates. Publicly, he demanded that Noriega conduct a free and open election and announced that he was appointing former President Jimmy Carter to lead an international team of observers.

Despite widespread fraud verified by Carter's team, the opposition soundly defeated the dictator's handpicked candidates. Noriega nullified the election, whereupon the opposition took to the streets in protest. On May 10, Noriega called out his paramilitary "Dignity Battalions" to put down the demonstrations. Presidential candidate Guillermo Endera and vice presidential candidate Guillermo "Billy" Ford were bloodied by iron bars wielded by Noriega's forces, and Ford's bodyguard was shot dead. Much of this was shown on television news programs in the United States.

In a meeting with his top national security advisers on the evening of May 10, Bush made it clear that he wanted Noriega driven from power. He ordered a marginal augmentation of U.S. forces in the Canal Zone, but he did not want to make Noriega a martyr; any direct action against Noriega should be taken by the Panamanian military. He would, of course, use U.S. forces to protect the lives of U.S. military personnel and civilians in Panama and to protect the Canal if it came to that.[3]

Meanwhile, like his hero Theodore Roosevelt (who had also augmented his charisma by forceful action in Panama), the President would take to the "bully pulpit" and help whip up the domestic and world outrage at Noriega's thuggery. In statements and exchanges with reporters on May 11 and May 13, he urged the Panamanians to rise up against their dictator—but held back specifying what help they could expect from the United States if they did so:

THE PRESIDENT: The United States stands with the Panamanian people. We share their hope that the Panamanian defense forces will stand with them and fulfill their constitutional obligation to defend democracy.[4]

          . . .

QUESTION: Aren't you calling for a coup on the part of the PDF [Panamanian Defense Forces]?
THE PRESIDENT: I would love to see them get him out. We'd love to see them get him out—not just the PDF, the will of the people of Panama.
QUESTION: It sounds like you're calling on the people of Panama to rise up and basically have a revolution. Is that what you're trying to say?
THE PRESIDENT: A revolution—the people rose up and spoke in a democratic election. . . . The will of the people should not be thwarted by this man with a handful of these Doberman thugs.
QUESTION: What do you think the people should do now?
THE PRESIDENT: The people . . . ought to just do everything they can to get Mr. Noriega out of there.
QUESTION: The people could see that as inflammatory, like a call . . . to revolt. Would you add any words of caution—
THE PRESIDENT: No, I would add no words of caution . . .
QUESTION: If they ask for military support—if the PDF asks for military help, how can we respond? What would we do?
THE PRESIDENT: If the PDF asks for support to get rid of Noriega, they wouldn't need support from the United States to get rid of Noriega. He's one man, and they have a well trained force. That's my—
QUESTION: What about if [the] opposition asked for military support?
THE PRESIDENT: I've outlined what we're doing. I'd love to see this be resolved diplomatically. And when you have overwhelming world opinion on your side, maybe something is possible in the short-range future that has not been possible over the difficult past.[5]

During the summer and early fall, contingency planning started in earnest in the Pentagon for assistance to a coup from inside the PDF to remove Noriega, which in some versions would involve a discrete involvement of U.S. special units to capture him. The main problem with these plans in the eyes of Secretary of Defense Cheney and his planners was that any neat and swift removal of Noriega would leave powerful pro-Noriega elements in the PDF intact. A large operation, visibly involving U.S. forces, was probably required to do away with the Noriega regime. Was the President ready to consider a major U.S. military intervention? Clearly, this was Bush's least preferred option, and he would consider it only as a response to a clear and present threat to U.S. citizens in Panama or to the Canal itself.

The Abortive October 1989 Coup

The discrete-coup scenario was tested during the first week in October when plotters within the PDF, led by Major Moises Giroldi (up to then a member of Noriega's inner circle), tipped off the CIA in Panama that they were about to move on Noriega. The coup plotters asked that U.S. forces set up a military roadblock to prevent loyalist PDF units from reaching Noriega's quarters at the Comandancia.

The commander of the U.S. forces in Panama, General Maxwell Thurman, was suspicious of a Noriega trick to lure the United States into what would look like an attempted coup which, when foiled, would embarrass Bush. General Thurman expressed his concerns to Secretary Cheney and the new Chairman of the Joint Chiefs, General Colin Powell, and recommended that the United States stay aloof.

Cheney and Powell suggested a course of action that would avoid embarrassment while helping to assure the success of the coup in case it was genuine: U.S. forces would openly stage a "normal exercise" on the road the coup plotters wanted blocked but the United States would watch the coup develop before publicly committing to its success or involving U.S. forces in any definitive way. Bush agreed.

On the morning of October 3, with the United States implementing the road-block "exercise," the Giroldi group reported from the Comandancia that they were holding Noriega captive but were looking for an honorable way for him to remain in Panama. The U.S. command wanted to take Noriega into custody and told those now in control to deliver him to U.S. military headquarters. But the coup leaders refused to turn him over.

That afternoon, while Cheney and Powell were deliberating whether to ask Bush for authority to order General Thurman to employ U.S. forces to go in and get Noriega, word was passed from the Comandancia that the coup had failed. Elite PDF units, not dependent on the blocked road for access to the Comandancia, had been able to storm the building and rescue their leader. Noriega soon appeared on television condemning the coup and naming the United States as co-conspirator.[6]

White House press secretary Marlin Fitzwater quickly tried to distance the President from the failed coup. He issued a statement claiming that the administration lacked advance warning, had only heard "rumblings" and had "not been directly informed." If the administration was in fact informed before the plotters moved, "the President doesn't know about it, the Secretary of State doesn't know about and the Secretary of Defense doesn't know about it," he averred.[7] But Fitzwater could not protect the President from charges that he had let a golden opportunity slip away. In defending himself, Bush invoked his favorite decision making concept—prudence:

What . . . some people seemed to have wanted me to do is to unleash the full military and go in and—quote—get Noriega. . . . But . . . what could a Commander in Chief have done? I supposed you could have gone to general quarters. But that's not prudent and that's not the way I plan to conduct the military or foreign affairs of this country.[8]

And when asked if he would be inclined to use force more rapidly the next time, he replied, "I wouldn't mind using force if it could be done in a prudent manner." He was absolutely determined to get Noriega out, he insisted, but he was not going to give a "carte blanche commitment" of U.S. forces to support the next coup. "I have at stake the life of American kids, and I am not going to easily thrust them into a battle unless I feel comfortable with it and unless those general officers in whom I have total confidence feel comfortable."[9]

The failed October coup and Bush's explanation for the passive U.S. role elicited bipartisan congressional criticism—much of it implying that a "wimp" factor in the White House resulted in the missed opportunity. Conservative columnist George Will published a column titled "An Unserious Presidency." The President resolved not to let Noriega slip his grasp again. He was not to be disappointed.

Operation "Just Cause"

After having foiled the October 1989 coup, Noriega declared himself "maximum leader." But aware that the U.S. government was now hatching schemes to capture him and bring him to the United States for trial, he ordered increased surveillance of U.S. citizens using roadblocks, arbitrary searches, and interrogations. The killing of a U.S. serviceman at one of these roadblocks set off the crisis Bush needed to justify thrusting "American kids into battle" in Panama.

On the night of December 16, 1989, a car carrying four off-duty U.S. servicemen made a wrong turn on a street near PDF headquarters and came upon a PDF roadblock. After PDF soldiers, with weapons drawn, tried to pull the U.S. servicemen from their car, they tried to speed away. But the PDF opened fire, fatally wounding one. This confrontation was witnessed by a U.S. Navy lieutenant and his wife who had been detained at the same roadblock. Immediately after the shooting, the couple were blindfolded and taken to PDF headquarters were the lieutenant was beaten and his wife was sexually threatened. They were released about 2 A.M. The lieutenant returned to the U.S. Naval Station and reported the incident.

All of this was relayed to Washington, where it was immediately passed up to the highest levels. Cheney and Powell, particularly in light of recent statements by Noriega that Panama was in a "state of war" with the United States, agreed that military intervention was justified as there was now a clear and present danger to U.S. personnel in Panama. Meeting with President Bush on December 17, they recommended the activation of contingency plan Blue Spoon contemplating the use of 24,000 U.S. troops to overwhelm the 16,000 PDF, only 3,500 of whom were assumed to be combat capable.

The President wanted to know why Noriega couldn't be captured with a smaller operation. General Powell explained that unless the PDF were destroyed Noriega would simply be replaced by another

PDF leader. The Secretary of Defense, the Secretary of State, and National Security Adviser Brent Scowcroft all supported this assessment and the President signed an order authorizing armed forces to apprehend and arrest Noriega and other Panamanians currently under indictment in the U.S. for drug-related offenses.

Renamed "Just Cause," the operation was publicly defined as being required to protect the lives of U.S. citizens and bring democracy to Panama. To satisfy international law and Latin American sensitivity to intervention, the winner of the May elections, Guillermo Endera, officially requested U.S. help. Endera would be secretly sworn in as President of Panama just before the invasion.[10]

Speaking from the Oval Office on the morning of December 20, the President informed the nation that U.S. forces, including new deployments from the United States, were engaged in action in Panama. "No President takes such action lightly," he said, but there were compelling reasons:

Last Friday, Noriega declared his military dictatorship to be in a state of war with the United States and publicly threatened the lives of Americans in Panama. The very next day, forces under his command shot and killed an unarmed American serviceman; wounded another; arrested and brutally beat a third American serviceman; and then brutally interrogated his wife, threatening her with sexual abuse. That was enough.

General Noriega's reckless threats and attacks upon Americans in Panama created an imminent danger to the 35,000 American citizens in Panama. As President I have no higher obligation than to safeguard the lives of American citizens.[11]

There had been some loss of life, said Bush, to soldiers on both sides and to innocent civilians. Fortunately, the key military objectives had already been achieved, and most organized resistance eliminated. But the operation was not yet a total success, Bush conceded, because General Noriega was still in hiding.[12]

The mission of subduing pro-Noriega units of the PDF, successfully completed in two days, had been as intense as it was rapid. Over 400 bombs were dropped on Panama City, some delivered by the new Stealth bomber. Apache helicopters disgorged combat teams firing automatic rifles. Tanks rolled through the streets, demolishing wooden structures in poor barrios. According to the U.S. Southern Command's initial casualty estimates, the military deaths were 314 Panamanians and 23 U.S. troops; the wounded troops numbered about ten times those numbers. Southcom's report of 202 Panamanian civilians dead was contradicted by later news reports of thousands of civilian deaths (there was never a final official U.S. accounting of the civilian casualties).[13]

After an additional two weeks of anxiety in the White House, Noriega surrendered at the residence of the Papal Nuncio in Panama City. Noriega, armed with two AK-semiautomatic rifles, had entered the nunciature on December 24, evidently hoping for asylum and help from the church in arranging for his safe passage out of the country. U.S. troops surrounded the building, in assault formations. From December 24 until January 3, Generals Thurman and Carl Stiner (the Joint Task Force commander) negotiated with the Papal Nuncio on arrangements for releasing Noriega into their custody, and on the rules of military engagement should Noriega become violent inside the nunciature. To prevent eavesdropping on the negotiations, General Thurman ordered his troops to blast heavy metal rock music at the nunciature (journalists at first thought they were witness to a unique form of psychological warfare). Noriega evidently felt he had been tricked into a humiliating surrender, for when he emerged from the building on January 3 in full military dress and was manhandled by the U.S. troops as if he were an ordinary criminal, he started shouting curses at the Papal Nuncio.[14]

Bush's sweet taste of personal victory, however, could not compensate for the loss of international respect the United States incurred in acting, once again, as a self-appointed policeman in Latin America. On December 29, a United Nations General Assembly resolution stated that it:

1. *Strongly deplores* the intervention in Panama by the armed forces of the United States of America, which constitutes a flagrant violation of international law and of the independence, sovereignty and territorial integrity of States;

   2. *Demands* the immediate cessation of the intervention and the withdrawal from Panama of the armed invasion forces of the United States.[15]

El Salvador was the only Latin American country to vote against the resolution (which passed by a vote of 75 to 20, with 40 abstentions) beside the U.S.-installed Panamanian government.

Within the administration there were second thoughts about whether the deaths, destruction, and diplomatic costs of "Just Cause," had been fully justified by the presumed threat to U.S. interests. Pentagon analysts admitted in internal assessments that the Canal could have been easily defended by U.S. forces already in the Canal Zone. Bush, remorseful at the destruction to civilian areas in Panama City, announced a special $1 billion aid package to "repair the wounds, repair the damage" to civilian areas in Panama City.[16] Months later, the hope for significant domestic reform in a post-Noriega Panama were fading. The drug trade had revived. Former members of Noriega's PDF were again in positions of influence in the domestic police force. And anti-U.S. sentiment was greater than it had been before the invasion.[17]

DEALING WITH SADDAM HUSSEIN

As Saddam Hussein escalated his verbal threats and deployed his forces on the Kuwaiti border in late July 1990, President Bush and other U.S. officials communicated their concerns in bland language couched in reassurances that the geopolitical interests the United States shared with Iraq in the region still constituted the controlling reality for Washington.

Saddam's impression that the United States considered Iraq a geopolitical partner had been nurtured in Washington throughout the 1980s. The common view among U.S. strategists was that Iraq's September 1980 reopening of its war with Iran had been the crucial determinant of Teheran's decision to settle the embassy hostage conflict with the United States. With the Khomeini regime in Teheran having become Washington's new bête noire in the Middle East, the U.S. government did what it could to assure that Iraq would win its war with Iran and emerge from that war in a superior economic and military position. In 1982, the Department of State removed Iraq from its list of terrorist countries, so that it could qualify for U.S. aid and credits. In 1984 full diplomatic relations (severed in the 1950s when Iraq became a Soviet client state) were reestablished between Washington and Baghdad. The White House encouraged its allies to sell Iraq conventional arms and high-technology equipment which Saddam used to develop ballistic missiles and chemical, biological, and nuclear weapons. A dramatic indication of how determined the Reagan administration was to secure Iraq as a counterweight to Iran was the mild reaction by the White House to the mistaken launching of a missile from an Iraqi jet aircraft against the U.S.S. *Stark* (which killed thirty-seven U.S. sailors and nearly sunk the ship).

By the time of George Bush's inauguration in 1989, trade between the United States and Iraq had grown to $3.6 billion a year. Despite allegations that Iraqi forces had used chemical warfare against the secessionist Kurds, reports of the worsening human rights situation in Iraq, and growing suspicions during 1989 that Iraq was attempting to develop nuclear weapons, President Bush resisted congressional efforts to get tough with Saddam Hussein. In January 1990 Bush signed an executive order certifying that it would be against the national interest of the United States to halt Export-Import Bank loans to Iraq.[18]

The developing cordiality in U.S. relations with Iraq was temporarily interrupted in April 1990, when Saddam threatened that in a renewed war with Israel he would use chemical weapons that would "eat up" half of Israel. High U.S. officials expressed dismay and a State Department spokesperson called Saddam's remarks irresponsible and outrageous. But relations were put back on track by a delegation to Baghdad of farm-state congressman and senators headed by Robert Dole. They assured Saddam of their support of the President's desire for friendly relations between the two countries (Iraq was the ninth largest customer for U.S. agricultural products).

When Iraq began to openly threaten military action against Kuwait in mid-July, 1990, the reaction of the Bush administration was ambiguous at best. Secretary of Defense Cheney told reporters on July 19 that American commitments, made during the Iran-Iraq war, to come to Kuwait's defense were still valid; and on July 23, the administration ordered its naval vessels in the region to engage in joint exercises with the United Arab Emirates. But on July 24, Department of State spokesperson Margaret Tutwiler told reporters that "we do not have any defense treaties with Kuwait, and there are no special defense or security commitments to Kuwait." In Baghdad, Saddam summoned U.S. ambassador April Glaspie for an interview in which the Iraqi president outlined his grievances with Kuwait, and the ambassador, following instructions from Secretary of State James Baker, assured Saddam that "we have no opinion on the Arab-Arab conflicts, like your border disagreement with Kuwait."[19] The Baker instruction to Glaspie reportedly asked her to remind the Iraqis that the United States would regard the use of force as "contrary to the U. N. Charter principles," but there is no evidence that she said this to Saddam during her interview.[20]

Two days later, with intelligence agencies reporting a huge buildup of Iraqi troops just across the border from Kuwait, President Bush sent a mildly worded cable to Saddam emphasizing his desire for improved relations and advising that Iraq's disputes with Kuwait be resolved peaceably. Defense Department officials tried to toughen up the tepid presidential message, but to no avail. Only three paragraphs long, the cable as dispatched read:

I was pleased to learn of the agreement between Iraq and Kuwait to begin negotiations in Jedda to find a peaceful solution to the current tensions between you. The United States and Iraq both have a strong interest in preserving the peace and stability of the Middle East. For this reason, we believe that differences are best resolved by peaceful means and not by threats involving military force or conflict.

I also welcome your statement that Iraq desires friendship, rather than confrontation with the United States. Let me reassure you, as my Ambassador, Senator Dole and others have done, that my administration continues to desire better relations with Iraq. We will also continue to support our other friends in the region with whom we have had longstanding ties. We see no necessary inconsistency between these two objectives.

As you know, we still have fundamental concerns about certain Iraqi policies and activities, and we will continue to raise these concerns with you in a spirit of friendship and candor, as we have in the past both to gain a better understanding of your interests and intentions and to ensure that you understand our concerns. I completely agree that both our Governments must maintain open channels of communication to avoid misunderstanding and in order to build a more durable foundation for improving our relations.[21]

On July 31, the Assistant Secretary of State for Near Eastern Affairs, John Kelly, testifying before the Middle East subcommittee of the House foreign affairs committee, was asked about Secretary of Defense Cheney's July 19 statement to reporters about U.S. commitments to Kuwait. Secretary Kelly's answer must have reassured Saddam: "I'm not familiar with the quotation that you just referred to, but I am confident in the administration's policy on the issue: We have no defense relationship with any Gulf country. This is clear." Kelly was pressed by the committee chairman to clarify what the U.S. policy would be in the event that "Iraq, for example, charged across the border into Kuwait . . . In that circumstance . . . is [it] correct to say . . . that we do not have a treaty commitment which would obligate us to engage U.S. forces there?" The Secretary confirmed that the United States did not have a treaty commitment to cover that circumstance.[22]

The very next evening (1:00 A.M. August 2, 1990 in the Persian Gulf), two of Saddam's Republican Guard armored divisions slashed into Kuwait followed by 1,800 tanks and 140,000 troops. By the end of the next day Kuwait was under the control of Iraq. Secretary of State Baker, in the Soviet Union conferring with Foreign Minister Eduard Shevardnadze, got the Soviets to cooperate with the United States in pushing a resolution through the United Nations Security Council at 6 A.M. on August 2 condemning the invasion and demanding "that Iraq withdraw immediately and unconditionally all its forces to the positions in which they were located on 1 August 1990."[23]

The Commitment to Reverse Iraq's Aggression

The Bush administration had been caught completely off guard by news of the invasion. Before convening the National Security Council early on August 2, the President told reporters that he did not believe the Iraqi move into Kuwait threatened other countries and that he was not contemplating intervention. But in the NSC meeting a more ominous interpretation was put on the events in the Gulf region: by taking over Kuwait, Saddam Hussein now controlled one-fifth of the world's oil reserves, and this would be doubled if Iraq also conquered Saudi Arabia. At a minimum, Saddam would have to be blocked from crossing over into Saudi territory. The President asked for military options. The Chairman of the Joint Chiefs of Staff, Colin Powell, contended that if U.S. force were to be used, the best option would indeed be to defend the Saudi border with Kuwait. The President, however, indicated that he was not at all comfortable with accepting the occupation of Kuwait as a fait accompli.[24]

In Aspen, Colorado on the evening of August 2 to attend a meeting on international affairs with Prime Minister Margaret Thatcher among others, Bush's public stance stiffened. He talked of Iraq's "naked aggression" and told the press that "We are not ruling any options in, but we are not ruling any options out."[25] And when he returned to Washington a few days later, he promised, "This will not stand. This will not stand, this aggression against Kuwait." He was determined "to reverse" it, he told reporters on the White House lawn. Then on August 6, buoyed by UN Security Council resolutions condemning the invasion and mandating comprehensive economic sanctions against Iraq, and standing side-by-side at the White House with Prime Minister Thatcher and NATO Secretary General Manfred Woerner, the President said that he was "ruling out nothing at all" when it came to implementing the sanctions. "These things will be enforced, whatever it takes."[26]

But in announcing the deployment of U.S. forces to Saudi Arabia on August 8, Bush was careful to delimit their mission to the "wholly defensive" one of deterring an attack on Saudi Arabia. "They will not initiate hostilities," he said. It "is not the mission to drive the Iraqis out of Kuwait." While the "overall objective" remained to get Saddam Hussein out of Kuwait, the "military objective is to see Saudi Arabia defended."[27]

Within the NSC there was great skepticism that economic and diplomatic sanctions alone could convince Saddam to withdraw from Kuwait; the view was that sooner or later he would have to be driven out by military force—or at best a credible threat to use military force. Those arguing for war preparations felt confirmed in their prognosis when on August 8, hours before Bush's public revelation of the decision to send U.S. forces to Saudi Arabia, Saddam's Revolutionary Command Council announced that the merger of Iraq and Kuwait was accomplished and irrevocable.

Operating from the premise that the United States might well have to go to war against Iraq to liberate Kuwait, the administration pursued a three-pronged political strategy over the next few months, consisting of:

1. efforts to gain United Nations legitimation for the use of force against Iraq;

2. efforts to internationalize the military operation against Iraq without constraining U.S. combat effectiveness or flexibility while getting other countries to join a U.S.-led military coalition; and

3. a campaign to generate popular support in the United States for punishing Saddam, so that Bush would have a free hand to order U.S. forces into action without congressional interference.

The Bush-Baker campaign to obtain UN resolutions condemning Iraq's invasion of Kuwait and to generate international support for possible military operations focused on Mikhail Gorbachev. Gorbachev's immense international popularity at the time as well as the

Soviet Union's veto power in the Security Council made him a special target of the President's efforts: his posture in the crisis would make a large difference in the kind of cooperation Washington could generate from other capitals and might even affect public attitudes in the United States toward the use of force in the Persian Gulf.

Despite Bush's considerable leverage with Gorbachev—the Soviet leader was in desperate need of Bush's cooperation in obtaining international financial help for perestroika—Secretary Baker understood it could be counterproductive to pressure the Soviets to rubber-stamp U.S. plans for dealing with Saddam. It would be enough at the outset to get Soviet support for an economic and weapons shipment embargo against their former client in Baghdad. To obtain this degree of Soviet cooperation, Baker reassured Shevardnadze on August 3 that Bush was not preparing to take unilateral military action against Iraq. The result was the U.S.–Soviet statement of August 3, read aloud at the Moscow airport by Baker with Shevardnadze standing at his side, "jointly calling upon the rest of the international community to join with us in an international cutoff of all arms supplies to Iraq."[28]

Soviet and U.S. diplomats at the United Nations worked together to formulate the Security Council resolution of August 6 instructing all members of the United Nations to cooperate in a comprehensive embargo on Iraq's oil exports and its export and import of other goods. Resolution 661—the most severe set of economic sanctions ever voted by the United Nations—stated that:

all States shall prevent:
(a) The import into their territories of all commodities and products originating in Iraq or Kuwait or exported therefrom . . .;
(b) Any activities by their nationals or in their territories which would promote . . . the export or transshipment of any commodities or products from Iraq or Kuwait . . .;
(c) The sale or supply by their nationals or from their territories or using their flag vessels of any commodities or products, . . . but not including supplies intended strictly for medical purposes, and, in humanitarian circumstances, foodstuffs, to any person or body in Iraq or Kuwait.[29]

The embargo resolution was passed by a vote of 13 to 0, with only Cuba and Yemen abstaining.

August 6, 1990 was also the day of Bush's historic decision to undertake the "Desert Shield" deployment of U.S. forces to Saudi Arabia—now made possible by King Fahd's agreement, which the royal family had been reluctant to give, to have a large and visible contingent of American troops on Saudi territory. Two days later, in announcing the dispatch of troops, the President claimed that their mission was "wholly defensive" and promised they "will not initiate hostilities." Bush was not yet ready to define Iraq's subjugation of Kuwait as sufficiently injurious to U.S. interests to warrant the use of military force to reverse it. This would only come after Saddam Hussein's defiant insistence, despite UN resolutions and economic sanctions, that Kuwait was now permanently a part of Iraq. In the weeks immediately following the invasion, Bush's threats to use U.S. force were restricted to the defense of Saudi Arabia, claiming that kingdom's "sovereign independence . . . is of vital interest to the United States." He talked of the crucial dependence of the U.S. economy on the region's oil. "A line has been drawn in the sand," he said. The troops were there to deter a move across the Saudi border.[30]

Expecting the Soviets would oppose the deployment of U.S. forces into Saudi Arabia, Bush and Baker had refrained from consulting Gorbachev or Shevardnadze in advance. When Baker phoned Shevardnadze on the eve of the deployment, the irritated Soviet foreign minister proposed that the military units should be placed under the aegis of the United Nations—specifically the military staff committee of the Security Council. Baker knew this would be unacceptable to Bush since it would give the Soviets an effective veto of U.S. military operations; but to deflect Shevardnadze's resentment, he promised to raise the idea with the President.[31]

The Baker-Shevardnadze exchange fueled worries in the U.S. and British governments that there was already too much of an apparent commitment by Bush to work through the UN, and that this could come back to haunt him in the event of actual U.S. combat operations (particularly an offensive attack into Kuwait) when maximum secrecy and flexibility were required. State Department legal experts, however, pointed out that the United States could maintain flexibility for any unilateral military actions Bush might authorize by obtaining a request from the Emir of Kuwait for United States military help under Article 51 of the Charter—the "self-defense" article—rather than defining the U.S. military operations as "collective security" actions (Articles 41 through 47), subject to direction and control from the Security Council.

U.S. diplomatic strategy henceforth was directed toward (a) securing a permissive mandate from the United Nations for the United States to use whatever means were necessary—including military action—to enforce the embargo and collateral UN resolutions demanding Saddam's unconditional withdrawal of his forces and (b) obtaining commitments from as many countries as possible to join or financially support a U.S.-led military operation to drive Iraqi forces out of Kuwait. Security Council Resolution 665 of August 25 authorized member states to use their maritime forces to ensure compliance with the economic embargo on Iraq established by Resolution 661. The maritime measures could include those "necessary . . . to halt all inward and outward maritime shipping in order to inspect and verify their cargoes and destinations."[32] Once again, the vote was 13 to 0 with Cuba and Yemen abstaining. To placate the Soviets and Chinese, a direct reference to "minimum force" was deleted from the final text and the phrase "with maximum use of political measures" was substituted.[33]

Bush and Baker were determined to avoid the pitfall of turning the anti-Saddam coalition into a predominantly NATO or "Western" grouping that would be seen as anti-Arab, anti-Islamic—which indeed was the way Iraqi propaganda was trying to portray the conflict in radio broadcasts to Arab masses throughout the region. Such a polarized definition of the conflict would not only discourage governments in the area from providing important basing, logistics, and communications support for the U.S. military buildup in the Gulf, but it would also make it virtually impossible to enforce the UN sanctions.

The task of inducing other Middle Eastern governments to join the coalition, or at least remain neutral, turned out to be easier than the White House expected, as Saddam had managed to severely alienate most of his neighbors over time. And within the previous year or so, with the Soviets no longer creating and actively sustaining Middle Eastern clients, even the region's traditionally anti-Western statesmen were prepared to accept United States action against Saddam Hussein.

In addition to Saudi Arabia, the most crucial players in the regional power alignment would be Egypt, Syria, Iran, Jordan, and

Israel. Each had its own set of considerations, which the Bush administration—concentrating on the imperative of organizing a balance of power against Iraq—tried to take into account.

For Egypt, joining the anti-Iraq coalition involved a reversal of President Hosni Mubarak's policy during the 1980s. Mubarak had provided Saddam with military supplies and economic support during the Iran-Iraq war, and in return Saddam had been the main champion of Egypt's reacceptance into the councils of Arab statecraft from which it had been excluded in reaction to the Israeli-Egyptian peace treaty of 1979. Mubarak felt personally betrayed, however, by Saddam's violation of his pledges in the spring and summer of 1990 not to attack Kuwait (Mubarak had previously represented Saddam's grievances and intentions toward Kuwait as understandable and deserving of negotiations).[34] The Egyptian president, now embarrassed and furious, was a ready participant in the coalition being formed by Bush; but he was adamant that Israel be kept out of the coalition and that Bush commit himself to putting new pressures on Israel after the current crisis to adhere to its promises to negotiate political autonomy for the Palestinians.

Putting aside Syrian President Hafiz Assad's terrible record on human rights and his notorious sponsorship of international terrorists, Bush and Baker were keen to exploit the longstanding and bitter rivalry between Assad and Saddam for pan-Arab leadership. According Syria a prominent role in the coalition would give the lie to the Iraqi dictator's claim that his confrontation with the United States over Kuwait was the latest expression of the historic clash between Arab nationalism and Western imperialism. "It is very important," Bush explained publicly, "that we cooperate with a major Arab country who happens to share the same goals that we do . . . on this very, very important issue."[35] Personal phone calls to President Assad from President Bush and visits to Damascus by high State Department officials, including Secretary Baker, produced a diplomatic initiative by Assad committing the Arab League to deploy an inter-Arab force, including some 15,000 Syrian troops, to Saudi Arabia. The Syrians also helped convince Iran (which Syria had supported in the Iran-Iraq war) to resist Saddam's efforts to now ally with him against the Americans, the Saudis, and the Israelis.

King Hussein of Jordan proved particularly difficult to deal with. Presiding over a population of ethnic Palestinians among whom

Saddam was wildly popular and over a weak economy highly dependent upon trade with Iraq, the normally pro-Western monarch was determined to keep out of the anti-Iraq coalition. From the outset of the crisis, the King offered himself as a mediator and tried to convince other regional leaders to effectuate an "Arab solution" instead of allowing the United States and its allies to reimpose a "Western imperial presence" in the region. He shuttled from capital to capital (including Washington) with various peace plans—essentially formulae for phasing Iraqi military withdrawals from Kuwait with the start of a negotiating process between the Iraqis and the Kuwaitis over the territorial and economic issues that were in dispute before the invasion. But the White House was totally opposed. Negotiations with Saddam could only take place, Bush insisted, following Iraq's complete and unconditional withdrawal from Kuwait. Anything else would be "to reward aggression." The White House and the State Department tried to deflect the impact of King Hussein's mediation efforts. But they quickly realized that the Jordanian monarch's role in any event would be marginal, for his credentials for stage-managing regional diplomacy had lost credibility over the years and, especially with every country in the region trying to enhance its own post–Cold War relations with the United States, now carried very little weight with the other Arab leaders.

The role to be played by Israel was vexing to the Bush administration from the outset, as it would continue to be for most of the war. One of Saddam's principal stratagems for sabotaging Washington's efforts to include key Arab states in the coalition was to link the conflict to Arab-Israeli issues. Hoping to provoke a visible Washington-Jerusalem embrace (and later, through his Scud missile attacks, to provoke Israel's entry into the war), Saddam also demanded a comprehensive "peace negotiation" encompassing a wide range of the region's unresolved disputes, including preeminently the future of the Palestinians.

Thus, on August 12, Saddam called for a resolution of the crisis by dealing with issues of "occupation" throughout the entire region; this would require a comprehensive regional agreement providing for "the immediate and unconditional withdrawal of Israel from the occupied territories in Palestine, Syria, and Lebanon, as well as the withdrawal of Syria, and the withdrawal of Iraq and Iran." These outstanding issues should be settled in sequence, that is, as a precondition for the settlement of the situation in Kuwait, which should take into consideration "the historic rights of Iraq to its territory and the choice of the Kuwaiti people."[36]

One of Secretary Baker's recurrent tasks during the next eight months was to dissuade members of the coalition from granting the legitimacy of such attempts to link (and to establish a moral equation between) Iraq's occupation of Kuwait and Israel's occupation of the West Bank and the Gaza Strip. It also involved waylaying Gorbachev's attempt to retrieve the Soviet Union's flagging influence in the Middle East by championing the idea of a general peace conference where Iraq's subjugation of Kuwait would be, in Shevardnadze's words, "one of several highly complex, interlocking problems."[37] At the September 9 meeting between Bush and Gorbachev at Helsinki, the U.S. Secretary of State and the Soviet Foreign Minister and their respective Middle Eastern experts were able to remove from the public communique any explicit calls for comprehensive multiple-issue Middle East negotiations in exchange for a secret promise by Bush to support such an international conference following the resolution of the current crisis over Kuwait.[38]

The Bush-Baker diplomacy toward America's other coalition partners was also careful to respect their various situations and definitions of national interest. The West Europeans and the Japanese had their own legacies of dealings with countries in the Middle East (France, for example, was Iraq's second largest military supplier next to the Soviet Union). Visible token military deployments from coalition partners were symbolically important, but, in fact, the U.S. military commanders were just as pleased to be able to run the show mainly with their own personnel and equipment—without having to deal with the tangled problems of command and control that substantial foreign military contributions would entail. From Germany and Japan, both constitutionally restricted from direct military participation, the Bush administration made it clear that it expected substantial financial contributions to help countries in the Middle East being economically hurt by the boycott of Iraq and to relieve the drain on the U.S. budget caused by the military operations.

Although the President and his national security adviser, Brent Scowcroft, had concluded in the first week of the crisis that the United States would probably need to use major military force to reverse Saddam's occupation of Kuwait, the Pentagon needed time to organize and put in place the military capabilities required. This required Bush to modulate his rhetoric in the interim, lest he provoke Saddam to attack the Desert Shield forces in Saudi Arabia before the local military balance shifted drastically against Iraq. Such an early attack by Iraqi forces against the outnumbered and still underequipped U.S. forces in the Saudi desert could inflict levels of casualties on U.S. troops that would divide the American public and perhaps make it impossible for Bush to persist in his determination to drive Saddam out of Kuwait.

In August, the Iraqi government prevented U.S. citizens and other foreigners from leaving Kuwait and Iraq—in effect, holding them as hostages to compel a lifting of the economic embargo and, even more starkly, as "human shields" at strategic sites to dissuade the United States and its allies from launching military attacks. The Iraqis also demanded that all countries close their embassies in Kuwait since it was no longer a sovereign state. The United States was among the countries that refused and ordered their embassy personnel to stay put. Another hostage crisis loomed. Saddam played his hostage card for its effects on public opinion in the West, inviting the media to interview the hostages in comfortable hotel accommodations. The administration tried to keep the names of the American hostages from the press and to minimize the publicity. As it turned out, however, the hostage ploy backfired on Saddam by undercutting whatever sympathy for the plight of the economically squeezed Iraqis he had been trying to generate. At the end of August, he announced that all foreign women and children were free to leave. Over succeeding weeks, the hostage issue was further diffused as each of a succession of dignitaries from Willy Brandt to Jesse Jackson was allowed to leave the country with some of the captives. (The remaining hostages were released in late November and early December.)

In October 1990, Bush had set in motion the Pentagon planning that would give the U.S. military an offensive option against Iraq, and by the end of the month he had approved the basic scenario that would be implemented the following January and February. Asserting the objectives of "complete and unconditional withdrawal of Iraqi forces from Kuwait . . . and restoration of security and stability in the Persian Gulf region," Bush announced on November 8:

I have today directed the Secretary of Defense to increase the size of U.S. forces committed to Desert Shield to ensure that the coalition has an adequate offensive military option should that be necessary to achieve our common goals.[39]

The term "offensive military option" was chosen with care, and the President would not allow reporters to push him into revealing that he had already decided for war. When asked "Are you going to war?" his response was evasive: "I would love to see a peaceful resolution . . . [but] I don't want to say what I will or will not do."[40]

Up to November 8, there had been solid public and Congressional support for Bush's expressed determination to take a stand against the Iraqi aggression. Influential members of both political parties and editorials in the major newspapers endorsed the deployment and stated mission of the Desert Shield forces. Suddenly, however—with the addition of the "offensive option"—the consensus broke, especially as the huge number of troops (over 200,000) in the augmentation were revealed.

Defense specialists critical of the apparent abrupt change in strategy, including Senate armed services committee chairman Sam Nunn, pointed out that maintaining the new Desert Shield level of over 400,000 troops would preclude rotating a significant portion of them in and out of the Saudi desert; this meant that the offensive option would have to be used within the next few months: the military tail was now wagging the political dog. But the decision to violently force Saddam out of Kuwait was the President's considered political decision.

Other critics testifying before the Senate Armed Services Committee at the end of November faulted the administration for not giving economic coercion enough time to work before resorting to military force. Among these were Paul Nitze, James Schlesinger, and two former chairmen of the Joint Chiefs of Staff, General David Jones and Admiral William Crowe, Jr. Crowe's admonitions against rushing into war were widely televised. The issue, he said, "is not whether an embargo will work but whether we have the patience to let it take effect." The U.S. was letting its dislike for Saddam crowd out other considerations, "selling our country short by jumping to the conclusion that we can't stare down our opponent." The bemedalled Admiral chided the "armchair strategists" who were counselling a near-term attack on Iraq for forgetting that "War is not neat . . . And once you resort to it, it's a mess."[41]

In the face of the intensifying domestic debate, Bush and Baker sought another UN resolution to give international legitimacy to the President's decision. State Department lawyers once again advised that it was unnecessary to obtain the Security Council's imprimatur: the United States could do all it wanted under the self-defense clause in Article 51. And Margaret Thatcher continued to counsel against the precedent of seeking approval from countries like Russia and China, which might hesitate to actually use force against an Arab client. But Bush hoped that with a special UN resolution authorizing the use of force to drive Saddam out of Kuwait, coalition members would be less likely to defect when the United States actually implemented its offensive option.

The original U.S. draft of the UN resolution contained an explicit authorization to employ "all necessary means, including the use of force." To assure the required majority in the Security Council, however, Secretary Baker settled for a more ambiguous yet sufficiently elastic wording. As passed on November 29, 1990 (with only Cuba and Yemen voting no and China abstaining), Resolution 678 stated that:

The Security Council . . . .

1. *Demands* that Iraq comply fully with resolution 660 (1990) and all subsequent relevant resolutions, and decides, while maintaining all of its decisions, to allow Iraq one final opportunity, as a pause of goodwill to do so;

2. *Authorizes* Member States, cooperating with the Government of Kuwait, unless Iraq on or before 15 January 1991 fully implements, as set forth in paragraph 1 above, the foregoing resolutions, to use all necessary means to uphold and implement . . . [these resolutions] and to restore international peace and security in the area.[42]

The phrase "as a pause of goodwill" as well as the deadline of January 15 (Bush wanted January 1) were concessions to Gorbachev's desire to allow Saddam to reconsider whether holding on to Kuwait was worth a war with the United States.[43]

To solidify support from the Soviets and other countries and to deflect the growing domestic criticism that the President had prematurely locked the country into a collision course, Bush announced on November 30 (just one day after the passage of the deadline resolution) that he was sending Secretary of State Baker to talk directly with Saddam Hussein. The announcement and press conference, more than any other public statement, revealed the President's thinking about why he had no alternative but to lead the nation into a war against Saddam Hussein. There was too much at stake:

We're in the Gulf because the world must not and cannot reward aggression. And we're there because our vital interests are at stake. And we're in the Gulf because of the brutality of Saddam Hussein. We're dealing with a dangerous dictator all too willing to use force who has weapons of mass destruction and is seeking new ones and who desires to control one of the world's key resources. . . .

Our objectives remain what they were since the outset. We seek Iraq's immediate and unconditional withdrawal from Kuwait. We seek the restoration of Kuwait's legitimate government. We seek the release of all hostages and the free functioning of embassies. And we seek the stability and security of this critical region of the world.

The President contended that it was futile to rely entirely on economic sanctions to achieve these objectives. Moreover, there were substantial costs to the coalition from continuing the embargo on Iraqi and Kuwait oil. "Those who feel that there is no downside to waiting months and months must consider the devastating damage being done every day to the fragile economies of those countries who can afford it least." The United States too was being hurt by the increase in oil prices: "Our economy . . . is at best in a serious slowdown, and if uncertainty remains in the energy markets, the slowdown will get worse." Bush insisted that no one wanted peace more than he did, and he remained hopeful that a peaceful resolution of the crisis could still be achieved. "But yesterday's U.N. resolution . . . properly says to Saddam Hussein: Time is running out. You must leave Kuwait. And we've given you time to do just that." Consistent with the terms of the Security Council's mandate, and "to go the extra mile for peace," said the President,

I will issue an invitation to Foreign Minister Tariq Aziz to come to Washington . . . to meet with me. . . . And I will suggest to Iraq's President that he receive the Secretary of State. . . . I will be prepared, and so will Secretary Baker, to discuss all aspects of the Gulf crisis. However, to be very clear about these efforts to exhaust all means for achieving a political and diplomatic solution, I am not suggesting discussion that will result in anything less than Iraq's complete withdrawal from Kuwait, restoration of Kuwait's legitimate government, and freedom for all hostages.[44]

When reporters pressed the President to say whether anything would be offered Saddam in these meetings in return for pulling out of Kuwait, Bush simply reiterated, repeatedly, that the only acceptable outcome would be Iraq's fulfillment of the terms of the UN mandate. What then was the point of the meeting, he was asked. "Are you just delivering ultimatums?" Bush rejected the word but then proceeded to make the proposed Baker-Saddam meeting sound precisely like such a confrontation:

[Saddam] has got to understand what the alternatives are to complying with the United Nations resolutions. And the best way to get that across is one on one— Baker looking him right in the eye. . . . [This] isn't a trip of concession. When you've done what he's done, I don't see there's room for concession, . . . for giving something to save face. That's not the way you treat with aggression.[45]

Despite such insistence, new alarms about Bush's steadfastness were raised by those who believed that, obsessed with the lack of a firm domestic consensus for war, Bush might succumb to a partial concession from Saddam. Henry Kissinger publicly warned Bush against the temptation to compromise. Richard Perle, a former Reagan administration strategist, speculated that from Saddam's point of view, a U.S. initiation of negotiations at this point might confirm the theory that Bush had a "tendency to buckle under pressure."[46] Israeli officials also expressed strong concerns, as did Saudi King Fahd who, having allowed his country to host an embarrassingly large Western military presence, now hungered to be vindicated in a swift desert war to liberate his northern neighbor. In attempting to allay these fears, National Security Adviser Brent Scowcroft revealed what the administration was really up to. "Basically the President has made up his mind," he told the Saudi ambassador. The diplomatic efforts were "all exercises."[47]

As it turned out, the "extra mile" offer failed to take James Baker to Baghdad. Saddam agreed to meet with the American Secretary of State, but not before January 12. Bush rejected the transparent ploy to extend the UN deadline by beginning "negotiations" just three days before its expiration. The final pre-war meeting took place in Geneva on January 9 between Secretary Baker and Iraqi Foreign Minister Aziz. Baker attempted to deliver a direct letter to Saddam from President Bush. When Aziz saw that the letter was essentially an ultimatum (comprising a forecast of defeat for Saddam's military and calamity for his country if he did not unconditionally relinquish his occupation of Kuwait), he refused to accept it. This bit of diplomatic theater was followed by a lengthy oral confrontation between Baker and Aziz in which both reiterated their set positions and exchanged warnings of the terrible destruction each would inflict in a war, including mutual threats of devastating retaliation in the event the other side used its weapons of mass destruction.[48]

Desert Storm and its Aftermath

Bush had all he required now to order U.S. forces into action against Iraq. He saw no need to ask the Congress for a declaration of war. The combination of the United Nations deadline resolution and his prerogatives as Commander in Chief would be sufficient. As head of state of a signatory country to the UN Charter, which had been duly approved by the Senate, Bush could claim to be already authorized by the Congress to use military force to implement a collective security decision of the Security Council—just as Truman did in the Korean War. As Commander in Chief, he had the duty to take military action to protect the U.S. forces in Saudi Arabia from being attacked, which he was prepared to claim was imminent in light of intelligence on Saddam's buildup of Iraqi forces across the border in Kuwait.

But Scowcroft and White House Chief of Staff John Sununu persuaded the President that he would be in a much stronger position internationally as well as domestically if he could get the House and Senate to give him the advance backing in this instance that the Congress gave Eisenhower in the Formosa Straits crisis and Johnson at the time of the Gulf of Tonkin crisis. Accordingly, on January 8, Bush formally sent letters to both houses of Congress requesting them to adopt a resolution authorizing his use of United States armed forces to compel Iraq to withdraw from Kuwait. This was the day before the Baker-Aziz confrontation in Geneva. The day after Geneva, the congressional debate began on Bush's request.

The main arguments had already been well rehearsed. The President's congressional supporters echoed his rhetoric demonizing Saddam as a madman armed with weapons of mass destruction, and predicting dire economic consequences from a perpetuation of the crisis. The opponents for the most part agreed that there was a compelling national interest to get Iraq out of Kuwait, but they argued for more time for economic sanctions and diplomatic pressures to bring Saddam to his senses before committing unpredictable numbers of American soldiers to die in a desert war of unpredictable duration.

The joint congressional resolution the White House wanted was approved overwhelmingly in the House on January 12 by a vote of 250 to 183 (the majority included House armed services committee chairman Les Aspin and 82 other Democrats), but in the Senate it carried by only three votes (with only 10 Democrats in favor). The preamble justifying the resort to force left the language of the White House draft virtually unchanged—citing Iraq's unprovoked aggression and occupation of Kuwait; its defiance of the United Nations demands for unconditional withdrawal and the January 15 deadline; and Iraq's chemical, biological, and nuclear weapons and ballistic missile programs and its "demonstrated willingness to use weapons of mass destruction." The authorization section was somewhat more assertive of continuing congressional monitoring than Bush preferred:

(a) *Authorization.*— The President is authorized, subject to subsection (b), to use United States Armed Forces pursuant to United Nations Security Council Resolution 678 (1990) in order to achieve implementation of Security Council Resolutions 660, 661, 662, 664, 665, 666, 667, 669, 670, 674, and 677.
(b) *Requirements for determination that use of force is necessary.* — Before exercising the authority granted in subsection (a), the President shall make available to the Speaker of the House of Representatives and the President pro tempore of the Senate his determination that (1) the United States has used all appropriate diplomatic and other peaceful means to obtain compliance by Iraq with the United Nations Security Council resolutions cited in subsection (a); and (2) that those efforts have not been and would not be successful in obtaining such compliance. [49]

Upon signing the resolution on January 14, Bush stated that "my request for congressional support did not, and my signing this resolution does not, constitute any change in the long-standing positions of the executive branch on the President's constitutional authority to use the Armed Forces to defend vital U. S. interests." The next day, January 15, 1991, with the expiration of the UN deadline, the President signed the national security directive authorizing the execution of war plans he had approved at the end of December. The directive was transmuted by Secretary of Defense Cheney and Chairman Powell into operational orders to General Norman Schwartzkopf, commander of the U.S. central command for the Middle East and Southwest Asia. On January 16 Desert Shield became Desert Storm. [50]

In his address to the nation on the night of January 16, Bush held Saddam personally responsible for the terrible destruction that U.S. bombers had already started to rain on Iraq, claiming that the Iraqi tyrant had "systematically raped, pillaged, and plundered a tiny

nation" and "maimed and murdered . . . innocent children." Moreover, he had met every overture of peace with open contempt. "No
president can easily commit our sons and daughters to war," said
Bush. But he wanted to reassure the American people that "this will
not be another Vietnam. . . . Our troops will have the best possible
support in the entire world and they will not be asked to fight with
one hand tied behind their back." Moreover, U.S. troops would be
sent into battle knowing that they were helping the United States,
once again, to do something great:

This is an historic moment. . . . We have before us the opportunity to forge for
ourselves and for future generations a new world order—a world where the rule of
law, not the rule of the jungle, governs the conduct of nations. When we are
successful—and we will be—we have a real chance at this new world order, an
order in which a credible United Nations can use its peacekeeping role to fulfill the
promise and vision of the UN's founders.

The President quoted a U.S. paratrooper in Saudi Arabia as saying:
"We're here for more than just the price of a gallon of gas. What
we're doing is going to chart the future of the world for the next
hundred years."[51]

The "new world order" was added to the rationale for using force
to help mobilize support for the changeover from Desert Shield to
Desert Storm. But like the other add-ons to the objective of extracting Iraq from Kuwait—disarming Iraq of its weapons of mass
destruction, offensive missiles, and capacity to launch any further
aggression; punishing Saddam for his aggression; getting the Iraqis
to depose him from power—it only created confusion on the part of
the military and public alike about the ultimate mission of the
U.S. forces.

Bush devolved the primary responsibility onto Cheney, Powell,
and Schwartzkopf for devising and carrying out the military missions
necessary to drive Iraqi forces from Kuwait. Most of the military
actions during the forty-four days of Desert Storm were publicly
justified as necessary for accomplishing this overriding objective as
quickly as possible with a minimum of U.S. casualties. The unrelenting and withering bombing of Saddam's military forces and mili-
tary-related infrastructure—both in Iraq and in Kuwait—were designed not only to hobble Iraq's ability to hold on to Kuwait against
the forthcoming coalition ground attack, but also to drive home to
Saddam that the longer he persisted the less he would be left with to

sustain his power within Iraq. Bush's most controversial decision of the war, his ordering Schwartzkopf to institute a cease-fire on February 27 (the fourth day of the massive ground assault into Kuwait), thereby allowing major elements of Saddam's elite Republican Guard with their tanks and helicopter gunships to be pulled back deeply into Iraq, was portrayed as the result of the President's determination to avoid an unnecessary climactic battle that would have multiplied U.S. casualties. (The final U.S. casualties were 148 killed and 148 wounded.[52])

The actual reasons for the way the war was conducted and terminated were more complex than was suggested throughout the crisis by the administration's rhetoric. Indeed, Brent Scowcroft was reportedly at odds with the President from the outset of the crisis on the consequences of branding Saddam a Hitler. He worried that Bush's verbal attacks on his enemy would create public enthusiasm that might later trap Bush into driving on to Baghdad.[53]

Feeling betrayed by Saddam, Bush wanted to get rid of him—but not through an American invasion and occupation of Iraq (no more Vietnam-type quagmires), nor through bringing about full-scale insurrections by the Shiites and Kurds (creating a Lebanon-type cauldron that would tempt intervention by Iran). The White House hoped that the punishment inflicted on Iraq proper would stimulate a "palace revolt" among Baghdad's military and political elite, disillusioned and angry with Saddam for stupidly bringing such a humiliating calamity on the country. Yet Bush's rhetoric, for example, his February 15 plea to the people of Iraq to "take matters into their own hands to force Saddam Hussein the dictator to step aside," continued to stimulate domestic hunger for a dramatic finale.

Privately, Bush kept his cool. He called a cease-fire at the end of February not simply to avoid having to occupy Iraq militarily, but also to avoid the total collapse of a viable Iraqi state able to balance Iranian power—the original motive for Washington's courtship of Baghdad after the Iranian revolution. Instead of completely smashing Saddam's elite legions and forcing him out of power, Bush settled for Iraq's acceptance of harsh cease-fire terms that subjected the country to an unprecedented degree of imposed disarmament and intrusive international control.

The cease-fire terms, incorporated in Security Council Resolution 687 (April 3, 1991), included the requirements that:

Iraq unconditionally accept the destruction, removal and rendering harmless, under international supervision, of:

(a) all chemical and biological weapons and all stocks of agents; and related subsystems and components and all research, development, support and manufacturing facilities;

(b) all ballistic missiles with a range greater than 150 kilometers and related major parts, and repair and production facilities . . . . [and] that Iraq shall unconditionally agree not to acquire or develop nuclear weapons or nuclear weapons-usable material . . . or components or . . . research, development, support or manufacturing facilities. . . . [and] to accept . . . urgent, on-site inspection and the destruction, removal, and rendering harmless of all [these] items.[54]

These disarmament requirements were supplemented by additional demands in Resolution 688, passed on April 5, that the government of Iraq cease the military repression of its civilian population in the Kurdish and Shiite areas and that it allow immediate access by international humanitarian organizations to all those in need of assistance.[55] Resolution 688 was as far as Bush wanted to go to intervene in Iraq's political affairs after the conclusion of the Gulf War—a considerable backtracking from his wartime encouragement of the people of Iraq to overthrow the Saddam dictatorship.

Despite the fact that Bush's earlier rhetoric was a major stimulus to the rebellions that broke out in the Kurdish and Shiite areas in March—a fact that critical editorial writers were now waving in his face—Bush insisted that his remarks about the people of Iraq throwing out Saddam had been misinterpreted. He had never implied that the United States would assist them militarily. It was important now to get humanitarian aid to the people of Iraq. "But I do not want one single soldier or airman shoved into a civil war that has been going on for ages." His consistent position, he claimed, was that the United States was not going to intervene militarily in Iraq's internal affairs and risk being drawn into a quagmire.[56]

But public outrage at the brutal slaughter of the Kurds prompted the Senate to pass, on April 11, a resolution stating that the United States had a "moral obligation" to help the UN enforce its demands that Saddam stop repressing the civilian population of Iraq. Responding to these pressures, and accepting the suggestions of the new British Prime Minister, John Major, Bush agreed to have some 5,000 U.S. troops join British, French, and Dutch military units in northern Iraq to secure "safe havens" (special encampments) for the

Kurds where they would be free from attacks by Saddam's forces and could receive food and medical help from relief agencies. The coalition also indicated that it was prepared to enforce "no-fly zones" above the 36th parallel and below the 32th parallel to prevent Saddam from using helicopters and other aircraft to harass the Kurdish and Shiite communities. All of this, Bush insisted, was "purely humanitarian," and did not contradict his determination to refrain from intervening in the internal political affairs of Iraq. But at the same time he continued to insist that "the most important thing . . . is to get Saddam Hussein out of there"—removed from power in Baghdad.[57]

During the 1992 presidential election congressional Democrats alleged that the Departments of Commerce and Agriculture had cooperated with private banks to finance prohibited Iraqi military purchases out of credits that were supposed to have been restricted to purchases of agricultural commodities. Not only did these new allegations, and the administration's attempt to rebut them, highlight the extent to which Reagan and Bush had assisted Saddam in the years prior to Iraq's invasion of Kuwait, but they called attention, once again, to the fact that more than a year after the cease-fire Saddam still ruled in Baghdad and was arrogantly acting in defiance of some of the terms of the cease-fire accords. By all accounts, Bush was sorely tempted to inflict additional punishment on Saddam in the fall of 1992, but was worried this might be viewed as motivated by electoral considerations—which could then only boomerang against him in November.

After the election Bush had nothing to lose by another show of force. His final flurry of missile strikes in January 1993 against Iraqi military facilities were necessitated, explained the President, by Saddam's continuing failure to live up to the UN cease-fire resolutions—the provocation being Saddam's moving around Iraqi surface-to-air missiles in a way that threatened U.S. aircraft monitoring the no-fly zones established to protect Shiite and Kurdish enclaves. Bush was not in the least apologetic about launching these largely symbolic parting blows at his nemesis in Baghdad. He was acting no differently than he had during the past four years, said Bush, and "I have no intention of changing that approach to life in the last six or seven days of my presidency."[58]

HUMANITARIAN INTERVENTION IN SOMALIA

Bush also waited until after the November 1992 election to commit United States power to control the deteriorating situation in Somalia. Since January 1991, the former Cold War client of the United States had been in a condition of virtual anarchy—the aftermath of a rebellion that had forced the U.S.-supported dictator, Siad Barre, to flee the country. Rival warlords were fighting to gain control of the country by preventing the people in their enemy's area from obtaining access to food.

By the summer of 1992, the situation had deteriorated to the point where some 30 percent of Somalia's 8 million people were on the verge of starvation. Attempts by international relief agencies to deliver food and medical supplies in convoys from the port city of Mogadishu were being blocked by armed gangs in the employ of the rival warlords. United Nations cease-fire efforts were being sabotaged. Scenes of little children dying of hunger and disease were on the nightly news.

Moved by Secretary General Boutros Ghali's complaint that the United States and the Europeans were evidently more willing to let Africans be the victims of enforced starvation than Yugoslavs (a reference to UN peacekeeping efforts in Bosnia), the Security Council on July 27 approved an emergency airlift of supplies into Somalia. The Bush administration cooperated by assigning U.S. Air Force cargo planes to fly food to the besieged towns. But efforts on the ground to distribute the supplies continued to be thwarted by the warlords' gunmen.

Into the fall, the administration received appeals from humanitarian organizations for the United States to participate more vigorously and visibly in the UN relief efforts—perhaps by contributing an American unit to the small UN peacekeeping operation in Somalia. But Bush's national security advisers, and the President himself, were not ready to deal with the prospect of American military personnel getting caught in the cross-fire of the rival gangs.

Once the presidential election was over, the administration began to look carefully at its options. On Thanksgiving eve, to the surprise of the State Department which had been arguing for a more modest approach, Bush decided to offer the use of U.S. combat troops to the

United Nations to help get the relief supplies to the Somali people. But upon the insistence of the Pentagon, he attached the condition that the force be under American command.[59] The result was the UN Security Council resolution of December 3 authorizing "the Secretary General and member States cooperating to implement the offer [by the United States] . . . to use all necessary means to establish as soon as possible a secure environment for humanitarian relief operations in Somalia."[60]

The day following the UN authorizing resolution, President Bush in a television address announced that he had ordered Secretary of Defense Cheney "to move a substantial American force into Somalia." Designated "Operation Restore Hope," this force (which background briefings revealed would comprise nearly 30,000 troops) was being dispatched for "humanitarian" reasons only. Its mission, in the words of the UN resolution, was "to establish a secure environment" against the armed warlord gangs that had been preventing international relief efforts from delivering food to the starving people in Somalia. The President made a point of reassuring the public that "the troops have the authority to take whatever military action is necessary to safeguard [their own] lives." Yes, he was again asking the men and women of the armed forces to take on a "difficult and dangerous job," but "It's now clear that military support is necessary to insure the safe delivery of food Somalis need to survive. . . . The people of Somalia, especially the children of Somalia, need our help. We're able to ease their suffering. We must help them live. We must give them hope. America must act. . . . When we see Somalia's children starving, all of America hurts."

Anticipating criticisms that he was establishing a precedent for the United States to intervene militarily all around the world where local political conditions are causing people to starve—Bosnia, most urgently, but also Haiti, Mozambique, and Burma—Bush insisted that he understood "the United States alone cannot right the world's wrongs, but we also know that some crises in the world cannot be resolved without American involvement, that American action is necessary as a catalyst for broader involvement of the community of nations." The American military units involved in this mission, said the President, were "doing God's work."[61]

MAXIMS FOR THE USE OF FORCE IN THE
POST–COLD WAR ERA

The presidency of George Bush, no longer facing an adversary capable of posing a clear and present danger to the survival and well-being of the United States itself, might have been expected to substantially reduce the weight given to military power in the country's foreign policy. Instead, what were supposed to have been the "kinder and gentler" Bush years featured a dramatic recrudescence of the reliance on force internationally. Indeed, George Bush ordered U.S. military forces into action abroad in more instances and in larger numbers than any president since the end of the Vietnam War. But Bush's justifications for each of the military operations he ordered lacked the clarity of purpose that had characterized official justifications for using force during the Cold War. In an attempt to rebut criticisms that his "moment-of-truth" decisions as Commander in Chief had been impulsive and not informed by the kind of moral reflection and strategic assessment that should govern the choice to sacrifice human lives, Bush at the end of his presidency delivered a speech at West Point on his "principles" for using military force.

The speech at the military academy on January 5, 1993 was trumpeted in advance by White House aides as likely to be equal in importance to other famous farewell addresses—Eisenhower's, possibly even George Washington's. The President would use the platform at West Point to counter allegations that his decisions on war and peace were arrived at in the absence of a well thought-out concept of the national interest and were motivated by either electoral politics or personal psychological needs.

Bush introduced his subject by talking of the mixed blessings of the end of the Cold War. It was a time of great promise: democratic governments had never been so numerous. The recently concluded U.S.–Soviet START II treaty diminished the likelihood of nuclear holocaust. But this did not eliminate the "specter of war," the "threats to be reckoned with." If the United States were to be passive and aloof, "We would risk the emergence of a world characterized by violence, characterized by chaos. One in which dictators and tyrants threaten their neighbors, build arsenals brimming with weapons of mass destruction, and ignore the welfare of their own men, women, and children. And we could see a horrible increase in international terrorism with American citizens more at risk than ever before." To prevent this from happening, the United States must lead the world in bringing about a "new world order—one of governments that are democratic, tolerant, and economically free at home and committed abroad to settling inevitable differences peacefully, without the threat or use of force."

The leadership required of the United States "should not be confused with either unilateralism or universalism," said Bush. "Nope, the United States should not seek to be the world's policeman." But in the wake of the Cold War, it was the role of the United States, "the only remaining superpower," to promote a democratic peace. "There is no one else."

Such world leadership required "a willingness to use military force" as a "useful backdrop to diplomacy, a complement to it, or, if need be, a temporary alternative." This was what he had done in the Gulf War, and was now doing in Somalia. These cases demonstrated "the wisdom of selected use of force for selective purposes." He then proceeded to offer his view of that wisdom:

In the complex world we are entering there can be no single or simple set of fixed rules for using force. Inevitably, the question of military intervention requires judgment. Each and every case is unique. . . . But to warn against a futile quest for a set of hard and fast rules to govern the use of military force is not to say there cannot be some principles to inform our decisions. . . . *Using force makes sense as a policy where the stakes warrant, where and when force can be effective, where no other policies are likely to prove effective, where its application can be limited in scope and time, and where the potential benefits justify the potential costs and sacrifice.*[emphasis added][62]

Editorials the next morning hailed this statement as a sophisticated improvement over the Pentagon's "all or nothing" conditions for using military power which had been articulated by Secretary Weinberger in 1984 and reaffirmed in recent policy debates by Secretary Cheney and Chairman Powell.

Upon closer inspection, the Bush principles are a set of abstract maxims against which no one could argue, but which did nothing to advance the policy debate about the legitimate use of military power in the post–Cold War world. The problem still remained of determining which "stakes warrant" the use of force and under what conditions "force can be effective." Moreover, no criteria of "effectiveness" were suggested. Given his failure to offer any substantive content to his maxims, Bush's final, bottom-line standard—"where the potential benefits justify the potential costs and sacrifice"—was an empty formula, providing no basis for judging whether the expected benefits of any contemplated use of force would indeed warrant the expected costs and sacrifice.

29

THE NEW WORLD ORDER

Let me assure you, the United States has no intention of striving for a Pax Americana. . . . *We seek a* Pax Universalis *built upon shared responsibilities and aspirations.*

—GEORGE BUSH

During the Persian Gulf crisis of 1990–1991, George Bush found a need for "the vision thing"—his disparaging term for the idealistic appeals politicians sometimes have to make to garner support. He needed it to help overcome the arguments from many quarters (including the Chairman of the Joint Chiefs of Staff) that Saddam Hussein's forcible annexation of Kuwait did not pose a sufficient threat to vital U.S. interests to justify going to war. "Oil"? "Jobs"? Saddam couldn't drink the additional oil he now controlled in Kuwait; if he charged too high a price, the industrial world could purchase its energy supplies elsewhere. Deter him from trying to grab control of Saudi oil (the justification for "Desert Shield"), but why sacrifice American blood and treasure to compel him to withdraw from Kuwait?

The President knew that his early determination to reverse Iraq's aggression was not just visceral, or a personal reaction to having been diddled and defied by the Iraqi dictator. Nor was it that, having publicly declared "this shall not stand," to let it stand would revive all of the "wimp" allegations. It was much more than any of these things, but as usual it was difficult for Bush to find the right concepts to express his larger view of the matter.

When Margaret Thatcher reminded him of the failure of the Western democracies to stand up to Germany prior to World War II, that rang a bell. So he compared Saddam to Hitler. And then there was Truman committing the United States to reverse the North Korean invasion of South Korea. But Iraq was no Third Reich and Kuwait was no democratic Czechoslovakia; nor was this a case anymore of a proxy or client of America's superpower rival expanding the patron's sphere of control. Something else was at stake: the rules of the game, the world order—the rules of international behavior for the post–Cold War era the world was now entering—the *new* world order.

HOMILIES IN SEARCH OF A SUBSTANTIVE CORE

In introducing the concept of a "new world order" to explain his overarching objectives in the Gulf, Bush presented a loose conglomeration of preachments that failed to distinguish the new world order from any of the usual goals of statecraft that are equally embraced in the rhetoric of democrats and despots, conservatives and radicals, imperialists and defenders of the status quo alike. The "new world order," he told a joint session of Congress on September 11, 1990, was to be "a new era—freer from the threat of terror, stronger in the pursuit of justice, and more secure in the quest for peace. An era in which the nations of the world . . . can prosper and live in harmony. . . . Today that new world is struggling to be born, a world quite different from the one we've known. A world where the rule of law supplants the rule of the jungle. A world in which nations recognize the shared responsibility for freedom and justice. A world where the strong respect the rights of the weak."[1]

At the end of the Gulf War, returning to address the Congress, he claimed to be able to see a new world coming into view—"A world in which there is the very real prospect of a new world order. In the words of Winston Churchill, a world order in which 'the principles of justice and fair play protect the weak against the strong.' A world where the United Nations—freed from cold war stalemate—is poised to fulfill the historic vision of its founders. A world in which freedom and respect for human rights finds a home among all nations. The Gulf war put this new world to its first test. And my fellow Americans, we passed that test."[2]

Amorphous as it was, Bush's new world order, when peeled back to its core—as revealed in his policy decisions and their more immediate justifications—was a revival of the old world order: the state-sovereignty system and its associated norms, which had been submerged for some four decades into the supranational coalitions organized by the Cold War superpowers.

With roots extending back three centuries, the traditional system now manifesting itself as the new world order emphasized the sovereign equality of states, the sanctity of state borders, and noninterference by states in each other's domestic affairs. It was an elitist order run, as ever, by and for the great powers—sometimes in informal concert (as in the Group of Seven industrial powers), sometimes through membership in international agencies (as in the United Nations Security Council, the International Monetary Fund, and the World Bank), and sometimes unilaterally. To the rest of the world it might appear that this world order contained a double standard: the sovereignty and borders of the great powers could never be violated; but the weaker powers were subject to intervention, albeit intervention authorized by the international agencies controlled by the great powers—yes, there might be occasions for such apparent compromises with the principle of the sovereign equality of states, but these would only be for the purpose of upholding the norms of the system itself against radical states and movements attempting to overthrow the legitimate order.

Bush identified Saddam Hussein's violation of the sovereign independence of Kuwait as the first major test to the new—revived old—world order. All necessary means could and should be used to restore the independence of Kuwait. But actually Bush was describing only the first half of the test. The second half came at the end of Desert Storm when the United States forces, having pushed the Iraqis back out of Kuwait, were ready to move on toward Baghdad, and Bush said no. This was followed during successive weeks and months by another test in the form of appeals from the Iraqi Kurds and Shiites to the United States to intervene on their behalf against the brutal repression they were suffering at the hands of Saddam's forces. In each of these situations, Bush was true to his view that the rights and obligations of states toward one another were the essence of world order, whereas how governments treated the people within their jurisdictions was, except in cases of actual or virtual genocide, normally their own business.

But, characteristically, he was not always consistent in acting according to the precepts of this world order philosophy. Success in the world of statecraft as well as in domestic politics often required the subordination of principle to prudence.

MORE THAN REALPOLITIK BUT LESS THAN GLOBAL LIBERALISM

Despite the shallowness and plasticity, Bush's self-concept as a statesman pursuing the new world order provided an orientation—both for policymakers within his administration as well as for others who would have to deal with him—to which considerations would move him to act vigorously in international relations. The concept also provided the President himself with the ballast he needed to stabilize his often oscillating impulses to be bold or cautious—and, not incidentally, with some after the fact justifications for actions he found difficult to explain while events were unfolding.

Rationalizing Tiananmen

The greatest embarrassment suffered by President Bush for his handling of foreign policy attached to his response to the Chinese government's brutal repression of pro-democracy, student-led demonstrators in Beijing's central Tiananmen square during the first week of June 1989. Chinese soldiers killed hundreds of civilians, wounded thousands, and arrested thousands more. As reports and video coverage of the brutal crackdown flooded U.S. television screens on June 3, President Bush issued a brief public rebuke to authorities in Beijing, deploring "the use of force against Chinese citizens who were making a peaceful statement in favor of democracy."[3]

The President wanted to let it go at that. "I know the Chinese," he is quoted as telling his aides, invoking his experience as the Ford Administration's envoy to Beijing in 1974 and 1975. "I know how to deal with them, and it's not through pressure or sanctions."[4] (Bush's first foreign trip as President in February 1989 had included a visit to Beijing. Despite vocal criticism by U.S. human rights groups and congressional Democrats of the regime's policies toward dissidents, Bush used the occasion to re-establish his old connections and to reassure his hosts that they had a good friend in the White House.

The principal issues between the two countries—China's missile sales to Middle Eastern countries and its textile marketing policies— were negotiable.)

To avoid being outflanked on the human rights issue by the Democratic opposition in Congress and by the ideological right wing of his own party, the President called a press conference on June 5 to express his disapproval of the Tiananmen massacre more strongly than in his June 3 statement, and to announce the imposition of a number of sanctions: suspension of U.S. weapons sales to China, suspension of technical exchanges between the military of the two countries, and suspension of visits by high-level U.S. and Chinese officials. Yet when asked why he wasn't also imposing economic sanctions, the President demurred:

THE PRESIDENT: On the commercial side, I don't want to hurt the Chinese people. I happen to believe that the commercial contacts have led, in essence, to this quest for more freedom. I think that as people have commercial incentive, whether it's in China or other totalitarian systems, the move to democracy becomes inexorable. So what we've done is suspend certain things on the military side, and my concern is with those in the military who are using force. . . .

QUESTION: Will you, Mr. President, be able to accommodate to the calls from Congress for tougher sanctions? Many lawmakers felt you were slow to condemn or criticize the violence in China before now, and many are pushing for much tougher action on the part of this country.

THE PRESIDENT: I've told you what I'm going to do. I'm the President. I set the foreign policy objectives and actions taken by the executive branch. I think they know, most of them in Congress, that I have not only a keen personal interest in China, but that I understand it reasonably well. I will just reiterate . . . my conviction that this is not the time for anything other than a prudent, reasoned response. . . . So I would argue with those who want to do something more flamboyant, because I happen to feel that this relationship is vital to the United States of America, and so is our adherence to democracy and our encouragement for those who are willing to hold high the banner of democracy. So we found, I think, a prudent path here.[5]

Privately, the President and his advisers considered even the limited sanctions policy—which they adopted reluctantly in response to domestic pressures—to be counterproductive. The suspension of high-level official exchanges prevented the administration from maintaining the dialogue with the Chinese leaders that Bush believed was crucial for inducing Beijing to pursue constructive policies internationally and to make further progress internally toward capitalism and democracy. Accordingly, in July 1989 Bush sent National Security Adviser Scowcroft and Deputy Secretary of State Lawrence Eagleburger on a secret mission to Beijing to reassure the Chinese leaders of Bush's desire to put Sino–U.S. relations back on track and to suggest practical steps for how this might be done. Scowcroft made another secret visit in December but this time the Western press discovered that the administration was acting in violation of its own sanctions and AP wire stories carried reports of a Scowcroft banquet toast to the Chinese leaders in which he referred to the "negative forces" in both countries that "seek to frustrate our cooperation." Secretary of State Baker compounded the domestic political damage by telling a television interviewer that this was the first time that any such high level visit to Beijing had occurred since Tiananmen, only to be discredited when CNN reported the July trip of Eagleburger and Scowcroft.[6]

Bush's determination not to let China's poor human rights record interfere with his administration's relations with the government in Beijing was periodically a subject of contention with Congress in connection with legislative efforts to suspend China's most favored nation (MFN) trading status. Bush repeatedly threatened to veto the punitive legislation and he felt strongly that he was doing the right thing by refusing to cave in to the popular view. The arguments for maintaining normal trading status for China were made time and again during the Bush administration: suspension of MFN would not only be perceived in Beijing as especially discriminatory against China (other countries with negative human rights ratings from the State Department still kept their MFN status) and produce a general worsening of U.S.–Chinese relations, but it would also hurt important U.S. economic groups, including aircraft manufacturers, wheat farmers, and fertilizer companies.[7] Paradoxically, the persistent congressional targeting of MFN actually helped the administration in some of its high-stakes international diplomacy with Beijing, especially during the Gulf War, by allowing it to credibly threaten the Chinese with the virtual certainty of a denial of MFN if they vetoed the key UN Security Council resolutions against Iraq.

Domestically, however, Bush continued to suffer the political liabilities of a China policy that lent itself to charges of being a throwback to Kissinger's realpolitik. In the presidential debates in the fall 1992 campaign, Bill Clinton recalled how "all those kids went out there carrying the Statue of Liberty in Tiananmen Square, and Mr. Bush sent two people in secret to toast the Chinese leaders and basically tell them not to worry about it." Bush's rebuttal was a charge that Congress and Governor Clinton wanted to isolate China. By "putting conditions on MFN and kind of humiliating them, . . . you . . . turn them inward, and then we've made a terrible mistake. I'm not going to do it. I've had to fight a lot of people that were saying 'human rights.' We are the ones that put the sanctions on and stood for it."[8]

Keeping Cool on Bosnia: Avoiding the Self-determination Quagmire

The Bush administration also found that the new world order concept (defined as the revived *old* world order) failed to adequately comprehend the post–Cold War rise of national self-determination movements. It was all very well to talk about the sanctity of borders and noninterference by nation-states in each other's domestic affairs as long as the location of borders and the identity of the "nation" was a settled matter. But these principles provided insufficient policy guidance for situations where an ethnic group within the jurisdiction of a presumably sovereign nation-state was challenging the legitimacy of its control by the nation-state and demanding political independence. Yet these were the situations that were reemerging on Bush's watch as a characteristic feature of international politics.

A purely realpolitik U.S. policy would simply remain aloof from secessionist crises and other issues concerning the legitimacy of other states' regimes—except in cases where the local instability might threaten America's own geostrategic or crucial economic assets, or put the lives of its citizens in danger. Such aloofness characterized Bush's early responses to the secessionist violence in Yugoslavia in the summer of 1991 even as it became clear that the federation was doomed to break up. (The first official U.S. response to Croatia's vote of May 21, 1991 to secede was a standard formal reaffirmation of support for the "territorial integrity of Yugoslavia within its present borders."[9]) For a time he could justify this posture as being consistent, or at least not inconsistent, with new world order principles since no aggression was taking place across established international borders.

Lagging behind the European Community, which by late 1991

and early 1992 had begun to recognize the independence of the seceding republics, the United States recognized Slovenia, Croatia, and Bosnia-Herzegovina as independent states on April 7, 1992. Up to then the Bush administration had contented itself with supporting UN mediation and peacekeeping efforts on behalf of a cease-fire between Serbs and Croats who had been fighting over disputed areas. But now that the United States had recognized the statehood of the former Yugoslav republics, Bush could not sit idly by—without compromising his new world order principles—as Serbia sent its military forces into newly independent Bosnia to help the ethnic Serbs in their own secessionist struggle against the predominantly Muslim Bosnians.

On May 30, 1992, while not taking sides on the merits of the territorial disputes, and insisting that these be resolved by peaceful negotiations, the United States supported the UN Security Council condemnation of the Serbian actions in Bosnia and the application of economic sanctions against the Serbian regime in Belgrade.[10] Unlike its reaction to Iraq's invasion of Kuwait, the Bush administration had no inclination to use U.S. troops in a military operation to push Serbia's forces out of Bosnia. The United States would provide logistics support for UN relief convoys attempting to reach besieged Muslim enclaves in Bosnia, but the administration refused to deploy its own combat forces to protect the relief convoys.

With popular outrage growing over the Serb policy of "ethnic cleansing" (forcible removal of Muslims to create Serb-majority areas in Bosnia), plus evidence of efforts to starve the people in Muslim enclaves and reports of mass rapes of Bosnian women, the Bush administration was hard pressed to keep to its policy of no direct U.S. military involvement. Editorial columnists and Democrats, including presidential candidate Bill Clinton, argued that the U.S. should at the very least provide air cover for UN relief operations. But Bush and his advisers feared such a commitment carried a high risk of escalating to a large-scale U.S. military involvement if the Serbs tried to shoot down U.S. aircraft; it also became clear that air cover by itself could not adequately protect the relief convoys from Serb ambushes on the ground.

It fell to Acting Secretary of State Lawrence Eagleburger to elucidate the administration thinking on the MacNeil/Lehrer News Hour on August 28. Asked to explain why it was appropriate for U.S.

aircraft to fly air cover for the Shiites in Iraq but not for the Bosnians, Eagleburger rejected the analogy:

The proper comparison with regard to Iraq . . . is the fact that the President stopped at a point. He didn't go chasing after Saddam Hussein through all of Iraq and getting us tied down; . . . there is a fundamental difference between [Bosnia and] the kind of activity that went on in [the Gulf War] . . . including the Iraqi invasion of another country. . . . [The Bosnian conflict] is in a sense a civil war— not that these aren't different republics and different countries now, but it is inter-ethnic conflict; it is massively mixed up; it is in territory that is extremely difficult to fight in.

The Secretary explained what U.S. Bosnian policy was and was not:

And the one thing we have decided clearly [that] we're going to do is [that] we will use all necessary force to get humanitarian supplies in to these people. And that is critically important. What we have also said is [that] we are not going to involve ourselves militarily in trying to make peace and force this conflict to an end.[11]

Eagleburger was being faithful to what he understood to be the "prudent" considerations in the White House: Bosnia was, if anything, not like Kuwait but like Lebanon—a cauldron of communal hatreds extending back centuries, in which politics was reduced to the most primordial of all issues, the ownership and control of land. Were the United States to involve itself as a military protector of any particular community, it would become the object of hatred and violent attacks by the others. If the United States did attempt to intervene with major military force to control the situation, it would find itself shooting at indigenous paramilitary units, even peasants (the Vietnam "quagmire"), not simply against the troops and aircraft of an invading country. Finally, the administration was fearful of setting a precedent, generating pressures for U.S. intrusion into similar ethnic conflicts exploding across the former Soviet Union— where the Russian government might employ its military forces on behalf of ethnic Russians who were contesting their subjugation by non-Russian regimes in the other republics—or even within the Russian Federation itself.

Eagleburger's comment about the Bosnian situation could be read as a metaphor for the administration's realization of the predicaments inherent in the new world order. "Until you've seen what kind of country it is," he said, "until you understand the terribly complex relationships between people in Yugoslavia, it is very dangerous to look for simplistic solutions."[12]

The new world order according to George Bush also differed from the realpolitik old world order when it came to international economic issues. The realpolitik model is essentially mercantilist: nation-states, especially the great powers, pursue self-sufficiency in at least their ability to make war, and therefore eschew the kind of economic interdependence (and specialization) that is supposed to result from an open world trading system. Yet Bush, like all of his post–World War II predecessors with the exception of Richard Nixon was ideologically committed to the doctrine of global free trade.

The concept of free trade, articulated with the greatest conviction by Ronald Reagan, holds that world and national prosperity and peace will be advanced to the extent that barriers are removed to the worldwide functioning of the economic laws of supply and demand; the greatest good for the greatest number of the world's peoples will result from a global free market favoring those producers and distributors who can manufacture and sell their goods and services at least cost to consumers; the specialization of national export and import lines that result as countries pursue their comparative advantages in providing particular categories of goods and services will increase interdependence among nations and thus give them a vital stake in preventing international conflicts and domestic strife that could disrupt the peaceful functioning of the world market.

With the end of the Cold War, the collapse of the bastions of Marxist socialism, and the stated acceptance of some form of market economics by the new leaders in most of the post-Soviet states, Bush could hope for an historic opportunity to finally put global free trade into practice. But free trade would be far from simple.

No longer united against a common enemy, the governments of advanced industrial countries were faced with increasing pressures from recession-hit sectors of their economies for continued subsidies. Protected sectors within the European Community (such as the French farmers) used their political power within their national governments to demand continuing protection against imports from countries outside the Community, especially the United States. The Japanese, increasingly excluded from the European market and facing competition from the newly industrializing countries of the Pacific rim, were less and less inclined to accede to insistence from Washington that they "voluntarily" limit their exports of automobiles to the United States. The Japanese were also more overtly resentful than they had allowed themselves to be during the Cold War (when they feared the loss of the U.S. security umbrella) of the persistent hectoring from the United States that they should provide greater hospitality to American investments. Recession-plagued sectors of the U.S. economy, particularly the automobile industry, were demanding that the administration get tough with the Japanese or else Congress would be forced to pass protectionist legislation.

Popular discontent with Bush's unwillingness to play economic hardball with the Europeans and the Japanese was deflected during and immediately following the Gulf War as the President basked in the public's approval of his leadership, which rose to over 70 percent in the opinion polls (even higher than Reagan's best ratings). But as the recession persisted and deepened in 1991 and 1992 the opinion polls registered a precipitous drop in approval. Many felt that the President was spending too much time on foreign affairs and neglecting domestic problems.[13]

Looking toward his forthcoming reelection campaign and trying to recast himself as now fully engaged with the country's domestic predicaments, Bush abruptly canceled a planned December 1991 trip to Japan and other Asian countries. The visit was to have coincided with the 50th anniversary of Pearl Harbor, and the Japanese had hoped to use the occasion to purge the residual bitterness from that historical tragedy. The American media portrayed the trip cancellation as a panicky and clumsy reaction to his negative poll ratings. The President hurriedly rescheduled his trip for January 1992, with his mission being to persuade the Japanese of the benefits of U.S. investments and imports. He was going as America's chief salesman, on behalf of American products. His trip, he said, was about "jobs, jobs, jobs."[14]

At the President's invitation, twenty-one business leaders, including the CEOs of the big three auto makers, joined him in his January visit to Japan to make the case for greater access to Japanese markets. If this was to be a media show for the audience back home, it failed dismally: the CEOs contradicted in public his claims of gaining significant guarantees from his hosts to sell American cars in Japan; and the media in both countries made his effort look like a whining plea to the Japanese to take pity on the United States for its competitive weaknesses.

At the state dinner in his honor, President Bush took sick, vomited on the Japanese Prime Minister who was sitting next to him, slumped to the floor, and was comforted by the PM, who cradled the President's head in his lap. The world media audience was treated to incessant replays of this all too symbolic scene for more than a week.

An authoritative study of U.S. trade policy recounts the aftermath of the Japan trip:

> It unleashed a torrent of Japan-bashing (and America-bashing) . . . , together with a grassroots 'buy America' campaign. Suddenly, U.S. trade policy seemed again up for grabs. The multilateral Uruguay round [of GATT negotiations] was again stalemated. . . . The President had both legitimized attacks on Japan and undercut his capacity to counter them.[15]

The administration viewed the signing of the North American Free Trade Agreement (NAFTA) between the United States, Mexico, and Canada as a success for President Bush in the economic sphere. In his announcement on August 12, 1992 that the 14-month negotiations had been successfully concluded, Bush related the accomplishment to the new world order. "The Cold War is over," he said. "The principal challenge now facing the United States is to compete in a rapidly changing, expanding global market."[16] In large measure a defensive reaction to the success of the European Community and to Japan's aggressive penetration of the markets of the Western hemisphere, NAFTA would create a regional trading bloc of 370 million people producing $6 trillion worth of goods and services each year, greater than the combined gross domestic product of the EC. Basically an incorporation of Mexico into the free-trade zone agreed to in 1988 between the United States and Canada, the new accord, in its main provisions, stipulated that:

- Customs duties between the three countries on nearly 10,000 products would be eliminated—some immediately, some in stages.
- Mexico's barriers to the import of cars, trucks, and vehicle parts would be phased out.

• U.S. and Canadian banks and securities firms could immediately acquire up to 10 per cent of the Mexican capital in such industries; by the year 2000 all Mexican limits on U.S. and Canadian ownership in the banking and securities field would be eliminated. There would be a similar elimination of all limits on U.S. and Canadian takeovers of Mexican insurance firms.

• Mexico would rapidly phase out requirements that Mexican state-owned enterprises reserve most of their contracts for Mexican companies.

Spokespersons for large U.S.–owned multinational manufacturing enterprises and financial institutions hailed the accord as opening up a great new economic frontier in North America. American officials pointed out the advantages to the ordinary consumer. Carla Hills, the United States Trade Representative, cited the increased choices in U.S. supermarkets as the tariffs against Mexican fruits and vegetables were removed. But various traditionally organized and specialized industries—in textiles, for example—were wary of being displaced by the mobile multinationals that could take advantage of the lower factor costs across the Mexican border to manufacture and then sell their now-cheaper finished products back in the United States. Leaders of the AFL-CIO said they would oppose congressional approval of NAFTA for exactly this reason, complaining that the accord would throw hundreds of thousands of U.S. laborers out of work as companies previously based in the United States set up factories in Mexico to take advantage of the lower wages there. Environmental groups criticized the incentives for manufacturing firms to escape U.S. environmental controls by moving south of the border where such controls were lax or nonexistent, labeling this "the export of pollution." Presidential candidate Bill Clinton said that while he favored NAFTA in principle, he would insist on adding provisions to ensure job protection for the U.S. worker and Mexican adherence to fair labor and environmental standards. In any event, he strongly objected to the Bush administration's effort to obtain "fast track" congressional approval of the accord before the end of Bush's term of office.

Sensing that a push for fast track approval of NAFTA would lose him votes with some constituencies, and listening to the worries of many congressional Republicans concerned about their own chances for reelection, Bush pulled back from his insistence on quick ap-

proval. It would fall to Clinton to bear the brunt of the controversies
during the ratification process—controversies reflective of the increasing intermeshing of domestic and foreign policies in the new
world "order."

OPPOSING A NEW WORLD ORDER FOR THE
GLOBAL ENVIRONMENT

The Bush administration's commitment to a global free market extended also to the environmental field, where most of the other
advanced industrialized countries and a majority of the Third World
countries had accepted the premise that the health and wellbeing of
their peoples required substantial international regulation of economic activity.

The isolation of the United States on issues of the global environment during the Bush years was starkly revealed at the United
Nations Conference on the Environment and Development (popularly called the "earth summit") attended by more than 100 heads of
state in Rio de Janeiro during the first two weeks of June 1992. The
leaders signed a collection of treaties and documents holding them
all accountable to a set of international rules (to that extent limiting
their sovereignty) on their activities affecting ecologies and environ-
ments that they shared in common. The earth summit reflected the
growing scientific and popular consensus that a laissez-faire, business as usual approach was no longer acceptable as population
growth and industrialization accelerated the depletion and abuse of
the world's air, water, fertile soil, and interdependent biological
species that have sustained human life on earth. Fears centered on
holes in the stratospheric ozone layer that filters out the sun's harmful ultraviolet rays, and the phenomenon of global warming resulting
from the buildup of carbon dioxide in the atmosphere (the "greenhouse effect").

The central theme of the Rio earth summit was the concept of
"sustainable development" developed by the World Commission on
Environment and Development (often called the Brundtland commission, after its chairperson, the former prime minister of Norway,
Gro Harlem Brundtland). The biologists, meteorologists, earth scientists, and economists who did the back-up studies for the Brundtland
commission and the earth summit maintained that the presumed
conflict between ecological care and economic growth was a myth:

economic development that was ecologically efficient and conserved the natural resources on which agriculture, industrial production, and the health of the planet ultimately depend would produce sustainable (meaning durable) economic growth; moreover programs to discover and implement such sustainable economic growth could themselves be designed and financed in ways that would stimulate job-creating enterprises and projects.

This was a logic that even the ideologically conservative Reagan administration, after some hesitation, had come to embrace in the negotiations leading toward the 1987 Montreal Protocol for phasing out substances that were depleting the ozone layer. When DuPont and other major U.S. companies developed efficient ozone-safe substitutes in response to domestic legislation, the State Department suddenly became a convert to internationally binding agreements that would limit other countries' production of ozone-damaging chlorofluorocarbons (CFCs), thus creating a ready market for the already developed U.S. substitutes.[17]

Bush's director of the Environmental Protection Agency, William Reilly, wanted to build on the experience of the Montreal Protocol to fashion progressive U.S. domestic and international policies and evidently took at face value Bush's 1988 campaign pledge to be the "environmental" President. But Reilly ran into determined opposition from others in the Bush administration, notably Chief of Staff John Sununu and Vice President Dan Quayle, head of the President's cabinet-level Council on Competitiveness (a group with a mandate to reduce the costs to businesses of government regulations). Outranking Reilly, they were able to persuade the President to oppose key aspects of a number of the treaties and resolutions being readied for the earth summit.

In the weeks leading up to his appearance at the June summit at Rio, Bush came out against the binding controls on CO_2 emissions in the draft Convention on Climate Change, claiming that more scientific research was needed on the "greenhouse effects" of CO_2 before states should be required to adhere to specific limits. He also opposed the Convention on Biodiversity, claiming that its provisions would stifle innovation in the biotechnology industry. Bush's positions on the draft agreements, accompanied by his rhetoric on the need to protect U.S. jobs, effectively pulled the rug out from under EPA chief Reilly in his role as principal U.S. representative and negotiator at the conference. Reilly was further undercut and publicly embarrassed when some of his opponents in the administration leaked to the press one of his confidential memoranda to the White House requesting authorization to agree to certain minor modifications in the Biodiversity Convention that would allow the President to sign it.[18]

To keep the American President from withdrawing entirely from the historic earth summit, the negotiators agreed to a watered down Framework Convention on Climate Change, which Bush did sign, along with an agreement on 17 nonbinding principles on the care and management of forests and a broad "Agenda" of nonbinding commitments to pursue a wide range of sustainable development objectives ranging from combating desertification and drought to safely managing the disposal of radioactive wastes.[19] Efforts to achieve a compromise on the Convention on Biodiversity failed, and Bush, alone among the major heads of state, refused to sign it— earning him the sobriquet of "the Darth Vader of the Rio Meeting."[20] Playing more to his home audience than to the delegates in Rio, Bush proclaimed to the conference that "America's position on environment protection is second to none, so I did not come here to apologize."[21]

EPA administrator Reilly put the best public face possible on the United States performance, focusing on the unprecedented range of the commitments by countries to cooperate with one another to protect the global commons. With the employees of his agency he shared his more candid assessment of the self-isolation of the United States at the Rio summit:

We assigned a low priority to the negotiation of the biodiversity treaty, were slow to engage the climate issue, were last to commit our President to attend Rio. We put our delegation together late, and we committed few resources. No doubt, this contributed to negative feelings toward the United States.

For me personally, it was like a bungee jump. You dive into space secured by a line on your leg and trust it pulls you up before you smash into the ground. It doesn't typically occur to you that someone might cut your line.[22]

Those in the administration who undercut Reilly opposed on ideological grounds the worldview that underpinned the earth summit. Sununu and Quayle were determined to prevent any U.S. acquiescence to what they regarded as the internationalist/socialist premises of the environmental movement—an internationalism that would erode the nation's sovereign independence and subject the United

States to decisions by world organizations run by groups hostile to the American way of life; and a socialism antithetical to free enterprise and market capitalism based on the profit motive. Sununu and Quayle deliberately attempted to sabotage Reilly's efforts to iden- tify the United States with the new global environmentalism. The fact that President Bush's views on the major environmental issues were unformed and ambivalent meant that, by default, the anti- environmental zealots would succeed in isolating the United States from the emergent global consensus in favor of interna- tional controls on environmentally damaging activities of states and firms.

START II

The new world order continued to have more coherence in the realm of superpower relations—but here too, it was more a departure from the Cold War system than a design for a successor system. Yet Bush was able to announce at the end of his tenure in office that he and President Yeltsin of Russia had come to an agreement unprecedented in the history of international relations: as a follow-on to the START I accord, the United States and Russia were taking another huge step to mutually divest themselves of the bulk of their massive strategic nuclear arsenals.

Signed in Moscow on January 3, 1993 by the two presidents, START II committed the United States and Russia to drastically slash their strategic systems and to have completed the process no later than January 1, 2003, retaining one-quarter of the nuclear warheads they had at the beginning of the 1990s. They would be left with 3,000 to 3,500 warheads each. As significant as the numerical limits was the new treaty's ban on the deployment of multiple-warhead ICBMs—the principal "first strike" weapons in each side's arsenal. This ban made real the standard claims that strategic forces existed only for the purpose of deterring a strategic attack from the other side.[23]

"Today, the Cold War is over," proclaimed President Bush at the signing ceremony—apparently forgetting that he had made that same proclamation on at least five major international occasions over the previous year and a half. But both Presidents had reason to wax hy- perbolic.

YELTSIN: In its scale and importance, the treaty goes further than all other treaties ever signed in the field of disarmament.

. . .

I would like to pay tribute to my colleague and friend, George. His remarkable personal and political qualities and competence have contributed to a successful transition from the cold war to a new world order.

. . .

BUSH: We meet at . . . a moment that is also a new era for our two nations and for the world. We stand together . . . at the threshold of a new world of hope, a widening circle of freedom for us and our children.[24]

The euphoria of the moment covered over the worries in the Bush administration during its last days that Yeltsin and his reformist policies—perhaps even his commitment to radical disarmament—were faced with growing opposition in Russia. Not the least of these concerns attached to the continuing inability of Yeltsin to get Ukraine and Belarus to implement the START I requirements that all former Soviet republics except Russia remove all strategic nuclear weapons from their territories. The increasing political instability in Russia and the problem of arms control in the former Soviet republics were part of the large agenda of unfinished new world order business Bush would have to pass on to his successor in the Oval Office.

PART IX

ENTER BILL CLINTON

When we took office . . . we found the agenda overflowing with crises and potential disasters.

—WARREN CHRISTOPHER

I didn't get hired to fix everything. . . . I got hired to do what I'm now trying to do, to set forth a vision. . . . But I think a President needs a little time to set forth the big framework of things.

—BILL CLINTON

30

FROM DOMESTIC POLITICIAN
TO GEOPOLITICIAN

I'm sure he's interested in foreign policy, but right now it's just not where he's focused. It's not where he's immersing himself in the details.
—A SENIOR AIDE TO PRESIDENT CLINTON

Alleging during his campaign for the presidency that George Bush had been too preoccupied with foreign policy and had squandered the opportunity provided by the end of the Cold War to reorder the country's priorities, Bill Clinton was ready to interpret his election as a mandate to devote most of his energies to neglected domestic needs. The principal threats to the security, well-being, and basic way of life of the people of the United States no longer came from foreign adversaries but from the worsening economic condition of the country. The domestic economic crisis and the spreading crime and drug problems tearing apart the social fabric of the country produced widespread cynicism about the capacity of the American democratic system to cope with the societal problems of the late twentieth century. The adverse international trade balance—targeted by the Democratic congressional leadership during the Bush years as one of the principal causes of the domestic economic crisis, and by some of Clinton's rivals for the Democratic nomination as the cause of the abnormally high levels of unemployment—was, for Clinton, a glaring symptom of the need for domestic economic restructuring. If the United States was falling behind Japan and the

European Community in the international economic competition, and if this was part of the reason why U.S. workers were losing their jobs, the remedies lay not so much in international trade policy (getting the Japanese and the Europeans to reduce their barriers to U.S. imports and investments) as it did in rejuvenating the U.S. economy to revive the competitiveness of U.S. products at home and abroad. The country was indeed in trouble, but sources of and remedies for the trouble were to be sought more in domestic policy than in foreign policy.

Consistent with his preoccupation with the country's economic condition, the president-elect's earliest choices for top posts in the new administration were in the domestic sector, or for those international functions primarily directed toward strengthening the country's domestic economy, such as secretaries of treasury and commerce. His choices for secretary of state, secretary of defense, national security adviser, and the director of central intelligence were announced just before the inauguration.

In a pre-inaugural address on foreign policy (echoed in numerous statements thereafter by Secretary of State Warren Christopher), president-elect Clinton pointed to "the economic security of our own nation" as "the first pillar" of his foreign policy; the second pillar would be a "restructuring of our armed forces" and the third, "the spread of democratic values."[1]

Yet the world as of January 20, 1993—though very different from what it was upon the inauguration of each of his predecessors— would demand the same close attention to international affairs from this president no less than it had of the Cold War presidents. And this domestically honed politician would be expected in his press conferences and in his daily contacts with his foreign counterparts to be no less informed about international developments affecting the interests of the United States than about the country's domestic situation. Foreign policy was not something he could delegate to the internationally knowledgeable vice president or to his top foreign policy team, no matter how competent; for only the president could authoritatively commit the country to courses of action abroad, and the electorate would properly hold him responsible for acts of commission or omission in the international arena that affected their daily lives.

Most of what was on Bill Clinton's uncomfortably full foreign policy agenda on day one of his administration was in the form of unfinished business passed on to him by the Bush administration:

- the issue of what responsibilities and burdens the United States should assume in helping Russia and the other former Soviet states in their turbulent transition from communism to democratic capitalism;
- the question of what role the United States should play in an international effort to terminate the bloody civil war in the Balkans;
- the problem of assuring that Saddam Hussein adhere to the terms of the cease-fire agreements that ended the Gulf War;
- the issue of how much to publicly disassociate the U.S. government from Israel's new belligerent confrontations with Lebanon, and how much pressure to put on the Rabin government to get the derailed Israeli-Palestinian negotiations back on track;
- the predicament in Somalia, where the withdrawal of U.S. forces that had been deployed by Bush to accomplish limited "humanitarian" missions would leave the United Nations without adequate power to accomplish its more comprehensive peacemaking mandate;
- the dilemma of how to restrict the flow of refugees into the U.S. from Haiti and other repressive regimes without contradicting what was supposed to be a renewed emphasis on human rights (and having to renege on promises made during the election campaign);
- the issue of how insistent Washington should be that Beijing substantially improve its human rights performance as a condition of the extension of normal commercial relations to China;
- the question of how much to demand of Mexico concerning labor conditions and environmental controls in new side agreements to the North American Free Trade Agreement (NAFTA);
- and, finally, the fundamental question of whether to engage in retaliatory or accommodative responses to the protectionist policies of the major economic competitors of the United States—Japan and the EC.

The new president could not blame these burdens of decision (and demands on his time and attention) on his predecessor. Clearly, the predicaments and dilemmas now facing Clinton emanated from developments and forces that were part of structural changes affecting virtually every country in the post–Cold War era. Instead of reducing the need of the U.S. to concern itself with the security and wellbeing of the wide array of countries allied with the U.S. against the USSR, the demise of the Cold War, by bringing the peoples of the erstwhile Soviet sphere into the world community, enlarged the circumference of practical interdependence and potential moral concern. Former wards of the Kremlin and its client regimes now looked to the United States and the other advanced capitalist countries to assist them with their sustenance and security.

CLINTON'S RUSSIA PROBLEM

Bill Clinton's hope to be first and foremost a domestic president was based on the assumption that the end of the Cold War would release both financial resources (the "peace dividend" from reduced military expenditures) and human resources within the policy community that could now be mobilized for the daunting task of restructuring the American economy. In his campaign for the presidency, Clinton had criticized George Bush for procrastinating and finally offering too little help to Mikhail Gorbachev and then Boris Yeltsin in their efforts to transform the Soviet system into a modern market-based economy and political democracy. But his complaints about the inadequacy of the Bush response to the needs of the former Cold War enemy were essentially rhetorical flourishes designed to tarnish Bush's image as a lustrous foreign policy president. Clinton carefully avoided creating the impression that he favored anything like the huge resource transfers proposed by champions of the "Grand Bargain" or other assistance programs modeled on the Marshall Plan.

The Cold War was over, and while the people of the United States might prefer the transformation of the ex-Soviet states into democratic capitalist societies, there was little popular support for the United States to assume the burden of this transformation as if it were a vital interest of the United States. The new wisdom in the policy community discounted the possibility of a renewal of the Cold War. Russia and the other republics might suffer economic dislocation and political instability in the process of reforming themselves but, apart from the hypothetical dangers of a breakdown in command and control of the former Soviet Union's strategic nuclear arsenal, such turbulence would not translate into dire threats against the United States and, in any event, would only further draw the energies of the ex-Soviet republics inward, denying them the capability for foreign adventures.

Yet after only two months in office, the Clinton administration appeared to have drastically revised its assessment of the importance to the United States of what was transpiring in Russia. Secretary of State Warren Christopher, not noted for overstatement, was now calling the task of helping the Russians to build a free society and a market economy "the greatest strategic challenge of our time." On March 25, in a major speech before the Chicago Council on Foreign Relations, Christopher argued that it was essential to "change our mindsets" concerning Russia and its fellow republics. For America and the world, "the stakes are just monumental," he said. "Bringing Russia . . . into the family of peaceful nations will serve our highest security, economic and moral interests. . . . If we succeed, we will have established the foundation for lasting security into the next century. . . . We must understand that helping to consolidate democracy in Russia is not a matter of charity but a security concern of the highest order."[2]

This sudden upgrading of the stakes was a response to the danger of the immanent collapse of the reform-minded government of Boris Yeltsin. As put by Christopher, "if Russia falls into anarchy or lurches back to despotism, the price that we pay could be frightening. Nothing less is involved that the possibility of renewed nuclear threats, higher defense budgets, spreading instability, the loss of new markets, and a devastating setback for the worldwide democratic movement."[3]

There was considerable worry in the Washington policy community about the risks in the Clinton administration's investing so much political capital in the survival of Yeltsin himself. But the administration stuck to its position. In his testimony on March 30 before the appropriations subcommittee of the Senate Committee on Government Operations, Christopher tied the implementation of START I and START II, and therefore the ability to substantially reduce the U.S. defense budget, to the success of democracy and market reforms in Russia—both of which, he said, would be likely to suffer a setback if Yeltsin were deposed.

But public opinion polls were running against the U.S. providing economic aid to Russia. A New York Times/CBS News Poll conducted from March 28 to March 31 showed that 51 percent opposed and 41 percent favored giving aid to help reform Russia's economy. When the question was whether economic aid should be given "to help Boris Yeltsin remain in power," 61 percent opposed and 21 percent were in favor. There was a 52 percent to 40 percent response in favor of giving economic aid to Russia "to help avoid a civil war there."[4]

On April 1, two days before traveling to Vancouver for a summit with Boris Yeltsin, President Clinton delivered a major address to the American Society of Newspaper Editors in which he tried to warm the country's still cool attitude toward a major program for helping Russia. Like the Secretary of State, he cast the issue not so much in altruistic terms of helping the plight of another people but rather in terms of the threats and opportunities posed to U.S. interests: especially the chance to "improve out own security," to reduce spending on defense, and to help create a vast new market for American business. It was essential, he said, that the U.S. act urgently "to strike a strategic alliance with Russian reform." Mindful of the need to support Yeltsin as well as of the risks of becoming too closely identified with his political success or failure, Clinton devoted only a few short phrases of this widely broadcast speech to the man he would be meeting that weekend, referring to him as "the man who stands as the leader of reform—Russia's democratically elected president, Boris Yeltsin." Clinton also avoided giving the impression that he was considering anything like a Marshall Plan aid package for Russia or the other former Soviet republics. His speech emphasized U.S. business investments and people-to-people technical assistance programs.[5] Allusions to financial aid were couched mostly in references to cooperative international efforts to be funneled primarily through the International Monetary Fund and the World Bank. In background briefings, administration officials informed the press that the package he would present Yeltsin in Vancouver would focus less on the infusion of money into the Russian economy and more on the exchange of goods, expertise, and training.[6]

Constrained by Clinton's commitment to reduce the federal deficit and by a public less enthusiastic about the dramatic experiments in democratization underway in the former Soviet Union, the Secretary of State nevertheless worked assiduously over the next few months with his counterparts from the Group of Seven industrial nations to put together a package of nearly $30 billion in pledged funds to assist in Russia's economic development. Much of the funding would be approved on a project by project basis by the parliaments of the donor countries or by the international lending agencies.[7] This portended continued debate in the U.S. government—including members of Congress—between those who were insistent on a credible and swift privatization of Russia's state run economy as a precondition for the release of funds (claiming this would give Yeltsin leverage over the Communist reactionaries) and those who saw the need to allow the Russians room to work out their own evolution into a market system (fearing that too much external pressure would galvanize an anti-Yeltsin, "red-brown" coalition between the Communists and traditional Russian nationalists).

How closely the U.S. government should associate itself with the fate of Yeltsin's leadership became a front burner issue again late in September 1993 as the Russian president, frustrated with legislative opposition to his economic reforms, summarily dismissed the Russian Parliament and called for new parliamentary elections in December. When Yeltsin's parliamentary opponents responded by naming their own leader "acting president" of Russia and the prospect of civil war loomed, Clinton and other high administration officials (correctly guessing that the Russian armed forces would not defect to the opposition) reiterated their support of Yeltsin. In the days following Yeltsin's military suppression of this revolt on October 4, the chorus of support for him from Washington was more unified and vigorous than ever.

There was also bad news from Poland, the presumed showcase for rapid transition to a market economy and democracy: the fall 1993 elections gave control of the Parliament to the Democratic Left Alliance, led by former officials of the Communist government, and the Peasant's Party, formerly a rural Communist organization. Together these parties had won over 35 percent of the popular vote and two-thirds of the seats in Poland's lower house, compelling President Lech Walesa to designate Aleksander Wasniewski, a minister in the former Communist government, as the country's prime minister.

Next came the surprising—and alarming—results of the December 1993 elections in Russia, which the Clinton administration had hoped would reestablish a popular mandate for Yeltsin's reforms. The new constitution strengthening the president's powers vis-à-vis the parliament was approved by a narrow margin, but in the balloting for the new parliament, the biggest winner was the party of ultra-

nationalist Vladimir Zhirinovsky (the "Liberal Democratic Party"),
garnering 24 percent of the party-preference vote. The principal pro-
Yeltsin bloc, Russia's Choice, obtained only 14.5 percent just ahead
of the Communists with 14 percent. Although a two-tier system
of apportioning seats (combining district returns with the party-
preference vote) gave Russia's Choice and various moderate parties a
slight plurality of the seats in the parliament, Zhirinovsky's supporters, if they combined with the Communists, could act as a blocking
coalition to stop reformist legislation—which might induce Yeltsin
to use the authoritarian powers granted the president in the new
constitution. The most worrisome aspect of the election results was
the apparent popularity of Zhirinovsky's chest-thumping nationalism: his threats to punish republics that mistreat their Russian
minority populations, his boasts of reestablishing the imperial span
of control of the former USSR and historic Russia, even (was it
simply a joke?) taking back Alaska from the United States! and, most
ominously, his warning that nuclear weapons might be used against
Germany and other countries that tried to prevent the restoration of
greater Russia's territorial integrity. The Clinton administration,
while reluctant to enhance Zhirinovsky's appeal by making a big
issue of his extremist views, once again affirmed its support for
Yeltsin and his commitment to democratic reform. Clinton himself
characterized the election outcome as most likely "a protest vote"
against the hardships inevitably associated with the transition to
democratic capitalism, and not really indicative of a widespread
endorsement of Zhirinovsky's ideas. But Vice President Gore, in
Moscow for a meeting with Yeltsin, told reporters (undoubtedly
having cleared it with the White House) that "The views expressed
by Zhirinovsky on issues such as the use of nuclear weapons, the
expansion of borders, the treatment of ethnic minorities, are repre-
hensible and [an] anathema to all freedom-loving people in Russia,
in the United States and everywhere in the world."[8]

   The political backsliding in Russia and Poland coincided with and
gave additional impetus to fresh questioning in Washington of the
efficacy of the "shock therapy" prescriptions of the International
Monetary Fund and other international lenders. Perhaps the West
had been naively optimistic about the popular acceptance in the ex-
Communist lands of the unemployment and inflation and new social
inequalities that would accompany the swift privatization of industry

and the decontrol of prices. Perhaps for the institutions and norms of the market and democracy to take root, they needed to be implanted more gradually and experimentally cultivated, respecting the indigenous cultural soil of each country—as Gorbachev had recommended for the Soviet Union and as the Chinese (with considerable foot-dragging on the democracy side) were attempting.

The growing uncertainty over the course of reform in Eastern Europe and the recrudescence of xenophobic nationalism in Russia also prompted second thoughts on the design for a post-Cold War European security system. Whereas previously the dominant view in Washington, carried over from the Bush administration, was that an enlarged NATO should be the core of the new European system—the enlargement to start with the admission of Poland, Hungary, and the Czech Republic—the revised view contemplated an extended period of quite limited association rather than membership for qualified East European countries, and possibly also for Russia. This diluted enlargement (named "Partnership for Peace") reportedly was urged on the Clinton administration by Strobe Talbott, the U.S. Ambassador at Large to the former Soviet republics, in response to President Yeltsin's need, following the abortive October coup, to cater to the Russian military. Yeltsin's new view was that his military were correct in regarding a NATO that included the East Europeans, and not Russia, as potentially hostile. The success of Zhirinovsky in the December elections, however, was invoked by champions of membership for the East Europeans as reason for including especially those states that previously had been threatened by Russia and might be once again. But Clinton's appointment of Talbott in late December 1993 as Deputy Secretary of State (second in command to Warren Christopher) was an indication that the alternative view—namely, that this was no time to exacerbate Russian fears of encirclement—was to be the premise of any NATO enlargment.[9]

WHETHER AND HOW TO INTERVENE IN THE BALKANS

Having criticized President Bush during the election campaign for not doing enough to arrest the Serbian "ethnic cleansing" campaign in Bosnia and to compel the warring ethnic groups to peacefully settle their disputes over the structure of the Bosnian state, Clinton began his presidency under considerable pressure to come forward with an activist policy to end the civil war. Each week that went by, the better-armed Serbs (having inherited most of the heavy arms and equipment from the disintegrated Yugoslav federation) were getting their way. At the start of February 1993, they had already captured about 70 percent of Bosnia and were starving out enclaves of Muslims who refused to leave the Serb-dominated areas. As many as 150,000 Bosnians had already lost their lives and 1.5 million had been driven from their homes during the past year of inter-communal strife.

Clinton thus inherited a set of interlinked dilemmas at least as painful as those which had paralyzed the Bush administration. On the political and diplomatic level, should the United States insist the Bosnian Serbs relinquish the bulk of the territory they had captured as a condition of a settlement? The Serbs were bound to reject this, making it necessary for outsiders (including the United States) to provide military assistance to the anti-Serb forces. Clinton was advised that such an equalization of fighting capability would likely prolong and intensify the civil war and that the only way to avoid this consequence would be to credibly threaten direct military intervention by the West with enough forces to decisively turn the tide of battle against the Serbs. Alternatively, should the United States give highest priority to an immediate cessation of hostilities—a cease-fire in place—and the negotiation of a compromise settlement (along the lines of a plan developed jointly by the UN mediator Cyrus Vance and the European Community mediator David Owen) that would in effect carve up Bosnia into essentially autonomous provinces based on current concentrations of the different religious groups? The Vance-Owen plan would appear to reward the Serbs' brutal aggression and to legitimize their holding on to much of the territory they had taken by force. Moreover, given the bitter grievances that such a partition of Bosnia would leave among minorities within each of the ethnic-majority provinces, the arrangement would require longterm enforcement by large and uniquely powerful international peacekeeping units.

On the military level, President Clinton's military advisers attempted to disabuse their new Commander in Chief of his notion, expressed during the election campaign, that limited and selected air-strikes against Serbian artillery or counter-air enforcement of "no-fly" zones against Serbian aircraft would be sufficient to break the Serbian siege of Bosnian Muslim enclaves. The French commander of UN peacekeeping and humanitarian relief forces also opposed these moves as likely to subject his lightly armed units to retaliatory attacks; and United Nations military authorities objected to lifting the arms embargo on supplies to the Bosnian Muslims on grounds that this would only encourage them to reopen hostilities against the Serbs in areas where the cease-fire was currently holding. The consensus among the military—national and international—was that any enforcement objectives had to be precisely defined and then provisioned with unambiguously sufficient forces to accomplish their missions. But whether the objective was the imposition of withdrawal demands upon the Serbs or the enforcement of a negotiated settlement, the military requirements would be large—at least 50,000 and as many as 200,000 ground troops, in addition to substantial air cover. Would the United States be willing to participate in this effort, contributing not just air support but also troops to a United Nations or NATO command?

The administration's procrastination on firm answers to either the political-diplomatic or the military questions would have the effect of contributing to an intensification of the civil war. Suggestions that Clinton found the Vance-Owen plan unfair to the Muslims, and the announcement that he was appointing his own mediator, Ambassador Reginald Bartholomew, to join the UN mediation effort had the unintended effect of delaying Muslim acceptance of a negotiated compromise, which in turn allowed the Serbs to intensify their military efforts to grab even more of Bosnia before the imposition of a firm cease-fire.[10]

The Bosnian crisis posed questions concerning the purposes and power of the United States in the emerging system of world politics for which the Clinton administration had no answers at the outset, and for which it would need to evolve an appropriate conceptual apparatus along the way. It had problematic ramifications for developments in other regions. Any overt definition of the Serbs as the U.S. or Western enemy in Bosnia could play into the hands of the anti-reform nationalists in Russia for whom a pro-Serbian policy was a cultural, religious, and geopolitical given; accordingly, Yeltsin and the pro-reform elements would be reluctant to support UN or NATO actions that punished the Serbs. But opposed to this con-

straint on U.S. policy was the growing frustration throughout the
Muslim world with the failure of the West to support their Bosnian
religious brethren against blatant aggression at the hands of the
Euro-Christian Orthodox Serbs and Catholic Croats—a potentially
dangerous polarization of attitudes that could undermine U.S. interests throughout the Middle East.

The crisis was at the center of the post–Cold War issue of the
extent to which the United States should identify itself on the one
hand with the national self-determination fever sweeping across the
region in the aftermath of the demise of the Soviet empire, and on
the other hand with federalist principles and structures for achieving
regional and global public order in an increasingly interdependent
world.

THE ROLE OF THE UNITED NATIONS

The problem of suppressing and containing the ethnic violence in
Bosnia also gave urgency to the question, deferred during the Gulf
War, of the military role of the United Nations in the post–Cold
War era. Even more than in Somalia, when it came to applying
military force to compel the warring communities in Bosnia to adhere
to cease-fires or a political settlement, the national security officials
in the Clinton administration insisted that the U.S. government
retain operational command and control of any U.S. deployed forces
(either directly or through NATO). But this posture would contradict an important aspect of the worldview that most of the Clinton
foreign policy team brought into office with them. One of their key
assumptions—highly congenial to a president intending to devote
most of his attention to domestic matters—was that the end of the
Cold War would simultaneously reduce the need for the United
States to take sides in virtually every important international conflict
and increase the availability of the United Nations as a neutral
presence.

During his election campaign, Cinton supported the concept of a
permanent UN rapid deployment force to which the United States
would commit military units, and Warren Christopher endorsed the
idea during his confirmation hearings. An early National Security
Council draft of a presidential directive on the subject contemplated
that the nationally-contributed units would be under the operational

control of the United Nations commander responsible to the UN Security Council via the United Nations Secretary General. But as international and domestic controversy heated up in the summer of 1993 precisely over the question of the international command and control of the UN peacekeeping contingents then in Somalia and being considered for Bosnia, National Security Adviser Lake asked for a redraft of the proposed presidential directive.

Advance notice that President Clinton's maiden address before the United Nations General Assembly would not be, as widely anticipated, a set of proposals for substantially enhancing the organization's peace and security functions, was provided in a speech by the Secretary of State on September 20. Countering allegations that Clinton had allowed himself to be captivated by the ideologues of "multilateralism" in his administration, Christopher averred that "This country will never subcontract its foreign policy to another power or person."[11] Clinton's September 27 address to the United Nations indeed did feature more reservations concerning the peacekeeping and peace enforcement operations than ringing endorsements of its role in the post Cold War world. The most quoted passages, cautioned that:

our nation has begun asking harder questions about proposals for new peacekeeping missions. Is there a real threat to international peace? Does the proposed mission have clear objectives? Can an exit point be identified for those who will be asked to participate? How much will the mission cost? From now on the United Nations should address these and other hard questions for every proposed mission before we vote and before the mission begins.

. . .

The United Nations simply cannot become engaged in every one of the world's conflicts. If the American people are to say yes to U.N. peacekeeping, the United Nations must know when to say no.[12]

And in a follow-up press conference the President revealed the more rigid criteria that, on the basis of the new deliberations in his administration and consultations with congressional leaders, would constrain his deployment of U.S. forces as a part of international peacekeeping efforts in Bosnia (or elsewhere):

I would want a clear understanding what the command and control was. I would want the NATO commander in charge of the operation. I would want a clear timetable for . . . the right to terminate American involvement. I would want a clear political strategy along with a military strategy. . . . And I would want a clear expression of support from the United States Congress. . . . We have to know how we are going to fund it, and then we would have to know that others were going to do their part as well.[13]

President Clinton's predecessors were intensely engaged with events in the Middle East for a combination of sometimes incompatible reasons: containing Soviet expansionism, maintaining access to the petroleum resources of the Persian Gulf, helping to maintain the viability of the state of Israel. This region—the scene of President Carter's most agonizing frustration (the embassy hostage crisis in Teheran) and his proudest triumph (the Israeli-Egyptian peace treaty), of President Reagan's greatest embarrassments (the massacre of U.S. marines at the Beirut airport and the arms-for-hostage deal with Iran), of President Bush's most popular undertaking (the Desert Storm operation to drive Saddam Hussein's forces from Kuwait)—topped the agenda of unfinished business passed on to Clinton's foreign policy team by the outgoing administration.

Dealing with Saddam

For George Bush, having demonized the Iraqi tyrant as another Hitler, amicable relations with the government in Baghdad were virtually intolerable as long as Saddam remained in power. A new president could have attempted to experiment cautiously with a normalization of relations—conditioned on a creditable adherence by Saddam to the U.N. cease-fire accords; but during the last month of the Bush administration, Bush and Saddam maneuvered themselves into a new confrontation that compelled the president-elect to define his alternatives more rapidly and rigidly than be might have preferred.

While supporting the military actions against Iraq that Bush ordered during the last week of his presidency (air strikes against Iraqi anti-aircraft missile sites in no-fly zones and the dispatch of a battalion of troops into northern Kuwait to prevent Iraqis from removing equipment), Clinton tried, but failed, to allow himself negotiating room. In an interview quoted in the January 14 edition of the *New*

York Times, Clinton said that his grievances were with Saddam's failure to implement the cease-fire accords and he was absolutely in accord with President Bush's insistence that they be adhered to. But the president-elect also insisted that he was "not obsessed with the man." He averred that "the people of Iraq would be better off if they had a different leader. But my job is not to pick their rulers for them. I always tell everybody, 'I'm a Baptist; I believe in deathbed conversions.' If he wants a different relationship with the United States and with the United Nations, all he has to do is change his behavior."[14]

Bush administration officials, editorial writers, and, privately, even members of Clinton's own foreign policy entourage immediately criticized Clinton for seeming to differentiate himself from President Bush in the midst of a new military confrontation and for giving the impression that the incoming administration might be willing to normalize relations with Saddam, thus undercutting Bush's coercive leverage. Clinton responded to these criticisms, claiming he had no expectation of normalizing relations with the Iraqi dictator and that it was a misinterpretation of his remarks to suggest that he had any such intention. "I said what I've said many times," Clinton insisted, "that I will judge him by his conduct. That's precisely what the Bush administration has done. . . . They decided to bomb him because he violated the United Nations cease-fire accord. That is my position."[15]

To underline his promise to be no less tough on Saddam than was Bush, Clinton authorized a continuation of the attacks for 24 hours following his inauguration. Television news reports juxtaposed the inauguration-night barrage on weapons facilities in the Baghdad suburbs with celebratory fireworks over the skies of Washington, DC.

On February 2, the Pentagon acknowledged the cessation of combat flights as of January 23, after Iraq turned off its target acquisition radars and in the absence of any direct challenge to U.S. and allied aircraft policing the no-fly zones. "The Iraqis have changed their behavior," the Pentagon spokesman said.[16]

A period of relative quiescence in which Iraq formally complied with the terms of the Gulf War cease-fire accords would face Clinton with a set of problems. Saddam was still in power: there was little chance that he would reform his brutal dictatorship or that he would allow substantial self-determination to the Kurds or Shiites; and he would surely insist that the United Nations at some point call off its intrusive inspections of potential Iraqi weapons facilities. But continuing to treat Iraq as a pariah while other countries in the region with terrible human rights records and a history of unscrupulous international power plays (Syria and Iran, for example) were granted full sovereign rights might create new sympathy for Saddam among Arab populations throughout the region. Moreover, to remove Iraq for the foreseeable future as a counterweight to the hegemonic pretensions of fundamentalist Iran would not augur well for regional stability.

There were press reports at the end of March 1993 that the British and U.S. governments were considering relaxing their stand against Saddam by indicating that a lifting of the sanctions on Iraq and eventually the restoration of normal relations would follow Baghdad's adherence to the terms of the U.N. war-terminating agreements. These were immediately denied by administrations spokespersons. Secretary of State Warren Christopher, testifying before the appropriations subcommittee of the Senate Government Operations Committee on March 30, insisted that there had been "no softening" of the government's position that it would be good if the people of Iraq themselves ended Saddam's regime. There would be "no relenting," he said, in the Clinton's administration's insistence that there be full and total compliance with the United Nations cease-fire resolutions.[17]

Israel and the Palestinians

While inexperienced in the intricacies of Arab-Israeli relations, Clinton, like any nationally-successful U.S. politician, was quite aware that there could be major domestic political ramifications from any positions he might take on the issues. He had deftly avoided some of the minefields during his campaign. But even before taking office, he had to deal with the expressed dissatisfaction of some domestic Jewish groups over his nominations of Warren Christopher as Secretary of State and Anthony Lake as National Security Adviser. Christopher and Lake had been high State Department officials in the Carter administration (Under Secretary and head of policy planning, respectively) and were suspected of carrying with them into the new administration the sympathies for the Palestinian cause harbored by the former president. To counter the discontent, Clinton personally phoned several Jewish members of Congress to assure them that he would be appointing some mainstream members of the Jewish establishment to senior sub-cabinet posts with major foreign policy responsibilities.[18]

Of course more than domestic politics was involved. The new administration's effectiveness in dealing with Iraq and a whole complex of issues in the region would be affected by its performance on the Israeli-Palestinian issue. Clinton's predicament was no different than that faced by his predecessors: to the extent that U.S. positions on the Palestinian question supported Israel against a solidifying camp of Muslim countries, it would weaken Washington's diplomatic influence with other countries in the region and indeed throughout the Third World. And to the extent that Washington revealed a lack of influence over the Arabs, it would lose its leverage over the Israelis, which in turn would feed back into a further loss of influence over the moderate Palestinians in the peace process.

Clinton faced this predicament from the very outset of his administration. The Arab-Israeli negotiations over the future of the West Bank and the Gaza Strip were at a standstill and threatening to collapse after Israel, on December 17, deported to Lebanon 415 Palestinians from the West Bank it accused of being Islamic terrorists. The Israeli authorities had summarily arrested the men at their homes, driven them in vans across the Lebanese border into the demilitarized security zone, and abandoned them there. The government of Lebanon and the Arab states denounced the action, refused to accept jurisdiction over the deportees, and demanded that Israel immediately take them back. The next day, Bush authorized the U.S. representative to the UN Security Council to vote along with the majority in support of a resolution condemning the deportation and demanding the immediate return of the deportees. Over the next few weeks the deportees captured worldwide public sympathy through media reports of their hunger and cold in the hills of Lebanon while the Israeli and Lebanese governments insisted it was the other's responsibility to care for them.

Upon being sworn in as Secretary of State, Warren Christopher engaged in urgent negotiations with the Israelis to soften their rigid stance on the deportation in the hope of deflecting the Arab states from bringing a resolution to apply sanctions against Israel to a vote in the Security Council. Prime Minister Rabin agreed to allow 101 of the deported Palestinians to return immediately and to initiate a review process that would repatriate the rest by December 1994. Meanwhile, Christopher tried to convince dissatisfied Arab governments to refrain from taking action in the United Nations that would force a U.S. veto.

An essential objective of the new administration's strategy on the deportation issue, as well as on the larger complex of issues involved in the Israel-Palestinian peace process, was to maintain the U.S. government's credibility as honest broker between the protagonists. Moderate Arabs and Israelis understood this, and would work cooperatively with U.S. diplomats, in the knowledge that the U.S. government would sometimes have to take positions in opposition to their preferences. By contrast, the extremists on both sides (including parts of the American Jewish community) were ever anxious to push the United States government to choose between the "right" and "wrong."

Then suddenly, at the end of August 1993, to the surprise of the White House no less than to the rest of the world, the Rabin government and Palestine Liberation Organization (PLO) chief Yasir Arafat revealed that they had secretly negotiated the basis for mutual recognition and peace. The honest broker had been neither the United States nor Russia (the cosponsors of the on-again-off-again Madrid/Washington peace negotiations between the Israelis and moderate Palestinians), but rather Norway, in the person of Foreign Minister Johan Jorgen Holst.

As when the Carter administration's peace initiatives were preempted in November 1977 by Anwar Sadat's dramatic démarche to initiate negotiations with Israel, the Clinton administration, initially embarrassed by being taken completely unawares, quickly regained its diplomatic composure and offered its blessings and services to the two sides to assist in the historic breakthrough. But this time the President had much less to do than did Carter, who played an active and ultimately crucial role in mediating the 1979 Egypt-Israel Peace Treaty and the associated Framework for Peace in the Middle East.

President Clinton hosted and officiated at the White House ceremony at which the two heretofore implacable enemies signed their Declaration of Principles for Palestinian self-government in the Israeli-occupied Gaza and the West Bank and mutually pledged to beat their swords into plowshares. U.S. diplomatic support in attempting to draw Jordan and Syria into a similar reconciliation with Israel would yet be crucial, as would be U.S. financial aid in giving incentives to the peoples of the region to cooperate in building webs of positive interdependence. Clearly, however, Clinton's role was more that of after-the-fact implementor and facilitator rather than of superpower impresario—a not unwelcome gift to a President who would rather concentrate on domestic affairs. This assumed, of course, that the enemies of the peace process in the Middle East did not again get the upper hand.

PROMOTING SOCIAL JUSTICE ABROAD

Clinton's embrace of the universal validity of human rights was a natural posture for a politician spawned by the Kennedy and Carter wings of the Democratic party. Like those presidents, he too would find it difficult to translate these impulses to do good in the world the democratic way into concrete policy and programs in unfolding, chaotic situations where human rights and democracy were obviously being violated, but it was not at all clear who were the offenders and who were the credible defenders of justice. Moreover, the dilemmas faced by Kennedy and Carter when it came to diverting resources away from domestic programs to "humanitarian" imperatives abroad would be compounded for Clinton. Denied the ability to fall back on the "national security" rationale given the end of the Cold War, he also faced a greater crunch than did his liberal predecessors in simultaneously having to deal with questions of poverty and human rights issues at home and not having the wherewithal to generate public funds to apply to these problems.

A new administration needs to take some time to develop its approach to dealing with these dilemmas (as the Kennedy administration did in working out its foreign aid program and Carter did in fashioning a pragmatic human rights policy), but Clinton would have no breathing space. There were too many unresolved, urgent "humanitarian" crises left over from the Bush administration—some of which Clinton, perhaps too rashly, had already taken positions on during his presidential election campaign.

The Haitian Refugees

As with so many other issues, the view from the Oval Office on the issue of how to deal with the boatloads of refugees from Haiti's repressive regime looked different than it had from the campaign bus.

The Haitian refugees had started coming in great numbers following the October 1991 military coup in Haiti against the elected President Jean-Bertrand Aristide. Amid persistent reports of brutal repression and abuse of Aristide's supporters by the military regime, more than 30,000 Haitians headed for the United States in small boats between the coup and the end of Bush administration. Approximately 20,000 of these were turned back while still outside U.S. territorial waters by the U.S. Coast Guard.

During the campaign Clinton had excoriated as "inhumane" and "immoral" Bush's policy toward the Haitians and Bush's rationalization that most of the boat people were not really political refugees seeking asylum but people fleeing economic hardship, whom the United States was in no position to absorb. Bush claimed that the proper way to deal with the Haitian exodus was to have U.S. authorities in Haiti screen all potential emigrés to the United States to determine whether they were indeed proper candidates for political asylum.

Clinton had pledged to modify the Bush refugee policy if elected president and also to intensify efforts to restore democracy in Haiti. But shortly after his inauguration, evidently worried that a more welcoming attitude toward the refugees might unleash a veritable flood of refugees upon Florida's shores, Clinton averred that he might have been "too harsh" in his criticism of the Bush policy and announced that he would continue the policy of interception "for the time being" but would make it "easier and safer" for Haitians seeking political asylum to apply through the U.S. embassy in Haiti. Meanwhile, he was putting his administration to work to arrange for a restoration of democracy on the island and to help Haiti with its economic development. White House spokesperson George Stephanopolous told reporters that administration lawyers had determined that the Bush repatriation policy was not in violation of U.S. or international law, and that the President had "reconsidered his position. . . . He believes that this is the right thing to do. It is the best way to save lives." [19]

Unfinished Business in Somalia

One of the large worries of the president-elect's foreign policy advisers was that Bush's public promise that the U.S. military deployment in Somalia was to be swiftly completed, a promise that Clinton had endorsed, would come back to haunt him. The premise of the Bush intervention was that once the U.S. forces had established a modicum of order by separating or partially disarming the warring warlord factions and had provided security for the delivery of humanitarian relief, the United Nations would take over the long-run peacekeeping and relief tasks. But Secretary General Boutros Boutros Ghali had disputed the Bush administration's timetable for the completion of the initial pacification efforts by the U.S. forces, claiming that the United Nations did not presently possess either an adequate mandate or the peacekeeping resources that would be required to substitute for the U.S. presence.

However, the UN Secretary General was faced by the determination of Clinton's administration to fulfill Bush's promise. The result was the Security Council's unanimous passage on March 26, 1993 of the U.S.-drafted resolution for turning over the basic functions (and more) of the U.S.-led Operation Restore Hope to the United Nations on May 1. The authorized United Nations operation in Somalia would be one of the largest and most ambitious peacekeeping or humanitarian operations in the organization's history. Costing an estimated $1.5 billion during its first year and involving a planned 28,000 blue-helmeted UN troops and another 2,000 civilians, the world organization's operation in Somalia would be mandated to virtually run the country. The UN military force would include an American contingent which—in a departure from the Bush administration policy of maintaining U.S. command and control of any U.S. forces—would be subject to the authority of the UN operation's commander, a general from Turkey. Operating under authority of Security Council resolutions ordering the capture of warlord Mohammed Aidid and the confiscation of his arms caches, the UN force was the target of increasing numbers of violent attacks in the summer and fall of 1993, in which U.S. soldiers were killed, wounded, or captured. At the time of this writing, Clinton was under growing pressure from members of Congress to withdraw the U.S. military personnel. But his first response was to augment the size and weaponry of those already there.[20] The UN's expanded mandate in Somalia now also included the repatriation of hundreds of thousand of refugees, clearing land mines, setting up a civilian police force, conducting peace talks on the setting up of a new government, creating jobs, rebuilding the economy, and building political institutions—an unprecedented grant of supranational authority to the world organization.[21]

Was Somalia a precedent for how the United States under Clinton would handle other situations of poverty and chaos around the world that, once the media spotlights were turned on them, would be shown to be no less threatening to the survival of the indigenous populations than was the situation in Somalia that prompted the Bush intervention? If so, even if they were financed and otherwise supported through the UN system, the financial contributions from the United States would be substantial, and would require the administration to bear the burden of proof before the Congress and the American people that the diversion of resources from tasks at home was in the national interest.

Clinton's China Problem

The competing demands of justice, world order, and national economic self-interest were particularly difficult for the new administration to manage—often embarrassingly so—when it came to dealing with China. Once again, the embarrassments were in large part a function of the gap between Clinton's rhetoric on the campaign trail, which had excoriated Bush for putting old-fashioned geopolitics ahead of human rights, and his more complicated view of the matter from the Oval Office.

Despite congressional and public criticism, the Bush administraion continued after the Tienanmen Square massacre to extend most-favored nation (MFN) trading status to China, while indicating that there should be an improvement in Beijing's performance on human rights if normal commerce was to continue. During the 1992 election campaign Clinton promised to pursue a much tougher policy toward the regime in Beijing: He definitely would deny MFN status to China unless there was *clear* evidence of *substantial* betterment of the human rights situation in the country. Consistent with his pledge, a few weeks after inauguration Clinton sent a strongly worded letter to the Chinese government stipulating various steps they had to take in order to qualify for a further extension of MFN privileges; but by late spring, he appeared to be moving much closer to the position of his predecessor.

Obligated to inform Congress by June of his position on a continuance of China's MFN status, the President worked out an agreement with Democratic congressional leaders in May to allow him to keep it alive for yet another year on condition that he would indeed cancel it in June 1994 in the absence of significant progress by Beijing on human rights. The new extension reflected the fact that Clinton's perspective on the problem was changing and he wanted some maneuvering room.

The end of the Cold War, to be sure, had erased the geostrategic imperative of keeping Beijing happy so it would concert its anti-Soviet policies with Washington. But at the same time it removed the need felt by Deng Xiaoping's regime to enlist U.S. power as a counterweight to Moscow's hegemonic aims in Asia; and the Chinese government was now telling the Americans in no uncertain terms that they should not think the post-Cold War situation gave them license to ride Beijing hard on the issue of human rights. China wanted access to the U.S. market, but U.S. firms also wanted access to the 1.2 billion consumers of the fastest growing economy in the world. Moreover, China was also emerging as a big player in the global arms trade and her cooperation was essential to the Clinton administration's policy of discouraging the sale of advanced weaponry to Third World clients, particularly long-range ballistic missiles that could be used to deliver chemical or nuclear weapons. On the basis of a CIA report that China was selling M-11 ballistic missiles to Pakistan, the administration in August 1993 prohibited U.S. firms from consummating the sale of about $1 billion worth of high-technology items contracted for by the Chinese; but by September this punitive response along with the overall mix of carrots and sticks in U.S. China policy was subjected to a full-dress reassessment for its efficacy by Clinton's national security council. The result was a basic shift in strategy—though not publicly announced as such—away from the reprimanding rhetoric and threats of withdrawing

MFN privileges and toward drawing China more fully into the world capitalist system. Consistent with the new strategy, Clinton agreed to meet with China's president, Jiang Zemin, in November at the Seattle summit of the 15-member Asia-Pacific Economic Conference in order to open a new high-level dialogue on improving Sino-U.S. relations.[22]

Critics might object that the meeting of the two presidents was a retrogression to the Bush realpolitik approach of befriending the world's power elite regardless of how brutally they treated their people; but the administration champions of the new "realism" were convinced that, like Clinton, the human rights liberals could be persuaded that over the long run the full integration of China into the global market was the best hope for transforming China into an open society, even a democratic one. For most of the administration's policymakers, of course, the clinching arguments had very little to do with such idealistic aims, and almost everything to do with U.S. access to the huge Chinese market. *Time* magazine's Michael Kramer captured the animating spirit in his quote of a White House aide's comment that "Every country in the world wants in—as soon as possible and big time. We [too] . . . want a piece of the pie, a big piece, and we aim to get it."[23]

PREVENTING THE SPREAD OF NUCLEAR WEAPONS: THE SPECIAL CASE OF NORTH KOREA

A nonalienated China has become one of the highest-value objectives of the Clinton administration for a crucial reason already alluded to: As one of the five officially recognized nuclear weapons states, each of which also has a veto in the United Nations Security Council, China is in a position to either obstruct or assist the United States in its effort to prevent the further spread of nuclear weapons—a post-Cold War imperative that has risen to the top of the list of the Clinton administration's international security interests. Russia and the other two nuclear powers, Britain and France, have cooperated with the United States and the International Atomic Energy Agency (IAEA) in disarming Iraq of its nuclear-weapons potential and also in bringing pressure on Kazakhstan, Belarus, and a recalcitrant Ukraine to transfer to Moscow's control those parts of the Soviet nuclear arsenal left in their jurisdictions upon the breakup of the

USSR. China, however, has not been a reliable ally in the global nonproliferation regime.

The issue suddenly became acute for the Clinton administration in March as the Communist North Korean government announced its intention to withdraw from the 25-year-old Nuclear Non-Proliferation Tready (NPT). Pyongyang was reacting to IAEA insistences on inspection routines that the North Koreans claimed were in violation of national sovereignty. (U.S. intelligence agencies and the IAEA had suspected for some time that North Korea was manufacturing enough plutonium to make a bomb; and Pyongyang's surprise announcement was read as a virtual admission that this was indeed the case.) As the first major defection from the NPT in the post-Cold War era, and given the implications for Japan, let alone South Korea, military and arms control experts in the United States were adamant in their advice to Clinton that he could not afford to let Pyongyang thumb its nose at the rest of the world. But was it feasible to get the regime of the aging dictator Kim Il Sung to reverse his decision, and if so, what would he ask in return?

Clinton was convinced that the United States had to play it tough. He demanded that the North Koreans submit to a new round of IAEA inspections to verify that they were not producing nuclear weapons. And in a trip to Japan and South Korea in July 1993 he issued a threat more chilling than anything heard from the top of the U.S. government in decades: "When you examine the nature of the American security commitments in Korea and Japan, to this region," warned the President, "it is pointless for them [the North Koreans] to try to develop nuclear weapons, because if they ever use them it would be the end of their country."[24] But pointless or not, insisted the President and other administration officials, the North Koreans had to accept an appropriate degree of IAEA inspection now, and if they refused, they would be subject to international sanctions of the strongest sort.

Pyongyang countered with tough statements of its own, implying that the United States was dangerously courting a reopening of the Korean War, in which North Korea would smash South Korea even if this meant once again having to fight against the nuclear-armed United States. If the United States was determined to remove the threat of war from the Korean peninsula as it claimed, argued the North Koreans, then why was it continuing to conduct joint military exercises each year with the South Koreans? And if it was anxious to denuclearize the region, then why didn't the United States offer to subject its military deployments in and around South Korea to international inspection?

During the rest of 1993 the war of words continued between Washington and Pyongyang, and it looked as if the two sides had locked themselves into a game of chicken likely to end in disaster. Hawks in the Clinton administration began to prepare military contingency plans, including the possibility of aircraft or missile strikes against North Korean facilities suspected of harboring the nuclear bomb or its components. Clinton himself would not publicly rule out any options. But beneath the level of the public histrionics, cooler heads in both countries and in the U.N. arena explored through quiet diplomacy various formulae for diverting the antagonists from an impending head-on collision.

A conflict-resolution package receiving serious consideration in both capitals at the beginning of 1994 would have North Korea freshly renounce any intention to acquire or develop nuclear weapons and open up its facilities to the kinds of IAEA verification required in return for a United States agreement to dispense with its annual joint military exercises with South Korea and to undertake normal commercial relations with the North. Hard-liners in the Clinton administration reportedly were counselling the President that in light of the impossibility of obtaining foolproof verification that the North Koreans were *not* hiding some bombs (the CIA speculated that they already had two), Pyongyang was probably engaged in a delaying ploy by seeming to accept international inspection while continuing to build its nuclear arsenal. Support for such an agreement was centered in the State Department, where the dominant view emphasized the need to slow down the escalating confrontation; the objective of avoiding a war in which everyone would lose was presumably worth the risk that Pyongyang was pursuing a strategy of systematic deception.[25] A major consideration, which could tip the scales toward or against a military showdown in the region, was whether or not China would be willing to join the United States in promoting the denuclearization and possible demilitarization of the Korean peninsula.

TRADE POLICY DILEMMAS

No president can avoid being subjected to cross-pressures on trade policy, for the national constituency is comprised on the one hand of sectors who are convinced they will benefit most by allowing foreigners to compete freely in the U.S. market (and by allowing Americans to freely export to other countries) and those who are convinced they will suffer declining income or loss of jobs from the reduction of tariffs and other import barriers. Not only would President Clinton not escape these cross-pressures, but he would take office in the midst of a major national debate over free trade vs. protectionism—a debate generated by the economic recession of the late 1980s and early 1990s, which many commentators attributed in large measure to the chronic trade deficits the United States had been running ($84.3 billion in 1992). The debate was exacerbated by the North American Free Trade Agreement (NAFTA), signed near the end of the Bush administration but not yet ratified.

In his campaign for the presidency, Clinton was compelled to relate to intense concerns of voters that their jobs were highly dependent upon the trade policies that would be pursued by the next administration.

Philosophically a devotee of international free trade, Clinton as a practical politician was nonetheless constrained to respond to the fact that, in the short-term at least, thousands of workers in vulnerable sectors of the economy were being laid off by firms that were losing out to foreign competition.

Candidate Clinton had been unwilling to go as far as some of his rivals for the Democratic nomination—especially Jerry Brown, Thomas Harkin, and Bob Kerry—and embrace the strong protectionist ideas being propounded by the leaders of organized labor. But he did come out against quick congressional approval of NAFTA and said he would insist on amendments to the accord to assure that U.S. workers did not lose their jobs to workers in Mexico because of the relocation of U.S. firms across the border where low wages and the lack of environmental standards reduced manufacturing costs. And while continuing to insist that the basic sources of the decline in the global competitiveness of U.S. products lay in the misguided domestic policies of the Reagan and Bush administrations, he promised (again following the lead of congressional Democrats and his rivals for the nomination) to work aggressively to get Japan to reduce its barriers to U.S. imports and services.

The new president's appointments to top economic policy posts reflected and perpetuated this ambivalence on free trade: Lloyd Bentsen, a relatively consistent supporter of free trade, as Secretary of the Treasury; Laura D'Andrea Tyson, a devotee of "managed trade" agreements, as Chairperson on the Council of Economic Advisers; and Mickey Kantor, the Clinton election campaign chairman, noted for a combative negotiating style, as United States Trade Representative.

During the first few months of his administration, Clinton's basic trade policy predicament—how to provide a "level playing field" for U.S. industries vis-à-vis their international competitors without provoking retaliatory protectionist measures from foreign governments—was manifest in debates among his advisers over how to handle the following issues: [26]

• Quotas and tariffs on Japanese cars and trucks: Should the United States adhere to the Reagan-Bush policy of relying primarily on "voluntary" Japanese export quotas or should these be supplanted by increased U.S. tariffs, or a credible threat of such tariffs, on the import of Japanese vehicles and other products?

• European subsidies to its aircraft manufacturers: Should the United States insist that European aircraft manufacturers be required to repay, with full interest, their government subsidies (thus equalizing the European firms' factor costs via-a-vis their disadvantaged U.S. competitors), or should the United States emulate the Europeans and subsidize its own aircraft producers?

• European farm subsidies: How completely and rapidly should the European Community be required to phase out its Common Agricultural Policy (CAP) subsidies to its farmers? And to what extent should retaliatory trade discrimination measures be invoked against the EC?

• Government contracting: Should the United States rely on friendly persuasion and GATT dispute resolution processes to get other countries to remove government contracting rules that discriminate in favor of their own national producers or should it impose retaliatory "buy USA" rules in its own government contracting?

• NAFTA: Should the free trade accord with Mexico and Canada be amended to require Mexican adherence to fair labor standards and environmental protective measures, or should the United States attempt to provide a more level playing field by unilaterally imposing compensatory taxes on various imports from Mexico (especially from U.S. multinational firms with subsidiaries south of the border)? Also, should the United States government provide special adjustment benefits to workers displaced by business relocations to Mexico?

However these particular issues were handled, the Clinton administration would not be able to avoid the larger question of the extent to which the United States—harboring huge budgetary and trade deficits—should soften the blow to sectors injured by free trade through an "industrial policy" of publicly funded worker-retraining programs and business-retooling incentives to encourage displaced firms to enter product lines in which they would be more competitive.

THE PERSISTENCE OF SUPERPOWERISM

With a degree of candor and directness uncharacteristic of high State Department officials, the worldview prevailing at the top levels of the Clinton administration during its first few months was conveyed to a luncheon gathering of Washington reporters on May 25, 1993 by Under Secretary of State Peter Tarnoff. Speaking on condition of anonymity (which held for no more than a day), Tarnoff spoke of the administration's policy of making "a case by case decision to limit the amount of American engagement" around the world. There was now "a very different context for American foreign policy" than that which determined U.S. commitments and action during the Cold War. It was a mistake to view the Gulf War as the first battle of the new world order, he said. Rather it was the last battle of the Cold War. With the collapse of the Soviet Union, "there are fewer heavyweight bad guys but more middleweight bad guys," who are "enormously complicated" to deal with. "We simply don't have the leverage," he admitted. "We don't have the influence. We don't have the inclination to use military force. We certainly don't have the money to bring to bear the kind of pressure which will produce positive results any time soon."[27]

A chorus of administration officials, including the Secretary of State himself, quickly disavowed Mr. Tarnoff's comments; insisting (as did Christopher in an interview) that "our need to lead, our determination to lead, is not constrained by our resources." The primary consideration determining U.S. foreign involvement will be, as always, "where our vital interests are threatened. . . .we will *find* the resources" to accomplish what needs to be done, either multilaterally or unilaterally. The Secretary added a special section in his May 27 address at the University of Minnesota, lamenting that "Some say . . . our nation is on a course of decline, that we can no longer afford to lead." Certainly, he said, "is it true that the United States faces many challenges unlike our nation has ever felt before in our history. But to me, that means that we must be more engaged internationally, not less; more ardent in the promotion of democracy, not less, and more inspired in our leadership, not less."[28]

The day after Christopher's speech, a *New York Times* editorial stated what most Washington insiders knew: Mr. Tarnoff's argument did indeed "describe what we've seen of the Clinton approach." The editorial averred that the Tarnoff doctrine was "defensible, even sensible" and "less foolish than the charade it provoked. . . . it needs to be acknowledged and explained by Mr. Tarnoff's bosses, Secretary of State Warren Christopher, and Bill Clinton."[29]

But Bill Clinton's strongest political instincts, having evolved in the hurly-burly of domestic politics, would not allow him to settle simply for the case-by-case pragmatism toward post Cold War developments that Tarnoff and other foreign policy experts were recommending. He understood better than those who had never run for public office that the here-and-now domestic interests with well-organized constituencies will win out over foreign commitments, even those derived from long-term geopolitical interests, in the competition for resources unless the international imperatives are spelled out to the public in a coherent and dramatic way. Like Truman, whose presentation to the Congress in March 1947 finally provided him with the moral authority and bipartisan support he needed to act effectively in a new era of world politics, Clinton too might require a "doctrine" to relate the country's irreducible interests and basic values to the changed world of the 1990s so as not to be paralyzed in particular cases by his own ambivalence or congressionally imposed gridlock.

Hard pressed from all sides after eight months of apparent flip-flops on issues such as Somalia, Bosnia, Haitian refugees, and trade with China, and challenged by a new crisis of democracy in Russia and an exciting new breakthrough toward peace in the Middle East, the administration fired off a fusillade of foreign policy concepts at the end of September 1993. In rapid succession in the course of the week Secretary Christopher, National Security Adviser Anthony Lake, United Nations Ambassador Madeleine Albright, and the President himself each gave major speeches obviously designed to counter criticisms that the Clinton foreign policy was rudderless.

The most comprehensive formulation was articulated by the National Security Adviser. Clearly inviting it to be labelled the "Clinton Doctrine" (though not applying the term himself), Lake told his audience at the Johns Hopkins School of Advanced International Studies that "The successor to a doctrine of containment must be a strategy of enlargement, enlargement of the world's free community of market democracies." The new strategy had four basic imperatives:

First, we should strengthen the community of major market democracies—including our own—which constitutes the core from which enlargement is proceeding.

Second, we should help foster and consolidate new democracies and market economies where possible, especially in states of special significance and opportunity.

Third, we must counter the aggression—and support the liberalization—of states hostile to democracy and markets.

Fourth, we need to pursue our humanitarian agenda not only by providing aid, but also by working to help democracy and market economics take root in regions of greatest humanitarian concern. [30]

Once again, as so frequently happened during the Cold War, starting with the Truman Doctrine, the temptation of domestically-responsible decision makers to garner popular support by simplifying and sloganizing the complexities of international relations trumped the objections of diplomats like George Kennan in 1947 and now Peter Tarnoff that the rhetorical bifurcation of the world into friends and foes would interfere with an intelligent and efficient pursuit of the national interest.

If the incongruence between simplistic doctrine and complex reality was excessive even during the Cold War, when there was at least a rough worldwide bipolarization of the Marxists and anti-Marxists, the gap between the new rhetoric of the Clinton administration and the actual post Cold War experimentation with very different political and economic systems was enormous. As Kennan prophesied, the rhetoric could nevertheless become self-confirming as statespersons attempt to close the gap by bending reality to match their doctrines—

a tendency that surfaced in the days following Lake's address in the form of the almost automatic endorsement by the Clinton administration of Russian president Boris Yeltsin's confrontation with his parliamentary opponents, explained on the grounds of Yeltsin's championship of market democracy.

A potentially problematical aspect of the new "enlargement" doctrine was its explicit obligation to *counter* or attempt to reform states "hostile to democracy and markets." Our policy toward these "backlash states," said Lake, "must seek to isolate them diplomatically, economically and technologically." And when the actions of such states directly threaten our people, our forces, or our "vital interests" (a term left undefined), "we clearly must be prepared to strike back decisively and unilaterally."[31]

In so conceptualizing Clinton's evolving foreign policy philosophy, the National Security Adviser was perhaps more revealing than he intended of the extent to which for this young President (face relatively unlined, mostly smiling, optimistic) geopolitics was still primarily U.S. domestic politics. But given the intense intermeshing of domestic and international interests—an unavoidable fact of the late twentieth century—this could get the country, and the world, into a lot of trouble. If moment-of-truth decisions fail to measure up to the domestically-oriented rhetoric because of a lack of national will or tangible resources to support the grandly-defined obligations, the country's will and commitments are likely to be doubted thereafter even when irreducible national interests are at stake. Alternatively, if overly-ambitious formulations propel the country's leaders into ventures in advance of adequate real-time assessments of the material and human costs, there will be hell to pay—not only internationally, but domestically—for years to come. At the conclusion of this writing project, the Clinton administration had yet to show it understood how to navigate between these extremes.

NOTES

1. CONSTANCY AND CHANGE SINCE WORLD WAR II

1. President George Bush, address of December 4, 1992, on decision to deploy U.S. troops to Somalia, in *Weekly Compilation of Presidential Documents,* 28(49):2329–31.

2. See, for example, Noam Chomsky, *What America Really Wants* (Berkeley: Odonian Press, 1992).

3. This formulation of the "irreducible national interest," originally presented in the 1968 edition of *The Faces of Power,* was recapitulated and fruitfully used by Alexander L. George and Robert O. Keohane in their essay "The Concept of National Interests: Uses and Limitations," in Alexander L. George, ed., *Presidential Decisionmaking in Foreign Policy: The Effective Use of Information and Advice* (Boulder: Westview Press, 1980), pp. 217–237.

4. Robert J. Art and Seyom Brown, "U.S. Foreign Policy in the Post–Cold War World: Introduction and Overview," in Robert J. Art and Seyom Brown, eds., *U.S. Foreign Policy: The Search for a New Role* (New York: Macmillan, 1992), pp. 1–7.

5. John F. Kennedy, Inaugural Address, January 20, 1961, *Department of State Bulletin,* February 6, 1961, pp. 175–76.

6. Jimmy Carter, question-and-answer session with a group of publishers, editors, and broadcasters, May 20, 1977, in *Public Papers of the Presidents of the United States: Jimmy Carter, 1977,* I:147.

7. James Schlesinger, "Quest for a Post–Cold War Foreign Policy," *Foreign Affairs* 72(1):17.

2. THE CHANGING ESSENCE OF POWER

1. A piece of mine that tapped into this evolutionary dynamic at about its midpoint—the early 1970s—is Seyom Brown, "The Changing Essence of Power," *Foreign Affairs,* 51(2):286–99.

3. THE SHATTERING OF EXPECTATIONS

1. A thorough scholarly account of the wartime diplomacy of Franklin D. Roosevelt and the first two years of the Truman administration is provided by John Lewis Gaddis, *The United States and the Origins of the Cold War, 1941–1947* (New York: Columbia University Press,

1972). See also James MacGregor Burns, *Roosevelt: The Soldier of Freedom* (New York: Harcourt Brace Jovanovich, 1970); and Daniel Yergen, *Shattered Peace: The Origins of the Cold War and the National Security State* (Boston: Houghton Mifflin, 1977), pp. 3–137.

2. See Harry S. Truman, *Memoirs: Year of Decisions* (New York: Doubleday, 1955), 1:332–412.

3. *Ibid.*, p. 70.

4. *Ibid.*, p. 71.

5. William D. Leahy, *I Was There* (New York: McGraw Hill, 1950), pp. 351–52.

6. Truman, *Memoirs,* 1:85–87.

7. See especially Gar Alperwovitz, *Atomic Diplomacy: Hiroshima and Potsdam* (New York: Simon and Schuster, 1965).

8. The quotations are from Truman's letter to Byrnes of January 5, 1946. Truman, *Memoirs,* 1:551–52.

9. Truman, *Memoirs: Years of Trial and Hope* (New York: Doubleday, 1956), 2:11.

10. Walter Millis, *The Forrestal Diaries* (New York: Viking, 1952), p. 102.

11. *Ibid.*, p. 129.

12. *Ibid.*, pp. 135–40.

13. Truman, *Memoirs,* 2:95.

14. *Ibid.*, pp. 96–97.

15. Truman, *Memoirs,* 1:551–52.

16. John C. Campbell, *Defense of the Middle East: Problems of American Policy* (New York: Praeger, 1960), p. 33.

17. Truman, *Memoirs,* 2:100. Actually, the Greek Communists and their local allies were prosecuting their insurrection against the Greek monarchy contrary to the wishes of Stalin. The Greek Communists were aided by Tito, with whom Stalin was having an altercation; and, in any event, Stalin preferred to keep his spheres-of-influence agreement with Churchill, consigning Greece to British control. On this, see Yergin, *Shattered Peace,* pp. 288–95.

18. Address by the Secretary of State at Princeton University, February 22, 1947.

19. Joseph M. Jones, *The Fifteen Weeks* (New York: Viking, 1955), pp. 138–41. Dean Acheson's account of the February 27, 1947, meeting in the White House is in his *Present at the Creation* (New York: Norton, 1969), p. 219.

20. Jones, *The Fifteen Weeks,* pp. 157, 162.

21. Address by President Truman to Congress, March 12, 1947.

22. W. W. Rostow, *The United States and the World Arena* (New York: Harper, 1960), p. 209.

23. *Department of State Bulletin* (May 11, 1947), 16:410, 920–24.

24. Quoted by Harry Bayard Price, *The Marshall Plan and Its Meaning* (Ithaca: Cornell University Press, 1955), p. 22.

25. Jones, *The Fifteen Weeks,* pp. 251–52. See also George F. Kennan, *Memoirs 1925–1950* (Boston: Atlantic, Little, Brown, 1967), pp. 335–45.

26. *Department of State Bulletin,* June 15, 1947, pp. 1159–60.

27. Price, The Marshall Plan and Its Meaning pp. 24–29; Rostow, The United States and the World Arena pp. 209–13.

28. X (George Kennan), "The Sources of Soviet Conduct," *Foreign Affairs* (July 1947), pp. 566–82.

29. *Ibid.*, passim.

4. THE IMPLEMENTATION OF CONTAINMENT

1. Walter Millis, *The Forrestal Diaries* (New York: Viking, 1951), p. 341.

2. This interpretation of Marshall's views relies heavily on Warner R. Schilling's thorough

study, "The Politics of National Defense: Fiscal 1950," in Warner R. Schilling, Paul Y. Hammond, and Glen H. Snyder, *Strategy, Politics, and Defense Budgets* (New York: Columbia University Press, 1962), pp. 5–266, passim.

3. Millis, *The Forrestal Diaries*, pp. 240, 350.

4. *Ibid.*, 350–51.

5. This review is the subject of a detailed monograph by Paul Hammond entitled "NSC-68: Prologue to Rearmament," and published in Schilling, Hammond, and Snyder, *Strategy, Politics, and Defense Budgets*, pp. 271–378. My account of the substance of arguments and activities surrounding NSC-68 relies heavily on the Hammond monograph.

6. See Edward S. Flash, Jr., *Economic Advice and Presidential Leadership: The Council of Economic Advisers* (New York: Columbia University Press, 1965), pp. 39–52.

7. Coral Bell, *Negotiations from Strength* (New York: Knopf, 1963), pp. 6–10.

8. Samuel P. Huntington, *The Common Defense: Strategic Programs in National Politics* (New York: Columbia University Press, 1961), pp. 59–61.

9. Harry S. Truman, *Memoirs: Years of Trial and Hope* (New York: Doubleday, 1956), 2:341.

10. *Ibid.*, p. 380.

11. *Ibid.*, pp. 387–88.

12. *Ibid.*, pp. 397–98.

13. *Ibid.*, p. 403.

14. *Ibid.*, p. 408.

15. *Ibid.*, p. 432.

16. U.S. Senate, Committee on Armed Services and Committee on Foreign Relations, *Hearings: Military Situation in the Far East*, 82d Cong. 1st sess., 1951, pp. 731–32, 1219.

17. Truman, *Memoirs*, 2:437.

18. See Robert E. Osgood, *NATO: The Entangling Alliance* (Chicago: University of Chicago Press, 1963), pp. 78–79.

19. *Ibid.*, pp. 70–71.

20. *Hearings: Military Situation in the Far East*, p. 732.

21. For the full text of Acheson's remarks see his January 12, 1950, speech before the National Press Club, Washington, D.C., in *Department of State Bulletin*, January 23, 1950, pp. 111–18.

22. Department of State, *United States Relations With China* (Washington: GPO, 1949), p. 383.

23. Quoted by Tang Tsou, *America's Failure in China, 1941–1950* (Chicago: University of Chicago Press, 1963), p. 363. Dr. Tsou thoroughly documents the prevailing U.S. consensus of the late 1940s that the stakes on the China mainland were not worth a U.S. military combat intervention.

24. Quoted by John C. Sparrow, *History of Personnel Demobilization* (Washington: Dept. of Army, 1951), p. 380. See also Tang Tsou, *America's Failure in China*, p. 366.

25. Harry S. Truman, press conference of November 30, 1950; see Truman, *Memoirs*, 2:395–96.

5. A NEW LOOK FOR LESS EXPENSIVE POWER

1. Edward S. Flash, Jr., *Economic Advice and Presidential Leadership: The Council of Economic Advisers* (New York: Columbia University Press, 1965), pp. 100–2.

2. Warner R. Schilling, Paul Y. Hammond, and Glenn H. Snyder, *Strategy, Politics, and Defense Budgets* (New York: Columbia University Press, 1962), pp. 356–86.

3. Eisenhower, radio address, March 19, 1953, in *New York Times*, May 20, 1953.

4. See Robert E. Osgood, *NATO: The Entangling Alliance* (Chicago: University of Chicago Press, 1963), pp. 89–90.

5. For details on the formulation and contents of NSC-162, see Snyder in *Strategy, Politics, and Defense Budgets*, pp. 406–10.

6. *Ibid.*, pp. 414–15.

7. *Ibid.*, pp. 436–38.

8. John Foster Dulles, "The Evolution of Foreign Policy," address to the Council on Foreign Relations, January 12, 1954, in *Department of State Bulletin*, January 25, 1964, pp. 107–10.

9. John Foster Dulles, "Policy for Security and Peace," *Foreign Affairs* (April 1954), pp. 353–64.

10. On Dulles' *Weltanschauung*, see Michael A. Guhin, *John Foster Dulles: A Statesman and His Times* (New York: Columbia University Press, 1972).

11. John Foster Dulles, "Report on the Near East," in *Department of State Bulletin*, June 15, 1953, pp. 831–35.

12. John C. Campbell, *Defense of the Middle East: Problems of American Policy* (New York: Praeger, 1960), pp. 49–62.

13. Eisenhower, press conference, April 7, 1954, in *New York Times*, April 8, 1954.

14. From Eisenhower letter to Churchill, April 4, 1954. Quoted by Eisenhower in *Mandate for Change: The White House Years 1953–1956* (New York: Doubleday, 1963), p. 346.

15. *Ibid.*, 354.

16. See Chalmers Roberts, "The Day We Didn't Go to War," *The Reporter* (September 14, 1954).

17. Eisenhower, *Mandate for Change*, p. 352.

18. *Ibid.*, p. 354.

19. Dulles, radio-TV address, March 8, 1955, in *Department of State Bulletin*, March 21, 1955, p. 463.

20. In *Department of State Bulletin*, March 28, 1955, pp. 526–27. Eisenhower, *Mandate for Change*, pp. 476–77.

22. Quotes are from February 1955 Eisenhower letters to Churchill, appearing in *Mandate for Change*, pp. 470–75.

23. Emmet John Hughes, *The Ordeal of Power: A Political Memoir of the Eisenhower Years* (New York: Atheneum, 1963), p. 208.

24. James Shepley, "How Dulles Averted War," *Life* (January 16, 1956), pp. 70ff.

25. *Ibid.*

6. WAGING PEACE: THE EISENHOWER FACE

1. Emmet John Hughes, *The Ordeal of Power: A Political Memoir of the Eisenhower Years* (New York: Atheneum, 1963), pp. 343–44. Eisenhower's role in controlling the less temperate members of his administration is well described in Robert A. Divine, *Eisenhower and the Cold War* (New York: Oxford University Press, 1981).

2. Quoted by Sherman Adams, *Firsthand Report: The Story of the Eisenhower Administration* (New York: Harper, 1961), p. 89.

3. Dwight D. Eisenhower, *The White House Years: Waging Peace, 1956–1961* (New York: Doubleday, 1965), 2:365.

4. Adams, *Firsthand Report*, p. 89.

5. Hughes, *The Ordeal of Power*, p. 109.

6. Dwight D. Eisenhower, *Mandate for Change: The White House Years 1953–1956* (New York: Doubleday, 1963), p. 149.

7. "The Chance for Peace," address by the President, April 16, 1953, to the American Society of Newspaper Editors, in *Department of State Bulletin*, April 27, 1953, pp. 599–603.

8. Eisenhower, *Mandate for Change*, p. 251.

9. *Ibid.*, p. 252.

10. *Ibid.*, pp. 251–55.

11. Adams, *Firsthand Report*, p. 112.

12. Quoted by Andrew Berding, *Dulles On Diplomacy* (Princeton: Van Nostrand, 1965), p. 24.

13. See Roscoe Drummond and Gaston Coblentz, *Duel at the Brink: John Foster Dulles' Command of American Power* (New York: Doubleday, 1960), pp. 134–39, for a vivid description of Dulles' reactions to the cheering throngs and Soviet embraces during the May 15, 1955, signing ceremonies in Vienna.

14. See Coral Bell, *Negotiation from Strength: A Study in the Politics of Power* (New York: Knopf, 1963), p. 127.

15. *Ibid.*, pp. 111–23, passim.

16. Adams, *Firsthand Report*, pp. 176–77.

17. Eisenhower, *Mandate for Change*, p. 506.

18. Address by the President, July 15, 1955, in Department of State, *American Foreign Policy, 1950–1955: Basic Documents* (Washington: GPO, 1955), 2:2005–8.

19. Robert J. Donovan, *Eisenhower: The Inside Story* (New York: Harper, 1956), pp. 345–46.

20. Adams, *Firsthand Report*, pp. 177–78.

21. Donovan, *Eisenhower*, pp. 348–49.

22. James Reston, *New York Times*, July 22, 1955.

23. Proposal by the President at the Geneva Conference of Heads of Government, July 21, 1955, in Department of State, *American Foreign Policy 1950–1955: Basic Documents*, 2:2842–43.

24. Statement by the President at the Geneva Conference of Heads of Government, July 23, 1955, ibid., p. 2014.

25. Adams, *Firsthand Report*, pp. 178–79.

26. Eisenhower, *Mandate for Change*, p. 530.

7. CRISES AND COMPLICATIONS

1. See Walt W. Rostow, *The United States in the World Arena* (New York: Harper, 1960), pp. 364–65.

2. Robert J. Donovan, *Eisenhower: The Inside Story* (New York: Harper, 1956), p. 388.

3. Sherman Adams, *Firsthand Report: The Story of the Eisenhower Administration* (New York: Harper, 1961), p. 245.

4. Anthony Eden, *Full Circle* (London: Cassell, 1960), pp. 374–75.

5. Dwight D. Eisenhower, *The White House Years: Waging Peace, 1956–1961* (New York: Doubleday, 1965), 2:33, 34n; and Townsend Hoopes, *The Devil and John Foster Dulles* (Boston: Atlantic, Little, Brown, 1973), pp. 330–44.

6. Eisenhower, *Waging Peace*, p. 50.

7. *Ibid.*, p. 38.

8. *Ibid.*, p. 53.

9. *Ibid.*, p. 80.

10. *Ibid.*, appendix, p. 680.

11. *Ibid.*, p. 91.

12. *Ibid.*, p. 91.

13. *Ibid.*, p. 90.

14. Dulles, speech to Council on Foreign Relations, October 6, 1952. Quoted in John Robinson Beal, *John Foster Dulles: 1888–1959* (New York: Harper, 1959), p. 312.

15. Quoted by Beal, *John Foster Dulles* pp. 311–12.

16. Dulles, radio-television address, in *Department of State Bulletin*, February 9, 1953, 28:711, pp. 207–16.

17. Message from the Allied Commandants in Berlin to the Representative of the Soviet Control Commission, June 18, 1953, and letter from the Allied Commandants in Berlin to the Soviet Military Commander in Berlin, June 24, 1953; texts in Department of State, *American Foreign Policy 1950–1955: Basic Documents* (Washington: GPO), 2:1744–45.

18. Dulles, press conference, June 30, 1953, in *American Foreign Policy 1950–1955: Basic Documents*, pp. 1745–46.

19. *American Foreign Policy 1950–1955: Basic Documents*, p. 1750.

20. Warren R. Schilling, Paul Y. Hammond, and Glenn H. Snyder, *Strategy, Politics, and Defense Budgets* (New York: Columbia University Press, 1962), pp. 407–9.

21. Eisenhower, *Waging Peace*, pp. 87–89.

22. Roscoe Drummond and Gaston Coblentz, *Duel at the Brink: John Foster Dulles' Command of American Power* (New York: Doubleday, 1960), pp. 180–81.

23. *Ibid.*, p. 181. See also Andrew Berding, *Dulles on Diplomacy* (Princeton: Van Nostrand, 1965), pp. 115–16.

24. See Arnold L. Horelick and Myron Rush, *Strategic Power and Soviet Foreign Policy* (Chicago: University of Chicago Press, 1966).

25. Radio-television address by the President, November 7, 1957; see *Waging Peace*, pp. 223–25.

26. The most complete description, compiled from numerous open sources, is by Morton H. Halperin in his "The Gaither Committee and the Policy Process," *World Politics* (April 1961), pp. 360–84.

27. Eisenhower, *Waging Peace*, pp. 219–23.

28. Halperin, "The Gaither Committee and the Policy Process," passim.

29. Samuel P. Huntington, *The Common Defense: Strategic Programs in National Politics* (New York: Columbia University Press, 1961), p. 94.

30. From Eisenhower's account of November 1957 NSC deliberations, *Waging Peace*, pp. 221–22.

31. Quoted by Huntington, *The Common Defense*, p. 101.

32. Eisenhower, *Waging Peace*, p. 222.

33. Department of State, *American Foreign Policy: Current Documents* (Washington: GPO, 1957), pp. 784–85.

34. *Ibid.*, p. 790.

35. *Ibid.*, pp. 787–90, passim.

36. Statement by the Secretary of State before the Committees on Foreign Relations and Armed Services of the Senate, January 14, 1957, in *ibid.*, pp. 796–97.

37. *Ibid.*, p. 800.

38. Public Law 85–87, Congress, 1st sess., H. J. Res. 117, *American Foreign Policy: Current Documents*, 1957, pp. 816–17.

39. Documents Nos. 298–303, in *ibid.*, pp. 1023–28. See also John C. Campbell, *Defense of the Middle East: Problems of American Policy* (New York: Praeger, 1960), pp. 127–31.

40. Eisenhower, *Waging Peace*, p. 196.

41. White House news conference of August 21, 1957, in *American Foreign Policy: Current Documents*, 1957, p. 199.

42. *Current Digest of the Soviet Press*, 9(2):23.

43. Department of State press release, September 10, 1957, in *Department of State Bulletin,* September 30, 1957.

44. Address by President Eisenhower to the nation, July 15, 1958. Also Special Message of President Eisenhower to the Congress, July 15, 1958. Both in *American Foreign Policy: Current Documents,* 1958, pp. 965–67, 969–72.

45. Campbell, *Defense of The Middle East,* pp. 142–44.

46. Eisenhower, *Waging Peace,* p. 290.

47. *Ibid.,* pp. 290–91.

48. Address by the President to the Third Emergency Session of the UN General Assembly, August 13, 1958, in *American Foreign Policy: Current Documents,* 1958, pp. 1032–39.

49. Res. XCIII, Tenth Inter-American Conference, Caracas, Venezuela, March 1–28, 1954, in Department of State, *American Foreign Policy, 1950–1955: Basic Documents,* 1:1300–2.

50. Edwin Lieuwen, *U.S. Policy in Latin America: A Short History* (New York: Praeger, 1965), pp. 88–92.

51. Eisenhower's candid discussion of the intervention in his *Mandate for Change: The White House Years 1953–1956* (New York: Doubleday, 1963), pp. 504–11, details most of the essentials.

52. Lieuwen, *U.S. Policy in Latin America,* p. 113.

53. Eisenhower, *Waging Peace,* p. 525.

54. Statement by the President, July 11, 1960, in *Department of State Bulletin,* August 1, 1960, pp. 318–19.

55. Statement by Under Secretary of State Dillon, September 6, 1960, in *Department of State Bulletin,* October 3, 1960, pp. 533–37.

56. Eisenhower, *Waging Peace,* p. 539.

57. *Ibid.,* p. 533.

58. Arthur M. Schlesinger, Jr., *A Thousand Days: John F. Kennedy in the White House* (Boston: Houghton Mifflin, 1965), p. 222.

59. For a description of the U.S. responses to procedural harassments on the access routes to Berlin during the spring and summer of 1958, see Jean Edward Smith, *The Defense of Berlin* (Baltimore: Johns Hopkins University Press, 1963), pp. 157–60.

60. Note from the Soviet Foreign Ministry, November 27, 1958, in *Department of State Bulletin,* January 19, 1959, pp. 81–89.

61. *New York Times,* November 27, 1958.

62. Quotations are from Eisenhower, *Waging Peace,* pp. 334–49, passim.

63. *Ibid.,* p. 342.

64. *Ibid.,* p. 341.

65. Western Proposal on Berlin (Draft Agreement), June 16, 1959, Department of State account of the Geneva Foreign Ministers' Meeting, May–August, 1959, pp. 312–13.

66. Eisenhower's own paraphrase of his confidential letter to Macmillan (sent sometime between July 15 and 20, 1959), in *Waging Peace,* p. 402.

67. *Ibid.,* pp. 405–12.

68. Text in *New York Times,* September 29, 1959.

8. ENHANCING THE ARSENAL OF POWER

1. N. S. Khrushchev, "For New Victories for the World Communist Movement," *World Marxist Review: Problems of Peace and Socialism* (January 1961), pp. 3–28.

2. Arthur M. Schlesinger, Jr., *A Thousand Days: John F. Kennedy in the White House* (Boston: Houghton Mifflin, 1965), p. 302.

3. See Theodore C. Sorensen, *Kennedy* (New York: Harper, 1965), pp. 629–33; and Schlesinger, *A Thousand Days*, pp. 340–42.

4. See Schlesinger, *A Thousand Days*, pp. 585–91.

5. Address by the President, March 13, 1962, in *Department of State Bulletin*, April 2, 1962, pp. 539–42.

6. State of the Union Message by the President, January 30, 1961. *Public Papers of the Presidents: John F. Kennedy 1961* (Washington: GPO, 1962).

7. *Ibid.*

8. *Ibid.*

9. Quoted by Sorensen, *Kennedy*, p. 408.

10. Address by President Kennedy to the Congress, January 25, 1962, in House Document 314, 87th Cong., 2d sess.

11. See early sections of the 1961 State of the Union Message for this catalogue of domestic deficiencies.

12. John F. Kennedy, *The Strategy of Peace*, edited by Allan Nevins (New York: Harper, 1960), p. 4.

13. *Ibid.*

14. Quoted by Sorensen, *Kennedy*, p. 528.

15. General Maxwell Taylor recounts these doctrinal battles and advances the doctrine of "flexible response" in his *The Uncertain Trumpet* (New York: Harper, 1960).

16. See William W. Kaufmann, ed., *Military Policy and National Security* (Princeton: Princeton University Press, 1956); Robert E. Osgood, *Limited War* (Chicago: University of Chicago Press, 1957); Henry A. Kissinger, *Nuclear Weapons and Foreign Policy* (New York: Harper, 1957); and Bernard Brodie, *Strategy in the Missile Age* (Princeton: Princeton University Press, 1959).

17. *Public Papers of the Presidents of the United States: John F. Kennedy, 1961*, p. 231.

18. See Henry A. Kissinger, *The Troubled Partnership: A Reappraisal of the Atlantic Alliance* (New York: Anchor Books, 1966), especially pp. 106–28. See also Raymond Aaron, *The Great Debate* (New York: Doubleday, 1965).

19. *Public Papers of the President: John F. Kennedy, 1961*, p. 385.

20. See Seyom Brown. "An Alternative to the Grand Design," *World Politics* (January 1965), pp. 231–42.

21. See Sorensen, *Kennedy*, p. 567; and Schlesinger, *A Thousand Days*, pp. 872–73.

22. Remarks of Secretary of Defense Robert S. McNamara at Commencement Exercises, University of Michigan, Ann Arbor, June 16, 1962, in Department of Defense News Release No. 980–62.

23. *Ibid.*

24. *Ibid.*

25. Press conference of the President of France, November 10, 1962, in *New York Times*, November 11, 1962.

26. I am indebted to Herbert Dinerstein for the domestic analogy.

27. *Public Papers of the Presidents: John F. Kennedy, 1963*, pp. 174–75.

28. Sorensen, *Kennedy*, p. 564; Kissinger, *The Troubled Partnership*, pp. 82–83.

29. Joint statement following discussions with Prime Minister Macmillan—the Nassau Agreement, December 21, 1962, *Public Papers of the Presidents: John F. Kennedy, 1962*, pp. 908–10.

30. Schlesinger, *A Thousand Days*, pp. 865–66.

31. Testimony of the Secretary of Defense before the Senate Committee on Armed Services, February 20, 1963.

32. Testimony before the House Subcommittee on Appropriations, 1963; quoted by William W. Kaufmann, *The McNamara Strategy* (New York: Harper, 1964), p. 95.

33. Testimony before House Committee on Armed Services, February 1, 1963.
34. Speech to American Society of Newspaper Editors, April 20, 1963.
35. Testimony before subcommittee of Senate Committee on Appropriations, April 24, 1963.
36. *Ibid.*
37. Testimony before Senate Committee on Armed Services, February 21, 1963.
38. Testimony before House Armed Services Committee, January 30, 1963.
39. Testimony before House Armed Services Committee, February 1, 1963.
40. "McNamara Thinks About the Unthinkable," *Saturday Evening Post* (December 1, 1962), pp. 13–19.
41. Testimony before Senate Committee on Armed Services, February 21, 1963.
42. *Ibid.*, February 20, 1963.
43. *Public Papers of the Presidents: John F. Kennedy, 1963*, pp. 890–94.

9. THE THIRD WORLD AS A PRIMARY ARENA OF COMPETITION

1. From an address at La Grande, Oregon, November 9, 1959, in John F. Kennedy, *The Strategy of Peace,* edited by Allan Nevins (New York: Harper, 1960), pp. 107–8.
2. The most comprehensive policy-oriented statement to come out of this group was the book by Max Millikan and Walt Rostow, *A Proposal: Key to an Effective Foreign Policy* (New York: Harper, 1957). A more theoretical treatise is Rostow's *The Stages of Economic Growth: A Non-Communist Manifesto* (London: Cambridge University Press, 1960). Some refinements are added by John Kenneth Galbraith, "A Positive Approach to Foreign Aid," *Foreign Affairs* (April 1961), pp. 444–57.
3. Arthur M. Schlesinger, Jr., *A Thousand Days: John F. Kennedy in the White House* (Boston: Houghton Mifflin, 1965), p. 592.
4. Task force quotations are taken from Schlesinger, *A Thousand Days,* pp. 195–96.
5. Address by President Kennedy at a White House Reception, March 13, 1961, in *Department of State Bulletin,* April 3, 1961, pp. 471–74.
6. *Ibid.*
7. Address by Secretary of the Treasury Douglas Dillon to the Inter-American Economic and Social Conference, Punta del Este, Uruguay, August 7, 1961, in *Department of State Bulletin,* August 28, 1961, pp. 356–60.
8. Theodore C. Sorensen, *Kennedy* (New York: Harper, 1965), p. 535.
9. Tad Szulc, *The Winds of Revolution: Latin America Today—and Tomorrow* (New York: Praeger, 1963), pp. 243–44.
10. Quoted by Sorensen, *Kennedy,* p. 535.
11. Address by President Kennedy at the White House, March 13, 1962, in *Department of State Bulletin,* April 2, 1962, pp. 539–42.
12. Evaluation of the First Year of the Alliance for Progress by the Ministerial Representatives of the Inter-American Economic and Social Council, meeting in Mexico City, October 22–27, 1962, in *Department of State Bulletin,* December 10, 1962, pp. 897–901.
13. *Ibid.*
14. Address by President Kennedy to the Inter-American Press Association, Miami Beach, Florida, November 18, 1963, in *Department of State Bulletin,* December 9, 1963, pp. 900–4.
15. Address by President Kennedy to the Congress, March 13, 1962, House Document 362, 87th Cong., 2d sess.
16. Schlesinger, *A Thousand Days,* p. 597.
17. Department of State, *Report to the President of the United States from the Committee to Strengthen the Security of the Free World: The Scope and Distribution of United States Military and Economic Assistance Programs,* March 20, 1963. (Washington: GPO).

18. Address in Salt Lake City at the Mormon Tabernacle, September 26, 1963, in *Public Papers of the Presidents of the United States: John F. Kennedy, 1963*, pp. 733–38. (Emphasis added.)

10. KENNEDY'S CUBAN CRISES

1. Arthur M. Schlesinger, Jr., *A Thousand Days: John F. Kennedy in the White House* (Boston: Houghton Mifflin, 1965), pp. 210–13.

2. Press conference, April 12, 1961, in *Public Papers of the Presidents: John F. Kennedy, 1961* (Washington: GPO, 1962), pp. 258–59.

3. Peter Wyden, *Bay of Pigs: The Untold Story* (New York: Simon and Schuster, 1979).

4. Historian Richard Reeves in his *President Kennedy: Profile of Power* (New York: Simon & Schuster, 1993) shows Kennedy believing he was deliberately deceived by advisers who wanted him to use U.S. forces (pp. 76–106).

5. Schlesinger, *A Thousand Days*, pp. 252–95.

6. *Ibid.*, p. 276.

7. Quoted by Schlesinger, *Ibid.* p. 251.

8. Sorensen, *Kennedy*, pp. 297, 307.

9. Address to the American Society of Newspaper Editors, April 20, 1961, *Public Papers of the Presidents: John F. Kennedy, 1961*, pp. 204–6.

10. See Arnold L. Horelick, "The Cuban Missile Crisis: An Analysis of Soviet Calculations and Behavior," *World Politics* (April 1964), pp. 363–89.

11. *Public Papers of the Presidents: John F. Kennedy, 1962*, pp. 897–98.

12. *Ibid.*, p. 898.

13. *Ibid.*, pp. 808–9.

14. Quoted by Elie Abel, *The Missile Crisis* (New York: Lippincott, 1966), pp. 64–65.

15. Sorensen, *Kennedy*, pp. 684–85.

16. Abel, *The Missile Crisis* pp. 80–81.

17. Quoted by Abel, *The Missile Crisis* in footnote p. 64.

18. Robert F. Kennedy, *The Thirteen Days: A Memoir of the Cuban Missile Crisis* (New York: W. W. Norton, 1969).

19. The title of an insightful essay on the missile crisis by Albert and Roberta Wohlstetter. See their "Controlling the Risks in Cuba," *Adelphi Papers* (April 1965), Institute for Strategic Studies, London.

20. Robert Kennedy continued to maintain that his brother could not order an air strike because the contemplated attack without warning against a small nation would offend the American conscience. See Abel, *The Missile Crisis* p. 88.

21. Abel, *The Missile Crisis* p. 101.

22. *Public Papers of the Presidents: John F. Kennedy, 1962*, p. 808.

23. Sorensen, *Kennedy* p. 715; see also Abel, *The Missile Crisis* p. 201.

24. Sorensen, *Kennedy* p. 710.

25. Abel, *The Missile Crisis* p. 174; Sorensen, *Kennedy* p. 710.

26. Sorensen, *Kennedy* p. 717.

11. BERLIN AGAIN

1. Jean Edward Smith, *The Defense of Berlin* (Baltimore: Johns Hopkins University Press, 1963), p. 230.

2. Theodore C. Sorensen, *Kennedy* (New York: Harper, 1965), pp. 584–86.

3. Quotations are from the text of the *aide-mémoire,* handed by Chairman Khrushchev to President Kennedy at Vienna on June 4, 1961, in Department of State, *American Foreign Policy: Current Documents* (Washington: GPO, 1961), pp. 584–86.

4. The President's television address of July 25, 1961, *Public Papers of the Presidents of the United States: John F. Kennedy, 1961,* pp. 533–40.

5. Quoted by Smith, *The Defense of Berlin* pp. 254–55.

6. *American Foreign Policy: Current Documents,* (Washington: GPO) 1961, pp. 619–20.

7. *Ibid.,* pp. 620–21.

8. Sorensen, Kennedy p. 594.

9. General Clay's virtuosity in brilliantly staging a "confrontation" to counter attempted Communist "salami slices" is well described in George Bailey's "The Gentle Erosion of Berlin," *The Reporter* (April 26, 1962), pp. 15–19.

10. Quoted by Arthur M. Schlesinger, Jr., *A Thousand Days: John F. Kennedy in the White House* (Boston: Houghton Mifflin, 1965), p. 399.

12. THE VIETNAM QUAGMIRE

1. Arthur M. Schlesinger, Jr., *Robert Kennedy and His Times* (Boston: Houghton Mifflin, 1978), pp. 709–11.

2. President Kennedy's interview with Walter Cronkite, *Public Papers of the Presidents of the United States: John F. Kennedy, 1963,* p. 652.

3. For details of the U.S. government's cooperation in the coup against Diem see *The Pentagon Papers: The Defense Department's History of United States Decisionmaking on Vietnam,* Senator Mike Gravell, ed. (Boston: Beacon Press, 1971), 2:212–20, 239, 253–54, 257–62, 734, 738, 789–92.

4. *Ibid.,* 3:3.

5. *Ibid.,* 3:141–52. See also Leslie H. Gelb and Richard Betts, *The Irony of Vietnam: The System Worked* (Washington: Brookings Institution, 1979), p. 102.

6. *The Gulf of Tonkin: The 1964 Incidents, Hearings Before the Senate Committee on Foreign Relations,* 90th Cong., 2d Sess. (Washington: GPO, 1968).

7. U.S. Congress, Joint Resolution of August 7, 1964.

8. Address to the American Bar Association, August 12, 1964, *Public Papers of the Presidents of the United States: Lyndon B. Johnson, 1963–64,* 2:953.

9. Remarks in Manchester, New Hampshire, September 28, 1964, *Public Papers of the Presidents of the United States: Lyndon B. Johnson, 1963–64,* p. 2:1164.

10. October 21, 1964, 2:1391.

11. Press conference by Secretary of Defense McNamara and Under Secretary of State Ball, February 7, 1965, in *New York Times,* February 8, 1965.

12. State Department Publication 7839, February 1965.

13. Address by President Johnson at Johns Hopkins University, April 7, 1965, in *Department of State Bulletin,* April 26, 1965, pp. 606–10.

14. See the President's message to Congress, May 4, 1965, *Public Papers of the Presidents of the United States: Lyndon B. Johnson, 1965,* 1:494–98.

15. In *Department of State Bulletin,* July 12, 1965.

16. *New York Times,* November 18 and 19, 1965.

17. In *Department of State Bulletin,* August 16, 1965, pp. 262–65.

18. *Ibid.*

19. In *New York Times,* January 29, 1966.

20. James Gavin, testimony before Senate Committee on Foreign Relations, *Hearings: Supplemental Foreign Assistance Fiscal Year 1966—Vietnam,* pp. 230–31.

21. George Kennan in *ibid.*, pp. 331–36.

22. The Declaration of Honolulu and accompanying statements are published in *Weekly Compilation of Presidential Documents*, February 14, 1966.

23. Draft memorandum for the President from the Secretary of Defense ("The McNaughton Draft Presidential Memorandum"). May 19, 1967, *The Pentagon Papers*, 4:477–89.

24. Townsend Hoopes, *The Limits of Intervention* (New York: McKay, 1969), p. 181.

25. Doris Kearns, *Lyndon Johnson and the American Dream* (New York: Signet edition, 1977), p. 357.

26. Hoopes, *The Limits of Intervention* p. 205.

27. *Ibid.*, p. 217.

28. *Ibid.*, p. 222, for background. President Johnson's March 31, 1968, television address in *Public Papers of the Presidents of the United States: Lyndon B. Johnson, 1968*, 1:469–476.

29. Kearns, *Lyndon Johnson and the American Dream* pp. 351–68, passim.

13. AVOIDING HUMILIATION IN INDOCHINA

1. Henry Kissinger, "The Vietnam Negotiations," *Foreign Affairs* (January 1969), 47(2):218–19; and Henry Kissinger, *The White House Years* (Boston: Little, Brown, 1979), pp. 227–29, 298.

2. Kissinger, *The White House Years*, p. 298. See also Richard Whalen, *Catch the Falling Flag* (Boston: Houghton Mifflin, 1972); and Marvin Kalb and Bernard Kalb, *Kissinger* (New York: Dell, 1975), pp. 142–50.

3. Albert H. Cantril and Charles W. Roll, Jr., *Hopes and Fears of the American People* (New York: Universe Books for Potomac Associates, 1971), pp. 37–38.

4. Nixon's autobiography, published by Doubleday in 1962, was called *Six Crises*.

5. For Kissinger's defense of the legality and morality of the secret bombing of Cambodia see *The White House Years*, pp. 239–54.

6. President Nixon, radio-TV address to the nation, April 30, 1970, in *Department of State Bulletin*, no. 1612 (May 18, 1970), 62:620.

7. *Ibid.*, p. 619.

8. Richard M. Nixon, "A Report on the Conclusion of the Cambodian Operation." *Department of State Bulletin*, no. 1621 (July 20, 1970), 63:65–74.

9. See William Shawcross, *Sideshow: Kissinger, Nixon, and the Destruction of Cambodia* (New York: Simon and Schuster, 1979) for the most elaborate version of the charge that the United States was to blame for Cambodia's tragedy. Kissinger's refutation is in *The White House Years*, pp. 433–521.

10. Kissinger, *The White House Years*, p. 974.

11. Richard M. Nixon, "A Report on the Military Situation in Vietnam and the Role of the United States," *Department of State Bulletin*, no. 1716 (May 15, 1972), 66:684.

12. *Ibid.*, p. 685.

13. *Ibid.*, p. 684.

14. Richard Nixon, address of May 8, 1972, in *Department of State Bulletin*, no. 1718 (May 29, 1972), 66:747–50.

15. *Ibid.*

16. See Roger Morris, *Uncertain Greatness: Henry Kissinger and American Foreign Policy* (New York: Harper & Row, 1977), pp. 184–86.

17. Kalb and Kalb, *Kissinger*, pp. 352–54.

18. Morris, *Uncertain Greatness*, p. 186.

19. Kalb and Kalb, *Kissinger*, p. 384.

20. In *The White House Years* Kissinger unequivocally endorses the Christmas 1972 bomb-

ing: "Nixon chose the only weapon he had available. His decision speeded the end of the war; even in retrospect, I can think of no other measure that would have" (p. 1461).

21. Address by President Nixon, January 23, 1973, in *Department of State Bulletin*, no. 1755 (February 12, 1973), 68:153.

22. "Texts of Agreements and Protocols on Ending the War and Restoring the Peace in Vietnam," *Department of State Bulletin*, no. 1755 (February 12, 1973), 68:169–88.

23. Kissinger, *The White House Years*, p. 1470.

24. Kissinger, *Years of Upheaval* (Boston: Little, Brown, 1982), pp. 369–70.

25. *Ibid.*, pp. 301–35.

26. *Ibid.*, pp. 306–308.

27. *Ibid.*, pp. 318–19.

28. *Ibid.*, p. 324.

29. *Ibid.*, pp. 332–37.

30. *Ibid.*, p. 327.

14. THE INSUFFICIENCY OF MILITARY CONTAINMENT

1. Henry Kissinger, *The White House Years* (Boston: Little, Brown, 1979), pp. 62, 66–67.

2. *Ibid.*, p. 217.

3. President Nixon's news conference on January 27, 1969, *Department of State Bulletin*, no. 1547 (February 17, 1969), 143.

4. Richard M. Nixon, *U.S. Foreign Policy for the 1970s: Building for peace* (Washington: GPO, 1971), pp. 170–71.

5. Richard M. Nixon, *U.S. Foreign Policy for the 1970s: The Emerging Structure of Peace* (Washington: GPO, 1972), p. 158.

6. The skirmishing over strategic arms policy inside the U.S. government is described in rich detail by Kissinger in *White House Years*, pp. 215–18, 539–51; and by John Newhouse, *Cold Dawn: The Story of SALT* (New York: Holt, Rinehart, and Winston, 1973), esp. pp. 133–65.

7. Treaty Between the United States of America and the Union of Soviet Socialist Republics on the Limitation of Anti-Ballistic Missile Systems (signed in Moscow May 26, 1972).

8. *Ibid.*

9. Interim Agreement Between the United States of America and the Union of Soviet Socialist Republics on Certain Measures With Respect to the Limitation of Strategic Offensive Arms (signed in Moscow May 26, 1972), U.S. Arms Control and Disarmament Agency, Arms Control and Disarmament Agreements: Texts and History of Negotiations (Washington: ACDA, 1979), pp. 131–52

10. Newhouse, *Cold Dawn*, pp. 234–36.

11. Secretary of Defense James L. Schlesinger's news conferences on August 17, 1973; January 10, 1974; and January 24, 1974, Department of Defense texts (processed).

12. Secretary of Defense James R. Schlesinger, *Annual Defense Department Report, FY 1976 and Transition Budgets* (Washington: Department of Defense, February 5, 1975), pp. 1–14.

13. *Ibid.*

14. Kissinger's news conference in Moscow on July 3, 1974, *Department of State Bulletin*, no. 1831 (July 29, 1974), 71:210.

15. See Thomas W. Wolfe, *The SALT Experience: Its Impact on U.S. and Soviet Strategic Policy and Decisionmaking* (Santa Monica, Calif.: RAND, R-1686-PR, September 1975), pp. 164–71, for the specifics of the Vladivostok agreement, many of which were left out of the cryptic summit communiqué and dribbled out in subsequent press conferences and background news stories.

16. Kissinger's version of the early moves toward China is in *The White House Years*, pp. 163–94. The Kalb brothers, reflecting Kissinger's pre-Watergate deference to Nixon, give the nod to the President and cite his 1967 article in *Foreign Affairs* as evidence. Marvin Kalb and Bernard Kalb, *Kissinger* (New York: Dell, 1975), p. 250.

17. Kissinger, *The White House Years*, pp. 163–65.

18. A. Doak Barnett, *China Policy: Old Problems and New Challenges* (Washington: Brookings Institution, 1977), pp. 4–5.

19. *Department of State Bulletin*, no. 1573 (August 18, 1969), 61:126.

20. Richard M. Nixon, *U.S. Foreign Policy for the 1970s: A New Strategy for Peace*, Report to Congress, February 18, 1970 (Washington: GPO, 1970), pp. 140–141.

21. Kalb and Kalb, *Kissinger*, pp. 263–64.

22. *Ibid.*, pp. 266–70.

23. Nixon, *U.S. Foreign Policy for the 1970s: Building for Peace* (1971), pp. 105–10.

24. Kalb and Kalb, *Kissinger*, p. 272. See also John G. Stoessinger, *Henry Kissinger: The Anguish of Power* (New York: Norton, 1976), p. 120; and William Safire, *Before the Fall: An Inside View of the Pre-Watergate White House* (Garden City, N.Y.: Doubleday, 1975), p. 372.

25. President Nixon's news conference on August 4, 1971, in *Department of State Bulletin* no. 1678 (August 23, 1971), 65:191.

26. Nixon, *U.S. Foreign Policy The Emerging Structure of Peace* (1972), p. 35.

27. Tillman Durdin, "Peking Explains Warmer U.S. Ties," *New York Times*, August 22, 1971.

28. Text of joint communiqué issues at Shanghai, February 27, 1972, in *Department of State Bulletin*, no. 1708 (March 20, 1972), 66:435–38.

29. *Ibid.*

30. *Ibid.*

31. Winston Lord, statement before the Subcommittee on Future Foreign Policy Research and Development, House Committee on International Relations, March 23, 1976. Full text in *Department of State Bulletin*, no. 1921 (April 19, 1976), 74:514–18.

32. Excerpts from "Interview with Kissinger: Eight Years in Washington Evaluated," *New York Times*, January 20, 1977.

33. "Basic Principles of Relations Between the United States of American and the Union of Soviet Socialist Republics," in *Department of State Bulletin*, no. 1722 (June 26, 1972), 66:898–99.

34. Richard M. Nixon, *U.S. Foreign Policy for the 1970s: Shaping a Durable Peace*, Report to Congress, May 3, 1973, pp. 31–35.

35. Peter G. Peterson, *U.S.–Soviet Commercial Relations in a New Era* (Washington: U.S. Department of Commerce, August 1972), pp. 3–4.

36. See Seyom Brown, *New Forces in World Politics* (Washington: Brookings Institution, 1974), pp. 67–78.

37. *Department of State Bulletin*, no. 1718 (May 29, 1972), 66:755. Kissinger also arranged a special meeting between the Soviet Trade Minister and President Nixon and key U.S. trade officials at the White House three days after the Haiphong mining was announced. The Kremlin, denounced the U.S. threats to Soviet shipping as a gross violation of freedom of navigation and demanded that the blockade be lifted immediately, but continued its preparations for the Moscow summit. See Kalb and Kalb, *Kissinger*, pp. 352–53.

38. Kissinger, September 19, 1974. *Department of State Bulletin*, no. 1842 (October 14, 1974), 71:505–19.

39. Helmut Sonnenfeldt, "U.S.–Soviet Relations in the Nuclear Age," *Department of State Bulletin*, no. 1923 (May 3, 1976), 84:581.

15. THE MIDDLE EAST AND THE REASSERTION OF AMERICAN COMPETENCE ABROAD

1. UN Security Council Resolution 242 (1967).

2. Secretary of State William R. Rogers, "A Lasting Peace in the Middle East: An American View," address delivered December 9, 1969, in *Department of State Bulletin*, no. 1593 (January 5, 1970), 62:8.

3. William B. Quandt, *Decade of Decisions: American Policy Toward the Arab–Israeli Conflict, 1967–1976* (Berkeley: University of California Press, 1977), pp. 89–90.

4. Israeli Cabinet statement, December 22, 1978, quoted by Quandt, *Decade of Decisions*. p. 91.

5. Richard M. Nixon, *RN: The Memoirs of Richard Nixon* (New York: Grosset & Dunlap, 1978), pp. 478–79. Nixon's claim of advance skepticism about the prospects for the Rogers Plan is borne out by the fact that the President failed to identify himself with the plan at the time either publicly or within the counsels of government. See Tad Szulc, *The Illusion of Peace: Foreign Policy in the Nixon Years* (New York: Viking, 1978), pp. 97–98.

6. Nixon, *RN*, p. 479.

7. *Ibid.* See also Kissinger, *The White House Years*, p. 560–61.

8. See Kalb and Kalb, *Kissinger*, p. 215; Quandt, *Decade of Decisions*, pp. 97–99.

9. Quandt, *Decade of Decisions*, pp. 100–101.

10. Kissinger, as quoted by Kalb and Kalb, *Kissinger*, p. 222.

11. Szulc, *Illusion of Peace*, pp. 317–20; Quandt, *Decade of Decisions*, pp. 106–8; Kalb and Kalb, *Kissinger*, pp. 225–26.

12. Kissinger, *White House Years*, pp. 567–91.

13. See Quandt, *Decade of Decision*, p. 113.

14. Szulc, *Illusion of Peace*, pp. 324–25.

15. Kalb and Kalb, *Kissinger*, pp. 228–29.

16. Quandt, *Decade of Decisions*, p. 114.

17. Nixon, *RN*, p. 483.

18. Kissinger, *The White House Years*, pp. 594–631, provides the most complete account of White House actions and considerations in the Jordanian crisis. Nixon devotes only a few cryptic paragraphs of his memoirs to the crisis.

19. Kalb and Kalb, *Kissinger*, pp. 236–38; Quandt, *Decade of Decisions*, pp. 116–19; Szulc, *Illusion of Peace*, pp. 329–31.

20. Nixon, *RN*, p. 920.

21. Kissinger, *Years of Upheaval* (Boston: Little, Brown, 1982), and Kalb and Kalb, *Kissinger*, pp. 510–19, provide most of the material on the indications of impending war. See also Szulc, *Illusion of Peace*, pp. 726–27, and Nadav Safran. *Israel: The Embattled Ally* (Cambridge, Mass.: Belknap-Harvard, 1978), pp. 467–75.

22. John Stoessinger, *Henry Kissinger: The Anguish of Power* (New York: Norton, 1976), p. 179.

23. Kissinger, *Years of Upheaval*, p. 477.

24. Kissinger's news conference on October 25, 1973, *Department of State Bulletin*, no. 1794 (November 12, 1973), 69:583–94.

25. See Edward R. F. Sheehan, *The Arabs, Israelis, and Kissinger: A Secret History of American Diplomacy in the Middle East* (New York: Readers Digest Press, 1976). Kissinger "recognized instinctively," says Sheehan, "that . . . if he allowed neither side to win decisively, then he might manipulate the result to launch negotiations, and—ultimately—to compose the Arab-Israeli quarrel. All of Kissinger's ensuing moves must be understood in this perspective" (p. 32).

26. On the details of the arms supply delay see Walter Isaacson, *Kissinger: A Biography* (New York: Simon and Schuster, 1992), pp. 512–24.

27. UN Security Council Resolution 338, October 22, 1973, in *Department of State Bulletin*, no. 1974 (November 12, 1978), 69:604.

28. Kissinger, *Years of Upheaval*, pp. 570–71, 601–11.

29. Kalb and Kalb, *Kissinger*, pp. 550–51.

30. Kalb and Kalb, p. 553; Quandt, *Decade of Decisions*, p. 196; Szulc, *Illusion of Peace*, p. 745; Nixon, *RN*, p. 938.

31. James Schlesinger's news conference on October 26, 1973, in *Department of State Bulletin*, no. 1796 (November 19, 1973), 69:617–26. See also Kissinger, *Years of Upheaval*, p. 584.

32. Kissinger, *Years of Upheaval*, p. 585.

33. *Ibid.*, 585–86.

34. Nixon, *RN*, pp. 939–40.

35. Kissinger's news conference on October 25, 1973, *Department of State Bulletin*, no. 1794 (November 12, 1973), 69:588.

36. *Ibid.*, p. 589.

37. *Ibid.*, pp. 604–5.

16. THE ANACHRONISM OF CONSERVATIVE REALPOLITIK

1. Henry Kissinger, *The White House Years* (Boston: Little, Brown, 1979), pp. 842–918.

2. Henry Kissinger, *Years of Upheaval* (Boston: Little, Brown, 1982), pp. 374–413; but see Seymour M. Hersh, "The Price of Power," *Atlantic Monthly* (December 1982) 250(6):31ff.

3. Kissinger, *The White House Years*, p. 950.

4. John B. Connally, remarks at the International Conference of the American Bankers Association, Munich, May 28, 1971 (Department of the Treasury news release).

5. Richard M. Nixon, television and radio address on August 15, 1971, in *Department of State Bulletin*, no. 1680 (September 6, 1971), 65:253–56.

6. Kissinger, *The White House Years*, pp. 955–62.

7. See Seyom Brown, *New Forces in World Politics* (Washington: Brookings Institution, 1974), pp. 29–44.

8. Kissinger, address delivered to the annual meeting of the Associated Press editors, April 23, 1973, in *Department of State Bulletin*, no. 1768 (May 14, 1973), 68:593–98. See also Alvin Shuster, "Europe Cool to U.S. Design for New Ties," *New York Times*, May 22, 1973.

9. Kissinger, *Years of Upheaval*, pp. 128–94.

10. For details on the consultations prior to and during the Washington energy conference of 1974, see *ibid.*, pp. 896–934.

11. Kissinger, address delivered February 11, 1974, to the opening session of the International Oil Conference, Washington, excerpts in *New York Times*, February 12, 1974.

12. See address by Kissinger at the World Food Conference in Rome, November 16, 1974, in *Department of State Bulletin*, no. 1851 (December 16, 1974), 71:821–29.

13. Interview with Secretary of State Kissinger, *Business Week*, January 13, 1975; full text reprinted in *Washington Post*, January 3, 1975.

14. Bernard Gwertzman. "Threat of Force Serves as U.S. Weapon," *New York Times*, January 20, 1975.

15. Kissinger, address delivered in Milwaukee, July 14, 1975, in *Department of State Bulletin*, no. 1884 (August 4, 1975), 73:149.

16. Daniel P. Moynihan, "The United States in Opposition," *Commentary* (March 1975), pp. 31–44.

17. See Seyom Brown, "The New Legitimacy," *International Journal* (Winter 1975–76), 31(1):14–25.

18. Kissinger, address read by Daniel P. Moynihan to the General Assembly of the United Nations, September 1, 1975, in *Department of State Bulletin*, no. 1891 (September 22, 1975), 73:425–41.

19. Anthony Lake, *The "Tar Baby" Option: American Policy Toward Southern Rhodesia* (New York: Columbia University Press, 1976).

20. National Security Council Interdepartmental Group for Africa, *Study in Response to National Security Study Memorandum 39: Southern Africa*, Document (AF/NSC-IG 69—August 15, 1969), reprinted in full in Mohamed A. El-Khawas and Barry Cohen, eds., *National Security Study Memorandum 39: The Kissinger Study of Southern Africa* (Westport, Conn. Lawrence Hill, 1976).

21. The report of the NSC Task Force on Angola is summarized by Nathaniel Davis, "The Angola Decision of 1975: A Personal Memoir," *Foreign Affairs* (Fall 1978), 57(1):109–24.

22. Kissinger, statement made January 19, 1976, before the Subcommittee on African Affairs of the U.S. Senate Committee on Foreign Relations, *Hearings on U.S. Involvement in Civil War in Angola*, 94th Cong., 2d sess. (Washington: GPO, 1976), pp. 14–23.

23. Statement by Senator Dick Clark, February 6, 1976, in *ibid.*

24. Kissinger, address delivered in Lusaka, Zambia, April 27, 1976, in *Department of State Bulletin*, no. 1927 (May 31, 1976), 74:672–79.

17. THE MANY FACES OF JIMMY CARTER

1. *Public Papers on the Presidents of the United States: Jimmy Carter, 1977* (Washington: GPO, 1977), 1:3–4.

2. *Ibid.*, pp. 444–50.

3. *Ibid.*, pp. 955–56.

4. Interview with Zbigniew Brzezinski, *U.S. News & World Report* (May 30, 1977), pp. 35–36.

5. Jimmy Carter, Address at the United States Naval Academy, June 7, 1978, *Weekly Compilation of Presidential Documents*, 14(23):1052–57.

6. Hodding Carter III, "Life Inside the Carter State Department," *Playboy* (February 1981), p. 215.

7. James Fallows, "The Passionless Presidency," *Atlantic*, May, 1979, pp. 33–46f.

8. Cyrus Vance, Commencement Address at Harvard University, June 4, 1981, *New York Times*, June 5, 1981.

9. Richard Burt, "Brzezinski Calls Democrats Soft Toward Moscow," *New York Times*, November 30, 1980.

10. Bernard Gwertzman, "Vance, Looking Back, Lauds Pact on Arms and Retorts to Brzezinski," *New York Times* December 3, 1980.

18. IDEALISM AS THE HIGHER REALISM

1. Cyrus Vance, "Human Rights and Foreign Policy," address at Law Day ceremonies at the University of Georgia Law School at Athens, April 30, 1977, in *Department of State Bulletin*, no. 1978 (May 23, 1977), 76:505–8.

2. Information on the role and decisions of the Interagency Group on Human Rights and Foreign Assistance is from Neil J. Kritz, "The Carter Human Rights Policy: An Analysis," manuscript, Brandeis University, 1981.

3. *Ibid.*

4. Mark L. Schneider, Acting Assistant Secretary of State for Human Rights and Humanitarian Affairs, statement to the Subcommittee on International Organizations of the House Foreign Affairs Committee, February 28, 1979 (Washington: Dept. of State, processed)

5. Cecil V. Crabb, Jr. and Pat M. Holt, *Invitation to Struggle: Congress, the President, and Foreign Policy* (Washington: Congressional Quarterly Press, 1980), p. 71.

6. See William M. LeoGrande, "The Revolution in Nicaragua: Another Cuba?" *Foreign Affairs* (Fall 1979), 58(1):28–50.

7. *Ibid.*, pp. 32–33.

8. Richard R. Fagen, "Dateline Nicaragua: The End of the Affair," *Foreign Policy* (Fall 1979), no. 36, p. 184.

9. Fagen, pp. 185–86; LeoGrande, "The Revolution in Nicaragua," p. 35.

10. Cyrus R. Vance, address to the Organization of American States in Washington, June 21, 1979, excerpts in *New York Times,* June 22, 1979.

11. Andrew Young, "The United States and Africa: Victory for Diplomacy," *America and the World 1980* (special issue of *Foreign Affairs,* 1981), pp. 649–66.

12. Jimmy Carter, remarks on signing H.R. 1746 into law, March 18, 1977, in *Public Papers of the Presidents: Jimmy Carter, 1977,* 1:451–53.

13. David Ottaway, "Africa: U.S. Policy Eclipse," *America and the World 1979* (special issue of *Foreign Affairs,* 1980), pp. 640–41.

14. White House briefing by the President for civic community leaders, April 30, 1980, in *Public Papers of the Presidents: Jimmy Carter, 1980–1981,* 1:801.

19. CAMP DAVID ACCORDS: CARTER'S FINEST HOUR

1. Brookings Middle East Study Group, *Toward Peace in the Middle East* (Washington: Brookings Institution, 1975).

2. *Ibid.*, p. 13.

3. *Department of State Bulletin* (November 7, 1977), 77(2002):639–40.

4. Sidney Drell and Uri Dan, "Untold Story of the Mideast Talks," *New York Times Magazine,* January 21, 1979, p. 20ff.

5. Secretary of State Cyrus Vance, Statement of February 14, 1978, *Department of State Bulletin* (March 1978), 78(2012):37.

6. Jimmy Carter, *Keeping Faith: Memoirs of a President* (New York: Bantam, 1982), pp. 327–403.

7. Drell and Dan claim that the bifurcation of the Sinai issues into a treaty and the other aspects of the Arab–Israeli conflict into a set of guidelines for future negotiations was at first opposed by Brzezinski and the State Department as too much a separate peace between Israel and Egypt that would alienate the rest of the Arab world; and that Carter had to overrule his advisers to save the Camp David process from failure. Part Two of "Untold Story of Mideast Talks," *New York Times Magazine,* January 28, 1979, p. 38.

8. *Ibid.*

9. Camp David accords, Sept. 17, 1978, *Weekly Compilation of Presidential Documents,* 114(38):1523–28.

10. Drell and Dan, Part Two of "Untold Story," p. 38.

11. Treaty signing ceremony, *Weekly Compilation of Presidential Documents,* 15(13):518–22.

20. HOSTAGES IN IRAN

1. Henry Kissinger, *The White House Years* (Boston: Little, Brown, 1979), p. 1262.

2. For U.S. policies toward Iran during World War II see Bruce R. Kuniholm, *The Origins*

of the Cold War in the Near East: Great Power Conflict and Diplomacy in Iran, Turkey, and Greece (Princeton: Princeton University Press, 1980), pp. 130–208.

3. See Barry Rubin, *Paved With Good Intentions: The American Experience in Iran* (New York: Oxford University Press, 1980), especially pp. 29–90.

4. *Ibid.*, pp. 116–23.

5. Kissinger, *The White House Years,* p. 1264.

6. Michael Ledeen and William Lewis, *Debacle: The American Failure in Iran* (New York: Knopf, 1981), p. 51.

7. Kissinger, *The White House Years,* p. 1264.

8. *New York Times,* January 2, 1978.

9. Zbigniew Brzezinski, *Power and Principle: Memoirs of the National Security Adviser 1977–81* (New York: Farrar, Strauss, 1983), pp. 358–78.

10. William H. Sullivan, "Dateline Iran: The Road Not Taken," *Foreign Policy* (Fall 1980), no. 40, pp. 175–86. Compare with Brzezinski, *Power and Principle,* pp. 376–82.

11. Jimmy Carter, news conference, December 7, 1978, in *Weekly Compilation of Presidential Documents,* 14(49):2171–83.

12. Sullivan, "Dateline Iran," p. 184. Compare with Carter, *Keeping Faith,* pp. 443–49.

13. Terrence Smith, "Why Carter Admitted the Shah," *America in Captivity: Points of Decision in the Hostage Crisis* (special issue of *New York Times Magazine,* May 17, 1981), p. 42.

14. Pierre Salinger, *America Held Hostage: The Secret Negotiations* (New York: Doubleday, 1981), pp. 15–17. See also Carter, *Keeping Faith,* p. 452.

15. Henry Kissinger, speech of April 9, 1979, at Harvard Business School dinner, quoted by Terrence Smith, "Why Carter Admitted the Shah," p. 42.

16. Warren Christopher, letter of August 18, 1979, quoted by Salinger, *America Held Hostage,* p. 18.

17. Smith, "Why Carter Admitted the Shah," p. 47. See also Carter, *Keeping Faith,* pp. 454–55.

18. See Salinger, *America Held Hostage,* pp. 26–27.

19. The details of the takeover, unknown by Washington at the time, were reconstructed by journalists on the basis of interviews with the released hostages in early 1981. I have relied principally on the account by Charles Mohr, "Events That Led Up to Takeover of U.S. Embassy on November 4, 1979," *New York Times,* January 21, 1981.

20. Carter, *Keeping Faith,* p. 459.

21. See Carter statement on the American hostage, December 7, 1979, *Weekly Compilation of Presidential Documents,* 15(49):2205.

22. Terrence Smith, "Putting the Hostages' Lives First," *America in Captivity* (special issue of *New York Times Magazine,* May 17, 1981), p. 78

23. The secret proximity talks of mid-November 1979 are described in Smith, "Putting the Hostages' Lives First," pp. 81–82.

24. Salinger, *America Held Hostage,* pp. 169–81.

25. Robert Shalpen, "Eye of the Storm," *The New Yorker* (June 9, 1980), 2:48–49.

26. See Drew Middleton, "Going the Military Route," *America in Captivity* (special issue of *New York Times Magazine*), pp. 103–12; also the accounts in *Time* and *Newsweek* of May 5 and 12, 1980.

27. "Poll: Use of Force in Iran Favored." *Washington Post,* April 20, 1980.

28. The story of the rescue mission has been reconstructed from the material in Carter's *Keeping Faith,* pp. 506–21; Brzezinski's *Power and Principle;* and from numerous journalistic accounts based on Pentagon briefings in the days following the raid. Particularly useful accounts appeared in the *New York Times,* April 27, 1980; *Time* and *Newsweek* April 5, 1980; and the Middleton article in *America in Captivity.*

21. AFGHANISTAN AND THE REASSERTION OF GEOPOLITICAL IMPERATIVES

1. Jimmy Carter, interviewed by Frank Reynolds of ABC News, December 31, 1979; text in *New York Times,* January 1, 1980.

2. The strongest hint of a "linkage" between U.S. support for SALT and Soviet good behavior in the Horn of Africa were Brzezinski's in February 1978. See Strobe Talbott, *Endgame: The Inside Story of SALT II* (New York: Harper and Row, 1979), pp. 146–47.

3. Carter, address at Wake Forest University, March 17, 1978, in *Weekly Compilation of Presidential Documents,* 14(12):529–35.

4. Carter, commencement address at the United States Naval Academy, Annapolis, Maryland, June 7, 1978, in *Weekly Compilation of Presidential Documents,* 14(23):1052–57.

5. Carter, television address, January 4, 1980, in *Weekly Compilation of Presidential Documents,* 16(2):25–27.

6. Carter, State of the Union Address, January 23, 1980, in *Weekly Compilation of Presidential Documents,* 16(4):194–203. Quote at p. 197.

22. HIGH PURPOSE AND GRAND STRATEGY

1. Ronald Reagan, Inaugural Address, January 20, 1981, in *Weekly Compilation of Presidential Documents,* 17(4):1–5.

2. Richard Halloran, "Reagan Aide Tells of New Strategy on Soviet Threat," *New York Times,* May 22, 1982; Saul Friedman, "Reagan Calls for Pressure on USSR," *Boston Globe,* May 22, 1982.

3. Richard Halloran, "Pentagon Draws up First Strategy for Fighting a Long Nuclear War," *New York Times,* May 30, 1982.

4. Ronald Reagan, *An American Life* (New York: Simon and Schuster, 1990), p. 267.

5. *Ibid.,* p. 268.

6. Ronald Reagan, statement on sanctions being applied to the Soviet Union, in *Weekly Compilation of Presidential Documents,* 17(53):1429–30.

7. Margaret Thatcher, remarks to the British House of Commons, July 1, 1982, quoted by James Feron, "Mrs. Thatcher Faults U.S. on Siberia Pipeline," *New York Times,* July 2, 1982.

8. Judith Miller, "Curb Sought on Equipment for Soviet," *New York Times,* October 2, 1982.

9. Ronald Reagan, press conference of January 29, 1981, in *Weekly Compilation of Presidential Documents,* 17(5):64–72.

10. Ronald Reagan, Address to Members of the British Parliament, Palace of Westminister, June 8, 1982, in *ibid.,* 18(23):764–770.

11. Ronald Reagan, address before the National Association of Evangelicals, Orlando Florida, March 8, 1983, in *Weekly Compilation of Presidential Documents,* 19(10):364–70. Lou Canon reports that Reagan's speechwriter for both the London and Orlando speeches, Anthony Dolan, was considered by the President's more pragmatic advisers to be "a wild man . . . far to the right of Reagan." But Canon correctly observes that the speeches faithfully reflected Reagan's longstanding views and points out that the President took an active role in editing the drafts. See Lou Canon, *President Reagan: The Role of a Lifetime* (New York: Simon and Schuster, 1991), p. 317.

12. Ronald Reagan, address to the nation, March 23, 1983, U.S. Department of State, *Current Policy,* no. 472. Full text also in *Weekly Compilation of Presidential Documents,* 19(12):442–48.

13. Reagan, *An American Life,* p. 550.

14. Lou Canon, *President Reagan,* pp. 287–91.

15. On the origins of the Strategic Defense Initiative, see Janne E. Nolan, *Guardians of the Arsenal: The Politics of Nuclear Strategy* (New York: Basic Books, 1989).

16. Canon, *President Reagan,* pp. 323–33.

17. Nolan, *Guardians of the Arsenal,* pp. 175–82.

18. Ronald Reagan, speech to the National Space Club, March 29, 1985, excerpts in U.S. Congress Office of Technology Assessment, *Ballistic Missile Defense Technologies,* OTA-ISC-254 (Washington: GPO, September 1985), p. 298.

19. Paul Nitze, speech to Philadelphia World Affairs Council, February 20, 1985, excepts in *Ballistic Missile Defense Technologies,* p. 301.

20. Joseph E. Persico, *Casey: From the OSS to the CIA* (New York: Viking, 1990), p. 264.

21. Ronald Reagan, State of the Union address, February 6, 1985, *Public Papers of the Presidents of the United States: Ronald Reagan, 1985* (Washington: GPO, 1988), p. 135.

22. Ronald Reagan, remarks at Bitburg Air Base, May 5, 1985, quoted by Jeane J. Kirkpatrick and Allan Gerson, "The Reagan Doctrine, Human Rights, and International Law," in Louis Henkin, Stanley Hoffmann, Jeane J. Kirkpatrick, Allan Gerson, William D. Rogers, and David J. Scheffer, *Right v. Might: International Law and the Use of Force* (New York: Council on Foreign Relations, 1989), p. 22.

23. Jeane J. Kirkpatrick, "Dictatorship and Double Standards," originally in the November 1979 issue of *Commentary,* reprinted in her *Dictatorship and Double Standards: Rationalism and Reason in Politics* (New York: Simon & Schuster for the American Enterprise Institute, 1982), pp. 23–52, extended quote from pp. 29–30.

24. Kirkpatrick, "Dictatorships and Double Standards," pp. 41–42.

25. *Ibid.,* pp. 49–51.

26. *Ibid.,* p. 52.

27. Jeane J. Kirkpatrick, "The Reagan Doctrine II": Address before the National Press Club, Washington, DC, May 30, 1985. Reprinted in Jeane J. Kirkpatrick, *Legitimacy and Force: Political and Moral Dimensions* (New Brunswick: Transaction Books, 1988), 1:432–39.

28. On disputes within the administration over publicizing the Reagan Doctrine, see Constantine Menges, *Inside the National Security Council* (New York: Simon and Schuster, 1988), pp. 243–49.

29. Ronald Reagan, news conference, February 11, 1986, in *Weekly Compilation of Presidential Documents,* 22(7):211–18.

30. Canon, *President Reagan,* p. 364.

31. On Reagan's reluctant eleventh-hour abandonment of Marcos, see Stanley Karnow, *In Our Image: America's Empire in the Philippines* (New York: Random House, 1989), pp. [complete cite].

23. THE TENSION BETWEEN FOREIGN AND DOMESTIC IMPERATIVES

1. Ronald Reagan, address to the Board of Governors of the World Bank and International Monetary Fund, September 29, 1981, in *Weekly Compilation of Presidential Documents,* 17(40):1052–55.

2. David A. Stockman, The Triumph of Politics: Why the Reagan Revolution Failed (New York: Harper & Row, 1986).

3. A dispassionate analysis of the differences and similarities in economic philosophy among Reagan's economic advisers is provided by William A. Niskanen, *Reaganomics: An Insider's*

Account of the Policies and the People (New York: Oxford University Press, 1988). Niskanen was a member of the Council of Economic Advisers from April 1981 through March 1985.

4. *Ibid.*, p. 286.

5. Stockman, The Triumph of Politics, p. 76.

6. *Ibid.*, p. 376–94; quotes from p. 377.

7. Laurence I. Barrett, *Gambling with History: Reagan in the White House* (New York: Penguin, 1984), pp. 175–76.

8. Stockman, *The Triumph of Politics*, pp. 290–91.

9. *Ibid.*, p. 296.

10. *Ibid.*, p. 299.

11. Benjamin Friedman, *Day of Reckoning*, (New York: Random House, 1988), p. 274.

12. Niskanen, *Reaganomics*, pp. 33–34.

13. Donald T. Regan, *For the Record: From Wall Street to Washington* (New York: Harcourt Brace Janovich, 1988), pp. 153–59, 293–99.

14. Niskanen, *Reaganomics*, p. 176–77.

15. See I. M. Destler, *American Trade Politics: System Under Stress* (Washington: Institute for International Economics, 1986), pp. 100–109.

16. Clyde V. Prestowitz, Jr., *Trading Places: How We Allowed Japan to Take the Lead* (New York: Basic Books, 1988), p. 253.

17. Ronald Reagan, remarks to business leaders and members of the President's Export Council and the advisory committee for trade negotiations, September 23, 1985, in *Weekly Compilation of Presidential Documents*, 21(39):1128–31.

18. Robert B. Reich, "The Economics of Illusion and the Illusion of Economics," *Foreign Affairs*, 66(3):520–21.

19. *Ibid.*, pp. 522–23.

20. Michael Howard, "A European Perspective on the Reagan Years," *Foreign Affairs*, 66(3):478–93, quote from p. 492.

24. MIDDLE EASTERN COMPLEXITIES: THE ARAB—ISRAELI CONFLICT, TERRORISM, AND ARMS FOR HOSTAGES

1. Alexander M. Haig, Jr., *Caveat: Realism, Reagan, and Foreign Policy* (New York: Macmillan, 1984), pp. 169–70.

2. Ronald Reagan, news conference of June 16, 1981, in *Weekly Compilation of Presidential Documents*, 17(25):632–41.

3. Congressional Quarterly, *The Middle East* (Washington: Congressional Quarterly, 1990), p. 58.

4. *Ibid.*, pp. 76–78.

5. Ronald Reagan, *An American Life* (New York: Simon & Schuster, 1990), p. 411.

6. *Ibid.*, p. 415. Steven L. Spiegal, *The Other Arab–Israeli Conflict: Making America's Middle East Policy, from Truman to Reagan* (Chicago: University of Chicago Press, 1985), p. 410, credits reports that Reagan was misinformed about the intensity of Begin's lobbying efforts in Congress during his September 1981 visit.

7. Reagan, *An American Life*, p. 416.

8. Congressional Quarterly, *The Middle East*, p. 59; Spiegel, *The Other Arab–Israeli Conflict*, p. 410.

9. Haig, *Caveat*, p. 328.

10. *Ibid.*, pp. 326–27.

11. *Ibid.*, p. 335.

12. *Ibid.*, p. 342.

13. Michael Deaver, *Behind the Scenes* (New York: William Morrow, 1987), p. 166.

14. Caspar W. Weinberger, *Fighting for Peace: Seven Critical Years in the Pentagon* (New York: Warner Books, 1990), pp. 143–44.

15. Ronald Reagan address on U.S. policy for peace in the Middle East, September 1, 1982, in *Weekly Compilation of Presidential Documents*, 18(35):1081–85.

16. Weinberger, *Fighting for Peace*, pp. 151–52.

17. General James Vesey quoted by David C. Martin and John Walcott, *Best Laid Plans: The Inside Story of America's War Against Terrorism* (New York: Harper and Row, 1988), p. 97.

18. Weinberger, *Fighting for Peace*, p. 160.

19. Congressional Quarterly, *The Middle East*, p. 61.

20. *Report of the DOD Commission on Beirut International Airport Terrorist Act, October 23, 1983* (Washington: Department of Defense, 1983), p. 32.

21. Reagan, *An American Life*, pp. 437, 458.

22. *Ibid.*, p. 458.

23. Ronald Reagan, address to the nation, October 27, 1983, in *Weekly Compilation of Presidential Documents*, 19(43):1500–1502.

24. *Report of the DOD Commission on Beirut International Airport Terrorist Act, October 23, 1983*, p. 134.

25. Canon, *President Reagan*, pp. 456–57.

26. Reagan remarks at White House ceremony on January 27, 1981, in *Weekly Compilation of Presidential Documents*, 17(5):49–52.

27. Alexander Haig, press conference of January 28, 1981, *New York Times*, January 29, 1981.

28. *Ibid.*

29. Haig, *Caveat, passim.*

30. *Weekly Compilation of Presidential Documents*, 17(5):50–66.

31. Press interviews of Secretary Haig, March 13–28, 1981, in *Department of State Bulletin*, 81(2050):1–17.

32. President Reagan's remarks quoted by Mary McGrory, "The Price of Retaliation," *Boston Globe*, June 21, 1985.

33. Secretary of State George Shultz, "Terrorism and the Modern World," address before the Park Avenue Synagogue, New York, October 25, 1984, Department of State, *Current Policy* no. 629.

34. *Ibid.*

35. *Ibid.*

36. Bernard Gwertzman, "Bush Challenges Shultz's Position on Terror Policy," *New York Times*, October 27, 1984.

37. Secretary of Defense Caspar Weinberger, address to the National Press Club, Washington, D.C., November 28, 1984, text in his *Fighting for Peace*, pp.443–45.

38. George P. Shultz, *Turmoil and Triumph: My Years as Secretary of State* (New York: Scribners, 1993), p. 650.

39. Martin and Walcott, *Best Laid Plans*, pp. 161–202.

40. Jane Mayer and Doyle McManus, *Landslide: The Unmaking of the President 1984–1988* (Boston: Houghton Mifflin, 1988), pp. 94–96.

41. Ronald Reagan announcement of hostage release, June 30, 1985, in *Weekly Compilation of Presidential Documents*, 21(27):866–67.

42. Reagan, speech before the American Bar Association, July 8, 1985, in *Weekly Compilation of Presidential Documents*, 21(27):876–82.

43. Bob Schieffer and Gary Paul Gates, *The Acting President* (New York: Dutton, 1989), p. 233.

44. *Report of the Congressional Committees Investigating the Iran–Contra Affair: Abridged Edition* (New York: Times Books, 1988) p. 150. See also Shultz, *Turmoil and Triumph*, p. 785.

45. *The Tower Commission Report: The Full Text of the President's Special Review Board* (New York: Bantam Books and Times Books, 1987), pp. 217–18.

46. Larry Speakes, *Speaking Out: The Reagan Presidency from Inside the White House* (New York: Avon Books, 1989), pp. 342–54.

47. Reagan address to the nation, November 13, 1986, in *Weekly Compilation of Presidential Documents*, 22(46):1559–61.

48. President Reagan, news conference, November 19, 1986, in *Weekly Compilation of Presidential Documents*, 22(47):1583–90.

49. Speakes, *Speaking Out*, p. 365.

50. Gary Wills, *Reagan's America* (New York: Penguin, 1988), quote from the epilogue in this edition, p. 476.

51. My rendering of the *Achille Lauro* incident relies heavily on the detailed account by Martin and Walcott, *Best Laid Plans*, pp. 235–57.

52. President Reagan, remarks on the *Achille Lauro* hijacking, in *Weekly Compilation of Presidential Documents*, 21(41):1234–37.

53. Mayer and McManus, *Landslide*, p. 140.

54. Reagan news conference, January 7, 1986, in *Weekly Compilation of Presidential Documents*, 22(1):22–29.

55. On the lack of conclusive evidence that the Libyans were directly involved in the La Belle disco bombing, see Seymour M. Hersh, "Target Qaddafi," *New York Times* Magazine, February 22, 1987, pp. 17ff.

56. *Ibid.*

57. Martin and Walcott, *Best Laid Plans*, pp. 309–11.

58. Ronald Reagan address to the nation, April 14, 1986, in *Weekly Compilation of Presidential Documents*, 22(16):491–92.

59. *Ibid.*

60. Admiral Crowe quoted by Martin and Walcott, *Best Laid Plans*, p. 313.

25. CONTRADICTIONS IN LATIN AMERICA

1. Special Report on Communist Involvement in the Insurrection in El Salvador, *Department of State Bulletin*, 81(2048):1–11.

2. Quoted in The Lawyers Committee for International Human Rights, "The Case of Four U.S. Churchwomen Murdered in December 1980," New York (1984, processed). Much of my documentation on the Reagan administration's policies toward El Salvador relies on Eran Rafael, *The Reagan Administration's Attitude Toward Human Rights Violations in El Salvador 1981–1983* (Waltham: Brandeis University, 1991)—a senior honors thesis written under my guidance.

3. *Ibid.*

4. Ronald Reagan, news conference of March 6, 1981, in *Weekly Compilation of Presidential Documents*, 17(10):246–50.

5. Assistant Secretary of State Thomas Enders, "U.S. Policy Options in El Salvador," *Hearings and Markup Before the Committee on Foreign Affairs*, September 24, 1981, 97th Congress, 2nd session (Washington: GPO, 1982), p. 15.

6. Report on Haig's testimony in the *New York Times*, March 29, 1981.

7. Jeane Kirkpatrck, quoted in Marvin Gettlemen, Patrick Lacefield, Louis Menashe, David Mermelstein, Ronald Radosh, eds., *El Salvador: Central America in the New Cold War* (New York: Grove Press, 1981), pp. 344–45.

8. Presidential Certification of El Salvador, U.S. Congress, Hearing Before the Subcommittee on Inter-American Affairs, February 2, 23, 25 and March 2, 1982 (Washington: GPO, 1982), p. 2.

9. Cited by Cynthia J. Arnson, *Crossroad: Congress, the Reagan Administration, and Central America* (New York: Pantheon, 1989), p. 84.

10. *New York Times,* February 4, 1982.

11. Tom Buckley, *Violent Neighbors: El Salvador, Central America, and the United States* (New York: Times Books, 1984), p. 28.

12. Eran Rafael, *The Reagan Administration's Attitude Toward Human Rights Violations in El Salvador,* pp. 35–36.

13. George Bush, toast at dinner in San Salvador, December 1983, text of remarks in Robert S. Leiken and Barry Rubin, eds., *The Central American Crisis Reader* (New York: Summit Books, 1987), pp. 546–47.

14. Organization of American States, *Annual Report of the Inter-American Commission on Human Rights, 1984–1985* (Washington, D.C.: OAS, 1985), p. 141.

15. Ronald Reagan, address before the British Parliament, June 8, 1982 in *Weekly Compilation of Presidential Documents,* 18(23):764–770.

16. Letter from the President to the Speaker of the House of Representatives and the President Pro Tempore of the Senate, October 25, 1983, in *Weekly Compilation of Presidential Documents,* 19(17):1493–94.

17. Ronald Reagan, address to the nation, October 27, 1983, in *Weekly Compilation of Presidential Documents,* 19(17):1501.

18. Reagan, *An American Life,* pp. 456–57.

19. My information on the Grenada invasion relies heavily on Robert Pastor, "The Invasion of Grenada: A Pre- and Post-Mortem," in Scott B. MacDonald, Harold M. Sandstrom, and Paul B. Goodwin, eds., *The Caribbean After Grenada: Revolution, Conflict, and Democracy* (New York: Praeger, 1988), pp. 87–105. The Pastor essay is an update of his testimony before House Committee on Foreign Affairs, *Hearings: U.S. Military Actions in Grenada: Implications for U.S. Policy in the Eastern Caribbean,* November 2, 3, 16, 1983, pp. 72–102.

20. British report quoted by Pastor, "The Invasion of Grenada," p. 88.

21. Pastor, pp. 92–95.

22. Reagan, *An American Life,* pp. 457–58.

23. Ronald Reagan, address to the nation, October 27, 1983, in *Weekly Compilation of Presidential Documents,* 19(17):1502–03.

24. On the bureaucratic infighting by and against Thomas Enders, see Roy Gutman, *Banana Diplomacy: The Making of American Policy in Nicaragua 1981–1987* (New York: Simon and Schuster, 1988). See also Constantine Menges, *Inside the National Security Council* (New York: Simon and Schuster, 1988).

25. U.S. Congress, Iran-Contra Report, [publication title and date] pp. 31–32. See also Theodore Draper, *A Very Thin Line: The Iran-Contra Affairs* (New York: Hill and Wang, 1991), p. 16.

26. For Reagan April 1983 quotes on adhering to the law, see U.S. Congress, Iran-Contra Report, p. 33.

27. Ronald Reagan, address to the Congress, April 27, 1983, in *Weekly Compilation of Presidential Documents,* 19(17):608–14.

28. U.S. Congress, Iran-Contra Report, p. 36.

29. Senator Goldwater's letter to Casey was later published in the *Congressional Record,* March 3, 1988, p. S 1865. Theodore Draper, *A Very Thin Line,* p. 20–21, quotes it in full.

30. U.S. Congress, Iran-Contra Report, p. 41.

31. McFarlane, quoted by Draper, *A Very Thin Line,* p. 30.

32. The information on the "third country" and private financial contributions is from U.S. Congress, Iran-Contra Report, pp. 37–103.

33. U.S. Congress, Iran Contra Report, p. 327.

34. George Shultz, October 7, 1986, quoted in U.S. Congress, Iran-Contra Report, p. 145.

35. Ronald Reagan, news conference, October 8, 1986, in *Weekly Compilation of Presidential Documents,* 22(41):1348–49.

36. Congressman Foley's exchange with Fawn Hall that elicited her "above the law" statement is quoted by Haynes Johnson, *Sleepwalking Through History* (New York: Norton, 1991), p. 359.

37. Ronald Reagan, news conference statement of November 25, 1986, in *Weekly Compilation of Presidential Documents,* 22(48):1604–05.

38. Attorney General Edwin Meese, news conference remarks of November 25, 1986, quoted by Draper, *A Very Thin Line,* p. 543.

26. THE REAGAN–GORBACHEV SYMBIOSIS

1. Ronald Reagan, radio-TV address on Soviet-American relations, January 16, 1984, in *Weekly Compilation of Presidential Documents,* 20(3):40–45.

2. *Ibid.*

3. The Pentagon's basic assessment as of early 1984 of the Soviet threat and U.S. policies needed to counter it are found in Caspar W. Weinberger, "Annual Report to the Congress, Fiscal Year 1985, February 1, 1984" (Department of Defense publication).

4. Ronald Reagan, State of the Union address, January 24, 1984, in *Weekly Compilation of Presidential Documents,* 20(4):92–93.

5. John Newhouse, *War and Peace in the Nuclear Age* (New York: Knopf, 1989), pp. 373–74.

6. Michael K. Deaver, *Behind the Scenes* (New York: William Morrow, 1987), p. 39.

7. Ronald Reagan, address before the 39th session of the United Nations General Assembly, September 24, 1984, in *Weekly Compilation of Presidential Documents,* 20(39):1352–58.

8. Deaver, *Behind the Scenes,* p. 120.

9. Nancy Reagan, *My Turn: The Memoirs of Nancy Reagan* (New York: Random House, 1989), 336–37.

10. Donald T. Regan, *For the Record: From Wall Street to Washington* (New York: Harcourt Brace Jovanovich, 1988), pp. 296–99.

11. Larry Speakes, *Speaking Out: The Presidency from Inside the White House* (New York: Avon Books, 1988), pp. 159–60.

12. Ronald Reagan, *An American Life* (New York: Simon and Schuster, 1990), p. 12.

13. *Ibid.,* p. 634.

14. Joint statement of Ronald Reagan and Mikhail Gorbachev at the United States—USSR summit in Geneva, November 21, 1985, in *Weekly Compilation of Presidential Documents,* 21(47):1422–24.

15. Speakes, *Speaking Out,* p. 173.

16. Regan, *For the Record,* pp. 112–13.

17. Nancy Reagan, *My Turn,* pp. 342–43.

18. Reagan, *An American Life,* pp. 707, 712.

19. Speakes, *Speaking Out,* p. 173.

20. Regan, *For the Record,* p. 344.

21. *Ibid.,* pp. 338–41.

22. Newhouse, *War and Peace in the Nuclear Age,* p. 394–95.

23. My summary of Gorbachev's opening proposal at Reykjavik relies heavily on Strobe

Talbott's account in *The Master of the Game: Paul Nitze and the Nuclear Peace* (New York: Knopf, 1988), pp. 315–16.

24. Regan, *For the Record*, p. 350. See also Newhouse, *War and Peace in the Nuclear Age*, pp. 395–96; Jane Mayer and Doyle McManus, *Landslide: The Unmasking of the President 1984–1988* (Boston: Houghton Mifflin, 1988), p. 283.

25. Reagan, *An American Life*, p. 677.

26. Regan, *For the Record*, pp. 351–52.

27. Speakes, *Speaking Out*, p. 183.

28. Reagan, *An American Life*, p. 675.

29. Regan, *For the Record*, p. 336.

30. James Schlesinger, "Reykjavik and Revelations: A Turn of the Tide?" *Foreign Affairs* 65(3):434.

31. Newhouse, *War and Peace in the Nuclear Age*, p. 398.

32. Ronald Reagan, remarks at the Brandenburg Gate, Berlin, June 12, 1987, in *Weekly Compilation of Presidential Documents*, 23(24):657–61.

33. Reagan, *An American Life*, p. 683.

34. Michael E. Gordon, "Negotiating the Arms Treaty: Verification Issue Proved Thorny," *New York Times*, January 28, 1988. See also Newhouse, *War and Peace in the Nuclear Age*, pp. 400–401.

35. Remarks on signing the treaty eliminating intermediate-range and shorter-range nuclear missiles, December 8, 1987, in *Weekly Compilation of Presidential Documents*, 23(49):1458.

36. *Ibid.*

37. Reagan, *An American Life*, pp. 707–708.

38. *Ibid.*, p. 708.

27. PRESIDING OVER THE END OF THE COLD WAR

1. Michael Beschloss and Strobe Talbott, *At the Highest Levels: The Inside Story of the End of the Cold War* (Boston: Little, Brown, 1993), pp. 3–4.

2. Mikhail Gorbachev, Address at the Plenary Meeting of the 43rd Session of the United Nations General Assembly, December 7, 1988 (Washington: Embassy of the USSR, 1988).

3. Beschloss and Talbott, *At the Highest Levels*, pp. 13.

4. Brent Scowcroft on "This Week," American Broadcasting Company, January 22, 1989.

5. George Bush, news conference, January 27, 1989, in *Weekly Compilation of Presidential Documents*, 25(4):121.

6. Scowcroft on "This Week," January 22, 1989.

7. Bush, commencement address as Texas A&M University, May 12, 1989, in *Weekly Compilation of Presidential Documents*, 25(20):699–702.

8. Fitzwater quoted by Beschloss and Talbott, *At The Highest Levels*, p. 73.

9. *Ibid.*, p. 74.

10. Bush, remarks at Mainz, West Germany, May 31, 1989, in *Weekly Compilation of Presidential Documents*, 25(22):812–16.

11. Roger E. Kanet and Brian V. Souders, "Poland and the Soviet Union," in Richard F. Staar, ed., *East-Central Europe and the USSR* (New York: St. Martin's Press, 1991), pp. 125–45.

12. Beschloss and Talbott, *At The Highest Levels*, pp. 85–88.

13. Karl Kaiser, "Germany's Reunification," *Foreign Affairs* 70(1):179–205; and Robert

Gerald Livingston, "Relinquishment of East Germany," in Staar, ed., *East-Central Europe and the USSR*, pp. 82–84.

14. Livingston, "Relinquishment of East Germany," p. 86.

15. Kaiser, "Germany's Unification," *Foreign Affairs* 70(1):179–205.

16. See Seyom Brown, "Explaining the Transformation of World Politics," *International Journal*, 46(2):207–19.

17. Graham Allison and Robert Blackwill, "America's Stake in the Soviet Future," *Foreign Affairs*, 70(3):77–97.

18. Beschloss and Talbott, *At the Highest Levels*, pp. 411–15.

19. Bush, address to the Ukrainian Supreme Soviet, August 1, 1991, in *Weekly Compilation of Presidential Documents*, 27(31):1093–96.

20. Bush, exchange with reporters in Kennebunkport, August 19, 1991, in *Weekly Compilation of Presidential Documents*, 27(34):1154–58.

21. *Ibid.*

22. Bush, statement on the attempted coup in the Soviet Union, in *Weekly Compilation of Presidential Documents*, 27(34):1159–60.

23. Bush, news conference of August 20, 1991, in *Weekly Compilation of Presidential Documents*, 27(34):1160–66.

24. Bush, address to the nation, December 25, 1991, in *Weekly Compilation of Presidential Documents*, 27(52):1883–85.

28. GEORGE BUSH AND THE RESORT TO MILITARY POWER

1. Kevin Buckley, *Panama: The Whole Story* (New York: Simon & Schuster, 1991), p. 146–57; Dole quote at p. 147.

2. *Ibid.*, pp. 155–56.

3. Bob Woodward, *The Commanders* (New York: Simon & Schuster, 1991), pp.86–87.

4. George Bush, news conference of May 11, 1989, in *Weekly Compilation of Presidential Documents*, 25(19):689–91.

5. George Bush, interview with White House press corps aboard Air Force One, May 13, 1989, in *Weekly Compilation of Presidential Documents*, 25(20):706–710.

6. Buckley, *Panama*, pp. 197–208; Woodward, *The Commanders*, pp. 119–25.

7. Fitzwater statement, quoted by Woodward, *The Commanders*, p. 125.

8. George Bush, exchange with reporters, October 6, 1989, in *Weekly Compilation of Presidential Documents*, 25(40):1514–15.

9. George Bush, News Conference, October 13, 1989, in *Weekly Compilation of Presidential Documents*, 25(41):1541–43.

10. Woodward, *The Commanders*, pp. 156–74.

11. George Bush, address to the nation, December 20, 1989, in *Weekly Compilation of Presidential Documents*, 25(51):1974–75.

12. *Ibid.*

13. Tom Wicker, "What Price Panama?" *New York Times*, June 18, 1990.

14. Woodward, *The Commanders*, pp. 190–95; see also Buckley, *Panama*, p. 253.

15. United Nations General Assembly Resolution 44.240, adopted 29 December 1989.

16. Bush statement on post-invasion aid to Panama quoted in *New York Times*, January 26, 1990.

17. John Weeks, "Panama: Still Teetering on the Verge of Anarchy," *Boston Globe*, March 26, 1990; Howard W. French, "Noriega's Troops Now Form Police With U.S. Aid, Panamanians Say," *New York Times*, July 24, 1990.

18. Jean Edward Smith, *George Bush's War* (New York: Holt, 1992), pp. 44–45.

19. *Ibid.*, pp. 52–57.

20. Leslie Gelb, "Mr. Bush's Fateful Blunder," *New York Times,* July 17, 1991.

21. Michael R. Gordon, "Pentagon Objected to a Message Bush Sent Iraq Before Its Invasion," *New York Times*, October 25, 1992.

22. Quoted by Smith, *Mr. Bush's War*, pp. 59–60.

23. United Nations Security Council Resolution 660, August 2, 1990 *United Nations Security Council Resolutions Related to the Crisis in the Gulf* (United Nations: Department of Public Information DP/1104-41090, November 1990), p. 3.

24. Bob Woodward, *The Commanders*, p. 229; see also U.S. News and World Report, *Triumph Without Victory* (New York: Times Books, 1992), pp. 49–51.

25. Lawrence Freedman and Efraim Karsh, *The Gulf Conflict 1990–1991: Diplomacy and War in the New World Order* (Princeton: Princeton University Press, 1993), p. 74.

26. George Bush, remarks and exchange with reporters, August 6, 1990, in *Weekly Compilation of Presidential Documents*, 26(32):1214–15.

27. George Bush, address to the nation announcing the deployment of United States armed forces to Saudi Arabia and follow-up news conference, August 8, 1990, in *Weekly Compilation of Presidential Documents*, 26(32):1216–23.

28. Beschloss and Talbott, *At the Highest Levels*, pp. 244–248.

29. Resolution 661, August 6, 1990, *United Nations Security Council Resolutions Relating to the Crisis in the Gulf*, pp. 3–4.

30. A selection of remarks on the Persian Gulf situation by President George Bush from August 5 through August 10, 1990, in *Weekly Compilation of Presidential Documents*, 26(32):1207–26.

31. Beschloss and Talbott, *At the Highest Levels*, pp. 250–51.

32. Resolution 665, August 25, 1990, *United Nations Security Council Resolutions Relating to the Crisis in the Gulf*, pp. 5–6.

33. Elaine Sciolino, "How U.S. Got U.N. Backing for Use of Force in the Gulf," *New York Times*, August 30, 1990.

34. Freedman and Karsh, *The Gulf Conflict*, pp. 97–98.

35. Statement by President Bush on Syria's cooperation, quoted by Smith, *George Bush's War*, p. 153.

36. Freedman and Karsh, *The Gulf Conflict*, p. 101.

37. Beschloss and Talbott, *At the Highest Levels*, p. 259.

38. *Ibid.*, pp. 260–65.

39. George Bush, news conference on the Persian Gulf crisis, November 8, 1990, in *Weekly Compilation of Presidential Documents*, 26(45):1789–95; quote from p. 1790.

40. *Ibid.*, p. 1791.

41. Smith, *George Bush's War*, p. 215.

42. Resolution 678, November 29, 1990, *United Nations Security Council Resolutions Relating to the Crisis in the Gulf* (Supplement to report cited in note 23).

43. Freedman and Karsh, *The Gulf Conflict*, p. 233.

44. Presidential news conference, November 30, 1990, in *Weekly Compilation of Presidential Documents*, 26(48):1948–56.

45. *Ibid.*

46. Freedman and Karsh, *The Gulf Conflict*, p. 241.

47. Woodward, *The Commanders*, p. 345.

48. Freedman and Karsh, *The Gulf Conflict*, pp. 254–60.

49. Joint Congressional Resolution of January 12, 1991. Text published as Appendix B in U.S. News and World Report, *Triumph Without Victory*, pp. 449–50.

50. Woodward, *The Commanders,* pp. 366–67.

51. George Bush, address to the nation announcing Allied military action in the Persian Gulf, January 16, 1991, in *Weekly Compilation of Presidential Documents,* 27(3):50–52.

52. Freedman and Karsh, *The Gulf Conflict,* p. 409.

53. Michael Duffy and Dan Goodgame, *Marching in Place: The Status Quo Presidency of George Bush* (New York: Simon & Schuster, 1992), pp. 150–51.

54. United Nations Security Council Resolution 687, April 3, 1991, *United Nations Resolutions Relating to the Crisis in the Gulf.*

55. United Nations Security Council Resolution 668, April 5, 1991, *ibid.*

56. George Bush, speech at Maxwell Air Force Base, April 13, 1991, and news conference of April 16, 1991, in *Weekly Compilation of Presidential Documents,* 27(16):431–35, 444–50.

57. *Ibid.,* at pp. 447–48.

58. Reports and excerpts from Bush's remarks on January 14, 1993, *New York Times,* January 14, 1993.

59. Michael R. Gordon, "Somali Aid Plan is Called Most Ambitious Option," *New York Times,* November 28, 1992.

60. United Nations Security Council Resolution, December 3, 1992, in *New York Times,* December 4, 1992.

61. President George Bush, address of December 4, 1992 on decision to deploy U.S. troops to Somalia, in *New York Times,* December 5, 1992.

62. President George Bush, speech at West Point Military Academy, January 5, 1993, Cable News Network Transcript (#107–1).

29. THE NEW WORLD ORDER

1. George Bush, address before joint session of the Congress, September 11, 1990, in *Weekly Compilation of Presidential Documents,* 26(37):1358–62, quote at p. 1359.

2. George Bush, address before joint session of the Congress on cessation of the Persian Gulf conflict, March 6, 1991, in *Weekly Compilation of Presidential Documents,* 27(10):257–60, quote at p. 259.

3. George Bush, statement on the Chinese government suppression of student demonstrations, June 3, 1989, in *Weekly Compilation of Presidential Documents,* 25(23):838–39.

4. Bush statement quoted by Michael Duffy and Dan Goodgame, *Marching in Place: The Status Quo Presidency of George Bush* (New York: Simon & Schuster, 1992), p. 182.

5. George Bush, news conference, June 5, 1989, in *Weekly Compilation of Presidential Documents,* 25(23):839–43.

6. Duffy and Goodgame, *Marching in Place,* p. 183.

7. Robert S. Ross, "U. S. Policy Toward China," in Robert J. Art and Seyom Brown, eds., *U.S. Foreign Policy: The Search for a New Role* (New York: Macmillan, 1993), pp. 338–57.

8. Presidential debate in St. Louis, October 11, 1992, in *Weekly Compilation of Presidential Documents,* 28(42):1914–15.

9. U.S. statement on the situation in Yugoslavia, May 24, 1991, quoted in Morton H. Halperin, David J. Scheffer, Patricia L. Small, *Self Determination in the New World Order* (Washington, D.C.: Carnegie Endowment for International Peace, 1992), p. 33.

10. United Nations Security Council Resolution 757, May 30, 1992, text in U.S. Department of State *Dispatch,* 3(23):448–50.

11. Lawrence Eagleburger, interview on MacNeil/Lehrer News Hour August 28, 1992, text in U.S. Department of State *Dispatch,* 3(7):13.

12. *Ibid.*

13. I. M. Destler, *American Trade Politics* (Washington, D.C.: Institute for International Economics, 1992), pp. 208–209.

14. Duffy and Goodgame, *Marching in Place*, pp. 243–44.

15. Destler, *American Trade Politics*, p. 209.

16. George Bush, remarks on trade agreement, August 12, 1992, in *Weekly Compilation of Presidential Documents*, 28(33):1421–24.

17. Richard Elliot Benedick, *Ozone Diplomacy: New Directions in Safeguarding the Planet* (Cambridge: Harvard University Press, 1991), pp. 30–31.

18. Keith Schneider, "White House Snubs U.S. Envoy's Plea to Sign Rio Treaty," *New York Times*, June 5, 1991.

19. Edward A. Parson, Peter M. Haas, Marc A. Levy, "A Summary of Major Documents Signed at the Earth Summit and the Global Forum," *Environment*, 34(8):12f.

20. Steven Greenhouse, "Ecology, the Economy and Bush," *New York Times*, June 14, 1992.

21. George Bush, address at the earth summit in Rio, June 12, 1992, in *Weekly Compilation of Presidential Documents*, 28(25):1043–44.

22. William Reilly, mid-July, 1992 memo to EPA employees, quoted in Richard N. Gardner, *Negotiating Survival: Four Priorities After Rio* (New York: Council on Foreign Relations, 1992), p. 13.

23. START II: Treaty Between the United States of America and the Russian Federation on the Further Reduction and Limitation of Strategic Offensive Arms, text and analysis in *Arms Control Today* 23(1) Supplement, p. 1–8.

24. Remarks at the START II signing ceremony on January 3, 1993 in Moscow, *New York Times*, January 4, 1993.

30. FROM DOMESTIC POLITICIAN TO GEOPOLITICIAN

1. Bill Clinton address to the diplomatic corps, Washington, D.C., January 18, 1993 in *Department of State Dispatch* (February 1, 1993) 4(5):57–58.

2. Warren Christopher, speech before the Chicago Council on Foreign Relations, March 22, 1993, in the *New York Times*, March 23, 1993.

3. *Ibid.*

4. New York Times/CBS News Poll, *New York Times*, April 2, 1993.

5. President Clinton address in Annapolis, April 1, 1993, to the American Society of Newspaper Editors, in *Weekly Compilation of Presidential Documents*, 29(13):508–10.

6. Gwen Ifill, "President Urges America to Back Help for Moscow," *New York Times*, April 2, 1993.

7. David E. Sanger, "Seven Nations Pledge $28 Billion Fund to Assist Russia," *New York Times*, April 16, 1993; Gwen Ifill, "Seven Nations Hasten to Aid Russia: Will Push for Growth and Trade," *New York Times*, April 9, 1993.

8. Elaine Sciolino, "Clinton Reaffirms Policy on Yeltsin," *New York Times*, December 16, 1963.

9. Michael R. Gordon, "U.S. Opposes Move to Rapidly Expand NATO Membership," *New York Times*,' January 2, 1994.

10. Mary Curtis, "Some see in Clinton policy a casualty of Balkan war," *Boston Globe*, March 25, 1993.

11. Elaine Sciolino, "U.S. Narrows Terms for its Peacekeepers," *New York Times*, September 23, 1993.

12. President Clinton's, Address to United Nations General Assembly September 27, 1993, *Department of State, Dispatch*, vol. 4, no. 39.

13. Bill Clinton, press conference of September 27, 1993, quoted by Thomas L. Friedman, "Clinton at UN Lists Stiff Terms for Sending U.S. Force to Bosnia," *New York Times,* September 28, 1993.

14. *New York Times,* January 14, 1993. Extended excerpts from Clinton's January 13 interview were published by the *New York Times* on January 15, 1993.

15. Thomas L. Friedman, "Clinton Affirms U.S. Policy on Iraq." *New York Times,* January 15, 1993.

16. Thomas L. Friedman, "U.S. Asserts Iraq Changed Behavior," *New York Times,* February 3, 1993.

17. Warren Christopher, March 30, 1993 testimony before Appropriations Subcommittee of the Senate Operations Committee, C-SPAN telecast.

18. Thomas L. Friedman, "Jewish Criticism on Clinton Picks," *New York Times,* January 5, 1993.

19. Pamela Constable, "Clinton in reversal, backs Bush on Haiti," *Boston Globe,* March 3, 1993.

20. R. W. Apple, Jr., "Clinton Sending Reinforcements After Heavy Losses in Somalia," *New York Times,* October 5, 1993.

21. "Security Council Votes to Set Up Somalia Force," *Boston Globe,* March 27, 1993.

22. Elaine Sciolino, "Clinton's Gamble: Embracing China's Leaders," *New York Times,* November 17, 1993; and Mary Curtis, "Amid Tensions over Korea, U.S. Softens Tone on China, *Boston Globe,* November 16, 1993.

23. Michael Kramer, "Putting Business First," *Time,* November 29, 1993, p. 40.

24. Clinton's warning to North Korea quoted by Gwen Ifill, "In Korea, Chilling Reminders of Cold War," *New York Times,* July 18, 1993.

25. Stephen Engleberg with Michael R. Gordon, "Intelligence Study Says North Korea Has Nuclear Bomb," *New York Times," December 26, 1993;* Mary Curtis, "Agreement on Korea is Foreseen," *Boston Globe,* January 4, 1994.

26. On the trade issues facing Clinton at the outset of his administration, see Keith Bradsher, "Clinton Gets Tough on Trade, But Policies Are Still Blurred," *New York Times,* March 30, 1993.

27. Mary Curtis, "U.S. Tells Allies it Won't Always Take the Lead on Regional Crises," *Boston Globe,* May 26, 1993; and Mary Curtis, "Shift in Role Abroad Quickly Disavowed," *Boston Globe,* May 27, 1993.

28. Stephen A. Holmes, "Christopher Reaffirms Leading U.S. Role in World," *New York Times,* May 28, 1993.

29. "A Brand X Foreign Policy," *New York Times* (editorial), May 28, 1993.

30. Anthony Lake, address at The Johns Hopkins School of Advanced International Studies, Washington, D.C., September 25, 1993, *Department of State Dispatch,* vol. 4, no. 39.

31. *Ibid.*

INDEX

2